D0909371

The Role of Law in Social Work Practice and Administration

The Role of Law in Social Work Practice and Administration

Theodore J. Stein

COLUMBIA UNIVERSITY PRESS ■ NEW YORK

Columbia University Press
Publishers Since 1893
New York Chichester, West Sussex

Library of Congress Cataloging-in-Publication Data
Stein, Theodore J.
The role of law in social work practice and administration / Theodore J. Stein.
p. cm.
Includes bibliographical references and index.
ISBN 978-0-231-12648-9 (cloth : alk. paper)
1. Social workers—Legal status, laws, etc.—United States. 2. Social service—United States. I. Title.
KF3721.S74 2004
344.7303′132—dc22

2003068810

Columbia University Press books are printed
on permanent and durable acid-free paper.
Printed in the United States of America

To my family: Gary, Gus, Sheila, Dianna
Angela, Melanie, Vince, Tony, Julie, Jake, and Fern

Contents

PART 2 97

List of Figures and Tables

FIGURES

TABLES

Preface

THIS BOOK is about social work and the law—the ways in which the law affects the day-to-day practice of social work; the creation, administration, and operation of social service agencies; and the ways in which social workers and attorneys collaborate to serve those in need. Written primarily for social work students and professionals, the material may be helpful to any professional who works with individuals, families, groups, and communities to prevent or resolve the myriad problems that result from poverty, discrimination, family violence, and physical and emotional disabilities, as well as those who administer social service programs.

Whether you practice in the public or not-for-profit sector, whether you conceptualize your practice with reference to populations served—the elderly or children, for example—or to problems that your clients confront, such as homelessness, hunger, inadequate health care, substance abuse, or mental illness, the law will affect the work you do. The effect can be all-encompassing, as when the agency for which you work is chartered or licensed by the state and the policies that direct your practice are set by federal and state legislators who allocate funds to support your work. Private practice involves a great deal of autonomy but is also affected by the law, which may require you to disclose information that you regard as confidential, because the information suggests that someone faces imminent danger of injury. The law also determines the conditions under which a client can sue you for malpractice, and it establishes rules governing third-party payments from a public or private insurer for the services that you render.

Some social workers are employed directly by the courts, law enforcement agencies, or law firms; others are members of multidisciplinary teams that include attorneys, medical and mental health professionals, accountants, and members of the clergy.[1] In such employment settings and working with other professionals, social workers interview clients, prepare reports for use in court, interpret social science information, and consult on how best to approach client problems. In addition, there has been a growth in what are called "social justice collaboratives," or multidisciplinary service centers, where social workers, attorneys, and other professionals assist clients in resolving problems that require legal and counseling services, medical services, and/or assistance in obtaining benefits such as food stamps, housing, and services for victims of domestic violence.[2]

In addition to focusing on the relationship between the professions of social work and law, my objective is to help you develop the knowledge that you will need to practice in a legal environment. To accomplish this objective I have divided the book into three parts.

Part 1 contains four chapters. In the first I describe the legal environment in which social work practice occurs and discuss some activities undertaken by social workers who practice in a legal environment. Chapter 1 also includes a discussion of the various ways in which social workers and attorneys collaborate, a case example of collaboration, and consideration of some issues that arise in collaborative relationships. Chapter 2 focuses on the sources of law with attention to constitutional law, statutory law, case law, and common law. Chapter 3 discusses the court system, including the similarities and differences in civil and criminal law and respective court procedures. How to conduct legal research is the focus of chapter 4.

The first three chapters of part 2 consider the ways in which the law regulates the profession of social work. The range of topics addressed includes the organization of social services, the licensing of social service agencies, and some ways in which the state regulates professional practice through licensing of social workers and through establishing rules governing the confidentiality of information and the privilege to withhold information in court. As you practice your profession, you are apt to have occasion to appear in court as a lay or expert witness. The material in chapter 6 will familiarize you with some of the varied roles that social workers play in the judicial system and some skills that you will need to become an effective player. Among the topics that I cover are forensic social work, evidence, burdens of proof, the use of case records in court, and the kinds of testimony that you may provide as a witness. Chapter 7 addresses professional liability, including the conditions that create the potential for malpractice liability and the conditions that provide social workers with immunity from suit.

The first five of the seven chapters in part 3 focus on family law. Chapter 8 addresses two issues: family formation through marriage, adoption, civil unions, and domestic partnerships, and child custody when parents divorce or elect to live apart. Chapter 8 also addresses how the law decides custody matters. Chapter 9 examines the education of children and considers the role of the federal government in public education, decisions of the U.S. Supreme Court that affect primary and secondary education, and the law concerning the education of children with disabilities. Chapter 10 discusses the legal procedures that the state follows when it acts to protect abused and neglected children or to control the behavior of status offenders and delinquent youth. Chapter 11 examines the laws that govern the adoption of children, including the different ways that children become available for adoption, the approaches used by adults to find children in need of permanent homes, and the legal processes that must be followed to make a child a member of a new family. In chapter 12 I review two types of family violence: domestic violence, which concerns violent acts between adults who are in an intimate relationship, and the abuse of elderly family members by their caretakers. I will consider (1) the ways in which the law responds to these forms of family violence; (2) the effect of domestic violence on child custody disputes; (3) whether domestic violence can be considered a hate crime; and (4) how states provide for reporting elder abuse.

The last two chapters deal with the legal protections available to a person seeking care for physical health problems (chapter 13) and the person seeking care for mental health problems (chapter 14). Common themes in both chapters include informed consent, patient competency, the right to receive treatment, and the right to refuse treatment. Unique to chapter 13 is a discussion of the obligation of parents to provide health care for their children and the obligation of the state to ensure that parents do so, as well as an examination of a minor's right to consent to medical treatment. Chapter 14 features a discussion of the law of civil commitment and the effect that mental health has on criminal law defenses.

A NOTE ON LEGAL CASES INCLUDED IN THIS TEXT

Throughout the book I present examples of judicial rulings, called case law. I have selected and edited this material to illustrate certain points. For example, a case in chapter 4 asks whether a social worker is immune from suit for actions taken while investigating a report of child abuse. As is common, this case involved multiple legal issues. For example, the individual who sued the social worker had previously sued the county agency that employed the social worker. The court addressed the earlier action at length, but I have deleted it because it does not bear on the central question of social worker immunity. In addition, with few exceptions, to simplify the task of reading cases I have deleted the lengthy citations that often appear in the text of a judicial ruling. I have selectively presented citations with each case to allow the interested reader to retrieve the case and to review the excised material.

Readers should be aware that cases often are published only because the party who lost at the trial court level files an appeal. Many cases that I have used in the text are appellate court rulings. Appellate courts have a variety of dispositional alternatives, including affirming the trial court decision, overturning or vacating the trial court decision, or sending the case back (remanding) to the trial court to reconsider an issue or issues. After a case is remanded, the parties involved may agree to a settlement, or a trial court may issue a ruling that is never published. For the reader, either of these outcomes may prove frustrating because the specific disposition of the case may not be known. Also, many laws that affect social workers—for example, laws that govern confidentiality, disclosure of client records, and practitioner negligence—vary by state, and social workers must become familiar with the laws of the state in which they practice. I have used cases from different states, but providing illustrations from all the states would have been impossible.

One final point. The phrase "United States" is used in the federal constitution and in some case examples that appear in the text. When used, the reference is to the federal, not state, government. When a court action involves a state, it uses the noun *state,* as in *State v. Smith,* or it names the state involved.

PART 1

The purpose of part 1 is to identify the ways in which the practice of social work is inextricably linked to the law. The goal is to help you understand why the study of law is critical to your ability to be an effective practitioner. To achieve this, chapter 1 introduces you to three subjects: why knowledge of the law is essential to social work practice; the legal environment in which social work practice takes place; and a number of issues that may arise when social workers and attorneys collaborate on a case. Chapter 2 reviews the sources of law, beginning with the relationship between federal and state government. Then the chapter turns to constitutional law, statutory law, and case law. Chapter 3 focuses on the court system and court processes, describing and distinguishing the federal and state court systems, as well as a variety of civil and criminal court processes. In the final chapter you will learn the basic steps involved in conducting legal research.

1

Introduction

THIS BOOK is addressed mainly to social work students and to professionals in the field of social work. It focuses on the ways in which the law affects practice and administration and on the working relationship between social workers and attorneys. My intention is to make the law accessible so that social workers, in whatever capacity they practice, will understand (1) the various ways in which the law affects their profession; (2) how to expand the knowledge from this text into your own ongoing research; and (3) some ways in which social workers and attorneys can collaborate to better serve clients.

The relationship of social work to the law has its roots in the midnineteenth century when private charity was a main source of public support for poor people. Advocates for the poor, mentally ill, and children recognized that private charity was limited in its ability to respond to social problems that affected large numbers of people. For this reason they turned to government at the state and federal level to seek assistance in providing for the poor. For example, in the midnineteenth century Dorothea Dix sought the help of Congress to provide for the care of the mentally ill, and in the late nineteenth and early twentieth centuries Settlement House workers lobbied for legislation to alleviate the problems caused by urban poverty, regulate labor by limiting the number of hours that children and adults could work each day, separate children from adults in prison and other institutions, and create a juvenile court system that would pay attention to the special needs of children.[1] The responsibility of government to provide for the poor was firmly established in 1935 when the Social Security Act was passed; for reasons that I elaborate on later in this chapter, this also cemented the relationship of social work to the law.

After discussing why knowledge of the law is essential to effective social work practice, we will examine the legal environment in which social work practice occurs as well as the subject of social workers and attorneys working together. This chapter includes an example of a case handled by social workers and attorneys, followed by a discussion of some issues that arise in collaborative working relationships.

WHY KNOWLEDGE OF THE LAW IS ESSENTIAL TO EFFECTIVE SOCIAL WORK PRACTICE

For a variety of reasons knowledge of the law is essential to effective practice and administration. First, public funds that are authorized when social welfare legislation is passed are the main source of support for most social welfare programs, whether they are operated by public or nonprofit agencies. Consequently, the development and implementation of social welfare programs, the day-to-day practice of social work, as well as program administration are affected by mandates issued by government officials. These officials determine (a) which programs will be established, (b) the level of funding that will be provided, (c) what services will be available, (d) which populations will be served, and (e) what rules social workers must follow when they provide services.

Second, many problems that clients bring to social service agencies can be resolved only through the joint efforts of social workers and attorneys. Third, social workers and other mental health professionals are vulnerable to being sued by clients who believe that they have been injured by a professional's acts or failure to act. I briefly review the first two issues in this chapter and revisit them in subsequent chapters. Chapter 7 examines vulnerability to a lawsuit.

The Legal Environment of Social Work Practice

In the United States each branch of government—the legislative, executive, and the judicial—plays a pivotal role in the creation of law, which consists of statutes, regulations, and judicial decisions. Chapter 2 covers the subject of lawmaking in depth. Here it is important to note that before public money is spent to develop social welfare programs, the legislative branch of government passes a new statute, or amends an existing one, to authorize program development and the expenditure of public funds. Once a statute is passed, an agency in the executive branch of government (1) issues regulations or rules (both terms have the same meaning and are referred to as administrative law) to guide the states in implementing federal law; (2) enforces the laws when one of its agencies audits programs to ensure compliance with legislative mandates; and (3) provides a forum where clients can appeal decisions that deny them benefits. The judicial branch interprets statutes and regulations and makes new law when a judicial officer interprets existing law in a novel way.

It is also important that you understand the interplay between the federal government and the governments of the states. In the United States responsibility for governance in most domestic matters is divided between the federal government and the governments of each state. One result is that some rules that determine who is eligible for benefits and what benefits are available vary by state. For instance, in the pages that follow, you will read about a ruling that was handed down by New York state's highest court, which decided that the state was obliged to provide for the health care needs of noncitizens who are legal residents. The federal government does not require that the states provide for the health care needs of noncitizens, and the ruling has no application beyond New York. If, after practicing in New York state, you took a position in another state, the difference in benefits available to nonresidents is only one of the differences that you might find in how the law affects clients. Understanding the authority that the individual states have in regulating social welfare benefits should caution you not to make generalizations about available benefits and should alert you to the importance of learning about the laws that govern social welfare programs in the state in which you practice.

It is important that you understand the interplay between statutes, regulations, and judicial decisions for two reasons. First, many years may pass after the legislative branch of government has enacted a statute and before the precise meaning of the words and phrases it contains are clarified by a regulatory agency or by the courts. Thus it may be years before the full effect of laws pertaining to social work practice and clients is known. The practitioner who understands the process of lawmaking has the opportunity to participate in and affect the laws that are made. Chapter 2 covers the regulatory process in detail. Here it is enough to say that before a federal or state agency can issue regulations that affect the public, the proposed regulations must be made available to the public, and the government agency must provide to interested parties the chance to present their views concerning the proposed rule.[2] Advocacy groups, such as the National Association of Social Workers (NASW), the American Association of Retired Persons, and the National Organization for Women monitor the *Federal Register,* where proposed rules are published. Advocacy groups may publish newsletters and operate websites to disseminate information to their members and to encourage them to make their views known by writing letters, testifying before legislative bodies, lobbying, and engaging in other direct activities such as organizing clients to participate in peaceful demonstrations.

The following example illustrates the interplay between statutes, regulations, and judicial decisions, and the interplay between the state and federal governments. In 1996 Congress enacted the Personal Responsibility and Work

Opportunity Reconciliation Act (PRWORA).[3] PRWORA has had a significant effect on a number of aspects of social welfare, and these are reviewed at different places in this book. Two aspects of the law are relevant here. It created a program called Temporary Assistance to Needy Families (TANF) to replace the program of Aid to Families with Dependent Children (AFDC), which funneled financial assistance to children and their adult caretakers. TANF provides for assistance for a maximum of sixty months. Also, the law provides that federally funded assistance is denied to immigrants for the first five years that they live in the United States.

The meaning of the term *assistance* in a program that provides cash benefits may seem obvious to you, but it took the federal government more than three years to issue regulations that define this term. In the fall of 1999 the Department of Health and Human Services ruled that the sixty-month time limit applies to cash benefits designed to meet a family's long-term needs for food, clothing, shelter, and the like. However, assistance that can be provided beyond the sixty-month limit includes (1) short-term cash assistance in the event of a family crisis, (2) payments to employers in the form of work subsidies to help cover the cost of wages paid to TANF beneficiaries, and (3) supportive services such as child care, transportation, counseling, and services to help recipients find work. By definition, the latter are not forms of assistance.[4]

Let us now turn to the question of benefits for newly arrived immigrants. In June 2001, almost five years after Congress passed PRWORA, twelve aliens, all lawfully residing in New York, filed a class-action suit. The state's highest court ruled that failure to use state funds to provide Medicaid benefits to noncitizens who were legally residing in the state violated the state and federal constitutions.[5] Henceforth, noncitizens residing in New York, but not necessarily in other states, would be eligible for Medicaid benefits—not because a federal or state legislature decided that this was the correct course but because a judicial ruling determined that it was.

SOCIAL WORKERS AND ATTORNEYS WORKING TOGETHER

Social workers and attorneys work together for a variety of reasons. First, Americans have engaged in a process of transforming an ever growing number of social problems into legal problems. Thus whether the issue is controlling the behavior of a rebellious teenager, settling a dispute between neighbors who cannot agree on whether to trim branches from a tree, or resolving a problem that arises when we believe that we have been treated badly because of our gender, sexual orientation, race, or physical disability, we often turn to the courts to seek redress for problems that might be resolved more efficiently and less acrimoniously by family, community, or informal means such as mediation. An increased reliance on judicial intervention to resolve social problems that involve, among others, children, the elderly, and people with disabilities increases the frequency with which social workers and attorneys encounter each other in a professional context. For example, family law, which involves matters such as marriage, divorce, child custody, and support, accounts for about 35 percent of all civil cases in the nation's courts. This area of the law constitutes the largest and fastest-growing part of any state's civil caseload.[6]

When family law involves children, the elderly, or problems such as domestic violence, problem solving often requires an interdisciplinary approach. For example, an unfortunate fact of family life is that children may become pawns in an acrimonious divorce. Judges are rarely trained to ascertain the truth of the allegations that parents hurl at one another, so they rely on mental health professionals to help them sort fact from the fiction. In addition, when both parents seek primary physical custody of a child, unless evidence is presented that one has been abusive or neglectful, nothing in the gender-neutral law of child custody determines conclusively which parent should have day-to-day physical custody.

In working with an attorney, a social worker's knowledge and skills may help resolve a client's legal problem. For example, a social worker may be asked to assess family dynamics when a child custody dispute arises, determine a client's competency to stand trial, or interpret a mental health evaluation or a social study. In addition, social worker assistance may be necessary to a client's well-being; for example, counseling services may be helpful to a client who is grieving the loss of a loved one, or a client who is having difficulty in obtaining financial aid or housing assistance may need an advocate. Such needs may be equal to the client's need to resolve a legal matter. Note also that just as an attorney may seek out the help of a social worker, so may a social worker turn to an attorney when a client is confronting legal as well as social problems. As I have already noted, the involvement of social workers in legal matters is not limited to the relationship between them and attorneys. Judicial officers also seek the expertise of social workers, to assess clients, conduct social studies, and interpret mental health evaluations.

Thus the frequency with which social workers and attorneys work together has increased because many problems that clients bring to either professional, especially to those who practice in settings that serve poor clients, cannot be wholly resolved by applying either legal or social work methods alone. Poor health, inadequate housing, lack of education, deficits in work skills, and social isolation are often the companions of poverty; these are difficulties that no single discipline, social system, or method of practice can hope to address in a satisfactory manner. Likewise, as the population of the United States ages, the demand for both legal and social work services to address the unique needs of the elderly is increasing. For instance, a person who is seeking legal assistance to settle the estate of a recently deceased partner or spouse may be as much in need of help in dealing with the emotional effect as with the legal ramifications of probating a will.

As I noted earlier, advocates for the poor and marginalized groups have recognized the need for a multidisciplinary approach to problem solving since the nineteenth century. Settlement House workers held degrees in economics, political science, law, medicine, and sociology. They understood that poverty was a complex matter and that bringing relief to poor people would require the efforts of people from different disciplines using various interventions.[7] In addition to providing practical assistance, such as child care and vocational training, these early "social workers" lobbied for legislation that would benefit those served. A multidisciplinary approach to problem solving was also a hallmark of the War on Poverty in the 1960s. Community-based multiservice centers, staffed by social workers, attorneys, and professionals from other disciplines, worked with and on behalf of poor people.[8]

Today social workers and attorneys collaborate in a variety of settings. Working relationships range from those where professionals in different organizations make referrals or provide consultation to one another to situations where social workers are employed by the courts, law firms, or multiservice centers to work alongside attorneys and other professionals as they seek to meet client needs.[9] Thus a social worker may need the help of an attorney (1) to obtain and enforce an order of protection on behalf of a client who is receiving services in a shelter for victims of domestic violence; (2) to determine whether a client who complains of workplace harassment has a basis for filing a complaint under federal or state law; or (3) to prepare to represent a client who is appealing a denial of benefits. Likewise, a lawyer may turn to a social worker upon recognizing that obtaining an order of protection is only the first step in helping someone resolve the complex issues arising from domestic violence, or that causing an employer to take action to eliminate workplace harassment will have limited results if employees are not trained to understand which of their behaviors are offensive and why, a task that social workers are uniquely qualified to undertake.

Collaborative working relationships offer a number of advantages, but difficulties may arise when people from different professions work with the same clients.

Collaboration: An Example

Hank and Maria were diagnosed with acquired immune deficiency syndrome (AIDS). Although the medications they were taking improved their health, they experienced side-effects that made it difficult for them to provide full-time care for Kevin, their physically active four-year-old. Hank and Maria decided that they wanted Kevin to live with Manny, Hank's brother, who agreed to this arrangement. Hank went to the Legal Aid Center to get help with resolving this problem.

On the center's staff were two full-time attorneys; one full-time and one part-time social worker, both with master's degrees; and social work and legal interns. Because the center could not serve all who sought assistance, new intake, except for emergency aid to avoid eviction, find housing, obtain food, and the like, was reviewed each Friday by the center's staff. Using information compiled at intake, the staff decided whether the center could accept a case or would have to refer it elsewhere. If it appeared that the staff could address a legal problem, staffers would decide at their Friday sessions whether the problem also called for social work assistance.

Hank had told the intake worker that he and Maria wanted Kevin to live with his brother, although the intake worker noted that Hank was hesitant in stating this goal. Hank reported that his brother was agreeable to this arrangement, but Hank was not clear in explaining why he had come to the center alone. For the purposes of staffing it was assumed that Hank had correctly conveyed Maria and Manny's position regarding Kevin's living arrangements. The staff agreed to accept the case, contingent on the results of an interview with the three adults. Because a child was involved, the staff determined that an attorney would conduct the initial interview, for reasons that I discuss later in this chapter.

The interview went well. The three adults were in agreement about Kevin's living arrangements, and the legal staff agreed to petition the family court to make Manny Kevin's legal guardian. (See chapter 12 for a more complete discussion of guardianship.) It was clear to the attorney who conducted the interview that the guardianship arrangement would reduce but not resolve Hank and Maria's problems. It was apparent that the decision to have Kevin move out of their home was emotionally difficult for Hank and Maria, not only because they would lose the care and day-to-day companionship of their son but also because the move was an acknowledgment of the severity of their illness. In addition, they would lose the financial stipend that the state provided for Kevin, as well as some of their food stamp allotment. Their financial situation was precarious, and these losses were significant. A social worker agreed to assist Hank and Maria on issues related to separation from their son, planning for ongoing visits with him, and ways to replace the financial and food losses they would suffer.

About eight weeks after Kevin moved to his uncle's home, Hank returned to the clinic and said that he wanted his son returned to his care. He reported that neither Maria nor his brother agreed with him, but he was adamant in his wish.

Hank had difficulty explaining his change of heart, but the center's legal staffers agreed that they were obligated to represent him if the situation required a return to court to seek revocation of the guardianship. The legal staff would have to clarify Maria's position and, if necessary, find an attorney to represent her, as well as Manny, if he opposed the change in Kevin's custody. In addition, in New York state, family court judges may appoint separate counsel for children when custody is in dispute.[10] However, the staff needed more information before returning to court. The social worker who had worked with Hank and Maria would speak with them as well as with Manny in an effort to clarify their wishes and to learn what she could about the reason for Hank's change of heart.

Fortunately for all concerned, the situation was resolved without returning to court. From her interviews with the adults, the social worker learned that Hank's decision arose from difficulties that he experienced in visiting with his son. The problem was this: After Kevin moved to Manny's home, Hank and Maria found a smaller apartment but did not discuss their move with the social worker, whose transportation plan for visits with Kevin was based on their old address. After their move they had to take three busses to get to Manny's home. When they arrived, they were too tired to enjoy their time with their son but never discussed this with anyone. The matter was resolved when Manny agreed either to bring Kevin to visit at Hank and Maria's home or to pick up Hank and Maria and drive them to his home.

ISSUES THAT ARISE IN SOCIAL WORKER AND ATTORNEY TEAMWORK

The situation that Hank and Maria presented highlights a number of issues that arise when social workers and lawyers work collaboratively. Collaborative work can result in improved services to clients and provide a broader perspective on client problems than is likely when difficulties are viewed through the filter of a single discipline. Attorneys are not trained to deal with a client's emotional problems and may not be comfortable in attempting to do so, nor are social workers trained to identify and resolve matters of a legal nature. Thus the initial collaborative effort resulted in the requested change of guardianship and in reducing the emotional impact that Hank and Maria suffered when Kevin left their home. In addition, the social worker was able to find alternative sources for financial aid and food support. The ultimate resolution of the case hinged on the efforts of the social worker, who was better trained than the attorney to conduct the kind of interview that elicited the information that led to solutions. The positive outcome of this case is reflected in the opinions of social workers and attorneys who, when queried, report that collaborative working relationships, although they involve certain difficulties, result in satisfactory outcomes for clients and in learning opportunities for the professionals involved.[11] But some difficulties do arise, and they may include issues involving confidentiality, ethics, confusion about the nature of the problem at hand, and role conflict.

Confidentiality

The obligation of social workers and attorneys to maintain client confidentiality is rooted in the ethical codes of each profession as well as in statutory law. Chapter 5 deals extensively with the subject of confidentiality, but here it is important to note that all states require social workers to report known or suspected child abuse and neglect but do not impose the same obligation on attorneys. Because Hank sought legal help in New York, where attorneys are not mandated reporters, a lawyer had to conduct the initial interview to avoid compromising the center's ability to help him. Stated another way, if a social worker had conducted the initial interview and had reason to suspect child abuse or neglect, the worker would have had to report this matter. Once a report is made, an investigation follows, and an attorney's ability to honor his or her professional obligation may be compromised by the disclosure of information that the client provided in confidence. You should note that a social worker who is employed by an attorney is covered by attorney-client privilege and may not be required to report abuse or neglect.[12]

Ethical Conflicts

The staff at the center questioned the wisdom of returning Kevin to Hank and Maria because of the limits that their illness placed on their ability to parent. Moreover, before sanctioning a return of custody, a judge would have asked for a social study that addressed Hank and Maria's parenting ability. In all likelihood, a judge would not have reversed the guardianship decision unless Hank and Maria had daily help in caring for Kevin.

Nonetheless, an attorney is bound to advocate for a client's wishes[13] as long as doing so does not result in disobeying a court order or in falsifying information provided to a court.[14] An attorney, acting as a legal counselor, should identify and discuss all available options with a client, and the center attorney encouraged Hank to leave Kevin with his brother and to arrange other means of fulfilling Hank's wish for greater contact with his son. However, an attorney cannot ethically substitute her or his judgment for that of the client, although some legal scholars argue that an attorney who is representing a client with a mental disability, or a child who is "disabled" due to young age, should work within a "best interest" model. According to this reasoning, the attorney defers to mental health experts or her or his own judgment about what is best for the client. According to some legal scholars, in such a model an attorney acts in the role of guardian ad litem, which is discussed more fully in chapter 10.[15]

Social work ethics are not as clear. Although social workers are admonished to promote the right of clients to select their own goals and to assist clients in doing so, social workers have the choice of limiting a "clients' right to self-determination when, in the social workers' professional judgment, clients' actions or potential actions pose a serious, foreseeable, and imminent risk to themselves or others."[16] It is not difficult to imagine that a social worker would, despite Hank's wishes and despite the ethical responsibility to promote client self-determination, recommend to a court that Kevin remain in Manny's custody with increased visitation for Hank. But despite her personal point of view, Hank's lawyer could not adopt the social worker's position.

What Is the Problem?

That an attorney cannot substitute his judgment for that of the client but social workers may do so is a potential source of tension between professionals. Cassie was fifteen when she was arrested for possession of cocaine. The arresting officer found the cocaine after conducting what her lawyer would later conclude was an illegal search. It was clear to both her court-appointed social worker and court-appointed attorney that Cassie had a drug problem, that it was likely, based on information she provided, that she was prostituting herself to obtain money to buy drugs, and that a drug rehabilitation program would be in her best interest. Cassie had no interest in entering a rehabilitation program, and she was clear in telling this to her attorney.

For Cassie's attorney the problem was straightforward. He had reason to believe that the police had violated Cassie's constitutional rights when they conducted an illegal search and that this could be remedied only if a judge declared the search illegal and dropped the charges against Cassie. In such a situation the lawyer assumes that the state's attorney will argue that the search was legal. In a courtroom the "truth" that emerges is produced by the adversarial contest between attorneys and by the evidence that each presents.

For Cassie's social worker the problem was equally straightforward but quite different: The young woman needed help, which she would receive only when a judge ordered her to enter a drug rehabilitation program. Disagreements about problem definition are not uncommon and may be an important by-product of collaborative working relationships to the extent that they result in discussion and debate, where the professional learn from each other, producing a better outcome for a client. When social workers and attorneys work together over a period of time, each will develop at least a respect for the different perspectives on problem definition that arise from their respective disciplines. But this can also be a source of tension and anger, with each considering the other to be acting against the client's best interest.

What Facts Are Important?

If each perceives the problem differently, it follows that each will consider different facts to be of importance and each will "select" those facts considered most salient to his or her position. For the attorney the salient facts lie in the police behavior that constituted the illegal search. For the social worker the salient facts lie in Cassie's substance abuse and the problems that will result if she is prostituting herself. These approaches point to an important professional difference between social workers and attorneys. In that part of a court proceeding where a person's guilt or innocence is the issue, the only salient facts are those that describe the behavior that brought the person before the court. Stated otherwise, attorneys and judges focus on the near past and do not consider future misconduct, although such may play a role when sentencing or disposition are at hand. By contrast, social workers, in addition to considering the facts that brought a client to their attention, may focus on the distant past and, most significantly, on predicting where any course of action will bring a client.

Who Is the Client?

In Hank's case, when he first sought legal assistance, his interests and those of Maria, Manny, and Kevin were harmonious. Hank and Maria agreed that their son needed care that they could not provide. Manny was willing and able to provide that care, and the parties agreed that Kevin's needs could best be met by a change of custody. Because all were in agreement, legal ethics permitted one attorney to represent all the parties. However, legal ethics do not allow an attorney to represent clients whose interests diverge, unless the clients understand the potential costs of such representation and agree in writing to have one attorney represent them, despite the conflict.[17] Therefore, once Hank decided that he wanted Kevin returned to his care, the potential for conflict arose as did the possibility that each party would require separate representation: Hank needed an advocate to advance his position regarding Kevin's custody, and Manny, whose interests were in conflict with those of his brother, required separate counsel. Maria's position was aligned with Manny's; while joint representation would have been possible, it would not have been a wise choice. Should one attorney agree to represent both Maria and Manny, and considering that either might later have a change of heart, the attorney who had been privy to confidences shared by both might have to withdraw, requiring the appointment of separate counsel and a needlessly drawn-out procedure. As I noted earlier, a family court judge may have thought it necessary to appoint counsel for Kevin too.

Social workers are in a different position than attorneys when it comes to determining who the client is. First, while the Code of Ethics of the National Association of Social Workers admonishes social workers to serve the well-being of their clients, the code does not provide clear guidance for deciding who the client is. As the code states:

> When social workers provide services to two or more people who have a relationship with each other (for example, couples or family members), social workers should clarify with all parties which individuals will be considered clients and the nature of social workers' professional obligations to the various individuals who are receiving services. Social workers who anticipate a conflict of interest among the individuals receiving services or who anticipate having to perform in potentially conflicting roles (for example, when a worker is asked to testify in a child custody dispute or divorce proceedings involving clients) should clarify their role with the parties involved and take appropriate action to minimize any conflict of interest.[18]

It is not uncommon for a social worker to represent diverse interests, and because social workers are trained to work with clients to negotiate differences of opinion without resorting to independent mediators, a worker may assist individuals whose interests diverge.

Thus where legal ethics would force an attorney to determine which of the parties she or he is ethically obligated to represent, social work ethics do not force such a choice, nor do they provide guidance to workers who believe that they can function only by deciding whose interests they represent.

Role Conflict

Social workers and lawyers have two main potential sources of role conflict. The first occurs when they disagree about who should perform specific tasks that are not clearly in the domain of either profession. The second source of conflict comes about when social workers and legal professionals stray beyond the boundaries of their professional competence.

There is a series of clearly defined tasks that must be performed when a case goes to court. When the matter involves unfit parenting, for example, someone must decide which charges or allegations to pursue, file a petition containing those allegations with the court, decide whether the child will testify, explain the reasons for the court action to the parents, and make a recommendation to the court about an appropriate custody arrangement for the child, whether in the child's own home or a substitute care setting.

Research has shown that social workers and attorneys disagree about who should perform specific tasks, such as deciding what allegations to make in a petition, explaining the reasons for a court hearing to parents, recommending where a child will live, and entering into agreements with parents or their agents regarding the disposition of a case.[19] Conflict is reduced when tasks fall clearly into the realm of either profession. For example, attorneys and social workers agree that conferring with collateral resources such as medical and police personnel, presenting social histories at court, and recommending psychological or psychiatric evaluations are clearly social worker responsibilities, while filing petitions, deciding who should testify at a hearing, asking witnesses to testify, and informing parties of the consequences of violating court orders are in the legal realm. Evidence exists that conflict may be reduced when social workers are trained in court-related tasks.[20]

The second source of conflict stems from the heavy reliance of juvenile court proceedings on sociological and psychological evidence. The court may be interested in information describing the environmental conditions in which a child lives, the emotional stability of the parents, the effects of parental behavior on the emotional and psychological well-being of the child, as well as with predicting how present conditions will affect the child in the long run. As a result, all the involved parties tend to stray beyond the boundaries of their professional competence—lawyers try to perform as social scientists, and social workers tend to think that they have more value than lawyers because of their social science training.

SUMMARY

Knowledge of the law is a key element of effective professional practice. This is so because (1) the development and implementation of social welfare programs and the day-to-day practice of social work are affected by laws enacted by legislative bodies that authorize the creation of and provide funding for social welfare programs; (2) the acts of judicial officers interpret laws and affect client rights; (3) the satisfactory resolution of some clients' problems may not be possible without the joint efforts of social workers and attorneys, as well as professionals from other disciplines; and (4) social workers are vulnerable to being sued by clients, and effective practice requires knowledge of the conditions that give rise to professional liability.

In addition, U.S. society has increased its reliance on judicial intervention to resolve social problems that involve children, the elderly, and people with disabilities, among others. Using judicial processes to resolve social problems increases the frequency with which social workers and attorneys encounter each other in a professional context.

Collaborative work can result in improved services to clients, and it can provide a broader perspective on client problems than is likely when difficulties are viewed through the filter of a single discipline. However, collaborative work may give rise to conflicts that stem from disciplinary differences, including (a) confidentiality rules that require social workers to report certain matters such as known or suspected child abuse but that often often do not apply to attorneys; (2) ethical conflicts that result from the duty of an attorney, with few exceptions, to advocate for a client's wishes, whereas social workers may substitute their judgment for that of the client. Also, conflict may arise different perceptions of the problem in need of resolution and different "filters" through which attorneys and social workers identify the facts that are relevant to defining the problem. Legal ethics require lawyers to determine who their client is, whereas the NASW Code of Ethics imposes no comparable mandate on social workers. Finally, role conflict can undermine cooperative working relationships. Conflict may exist when social workers and lawyers disagree about who should perform specific tasks that are not clearly in the domain of either profession, or when members of either profession stray beyond the boundaries of their professional competence by taking on tasks for which they are not trained.

2

Sources of Law

IN CHAPTER 1, I said that the development, implementation, and administration of social welfare programs and the day-to-day practice of social work are affected by the law. Your in-depth exploration of the ways in which the law affects programs, practice, and administration begins with the material in this chapter. We shall start with a definition of the law and then review six topics. The first three will address constitutional law, covering (1) federal and state constitutional law; (2) the U.S. Constitution and states' rights; and (3) constitutional law and the provision of social welfare. Next, our attention will turn to the role of the legislative, executive, and judicial branches of government in lawmaking, including the making of (4) statutory law; (5) executive orders, administrative law, and treaties; and (6) case law. Unless otherwise noted, all references to the Supreme Court are to the U.S. Supreme Court.

THE LAW DEFINED

The law consists of a series of rules that govern the behavior of people in a society, that allow for resolution of disputes between the members of a society and between individuals and the government, and that provide a means for the state to control the behaviors of its citizens.

But the law is more than a set of rules governing behavior and defining remedies for violations of these rules. The law embodies a philosophy of humankind and of the relationship between government and the members of society. For social work the law is important because it reflects an idea of the proper role of the state in caring for individuals and in protecting human welfare.

The rules of law in any society cannot be understood outside the social context in which they were formed and that sustains them. In the United States we are preoccupied with the individual, to whom all rights devolve and for whose protection the Bill of Rights was formulated. This does not mean that the collective good is not of concern but that questions of rights take as their starting point the individual and ask what harm will come to the individual if the state acts to curtail one person's freedom.

Countries that emerge after a struggle to overcome a colonial past, such as the United States, South Africa, and India, develop bills of rights to assure their citizens that they are protected from the tyrannies that characterized their colonial past. Some countries do not have a bill of rights, and others, such as Great Britain, did not develop a written bill of rights until the dawn of the twenty-first century, when the Human Rights Act gave British citizens their first unambiguous statement of their basic legal rights.[1] A bill of rights is significant. It empowers the individual to sue the government if it tries to limit the rights expressly granted; it also limits the power of a legislative body, such as the U.S. Congress or Parliament, to pass a law that conflicts with clearly established individual rights.

FEDERAL AND STATE CONSTITUTIONAL LAW

The U.S. Constitution is the supreme law of the land.[2] This means that laws that are made to carry out the purposes expressed in the U.S. Constitution, for example, to protect our right to free speech or to ensure that due process under the law is the supreme law of the land; any state laws that are in conflict with the Constitution will not survive if they are challenged.

In addition to the U.S. Constitution and the Bill of Rights, each of the fifty states has its own constitution, and many have their own bills of rights. The U.S. Constitution is divided into articles and amendments. The articles describe the division of responsibility between the legislative (Article 1), executive (Art. 2), and judicial (Art. 3) branches of government. At the state level these responsibilities are described in state constitutions. In simple terms, the authority to enact laws is reserved to the legislative branch of government, the authority to administer the law to the executive branch, and the authority to interpret and apply the law to the judicial branch. The first ten amendments to the U.S. Constitution are the Bill of Rights.

Amending Constitutions

Constitutions are difficult to amend, which is a good thing, because they set forth our basic freedoms, such as freedom of speech and freedom of religion, and because they limit the power of government to interfere in our lives without due process of law. An amendment to the U.S. Constitution requires that two-thirds of the members of both houses of Congress support the proposal, which can become final only if ratified by three-fourths of the states.[3]

State constitutions can be amended in different ways. The most common method is by an act of the legislature. However, legislative amendments cannot become law unless approved by the voters in a referendum, which is a mechanism that confers on the electorate the power to approve or reject statutes enacted by the legislature. In some states a constitutional convention may be called for the purpose of deciding whether to propose amendments to a state constitution. New York has such a mechanism, but a constitutional convention cannot be called unless approved by the voters. A third approach to amending state constitutions, found in twenty-two states and the District of Columbia, is the voter initiative. The initiative enables the public to command the passage of legislation. Voters have availed themselves of the initiative to end affirmative action in California and the state of Washington, to end the use of bilingual education in California, and to deny health care benefits to noncitizens. Use of the initiative requires that a specified percentage of the state's registered voters sign a petition to place the initiative on the ballot at the next general election. If approved by the voters, an initiative is subject to legal challenges and may be overturned by a court. In 1992 voters in Colorado approved an amendment to the state constitution that prohibited any legislative, executive, or judicial action that would provide protection against discrimination in employment or housing based on sexual orientation. The U.S. Supreme Court ruled that the amendment violated the equal protection clause of the Fourteenth Amendment because it denied to lesbians and gays, but no other group, the right to participate in the political process. Stated otherwise, the Colorado Constitution would have prevented lesbians and gays from petitioning their representatives for legislative action.[4]

THE U.S. CONSTITUTION AND STATES' RIGHTS

Federalism refers to the relationship between the national government and the government of the states and asks, "What power does each branch of government have to establish the rules by which we live our lives?" This question directs attention to two aspects of federal-state relations. The first is concerned with the applicability of the Bill of Rights to actions taken by the states. The second focuses attention on the powers that the U.S. Constitution grants to the national government and to the states. Before continuing this discussion, it is worth noting that for social workers, a discussion of federalism is more than an abstract discourse on the constitutional division of power. As I shall review in this chapter and elsewhere throughout this book, in a federalist system there is an ongoing debate about the role of each level of government in providing for the welfare of the people. While no one would seriously argue that government has no responsibility for social welfare, people of goodwill disagree about the extent of governmental obligation. The outcome of any debate on this matter will have a profound effect on public life because it will determine what social welfare obligations are taken on by the federal government and by state governments and those that they will not assume.

The Bill of Rights and State Action

The adoption of the Bill of Rights in 1791 placed limits on the federal government's authority to interfere with individual rights, but it did not offer protection to individuals whose rights were restricted by an action of state government.[5] After the Civil War some former Confederate states sought to limit the rights of newly freed slaves by passing laws that created a race-based caste system. Because the U.S. Supreme Court had made it clear that the Bill of Rights did not apply to state actions, the federal government had no way to intervene on behalf of the African American population.[6] Congress acted to remedy the situation by passing the Civil Rights Act of 1866, which was codified in 1868 as the Fourteenth Amendment to the Constitution. The Fourteenth Amendment made the protections in the Bill of Rights applicable to the states by providing that "No State shall make or enforce any law which shall abridge the privileges or immunities of citizens of the United States; nor shall any State deprive any person of life, liberty, or property, without due process of law; nor deny to any person within its jurisdiction the equal protection of the laws."[7] Despite passage of the amendment, the Supreme Court was reluctant to rule in favor of individuals who brought suit against a state for alleged violations of their rights.[8] Almost ninety years would pass before the High Court would sanction the Fourteenth Amendment's promise to hold the states accountable to the Bill of Rights. The latter process began in the mid-1950s when the Court ruled, in *Brown v. Board of Education,* that race-based segregation in public schools violated the equal protection clause of the Fourteenth Amendment.[9] For more than a decade after its decision in *Brown,* the Court would find other violations of the Fourteenth Amendment when a state (1) apportioned voting districts in a manner that diluted the votes of minority groups[10]; (2) denied to nonresidents of a state the welfare benefits that were available to residents[11]; (3) restricted access to contraceptive devices[12]; (4) labeled a person as a criminal based on his or her addiction to narcotics, rather than on behavior that violated the law[13]; (5) failed to provide legal counsel to an individual accused of a crime[14]; and failed to provide a speedy trial by an impartial jury.[15]

The State Action Requirement
The U.S. Constitution affects our relationship as individuals to government and offers us protection against government actions that arbitrarily limit the rights guaranteed by the Constitution. To win a claim that your constitutional rights have been violated, you must show that the alleged violation was the result of state action. The "state action requirement," as it is called, means that the Constitution does not protect us from each other as private citizens.

Federal Compared to State Power

The Tenth Amendment to the Constitution provides that the powers of the federal government are limited to those expressly enumerated in the Constitution and that powers not delegated to the federal government are reserved to the states. The federal government's responsibilities include (1) defending the nation (Art. 1, Section 8); (2) regulating commerce with foreign nations, Indian tribes, and among the states (Art. 1, Sec. 8); (3) entering into treaties with foreign nations (Art. 2, Sec. 2); and (4) establishing rules for naturalization (Art. 1, Sec. 8). The latter authority extends to setting rules that govern emigration to the United States.[16] However, the suggestion that federal powers are limited to those in the Constitution must be viewed with caution, lest this lead to the conclusion that a review of that document would make clear what powers belong to the federal government and what powers are reserved to the states. For purposes of illustration, consider the concept of commerce. *Black's Law Dictionary* defines *commerce* as "trade, traffic, commerce, transportation, or communication among the several states." When you think of commerce between the states, you may have an image of trucks rolling down an interstate, bringing goods manufactured in one state to customers across the country, and you would be correct. But if commerce is so limited, you might ask how the Supreme Court concluded that racial discrimination practiced by a two-hundred-room motel in Georgia affected interstate commerce or why commerce was affected by a New York City law that established literacy requirements as a condition for voting. You might also ask why possession of handguns in a school zone and violence against women did not affect interstate commerce.[17] The answers require that we cover several topics. First, we must consider what tools Congress has available when it chooses to affect state action, and then we must consider the effect that social conditions have on judicial interpretations of the Constitution.

How Congress Affects State Action

Congress acts to affect the behavior of state officials in different ways. A common approach involves a carrot-and-stick arrangement, whereby the federal government offers to pay part of the cost of providing benefits or services in exchange for the state's conformity to federal regulations. When Congress enacts a cost-sharing program, any state that disagrees with the federal rules can elect not to participate in the program. However, because the issues addressed by cost-sharing programs, such as the provision of health care for the poor and the elderly or foster care for children, are matters with which the states must contend, rejecting federal funds would force the state to carry the full fiscal burden of providing services.

When Congress seeks to compel state compliance with federal law, cost-sharing programs aside, it must find a source of authority in the Constitution to support its actions. The most frequently cited source for congressional authority for this is the commerce clause (Art. 1, Sec. 8) of the Constitution.[18] The Supreme Court has ruled that the commerce clause grants to Congress the authority to regulate the "channels" of interstate commerce (e.g., commercial pathways such as highways or airways); the "instrumentalities" of interstate commerce (e.g., the "persons or things" needed to carry out interstate commerce so that both a truck and the actions of its driver can be regulated); and intrastate activities that substantially affect interstate commerce. The last is known as the "Affectation Doctrine," which speaks to the cumulative effect on commerce of a series of discrete actions, whether direct or indirect. Thus the Supreme Court sanctioned a federal law that affected loan-sharking, even though the law applied to an intrastate activity; the justices based their ruling on congressional findings that using extortion to collect payments due on loans affected interstate commerce because the behavior involved organized crime and its reach across state lines.[19]

Social Conditions and Judicial Interpretation of the Constitution

For most of American history the Supreme Court was reluctant to sanction federal action that interfered with state autonomy and thus limited severely Congress's commerce clause authority. For example, in 1918 and again in 1922 the Supreme Court ruled that federal laws that were intended to regulate child labor were unconstitutional, even though the products that were manufactured by children were introduced into commerce.[20] In 1933 the Court ruled that the Agricultural Adjustment Act, enacted by Congress to provide financial subsidies to farmers as part of the federal effort to ameliorate the effects of the Great Depression of 1929, was unconstitutional.[21] In both cases the Court reasoned that federal action violated state authority.

However, in 1937 the direction of the Court changed. Newly appointed justices had a different perspective than their predecessors of federal efforts to act in areas previously reserved to the states. In part, this shift reflected a different view of the Constitution that the new justices brought to the Court, and in part it reflected the reality that the federal government had to act to relieve the suffering caused by the depression. This new direction was reflected in the Court's decision in *Steward v. Davis*,[22] where it ruled that the unemployment insurance provisions in the Social Security Act of 1935, which imposed a tax on employers to be used to fund unemployment benefits, was not a violation of the Tenth Amendment's reservation of powers to the states. The new interpretation laid the groundwork for the American welfare state. The jurisprudential shift continued in a ruling of the Supreme Court in 1941, when it declared that the Tenth Amendment was more in the nature of a declaration of the "relationship between national and state governments" than it was a substantive restraint on federal authority.[23] For more than half a century the Supreme Court would adhere to this view, supporting federal efforts to control what happened within the states. Using its commerce clause power, Congress passed laws as far-ranging as those that protect civil rights, prohibit people from creating obstacles to a woman's effort to gain access to abortion clinics, and criminalize failure of a noncustodial parent to make child support payments.[24]

How the commerce clause could apply to the actions of a Georgia motel but not violence against women is related more to the personal views of the justices,[25] and how changing social conditions affect interpretations of the law, than to the documented effect on commerce.

An example of how social conditions have affected the Court's decisions can be seen in decisions separated by almost sixty years. In 1896 in *Plessy v. Ferguson* the Supreme Court legitimized racial segregation.[26] The Court found that legislation segregating the races was constitutional because segregation did not constitute a "badge" of slavery, which was outlawed by the Thirteenth Amendment. In 1954 in *Brown v. Board of Education* the Court overturned *Plessy*, finding that segregated schools were unconstitutional because segregating children on the basis of race violated the equal protection clause of the Fourteenth Amendment. The language of the Constitution did not change between the decisions, so interpretation alone cannot logically explain both decisions, which were diametrically opposed. Thus the Court must reconcile the different rulings with a reasoned argument. When *Brown* was decided, the Court distinguished it from *Plessy* by referring to the importance of public education in the mid-1950s in comparison to 1896, when the latter case was decided.[27] It follows, therefore, that whether a state's action represents a violation of the equal protection clause may be subject to the Court's understanding of changing social conditions. *Brown v. Board of Education* is not the only example of this.[28]

Eventually, Congress's use of the commerce clause to enact legislation affecting a wide a range of matters became a source of dissatisfaction to many who regard the practice as eviscerating the concept of states' rights. In the mid-1990s the political climate provided a forum for those who sought to increase states' rights and to limit federal control. In 1994 the Republican Party won control of both houses of Congress for the first time in fifty years, setting the stage for the welfare reform amendments of 1996. At the same time the Supreme Court had a conservative majority, which was able to give effect to its concern that Congress had gone too far in substituting federal control for states' rights. In 1995, for the first time since 1937, the Court ruled that Congress had exceeded its commerce clause authority when it enacted the Gun-Free School Zones Act, which prohibited possession of a firearm in a school zone; the Court found the act was unconstitutional. The Court ruled that possession of guns in school zones failed to qualify as an economic activity and that such possession did not substantially effect commerce.[29] After its 1995 decision the Court handed down a series of rulings that limited Congress's authority to enact legislation affecting the states, including (1) provisions in the Age Discrimination and Employment Act that had prevented the state as an employer from discriminating on the basis of age[30]; (2) provisions in the Brady Handgun Violence Act that had required state officials to conduct background checks on prospective handgun purchasers[31]; and (3) provisions in the Violence Against Women Act that had given federal courts jurisdiction over crimes committed against women, which meant that women would have been able to sue their attacker in federal court.[32]

The U.S. Constitution, State Constitutions, and Social Welfare

For social workers and other human service providers, an important aspect of constitutional law is the relationship between the U.S. Constitution, state constitutions, and social welfare benefits.

The guarantees in the U.S. Constitution are "negative rights," meaning that they limit the ability of government to restrict our behavior in areas such as speech and freedom of worship while limiting the ability of government to deprive us of life, liberty, or property without due process of law. State constitutions differ from the U.S. Constitution in two ways. First, many create positive rights, or "affirmative duties," meaning that they impose obligations on the state to assist residents who are in need. Second, a number of state constitutions afford greater protections than those provided by the U.S. Constitution. For example, in 1980 the U.S. Supreme Court ruled that a federal law that prevented the use of federal monies to fund abortions did not violate the Constitution,[33] but the Supreme Court of Minnesota, noting that there is no reason that a state constitution cannot provide more, ruled that denying payments for abortion services infringed on a woman's fundamental right to privacy under the state constitution.[34]

Article 1, Section 8 of the Constitution provides that Congress may spend money in aid of the "general welfare." Advocates for the poor have argued that the general welfare provision is a source of authority for federal involvement in providing welfare benefits.[35] Indeed, the Supreme Court sanctioned the use of federal funds for the general welfare in 1937, when the government intervened to mitigate problems caused by the depression, because they were national in scope and thus beyond the ability of any one state to resolve.[36] The Court has also sanctioned Congress's use of its general welfare authority to further broad policy objectives. For example, the Court sanctioned a federal law that requires that a percentage of federal funds used for public works projects be awarded to minority-owned firms.[37]

However, except for its depression-era willingness to interpret the "general welfare" clause as a source of authority to sanction the provision of aid to the poor,[38] the Court has stated in unambiguous terms that "welfare benefits are not a fundamental right, and neither the states nor the Federal Government is under a constitutional obligation to guarantee minimum levels of support."[39] The Court made its position clear in a series of cases that it heard between 1969 and 1979. Its position can be summed up as follows. If a statute provides for welfare benefits, eligibility rules cannot violate constitutional protections and must be applied in a uniform manner. In addition, the Fourteenth Amendment provides certain due process safeguards, such as the right to a hearing before benefits can be terminated, but the Constitution does not, in and of itself, provide any substantive right to welfare. Several examples will help to clarify this matter.

In the late 1960s Connecticut, Pennsylvania, and the District of Columbia denied welfare benefits to individuals with less than one year of residency.[40] Applicants for assistance under the Aid to Families with Dependent Children (AFDC) program and under a program that assisted individuals with disabilities sued after they were denied financial assistance. The Court ruled in their favor, finding that classifying people on the basis of residency violated the equal protection guarantees of the Fifth and Fourteenth amendments.[41] The Court was concerned that one result of the classification scheme was to deny citizens the right to travel from state to state and that the only reason for the residency requirement was to inhibit the movement of poor people across state lines.[42] One year later the Court heard another case concerning welfare benefits that asked whether a state was required to provide notice and a hearing before terminating statutorily conferred welfare benefits.[43] Once again the plaintiffs prevailed. The Supreme Court ruled that the Fourteenth Amendment guarantees of procedural due process require that a hearing be held before denying public assistance payments. Furthermore, the Court ruled that recipients have a right to appear at the hearing, with or without counsel, and that they have the right to present evidence and to confront or cross-examine witnesses. What these cases have in common is that the Court held that the states' actions violated constitutional protections guaranteed to all citizens.

However, in the same year that the Court ruled that a state had to hold a hearing before denying welfare benefits, it limited constitutional claims to welfare benefits. In *Dandridge v. Williams* residents of Maryland who participated in the AFDC program sued to prevent the state from enforcing a regulation that limited the amount of an AFDC grant to $250 per month, regardless of family size.[44] The plaintiffs argued that the state's system placed families in categories defined by family size and that such a classification violated the equal protection clause of the Fourteenth Amendment. The Court disagreed. It ruled that as long as the state provided some aid to all eligible families, it had great latitude in determining the size of an AFDC grant and that as long as the state's system of classification was rationally related to a legitimate state interest—here, preserving funds—that the system would withstand constitutional scrutiny. The Court summed up its view when it opined that the subject of welfare benefits raises "intractable economic, social and even philosophical problems [that] are not [its business]."[45] In later cases the Court rejected claims that the Constitution confers a right to housing,[46] public education,[47] and medical services.[48]

State Constitutions and Social Welfare

Although the U.S. Constitution does not provide any guarantee of welfare payments, some state constitutions do. The Alabama Constitution, for example, provides that "it is the duty of the legislature . . . to make adequate provision for the maintenance of the poor"[49]; that of Kansas, that the counties shall provide for residents who due to "age, infirmity or other misfortune may have claims upon the aid of society"[50]; and that of New York, that the "aid, care and support of the needy are public concerns and shall be provided by the state . . . in such manner and by such means, as the legislature may from time to time determine."[51] However, no doubt because of a concern that mandatory welfare provisions in state constitutions could be interpreted to give the poor an endless claim to state fiscal resources, Montana amended its constitution by changing the imperative in its social welfare provision from *must* to *may,* and in other states courts have ruled that the state legislature has the prerogative to determine how best to meet a constitutional mandate for welfare.[52] For example, in the mid-1970s three plaintiffs younger than twenty-one challenged an amendment to the New York Social Service Law that barred financial aid to those younger than twenty-one who were not living with a legally responsible relative. The only way such young people could obtain assistance was to first bring a support proceeding against the legally responsible adult and obtain an order of support. New York's highest court held that the state constitution imposed an affirmative obligation on the state to aid the needy. Thus providing aid "is not a matter of legislative grace; rather, it is specifically mandated by our Constitution."[53] However, the court ruled that the legislature may determine the amount of aid. The effect of the constitutional provision is to prevent the legislature from simply refusing to aid those whom it has classified as needy, but in the absence of a legislative act, the needy have no basis for a public claim on welfare benefits.

STATUTORY LAW

Congress and the legislatures of each state make statutory law. The majority of social welfare programs are created because a legislative body passed a law to channel public funds to programs that assist people in need. Statutory and constitutional law are connected. The U.S. Constitution, as well as some state constitutions, require that similarly situated people be treated alike. Thus classification schemes that allocate benefits to specific groups, such as the elderly or children, are acceptable so long as they do not violate the constitutional prohibition against classifying people on the basis of race, national origin, or alienage. And, as I noted earlier, the statutory provisions that require a hearing before welfare benefits are terminated follows from the due process requirements in the U.S. Constitution and in those of the states. In addition, some state constitutions place an affirmative obligation on the state to assist people in need, and this obligation will invariably be expressed in an act of a legislative body.

The Legislative Process

Bills originate in the House or the Senate. Members of either chamber may introduce a bill of interest to them, one that has been proposed by the executive branch, or one that has been proposed by a special interest group that has lobbied for its introduction. When legislation is introduced, it is "read into" the *Congressional Record* of the House or the Senate. The *Record,* published each day that Congress is in session, is the first place that the text of a newly proposed bill appears. The *Record* often contains opinions about the bill that are expressed by members of Congress and that do not appear elsewhere.

Regardless of the chamber in which the bill is introduced, it follows a similar path. The bill is assigned to a committee, which may in turn assign the bill to a subcommittee. Committees have specific areas of jurisdiction, and bills are assigned accordingly. Thus bills introduced in the Senate that address social welfare matters are assigned to the Committee on Health, Education, Labor and Pensions, whereas those introduced in the House are assigned to a subcommittee of the House Ways and Means Committee. Committees calculate the cost of proposed legislation, and standing committees may "kill, alter or report unchanged" the bills that have been assigned to them.[54] Committee staff members are often subject-matter experts, able to fine-tune legislative proposals.

At times Congress wants guidance from experts on the subject of the proposed legislation and holds hearings. Experts in social welfare or other fields testify about the substance of the legislation under consideration. The testimony may result in a bill's modification, and it may affect the bill's chances of passage.

If a bill is voted out of committee, it becomes the subject of floor debate in the chamber in which it was first introduced. If supported by a majority of the members, the bill is submitted to the other chamber, where the deliberative procedure is repeated. If both House and Senate support a bill without change, Congress sends it to the president for signature.

If a bill is supported with modifications, a conference committee comprised of members of the House and the Senate is convened and charged with ironing out the differences between the versions. Assuming that the committee resolves the differences, both chambers will reconsider the revised bill; if both chambers approve it, it goes to the president. If the president signs it, the becomes law; if he vetoes, it becomes law only if a two-thirds majority in each chamber votes to override the veto.

At times, different versions of the same legislation are introduced simultaneously in the House and Senate. If this occurs, each considers the bill as described here; bills that win passage are reconciled to achieve a consensus bill.

THE EXECUTIVE BRANCH OF GOVERNMENT AS A SOURCE OF LAW

At both the federal and state levels the executive branch of government participates in lawmaking in three ways. The first, which I have already discussed, occurs when a bill of interest to the president or governor is introduced by a member of the executive's political party. In the second method the president or a governor engages directly in lawmaking by issuing executive orders. The third method involves the administrative agencies that are a part of the executive branch, such as the U.S. Department of Health and Human Services and the U.S. Department of Education, and similar agencies at the state level, all of which issue regulations or rules (the terms are synonymous and are referred to as administrative law) to guide those who are responsible for implementing legislation. Federal rules ensure that all the states carry out the intent of the legislature in a uniform manner. The executive branch of the federal government also may make law by entering into treaties with other nations, an option that is not available to governors.

Administrative law is of central importance to human service providers, because the rules that govern the day-to-day operation of social welfare programs, such as those that establish a client's eligibility for services and a social worker's responsibilities in serving a client, may be set forth in the regulations.

Administrative Law

Administrative law is a compilation of rules that govern the behavior of government officials in developing, implementing, and administering programs that are funded with public monies.

Although the Constitution reserves to Congress the authority to make laws, the Supreme Court has ruled that Congress does not give up its role as lawmaker when it delegates to the executive branch the authority to make rules that do no more than secure the result that Congress intended when it enacted a statute. A congressional delegation of authority to an agency of the executive to make rules will withstand constitutional scrutiny so long as it is possible "to ascertain whether the will of Congress had been obeyed."[55]

The extensive grant of authority to agencies of the executive branch is a necessity. First, members of Congress are not likely to have the time or the expertise needed to issue the specific and detailed rules required to guide state officials in implementing the law. Also, the regulatory process has the potential to be more flexible than the legislative process because it does not involve the extensive debate and deliberation that often take place before a bill is passed.

The Administrative Procedures Act

Administrative agencies are vested with some of the powers otherwise reserved to the legislative, executive, and judicial branches of government. When administrative agencies issue regulations, they make law, a task that the Constitution assigns to Congress; when the agencies investigate violations of the law, they are undertaking a task assigned to the executive; and when they, along with the judiciary, adjudicate disputes—when, for example, clients file an appeal claiming that the agency unfairly denied them benefits—the agencies are doing work that the Constitution assigns to the judiciary. For example, the Social Security Administration (SSA) operates the Supplemental Security Income (SSI) program, which provides cash benefits to eligible people with disabilities. The SSA makes law when it creates the list of conditions that define disability and establishes the rules for determining whether a client is eligible for benefits. The SSA has the power to investigate whether the states are applying its rules in a uniform manner. And the agency acts as judge and jury when its administrative law judges adjudicate a client's appeal of a denial of benefits.

Administrative agencies derive their authority primarily from the Administrative Procedures Act (APA) of 1946, which establishes a framework for an administrative agency to carry out its rule-making and adjudicatory functions.[56] Section 553 of the act describes the procedures that administrative agencies must follow when they make rules, defined as agency statements "designed to implement, interpret, or prescribe law or policy." Proposed rules must appear in the *Federal Register* (which is published five days a week) at least thirty days before the rule is to take effect. When the rule is finalized, it is published in the *Code of Federal Regulations,* which contains all administrative rules.

The notice that appears in the *Federal Register* identifies by name the statute that the rule is meant to implement and informs the public of any hearings to be held for gaining public comment.[57] The APA requires that the administrative agencies provide to interested parties the chance to "participate in the rule making through submission of written data, views, or arguments with or without opportunity for oral presentation."[58] Administrative agencies must consider public comment and include in the final rule a brief statement of the purpose of the rule and why, in light of the feedback provided, the rule took its final form. Some statutes require that rules be made "on the record," meaning that the agency must hold a full hearing that provides interested parties with the opportunity to present evidence and cross-examine witnesses.[59]

Executive Orders

Executive orders are directives that the president or governor issues for the purpose of making law. The *Federal Register* publishes the executive order, thereby providing the public with notice of the intention of the president to make law, but such orders must be published only when they are designated as executive orders or presidential proclamations,[60] are meant to have the force of law, and affect the general public.[61] After they are published in the *Federal Register,* executive orders appear in the *Code of Federal Regulations.*

Authority for the Use of Executive Orders

Presidents since George Washington have used the executive order to make law, although nowhere in the Constitution is the president granted lawmaking power.[62] Executives justify their actions by (1) referring to a statute in which Congress has empowered the president to act unilaterally in times of national emergency and (2) to "the powers vested [in the office of the president] by the Constitution and laws of the United States."[63]

Conditions for Use of Executive Orders

Doubtless, a president has any number of reasons to choose to make law by using an executive order rather than by proposing that Congress enact legislation. When a president wants a result that Congress is not likely to effect, such as desegregating the armed forces after World War II, an executive order will accomplish this end, as did the order issued by President Harry Truman in 1948. Also, like the regulations of an administrative agency, executive orders can be issued quickly because they bypass the lengthy committee and debate process in Congress. Thus after the attack on the World Trade Center in 2001, President George W. Bush quickly established the Homeland Security Agency by executive order as a means of dealing with domestic terrorism.

Ending Executive Orders

A president may repeal or modify an order that he has issued, or a subsequent president may repeal it. Some executive orders have an expiration date, and others expire when the conditions that caused their issuance have passed. An order may be overturned after judicial review, or Congress may enact a statute that has the effect of overturning an executive order. In 1952 the Supreme Court overturned an executive order issued by Truman. While the country was engaged in the Korean War, steelworkers threatened to strike. Basing his order on the perceived threat to the war effort that a strike would cause, Truman ordered the secretary of commerce to take control of and operate most steel mills in the United States. The Court overturned the president's order because the Constitution did not confer on him the power to take control of private property, despite the emergency.[64]

Treaties

Article 2, Section 2 of the Constitution allows the president, with the advice and consent of the Senate, to enter into treaties, which are agreements between two or more sovereign nations. Treaties are relevant to social workers because of the International Law of Human Rights (ILHR).

The ILHR was created after World War II in reaction to wartime atrocities. The origins of the treaty are linked to the creation of the United Nations in 1945. The U.N. Charter refers, in part, to the dedication of its member nations to uphold

> The right to self-determination of people . . . respect for human rights and fundamental freedoms, respect for the equal rights of all without distinction as to race, sex, language, or religion, and international cooperation in solving international problems of an economic, social, cultural, or humanitarian character.[65]

Three years later the U.N. General Assembly adopted the Universal Declaration of Human Rights. The Declaration, which is part of the larger ILHR, proclaims that all people have the right to pursue life, liberty, and property. As with the Fourteenth Amendment to the U.S. Constitution, these rights are conferred on people regardless of gender, race, color, national origin, or religion.[66] Also like the U.S. Constitution, the Declaration offers no protection for individuals on the basis of sexual orientation.

Enforceability of International Human Rights Law

The ILHR is a statement of basic principles supporting an individual's right to self-determination and respect based on our common humanity. However, the ILHR does not confer any specific rights—for example, it does not guarantee a right to freedom of speech or religion or due process of law.

Statements of principle are moral pronouncements. They make clear the position of the signatories on the issues that are covered, but they cannot be enforced under U.S. law without supporting legislation unless the document itself is "self-executing." To be self-executing, and therefore enforceable, the treaty must "without amplification or implementation . . . establish specific rights and obligations in individuals,"[67] and it must be clear that the parties who framed the treaty intended to set forth a rule that, standing alone, would be enforceable.[68]

Efforts by individuals to seek justice under the ILHR have failed. Thus a person of Japanese origin could not enforce his claim of ownership to land in California because the U.N. Charter was not self-executing,[69] nor, for the same reason, could Mexican children who were not legal residents of the United States claim a right to an education under a treaty between the United States and countries of South America (although the U.S. Supreme Court would later support the children's claim on equal protection grounds).[70]

THE JUDICIAL BRANCH AS A SOURCE OF LAW

Rulings issued by judges are a major source of law. Judicial rulings are set forth in case law, which refers to the aggregate of reported cases covering a particular subject, such as adoption, confidentiality, or employment discrimination. Case law is critical to practitioners who want to know how the courts have ruled on issues that affect their practice and matters that affect clients, such as a client's obligations to work under an income maintenance program. Let us begin by exploring the tools that judges have available to them to develop case law.

The Common Law

English common law was brought to the early colonies and was, to a significant extent, the only source of law in the states until the twentieth century, when statutory law began to replace the common-law approach to deciding cases.[71]

When judges use their common-law power to decide cases, they are engaging in lawmaking and policy making, tasks ordinarily undertaken by the legislative branch of government.[72] The rules that form the common law are derived from the aggregate of human wisdom, embodied over time in cases that form a "stable body of rules" for settling disputes and for guiding future behavior.[73] The accumulation of rules is what the term *precedent* refers to. Precedent is comprised of past decisions that guide, and to an extent restrain, a judge from engaging in freewheeling lawmaking while providing a great deal of latitude to interpret rules in light of current realities and individual beliefs. A legislative body may enact a statute that overturns a decision based on common law, but unless that occurs, the common law provides state judges with a significant amount of latitude to make law.[74]

For example, in 1974 the Supreme Court of California ruled that a therapist has a duty to warn a third party who has been threatened by a patient, thus creating an exception to the rules that govern confidentiality. To establish the rule the court referred to the common-law concept of "special relationship" and held that a special relationship existed between a therapist and a third party who was in danger; the court imposed on the therapist a duty to act to protect that third party.

At times the courts step in and apply the common law to develop public policy because the state legislature may be avoiding a controversial issue. This has occurred with the so-called right to die cases that pit the state's interest in preserving life against an individual's common-law right to refuse medical treatment.[75] New York's Court of Appeals, the state's highest court, held that a competent adult had the right to elect an appropriate course of treatment and that this right included the right to refuse treatment.[76]

The precedents that evolve through judicial rulings are critical in guiding judges and attorneys, and the uniform application of precedents is necessary to sustain public confidence that the law consists of a set of rules applied in a uniform manner. However, the dictum that judges "adhere to precedent," called *stare decisis,* is not an "inexorable command."[77] Judges do overturn established laws. For example, I referred earlier to the Supreme Court decision in *Brown v. Board of Education,* in which the High Court overruled its earlier decision sanctioning race-based discrimination. The Supreme Court's departure from precedent can be explained in different ways. Changing social conditions may cause a judge to conclude that a departure from precedent is called for—certainly this factored into the High Court's ruling in *Brown*—or judicial bias may cause a judge to conclude that the case that established the precedent was wrongly decided. This may influence a judge to support, narrow, or overrule the precedent-setting case. Judges are also influenced by a preference for one or another party or lawyer. Conversely, a judge may support a disfavored precedent because it has become an integral part of subsequent case law and because individuals have relied on a precedent to advance important ends in their lives. For example, some members of the Supreme Court think that *Roe v. Wade* was wrongly decided because the Constitution does not contain an explicit right to privacy, which is the foundation for the Court's ruling that a woman has the right to terminate a pregnancy.[78] While the Court has sanctioned laws that have narrowed the scope of *Roe,* it has not altered the basic law. Justice Sandra Day O'Connor explained the Court's unwillingness to overturn *Roe* when she wrote that the availability of abortion has influenced the ways in which people have organized their lives and has "affected the ability of women to participate equally in the economic and social life of the Nation. . . . The Constitution serves human values, and while the effect of reliance on *Roe* cannot be exactly measured, neither can the certain costs of overruling *Roe* for people who have ordered their thinking and living around that case be dismissed."[79]

JUDICIAL REVIEW

Judicial review refers to the power of the courts to review decisions made by other branches of government, to overturn those that violate the U.S. Constitution or the constitution of a state, or, in the case of administrative law, to rule that regulations are not supported by the statute that they seek to clarify. Judicial review is a powerful tool because it allows a court to substitute its judgment for that of elected officials. This was illustrated in the earlier discussion of those decisions that the Supreme Court rendered in the mid-1990s that went against almost sixty years of deference to congressional use of the commerce clause to enact legislation affecting the states. Courts use a variety of methods when they review decisions of other branches of government.

Constitutional Interpretation

Courts have the final say in constitutional interpretation. Whereas a legislative body can rewrite a statute to overrule a disfavored statutory interpretation, it cannot affect a court's interpretation of a constitution without undertaking the difficult and lengthy process of amending the constitution. Thus courts have the greatest degree of lawmaking power through constitutional interpretation.

Consider the following example. The U.S. Constitution does not expressly mention the concept of privacy. This right was first inferred as an aspect of "liberty" in the due process clause of the Fourteenth Amendment in 1965 when the Supreme Court overturned a Connecticut statute that banned the use of contraceptives.[80] The 1965 decision is significant in several respects. First, the Court overturned a law made by elected officials and substituted its judgment. The justices did not base this decision on a violation of an express constitutional provision, where, for example, a legislature passed a law limiting freedom of speech or religion, but on their understanding of what the concept of liberty means. The 1965 decision had far-reaching consequences because it set the stage for future decisions that rested on an expanded notion of privacy, including the Court's decision that overturned a Texas law that banned abortions (*Roe v. Wade*[81]) and by implication the law in any state that banned abortion; its decision supported a claim that an individual has a right to privacy in her or his medical records (*Whalen v. Roe*[82]).

Terms such as *liberty* and *equal protection* are not self-defining. The term *liberty* in the due process clause of the Fourteenth Amendment means more than freedom from confinement or physical restraint. Over time the Supreme Court has interpreted the fundamental right to liberty to include matters as diverse as (1) a parent's right to send a child to a private school[83]; (2) the right to marry, including the right to marry a person of another race[84]; and (3) the right to right to procreate, to use contraceptives to prevent procreation, and the right to terminate a pregnancy.[85]

Some legal scholars think that the role of the Court in constitutional or statutory interpretation should be limited to discerning the intent of the Framers and ratifiers of the Constitution. From this perspective the privacy cases were wrongly decided: If the Framers had intended the Constitution to include a protected right to privacy, they would have expressly included such a right.[86] Thus when judges interpret the Constitution, creating new rights and policies for the nation, they are crossing the line into the realm of legislative behavior, which the Constitution assigns to elected bodies. Another point of view holds that discerning the intention of the Framers is not possible, especially with respect to the more general constitutional phrases such as due process and equal protection. This point of view draws attention to the difficulty of identifying the intention of the individual Framers of the Constitution as well as the aggregate intention of all who ratified the Constitution.[87]

On the other hand, judges who take an expansive view of the language in the Constitution are more likely than others to view the law in functional terms, where the task is to ensure that the law achieves social justice.[88] Judges who apply this point of view are less likely than others to defer to the decisions of legislative bodies, and they are not overly concerned with the idea that policy is being made by officials who were not elected. A functional approach to constitutional interpretation was the dominant approach that the Supreme Court used when Earl Warren was chief justice. The "Warren Court" was responsible for major civil rights decisions, beginning with *Brown v. Board of Education* in 1954 and continuing with *Roe v. Wade* two decades later and into the mid-1980s. As I noted earlier in the discussion of the limitations that the High Court has placed on Congress's use of the commerce clause to affect state behavior, the composition and functional approach of the Court changed by the mid-1980s, and this change has affected decisions regarding federal and state relations.

Statutory Interpretation

When the language in a statute is precise and its meaning plain, unless it violates the U.S. Constitution or that of a state, courts are bound to adhere to the dictates of the legislative branch of government. But judges are advised "not to make a fortress out of the dictionary . . . [they] must remember that statutes always have some purpose or object to accomplish, whose sympathetic and imaginative discovery is the surest guide to their meaning."[89] When terms are vague or subject to differential meaning, courts must interpret the unclear terms if they are to provide guidance to those responsible for implementing the law and to lower courts whose decisions may reflect disagreement about the meaning of key terms. If the legislative branch does not support a judicial decision, it may, unless the issue involves constitutional interpretation, rewrite the interpreted legislation to reflect more clearly its intent.

Judith Kaye, the chief judge of New York's Court of Appeals, provides an example of statutory interpretation that reflects an effort to remain faithful to the intent of the legislature. In her discussion Kaye refers to a case in which her court had to interpret the phrase "currently dangerous" in a statute that addressed whether a person found not responsible for attempted murder by reason of a mental condition should remain confined in a secure mental health facility. The word *currently,* meaning "right now, at this moment," is clear, she wrote, but to apply the word strictly supports the illogical conclusion that a person who is restrained and surrounded by armed guards is not currently dangerous. Because this conclusion could not have been what the legislature intended, the court sought to give the term *currently* a meaning that would comport with common sense. The term could not permit an interpretation that *current* referred to the condition of a person who was confined and not dangerous for that reason. So literal an interpretation would have made it impossible to be faithful to the basic legislative goal of protecting the public from a potentially dangerous person.[90]

When judges undertake the task of interpreting statutes, they seek guidance from a variety of sources. First, rather than delving into the minds of legislators to discern their intent, a court may, as in the New York example, consider the purpose of the statute and give meaning to its unclear or contradictory terms to carry out that purpose. Next, courts must consider any specific rules of interpretation that a legislative body provides. For example, the Americans with Disabilities Act of 1990 (ADA) uses terms similar to those found in the Vocational Rehabilitation Act (VRA) of 1975. In passing the ADA, Congress expressly stated its intention that the body of case law developed under the VRA should guide the courts in interpreting the new law; doing so would provide disabled people with the same standard of protection that had been applied under the VRA.[91]

Legislative history, found in the reports issued by legislative committees and subcommittees, and the minutes of the floor debates that precede passage of a bill are two other sources of information for discerning legislative intent. Some jurists argue that legislative history has little value in discovering legislative intent because it is biased and "unauthoritative."[92] This is so, the argument goes, because the information that is contained in the documents that comprise the history of a specific piece of legislation may reflect the bias of a committee staff member or that of a lobbyist.[93]

Nevertheless, a search for legislative intent is necessary when statutory language is vague or, as in the New York example, the law as written could produce an illogical result. Floor debates may not be useful because they are not the forum in which words are fine-tuned; therefore, committee reports, limitations aside, may be a primary source to which judges turn.

Judges may also have to "choose among competing policies in order to fill the gaps" and therefore considerations of social welfare and public policy may enter into the decisions that they make.[94] In 1989 the New York Court of Appeals held that the term *family* in the noneviction provisions of the New York City rent control statute of 1946 include the deceased tenant's homosexual partner.[95] The legislation did not contain a definition of *family*, nor was there legislative history that addressed the issue of what *family* meant for purposes of the law, although it is reasonable to conclude that in 1946 the term referred to people with a legal relationship. The Court reasoned that the term *family*

> should not be rigidly restricted to those people who have [legally] formalized their relationship. . . . The intended protection against sudden eviction should not rest on fictitious legal distinctions or genetic history, but instead should find its foundation in the reality of family life. The . . . rent-control statute [seeks] . . . to protect occupants from the sudden loss of their homes

> and requires the result reached. In the context of eviction, a more realistic, and certainly equally valid, view of a family includes two adult lifetime partners whose relationship is long term and characterized by an emotional and financial commitment and interdependence.[96]

Standards of Review and Equal Protection

Many cases that come before the Supreme Court that address matters of concern to social workers involve the equal protection clause of the Fourteenth Amendment. The equal protection clause provides that the states shall not deny to any person the equal protection of the laws.[97] The offered protection is a safeguard against classification schemes that are invidious because they treat differently people who are in similar situations. However, the government frequently classifies us, for example, on the basis of age, income, physical ability, marital status, employment status, and the like; and government benefits, whether income support through a social welfare program or tax breaks through the Internal Revenue Code, are often available on the basis of one's membership in a category.

Because classification is key to the allocation of social welfare benefits, the question of concern is how the courts determine when a classification scheme violates the Constitution. Discussing this issue, Justice William J. Brennan said that the Court seeks to ensure that the classification at issue bears some fair relationship to a legitimate public purpose.[98] Those classifications that cause concern for the courts are those that disadvantage a suspect class or that interfere with the exercise of a fundamental right.

Certain classifications are suspect, Brennan wrote, because they "reflect deep-seated prejudice rather than legislative rationality in pursuit of some legitimate objective." Stated otherwise, classifications that are suspect "tend to be irrelevant to any proper legislative goal."[99] With reference to fundamental rights, the Court looks to see whether the Constitution explicitly or implicitly refers to the right. Explicit rights include freedom of speech and of religion and matters concerning due process. Implicit rights are those that the Court finds necessary to effectuate the purposes of the Constitution, such as the right to privacy that has been inferred from the liberty clause of the Fourteenth Amendment, and the right to travel, which I discussed earlier and is not expressly mentioned in the Constitution.

Thus we can say that the protection that the Constitution offers us is protection from discriminatory classifications that are made without good reason. To determine whether a state-applied system of classification is permissible, the courts analyze the system by using one of three standards of review: strict scrutiny, intermediate scrutiny, and rational basis.

Strict scrutiny applies to any law that classifies people on the basis of race, alienage, or national origin, as it does to laws that restrict our basic freedoms such as freedom of speech or freedom of religion. When a state passes a law that classifies people on the basis of a prohibited characteristic or one that limits a fundamental freedom, the state must show that the law serves a compelling state interest and is narrowly tailored to achieve that interest. Justifying a race-based classification system is virtually impossible, especially because putting an end to such systems was a driving force behind passage of the Fourteenth Amendment. However, the Supreme Court will sanction race-based classifications under limited circumstances, as it did when it sanctioned internment of Japanese people during World War II, accepting the government's argument that this was a necessary precaution against sabotage and espionage.[100] It did so again as a remedy after a finding of "pervasive, systematic, and obstinate discriminatory conduct" in employment practices.[101]

Race is the paradigmatic classification that triggers rigorous judicial review. In large measure this is because of the history of race-based discrimination in the United States but also because there is rarely a legitimate basis for categorizing people according to their race. In modern times the law has come to recognize other classifications as suspect that in earlier periods of history would not have been so judged. The notable classifications here are those based on gender and a newborn's status as "legitimate." When a law classifies people for one of these reasons, the standard of review is intermediate (sometimes called heightened scrutiny) where the state must show that the classification is substantially related to an important government interest, a much lower threshold than is imposed by strict scrutiny. The Supreme Court has. struggled with classifications based on gender and is most likely to find unconstitutional a statute that rests on stereotypes of women. Thus the Court found that the Social Security Administration discriminated against women by assigning their survivors' benefits, which are based on earnings, only to their children and not to their widowers, whereas survivors' benefits based on a man's earnings were available to both a child and a widow. The Court found that this practice violated equal protection because the benefit-distribution system rested on the assumption that men are more likely than women to be the primary supporters of their spouses and children. This reasoning could not justify "the denigration of the efforts of women who do work and whose earnings contribute significantly to their families' support," the High Court found.[102] On the other hand, the Supreme Court would not disturb a California law that punished men, but not women, for the crime of statutory rape. The Court reasoned that the gender-based classification scheme was acceptable because the state had a significant interest in reducing the number of out-of-wedlock teenage pregnancies and because the sexes are not similarly situated in all circumstances.[103]

A state law that does not involve classifying people on impermissible grounds and that does not infringe on a fundamental freedom will survive judicial review if the law is rationally related to achieving a legitimate government interest. This standard of review is highly deferential to state government. Those who attack the rationality of a legislative classification have the burden "'to negative [*sic*] every conceivable basis which might support it.'"[104] Thus in striking down provisions in the Age Discrimination in Employment Act, the Supreme Court opined that unlike "race [which] would not pass muster as a basis for classification and gender rarely so," classifications that are based on age "cannot be characterized as so seldom relevant to the achievement of any legitimate state interest that laws grounded in such considerations are deemed to reflect prejudice and antipathy."[105] States are free, the Court ruled, to engage in age discrimination that is rationally related to a legitimate state interest, because age can be a proxy for other characteristics, such as productivity.

SUMMARY

The U.S. Constitution protects our most basic rights, including freedom of speech and religion, and it guarantees due process of law. State constitutions contain similar protections; whether at the federal or state level, constitutions describe the division of responsibility among the legislative, executive, and judicial branches of government.

For social workers an important aspect of constitutional law lies in the relationship of the U.S. Constitution, state constitutions, and social welfare. The Supreme Court has sanctioned the use of federal funds for social welfare purposes when the problems to be resolved are national in scope and when Congress conditions the receipt of federal funds upon compliance, by the recipient, with federal rules. Moreover, if a statute provides welfare benefits, its eligibility rules cannot violate constitutional protections and must be applied in a uniform manner. Finally, the Constitution provides certain due process safeguards, such as the right to a hearing before benefits can be terminated, but the Constitution does not, in and of itself, provide any individual right to welfare. State constitutions are different in that they may contain provisions that obligate the state to provide for the social welfare of its citizens.

Most social welfare programs come into being after a legislative body has enacted a statute authorizing the program and providing money for its operation. A majority of welfare programs are funded jointly by the federal government and the states. The federal government often uses a carrot-and-stick arrangement whereby it offers to pay part of the cost of providing benefits or services in exchange for the state's conformity to federal regulations issued by such agencies in the executive branch of government as the Department of Health and Human Services.

Regulations are a main source of law. The rules are established to govern the behavior of government officials in developing, implementing, and administering programs funded with public monies. The rules also govern the behavior of social workers, whose responsibilities in serving clients are often set forth in regulations that provide a framework for determining whether a client is eligible for benefits. The process of issuing regulations is spelled out in the Administrative Procedures Act (APA), which requires that proposed rules appear in the *Federal Register* before the rule takes effect. The APA requires that interested parties be allowed to submit written comments about the proposed rules, and the agency that proposed the rule must review the comments. Final rules are published in the *Code of Federal Regulations.*

Executive orders are directives issued by the president or a state governor. Executive orders, or presidential proclamations, as they are sometimes called, are published in the *Register.* Finally, the executive may enter into treaties, which are agreements between two or more sovereign nations. Treaties that involve human rights, such as the United Nations Declaration of Human Rights, are important statements of principle, but the rights to which they refer rarely create enforceable claims.

Judicial rulings embodied in case law are critical to social workers who want to know how the courts have ruled on issues that affect their practice. State judges affect social work practice when, using their common-law authority, they interpret cases in light of current social conditions and issue rulings that govern the day-to-day practice of social workers. For example, in some states a social worker must warn someone against whom a client has made a threat, and this obligation is rooted in common law.

Judges may review decisions that are made by other branches of government. They may overturn those that violate the U.S. Constitution or that of a state, or, in the case of administrative law, a court may rule that regulations are not supported by the statute that they seek to clarify.

Courts interpret constitutional and statutory law when they are asked to determine the meaning of the words and phrases that legislators have used or when they are asked to find that the law violates the constitutional rights of an individual or a group. Interpretation is critical insofar as terms such as *liberty* and *equal protection* are not self-defining, and their meaning may change over time in relation to changing social conditions.

When reviewing cases, the courts use different standards depending upon the issue before them. When the law classifies people on the basis of race, national origin, or alienage, or seeks to limit a basic freedom such as freedom of speech or the right to due process, the court will closely scrutinize the law to ensure that the state has a compelling interest in the classification scheme or limitation and that the chosen scheme is narrowly tailored to serve the state's interest.

Some classification schemes, for example, those based on gender and on a child's status as "legitimate" or "illegitimate," are scrutinized using a lower standard of review, because the state may have a proper reason for the classification. For this standard of review, called intermediate review, the state must show that the classification is substantially related to an important government interest. The courts are most likely to find gender-based classifications unconstitutional if the scheme rests on stereotypes of women. When a state law does not involve classifying people on impermissible grounds and does not infringe on a fundamental freedom, it will survive judicial review if it is rationally related to achieving a legitimate government interest. This standard of review is highly deferential to state government, and those who attack the rationality of a legislative classification have the burden "to negative [*sic*] every conceivable basis which might support it."

3

The Justice System and an Introduction to Criminal and Civil Law

MANY OF YOU will have contact with the justice system in the course of your practice. You may be employed by the courts, law enforcement agencies, or law firms, or you may be hired to consult with any of these entities. Whether as an employee or consultant, you may conduct interviews, prepare reports, and interpret social science information for use in court. In addition, you may testify in court as an expert witness, and if you engage in direct practice, you may be subpoenaed to testify about one of your cases, or you may find yourself enmeshed in litigation initiated by a dissatisfied client.

To participate effectively in any of these ways, you should have a basic understanding of (1) how the federal and state court systems are organized, including matters of jurisdiction and the precedent-setting and binding nature of court decisions; (2) the difference between civil and criminal law and the role of the federal government and that of the states; (3) how cases get to court, including constitutional and statutory protections that come into play when a person is charged with a crime or becomes involved in the civil court system; and (4) how civil and criminal proceedings unfold. These matters will be addressed in the following pages. Greater detail to the role of social workers in the court system will be the subject of Chapter 6 and aspects of criminal and civil law are revisited throughout the text.

Before starting, I want to make one point. In many states the organization of social services is local, meaning that one may be employed by a county, city, or town; thus lawsuits may refer to a local unit of government rather than to the state. For the sake of simplicity, I use *state* to embrace units of government other than the federal government when both federal and state are implicated, and *federal* when the discussion is limited to the national government.

THE FEDERAL AND STATE COURT SYSTEMS

Constitutions describe the organization of courts. Article 3 of the U.S. Constitution calls for one Supreme Court and such other courts as Congress deems necessary. The federal system is uniform across the country, whereas each state has its own court system whose organization is described in the state's constitution.

The basic organization of the federal and state court systems is the same (see table 3.1); the exception is that the federal system does not have local courts. As a rule both federal and state levels have trial courts that are courts of general subject-matter jurisdiction, meaning that they are authorized to hear any type of criminal or civil case. Losses in trial court may be appealed to an intermediate appellate court and, in certain circumstances, to the state's highest court or to the U.S. Supreme Court.

Local courts, such as juvenile or family court, and specialized courts, such as drug courts or mental health courts, have limited subject-matter jurisdiction, meaning that they hear specific types of cases, such as those involving neglect

TABLE 3.1 Hierarchy of Federal and State Courts

FEDERAL COURTS	STATE COURTS
U.S. Supreme Court	**State Supreme Court**
Court of final jurisdiction on questions of federal law	Court of final jurisdiction on questions of state law
Intermediate Appellate Courts	**Intermediate Appellate Courts**
Eleven circuits and Court of Appeals for the District of Columbia hear appeals from federal district courts	Hear appeals from state trial courts
General Trial Court	**General Trial Court**
Denominated federal district court with general jurisdiction over federal matters	Denominated district or superior courts with general jurisdiction over state matters
	Local Courts
	Juvenile, family, or domestic relations court; probate and small claims courts

and abuse of children (juvenile or family courts), or cases where a defendant requires treatment for substance abuse or mental health problems to reduce the likelihood of recidivism. Losses at the local court may be appealed to a state-level appellate court.

Cases rarely cross the boundary between the state and federal systems, although they may do so when the matter at hand concerns a federal question, meaning that the issue involves a possible violation of the U.S. Constitution, an act of Congress, or a treaty.

Jurisdiction

Jurisdiction has two aspects. The first concerns subject-matter jurisdiction and asks which court is empowered to hear the type of case that I am bringing.[1] The second aspect is personal jurisdiction, which asks whether a particular court has the authority to order a person to appear before it. Generally, a court has personal jurisdiction over people living in the state in which the court is located, and in some circumstances a court has the authority to hold accountable people who do not reside in the state but who do business there.

State constitutions and or statutes describe the subject-matter jurisdiction of courts. For example, New York's Family Court has subject-matter jurisdiction over all matters concerning the care and custody of children, including allegations that a child has committed a crime or that she or he is a status offender or the victim of abuse or neglect. Foster care proceedings are initiated in Family Court, which retains jurisdiction to review periodically the cases of children in care. And the Supreme Court of New York, which has subject-matter jurisdiction over divorce, may refer a family to Family Court to resolve a dispute about child custody or visitation.

In civil matters personal jurisdiction is generally obtained by serving a summons and complaint, also called a petition, on the person involved. In criminal matters an arrest warrant may be the first notice to a person that she or he is being charged with a crime.

There is a preference for serving people in person, although service may be effected in other ways, for instance, by serving a person's attorney, through newspaper publication when a person's whereabouts are not known, or by mailing the summons and complaint to the concerned party. The summons informs the person on whom it is served that she or he must appear in court and includes the time, date, and place of appearance, as well as why the action was brought. The listed reasons are referred to as the cause(s) of action. A cause of action may be an allegation that the complaining party suffered a physical injury when struck by an automobile allegedly driven by the person served, or it may contain an allegation that a professional was negligent when providing treatment. The injury would be identified, as would the remedy sought, for example, monetary compensation for injuries suffered. People charged with a crime will be informed of the specific charges at a preliminary hearing.

The Binding Effect of Court Decisions

Whether a court's rulings are binding, meaning that they must be followed by other courts, depends upon (1) the court's location in the judicial hierarchy, (2) the geographical jurisdiction of the court, and (3) whether the issue can be resolved under federal or state law. As a general rule, decisions made by the U.S. Supreme Court are binding on the nation as a whole, and the decisions made by the highest court of any state are binding on the state as a whole.

To understand the binding nature of appellate decisions, it is important to consider geography. The federal level has eleven circuit courts and a circuit court for the District of Columbia. Each circuit has jurisdiction over appeals from specific states, with the reach of the Court of Appeals for the District of Columbia limited to that jurisdiction. For example, the decisions of the U.S. Court of Appeals for the First Circuit are binding on federal courts in Massachusetts, Maine, New Hampshire, Rhode Island, and Puerto Rico. Those of the Fourth Circuit are binding on Virginia, Maryland, West Virginia, and North and South Carolina.[2] To illustrate the issue of geography and the binding nature of state court decisions, consider New York. For purposes of the judiciary the state is divided into four departments, each of which has its own appellate division. Each appellate division has jurisdiction over specific counties, and rulings bind only the courts within the counties that make up each department. An important effect of geography on the binding nature of court decisions is that rulings may differ both within a state and across the states. When disagreement exists, the likelihood is increased that the U.S. Supreme Court or the highest court within a state will hear a case on appeal to resolve the disagreements among lower courts. For example, before 1998 federal courts disagreed about whether a person who was infected with human immunodeficiency virus (HIV)—but had never developed symptoms associated with acquired immune deficiency syndrome (AIDS)—was disabled for purposes of the Americans with Disabilities Act (chapters 9 and 14). Because this question was an important one and because lower federal courts disagreed, the U.S. Supreme Court accepted for review a case that raised this issue. The justices answered the question in the affirmative, resolving this point.[3]

To understand whether a state or federal court should hear a particular case, recall the discussion in chapter 2 about constitutional law. There I said that a state court can confer greater rights on its own citizens than the U.S. Supreme

Court has conferred on the nation as a whole. For example, in 1976 the U.S. Supreme Court ruled that the Constitution's guarantee of free speech did not confer on striking workers a protected right to demonstrate in a shopping mall that was private property, thus limiting the reach of First Amendment protections to public spaces.[4] In the early 1990s a similar case came before the New Jersey Supreme Court when a group of citizens asked it to find that the New Jersey Constitution provided greater protection to speech in shopping malls than the U.S. Constitution does.[5] The court agreed, thus creating greater free-speech rights for citizens of New Jersey than citizens have in other states whose courts have not ruled on this issue under their own constitutions.

Specialized Courts

Individuals who appear before criminal and civil courts can be described with reference to the charges brought against them, such as assault, robbery, or negligence, or with reference to the special social problems that are presumed to be causal to the charges, such as substance abuse problems and mental health problems. Whether due to an increase in the number of people who appear to have such special problems, an increased awareness of these problems, or the limits of traditional judicial procedures to effect a change in the lives of those involved, specialized courts have evolved that go by various names, including (a) mental health courts, (b) drug courts, (c) family treatment courts, (d) domestic violence courts, and (e) specialized juvenile courts that focus on a juvenile's use of guns or drugs. Mental health courts provide a good illustration of the unique aspects of special courts.

The U.S. Department of Justice operates a program through which federal funds are made available to develop and implement mental health courts to serve nonviolent offenders and those who are charged with misdemeanors.[6] State and local units of government and native American tribal governments may apply for grants. Specialized courts combine the authority of the court with the provision of services such as mental health counseling. The goal of specialized courts is to reduce the high rates of recidivism that are associated with the special problems that these courts seek to treat. Defendants who appear before specialized courts are offered a reduced charge or a dismissal of charges in exchange for their willingness to participate in a treatment program and to submit to continued court supervision.[7]

Working cooperatively, judges, attorneys, probation officers, social workers, and other professionals coordinate service delivery. Services may include (a) comprehensive intake assessments, (b) mental health treatment, (c) life skills training, (d) assistance in obtaining housing, (e) educational opportunities such as vocational rehabilitation and job placement services, (f) health care, (g) case management to coordinate the work of the court with that of service providers, and (h) judicial supervision of the defendant's progress in treatment.[8]

CIVIL AND CRIMINAL LAW

Nations have criminal laws, civil laws, and procedural rules that must be followed, whether by the state in pursuit of the public interest or by private parties in pursuit of their rights. A nation's substantive law is its basic law of rights and duties. Substantive criminal law identifies behaviors that society views as antisocial to a degree that subjects the person who engages in the prohibited behavior to punishment, and the law prescribes the range of punishments associated with different crimes, including the possibility of incarceration. Substantive civil law identifies those behaviors that affect private rights and interests as well as remedies that are available to compensate injured parties. Examples include laws that provide remedies for violations of a person's civil rights, professional malpractice, or neglect or abuse of children. Violations of civil law are called torts, which are losses or harms sustained by the acts of another that do not reach the level of harm necessary to constitute criminal acts.

Procedural law includes constitutional protections that come into play when government acts threaten to deprive us of life, liberty, or property. It also includes statutory rules, such as those that govern how a summons and complaint are served. When government action could result in the loss of life, liberty, or property, the due process clauses of the Fifth and Fourteenth Amendments require that the affected person receive notice of the action taken and have the opportunity to respond to the charges.

The process for civil proceedings is less rigorous, in part because the consequences are viewed as less serious than those of a criminal proceeding. For example, the U.S. Supreme Court suggested that welfare recipients have a "property" interest in their cash benefits that cannot be terminated without a hearing (see chapter 2). A beneficiary has a right to present evidence, to confront and cross-examine witnesses, and to appear with or without counsel.[9] However, unlike criminal procedures, where counsel must be appointed to represent indigent defendants, there is no right to appointed counsel at a hearing concerned with benefits termination. And when a civil proceeding results in confinement, for mental illness, for example, the state has an obligation to provide some treatment to compensate for the loss of liberty (see chapter 14). Before we move on, you should know that criminal and civil litigation can be brought at roughly the same time. For example, a victim of a criminal assault may sue the assailant for monetary damages. Because the burden of proof in a civil case is less than in a criminal matter, the state may lose the criminal court case because of insufficient evidence, but the victim may prevail in civil court.

Federal and State Laws

Both federal and state laws address criminal and civil matters. In criminal matters the jurisdiction of the federal government extends to acts that are committed (a) on federal land, which includes military bases, post offices, and national parks; (b) in the District of Columbia and the U.S. territories; and (c) by U.S. citizens on foreign soil.[10] When crimes are committed within the states, the federal government may assert jurisdiction where (d) the harm is to the federal government, for example, crimes that involve treason or espionage; (e) affect interstate commerce; or (f) involve narcotics or gambling [11]; (g) flight across state borders, or (h) use of the U.S. mail to facilitate a criminal act.

States may criminalize whatever conduct they choose, so long as they do not legislate in an area that the U.S. Constitution has reserved to the federal government, such as the regulation of interstate commerce; state law may not conflict with federal law. For example, in 1992 Congress enacted the Child Support Recovery Act (CSRA), which provides that a failure to make court-ordered child support payments is a federal crime when the parent and child live in different states and the parent owes more than $5,000 or where a lesser amount has remained unpaid for more than a year.[12] When it enacted the CSRA, Congress criminalized behavior that in some states had been subject only to civil penalties, and states had to amend their statutes to conform to federal law. In addition to illustrating how states may be required to modify their laws, the CSRA is an example of how both state and federal courts may have jurisdiction over the same matter. State law would cover failure to pay child support by a parent living in the same state as the child, whereas federal law covers the same behavior when the parent and child live in different states. Finally, state laws cannot undermine rights that are guaranteed by the U.S. Constitution, such as the right to free speech, due process, and equal protection.

THE ROAD TO COURT: CONSTITUTIONAL AND STATUTORY LAW

Criminal and civil cases proceed to court in both similar and different ways. I will begin this discussion by focusing on investigations to determine whether to proceed to court. Our interest is limited to investigative devices that implicate a constitutional or statutory right of the suspect, for example, those investigatory acts that require a search warrant. Then I will review procedures that are used to prosecute a criminal or civil matter. Note that some aspects of criminal and civil investigations do not raise questions about an individual's constitutional rights. For example, officials are free to study information gathered at a crime scene and to review laboratory reports describing such evidence, although they must take care not to contaminate evidence if they wish to preserve it for use in court. In addition, whether the matter is civil or criminal, investigators are free to interview those who wish to volunteer information, and attorneys engaged in civil litigation compile information from public records. Note also that a case may proceed to court without an investigation, for example, when a police officer issues a summons to a person for a traffic violation or for committing a public offense such as loitering or vagrancy. The summons will specify the date, time, and place for a court appearance or procedures for entering a guilty plea and paying a fine through the mail.

Custodial Interviews—Criminal Law

The police may interview people without advising them of their Sixth Amendment right to counsel or Fifth Amendment right to remain silent so long as the interviewee is free to leave at any time. Once the interview becomes custodial, the police must inform the individual of these rights by providing a Miranda warning. The police must caution the interviewee of the right to remain silent, that anything said can be used in court against the speaker, and that the interviewee has the right to have an attorney present, including the right to a court-appointed attorney if private counsel is not affordable.[13]

Determining when an interview has crossed the boundary from noncustodial to custodial is not always easy. An interview may become custodial (1) when the police intend that it be so because they have probable cause to arrest the interviewee; (2) because the police believe that the interviewee committed the crime and the purpose of the interrogation is to gather information to support that belief; or (3) when the person interviewed believes that he or she is in custody and cannot leave.[14] When any of these factors comes into play, the police are required to "Mirandize" their suspect in order to safeguard that person's constitutional rights and because being interviewed by the police is frightening and "inherently coercive," possibly leading to a coerced admission of guilt.

An individual may exercise the right to remain silent or to consult with an attorney at any time during an interrogation; if the interviewee asks for an attorney or refuses to speak, the questioning must stop.[15] However, the person being interviewed may "knowingly and intelligently" waive his or her rights and talk to the police. However, if the case goes to trial and the defendant argues that he did not waive his rights, the prosecution will have to demonstrate that the police gave the Miranda warning and the suspect waived his rights; otherwise, evidence gathered during the interview will not be admissible for use against the defendant.

Custodial Interviews—Civil Law

Social workers conduct interviews as a normative part of practice, although a worker is not likely to refer to an interview as an interrogation. Several courts have addressed the question of whether social workers who conduct child abuse investigations have to give a Miranda warning to the person interviewed. This question has not been conclusively decided, but the answer in general is no if (1) the worker is conducting an interview in the family home or her office; (2) she or he is acting as an agent of a state department of social services rather than an agent of the police to gather evidence to aid a criminal investigation; and (3) when interviewing a parent and the parent is able to leave the interview situation at any time. A social worker may have an obligation to give a Miranda warning when interviewing a parent who is in police custody or when the purpose of the interview is to gather evidence for criminal prosecution.[16]

The latter issue is one of concern because social workers are cooperating with police with increasing frequency in investigations of family violence, including child abuse, and workers may be acting as an "extension" of the police, not simply as providers of social services. Moreover, many investigative functions performed by the police in criminal matters are performed by social workers when they investigate reports of child abuse. This has caused some legal scholars to argue that the investigative actions of social workers are comparable to those of the police and should be similarly viewed when questions of Fourth Amendment rights arise.[17] The dissenting opinions in a 1997 ruling of the New Jersey Supreme Court highlight this issue and may be a harbinger of the way in which courts will view a social worker's responsibility to inform clients of their rights. The question before the court was whether incriminating statements made to a social worker during an investigation into a report of child abuse were admissible in a criminal trial, because the defendant had not received a Miranda warning. Two lower courts had ruled that the statement was inadmissible. In a split opinion the New Jersey Supreme Court overturned the lower courts, finding that a Miranda warning was not called for because social workers should not be constrained in their efforts to protect children. Two justices dissented, arguing that the social worker was "a dual agent" for the Department of Children and Family Services and the prosecutor's office. The dissent expressed the view that the social worker's concern went beyond the child's welfare to a wish to obtain statements from the defendant that would be admissible in court.[18]

Right to Counsel—Criminal Investigation

A Miranda warning includes a caution that a person has a Sixth Amendment right to counsel. But this right applies only when a person is charged with a crime that might result in a deprivation of liberty.[19] The individual who is charged with a minor offense—one that is punishable by no more than a fine—does not have a constitutionally protected right to counsel. If there is a right, it "attaches" at the initiation of adversarial judicial proceedings "whether by way of formal charge, preliminary hearing, indictment, information, or arraignment."[20] When indigent people are charged with a crime that is likely to result in incarceration, they are entitled to representation by an court-appointed attorney.

Right to Counsel—Civil Investigation

The right to counsel in a criminal matter is straightforward because it is derived from the Constitution, and it applies when the penalty upon conviction could be incarceration. If the result of a civil proceeding is a loss of liberty, for example, when an adult is committed to a mental institution or a juvenile to a detention facility, the right to counsel applies, although minors whose parents commit them for inpatient psychiatric care have no such right.[21]

Whether a defendant has a right to counsel in other civil proceedings depends upon several factors, including whether a statute confers such a right and, if so, what conditions are imposed on the exercise of this right. The right to counsel also depends upon the discretion of the court. For example, a federal statute provides that a judge may appoint an attorney to represent a person in a civil rights action[22] if "exceptional circumstances" exist.[23] Exceptional circumstances take into account the complexity of the case, whether the complaining party is able to conduct an investigation and present a case in court without the assistance of counsel, and the likelihood that the complaining party will prevail without the assistance of counsel, a judgment made in light of the availability of counsel to the opposing party.

Search and Seizure—Criminal Law

The Fourth Amendment of the Constitution prohibits government agents from acting unreasonably by (1) searching our property or our person without a warrant; (2) seizing our property without a warrant; and (3) arresting us without a warrant, although exceptions apply when matters of national security are at issue.[24] A judicial officer may issue a warrant when the request is supported by probable cause[25], which means that it is likely that evidence of a crime is in a particular place[26], or when police have current knowledge of facts and circumstances that an "offense has been or is being committed by the person arrested."[27]

Reasonableness is the key to understanding whether the action of a government agent will survive judicial scrutiny. A search is not reasonable if the person searched had a subjective expectation of privacy that was objectively reasonable, meaning that the expectation of privacy is one that society recognizes as reasonable.[28] Thus a judge excluded from evidence drugs that a border patrol agent found when he "squeezed" an opaque bag that a bus passenger had placed in an overhead rack. The passenger would have expected a bus employee or another passenger to handle his luggage, but he had an expectation of privacy, evidenced by the opaque bag, which he placed directly over his seat, that was violated when a law enforcement officer handled his bag in an exploratory manner.[29] Vague suspicions, for example, that drug addicts are prone to stealing things, will not suffice to justify an officer's search of a patient's medical records at a substance abuse clinic.[30] However, a judge found that a resident had no reasonable expectation of privacy and that a warrantless search was permissible because the interior of the home was open to public view through uncovered windows and a police officer observed what he thought to be illegal gambling.[31] Another defendant, who conducted illegal drug activity in a shed behind his house, did not have a reasonable expectation of privacy when he used the shed to conduct a legitimate business.[32] When evidence is seized without a warrant, the remedy for the improper seizure is to exclude the evidence at trial.[33]

A seizure of our person occurs when, considering all the circumstances, we reasonably believe that we are not free to leave an encounter with a government official. A seizure of our property occurs when a government intrusion interferes with our freedom to make use of our property.[34] A person who is arrested will be processed at a police station. Processing, commonly called booking, generally involves photographing and fingerprinting the arrested person, who may then be released with a summons to appear on a certain date and at a certain time or face incarceration.

Search and Seizure—Civil Law

The Fourth Amendment protection against unreasonable search and seizure applies to civil as well as criminal searches. However, in the civil arena the U.S. Supreme Court has carved out situations where special needs sanction warrantless searches. Warrantless searches have been sustained when (1) school officials, seeking to maintain order, searched a student's purse for cigarettes[35]; (2) a government official who supervised and controlled the workplace searched the office of an employee who was accused of sexual harassment[36]; (3) school officials, to reduce drug use by students who participate in competitive extracurricular activities, required such students to submit to drug testing[37];

and (4) when management sought to increase railroad safety by requiring drug and alcohol testing of railroad employees.[38] In addition, an arrest warrant is not required when the police believe that a suspect is mentally ill and a danger to himself or others, thus requiring inpatient hospital care.[39] However, the special needs exception does not apply when the search is conducted to gather information for use in a criminal prosecution. For this reason the High Court has ruled that a hospital's actions in conducting urine tests on pregnant women and then reporting the results to the police amounted to an unconstitutional search, even if the ultimate goal was to get the women off drugs and into treatment and to protect their fetuses.[40]

Several courts have considered whether social workers have to obtain a search warrant when they are conducting an investigation pursuant to a report of child abuse or neglect. The question has arisen when social workers conducted visual inspections of a child's body to look for signs of maltreatment or entered a family home without permission. Four U.S. Courts of Appeals for for circuits have addressed this matter, and all have ruled that such searches qualify for Fourth Amendment protection.

The U.S. Court of Appeals for the Seventh Circuit found such circumstances and ruled that visual inspections of unclothed children conducted by social workers would survive constitutional scrutiny because the objective was to protect children. However, the court cautioned social services officials not to assume that the exigent circumstances that justify such a search are present simply because they have a report of suspected child abuse. It might be necessary, the court said, for a department of social services to establish criteria for intrusive searches, for example, by requiring that workers verify reports made by anonymous callers or when the report was suspect for other reasons.[41] And, the appellate court for the Fifth Circuit, after discussing the necessity for warrants or exigent circumstances, found that because the parents had sanctioned the social worker's entry into the home, no Fourth Amendment violation existed.

Appellate courts for both the Third and Ninth Circuits considered whether a report made to child protective services constituted a reason to assume the existence of exigent circumstances; both courts concluded that the social workers had overstepped their bounds. In one case the federal appellate court rejected the argument that officials could make a warrantless entry to the home of a child abuse suspect based on a single anonymous report made twenty hours before an investigation began, where the only allegation was that someone had seen a seven-year-old on one occasion with bruises of unspecified severity.[42] In another case the appellate justices refused to sanction as exigent circumstances a search that commenced after an anonymous telephone tip.[43]

However, the lower standard of suspicion that applies to the conduct of a social worker who is concerned with a child's safety does not justify a police officer's body search of a child. Police know that probable cause is required for a search warrant, and an officer's actions often seek to advance a criminal investigation, not to advance mainly child safety considerations.[44]

The Decision to Prosecute—Criminal Prosecutions

Prosecutors have broad discretion to initiate and conduct criminal prosecutions and to seek an indictment from a grand jury so long as their actions are not selective (based on race, religion, or some other characteristic) or vindictive (based on a wish to punish a person for exercising a constitutional or statutory right).[45]

The Decision to Prosecute—Civil Actions

Unlike criminal prosecutions, which are brought only by law enforcement officials, civil actions may be brought by a unit of government, for example, when the U.S. Department of Justice files a civil rights suit alleging discrimination against an individual or group, or by private parties. Civil actions brought by private parties are diverse and include (1) negligence claims that arise from injuries sustained by a person who slipped on an icy sidewalk; (2) malpractice claims brought by a person who thinks that she was harmed by her physician or therapist; (3) suits that parents fighting about child custody bring against each other; and (4) suits filed by groups of prisoners or the mentally ill against a unit of government that they charge has violated their Eighth Amendment right to be free of cruel and unusual punishment.

Social workers are involved in decisions that result in loss of liberty through commitment of the mentally ill, and those who practice in a child welfare setting often must decide whether to bring a case to court when child abuse or neglect is believed to be a factor. State law or agency policy may require that a petition be filed with the family or juvenile court when certain factors are present, for example, whenever evidence of severe physical or sexual abuse exists. Absent guidance from statute or policy, social workers and their supervisors determine whether to file a court petition. If parents will not accept services voluntarily, social workers believe that parents who agree to work cooperatively will not do so, or clients withdraw from services and doing so creates risk for a child, social workers may decide to petition the court.

Criminal Indictments

Federal law authorizes the U.S. attorney to initiate a prosecution by filing a complaint, requesting an indictment from a grand jury, or by filing an "information." When the offense is capital, or an otherwise "infamous crime," the Fifth Amendment requires that the prosecution be initiated by "a presentment or indictment of a Grand Jury."[46] An indictment is a formal written accusation that a grand jury issues, referred to as a true bill. Infamous crimes are defined by their punishment, not by the act committed, and any crime that may be punished by more than one year in prison is an infamous crime.[47]

An information is an accusation of criminal behavior that differs from an indictment only in that it is presented by a public official instead of a grand jury. An information may be used when the defendant has waived an indictment or when the punishment for the crime is less than one year in prison.[48]

Gathering Evidence Before Trial—Criminal Matters

In a criminal proceeding the evidence that the state will use at trial is gathered mainly during the investigation. This information will be used to support requests for warrants and to obtain an indictment. The defense does not have a right to obtain statements from government witnesses before trial, and its ability to discover information in the control of the prosecution is often limited to what is disclosed at an arraignment or probable cause hearing.[49] However, certain information is subject to discovery. The U.S. Supreme Court has ruled that the prosecution violates due process if it withholds evidence that is favorable to the accused when the withheld evidence is material to establishing guilt or to deciding punishment.[50] The Court also has ruled that a federal prosecutor has a duty to volunteer exculpatory information to the defense, even if the defense has not requested the information.[51] Evidence is material if the outcome of a proceeding would have been different had the information been disclosed.[52]

Gathering Evidence Before Trial—Civil Matters

Lawyers preparing to file a civil suit are limited in their ability to gather information during an investigation. Lacking the authority to issue warrants, to subtly coerce those with information to speak with them, or to compel the disclosure of documents, civil attorneys rely on information in the public record, such as reports to a legislative body that describe the operations of a state social services agency, and on the goodwill of individuals to speak with them and to provide information in their possession. Once a suit is filed, the attorney prosecuting a civil matter is likely to petition the court for orders to compel discovery, which is a process that allows each party to obtain information that the other party has, to aid in preparing for trial. Plaintiffs in a civil case are entitled to discover almost any information that they wish to pursue if it seems likely that the search will lead to uncovering evidence admissible in court.[53] Your case records and notes, e-mail communications, and the hard drive from your computer are subject to discovery.[54] Likewise, the defendants in a civil matter will be able to review certain information compiled by opposing counsel in an effort to discern the strengths and weaknesses of the case and to prepare their response to the charges. Information pursued during discovery excludes privileged information, such as communications between attorneys and their clients, or an attorney's "work product." The latter includes documents that outline the legal theory being pursued, the strategy that attorneys plan to use, and communications between attorneys and their experts that pertain to expert testimony. Opposing counsel is likely to object to requests for information on the basis that it is confidential or covered by the work product privilege and might also argue that compiling information is so time consuming and costly that the court should deny the request by issuing a protective order that limits the scope of discovery or stops the process altogether. For example, an attorney who is prosecuting a class action on behalf of all incarcerated in a state prison may ask for the records of a random sample of inmates, and attorneys for the state may argue that it would be too costly and too time consuming to produce the documents sought.

Attorneys employ a variety of techniques to compile information during discovery, including the use of (1) interrogatories, which are questions submitted by either party that the opposing side must answer in writing and sign under oath; (2) depositions of those believed to have information material to the matter being litigated, wherein deponents answer questions under oath and a verbatim transcript is made of the proceeding; (3) case record reviews conducted by experts who are qualified to gather and analyze social science data; and (4) review of other documents, for example, an agency's policy and procedures manuals, computer tapes, and reports prepared internally and by outside consultants.

CRIMINAL PROCEEDINGS

The term *proceedings* refers to the form and manner of conducting judicial business and may include all the steps that take place from the time that a petition or complaint is filed through a judicial ruling. Criminal proceedings will be reviewed first, followed by civil matters.

Pretrial Hearings—Criminal Law

The events that unfold before a trial will vary as a function of the conditions under which an arrest took place and according to whether a defendant was detained or released. The person who is arrested without a warrant and detained by the police has a Fourth Amendment right to a hearing[55] within forty-eight hours of arrest.[56] At the hearing a judicial officer must determine whether there is probable cause to believe that the defendant committed the crime charged. This hearing is not constitutionally required if an arrest was made pursuant to a warrant, because the issuance of a warrant means that probable cause has already been determined, nor is it required if the defendant is not detained. However, some states have statutes that require such a hearing whenever a defendant is charged with a felony, which is a crime punishable by death or by a term of imprisonment exceeding one year.

Assuming that probable cause has been determined, either by warrant or at a hearing after an arrest, a defendant has a right to an arraignment (also known as an initial appearance), whether the person was detained or not. At arraignment the court must inform the defendant of the charge or charges lodged; of his or her rights (a) to remain silent, (b) to retain counsel or, if indigent, to have court-appointed counsel; and (c) to gain a postponement if needed to obtain and confer with counsel. The court also informs the defendant of the conditions under which she or he may be released before trial. At the end of the hearing bail must be set or denied.

Pleas

A defendant must enter a plea at the arraignment. In general, the pleas available in federal court are guilty, not guilty, or, with approval of the court, nolo contendere, which means that the defendant forgoes the right to a trial in exchange for neither contesting the charges nor admitting to them.[57] The court will enter a plea of not guilty for a defendant who refuses to enter a plea, and a court may allow a defendant who shows good cause to change an earlier plea. Defendants who intend to raise an insanity defense must notify the state of the intention to do so before trial.[58]

A plea bargain is a contract between the defendant and the state. A defendant enters into a plea agreement before trial because the prosecutor agrees to recommend to the court that charges be dismissed or to recommend a lighter sentence than what the defendant could expect if found guilty. Either side may try to bargain for a plea after the trial begins if it thinks that the case is going against its interests. The court may accept or reject the recommendation.[59]

A guilty plea is an admission to the crime charged and a waiver of basic constitutional rights, such as the right to a trial by jury and the right against self-incrimination. Because of the implications of waiving one's constitutional rights, the court will ensure that the plea is made knowingly and voluntarily, and as a rule it will not accept a guilty plea before advising the defendant of the consequences of entering such a plea.[60]

Pretrial Dispositional Alternatives

Dispositional alternatives available to the court before trial include(1) releasing a person on his or her own recognizance, meaning a bond is not required; (2) requiring the posting of a bond[61]; (3) detaining a person whom the court believes is a flight risk or whose detention is necessary to ensure the safety of others in the community; or (4) releasing a person and setting conditions for release. These conditions may require that the defendant (a) remain with a person designated by the court; (b) maintain or seek employment or undertake an educational program; (c) remain within a specified geographic area; (d) live in a designated setting such as a group home; (e) stay away from named individuals; (e) report on a regular basis to a designated law enforcement agency, pretrial services agency, or other agency; or (f) undergo medical, psychological, or psychiatric treatment, including treatment for drug or alcohol dependency.[62]

Criminal Trials

Under the Sixth Amendment a defendant in a criminal case has (1) the right to a speedy trial; (2) the right to a public trial; and (3) the right to be tried by an impartial jury, meaning that the jury selection process cannot be conducted so as to intentionally exclude people on the basis of a characteristic such as race or gender. Historically, juries in criminal trials had twelve members, but the U.S. Supreme Court has ruled that juries of six or more satisfy the Constitution.[63]

Sixth Amendment rights apply only to those charged with a "serious" crime, which is any crime that carries a sentence of more than six months in prison.[64] The U.S. Supreme Court has never defined the term *speedy*, holding that whether a delay is unreasonable is determined on a case-by-case basis, taking into account (1) the length of and reason for the delay, (2) whether the defendant asserted his or her right to a speedy trial, and (3) whether the delay was prejudicial to the defendant.[65]

When trials are open to public view and subject to press coverage, there is an assumption of fairness that would not exist if trials were closed to public scrutiny. However, a judge may exclude the public from a portion of a trial, for example, when a child victim of sex abuse testifies. However, the decision to exclude must be made on a case-by-case basis, because shielding all or part of a trial from public scrutiny implicates a defendant's Sixth Amendment rights, as well as the First Amendment rights of the press. In closing a trial to public view, the government must assert a compelling interest, and the remedy of closure must be narrowly tailored to serve that interest.[66]

Elements of a Crime

To obtain a conviction the prosecution must establish the concurrence of a criminal state of mind, or mens rea, with the commission of the act, *actus reus*, that the law defines as criminal. Criminal statutes use adverbs to refer to a defendant's state of mind, for example, *willfully, purposely, intentionally, knowingly,* or *recklessly.* For example, the crime of burglary is defined as breaking or entering (the act) into a building, such as a home, office, or store, with the intent (state of mind) to steal. Some crimes contain an element of harm. For example, a charge of murder, in addition to requiring an act and a state of mind, requires a particular result: the death of a human being.

Consider an example of how the elements of a crime interact. Amy is charged with the intentional murder of John. The state must prove that (1) Amy had the requisite state of mind, which might be shown if she told others of her intent, or might be inferred if Amy carried a loaded gun to a meeting with John; (2) Amy acted by pointing the gun and pulling the trigger, proof of which might come from eyewitness testimony or forensic evidence such as gunpowder residue on Amy's hands; (3) Amy's actions caused a specific harm that requires that "but for" her act of pointing a loaded gun and pulling the trigger, the bullet would not have caused John's death. If John suffered a heart attack when he saw Amy point her gun, and if it were proved that he died of the heart attack, Amy might be charged with attempted murder, but since her act did not cause John's death directly, the state would not be able to make its case that Amy murdered John.

Motive is not an element of a crime, but a legislative body can enact a statute making it so. Because motive is not an element, a prosecutor need not introduce evidence of it. However, consideration of motive might influence a prosecutor's decision about whether to bring charges, as well as affecting what charges are brought. Certainly, juries want to know why a person committed an act, and a defense attorney whose client might be viewed sympathetically because he or she acted to end the suffering of a terminally ill relative, for example, would want motive evidence introduced at trial in the hope that jury might vote for acquittal.

Motive may come into play at the sentencing phase of a trial, where, unless the crime is punishable by death, the standard of proof is lessened and where hearsay evidence, which is evidence adduced outside the courtroom and not subject to proof by cross-examination, may be acceptable. A sentence may be increased or decreased depending upon the amount of sympathy that a defendant can elicit by evidence concerning motive.

Standard of Proof

Standards for proof instruct a fact finder, be it a judge or jury, regarding the degree of confidence that society thinks that the fact finder should have in the conclusions that it draws.[67] At a criminal trial the state bears the burden of proof, which requires that the state produce evidence of all the required elements of the crime—for example, the state must prove that the crime was committed and that the defendant had the requisite state of mind—and it must prove each element beyond a reasonable doubt. In a jury trial the judge instructs the jury about the meaning of this standard before it begins its deliberations. As I noted earlier, the standard of proof is lessened at the sentencing phase of a noncapital case, because the defendant has already been convicted and because the court may want to hear victim testimony and evidence in presentence reports.

Defenses

Because the burden of proving each element of the crime falls on the state, the defense has no obligation at trial beyond endeavoring to weaken the state's case by planting a seed of doubt in the mind of the fact finder. The defense does this through cross-examination of the prosecution's witnesses and by having its own witnesses testify, for example, to provide an alibi for the defendant or, in the case of experts, to cast doubt on evidence presented by the prosecutor. An exception to the rule occurs when the burden of proof shifts to the defendant. It comes into play when a defendant mounts an "affirmative defense" by acknowledging that she or he committed the crime but argues justification. Affirmative defenses include (a) insanity and diminished capacity (see chapter 14), (b) self-defense, and (c) "symptom" defenses such as battered spouse syndrome and battered child syndrome (see chapter 6).

Sentencing

If a person is found guilty at trial or has entered a guilty plea, sentencing must take place. Sentences meted out in federal courts are determined by guidelines established by the U.S. Sentencing Commission.[68] Some states use sentencing guidelines, and some, along with the federal government, use "three-strikes" rules, which enhance sentences for those who commit serious felonies and have a prior record of serious felonies.

Guidelines were implemented to reduce sentencing disparities that resulted when judges could impose any sentence up to the statutory maximum specified for a crime. Federal sentencing guidelines instruct judges to use "sentencing tables," which guide the decision by taking into account such factors as (a) the offense committed; (b) the harm caused; (c) the role that the defendant played in the crime for which he or she was convicted; (d) the defendant's criminal history, which includes a determination of whether the defendant is a "career criminal"[69]; and (e) whether the defendant accepts responsibility for his or her actions. A judge may depart from the guidelines by increasing the sentence if there are aggravating circumstances. For example, courts have departed from the guidelines to increase a sentence in cases where a defendant murdered four people during a carjacking, targeted elderly people with a scheme to defraud them of their savings, or had an extensive criminal record and a tendency to repeat crimes of violence. Likewise, sentences can be less than what the guidelines call for in cases where a defendant provided substantial assistance to the government during a criminal investigation, grew marijuana solely to help relieve chronic depression and to avoid greater risk of suicide, or entered the country illegally to ensure that his girlfriend received medical care.[70]

Social Reports I use the term *social reports* generically to refer to any report prepared by a social worker or other mental health professional at the direction of a judge or attorney. Federal law requires such a report, known as the presentence investigation report, before a sentence is handed down. Federal judges rely heavily on social reports as an aid in applying some factors in the sentencing guidelines, as do judges in state courts whose sentencing decisions are not always constrained by the strict rules found in guidelines.

The presentence report, in addition to containing information describing the crime committed and the sentence range in the guidelines, must contain information about the defendant's (1) history and characteristics, including any prior criminal record; (2) financial condition; (3) any circumstances that, because they affect the defendant's behavior, may be helpful in imposing sentence or in correctional treatment; and any other information thought to be applicable to the defendant's case, including (4) identification of factors that may suggest a different sentence than that provided in the guidelines; (5) an assessment of the financial, social, psychological, and medical effects on any victim; and, (6) where appropriate, information about the nature and extent of nonprison programs and resources available for the defendant.[71]

Mitigating and Enhancing Factors at Sentencing Defendants may call witnesses to provide background and character information in the hope that a decision maker will take into account mitigating factors in their past, such as childhood abuse and factors attesting to good character, and consequently reduce the sentence. Likewise, victims or their family members may testify about the effect that the crime has had on them, and prosecutors may in their closing arguments at the sentencing phase comment on the continuing effects on the victim's family.[72] When a crime involves violence or sexual abuse, federal law requires that the court, at sentencing, address "any victim who is present . . . and . . . permit the victim to speak or submit . . . information about the sentence. Whether or not the victim is present, a victim's right to address the court may be exercised by a parent or legal guardian, if the victim is younger than 18 years or is incompetent; or another family member(s) . . . if the victim is deceased or incapacitated."[73]

Dispositional Alternatives

In addition to a term of imprisonment, the sentencing options available to a judge include restitution, probation, supervised release, community service, work release, or suspended sentence.

Restitution Restitution requires the person convicted of a crime to compensate the victim. Restitution may be required in addition to other sentencing options. Factors that come into play in ordering restitution include the loss sustained by a victim, the defendant's financial resources, and the financial needs and earning ability of the defendant and any dependents.[74]

Suspended Sentence A sentence may be imposed, then suspended for a specified period of time, allowing the person who was convicted to remain free. A record may be expunged if during the period of suspension the person engages in no criminal activity or successfully completes a treatment program.

Probation Probation is release before serving any time. Conditions may be imposed on the probationer, including participation in a treatment program or in a community service program for a specified number of hours per day or per week to provide such community service as serving food in a homeless shelter. Restrictions may be placed on the probationer's freedom to travel, association with others, choice of residence, and other freedoms as the court sees fit.[75]

Work Release Work release programs allow a person to remain in the community for specified periods of time, during the workweek, for example, with the requirement that the person return to jail on the weekends.

Supervised Release Supervised release requires that after prisoners have served their sentence, they must serve an additional term under the supervision of a probation officer.[76] As is the case with probation, a court is free to impose restrictions during the period of supervision.

Prisoner Rights

Prisoners retain limited constitutional rights. Limits are set by the need of prison authorities to maintain order and discipline,[77] and the latter justification has been used to deny to prisoners a blanket Fourth Amendment protection against unreasonable search of prison cells and seizure of contraband found in cells and against physical searches of the prisoners themselves. Prisoners retain the following limited rights because they do not threaten order and discipline: (1) assistance in preparing and filing legal documents, which can be met only if the prison has a law library or some agency provides assistance from people trained in the law; (2) correspondence with members of the press but not to have face-to-face interviews with media representatives; (3) marriage, but authorities may dictate the circumstances under which the ceremony takes place and may deny conjugal visits; and (4) freedom from cruel and unusual punishment. The latter would include (a) prolonged isolation in unsanitary isolation cells; (b) denial of food as punishment for violating prison regulations; (c) being forced to remain outdoors for several days while the prison was searched and inmates were deprived of food, water, protection from elements; and denial of access to toilets, as well as (5) denial of adequate medical treatment; and (6) denial of an adversarial hearing before being transferred from prison to a mental hospital or of a review procedure before being forced to take medication.

RELEASE FROM PRISON

Parole

Parole refers to release from jail or prison after serving part of a sentence. Prisoners have a constitutionally protected interest in receiving parole when a statute provides that a prisoner "shall" be released unless the parole board determines otherwise. Such mandatory language leads a prisoner to expect parole and creates a "liberty interest" that is entitled to some constitutional protection. The U.S. Supreme Court has held that an informal hearing addressing the parole decision, together with a statement of the reasons why parole is denied, satisfies due process.[78] Due process comes into play when parole is revoked and gives rise to a requirement for a hearing.[79]

Preventive Detention

Preventive detention allows the state to incarcerate or severely limit the freedom of movement of a person beyond the statutory maximum for the crime committed; this mechanism is based on the assumption that the person poses a predictable risk to the community. Preventive detention assumes that it is possible, based on a past record of bad behavior, to predict the likelihood of future criminality.

Sentence enhancement, for example, three-strikes rules, are a form of preventive detention, because their application increases a person's period of incarceration beyond what the legislature has determined is appropriate for a given crime.[80] Likewise, the trend toward prosecuting juveniles as adults (see chapter 10) is a form of preventive detention, because youngsters sentenced under delinquency statutes can be incarcerated only until they reach the age of majority, whereas those sentenced under adult laws are subject to prolonged periods of imprisonment.

Sexual predator laws, which are invoked after a person has served the sentence meted out at trial, are another form of preventive detention. A sexual predator is a person who is not mentally ill and who is "untreatable" using existing treatment modalities. In 2002 the U.S. Supreme Court ruled that civil commitment of sexual predators is permissible under the Constitution when a court has determined that the person is a dangerous sexual offender who has "serious difficulty" in controlling his behavior. In the case considered by the Court, the defendant was a convicted pedophile, which the psychiatric profession classifies as a serious mental condition, and he admitted that he was not able to control his behavior, thus reinforcing the idea that he would commit another crime.[81]

Community Notification of a Sex Offender's Release from Prison

Community notification statutes were born of a concern that sex offenders pose a risk to members of the community in which they reside after the offenders are released from prison. In 1994 Congress enacted the Jacob Wetterling Crimes Against Children and Sexually Violent Offender Registration Act, which encouraged the states to establish systems for registering sex offenders who targeted children.[82] The act provided for the release of "relevant information" to protect the public. Congress amended the act twice in 1996, first with the passage of Megan's Law, which mandated release of information necessary to protect the public; it was named after a seven-year-old who was murdered after a sexual assault.[83] Megan's Law was followed by passage of the Pam Lychner Sex Offender Tracking System.[84] This law provides for a federal system for registering sex offenders and allows the U.S. attorney general to establish a national database in the Federal Bureau of Investigation.

Forty-five states have statutes that provide methods whereby members of a community may learn that a released sex offender has taken up residence where they live.[85] Community notification laws should not be confused with sex-offender registration laws, which require released sex offenders to register with the police in the community where they will reside but carry no imputation of notification to the community.[86]

Several cases have challenged the constitutionality of community notification laws. It has been argued that they represent a form of double jeopardy, violate a released prisoner's right to privacy, violate due process, and constitute cruel and unusual punishment.[87] Most challenges have been unsuccessful, because the courts have found that notification laws are civil, not criminal, meaning that the intent is not to punish or further restrain a released offender.

Methods used to notify communities include (a) postings on websites, (b) sending notices to the media and to such organizations as school boards and child care facilities, (c) providing telephone numbers that people can call for information, and (d) creating a sex-offender registry with public access. The information released differs from state to state but may include the name (as well as aliases), address, and telephone number of the released offender; sex and race; photograph; physical description; date of birth; and the offense for which the person was convicted.

Some communities use a ratings scale, assigning scores to various factors in an effort to create a "likelihood of recidivism" score. The information provided to the community, as well as the methods used to notify community members, will vary as a function of the assigned score.

CIVIL PROCEEDINGS

Pretrial Hearings

Events that transpire before trial in a civil matter will vary according to the circumstances under which a petition or complaint was filed (hereafter, the petition). Some petitions refer to emergencies, such as when a social worker asks the court to sanction the immediate removal of a child who was subject to maltreatment, when an individual asks the court to issue a temporary order of protection to restrain another from attempting contact, or when tenants seek to prohibit a property owner from executing an eviction. In such situations emergency hearings may take place ex parte, meaning with only one side present. The court may issue an order and direct that the party who is not present be served with notice of the charges. A second hearing will be scheduled, at which time the court will inform the other party of the specific charges and give the person an opportunity to respond. The second hearing is similar in purpose to an arraignment in a criminal matter.

In nonemergency situations a civil proceeding begins when the complaining party files a petition in court and serves notice and a copy of the petition on the other party. The person served must respond to the petition and may do so before a court date is scheduled. The response may be in the form of an "Answer" in which the party denies, admits, or affirmatively defends each point raised in the petition.

For example, assume that you are being sued for malpractice by a client who alleges that you failed to warn her of a threat that one of your clients made against her. You may admit that you are a social worker in private practice, refuse for reasons of confidentiality to admit that the party who allegedly threatened another was a client, and/or deny that your practice ever fell below accepted professional standards.

In lieu of an Answer you may file a motion to have the suit dismissed. You might assert that the person alleged to have made a threat was never a client. Another option is to file a motion for summary judgment. The party who moves for summary judgment is arguing that no factual issue exists for a judge or jury to decide. A factual issue exists only when the particulars of a case are subject to interpretation in different ways.

Continuing with the malpractice example, the injured party may argue that you never warned him that a threat had been made, and you may counter that you met your responsibility to warn by notifying the police in the community where the threatened person resides. When confronted with a disagreement about what did or did not happen, a court that is considering a motion for summary judgment will probably rule that the dispute should go to trial. However, let us assume that you practice in a state where you are permitted, but not required, to disclose confidential information when it involves a threat of harm to a third party. In your motion for summary judgment you might argue that because the statute is permissive, you were not under an obligation to provide a warning, and therefore no factual dispute exists. If a petition survives either an effort to have it dismissed or a motion for summary judgment, the case will proceed to trial unless it is settled out of court. Discovery may take place before trial.

Pleas and Settlements

A parent who is charged with child abuse or a youngster who is charged with chronic truancy will enter a plea to the charges at a preliminary hearing or arraignment. In some civil courts the term *admit* is used in lieu of *guilty*, and *deny* is used in lieu of *not guilty*.

As with criminal trials, pleas may be made before or during a trial. Plea bargaining in civil court is similar to plea bargaining in a criminal court in that pleas are (1) contracts between the defendant, referred to in civil court as the respondent, and the state, referred to as the petitioner; (2) entered into because the petitioner agrees to recommend to the court that charges be dismissed or to recommend a sentence more favorable than what would be expected at the outcome of a trial; and (3) subject to being accepted or rejected by the court. As in criminal court, a guilty plea is an admission to the act charged and a waiver of basic constitutional rights. The court will ensure that the plea is made knowingly and voluntarily, and it will advise the respondent of the consequences of a plea of guilty before accepting the plea.

Settlements are another way of resolving civil cases, and the parties may propose a settlement any time before a judicial order is issued. Settlements are in some ways similar to, and in some ways different from, plea bargains. Settlements come into play to resolve a variety of disputes, for example, between divorcing parties or to settle claims of negligence or breach of contract.

A settlement is like a plea bargain in that the agreement is a contract between the parties that must be approved by the court. The settlement will describe the remedy for the alleged violation, but unlike a plea bargain a settlement may contain a provision that the exact terms of settlement remain confidential. Another way in which a settlement differs from a plea bargain is that one condition for resolving a dispute may be that the party charged with wrongdoing not make an admission of guilt; rather, the settlement may stipulate that it is not an admission of guilt and that the matter is being settled to avoid a lengthy trial and the costs associated with going to trial.

Pretrial Dispositional Alternatives

The subject of bail arises in civil proceedings when incarceration is possible. The adult who is charged with domestic violence or severe physical or sexual abuse of a child, or the juvenile who is charged with delinquent behavior, is entitled to have the court consider bail. If bail is set, the court may impose conditions for release, requiring that the released person report to a probation officer or attend counseling. If the matter involves family violence, the court will likely issue a protective order to restrain the defendant from contacting the threatened or injured party.

Courts may require litigants to participate in some form of alternative dispute resolution (ADR) before going to trial. In 1998 Congress passed the Alternative Dispute Resolution Act to reduce the backlog of cases in the federal courts and to move cases toward speedy resolution. Likewise, a number of states have statutes that provide for a form of ADR. ADR is defined as any process or procedure, other than judicial adjudication, where a neutral third party assists litigants to resolve their disagreements. ADR takes different forms, including "early neutral evaluation, mediation, minitrial, and arbitration."[88]

The ADR requires federal courts to develop programs and to mandate participation in civil cases under certain circumstances, including those that individual courts choose to carve out. Courts cannot mandate participation in arbitration, nor can they permit participation in arbitration for cases that involve (1) alleged violations of the Constitution, (2) monetary damages in excess of $150,000, or (3) civil rights violations.[89]

Another pretrial matter is that one party may want the court to issue a pretrial order. For example, a parent whose child was placed in foster care may want the court to order visitation while the matter is pending; the party against whom a protective order was issued may ask the court to permit supervised visits with a child; and the party whose neighbor threatens to cut down a tree may ask the court to issue a temporary order restraining tree cutting. Likewise, a social worker may ask the court for a temporary order directing a parent to cooperate with service providers as a condition for continued visits with a child placed in foster care.

Civil Trials

The terms *fact-finding hearing* and *adjudicatory hearing* refer to the trial phase in a civil proceeding. Regardless of the term used, the purpose is to determine whether the evidence is sufficient to support the allegations in a petition. The party that initiated the litigation, whether the state in a proceeding against a parent for neglect or abuse or a private party who sues a therapist, bears the burden of proof.

Civil proceedings are most akin to criminal proceedings when they involve delinquent behavior, because the youth who is charged has all the due process rights afforded an adult in criminal court, except the right to a jury trial.[90] Extensive constitutional guarantees do not affect neglect and abuse hearings. Unlike delinquency proceedings, the outcome of which threatens a young person's liberty because incarceration is possible, neglect and abuse hearings affect custody. Because the family settings in which most children are placed are seen as less restrictive than institutional settings, fewer constitutional safeguards are seen as necessary.

In civil matters that involve monetary damages, the right to a jury trial is found in the Seventh Amendment to the U.S. Constitution, in some state constitutions, and in some statutes. Thus when a suit alleges malpractice, breach of contract, or employment discrimination, it may be heard by a jury, but the parties have no right to a jury trial when the petitioner seeks equitable relief, which I discuss at the end of this chapter.

Elements and Standard of Proof

In discussing criminal law, I said that the prosecution carries the burden to prove each element of a crime and that the standard of proof requires that each element be proved beyond a reasonable doubt. In civil matters this standard and burden of proof apply only when a young person is charged with a crime.[91] Otherwise, what must be proved and the applicable standard differ according to the matter adjudicated. Consider some examples.

When a parent is charged with child abuse, the elements that the state must prove may include (1) that the charged adult is the child's parent or caretaker; (2) that the parent harmed or allowed another person to harm the child or to place the child at risk of injury; and (3) that the harm was not accidental. The state must prove its case by a "preponderance of the evidence," the most common standard of proof in civil cases. This standard requires that the evidence that is offered in support of the allegation be greater or more convincing than the evidence offered in opposition to it.

When a practitioner is charged with negligence, the elements that must be proved differ and include proof (1) that the person bringing suit was a client, (2) that the practitioner breached a duty of reasonable care owed to clients, and (3) that the breach caused harm to the client (see chapter 7).

In some civil cases the standard of proof is greater than the "preponderance of the evidence" standard. For example, in disputes about child custody, where the petitioner is a relative of the parent[92]; in some civil matters such as disputes about the title to property[93]; and when the state petitions to terminate parental rights, the courts require that the petitioner prove its case by "clear and convincing evidence." This standard is equated with proof that results in a "reasonable certainty," or high probability, that the facts asserted are true.[94] While more stringent than the preponderance of the evidence standard, this standard is less stringent than beyond a reasonable doubt.

Defenses

A young person who is charged with delinquent behavior may raise any of the defenses discussed earlier in the section on criminal law. When a parent is charged with child abuse, the defense attorney probably will try to weaken the state's case, for example, by putting on expert witnesses to dispute the evidence presented by the state or through rigorous cross-examination of the state's witnesses. Defenses that are used in a criminal case would ill serve a parent because most would support the argument that the parent was not able to care for the child. Some states allow a battered spouse to raise the affirmative defense of spouse battering to a charge of "derivative" neglect or abuse where the parent's culpability derives from a failure to protect a child from the acts of another family member or paramour.

Because allegations of malpractice require proof that the practitioner's behavior fell below a standard of professional care, the most common defense strategy is to call experts who will testify that the methods used by the practitioner met professional standards.

Civil Remedies

The prevailing party in a civil suit may receive monetary awards or equitable relief. Equitable relief is provided where monetary damages do not suffice to correct an injustice or where the petitioner's goal is to reform the institution that caused the damage (see chapter 7). Assume, for example, that a group of children who were placed in state-supervised foster care sustained injuries at the hands of their foster parents and that the children sue the state for failing to properly supervise their placement. People who claim such injuries due to the negligence of another typically want monetary damages. However, if the only relief provided to children who are injured in foster care is monetary compensation, children placed later still could suffer similar injuries. Stated otherwise, unless the relief includes provisions for ensuring that the state supervises closely the homes in which it places children, the result will not be equitable or fair to other children.

APPEALS

An appeal is a plea to a higher court to overturn all or part of a decision of a lower court (see table 3.1). Federal and state laws set rules for appealing a decision. Some decisions may be appealed "as of right," meaning that the person who loses at trial has a legal right to file at least one appeal, whereas other appeals are by permission, meaning that the appellant must ask the court's permission to file an appeal. Appellate courts have discretion in deciding which cases they will review. The U.S. Supreme Court receives more than five thousand petitions for review each year; the Court accepts approximately 5 percent. Appeals are difficult to win because appellate courts are loathe to second-guess trial courts and to upset the rulings that they make.

As a general rule, an issue can be raised on appeal only if it was "preserved" at trial. Issues are preserved when lawyers raise objections to judicial rulings. For example, if an attorney objects to a judicial ruling to allow testimony that he believes is unduly prejudicial to a client, this issue may be raised on appeal, and the attorney is likely to argue that, but for the prejudicial testimony, the result of the trial would have been different.

Appeals are made on the merits and on the law. An appeal on the merits raises questions about the factual basis of a judicial ruling. Judges make "findings of fact," meaning that in their rulings they refer to the evidence and the testimony presented at trial. An attorney who appeals a case on the merits argues that the evidence was not sufficient to support the conclusion reached; or, if more than one witness testified to the same matter, the attorney would argue that the testimony was so contradictory that the conclusion reached by the court cannot be sustained. It is very difficult to win an appeal on the merits. Appellate courts defer to decisions made at the trial level, where the judge has the opportunity to observe the witnesses and to judge the credibility of each. While there are exceptions, the question of whether evidence is admissible is left mainly to the trial judge.

Appeals on the law argue that the decision made at trial cannot be supported as a matter of law or, stated otherwise, that the law does not allow the conclusion that was reached. For example, a person who is convicted in a criminal matter may argue that the state failed to prove each element of the crime and that the judgment against him cannot be sustained as a matter of law. Or a parent whose rights were terminated may argue that the court reached its decision on a preponderance of the evidence, which, as a matter of law, is the wrong evidentiary standard.

SUMMARY

The federal and state court systems have similarities and differences in their organization. Each has three tiers, consisting of a trial court and two higher appellate courts, but local courts, such as juvenile or family court, which exist in each state's judicial system, are not found in the federal judiciary. Trial courts hear cases that arise under criminal law, which is concerned with behavior that society may choose to punish with imprisonment, and under civil law, which is concerned with behavior that affects private rights where the objective is to compensate the injured party, not to imprison a wrongdoer.

This chapter focused on certain procedural aspects of criminal and civil law, paying attention to the constitutional and statutory protections that come into play when the state seeks to deprive an individual of life, liberty, or property, and with rules that govern the procedures for filing a civil lawsuit and for proceeding in court. A key to distinguishing criminal from civil procedure lies in the different consequences that might result from a loss at trial. Because criminal proceedings may result in a loss of liberty, the constitutional and statutory protections afforded the individual are greater than in a civil matter. Despite the magnitude of loss that an individual may experience, civil cases carry no threat of incarceration, although civil procedures that seek to commit a person who is mentally ill or a juvenile charged with a crime could result in a loss of liberty. Such cases carry a greater degree of statutory and constitutional protection than the ordinary civil matter.

In criminal matters, when the state has probable cause to believe that a person has committed a crime, unless the person is about to flee the jurisdiction or to commit another crime, the state should not (1) arrest the suspected individual without a warrant; (2) conduct a search or seizure of property without a warrant; (3) interview individuals in custody without informing them of the right to remain silent and the right to counsel; (4) file criminal charges in a case brought under federal law without obtaining an indictment from a grand jury; (5) deny a probable cause hearing to a person who has been detained for more than forty-eight hours after a warrantless arrest; (6) deny to the person charged with a serious crime (a) the right to have a judicial officer consider pretrial release, (b) the right to a speedy trial, (c) the right to a public trial; and (d) the right to trial by an impartial jury; and (7) obtain a conviction without proving each element of the charged crime beyond a reasonable doubt.

In civil matters the law gives wide investigative latitude to social workers whose actions are governed by a wish to protect children from abuse or neglect, just as it does to school officials whose warrantless searches of student property are sanctioned by the need to maintain order. However, constitutional protections do exist in civil matters, although the state's obligation is less than when criminal charges are brought. When, for example, the state seeks to terminate parental rights, the parents have a right to counsel, but unless a statute obligates the state to provide counsel to the indigent, the state has no constitutional obligation to do so. Juveniles who face incarceration for delinquent behavior have many constitutional guarantees afforded adults in a criminal trial, but the juvenile who is facing incarceration does not have a right to a jury trial.

Sentences meted out in federal court, and in some state courts, are determined by guidelines established by the U.S. Sentencing Commission. Sentencing tables guide the court's decision, directing it to consider factors such as (a) the offense committed, (b) the harm caused, and (c) the role that the defendant played. This information is weighed in a context that includes information contained in social reports that may concern the history and characteristics, including any prior criminal record, of the defendant, and other relevant information. The sentence handed down may be increased when the crime is especially heinous or reduced by factors that include good character and assistance provided to law enforcement.

Civil remedies may be in the form of monetary awards or equitable relief. The latter is provided where monetary damages do not suffice to correct an injustice, for example, where extensive training of newly hired social workers is seen as producing a more just outcome for clients than would be achieved by awarding monetary damages.

Court rulings may be appealed. Appeals are made on the merits and on the law. Appeals based on the merits raise questions about the factual basis of a judicial ruling, whereas those based on the law contend that the law does not allow the conclusion that the court reached. Appellate courts are loathe to overturn the decisions of trial courts unless a trial judge makes a serious error in interpreting the law. Thus the likelihood of prevailing on appeal is greatest where, for example, a wrong evidentiary standard was applied, such as would be the case if a court terminated parental rights based on a preponderance of the evidence rather than clear and convincing evidence.

4

Legal Research

STUDENTS ACCUSTOMED to conducting research in the social or behavioral sciences or the humanities often find the conduct of legal research intimidating. This chapter is an introduction to this subject. We will begin with an example of how one might approach researching a legal issue, followed by a general discussion of how to conduct research in the areas of statutes, regulations, and case law. The chapter also covers computerized legal research.

LEARNING ABOUT A LEGAL ISSUE

Assume that you are newly employed in a public agency. You learn that a coworker is being sued by a party who claims that the coworker acted inappropriately when investigating a report of child abuse. In discussing this matter with others, you hear the phrase "qualified immunity," and office scuttlebutt is that your coworker will prevail in court because he has qualified immunity. Your curiosity is piqued. You decide to do some research to learn about this subject.

You may begin your research as you would any other kind of research, by a search of subject areas. Either of two legal encyclopedias, *American Jurisprudence* or *Corpus Juris Secundum,* provides a good starting point. Let us assume that you begin by using the subject index to *American Jurisprudence,* where you locate the phrase "qualified immunity." It refers you to "Section 309—Qualified Immunity, Generally."

From your review of section 309 you learn that qualified immunity protects "public officials" from being sued for monetary damages for judgment calls made in a "legally uncertain environment." Qualified immunity applies to actions performed in the context of a "discretionary function" but only when taken in "good faith" and within the "scope" of one's authority. As you continue, you begin to understand why your colleagues are not concerned about the lawsuit: You read that "qualified immunity protects all but the incompetent or those who knowingly violate the law . . . [and that] immunity [may be] destroyed by malice, bad faith or improper purpose."

You find that you need to learn the definitions of some terms used in the encyclopedia. You start by looking them up in a law dictionary. Using *Black's Law Dictionary,* you find the phrase "public official," but the definition does not tell you whether a social worker in public employment is covered, and the phrase "legally uncertain environment" does not appear in the dictionary. You have better luck with "good faith," "discretionary function," and "scope of authority." You learn that (a) good faith encompasses an "honest belief" in the goodness of one's actions, together with an absence of malice or intent to take advantage of another; (b) discretionary functions are actions not governed by hard-and-fast rules; and (c) "scope of authority" refers to the tasks delegated by law or policy to a person's position in an agency.[1]

If you return to the subject index of *American Jurisprudence* and search for the heading "public officials," you will learn that social workers who practice in child welfare settings are viewed as such, and from a review of case law you learn that a legally uncertain environment is one where the rights of the parties are not clearly established.[2] For example, recall the discussion of search warrants in chapter 3. There I said that social workers, who are not trained in matters of criminal procedure and constitutional law, would not be expected to know that a search warrant might be required before conducting a body search of a child. Moreover, the law holds social workers to a lower standard than police officers when a worker is conducting a search for the purpose of protecting a child whom the worker reasonably believes is in danger. Because of their training, police know the rules that govern when they must obtain a search warrant, and more is expected of them.

Returning to section 309 of the encyclopedia, in addition to learning the definition of "qualified immunity," you will find citations to case law where the issue of qualified immunity has been adjudicated. Each case cited is followed by an abstract that you may review to decide whether any of the cited cases are relevant to your research interests. We will return shortly to the subject of case law.

CASE-FINDING TOOLS

The lawsuit brought against your colleague falls within the law of negligence, which covers malpractice. Let us assume that you want to know more about malpractice actions brought against social workers. You may find information in textbooks that are organized by subject area, such as negligence or malpractice, as well as by legal topics, such as family law or civil rights law. In addition, continuing legal education material is available, and as with textbooks, this material is organized by subject area or legal topic. Texts and similar materials are updated periodically with supplements or "pocket parts," which can be inserted in "slits" in the back cover of legal texts. Updates are organized by section numbers and headings that correspond to numbers and headings in the text. For example, a text on disabilities law has a section "6.02" that describes the law requiring modifications to buildings to provide access for people with disabilities. If the law has changed because a court has interpreted it in a novel way, or because a legislative body has amended the law, information concerning the interpretation or amendment will be reported in supplementary material that will be cross-referenced to the section in the text by the number 6.02.

Other "case-finding tools" include legal encyclopedias, digests, looseleaf services, and citators. These resources are secondary sources of law that report information abstracted from primary sources, such as constitutions, statutes, regulations, and court rulings.

You may locate information in a case-finding tool by a search of subjects rather than having to know and to look first for specific cases. Case digests organize subject matter alphabetically and cite relevant court decisions chronologically. A list of topics and subtopics covered in a digest appears as a table of contents. Once you select a topic and/or subtopic of interest, you go to that section of the digest in which cases are abstracted.

American Law Reports (*ALR*) is one such digest. If you search the subject index for the phrase "social worker malpractice," you will find a reference to volume 58, which is titled "Social Worker Malpractice." The introduction informs you that this volume contains state and federal case law where courts have addressed what actions constitute malpractice by a social worker. The *ALR* contains an index of cases organized by state, abstracts that provide sufficient information for you to determine whether any of the cited cases apply to your concern, as well as full case citations that allow you to look up any case of interest. In addition, you would find references to other publications on the topic; for example, it is common for the "research" section of a volume of *ALR* to cite law journals on the subject of interest and to contain references to encyclopedias.

Looseleaf services are legal texts bound in three-ring binders to permit the insertion and deletion of pages as the law is updated. Looseleaf services provide a convenient way of finding relevant court decisions and statutes. Looseleaf services are organized by subject area, such as family law, malpractice, Medicaid, and Medicare. The *Looseleaf Series on Family Law*, published by Looseleaf Law Publications, Inc., for example, contains (1) relevant statutes such as a state's laws on adoption; (2) court rules, which describe how court hearings are to be conducted; (3) a description of a state's organizational hierarchy for administering social services; and (4) procedural requirements, for example, for receiving and investigating reports of child abuse and neglect.

West's digests allow you to locate information (1) by topic; (2) through a table of cases, if you have already identified a specific case; (3) by use of descriptive words that reflect commonly used terms; or (4) by "key numbers."

In the body of the digest you will find summaries, called "squibs," which are abstracts containing relevant sections of court rulings. Each abstract summarizes a point of law, and each topic is assigned a key number. The topic "immunity" will be found as a subtopic in more than one place, for example, under the topic of "Infants" or, as shown in figure 4.1, under the topic of "Civil Rights."

Number 78 is assigned to the topic "Civil Rights," number 78k211 to the subtopic "Privilege or Immunity; Good Faith and Probable Cause," and number 78k214 to the subtopic "Governmental Agencies." Each squib contains a rule of law that was applied in the case cited at the end of the squib; note that the squib identifies the department in which the case was decided, so that New York practitioners, for example, can select cases that apply to the county in which they practice (see the discussion of geography and the binding nature of court decisions in chapter 3).

West's digests are associated with West's regional reporter system (table 4.1). Figure 4.1 contains a series of squibs from West's *New York Digest.* Not shown in the figure are a variety of other subtopics under "Civil Rights." If you were to search by using the subtopic number, you would produce the squibs shown in figure 4.1, among others. Each squib also identifies the case from which it was taken. Searching key number 78k214 produces one squib that is pertinent to the question of concern to you. The squib includes this information:

> Police officers and protective service caseworkers were entitled to qualified immunity in civil rights action based on alleged improper interrogation and physical examination of three-year-old plaintiff without her parents' knowledge and consent during child abuse investigation; defendants [police and caseworkers] were acting pursuant to custom and practice of sex crimes squad to interview child outside the home and family during child abuse investigation, and there was no evidence that they acted incompetently or with malice.
>
> *Galante v. County of Nassau,* 720 N.Y.S.2d 325 (2000).

LOCATING AND READING CASE LAW

When reading cases, it is a good idea to confine yourself initially to a review of cases in the state where you practice. This will allow you to become

FIGURE 4.1

New York Digest Headnotes

78 CIVIL RIGHTS
78k211 Privilege or Immunity; Good Faith and Probable Cause
78k214 Governmental Agencies
N.Y.A.D. 3 Dept., 2001
A government official performing a discretionary function is entitled to qualified immunity provided his or her conduct does not violate clearly established statutory or constitutional rights of which a reasonable person would have known. Kravitz v. Police Dept. of City of Hudson, 728 N.Y.S.2d 267

78 CIVIL RIGHTS
78k211 Privilege or Immunity; Good Faith and Probable Cause
78k214 Governmental Agencies
N.Y.A.D. 3 Dept., 2001
To establish defense of qualified immunity, the government official must establish that he or she had an objectively reasonable belief that his or her act violated no clearly established rights. Kravitz v. Police Dept. of City of Hudson, 728 N.Y.S.2d 267

78 CIVIL RIGHTS
78k211 Privilege or Immunity; Good Faith and Probable Cause
78k214 Governmental Agencies
N.Y.A.D. 3 Dept., 1997
Defense of qualified immunity required proof establishing that it was objectively reasonable for police officer to believe that his conduct was appropriate under circumstances, or that officers of reasonable competence could disagree as to whether his conduct was proper. Baez v. City of Amsterdam, 666 N.Y.S.2d 312

78 CIVIL RIGHTS
78k211 Privilege or Immunity; Good Faith and Probable Cause
78k214 Governmental Agencies
N.Y.A.D. 3 Dept., 1997
Employee of county department of social services who helped pregnant minor find shelter in local hotel acted in objectively reasonable manner, and was therefore entitled to defense of qualified immunity in action by minor's mother alleging violations of her civil rights arising from provision of assistance to her daughter, where assistance provided to minor did not interfere with mother's parental rights. Kubik v. New York State Dept. of Social Services, 664 N.Y.S.2d 365

78 CIVIL RIGHTS
78k211 Privilege or Immunity; Good Faith and Probable Cause
78k214 Governmental Agencies
N.Y.A.D. 1 Dept., 1995
To determine whether public employee is entitled to qualified immunity, court must determine (1) what specific right was allegedly violated, (2) whether that right was so

"clearly established" as to alert reasonable official to its constitutional parameters, and (3) whether reasonable official could have believed that particular conduct at issue was lawful. Liu v. New York City Police Dept., 627 N.Y.S.2d 683

78 CIVIL RIGHTS
78k211 Privilege or Immunity; Good Faith and Probable Cause
78k214 Governmental Agencies
N.Y.A.D. 1 Dept., 1995
Government official will prevail on qualified immunity claim if right asserted by claimant was not "clearly established" at time that official acted, or if official reasonably believed his particular conduct was lawful. Liu v. New York City Police Dept., 627 N.Y.S.2d 683

familiar with how the courts in the city or town where you practice define such concepts as the "best interest of the child" and how they view problems, such as domestic violence, that you encounter in everyday practice. But before we examine a case, you should become familiar with the sources in which cases are published.

Court Decisions

The majority of court decisions are published by commercial publishers, some in cooperation with the federal court system or the court system of a state, whereas others publish decisions independent of the judiciary. The federal government publishes the decisions of the U.S. Supreme Court in *United States Reports;* Supreme Court decisions also appear in *United States Supreme Court Reports,* published by Lawyers Co-Op, and the *Supreme Court Reporter,* published by West. Today the decisions of many courts, both federal and state, are available on line, and I will discuss computerized legal research at the end of this chapter.

The government does not publish the decisions of federal district and appellate courts; these can be found in West Publishing Company's National Reporter System (see table 4.1). The National Reporter System divides the country into seven regions and produces seven regional reporters, as well as separate reporters for California and New York. Thus, if you are interested in finding cases that deal with procedures for civil commitment of the mentally ill and you practice in Massachusetts, you would find cases of importance in the *North*

TABLE 4.1 West's National Reporter System

REGIONAL REPORTER	STATES COVERED
Atlantic Reporter	Conn., Del., Maine, Md., N.H., N.J., Pa., R.I., Vt., and the Court of Appeals for the District of Columbia
North Eastern Reporter	Ill., Ind., Mass., N.Y., Ohio
North Western Reporter	Iowa, Mich., Minn., Neb., N.Dak., S.Dak., Wis.
Pacific Reporter	Alaska, Ariz., Calif., Colo., Hawaii, Nev., N. Mex., Okla., Ore., Utah, Wash., Wyo., Idaho, Mont., Kans.
South Eastern Reporter	Ga., N.C., S.C., Va., W.Va.
South Western Reporter	Ariz., Ky., Mo., Tenn., Tex.
Southern Reporter	Ala., Fla., La., Miss.
New York Supplement	
California Reporter	
FEDERAL REPORTERS	**COURTS COVERED**
Federal Reporter	U.S. Courts of Appeals, U.S. Tempo rary Emergency Court of Appeals, U.S. Court of Appeals for the Federal Circuit, U.S. Court of Federal Claims
Federal Supplement	U.S. District Courts, U.S. Court of International Trade
Federal Rules Decisions	Federal Rules of Civil and Criminal Procedure
Supreme Court Reporter	U.S. Supreme Court

Eastern Reporter, and if you practiced in Kansas, you would find cases from that state in the *Pacific Reporter*.

In addition to regional reports, West also publishes federal reporters that contain decisions made by federal district courts (*Federal Supplement*); U.S. Courts of Appeals, U.S. Temporary Emergency Court of Appeals, U.S. Court of Appeals for the Federal Circuit, and U.S. Court of Federal Claims (*Federal Reporter*); and the U.S. Court of International Trade (*Federal Supplement*). Federal court decisions that deal with civil and criminal procedural matters, such as rules of evidence, expert witness testimony, and appeals procedures, are reported in West's *Federal Rules Decisions.*

FINDING REPORTED CASES

Let us say that you are interested in cases decided in New York state that deal with the subject of social worker immunity. Your interest is confined to immunity that is granted in the context of investigating a report of child abuse or neglect. Assume that the abstract from *Galante v. County of Nassau,* presented in figure 4.2, is of sufficient interest to cause you to want to read the case. To find the case you first have to know how to read legal citations.

Reading Legal Citations

All legal citations begin with the case name, followed by the volume number of the reporter in which the case may be found, the name of the reporter, the number of the page on which the case begins, and the year in which the decision was made. Note that the *Galante* case has two citations. The abbreviation "Misc." stands for *New York Miscellaneous Reports,* which contains cases from the state's supreme courts, family courts, and some appellate rulings. The second citation is to West's *New York Supplement* (see fig. 4.2).

CASE NAME	VOL. NO.	ABBREVIATION FOR VOLUME IN WHICH CASE IS REPORTED	PAGE NUMBER WHERE CASE BEGINS	YEAR DECIDED
Galante v. County	186	Misc. 2d	733	2000
	720	N.Y.S. 2d	325	2000

Some legal citations appear to be complicated because a case has wound its way through the appellate process. Consider the following citation. This case involved a class-action lawsuit brought against the District of Columbia by a group of children in foster care. The full citation is as follows:

> ***LaShawn A. v. Dixon,* 762 F. Supp. 959, 59 U.S.L.W. 2651 (D.D.C. Apr. 18, 1991), *Decision Affirmed and Remanded by LaShawn A. v. Kelly,* 990 F.2d 1319, 301 U.S. App. D.C. 49 (D.C. Cir. Apr. 16, 1993), *rehearing and suggestion for rehearing en banc denied* (Aug. 9, 1993) *Certiorari Denied by Kelly v. LaShawn A.,* 510 U.S. 1044, 114 S. Ct. 691, 126 L. Ed. 2d 659, 62 U.S.L.W. 3446, 62 U.S.L.W. 3451 (U.S. Jan. 10, 1994).**

FIGURE 4.2

Reading Cases: An Example

Supreme Court, Nassau County, New York. Dec. 12, 2000. 1st Dept.
186 Misc.2d 733, 720 N.Y.S.2d 325
Galante, an Infant, by Her Mother
v.
County of Nassau

Summary of Action
Civil rights action was brought against county [agencies and individual] . . . police officers, and protective services caseworkers, based on interrogation and physical examination of three-year-old child during child abuse investigation. . . . The Supreme Court, Nassau County held that officers and caseworkers were entitled to qualified immunity.

West Headnotes

Civil Rights k214(6)
78k214(6)
Police officers and protective services caseworkers were entitled to qualified immunity in civil rights action based on alleged improper interrogation and physical examination of three-year-old plaintiff without her parents' knowledge and consent during child abuse investigation; defendants were acting pursuant to custom and practice of sex crimes squad to interview child outside the home and family during child abuse investigation, and there was no evidence that they acted incompetently or with malice. 42 U.S.C.A. 1983.

Civil Rights k214(2)
78k214(2)
The "objectively reasonable" standard is met and a defendant is entitled to qualified immunity if officers of reasonable competence could disagree on the legality of the defendants' conduct.

Procedural History
Both sides agree that plaintiff Kaia Galante previously alleged a claim for violation of her civil rights pursuant to 42 U.S.C. 1983. The previous claim was based on the same incident as [this] claim . . . namely, the alleged improper interrogation and physical examination of her at the age of three by defendants, without her parents' knowledge or consent. [The] . . . civil rights claim was dismissed after trial in the prior action and [county agencies] seek dismissal of [this] claim . . . on the basis of *res judicata* which is "grounded on the premise that once a person has been afforded a full and fair opportunity to litigate a particular issue, that person may not be permitted to do so again."

Issue and Facts

Police and protective service defendants were not parties to the prior action. Consequently, they do not seek dismissal on the grounds of *res judicata*. Rather, they claim that they are shielded from plaintiff's federal civil rights claim on the grounds of qualified immunity. Again, the conduct at issue is the interrogation and physical examination of the then three-year-old plaintiff without parental consent or court approval, in the context of a child abuse investigation. Plaintiff argues in opposition that because of a decision changing the law in August, 1990, the qualified immunity defense is not available to these defendants.

The Law

Plaintiff relies upon the case of *Tenenbaum v. Williams*, 193 F.3d 581, 596 (2d Cir. 1999) . . . wherein the test for qualified immunity to federal civil rights claims was stated as follows: Government officials "enjoy qualified immunity when they perform discretionary functions IF EITHER (1) their conduct did not violate clearly established rights of which a reasonable person would have known, OR (2) it was objectively reasonable to believe that [their] acts did not violate these clearly established rights." In *Tenenbaum* caseworkers were sued in connection with the removal of a 5-year-old child from school and the subsequent physical examination of the child for signs of abuse without parental approval or court order. The court held that the individual defendants were entitled to the qualified immunity defense under the first prong of the aforementioned test. The *Tenenbaum* court reasoned that the law was not clear until August 1990 that subjecting a child to invasive investigatory medical examination in the course of an abuse investigation requires a court order absent parental consent.

Reasoning and Holding

As the conduct at issue in this case took place in 1992, plaintiff . . . insists that under *Tenenbaum* . . . defendants cannot meet the first prong of the qualified-immunity test. However, plaintiff . . . fails to take into account the . . . second prong of the test. Even the *Tenenbaum* court acknowledged that there remains substantial protection for caseworkers under the second prong of the qualified immunity test, so long as it is "objectively reasonable [for them] to believe that [their] acts [do] not violate these clearly established rights." [citation omitted]

. . . [I]n qualified immunity cases the issue is not the correctness of defendants' conduct, but the objective reasonableness of their chosen course of action given the circumstances confronting them at the [time]. The judge is required to resolve questions of reasonableness on summary judgment in qualified immunity cases where the material facts are not in dispute because of the broad purpose of providing government workers with immunity from defending lawsuits, as well as immunity from liability.

Decision

Here, the brief interrogation and the physical examination of the plaintiff was made in the course of the ongoing child abuse investigation of plaintiff's father. According to the trial testimony . . . when a parent is a suspect in a child abuse investigation, it was the custom and practice of the sex crimes squad to interview the child outside the home and family. The record is barren with respect to evidence of incompetence or malice. By way of comparison, state law would afford these defendants qualified immunity from state claims because defendants were acting within the scope of their employment and did not engage in willful misconduct or gross negligence. Under all of the circumstances of this case and the *Tenenbaum* directive that qualified immunity should continue to enable protective services caseworkers the necessary latitude to exercise their professional judgment in matters of child welfare . . . the court finds that the conduct of the . . . [police and protective service] defendants . . . meets the objective reasonableness standard. Based on this finding, the qualified immunity test is satisfied and this defense is available to the . . . defendants. Accordingly, the individual defendants are entitled to summary judgment dismissing the complaint.

Let me break this citation down into its various segments and explain how to read it:

***LaShawn A. v. Dixon,* 762 F. Supp. 959, 59 U.S.L.W. 2651 (D.D.C. Apr. 18, 1991).**

The first citation is to the original ruling of the trial court. From what we have learned so far, we know that the italicized portion of the citation is the case name: LaShawn is the child who came to represent the class of children in foster care, and Dixon was the director of children's services when the suit was filed. From a review of the information in figure 4.2 we know that F. Supp. is the West reporter in which decisions of federal district courts are reported. U.S.L.W., a publication of Lawyers Cooperative, contains the same basic information, except that the headnote, shown in figure 4.2, appears only in documents published by West. "D.D.C." means District of the District of Columbia.

***Decision Affirmed and Remanded by LaShawn A. v. Kelly,* 990 F.2d 1319, 301 U.S. App. D.C. 49 (D.C. Cir. Apr. 16, 1993) rehearing and suggestion for rehearing en banc denied (Aug. 9, 1993)**

This citation provides two important pieces of information: first, that the case was referred to an appellate court and that the appellate court affirmed the ruling of the trial court. In some citations you will see the abbreviation *aff'd* for *affirmed* and *rem'd* for *remanded. Remanded* means that the case was sent back to the trial court for reconsideration of some issue discussed in the ruling of the appellate court. *Kelly* here has replaced *Dixon,* which means that children's services had a new director when this appeal went forward. F.2d is the West reporter that contains decisions of the U.S. Courts of Appeals; the second reference is to a Lawyer's Cooperative publication in which appellate decisions for the District of Columbia are published. D.C. Cir. in parentheses tells us that the appellate court was the Court of Appeals for the District of Columbia. Appeals court decisions for other circuits are reported by circuit number. For example, 9th Cir. refers to the U.S. Court of Appeals for the Ninth Circuit, which has jurisdiction over California, Hawaii, Alaska, and other western states (see note 2, chapter 3). Appellate courts consist of "panels," each of which is made up of specified number of appellate court justices. Generally, the panels handle appeals, but an appellant may request a hearing "en banc," which means a hearing by the full court. The reference makes clear that the request for an en banc hearing was made and denied.

> ***Certiorari Denied by Kelly v. LaShawn A.* 510 U.S. 1044, 114 S. Ct. 691, 126 L. Ed. 2d 659, 62 U.S.L.W. 3446, 62 U.S.L.W. 3451 (U.S. Jan. 10, 1994)**

Certiorari, at times abbreviated as "cert.," is a request to an appellate court to review a lower court's decision. The information here tells us that an appeal was filed with the U.S. Supreme Court and that the Court denied the request. Each reference identifies a reporter: U.S. stands for *United States Reports,* the reporter published by the government that prints decisions of the U.S. Supreme Court. This citation is followed by citations to commercial publishers.

This section of the citation for this case contains two anomalies that sometimes occur. First, note that "Kelly," who was the defendant in the original case, is named first. Placing the defendant first, although the defendant was not named first in the second part of the citation, is simply a quirk in the way case names are reported. Next, it is clear that the defendant named has reverted to Kelly from Dixon. This is just another oddity in the way that case names may appear.

Other terms that appear in citations but are not included in the example are *reversed* and *vacated;* the former means that a higher court has reversed the finding of a lower court, which means that the decision was set aside or voided, which is also the meaning of *vacated.* At times you will see information in parentheses at the end of a case that tells you about the geographic location of the court. For example, you may see S.D.N.Y., which means the southern district of New York, or W. Pa., which means western Pennsylvania.

Finally, when the parentheses at the end of a case contain the name of a state and provide a date, such as "(Me. 1966)," this means that the ruling came from Maine's highest court. When the ruling is from a state appellate court, it will generally be cited with the abbreviation App., with the state name abbreviated. So a decision from an appellate court in California will appear as Cal. App. and from the Illinois Appellate Court as Ill. App. Ct. At times you will see a reference to Dept. or Div., for example, "Cal. App. 3d Dept." This recognizes some states are divided into geographic divisions or departments, each with its own appellate court.

Reading Cases

Now assume that after reviewing the abstracts from the *New York Digest* (fig. 4.1), you decide to read *Galante v. County of Nassau*. Using the case citation reported with the abstract, and with access to either *New York Miscellaneous Reports* or the *New York Supplement* (see table 4.1), your search for *Galante* would produce the case that appears in figure 4.2.

The first paragraph in a case is a descriptive summary that provides just enough information for the reader to decide whether the case is of sufficient interest to read on. Here we learn that the action is classified as a "civil rights action"; that the claim is based on actions taken during a child abuse investigation by police officers and protective service workers; and that these public officials prevailed because they were entitled to qualified immunity. Before I continue, we need a brief digression to explain why this suit was filed as a civil rights suit.

In certain circumstances attorneys have the option of pursuing a claim under state or federal law. An attorney will select whichever course of action is more likely to favor her or his client. The civil rights law at issue here (discussed in detail in chapter 7) allows an individual to sue public officials who, acting in their official capacity, allegedly deprived the plaintiff of a right guaranteed by the Constitution or by a federal statute. Jumping ahead for a moment, if you read the text under the heading of "Decision" in figure 4.2, you will see that New York law was clear that the social workers and police had qualified immunity, so a claim filed under state law probably would be dismissed. The attorneys' only option was a civil rights claim.

Returning to figure 4.2, the first headnote should be familiar to you, for it is the abstract that turned up in the earlier search of *New York Digest.* The points of laws contained in the headnote apply directly to the case in which they appear.

Issues

An issue is a question of law presented to a court, and cases often present more than one issue. Here the court was asked (1) whether the plaintiffs, who had already sued the county agencies on the same issue, could relitigate this matter, and (2) whether plaintiffs could prevail in a suit against individual police officers and protective service workers not identified in the previous suit. The answer to the first question appears in the first paragraph in the section headed

"Procedural History." The procedural history of a case includes historical information, such as previous court rulings in the case as well as information about motions filed by attorneys. The court will report only those aspects of procedural history relevant to the decision being rendered. Here the earlier claim was a key issue, and the court's discussion includes both the facts and its holding that the issue cannot be relitigated.

Issue and Facts

As stated in the procedural history, neither the social workers nor the police officers were named as defendants in the earlier action, so the case was allowed to proceed against these parties. In their defense the police and social workers argued that they had qualified immunity and could not be sued. The plaintiff responded that the law on this matter was not settled in 1992 when the investigation in question took place.

The Law

In the section of figure 4.2 headlined "The Law," the summary refers to the *Tenenbaum* case, which the plaintiffs relied on in arguing that neither the police nor social workers were immune from suit. Citing *Tenenbaum*, they argued that in 1992, when the child abuse investigation took place, the law was clear: police or social workers needed a court order or the consent of a parent to conduct an "invasive investigatory medical examination in the course of an abuse investigation." Thus the child's mother argued that the social workers and police "failed" under the first part of the test because their conduct violated a clearly established right.

Reasoning and Holding

The discussion of the law, under the heading "Reasoning and Holding," makes clear that the test for determining whether qualified immunity applies has two parts, and the court focused on the second part of the test. That part provides that immunity attaches if it was "objectively reasonable" for the state agent to believe that her or his actions did not violate clearly established rights.

Decision

The discussion in the section headlined "Decision" makes it clear why plaintiffs filed their suit under a federal civil rights statute rather than New York law. The court concluded that the behavior of the police and protective service workers was "objectively reasonable," thus satisfying the second part of the *Tenenbaum* test. In reaching its conclusion, the court took into account that it was the "custom and practice" of the sex crimes squad to interview the child outside the home, that the court had no evidence to suggest incompetence or malice on the part of the police or social workers, that their behavior was lawful in New York, and that the purpose of the law was not to thwart protective service caseworkers as they exercised their professional judgment to safeguard children.

A Note on Opinions

The *Galante* ruling was issued by a trial judge. Appellate courts, unlike trial courts, consist of panels of judges. A panel may render a unanimous decision, a majority decision, or a plurality decision, and appellate judges may file both dissenting and concurring decisions. To illustrate, consider the U.S. Supreme Court, which has nine justices. By definition, a unanimous decision is one in which all nine concur, and a majority decision is one in which at least five reach agreement. A plurality decision is one in which the ruling rests on the decision made by the greatest number of judges in agreement but where that number is less than a majority. Thus, if the court splits, such that four judges support one opinion, three judges support another opinion, and the two remaining judges support a third opinion, you would have a plurality ruling.

The majority decision reflects the law of the case, and a decision carries the greatest weight when it is unanimous, with decreasing weight as we move down the hierarchy to majority and plurality rulings. Concurring opinions are those in which the author agrees with the outcome reached by the majority by not necessarily with the reasoning that produced the outcome. Dissents and concurring opinions may be intellectually interesting and may in the future become the opinion of the majority, but until such time they do not have the weight of precedent.

UPDATING CASE LAW

When reporting legal research, you should know the current status of the law that you are reporting. Court decisions may be revised, overruled, and given special interpretation, and statutes may be amended. *Sheppard's Citators* and Westlaw's Key Cite System provide both "positive history"—cases that reached the same conclusion as the case that you are checking—as well as "negative history"—cases that disagreed with part of the case that you are checking or a case that overturned the case that you are checking.

FEDERAL STATUTES AND REGULATIONS

The *Congressional Record* is published each day that either the House of Representatives or the Senate is in session. The texts of bills that are introduced in either the House or the Senate are reported in the *Record*, which may also include debates about bills that have been introduced. When legislation is passed, it is issued first in pamphlet form (called slip laws) by the U.S. Government Printing Office. At the end of each legislative session, the printing office compiles slip laws and publishes them in a series of volumes called *Statutes at Large*, also referred to as "session laws," meaning that the volume contains all the legislation passed in any legislative session. The *United States Code Congressional and Administrative News* and the *United States Code Annotated (U.S.C.A.)*, both published by West, and *United States Code Services (U.S.C.S.)*, published by Lawyers Co-op, are unofficial sources in which you may find legislation.

Regulations issued to guide the implementation of public policy are published in the *Federal Register* when they are first proposed and when they are finalized (see chapter 2). The *Register* identifies the agency proposing the regulations, for example, Health and Human Services, and cites the legislation to which the regulations would apply. Final regulations are published in the *Code of Federal Regulations.*

Figure 4.3 provides the text of House Bill 3443, introduced in November 1999. The text begins with congressional "findings" derived from various sources, such as written testimony submitted to Congress, oral testimony provided at congressional hearings, the research of congressional committees, and reports prepared by scholars at think tanks, such as the Urban Institute or the American Enterprise Institute. Findings provide a rationale for the expenditure of public funds, and they inform the public at large of the purpose that Congress seeks to achieve when it passes legislation and funds programs. The first paragraph tells us that the legislation is intended to benefit "older children" as they make the transition from foster care to independent living. By reading the first and fifth paragraphs in combination, we learn that the benefits provided are educational and include job training, assistance in finding employment, and financial support and that these services should be provided before high school graduation and may continue until the recipient turns twenty-one. The second paragraph addresses the importance that Congress assigns to placing children in adoptive homes by making clear that the receipt of independent living services should not preclude efforts to find such homes. The third and fourth paragraphs describe the problem to be resolved by the legislation.

The information contained in the section headed "Purpose" both elaborates on the purpose of the statute and provides greater detail about the kind of benefits that Congress had in mind. The section headed "Applications" addresses what states must do to qualify for funding, including submitting a state plan, which must (1) describe how programs will operate; (2) ensure that the criteria used to determine program eligibility are objective and fair, and (3) provide ways to cooperate in national evaluations of independent living programs. The

FIGURE 4.3

Legislation Introduced into the House of Representatives

H.R. 3443—November 1999
Foster Care Independence Act of 1999

TITLE I—IMPROVED INDEPENDENT LIVING PROGRAM
Subtitle A—Improved Independent Living Program
SEC. 101. IMPROVED INDEPENDENT LIVING PROGRAM.

(a) FINDINGS—The Congress finds the following:

(1) States are required to make reasonable efforts to find adoptive families for all children, including older children, for whom reunification with their biological family is not in the best interests of the child. However, some older children will continue to live in foster care. These children should be enrolled in an Independent Living program designed and conducted by State and local government to help prepare them for employment, postsecondary education, and successful management of adult responsibilities.

(2) Older children who continue to be in foster care as adolescents may become eligible for Independent Living programs. These Independent Living programs are not an alternative to adoption for these children. Enrollment in Independent Living programs can occur concurrent with continued efforts to locate and achieve placement in adoptive families for older children in foster care.

(3) About 20,000 adolescents leave the Nation's foster care system each year because they have reached 18 years of age and are expected to support themselves.

(4) Congress has received extensive information that adolescents leaving foster care have significant difficulty making a successful transition to adulthood; this information shows that children aging out of foster care show high rates of homelessness, non-marital childbearing, poverty, and delinquent or criminal behavior; they are also frequently the target of crime and physical assaults.

(5) The Nation's State and local governments, with financial support from the Federal Government, should offer an extensive program of education, training, employment, and financial support for young adults leaving foster care, with participation in such program beginning several years before high school graduation and continuing, as needed, until the young adults emancipated from foster care establish independence or reach 21 years of age.

INDEPENDENT LIVING PROGRAM

(a) PURPOSE—The purpose of this section is to provide States with flexible funding that will enable programs to be designed and conducted—

(1) to identify children who are likely to remain in foster care until 18 years of age and to help these children make the transition to self-sufficiency by providing services such as assistance in obtaining a high school diploma, career exploration, voca-

tional training, job placement and retention, training in daily living skills, training in budgeting and financial management skills, substance abuse prevention, and preventive health activities (including smoking avoidance, nutrition education, and pregnancy prevention);

(2) to help children who are likely to remain in foster care until 18 years of age receive the education, training, and services necessary to obtain employment;

(3) to help children who are likely to remain in foster care until 18 years of age prepare for and enter postsecondary training and education institutions;

(4) to provide personal and emotional support to children aging out of foster care, through mentors and the promotion of interactions with dedicated adults; and

(5) to provide financial, housing, counseling, employment, education, and other appropriate support and services to former foster care recipients between 18 and 21 years of age to complement their own efforts to achieve self-sufficiency and to assure that program participants recognize and accept their personal responsibility for preparing for and then making the transition from adolescence to adulthood.

(b) APPLICATIONS—

(1) IN GENERAL—A State may apply for funds . . . for a period of five consecutive fiscal years. . . .

(2) STATE PLAN—A plan meets the requirements of this paragraph if the plan specifies which State agency or agencies will administer, supervise, or oversee the programs carried out under the plan, and describes how the State intends to do the following:

(A) Design and deliver programs to achieve the purposes of this section.

(B) Ensure that all political subdivisions in the State are served by the program, though not necessarily in a uniform manner.

(C) Ensure that the programs serve children of various ages and at various stages of achieving independence.

(D) Involve the public and private sectors in helping adolescents in foster care achieve independence.

(E) Use objective criteria for determining eligibility for benefits and services under the programs, and for ensuring fair and equitable treatment of benefit recipients.

(F) Cooperate in national evaluations of the effects of the programs in achieving the purposes of this section.

(c) REGULATIONS—Not later than 12 months after the date of the enactment of this Act, the Secretary of Health and Human Services shall issue such regulations as may be necessary to carry out the amendments made by this section.

FIGURE 4.4

Reading Statutory Citations: An Example

Foster Care Independence Act of 1999
106th Cong., 1st sess.
113 Stat. 1822
Pub. L. No. 106-169
42 U.S.C. 670 et seq.

final paragraph delegates responsibility to the secretary of Health and Human Services to develop regulations to guide program implementation.

Reading Statutory Citations

The statute that we just reviewed was signed into law by President Clinton in December 1999. The citation to this bill appears in figure 4.4. The first line after the title of the act identifies by number the Congress that enacted the bill (the 106th Congress was in session in 1999 and 2000) and the session of Congress in which the bill was enacted. Each session begins in January and runs for the calendar year.

The next line refers to *Statutes at Large,* discussed earlier. The first set of numbers refers to the volume in which the Foster Care Independence Act appears, and the second set refers to the hierarchal placement of this bill. Thus, "113 Stat. 1822," tells us this law is found in volume 113 and is the 1,822d law found in this volume. Next, we find the statute's public law number. To digress briefly public laws concern the organization of the state and describe the relationship between the state and the citizenry. Public law consists of constitutional, criminal, and administrative law and is distinct from private law, which is concerned with the relationships among individuals and organizations.[3] Returning to the citation, the first three numbers identify the Congress in which the bill was enacted, while the second set of numbers identifies the bill in the hierarchy of bills enacted during the session. Thus this act was the 169th law enacted by the 106th Congress. The *U.S. Code* is the official version of federal statutes. The code is organized first by titles. Title 42, for example, contains legislation concerned with public health and welfare. Each title is broken down into sections. If you look up Title 42, section 670, you will find the Foster Care Independence Act; Section 671 contains information concerning the required state plans. *Et seq.*

means "and the following" and is used when the legislation is spread out over several sections.

From a researcher's standpoint the *U.S. Code*, organized by subject matter, is easier to use than *Statutes at Large*, which organizes the law chronologically. The text of public laws also appears in commercial publications such as West Publishing Company's *United States Code Annotated (U.S.C.A.)* and Lawyers Co-op's *United States Code Services (U.S.C.S.)*. The *U.S. Code*, as well as commercial publications, contains historical information about statutes; for example, if a statute has been amended over time, each amendment is cited. Commercial codes contain additional information, such as references to legal encyclopedias and law reviews that discuss the subject of the statute, cite cases, and provide abstracts for each case cited. For example, if you were to look up Title 42, section 670 in *U.S.C.A.*, you would find that court decisions have clarified the purpose of the act, as well as the meaning of timely plan development.

State Statutes and Regulations

Every state compiles and publishes the laws passed during each legislative session. These collections are similar to those published in *Statutes at Large* and, like *Statutes at Large*, they are published in chronological order. However, all states compile their statutes by subject matter in a publication similar to the *U.S. Code*. Sheppard's also compiles a citator to state laws, and Looseleaf Services are a useful source for identifying major elements of state law and regulations and for directing you to original source documents.

Two guides locate state regulations. If the regulations are published (they are not published in all states), they should be available in any library that compiles state documents. It is beyond the scope of this text to name all the publications in which state regulations may be found. To learn whether your state publishes regulations, you must ask a reference librarian. Alternatively, you might seek copies of regulations from the secretary of state or the state agency that administers the program whose regulations interest you.

COMPUTERIZED LEGAL RESEARCH

You may conduct computerized legal research using CD-ROMs, subscription services such as Westlaw or Lexis, and the Internet. CD-ROMs are available from commercial vendors. They contain various data bases, including federal and state statutes, regulations, and court rulings. Unless you work for an organization that subscribes to a CD-ROM service, they are likely to be prohibitively expensive, in part because they have to be supplemented as the law changes. Likewise, commercial databases available through Lexis and West Group are costly, although many universities and your employer may subscribe to either service or to a service that provides CD-ROMs. Regarding the Internet, several words of caution are in order. First, websites come and go. Next, a website is unlikely to offer a comprehensive legal library on a given topic. Thus, if you search for cases dealing with social worker immunity or any other issue, you cannot be sure that the cases your search retrieves would include all the cases decided in the state or federal jurisdiction in which you are searching. Also, there is no way to predict how long it will take for a statute, regulation, or case to be published on line. Finally, web pages may be redesigned, so the guidelines that follow may be out of date. With these cautions in mind, here is a brief example of how to conduct computerized legal research on the subject of independent living.

Congressional Record

Recall that I said that the Record is published each day that either the House or Senate is in session and that it carries the text of bills that have been introduced. If you know that a bill concerning independent living was introduced in the House sometime in 1999 and you want to know what the bill was about, you could obtain a copy at the site www.access.gpo.gov. In the following order, select "Congressional Record," select "House," and in the date section type "01/01/99 [thru] 12/31/99," then type—in quotation marks—the phrase "independent living." You will retrieve a copy of the bill that appears in figure 4.4.

You can also obtain federal regulations at this website. To do so, select "federal regulations," then select "keyword search." Type "independent living foster care" as a phrase, and your search will produce the regulations for the independent living legislation that I have been discussing.

House of Representatives and the Senate

Each chamber of Congress maintains its own website, with the House accessible at www.house.gov and the Senate at www.senate.gov. At either site you can search by keywords, for example, "independent living," to find the legislation that I have been discussing.

Federal Appeals Court Decisions

If you go to www.uscourts.gov, you will find links to all the federal circuits; if you select "all court sites," you will find links to federal district courts in each circuit. For example, if you select "second circuit," you will find references to federal district courts in Connecticut, New York, and Vermont, and by selecting a state, you will find some court decisions. Finally, a number of universities have excellent law libraries on line, and they are available to anyone. By accessing the on-line libraries at Yale, Cornell, or Emory universities, for example, you can access statutes, including the U.S. Constitution, regulations, and some case law.

SUMMARY

In this chapter I have reviewed primary and secondary sources of law. Secondary sources, or "case-finding tools," include encyclopedias, digests, looseleaf services, and law reviews. A search of secondary sources will produce an overview of the area of law researched and references to additional secondary sources, as well as primary sources such as statutes or court decisions.

You must know how to read legal citations in order to locate cases or statutes. If you follow the directions provided in this chapter, you will find the cases or statutes that you seek. Learning how to read cases requires patience, in part because you have to become familiar with the language of a new discipline and in part because judges do not use a standard format for reporting their decisions. The lack of format often means you must read an entire opinion to understand the factual and legal issues involved. With these caveats in mind, a case can be organized by categories of information, including the (1) procedural history, (2) issues presented for resolution, (3) factual background, (4) legal principle or principles applied to resolve the matter, (5) holding or decision, and (6) reasoning or logic that led the court to rule as it did.

The *Congressional Record* is an excellent source for reviewing legislation soon after its introduction; it often contains commentary by members of Congress that provides some insight into the thinking behind the legislation. The most efficient way to conduct statutory research after legislation is enacted is to research the *U.S. Code*, published by the federal government, or the U.S. Code as published by a commercial publisher. As with case law, the guidelines provided for reading a statutory citation will help you in your research efforts.

Computerized legal research using CD-ROMs or the services of a commercial publisher simplifies legal research, as does use of the Internet. The latter has limits, the most significant of which is the lack of comprehensive coverage. Nevertheless, on-line access to government websites where you may search in the *Congressional Record*, the *U.S. Code*, and the *Code of Federal Regulations* where reported court decisions are found can facilitate your research. To be sure that your work is comprehensive, you will have to supplement your on-line efforts with library work.

PART 2

In chapter 1 reasons why knowledge of the law is essential to social work practice were reviewed. Public funds authorized when social welfare legislation is passed are the main source of support for most social welfare programs. Their development, implementation, and administration are affected by mandates issued by government officials who determine (a) what programs will be established; (b) what level of funding will be provided; (c) what services will be available; (d) what populations will be served; and (e) many of the rules that social workers must follow when they provide services.

In addition, the creation of public and voluntary social service agencies is governed by law, and the use of public funds to support service provision by voluntary agencies is sanctioned by law. Add to this list the following facts: standards set by professional organizations, legislative enactments, and court rulings (1) govern the use of a professional titles such as "clinical social worker" or "psychotherapist"; (2) control the exchange of confidential information; (3) afford to some the right to withhold information in a court of law; (4) in certain circumstances shield practitioners from suit for errors of judgment made while acting in good faith; and (5) expose to liability practitioners who fail to adhere to professional standards of practice and who fail to serve eligible clients without regard to personal characteristics such as race, gender, and physical disability.

These matters will be covered in the three chapters that comprise part 2 of this text. In chapter 5 the organization of social services will be discussed as will be some ways in which the law affects the development, implementation, and administration of social welfare programs and the practice of social work. Chapter 6 will ask the question, "What does a social worker have to know to be an effective participant in the court process?" and chapter 7 will focus on some conditions that give rise to malpractice liability.

5

The Organization of Social Services and the Regulation of the Profession

THE PUBLIC and private sectors provide an array of social services, including educational, health, and mental health services, in such diverse settings as social service agencies, schools, and hospitals. The private sector includes nonprofit agencies, for-profit entities, and private practitioners. Most social workers who are members of the National Association of Social Workers (80 percent) are employed in agency settings, with approximately 34 percent in the public sector (state, local, and federal agencies), 38 percent in the private nonprofit sector, and 28 percent in the for-profit sector.[1]

PUBLIC AGENCIES

Public agencies in each state administer a variety of social welfare programs, including but not limited to (1) those that determine a client's eligibility for financial, food, or medical assistance; (2) those that provide protective services, foster care services, and adoption services for children; (3) counseling and shelter to victims of domestic violence; (4) treatment to individuals addicted to alcohol or drugs; and (5) assistance in obtaining housing and job training.

The authority of social service programs is described in state statutes that identify the organizational unit within state or local government responsible for administering programs and for providing direct services. For example, the New York State Office for the Prevention of Domestic Violence was created by statute. The statute grants to this office diverse responsibilities, such as (1) advising the governor and the legislature on how best to respond to the problem of domestic violence; (2) developing and implementing policies and programs to assist victims of domestic violence and their families; (3) disseminating information concerning this social problem; (4) developing and coordinating outreach and educational programs across New York state; and (5) developing and delivering training to professionals working in the field of domestic violence.[2] In addition, the state office awards contracts for "batterers' programs" to private-sector agencies to provide services to victims of domestic violence.

Statutory changes may alter the operation of public programs and of private agencies supported by public funds. For example, in 1996 Congress reformed public assistance programs when it enacted the Personal Responsibility and Work Opportunity Reconciliation Act (PRWORA), which includes the program called Temporary Assistance to Needy Families (TANF). As was the case with its predecessor program, Aid to Families with Dependent Children (AFDC), TANF provides cash assistance to dependent children and their caretakers. However, AFDC was an entitlement program, meaning all who met the program's eligibility requirements had a legally enforceable claim to benefits. Entitlement programs operate within a legal structure made necessary because clients have a legal claim to benefits. The structure supports adherence to rules that, if ignored, increases the states' costs of defending claim denials. The entitlement ended when TANF was enacted, and when an entitlement ends, rules are often relaxed.[3] For example, parents who participate in TANF are required to work within twenty-one months of the time that they become program participants. New York City implemented its TANF program in 1997, after which income maintenance centers became "job centers" where social workers were charged with hastening the process of putting TANF recipients to work. In an effort to hasten recipients' transition to work, applicants were prevented from applying for food stamps and medical assistance at their first visit to a job center, and notices to clients of their benefit determinations were delayed. In late 1998 a lawsuit was filed on behalf of job center applicants, asserting that the city's actions ran counter to federal rules. The court agreed with the claim and ordered the city, among other things, to allow applicants to apply for cash, food stamps, and medical benefits on their first visit to a job center and to process all applications within the time frames required by law.[4]

NONPROFIT AGENCIES

Nonprofit agencies are generally organized as corporations, which are chartered by the secretary of state. Charters identify the purpose of the agency with regard to services offered and clients served, specify its organizational framework, and name its officers. To provide certain services such as child care and adoption services, nonprofit agencies must obtain a license from the state in addition to their charter. The granting of a license requires that the agency meet certain standards, for example, standards set for fire safety and teacher-student ratios.

Purchase of Service

Historically, nonprofit agencies have been supported by endowments, the interest earned from endowments, fees for service, contributions from the general public, and corporate gifts. In 1962 and again in 1968 Congress amended the Social Security Act to allow public agencies to enter into contracts to purchase from nonprofit agencies services that the public agency had provided. The New York law that established batterers' programs provides that the New York State Office for the Prevention of Domestic Violence enter into contracts with community agencies to provide this service. Today government is the single largest source of funding for nonprofit social service agencies, providing approximately 50 percent of agency income for employment, training, social services, and mental health services.[5]

To increase the number and diversity of agencies eligible to bid for contracts to provide social services, Congress enacted what are called the "charitable choice" provisions of the PRWORA.[6] The purpose of charitable choice is to improve access to federal funding for faith-based organizations by prohibiting states from discriminating against such organizations when they award contracts. To support charitable choice President George W. Bush signed two executive orders in January 2001. He established the Office of Faith-Based and Community Initiatives in the White House and assigned to it the task of setting policies to guide the federal effort to increase the role of faith-based and other community organizations in the provision of social services.[7] At the same time he ordered the creation of Centers for Faith-Based and Community Action in the Departments of Justice, Education, Labor, Health and Human Services, and Housing and Urban Development. Each executive-branch agency was charged with identifying barriers to the participation of faith-based organizations in the provision of social services and with proposing initiatives to eliminate barriers identified. In addition, agencies in the executive branch were charged with developing demonstration programs to increase the participation of faith-based organizations and conducting outreach to inform such organizations of their eligibility to bid for government contracts.

The effect of policy directives on social work practice is not limited to public agency workers but affects social work practice in any setting where the service provided is paid for with public funds. For example, in New York City a significant percentage of the children in foster homes are served by voluntary nonprofit agencies, many of which are operated by religious organizations under contract to the city. If services are supported by public funds, the agency is acting as an agent of the state, and it must adhere to the same rules and regulations imposed on public agencies.[8] Clients are entitled to the same benefits that they would receive if served directly by the public agency. Thus agencies operated by the Catholic Church cannot for reasons based on religious convictions deny to foster children the right to family planning information and contraceptive devices.

FOR-PROFIT ENTITIES

For-profit entities include corporations, partnerships, and solo practitioners, who are licensed to provide services such as medical services, counseling, or day care. Rules governing the formation of a business vary by state. As a general rule, corporations and partnerships register with a designated state office and identify the purpose of their business and the services that they will offer. In contrast, if you are a licensed social worker conducting a solo practice, chances are that you may practice solely on the basis of your professional license. If, however, you should form a partnership or corporation, you will probably be required to register your practice.

Privatization

When the Social Security Act was amended in the 1960s to allow public agencies to enter into contracts with nonprofit agencies, the movement to "privatize" services—to shift service provision from the public to the private sector—began. The movement gained momentum in the 1980s when President Ronald Reagan established a series of commissions and charged each with studying ways to reduce federal expenses and to increase the role of the private sector in performing functions traditionally performed by government.[9] Today legislative support for privatization is found throughout federal law. For example, the welfare reform legislation enacted in 1996 provides that the states may administer and provide services themselves or they may contract with charitable, religious, or private organizations for services for recipients of TANF, Supplemental Security Income, and food stamps.[10] Further evidence that the federal government hopes to increase the role of the private sector in service provision can be found in the Federal Activities Inventory Reform Act of 1998.[11] This act encourages governmental contracting with the private sector, except for matters of concern to national security and for functions that are inherently governmental. The latter are services traditionally carried out by government. Contracting is encouraged unless better value can be obtained by direct government provision or where the private sector lacks the capacity to provide the goods or services required.[12]

A 1997 decision of the U.S. Supreme Court may pose a barrier to efforts to privatize public services. In *Richardson v. McKnight* Ronnie Lee McKnight, a prisoner at a private correctional facility in Tennessee, sued the firm that operated the prison, including two prison guards in its employ, by claiming that his constitutional rights had been violated by the use of "extremely tight physical restraints."[13] The firm argued that it was immune from suit. Traditionally, public employees are immune from suit as long as their actions do not violate a clearly established statutory or constitutional right that the employee was aware of or should have been aware of. In *Richardson* the U.S. Supreme Court was asked to extend qualified immunity to prison guards employed by a private firm. The Court held that the guards were not entitled to qualified immunity because (1) there was no historical precedent for extending the principle of immunity to privately employed prison guards; (2) the private firm received little governmental supervision in its operation of the prison; (3) the task of running the prison had been undertaken for profit; and (4) the purpose of a qualified immunity defense is to protect public officials acting in their official capacity from being sued for civil damages. We shall return to this issue in chapter 7.

POLICY AND PRACTICE

The law and professional standards of practice may affect your work in various ways, for example, by setting rules that govern professional certification and licensing, the use of professional titles, your responsibility to maintain information as confidential, and your obligation under certain circumstances to disclose otherwise confidential information.

Professional Certification and Licensing

The Office of Quality Assurance of the National Association of Social Workers (NASW) sets and promotes standards and confers credentials for the professional who has met minimum educational and practice standards. The office administers four programs, each of which confers a different credential, including the ACSW conferred by the Academy of Certified Social Workers, the SSWS certifying the holder as a School Social Work Specialist, the QCSW (Qualified Clinical Social Worker) credential, and the Diplomate in Clinical Social Work.

In addition to an earned master's degree from an accredited school of social work. the applicant to these NASW programs must have at least two years of postmaster's supervised professional experience and must successfully complete an examination. Certain credentials require that the applicant pass a special test. For example, to be credentialed as a School Social Worker Specialist you must pass the School Social Worker Specialty Area Test, and to retain your credential you must participate in continuing professional education and earn a minimum of thirty hours of continuing professional education every three years. The applicant for the Qualified Clinical Social Worker credential must also hold a valid state social work license or certificate, and the applicant for the Diplomate must have three additional years of advanced clinical practice in addition to the two years of practice experience required for all credentials. Holders of the Diplomate must also have the highest level of social work license or certification available in their state, and they must successfully complete the NASW Diplomate Clinical Assessment Examination.

Certificates issued by professional organizations are not to be confused with state-issued licenses. Licenses are not necessary for the social worker who chooses to practice in an agency under the agency's license. Individual licenses confer the right to engage in private practice and the exclusive right to use designated professional titles. For example, in Minnesota and Florida only state-licensed social workers and those whom they supervise may call themselves "psychotherapists," and only licensed social workers are deemed to be qualified mental health professionals. Colorado and Alabama restrict the "private, independent practice of social work and the right to use the title licensed social worker, independent social worker and social worker" to holders of state licenses.[14]

Requirements for states licenses vary, but in general states set a minimum age for the applicant, who must hold a master's or doctoral degree from an accredited institution, have a minimum number of hours of practice experience, and must pass a state-administered examination. A number of states require a state-issued license as a basis for the practitioner to receive third-party payments from insurance companies.

It is your individual responsibility to be familiar with the licensing laws of the state in which you practice, because misuse of a professional title may subject you to legal liability.[15]

Confidentiality

The terms *confidentiality, privilege,* and *privacy* are often used interchangeably. For our purposes *confidentiality* refers to ethical guidelines and to statutory rules. An example of the former is the NASW *Code of Ethics*, which admonishes social workers to safeguard the "confidentiality of all information obtained in the course of professional service, except for compelling professional reasons."[16] Statutory rules are developed because information must be shared and rules are needed to control the conditions under which information is shared.

Privilege refers to the right to withhold confidential information in a court of law. Privilege is conferred by the legislature or the courts. You cannot refuse to testify in court by claiming that the information requested is confidential: to do so is to place yourself at risk of being held in contempt of court. You can withhold information only if the privilege to do so is granted by law to you as a member of a professional group. Most states extend privilege to social workers, although the privilege may be limited to certified or licensed social workers. In 1996 the U.S. Supreme Court extended to licensed social workers the privilege to withhold testimony in federal court.[17]

Privacy embraces confidentiality but is broader. Privacy

> protects the solitude necessary for creative thought. It allows us the independence that is part of raising a family. It protects our right to be secure in our own homes and possessions, assured that the government cannot come barging in. Privacy also encompasses our right to self-determination and to define who we are. Although we live in a world of noisy self-confession, privacy allows us to keep certain facts to ourselves if we so choose. The right to privacy, it seems, is what makes us civilized.[18]

Social workers are obliged to maintain the confidentiality of client information, yet the quality of social services often depends upon the exchange of information with others. The general rule is that a client or a client's legally authorized representative must consent to the release of records whose privacy is protected by a patchwork of federal and state statutes and court rulings. But there are notable exceptions to the general rule.

The U.S. Supreme Court in *Whalen v. Roe* responded to a challenge to a New York statute that provided for the creation of a centralized databank for storing personal identifying information about individuals receiving prescriptions for drugs such as opium, cocaine, and amphetamines. The Court ruled that the Fourteenth Amendment confers on the individual an "interest in avoiding disclosure of personal matters,"[19] yet in balancing the state's wish to prevent the flow of drugs to unlawful channels (the reason why the databank was created) against the individual's privacy rights, the Court decided that the patient-identification system was a reasonable exercise of state power. In issuing its ruling, the Court noted there was no evidence to sustain the allegation that the plaintiffs' constitutional rights to privacy were threatened. There are other examples where disclosure of otherwise private information is sanctioned for the public good. For example, most states require that physicians and or laboratories report confirmed cases of sexually transmitted diseases to public health officials so the sex partners of the infected person can be notified and tested and treated if necessary. All states permit disclosure of otherwise confidential information when disclosure is ordered by a court.

Concern with maintaining confidentiality has increased in recent times in relation to the use of computers as a primary tool for recording, storing, and transmitting information. As long as paper records stored in offices was the primary means of recording and maintaining information, and as long as the exchange of information required contact between individuals who exchanged information verbally or by transmitting documents, there was a sense of security among clients and professionals concerning confidentiality. Electronic storage and transmission means that information may be disclosed with the push of a button, and such information may be shared with countless individuals and organizations. Proponents of electronic storage and transmission argue that the ease with which information can be exchanged benefits the individual, who may be served more expeditiously because a provider has access to information concerning the client's previous assessment and treatment as well as information describing treatment outcomes. This may be especially important in emergency situations.[20] But the transition from paper to electronic recording and transmission increases the risk that people not entitled to access confidential information will gain access. For these reasons there have been legislative efforts to control the flow of electronic information. We will return to this subject later in this chapter.

At present, statutes that govern confidentiality vary by state, often focusing on protecting health information that relates to stigmatizing conditions, such as HIV/AIDS, other sexually transmitted diseases, mental illness, and substance abuse.[21] Some states have adopted versions of the federal Privacy Act (discussed further on). Others have adopted the Uniform Health-Care Information Act, a model law promulgated by the National Conference of Commissioners on Uniform State Laws that seeks to establish national standards for the maintenance and release of confidential health and mental health information.[22] What follows is (1) an overview of federal rules; (2) an example of two state statutes, one governing confidentiality, the other privilege; and (3) a court decision that illustrates how courts interpret privilege.

Before beginning, a caveat is in order. It is not always easy to determine exactly what information is subject to protection and when information may be disclosed. Caution suggests that you consult an attorney before disclosing information when you are uncertain. Consider the following: A patient told a nurse that he had tested positive for the HIV. She disclosed this information to a physician, who recorded the information in the patient's medical record, which was distributed to others, including a number of employees at the patient's insurance company. The patient sued, arguing that the disclosure violated his rights. The court disagreed, reasoning that the California confidentiality statute at issue was limited to disclosures of information contained in a medical record describing the results of a blood test and that the patient's self-disclosure did not constitute the kind of behavior that the statute proscribed.[23] Relying on this decision, an appellate court in Wisconsin held that disclosure of a prisoner's HIV status by employees of a county jail was not a prohibited disclosure, because they learned of the prisoner's HIV status from a medical report that the prisoner brought with him to the jail and not from the contents of the prisoner's actual medical record.[24] The prisoner's actual medical record was the only information source covered by the statute.

Federal Statutes and Client Confidentiality

The provisions in federal statutes that require service providers to maintain client records in a confidential manner and that concern the conditions under which information in client records may be released range from the general to the specific and are spread across a series of statutes.

The Ryan White Comprehensive AIDS Resources Emergency Act (CARE Act) requires each state receiving federal funds to provide for the confidentiality of information concerning a patient's health status but leaves it to the states to develop specific laws concerning maintenance of records and release of information.[25]

The Americans with Disabilities Act (ADA) has somewhat greater detail than is provided in the CARE Act. The ADA provides that medical information acquired in the course of a pre-employment medical examination cannot be disclosed and requires further that an employer maintain such information on separate forms in a separate medical file and treat the information as confidential.[26]

Public Health Service regulations that govern release of information about clients who have received treatment for alcohol or drug abuse are the most restrictive federal rules on the subject of confidentiality. Federal rules contain a form that may be used when information is requested. Information is not to be released unless the voluntary consent form (1) names the program or person permitted to release information; (2) names or provides the title of the person or organization to which disclosure is to be made; (3) names the patient, whose signature and date of signature are required, unless the patient is not competent to give consent, in which case consent must be given by a person designated to act on behalf of the patient; (4) states the purpose for which the disclosure is to be made; (5) identifies with specificity how much and what kind of information is to be disclosed; (6) states that the consent may be revoked at any time before the program or person to whom the information was released relied on the information to make a treatment decision; and (7) states a date, event, or condition upon which the consent will expire if not revoked beforehand. The law specifies also that consent forms cannot last any longer than is reasonably necessary to serve the purpose for which consent was given.[27]

The Restatement of Bill of Rights for Mental Health Patients contains a congressional directive to the states, which are to review and revise laws to protect mental health patients in a variety of areas, including laws to protect the confidentiality of records and provisions whereby a mentally ill person has access to her or his records.[28] Congress has asked the states to provide by statute for a patient's right to access her or his own records unless (1) the record contains information provided by a third party who was assured that the information would remain confidential or (2) the "health professional" responsible for mental health services determines in writing that access would be detrimental to the patient. If the latter occurs, the material should be made available to another "licensed health professional" selected by the patient, who may elect to provide access to the patient. Patients are also to be informed of these rights, including the right to pursue a grievance with respect to access to their records and the right to a "fair, timely, and impartial" grievance procedure.[29]

The federal Administrative Procedures Act includes the Privacy Act & the Freedom of Information Act. The Privacy Act protects individual privacy with regard to information maintained by federal agencies, but the conditions for sharing information are broad and provide less protection than the title of the act suggests. Records, which are defined to include any item of information, such as a person's educational, financial, medical, criminal, or employment history, are to be disclosed "pursuant to a written request by, or with the prior written consent of, the individual to whom the record pertains."[30] Nevertheless, there are numerous exceptions to this provision. For example, records may be disclosed under a variety of circumstances, including disclosure to personnel who work in the agency that maintains the record and who need the record in the performance of their duties. Thus medical records could be disclosed to persons responsible for determining whether a patient is entitled to insurance payments, to a colleague with whom one is sharing case-management responsibility, or to a supervisor or group of supervisors who are responsible for supervising the record keeper or the person described in the record. Records are also accessible for law enforcement activities and pursuant to a court order.[31] Of the various exceptions in the Privacy Act, the "routine use" exception is the most troublesome. For example, the Veterans Administration has created no fewer than thirty-eight "routine" uses, some exceedingly broad, for its patients' medical records.[32] The Freedom of Information Act (FOIA) establishes rules for accessing records maintained by the federal government.[33] FOIA may be in conflict with the Privacy Act, because FOIA allows access to any information maintained by a federal agency that is not covered by one of nine enumerated exemptions. Of the nine exemptions, the only records of concern to the providers of social services expressly exempted from disclosure are medical records. Another exemption provides that an agency may refuse a FOIA request when the materials sought are exempted from disclosure by another statute. On its face this exemption implies that records protected under the Privacy Act are automatically exempt from FOIA disclosure. However, because this provision is not specific as to the protected records, ongoing court interpretation is required to determine whether records in any set of circumstances are protected or must be disclosed.[34]

The Health Insurance Portability and Accountability Act of 1996 (HIPAA) brings us back to our earlier discussion of electronic storage and information transfer. A main goal of HIPAA is to facilitate the exchange of medical information by using electronic technologies where a "universal patient identifier" would link a patient's files throughout the nation's health care system while simultaneously quieting consumer concerns about privacy violations by establishing rules for the exchange of information.[35] When HIPAA was enacted, Congress directed the Department of Health and Human Services (HHS) to issue regulations to govern the act's implementation. While HHS has issued some regulations, it has not done so concerning the identifiers.[36] In fact, Congress appears to be backing off of the use of identifiers by directing HHS not to use any of the funds allocated by Congress to develop or adopt an identifier system. In May 2001 HHS stated that the development of a patient identifier system was on indefinite hold.[37]

Commenting on the use of patient identifiers, the National Research Council of the National Academy of Sciences stated that the use of a patient identifier has to be balanced against patient privacy and that such use has to be backed by policies that define proper and improper access and impose sanctions against abusers.[38] HIPAA admonishes health care providers, defined to include insurance companies and "clearinghouses" that maintain or transmit health information,[39] to "maintain reasonable and appropriate administrative, technical, and physical safeguards to ensure the integrity and confidentiality of the information; to protect against any reasonably anticipated threats or hazards to the security or integrity of the information; and [protect against] unauthorized uses or disclosures of the information."[40]

State Examples

Figures 5.1, 5.2, and 5.3 contain, respectively, (a) an Illinois confidentiality statute, (b) an Illinois statute conferring privilege, and (c) an Illinois court ruling on the subject of privilege.

The statute represented in figure 5.1 governs the maintenance and release of confidential information by licensed social workers. The statute takes into

FIGURE 5.1

Confidential Communication

No licensed clinical social worker or licensed social worker* [Hereafter, licensed social worker] shall disclose any information acquired from persons consulting the social worker in a professional capacity, except that which may be voluntarily disclosed under the following circumstances:

(a) In the course of . . . consulting with . . . superiors, colleagues or consultants who share professional responsibility . . . all recipients of . . . information are . . . bound to regard the communication as privileged;

(b) With the written consent of the person who provided the information;

(c) In case of death or disability, with the written consent of a personal representative . . .

(d) When a communication reveals the intended commission of a crime or harmful act and . . . disclosure is judged necessary . . . to protect any person from a clear, imminent risk of serious mental or physical harm or injury, or to forestall a serious threat to the public safety;

(e) When the person waives the privilege by bringing any public charges against the licensee; or

(f) When the information is acquired during the course of investigating a report or working on a case of elder abuse, neglect, or financial exploitation and disclosure of the information is in accordance with the provisions of the Elder Abuse and Neglect Act.

(g) When the person is a minor under [state law] and the information acquired by the licensed clinical social worker indicates the minor was the victim or subject of a crime, the licensed social worker may be required to testify in any judicial proceedings in which the commission of that crime is the subject of inquiry and when, after in camera review of the information that the licensed social worker acquired, the court determines that the interests of the minor in having the information held privileged are outweighed by the requirements of justice, the need to protect the public safety or the need to protect the minor, except as provided under the Abused and Neglected Child Reporting Act.

(h) Any person having access to records or any one who participates in providing social work services or who, in providing any human services, is supervised by a licensed social worker, is similarly bound to regard all information and communications as privileged.

(i) Nothing shall be construed to prohibit a licensed social worker from voluntarily testifying in court hearings concerning matters of adoption, child abuse, child neglect or other matters pertaining to children, except as provided under the Abused and Neglected Child Reporting Act.

---

*A licensed clinical social worker must have a master's or doctoral degree in social work and at least three years of supervised clinical social work practice after obtaining a master's degree (IL ST CH 91 5/1–122.1). A licensed social worker holds a master's or bachelor's degree in social work, and the holder of a bachelor's degree must have at least three years of supervised experience (IL ST CH 111 20/9A). Only a licensed clinical social worker may engage in independent practice.

Source: IL ST CH 225 20/16. Edited by the author.

account the necessity of sharing information with others, especially when consulting for the good of the client (section a) or for the good of identified others such as the elderly (section f), or children (sections g and i), as well as for the good of the public at large when the client indicates the intention to commit a harmful act (section d). *In camera* means in private; and when a statute does not preclude an in camera inspection by the court, the privilege is qualified, meaning that the court might rule that the interests of justice demand that the otherwise privileged information be disclosed. By eliminating the possibility of an in camera inspection, the legislature converts the qualified privilege to an absolute privilege.

All statutes governing the maintenance and release of confidential information will provide for its release with the client's consent or the consent of the client's representative (sections b and c). The provision in section (e) for disclosing information when charges are brought against a professional is another element common to confidentiality statutes, as is the provision in section (h) that others with whom information is shared are bound by the confidentiality provisions in the statute.

Excerpts from the Illinois statute governing privileged communication between a rape crisis counselor and a victim appear in figure 5.2. Privilege to withhold information in a judicial proceeding raises the possibility that a defendant's constitutional rights under the Sixth and Fourteenth Amendments will be adversely affected, because the defendant's ability to mount a defense may be compromised. (See fig. 5.3 and the discussion about it.) Thus privilege is not granted lightly,Withholding information must serve a public good that exceeds the possible cost to the person charged with a crime.

After defining "rape crisis counselor" and "confidential communication," the remainder of the statute deals with the waiver of privilege. It is important to review closely the definition of *confidential communication* because it sets boundaries around the communications that are protected. Earlier we discussed court rulings that sanctioned disclosure of a person's HIV status because the statute limited only disclosures of information contained in medical records; thus the language of the statute presented in figure 5.2 could be construed to protect only those exchanges that serve the purpose of "providing information, counseling and advocacy" (paragraph c). Thus a casual exchange in a public place might not be covered nor might exchanges that take place in the context of a general conversation that does not serve an informational, counseling, or advocacy function.

As sometimes happens, a third party is present when a client communicates with a professional. Information disclosed in the presence of a third party may not be covered by rules of confidentiality or privilege. Here an exception is made (paragraph d), no doubt in recognition that victims of violent crimes may benefit from the support provided by a friend whom the victim has asked be present at an interview or by participants in a therapy group.

FIGURE 5.2

Privileged Communications Made to Rape Crisis Personnel

(a) This section is intended to protect victims of rape from public disclosure of statements they make in confidence to counselors of organizations established to help them. . . . Because of the fear and stigma that often results from [rape], many victims hesitate to seek help even where it is available at no cost. . . . [Thus] they not [do not] receive needed medical care and emergency counseling, but may lack the psychological support necessary to report the crime and aid police in preventing future crimes.

(b) A "Rape crisis counselor" is a psychologist, social worker, employee, or volunteer. . . .

(c) "Confidential communication" means any communication between a victim and a rape crisis counselor in the course of providing information, counseling, and advocacy. The term includes all records kept by the counselor or by the organization in the course of providing services to an alleged victim concerning the alleged victim and the services provided.

Waiver of privilege.

(d) The confidential nature of the communication is not waived by: the presence of a third person who . . . expresses the interests of the victim . . . ; group counseling; or disclosure to a third person with the consent of the victim when reasonably necessary to accomplish the purpose for which the counselor is consulted.

(e) Except as provided in this Act, no rape crisis counselor shall disclose any confidential communication or be examined as a witness in any civil or criminal proceeding as to any confidential communication without the written consent of the victim or a representative of the victim.

(f) A rape crisis counselor may disclose a confidential communication without the consent of the victim if failure to disclose is likely to result in a clear, imminent risk of serious physical injury or death of the victim or another person. A rape crisis counselor . . . [whose disclosure is] in good faith . . . shall have immunity from any liability, civil, criminal, or otherwise. . . . The good faith of any rape crisis counselor or rape crisis organization who disclosed the confidential communication shall be presumed.

(g) Any rape crisis counselor who knowingly discloses any confidential communication in violation of this Act commits a . . . misdemeanor.

Source: IL ST CH 735 S 5/8–802. Edited by the author.

The most important provision is found in paragraph (e): that a rape crisis counselor need not disclose in court any confidential communication and may not be examined as a witness without the consent of the victim or the victim's representative. The latter point recognizes that the client, not the social worker or other counselor, is the holder of the privilege and only she or he may waive the privilege. Paragraph (f) provides for disclosure, as did section (d) in the confidentiality statute, for the good of the public when the client indicates intention to commit a harmful act. Paragraph (g) also provides that a counselor cannot be held liable for disclosures made in good faith, and that disclosures made in violation of the statute are misdemeanors.

When a defendant is denied access to information that he or she believes is essential to mounting a defense, the person charged with a crime may, as was the case in *People v. Foggy* (figure 5.3), petition the court to release the information sought. In discussing figure 5.1, I said that the Illinois legislature eliminated the possibility of an in camera inspection of records, thus converting the qualified privilege to an absolute privilege. In the "Summary of Action" section in figure 5.3, the court reports that this issue was raised by the defendant in his appeal, but the court found that argument to be lacking because the privilege was absolute. The legal issue is repeated in this and the next paragraph, which is followed by a brief summary of the facts, including that the victim had been abducted and sexually assaulted and that a store clerk had noted the license plate number of the person who was subsequently arrested.

FIGURE 5.3

A Request to a Court to Release Confidential Information

People v. Foggy, 149 Ill. App. 3d 599, 500 N.E.2d 1026 (Ill. App. Ct. 3d Dist. 1986).

Summary of Action:
Defendant was convicted . . . of aggravated criminal sexual assault. . . . He appealed. Held: refusal to conduct *in camera* hearing to determine whether relevant statements may have been made by rape victim to rape crisis counselors which would be exculpatory . . . or could otherwise impeach victim's testimony, which refusal was based on absolute privilege afforded by statute to confidential communications between rape victims and rape crisis counselors, did not unconstitutionally impair defendant's rights to due process and to confront witnesses against him. Affirmed.

Issue:
Defendant asks whether the privilege afforded confidential communications between rape victims and rape crisis counselors . . . unconstitutionally impairs his 6th and 14th Amendment rights to due process and to confront witnesses against him.

Facts:
The victim . . . complained that the defendant . . . abducted her and performed an act of sexual intercourse. . . . [A] store clerk [noted the] defendant's license plate [number]. [Victim] . . . phoned the police. . . . A complaint was filed . . . and a warrant for defendant's arrest was issued and executed.

Procedural History:
Defendant served a subpoena *duces tecum* . . . on the . . . Counseling Program seeking discovery of communications between [the victim] and [a] Rape Crisis Counselor. [Efforts to quash] . . . the subpoena [were successful]. . . . The confidential communications were absolutely privileged . . . and . . . [the victim] had not waived the . . . privilege . . . and the legislation [conferring the privilege] was not unconstitutional.

In [his] appeal, defendant renew[ed] his challenge to the constitutionality of the absolute privilege [and] contends that the privilege [violates] his 6th and 14th Amendments rights since it precludes . . . an *in camera* review [to determine] whether [the] victim [made] exculpatory statement . . .

Law:
. . . a defendant in a criminal prosecution enjoys a fundamental right to confront adverse witnesses . . . and to cross-examine them. The defendant's right to cross-examine . . . is not absolute and must at times "bow to accommodate other legitimate interests in the criminal trial process."

Holding & Decision:
[W]e believe that the nature of the privilege . . . considering the explicit statement of legislative intent embodying a strong public policy favoring an absolute privilege, requires [that we affirm]. . . .

Reasoning:
The privilege . . . was not enacted merely to protect the witness from public embarrassment or loss of reputation. . . . It was enacted [for] the . . . purpose of promoting the prosecution of sex offenders. . . . The relationship and open communication promoted by the privilege of confidentiality [may] represent . . . the first step taken by the victim [to] pursu[e] . . . justice. . . . The counselor coordinates interviews between the victim and the prosecutor and accompanies the victim . . . to the . . . attorney's office and to court. All services are provided with the assurance . . . [of] confidentiality. . . . The privilege . . . promotes the judicial process. . . .

We believe it . . . significant that . . . the statute . . . eliminate[s] *in camera* disclosure . . . [thus] convert[ing] a conditional privilege . . . into an absolute privilege. . . . The legislature intended to promote the strong public policy favoring the pursuit of justice on behalf of rape victims.

Source: *People v. Foggy,* 149 Ill. App. 3d 599 (Ill. App. Ct. 3d Dist. 1986). Edited by the author.

The section headed "Procedural History" refers to a subpoena *duces tecum,* which is a demand that the person ordered to appear in court bring documents identified in the subpoena. Here we note that counsel for the defendant issued such a subpoena, which the counseling center was successful in having "quashed," or vacated, overthrown, or annulled, because the communications were absolutely privileged and because it was determined that the privilege did not undermine any constitutional right of the defendant.

In the next two sections of the decision, the "Law" and the "Holding and Decision," the court makes clear that a defendant has a fundamental right to confront and cross-examine witnesses, but as with most rights, the protection is not absolute. There are situations, as here, where a person's right must give way to the public good that the legislature sought to achieve when it conferred privilege on the client's communication to a rape crisis counselor. In the final "Reasoning" section the court discusses why the privilege was granted. The privilege is conferred to protect a victim from the public embarrassment of having certain facts reported in open court and to increase the likelihood of prosecuting offenders. The underlying assumption is that, without the cloak of privilege, rape victims would not come forward.

Disclosure of Confidential Information

Sharing personal information, especially in large organizations, is not as regulated as we might expect. Even when protections exist—those found in the federal Privacy Act, for example—people may be unaware of the extent to which their personal information is shared with others.

Concern for the confidentiality of records was expressed by the National Research Council of the National Academy of Sciences when it reported that individuals might be surprised at the "electronic access now available to doctors, hospitals, insurers, prescription plans and state health agencies."[41] The panel urged that providers adopt practices to reduce unauthorized access to information, including the use of unique passwords for any employee authorized to access a patient's record, systems that are programmed to shut down if a work station is left idle for a set period of time, routine audits to track all accesses to confidential information, and a zero-tolerance policy for violators because most hospitals allow doctors and nurses to access the files of all patients, including those not under their care. The frequent use of e-mail raises concerns regarding confidentiality, since e-mail directed to a person in an organizational setting may be accessible by others. It may be necessary to encrypt messages to ensure that confidential information is not disclosed.

Countering the position of the academy are those who argue that the provision of high-quality health care services might be seriously impaired by rules limiting access to information. They argue that proponents of restrictive rules fail to recognize that health care is provided in an "integrated marketplace" where sharing of information in multiple directions is a daily occurrence. Patients are ultimately put at risk if privacy provisions require that patients decide to whom their information should be available. Proponents of more open access argue that current privacy rules hinder the provision of health care and increase its costs.[42]

These general concerns aside, there are a variety of circumstances in which confidential information may be disclosed without the consent of the client or patient. In general, when the state can demonstrate a need for information that overrides an individual's right to privacy and confidentiality, the state's need will trump the individual's right.

An example of overriding the individual's right to privacy appears in figure 5.4, a mental health confidentiality statute from Florida. After stating a general rule regarding the confidentiality of clinical records (paragraph 1), the statute provides for both the mandatory release of information (paragraph 2) and the permissive release of information (paragraph 3). As stated in parts (a) through (c) of paragraph 2, information "shall" be released when (a) a release is authorized by the patient or the patient's guardian; (b) needed by the patient's attorney; or (c) ordered by a court after it has weighed the good to be achieved by a release against possible harm to the person whose records are released. Paragraph 3 says that disclosure is permitted when a patient threatens another with harm or, with the approval of an official, when needed for (a) research, (b) treatment, (c) records maintenance, (d) planning, (d) program evaluation, or (e) by the state for monitoring purposes.

Provisions for release of otherwise confidential records for research purposes are commonly found in confidentiality statutes, which may require that identifying information such as a patient's name be deleted before records are released. Note that the provisions for release in paragraphs 3(b) and 4 are extensive, suggesting the breadth of release cited earlier by the National Academy of Sciences.

The concluding sections of this statute provide for the continued confidentiality of released records (paragraph 5), protection against civil or criminal liability when records are released in good faith (paragraph 6), and provisions for a patient to access her or his own records (paragraph 7).

Thus far we have considered situations in which disclosure of otherwise confidential information is permitted. There are circumstances in which disclosure is required. For example, with few exceptions, all states require social workers to report known or suspected child abuse to state officials.

In 1974, in *Tarasoff v. Regents of the University of California*, the Supreme Court of California ruled that when a doctor or a psychotherapist determines, or through the exercise of reasonable professional judgment should determine, that a patient poses a danger to another, who is not a patient, a duty arises obligating the professional to warn the person who is endangered (*Tarasoff* I).[43] The *Tarasoff* case arose in the late summer of 1974 after a voluntary outpatient at a mental health clinic at the University of California at Berkeley told his therapist that he was going to kill his girlfriend. Although the young woman was not identified by name, the young man provided enough information so that her

FIGURE 5.4

Confidentiality and Release of Clinical Records

Florida Mental Health Act. Clinical Records—Confidentiality

(1) A clinical record shall be maintained for each patient. . . . A clinical record is confidential. . . . Unless waived by express and informed consent [of] the patient . . . the patient's guardian or . . . the [deceased] patient's . . . representative, . . . the confidential status of the . . . record shall not be lost by . . . disclosure. . . .

(2) The clinical record shall be released when:

(a) The patient or the patient's guardian authorizes the release;

(b) The patient is represented by counsel and the records are needed by the patient's counsel for adequate representation.

(c) The court orders such release. In determining whether there is good cause for disclosure, the court shall weigh the need for the information to be disclosed against the possible harm of disclosure to the person to whom such information pertains.

(3) Information from the clinical record may be released when:

(a) A patient has declared an intention to harm other persons.

(b) Approved by a [proper official] to a qualified researcher; aftercare treatment provider, or employee . . . of the department . . . for treatment of the patient, maintenance of adequate records, compilation of treatment data, aftercare planning, or evaluation of programs.

(4) Information from clinical records may be used by the [State to] . . . monitor facility activity and complaints. . . .

(5) Any person [or] agency receiving information pursuant to this section shall maintain . . . information as confidential. . . .

(6) Any facility or private mental health practitioner who acts in good faith in releasing information pursuant to this section is not subject to civil or criminal liability. . . .

(7) Patients shall have reasonable access to their clinical records, unless . . . access is determined by the patient's physician to be harmful to the patient. [A] restriction of a patient's right to inspect his or her clinical record shall expire after 7 days but may be renewed, after review, for subsequent 7-day periods.

Source: FL ST S 394.4615. Edited by the author.

identify could be easily ascertained. The young man was taken into custody, then released when the campus police became convinced that he was rational and received his promise to stay away from his girlfriend. He killed his girlfriend after her return from summer vacation.

The *Tarasoff* ruling raised concern among mental health professionals, who resisted the notion that they were able to predict who was and who was not dangerous. They argued that therapists, rather than face a lawsuit, would engage in defensive practices by issuing unnecessary warnings and that the therapist-patient relationship would be severely undermined if clients knew that their disclosures could be made public.

The outcry from the professional community caused the California Supreme Court to reconsider *Tarasoff.* In July 1976 the court vacated its 1974 ruling and, after rehearing, clarified the duty that therapists owe to third parties who are the subject of a patient's threat (*Tarasoff II*).[44] The therapist's duty is to act reasonably under the circumstances, the court said. This duty may be discharged in several ways, including warning the person threatened or informing others who are likely to apprise her, notifying the police in the vicinity where the threatened person lived, or committing the patient or taking other steps reasonable under the circumstances.

In the summer of 1980 the California Supreme Court had occasion to revisit and further clarify its *Tarasoff* ruling in *Thompson v. Alameda County.*[45] *Thompson* concerned an incarcerated juvenile offender who said that when he was released, he would kill a child in his neighborhood. While on leave he did so. California's high court distinguished *Thompson* from *Tarasoff* and dismissed the suit brought by the murdered boy's parents. Unlike the victim in *Tarasoff,* there was no "readily identifiable" victim in *Thompson.* The victim could have been any one of the children in the neighborhood where the patient lived. Not only would warnings be difficult to give, but they would serve little purpose because parents could do no more than exercise ordinary vigilance over their children.

Since the *Tarasoff* ruling, a majority of states have established rules, through statute or court decisions, that address the issue of a professional's duty to warn. The majority of states use the phrase "mental health professional" in discussing who is obligated to provide a warning. States using this phrase include social workers in their definition of mental health professional, although in some states the duty to warn is limited to "licensed" or "board-certified" social workers.[46]

With several exceptions, the rules established by the various states have in common that (1) the client must make an explicit threat to an identified or identifiable victim; (2) the therapist has no express duty to warn the threatened victim, but a general duty to warn that may be satisfied in the ways spelled out by the California court in *Tarasoff* II; and (3) the professional is immunized against suit for disclosing confidential information.[47]

Texas and Wisconsin do not require that a specific victim be identified but that the therapist warn everyone within the "zone of danger" who may, depending upon the threat that is made, include all members of a person's family or all who work with the client.[48]

The kind of warning required by California and other states that have a rule similar to *Tarasoff* rest on the assumption that the special relationship that exists between therapists and their clients extends to third parties who are threatened by a client. Courts in New York, Florida, Virginia, and Kansas have not been willing to expand the notion of special relationship in so broad a manner.[49] Thus New York's high court allowed the parents of an infant to sue a pediatrician and the manufacturer of polio vaccine for injuries suffered by the infant's father, who was exposed to the virus in providing care to the infant. The risk of parental "contact" polio was well known, and the court found that a special relationship existed between the parents and the physician, who knew or should have known that the parents relied on his special medical expertise and who should have warned them of the risk of exposure.[50]

In contrast, a New York court rejected a wife's claim against her husband's physician in which she argued that the physician was negligent because he failed to warn her that her husband had tuberculosis.[51] The court held that a physician's duty is owed to the patient. The wife is a member of the community at large. She may also be a member of that class of people whom the physician knew or should have known were relying on him. However, the court reasoned that if it extended a duty of care, there would be no line of demarcation. Stated otherwise, there is no point where that duty would end. If there is a duty to a patient's spouse, why not extend the duty to other individuals with whom the patient had close contact, such as other relatives, coworkers, or even fellow commuters?

New York relies on the "professional judgment rule," whereby a physician or mental health professional will not be held liable if he has used his best judgment in making treatment decisions. Courts will not find professional liability for simple errors of judgment.[52] Thus the professional judgment rule has been used to exculpate psychiatrists from liability for diagnostic decisions,[53] treatment decisions,[54] decisions to release hospital patients who later harm themselves or others,[55] and decisions denying hospital admission.[56] New York courts will not apply the professional judgment standard to immunize psychiatric decisions where there was a failure to evaluate the condition of potentially dangerous patients before discharging them from the hospital[57]; or where there was a failure to keep detailed and proper medical notes preventing a determination whether an evaluation of the patient had been made by a qualified psychiatrist.[58]

SUMMARY

In this chapter some of the ways in which the law affects the organization and practice of social work have been reviewed. The former recognize that social services are provided by the public and the private sectors, including both nonprofit agencies and for-profit agencies in the private sector. The services provided by public agencies are described in the statutes that create them. Those provided by private agencies are described in documents that each agency files with an official agency in its home state, the secretary of state, for example.

Public agencies typically purchase from the private sector a broad array of services, such as counseling services, medical and mental health services, and foster care services. Beginning in the 1980s, the move gained momentum to privatize social services by contracting with private organizations to operate programs previously run by the state. Today legislative support for privatization is found throughout federal law.

Public policy affects the practice of social work practice in different ways. In the preceding pages we have considered policies that control professional certification and licensing, policies that control confidentiality of client information, rules that grant to social workers and other professionals the privilege to withhold information in a court of law, and rules that require under certain circumstances the disclosure of otherwise confidential information.

The National Association of Social Workers offers several credentials, all of which require the applicant to possess a master's degree from an accredited school of social work and a defined minimum of practice experience. Licenses that are issued by state government confer the right to engage in private practice and the exclusive right to use designated professional titles, such as "State-Licensed Social Worker."

Professional ethics and an array of policies limit disclosure of information concerning a person's health, mental health, illegal use of controlled substances, and general information maintained in records of federal agencies, including information concerning a person's educational, financial, medical, criminal, or employment history. The U.S. Supreme Court has ruled that individuals have a constitutionally protected interest in preventing disclosure of personal matters.

Concern with maintaining confidentiality has increased in recent times, along with the practice of relying on computers as a primary tool for recording, storing, and transmitting records and along with a decreased reliance on paper records stored in offices. The ease with which electronically stored information can be transmitted to countless individuals adds to the concern that information will fall into the wrong hands.

Proponents of electronic storage and transmission argue that the ease with which information can be exchanged benefits the individual who may be served more expeditiously because a provider has access to information concerning the client's previous assessment and treatment, as well as information describing treatment outcomes. This may be especially important in emergency situations. But the transition from paper to electronic recording and transmission increases the risk that people not entitled to access confidential information will gain access. For these reasons there have been legislative efforts to control the flow of electronic information.

There are numerous exceptions to rules that purport to protect confidential information from disclosure. Records may be disclosed to personnel in an agency on a need-to-know basis; to those outside an agency who oversee insurance payments; to colleagues who share case-management responsibility for serving clients; to a supervisor or group of supervisors responsible for supervising the record keeper; to quality control units that monitor agency compliance with professional standards and applicable law; and of course to the person described in the record. Records are also accessible for law enforcement activities and pursuant to a court order.

Privilege to withhold information in a judicial proceeding can be granted only by act of a legislative or judicial body. Withholding information in court raises the possibility that a defendant's constitutional rights under the Sixth and Fourteenth Amendments will be adversely affected, because the defendant's ability to mount a defense may be compromised; thus privilege is not granted lightly and only when withholding information serves a public good that exceeds the possible cost to the person charged with a crime.

There are situations where policy mandates disclosure without client consent, including a social worker's obligation to report known or suspected child abuse or neglect and, in some states, to warn a third party who is not a client that his or her life has been threatened by a client.

6

Social Workers and the Courts

AS A SOCIAL WORKER, you may be employed by the courts, law enforcement agencies, or law firms, or you may be a member of a multidisciplinary team that includes attorneys, medical and mental health professionals, accountants, and members of the clergy. In any of these ways you may have regular contact with the judicial system; you also may have such contact if your practice involves working with children and their parents, young adults, victims of domestic violence, or the mentally ill. Your work may require that you interview clients to gain information for attorneys, to prepare reports for use by a judge, or to prepare yourself to testify in court. In addition, you may be required to interpret social science information for members of the legal profession, to consult on how best to approach client problems, or to testify in court as either a fact witness or an expert witnesses.

In some practice settings you will have access to legal counsel whose advice you may seek when questions arise about what evidence to gather, how to document your observations, and what evidence is admissible in court. Attorneys will review your records before they are presented in court, and they will prepare you before you testify. However, in day-to-day practice, the likelihood that a case will go to court will not always be foremost in your mind. Many months, even years, may pass between the time you began to work with a client and the onset of litigation. For this reason it is important you be knowledgeable of legal issues that bear on your role as a participant in the legal process and that you conduct your practice with an eye to the future.

This chapter will begin with a discussion of forensic social work. Next, in the first of three parts, evidence and the admissibility in court of different kinds of evidence, will be discussed. Issues related to providing testimony will be the focus of part 2. There our attention will be on such topics as qualifying as an expert and the admissibility of expert testimony. The subject of providing testimony in court will be covered in part 3.

FORENSIC SOCIAL WORK

Forensic social workers apply the principles and practices of their discipline to the purpose of law. Forensic work is limited by the requirements of law, but at the same time it has the potential to embrace the entire range of practices that characterize any discipline.[1] Some social workers specialize in forensic work, while others undertake forensic activities as the need arises.[2]

Acting as a forensic specialist you may engage in any of the activities that typify social work practice, including (1) interviewing, (2) assessment, (3) evaluation, (4) testifying in court, (5) consulting, (6) preparing reports, and (7) supervising others. However, these activities are undertaken with knowledge of the legal framework that surrounds particular areas of practice and applicable legal principles, including (a) legislation, such as that addressing child abuse and neglect, child custody, adoption, domestic violence, witness competency to testify, and mental health commitment; (b) the legal processes involved in achieving certain outcomes, such as adoption and civil commitment of the mentally ill; (c) the structure and functioning of the social service and court systems in the state where you practice; (d) the roles played by the various parties in a court proceeding, such as judges, attorneys, those who represent children, and witnesses; and (e) a general understanding of what evidence is admissible and how evidence is used in court. And effective forensic practice requires information from the social sciences specific to the area in which you specialize and may include information on child development, memory, and communication and on the conditions that constitute physical disabilities and those that define mental illness.

Interest in forensic social work was spurred in part by the role that social workers played in the criminal prosecutions of teachers and administrators who were charged with sexually abusing children in day-care settings in the 1980s. The McMartin Preschool case in Los Angeles and the Margaret Kelly Michaels preschool case in New Jersey are the most famous of these cases.

The McMartin case began in August 1983 when the mother of a child at the preschool informed the police that her son's "bottom was red" and that he had made reference to a man who worked at the school. Concerned that the child's condition was the result of sexual misconduct by an adult, parents whose children attended the school were alerted to check their children for signs of molestation. Prosecutors eventually alleged that school officials and teachers had molested hundreds of children over five years. The trial was the longest and most costly in U.S. history, lasting for thirty-three months and costing California more than $15 million. The case was dismissed in January 1986 for insufficient evidence and without any convictions.[3] The Kelly Michaels case, like the McMartin case, involved allegations of sex abuse of children in day care. Unlike the McMartin case, Michaels was the sole defendant. She was convicted and spent approximately five years in prison before a New Jersey appellate court overturned her conviction.

The McMartin and Michaels cases have in common that the techniques used to gather information from the children were suspect. Jurors in the McMartin case said they voted for acquittal because they viewed the techniques used to interview the children as improper. Likewise, when the New Jersey Superior Court overturned the conviction of Margaret Kelly Michaels, it referred to inappropriate interviewing techniques. Besharov (1990) echoes this point in his discussion of the McMartin case. He tells us that jurors expressed concern that the only evidence linking the defendants to the alleged incidents of abuse was the children's statements, which a series of investigative and prosecutorial missteps had undermined. Jurors said that "there was not enough reliable evidence to decide whether the children had actually gone through the horrible things they described—or imagined them following the unintentional prompting of adult investigators and therapists."[4] Focusing on investigative techniques, the New Jersey appellate court said that the manner in which the interrogations were conducted was "highly improper [and that] the children's accusations were founded upon unreliable perceptions, or memory caused by improper investigative procedures."[5] According to Bruck and Ceci (1995), interviewers in the Michaels case had preconceived notions that the children had been abused. The authors based this conclusion on information provided by the interviewers, who believed that their major objective was to get the children to admit to sexual abuse.

The observation that the testimony of children may have been unduly influenced by interviewers who "suggest" answers that they wish to hear is not a new one. In 1985 in Minnesota parents accused of sexually abusing their children sued various government officials, alleging in part that their children were "worn-down and brainwashed" into making accusations against them.[6] The defendants, including county attorneys, sheriff's deputies, therapists, and social workers, were said to have coerced the children to give the responses they desired by differentially reinforcing children through verbal and nonverbal cues for providing "correct" answers.

These cases have called into question the credibility of child witnesses. Professionals have exacerbated the problem by claiming, notwithstanding the lack of empirical support, that young children do not lie about sexual abuse, because it involves matters that are outside their knowledge, and that young children are not vulnerable to having their testimony influenced by interviewer behavior.[7] Believing either proposition, an interviewer may deem as factual statements that are the product of her or his interview technique, not of the child's experience, or the interviewer may assume that the child who has recanted earlier testimony must have done so out of fear rather than recognizing that a child may have reconsidered the truth of her story.

In 1993 Ceci and Bruck reviewed all the research conducted in the twentieth century on the suggestibility of young children, and in 2000 Ceci and Friedman updated this review. The final conclusion that they reached, although disputed by some,[8] is that children are suggestible when (1) clinical interviewing techniques are used that prompt or suggest to the child the answer sought; (2) rewards are provided during the interview; (3) closed questions are repeated throughout the interview and across interviews; (4) interviewers use differential reinforcement where by tone of voice or facial expression they reward children for providing information sought and show disapproval when the answer does not correspond to the interviewer's expectations; and (5) interviewers engage in "stereotype induction," wherein the child being interviewed is repeatedly told that the person who is the subject of the questioning. such as a teacher, is a "bad" person.[9]

Therapeutic and Forensic Interviewing

The goals of therapeutic and forensic interviews are different.[10] The forensic investigator is concerned with collecting facts relevant to the case that will be presented in court. The work of the forensic investigator is to facilitate the fact-finding role of the court without presenting information that is either unfairly prejudicial or confusing.[11] This is in contrast to the emphasis on problem solving that is common to a therapeutic interview. Material derived from a therapeutic, or clinical, interview may or may not be based in objective reality and subject to verification. Because this distinction in roles is an important one, several professional organizations have adopted guidelines explicitly stating that the forensic and clinical roles should be filled by different individuals, and professional organizations have developed guidelines for forensic evaluations of children.[12]

Some states have enacted statutes to govern the questioning of child witnesses by requiring that (1) investigators receive special training; (2) the number of interviews be limited; (3) the amount of time a child spends on the witness stand be limited; and (4) safeguards be put in place to protect children from the harassment that may result when interviewers pressure children to provide desired responses.[13] For example, California law provides for investigations by "court-appointed investigators," including "child custody evaluators" who must receive special training and whose evaluations must conform to statutory guidelines.[14] A number of states have implemented "advocacy centers," which contain both treatment and interviewing rooms designed for children.[15] Conferees at an international meeting sponsored by the Family Law Section of the American Bar Association expressed their wish that the legal and mental health systems develop means to reduce the impact of contentious cases on children. They recommended that efforts be made to improve parent evaluations and evaluations of children to ensure that evaluators meet qualifications established by courts or a legislative body and that evaluators (1) receive training and continuing education on how to conduct a neutral and objective interview; (2) receive training and continuing education on topics, including child and adult development, interview techniques, domestic violence, child abuse and neglect, and family law; (3) provide reports that are "jargon free" and that reflect both positive and negative traits of the person evaluated; (4) distinguish clearly between clinical judgments, research-based opinions, and philosophical positions; (5) summarize their data-gathering procedures, identify their sources of information, and the amount of time spent exploring each source; (6) specify the limitations of their reports that result from their inability to obtain certain information, such as a party's failure to cooperate or other circumstances; and (7) have the skills to negotiate and resolve, before court appearance, differences with other evaluators if reports are conflicting.[16]

PART 1—EVIDENCE

Evidence refers to the different kinds of proof admitted in court to convince a judge or a jury of the truth of the matter being heard. The federal court system and that of the states (see chapter 3) have a body of law, called the law of evidence, which contains rules that judges apply to determine whether evidence is admissible and that govern the circumstances under which evidence is or is not admissible. The *Federal Rules of Evidence* governs the kinds of proof admissible in federal courts. Some states have adopted these rules, while others have their own rules of evidence.

Direct Evidence

Direct evidence comes from firsthand knowledge. It consists of facts describing what you heard, saw, said, and did. The following is an example of how you might record direct evidence after beginning an investigation into a report of child neglect:

> I arrived at the Phillips home at 2:30 *p.m.* Within five minutes of my arrival, I knocked on the door three times, each time waiting for someone to open the door. After the third time a child who appeared to be five years of age opened the door. She said that she was home alone. She said that her mother had gone to the grocery store and would home in a "coupla minutes." I waited outside for ten minutes. Mrs. Phillips did not return. I then knocked on the door of the next apartment. The door was answered by a woman who identified herself as Mrs. Garcia. Mrs. Garcia said that she did not know where Mrs. Phillips was. I requested and was given permission to use Mrs. Garcia's telephone. I telephoned the Fifth Precinct and requested an officer's assistance in taking the child into protective custody. Officer Steven Washington arrived within fifteen minutes. After I knocked at the door of the Phillips apartment, the child again opened the door. We talked with her for approximately five minutes, following which Officer Washington and I took the child to the offices of the Department of Social Services.[17]

Real Evidence

Documents and photographs are real evidence. A copy of school attendance records showing a high rate of absenteeism and certified by school authorities is one type of real evidence that may be presented to the court to support an allegation of educational neglect. X-rays and photographs may be important evidence in substantiating allegations of physical abuse or domestic violence. Letters sent to clients and returned by the post office bearing the legend "moved, no forwarding address" show efforts to locate parents and may be used to support an abandonment petition.

Circumstantial Evidence

Circumstantial evidence consists of deductions drawn from other kinds of evidence. For example, in one case, after photographs showing injuries sustained by a victim of domestic violence were introduced as real evidence, the following circumstantial evidence was offered to show the defendant struck the victim with a baseball bat: (1) the victim's testimony that the defendant was holding a bat when he hit her and that he hit her with something in his hand which was "hard"; (2) testimony from police officers who reported finding a bat with blood on it in the bedroom of the defendant's home; and (3) testimony from a physician who reported that the victim's injuries were consistent with having been hit with a baseball bat.[18]

Hearsay Evidence

Hearsay is secondhand information whose truth cannot be ascertained through cross-examination. The person whose observation is being reported is either unable, unwilling, or unavailable to testify, as in the baseball bat assault. If you were to testify that a neighbor saw the defendant hit his wife with a bat, this statement would be hearsay and would not be admissible in court. The statement may or may not be true. While true, it may exaggerate the situation and not reflect accurately the events that it purports to describe. There are exceptions to the hearsay rule.

Excited Utterances

These are statements made while the declarant is under stress caused by a startling event or condition. An excited utterance is presumed to be reliable because it is spontaneous and uncalculated. In *State v. Fortin* the court ruled that the out-of-court statements made by a rape victim to her former roommate and a police officer immediately after the sexual assault were admissible under the excited utterance exception to the hearsay rule.[19] And in *Hunt v. State* the court allowed the testimony of the mother of an eleven-year-old; the mother described a conversation with her daughter, who had been sexually assaulted by a friend of the child's father.[20] Several months after the child in *Hunt* was assaulted, she was watching a television program about a young rape victim and she began to sob hysterically. On questioning, she told her mother about the assault. The child testified at trial, where she reported that watching the television program caused her to become fearful that she might be pregnant, and her mother testified about her conversation with her daughter. Despite the passage of time and the fact that the event that triggered the excited utterance was not the attack itself, the court sanctioned the admission of the hearsay testimony, finding that the shock of seeing the television news program was sufficient to trigger the victim's out-of-court statements, and that her fear of pregnancy was startling enough to produce a state of nervous excitement so as to render her subsequent remarks spontaneous. But in *Glover v. State* the court ruled that hearsay testimony offered by the mother of a statutory rape victim did not qualify as an excited utterance because the statement was not made under the stress of the assault but under stressful conditions induced by the mother, who questioned her daughter by confronting her in an intentionally stressful way that was calculated to elicit a confession.[21]

Medical Exception

A second exception to the hearsay rule is evidence given to a medical person for the purpose of receiving treatment, because it is assumed that a person who needed treatment would not lie to a medical person. When courts consider whether to allow testimony under this exception to the hearsay rule, the question of concern is whether the patient believed that the information was given in expectation of receiving a medical benefit. In *State v. Ashford* statements made by a child to a triage nurse were allowed under this hearsay exception, since they described a sexual assault on the child.[22] But in *Cassidy v. State,* hearsay presented by a physician was disallowed. The court ruled that it was not admissible because the child was too young to understand the purpose of giving accurate information for medical treatment.[23]

Whenever hearsay evidence is allowed in court, a defendant's Fourteenth Amendment right to confront and cross-examine witnesses is compromised. For this reason the U.S. Supreme Court has ruled that if the witness whose testimony is entered into evidence is not available to testify, hearsay will be allowed only if it is sufficiently reliable to protect the defendant's constitutional rights.[24] Both the excited utterance and medical exceptions to the hearsay rule are considered reliable and trustworthy. For this reason in *White v. Illinois* the U.S. Supreme Court ruled that the Sixth Amendment rights of the defendant were not violated when a four-year-old's out-of-court statements describing her sexual abuse were admitted under both the excited utterance and medical exceptions and reported in court by the child's babysitter, mother, an investigating officer, and medical personnel.[25]

Prior Recollection Recorded

You may have made notes about an incident when it occurred. Notes may be read aloud at a trial, if you testify that (1) you had firsthand knowledge of the event when you made the notes; (2) you do not now remember the event; (3) the notes were made when your memory of the event was fresh; and (4) the notes were accurate when they were made.

Admissions

Admissions are statements made by a party to a legal action. A party is a person whose interests are at risk in the legal proceedings. If a parent tells you that he abused his son, you may repeat this statement in court. This admission is allowed as evidence to prove that the parent committed the act. If a neighbor told you that she abused the child in question, you cannot repeat her statement in court if she is not a party to the proceeding. An admission cannot be self-serving. For example, the statement "I did not abuse my son" would not be permitted under this exception.

Admission by Silence

If, in an interview with the parents of an allegedly abused child, the mother tells you that the father "always uses his belt to discipline their son," you could testify to this in court (1) if the statement was made in the father's presence, and (2) if it can be shown that he heard the statement, understood it, and did not object to it. His silence is construed as agreement with what was said by his wife. This testimony would not be admissible if the father (1) was not present; (2) did not hear the statement made; or (3) had consulted with an attorney and was acting on his attorney's advice not to talk about the incident.

Official Records

Birth and death certificates, official registries such as a sex-offender or child-abuse registry, and school or hospital records are allowed into evidence as exceptions to the hearsay rule. These records are admissible because it is assumed that a public official has no motive to create a false record because the public official did have not a direct connection to the people or events to which the records refer.

Catchall, or Residual Hearsay, Exceptions

A judge may make an exception to the hearsay rule, under the "catchall," or residual hearsay, exception if the nature and circumstances under which a statement was made offer strong assurances of its accuracy and the witness is not available to testify. Unavailable witnesses are those (1) not present, (2) not willing to testify, (3) exempt from testifying by reason of privilege, and (4) not able to remember the event. In *State v. Sorenson* (1988) the Wisconsin Supreme Court upheld hearsay statements made by a child to a social worker.[26] The court considered five factors in determining whether the statements were reliable: (1) attributes of the child, such as age, ability to communicate, and ability to know the difference between truth and falsehood; (2) the relationship of the victim to the person told and the motivation of that person to falsify or distort contents; (3) the circumstances of the disclosure; (4) the content of the statement, that is, whether it alludes to knowledge of sexual matters not ordinarily known by children of the victim's age; and (5) other corroborative evidence such as physical evidence.

In *Idaho v. Wright* (1990) the U.S. Supreme Court ruled that in a criminal trial corroborating evidence cannot be admitted under the catchall, or residual hearsay, exceptions unless "particularized guarantees of trustworthiness" can be shown, because it cannot be assumed that these exceptions contain the guarantees of trustworthiness found in the medical and excited utterance exceptions.[27]

The *Wright* case involved charges that a mother had molested her two young daughters. At trial statements made by Wright's two-year-old daughter to a pediatrician were admitted under Idaho's "residual or catchall" hearsay exception to corroborate that abuse had occurred. The Idaho Court of Appeals overturned the mother's conviction because the corroborative evidence provided by the pediatrician was not sufficiently reliable. The interview techniques used by the pediatrician were in and of themselves unreliable, the court ruled. He had not tape-recorded the interview, he had used leading questions, and he may have differentially reinforced, through the use of verbal and nonverbal behaviors, those statements most likely to support his conviction that the child was sexually abused.

Affirming the decision of the Idaho court, the U.S. Supreme Court ruled that the reliability of hearsay statements admitted under a residual, or catchall, hearsay exception must be judged with reference to the context in which the statements were made. Relevant contextual issues include (1) the spontaneity with which the child made the statement offered into evidence; (2) consistent repetition of the facts reported; (3) the mental state of the person making the statement; (4) the use of terminology unexpected of a child of similar age; and (5) the absence of a motive to fabricate.

A decision by the U.S. Court of Appeals for the First Circuit in *United States v. Ellis* illustrates how admitted evidence may be deemed reliable and admissible under this hearsay exception. In the *Ellis* case the court overruled objections to a social worker's testimony that was admitted under a residual exception. The social worker repeated statements made by a two-and-one-half-year-old who was at play with anatomically correct dolls. In deciding whether the child's statement had particular guarantees of trustworthiness, and focusing on the context in which the child made the statement, the court discussed the social worker's behavior in interviewing the child. Beyond asking the child whether "daddy" hugged her, the social worker asked virtually no questions. The youngster's gesture with the male "daddy" doll's hand toward the child doll's vagina was spontaneous. The child was not asked to reenact a situation but was simply given the dolls to play with. On cross-examination the social worker confirmed that she had not asked the child to do anything with the dolls but simply waited until the child did something. Also indicative of the child's truthfulness was her subsequent negative answer to the social worker's question, "Did daddy ever ask you to touch his she-she [the child's name for penis]?" Finally, the court noted that it might have been desirable to videotape the child's play in front of the social worker but that it did not find this to be essential to a finding of trustworthiness.

Corroborating Evidence

Judges are often reluctant to have young children testify in cases that involve physical or sexual abuse. Thus in a number of states the rules of evidence have been relaxed to allow a social worker or other professional to testify to what a child said out of court and thereby to provide evidence that corroborates or makes more certain other evidence of child abuse. Testimony concerning abuse that a child has suffered or observed that is not admissible under an existing hearsay exception may be permitted under a special "child hearsay" exception.

Special exception may be made if the child is very young, for example, younger than ten or twelve, and a judge finds that (a) the time, content, and circumstances of the statement provide sufficient guarantees of trustworthiness; and (b) the child either testifies at the proceeding or is unavailable to testify.

Several courts have held that the person who presents corroborating evidence must (a) be a highly qualified social worker, clinical psychologist, or psychiatrist; (b) use a reliable methodology or system of analysis such as play therapy and carefully phrased questions; and (c) be able to articulate precisely how the conclusions were a product of the methodology. For example, an expert may say that the child had a good capacity for accurate recall, her story was clear and coherent, she behaved in an age-appropriate manner, and her emotional reactions to the interview included manifestations of anxiety and shame consistent with posttraumatic stress.[28]

Standard of Proof

In Chapter 3 standards for proof in criminal and civil cases were reviewed. Because standards of proof are important to an understanding of social work practice in a legal environment, they bear repeating.

A standard of proof is established to provide guidance to a judge or jury regarding the degree of confidence that society thinks it should have in the correctness of the conclusions that the judge or jury draws. At a criminal trial the state bears the burden of proof, which requires that it prove each element of the crime, for example, that the defendant had the requisite state of mind, and it must prove each element beyond a reasonable doubt.

In civil matters this high standard of proof applies only when a young person is charged with a crime. Otherwise, what must be proved and the applicable standard differ according to the matter adjudicated. For example, when a parent is charged with child abuse, the state must prove that (1) the charged adult is the child's parent or guardian; (2) the parent harmed or allowed another to harm the child or to place the child at risk of injury; and (3) the harm was not accidental. The state must prove its case by a "preponderance of the evidence," the most common standard of proof in civil cases. This standard requires that the evidence offered in support of the allegation be greater or more convincing than the evidence offered in opposition to it.

When a practitioner is charged with negligence, the elements that must be proved are different and include proof that (1) the person bringing suit was a client; (2) the practitioner breached a duty of reasonable care owed to clients; and (3) the breach caused harm to the client.

There are civil cases where the standard of proof is greater than the preponderance-of-the-evidence standard. For example, in disputes about child custody where the petitioner is a relative of the parent; in some civil matters such as disputes about the title to property; and when the state petitions to terminate parental rights, the courts require that the petitioner prove its case by "clear and convincing evidence." This standard is equated with proof that results in a "reasonable certainty" or high probability that the facts asserted are true. While more stringent than the preponderance-of-the-evidence standard, this standard is less stringent than beyond a reasonable doubt.

PART 2—PROVIDING TESTIMONY

You may testify as either a fact witness or as an expert witness. As a fact witness, your testimony will be based on firsthand knowledge of events, for example, what you were told in an interview and what you observed. Thus you may testify that a woman told you that her partner hits her when he has had too much to drink. You may report that you observed welts and bruises on her face and arms, but you would not be allowed to draw the conclusion that the welts and bruises are evidence of domestic violence. Expert witnesses are allowed to offer their opinion in the area in which they are qualified as an expert. Thus you may testify regarding child development, client competency, or "syndrome" evidence, which will be discussed later in this chapter.

Qualifying as an Expert

If you are called to testify as an expert, you must be qualified and found acceptable by the court. The attorney for whom you are testifying will ask a series of questions to establish your credentials. You are likely to be asked to (1) name each institution of higher education that you attended; (2) identify by discipline the degrees that you have received; (3) identify any continuing education courses and the subject matter; (4) list the licenses or certifications you hold; (5) identify by name the professional organizations to which you belong; (6) identify your published work by name and source; (7) state how long you have been employed as a social worker or how long you have been in private practice; (8) report your work responsibilities; (9) state how many years of experience you have had with the type of case at issue; (10) specify how often you have testified as an expert and whether your previous testimony has been for the prosecution, the defendant, or both.

The Basis of Testimony

Both fact witnesses and expert witnesses may rely on information gathered in interviews, observed of clients, or recorded in a case file, although expert testimony may rest on information compiled specifically for court. The information in a case record may determine whether evidence is sufficient to file a lawsuit. For these reasons a brief digression to consider the topics of building a case record and using a case record is in order.[29]

Building a Case Record

The objective in building and maintaining case files is to record information descriptive of all transactions that occur between the client and agency representatives throughout the process of service delivery. The case record is the core of an information network. It is often the single repository of data on clients and the focal point for both storing and retrieving information. The record may be the only constant in a client's experience with a social service agency. It is what is "left" after workers and collaterals depart and everyone involved in service delivery has long forgotten the particulars of a case.

Social workers tend to assign a low priority to record keeping, seeing it as less important than direct work with clients. This position is understandable. But it is important to recognize that you may shortchange yourself and your clients if you fail to maintain thorough records. Recorded information may be your only resource for preparing yourself to testify, the contents of records may be used against you if information is incomplete, and your clients may not achieve their goals because your records do not provide support for requests made to the court.

Case records that document and describe your work with clients comprehensively will serve you well. Descriptive writing serves a client's best interests. Labels, while professionally expedient, suggest more than the facts will support. They facilitate the creation and maintenance of stereotypes, and, as such, their use is a disservice to the person labeled. But the best practices poorly documented provide little defense in court. If records are poorly kept, there will invariably be a contradiction between what is recorded and what you will recall when testifying. Presenting contradictory information can do little to enhance either your position or that of your client. The usefulness of your records will be increased if you record the information in the categories that follow.

Assessment Information

It is important to show that you selected services based on a thorough assessment of family circumstances. You should document the methods that you use to gather assessment information, for example, interviews and direct observation of clients, the number of sessions, their duration, and their location. Assessment often requires the skills of others, including medical personnel, psychologists, and psychiatrists. Your records should identify others involved, the reasons for their involvement, and the outcome of their efforts.

Referrals for Service

Referrals for service are a normative part of social work practice. Concerns that may arise in court about referrals are (1) whether clients are simply instructed to go to a service provider or have appointments made for them; (2) whether assistance is offered with transportation and, if necessary, child care; and (3) whether there is follow-up contact to ensure that the client has kept appointments and is receiving needed services.

Acceptability to the Client

Your records should show that you considered whether a service was acceptable to the client and that you took client concerns into account in developing plans for service. Clients have a right to know (1) what is expected of them; (2) what will be done to assist them in reaching their goals; (3) what they can expect as an outcome of their involvement with service providers; and (4) the consequences of their failure to remain involved in service programs. Your records should report your discussions with clients, note their acceptance or lack of acceptance thereof, and your efforts to accommodate a client's wishes.

Coordination of Effort

Many clients will receive help from multiple providers. Coordination of services is critical to ensure that each provider understands her or his role in helping clients to achieve goals, is working toward goal attainment within an agreed-upon time frame, is willing to participate in meetings to review client progress and to resolve problems, and is willing to maintain records needed by your agency and by the court. If there is no plan for coordination of services, each provider is free to pursue his or her own agenda, which may work at cross-purposes to your and your client's agenda. When clients receive conflicting advice and become "victims" of competing service directives, information needed for court reports may not be available.

Monitoring Service Provision

Monitoring refers to compiling information about a client's progress in problem solving. Collaterals to whom clients are referred must agree to monitor the client's progress and to file reports on a regularly scheduled basis. Monitoring is the only way that you will have of knowing whether clients are making progress in problem solving. Data describing progress toward goal attainment will alert you to possible difficulties and will cue you to intervene when progress does not occur. Be sure to record all contacts with clients, including unsuccessful efforts to contact clients, and all contacts with collateral resources providing services to your client. You should record the (1) date and time of each contact; (2) type of contact made, for example, in person or by telephone; (3) place of contact, for example, client's home or your office; (4) people in attendance;

(5) purpose of the contact, for example, to develop a service agreement with parents; and (6) results, for example, service agreement developed.

Use of Case Records in Court

The information in case records is hearsay, which as a rule is not admissible in criminal proceedings or at the adjudicatory phase of juvenile or family court proceedings. However, case records and reports prepared for court are admissible at dispositional hearings to help a judge determine sentencing in a criminal case or dispositional matters in a civil case, for example, what provisions to include in an order of protection, which parent should have custody of a child, where a child who is entering foster care should be placed, and matters concerning parent and child visitation.

Since a record often contains information recorded by social workers who preceded you, from service providers in other agencies, from laypeople whom you interviewed, and court reports, you can easily see why a record meets the definition of *hearsay* because the information is second hand and its truth not ascertainable through cross-examination. Nevertheless, records are admissible in court under the "business records exception" to the hearsay rule. To qualify for this exception the person who offers the record into evidence must testify that (1) the information in the record was maintained in the regular course of business; (2) the making of such records was part of the regular course of the business; and (3) the information was recorded when the event occurred or in close temporal proximity. This "regular course of business provision" may be interpreted to mean that information added to the record for the purposes of the court appearance may not be admitted. The fact that you may not have personal knowledge of all the information in the record, for example, a recording made by other professionals, may influence the weight that the court assigns to the evidence, but the record is nonetheless admissible. To address the importance that records may play in court, consider a brief example.

Assume that your agency has petitioned the court to terminate the rights of the parents of a child in foster care. Assume also that you were the social worker on the case when the child came in to foster care and that your recording was thorough and accurate as to the parental behaviors that necessitated out-of-home placement. Recall an earlier discussion of standards of proof, where I said that the standard for terminating parental rights requires the petitioner to prove its case by "clear and convincing evidence" and that this standard is more stringent than preponderance of the evidence, which is the standard that applies to finding that a child has been abused or neglected. This different standard suggests that the evidence that you compiled before the child's placement in foster care may not be sufficient to satisfy the more stringent standard required for termination. In a proceeding to terminate parental rights, a court probably will look for detailed and specific information concerning your efforts to assist the parent to regain custody of the child, including your efforts to facilitate parental participation in service provision and parent and child visits, as well as information descriptive of the parent's response to your efforts.

Thorough documentation of these matters is especially important, since an attorney for the biological parents will likely argue that you did not make efforts to help the parents regain custody of their child or that the efforts you made were not sufficient. In fact, you made diligent efforts to locate services for the family. You spent many hours on the telephone trying to find programs with space available for your clients. Unfortunately, you did not document each contact made, its date, the person with whom you spoke, and that person's response to your request that services be provided. In trying to juggle the demands of a heavy caseload, you decided that "something had to give," and you chose to assign the lowest priority to record keeping. While some information in the record describes your actions on behalf of this family, it is sketchy. Standing alone, the record does not support your contention that you made reasonable efforts to reunite the parents and child. The attorney for your agency will prepare you for your testimony. Preparation will include efforts to recapitulate information that you did not record. If you are lucky, some of the sources you contacted may have kept thorough records, which will be of value to you in sustaining your argument that you worked diligently to help your client. It is likely, however, that under a rigorous cross-examination by parents' counsel, your weak record-keeping practices will be highlighted to suggest a general sloppiness on your part, and if the records of collateral agencies are no better than your own, you will have an extremely difficult time defending your position.

Expert Testimony

The *Federal Rules of Evidence* state:

> If scientific, technical, or other specialized knowledge will assist the trier of fact to understand the evidence or to determine a fact in issue, a witness qualified as an expert by knowledge, skill, experience, training, or education, may testify thereto in the form of an opinion or otherwise, if (1) the testimony is based upon sufficient facts or data, (2) the testimony is the product of reliable principles and methods, and (3) the witness has applied the principles and methods reliably to the facts of the case.[30]

There is no precise rule concerning the "knowledge, skill, experience, training, or education" necessary to qualify as an expert, and a court is free to "trade off" factors, giving more credit to experience than education and scholarship or vice versa. For example, one court accepted as an expert a social worker with a bachelor of science degree in business, approximately fifteen hours of graduate study in psychology or sociology, and eleven years of experience in the field.[31]

If you are qualified as an expert witness, you may describe the behavior of a victim of domestic violence to help a judge or jury understand why an abused person might retaliate against an abuser. Likewise, you may describe the behavior patterns of sexually abused children to help the jury understand that certain behaviors, such as recanting testimony and presenting conflicting versions of events, may be characteristic of sexually abused children, lest the jury interpret these behaviors as reflecting inaccurate recall or prevarication. But experts may not testify that the victim was telling the truth. Thus in *Commonwealth v. Seese,*[32] when an expert witness testified that it was very unusual for young children to lie about being sexually abused, the witness usurped the jury's credibility-determining function, as did a child psychologist who testified that children who had not been involved in any type of sexual activity usually did not fantasize about sexual experiences.[33] An expert may say that children who are abused tend to act in certain ways but may not conclude that the actions of the alleged victim should be interpreted as being truthful, nor may you suggest, as did the witnesses who testified in *Commonwealth v. Seese,* that it is unusual for young children to lie or to have sexual fantasies, that the child is telling the truth. The determination of truthfulness lies solely within the province of the judge or jury.

You may testify during the "case-in-chief," which is that part of a trial where the party that bears the burden of proof—the state if prosecuting a criminal case or civil matter that involves child maltreatment, or a private party who is suing for divorce or child custody—presents its evidence, or you may testify as a rebuttal witness. Testifying as an expert during the state's case-in-chief, you may describe the behaviors characteristic of rape trauma syndrome to help the judge or jury understand why a victim failed to file a report in a timely fashion with the police, or you may help to counter a defense of consent. You may testify as a rebuttal witness in order to explain or counteract evidence given by an opposing party or to rehabilitate a witness whose testimony was weakened by a rigorous cross-examination. Thus an expert on child sexual abuse accommodation syndrome (CSAAS) was called as a rebuttal witness to describe characteristics of the syndrome common to sexual abuse victims.[34] The expert's testimony was needed because the victim's ability to recall and to recount the incidents of sexual abuse had been vigorously challenged on cross-examination.

Those whose testimony is offered as expert opinion must be qualified by the court. Social workers have been qualified as experts on diverse topics, including (1) common symptoms of CSAAS[35]; (2) the Indian Child Welfare Act and adoption[36]; (3) battered women's syndrome[37]; (4) sexual harassment in the workplace[38]; (5) emotional distress suffered by a client when a medical center released her medical records without her consent[39]; and (6) the administration of statewide child welfare systems.[40]

Is Expert Evidence Admissible?

Earlier I said that the federal and state court systems have a body of law called the law of evidence. It contains rules that judges apply to determine whether evidence is admissible and that govern the circumstances under which evidence is admissible. In general, evidence is admissible if it is relevant to the issue before the court and likely to make the existence of a fact material to the case "more probable or less probable than it would be without the evidence."[41] Thus the testimony of a certified social worker, who was qualified as an expert witness, was relevant in litigation against a hospital. The social worker's testimony concerning the plaintiff's mental disorders was critical to the plaintiff, who had to prove "severe emotional distress" to prevail in her suit.[42] Notwithstanding the rule regarding relevance, a judge may exclude evidence if its value is substantially outweighed by its tendency to prejudice a party or delay a trial.[43]

When an attorney offers expert testimony based on evidence gathered by using scientific or technical data-gathering techniques,[44] as opposed to expert opinion based on experience, courts apply one or two tests to determine admissibility. In all federal courts and in some state courts, a judge determines whether evidence compiled by scientific or technical methods is relevant and reliable. *Relevant* means the evidence is pertinent to the matter before the court. Reliability directs attention to evidence-gathering procedures, including those that take place in laboratories; those that take place in the natural environment using social science methodologies[45]; those that make use of clinical techniques such as interviewing, observation, and testing; and those that make use of an expert's technical expertise. The court is concerned with whether the data-gathering procedures conform to acceptable professional standards, thus providing some assurance that the evidence is not mere opinion or bias offered in the guise of science. Issues that a court may consider in determining whether the evidence-gathering procedures are reliable take into account (a) whether the theory or technique in question has been tested; (b) whether it has been subjected to peer review and publication; (c) its known or potential error rate; (d) whether the procedure has attracted widespread acceptance within a relevant scientific community[46]; and (e) whether the methodology was correctly applied when the evidence offered was gathered.

In some state courts the admissibility of evidence offered by experts is determined by another test, known as the Frye Test, where the judge probably will admit into evidence testimony based on evidence culled from scientific studies if a reliable body of scientific opinion supports a particular theory.[47] The theory need only have general acceptance in its field, not the unanimous endorsement of the broader scientific community. Evidence that a method is acceptable to a professional community is offered by introducing scientific or legal articles, by evaluating the reliability of the methodology used to arrive at the conclusions, or by presenting expert-witness testimony concerning the reliability and general acceptance of the methodology. Despite some differences in the "tests" that the courts apply, they are similar enough that their practical application may yield similar results.

However, when expert testimony rests on opinion based on personal experience and training, the inquiries suggested by the foregoing discussion are not applicable. Thus a witness could testify concerning the sexual acting-out of abused children and their experiences with nightmares, based on the witness's professional experience and observations, if a foundation was set to support the testimony.[48]

Syndrome Evidence

A syndrome is a constellation of symptoms that occur together and are characteristic of a specific condition. As used in the professional literature, syndromes refer to reactions to stressful events. For example, the rape trauma syndrome consists of a series of "somatic, cognitive, psychological, and behavioral symptoms" that occur in reaction to a life-threatening situation.[49]

The legal literature is replete with references to syndromes offered in court to explain unusual behavior, including "false memory syndrome," "urban survival syndrome," "Vietnam veteran syndrome," "battered parent syndrome," and "parental alienation syndrome."[50]

The syndrome evidence of concern to us here has been offered in court to explain the behavior of adult victims of domestic violence, victims of rape, and victims of child abuse. You should know that courts sometimes use different terms to refer to similar syndromes and that the term *profile* has been used in lieu of *syndrome.* For example, one court referred to the child sexual abuse syndrome (CSAS) when it meant the child sex abuse accomodation syndrome (CSAAS); and the "battered woman syndrome" has been referred to as the "battered women," "battered spouse," "battered housemate," and "battered wife" syndrome. Regarding the latter, whatever term is used, the basic characteristics are the same, and assigning one or another designation is a matter of semantics.[51]

Battered woman syndrome Battered woman syndrome is a subcategory of posttraumatic stress disorder, which is a "collection of thoughts, feelings, and actions that logically follow a frightening experience that one expects could be repeated."[52] The symptoms that define battered woman syndrome are typically exhibited by a woman who has been exposed to repeated physical and emotional abuse at the hands of a spouse.[53] Expert testimony is permitted to help the finder of fact understand why a woman who has suffered repeated abuse would remain with her abuser despite her ongoing fear of serious bodily harm or would recant her testimony that she has been abused.

Testimony based on this syndrome has been allowed in a divorce action where the wife argued that the division of marital property should take into account her need for financial assistance to provide for ongoing counseling services made necessary by her husband's abuse.[54] It also was allowed in a dispute about child custody, where the court found this testimony helpful to further its understanding of the wife's behavior and its decision to award custody to her.[55] Battered woman syndrome may be offered as an affirmative defense (see chapter 3) to support a claim that a defendant's act of seriously injuring or killing another was self-defense. The majority of jurisdictions in the United States will allow expert testimony on this matter, unless the harm inflicted by the victim is out of proportion to the harm suffered or the perceived threat of harm or where the harm was not imminent.[56]

Evidence of battered woman syndrome will not be admitted to explain the behavior of a person outside the context of a battering relationship. Thus a court was justified in denying a defendant's motion to admit testimony that his actions in killing a stranger could be explained because he demonstrated symptoms similar to that of a battered spouse.[57] And a woman charged with selling cocaine was denied the opportunity to present expert testimony on battered woman syndrome, which she offered to explain the relationship between her criminal behavior and her history of being abused and why the latter made her vulnerable to being coerced by an undercover police officer.[58]

Rape Trauma Syndrome Like the battered woman syndrome, rape trauma syndrome is a subset of posttraumatic stress disorder, and as with any syndrome evidence, it will not be admitted (1) to prove that rape occurred[59]; (2) if a court determines that the evidence is more prejudicial than probative[60]; or (3) if a court determines that rape trauma syndrome is not scientifically reliable.[61]

Testimony concerning rape trauma syndrome has been admitted to help jurors understand the behavior of a rape victim.[62] For example, if a victim delays making a report or, after lodging a complaint, attempts to retract it, syndrome evidence may be admitted to help the judge or jury understand that such behavior is not inconsistent with the actual occurrence of such an event.[63] Testimony is also admissible when it is offered to suggest that women who exhibit the emotional and psychological trauma that defines rape trauma syndrome could not have consented to sex.[64]

Battered Child Syndrome Battered woman syndrome and rape trauma syndrome are not diagnostic tools. Stated otherwise, both were developed to facilitate treatment, but neither can be used to determine that the abusive event to which they refer took place. For this reason testimony based on either syndrome is limited to describing the characteristics of those who have suffered a particular form of abuse but not to prove that the abuse took place. However, battered child syndrome is diagnostic, and testimony resting on evidence of battered child syndrome can be used to establish that a child's injuries could not have been sustained accidentally. The courts accept testimony based on this syndrome because it has been extensively studied by medical science and is accepted within the medical profession. Medical testimony is based on x-rays and other diagnostic techniques that allow the medical expert to conclude that a child was injured by nonaccidental means. Elements of battered child syndrome include (1) a child who is younger than three; (2) x-rays and other diagnostic evidence showing untreated injuries or injuries that could not have been sustained at play because of the child's age; and (3) an account of how the child was injured that does not comport with the injuries sustained.[65]

Battered child syndrome is used mainly to establish that abuse occurred. In recent years, however, battered child syndrome has been used to support a claim that a young person who faced criminal charges after assaulting or killing a parent acted in self-defense. In *State v. James* the court allowed expert testimony to support a seventeen-year-old's claim that he shot and killed his mother's paramour in self-defense.[66] Experts testified that the teen suffered from "chronic and enduring abuse that he received as a child and as an adolescent."[67]

Other Child Abuse Syndromes Court rulings vary in regard to the admissibility of evidence describing other syndromes. An appellate court in California ruled that evidence presented by two psychologists about the "child molest syndrome" was inadmissible because the syndrome lacked acceptance in the professional community,[68] but another court admitted testimony based on this syndrome to describe the characteristics of abused children.[69] Testimony based on observations of children at play with anatomically correct dolls is accepted by some courts but not others[70]; courts have excluded as prejudicial expert testimony that children were sexually abused, because the testimony was based on observations of the children, not on reliable and scientifically accepted measures.[71]

CSAAS has received a great deal of judicial attention. Most courts reject testimony based on this syndrome as offers of proof that abuse has occurred, but they sanction its use to rehabilitate a child witness whose credibility has been damaged by a delay in reporting, to explain why a child kept the abuse secret, or to explain why a child has recanted previously offered testimony.[72] A key problem that courts have in admitting testimony based on the CSAAS is the lack of evidence that the syndrome can discriminate between children who have been sexually abused and children whose problems stem from other sources.[73] Some courts have ruled CSAAS inadmissible, finding that it has not been generally accepted by the scientific community.[74]

PART 3—TESTIFYING IN COURT

The concept of privilege is key to a discussion of testifying in court.[75] Although I discussed privilege in chapter 5, key points bear repeating here:

- The legislature or the courts confer the right to claim that communications with a client are privileged and to withhold information in a court of law.
- Privilege allows the exclusion of testimony from the fact-finding process. Thus a claim of privilege can have serious consequences for a person accused of a crime who believes that mounting a proper defense requires the information being withheld.
- In determining whether a relationship is governed by privilege, (1) the communications must have originated in a confidence that they would not be disclosed; (2) protection from disclosure must be essential to the full and satisfactory maintenance of the relation between the parties; (3) the relationship must be one that, in the opinion of the community, should be seditiously fostered; and (4) the injury that would inure to the relationship by disclosing the information must be greater than the benefit thereby gained.
- The child abuse and neglect reporting requirements of most states waive privilege.
- Clients are the primary holder of the privilege, and they may waive this right.
- By introducing privileged material into the litigation, a client waives the right to claim subsequent privilege for the material introduced.
- A judge may require testimony about otherwise privileged communication if society's need for full information in a particular legal proceeding outweighs the client's right to claim privilege.
- When minors commit crimes, are used by adults as accessories in illegal activities, or are the victims of criminal activities, most states require that the information be reported.
- Privilege does not cover information learned outside the therapeutic relationship.
- Information communicated in the context of group therapy is a vague area of privilege. Because the client has shared information with others in the group, courts have been equivocal as to whether privilege pertains.
- The right of privilege is not extended from one state to another.

Being a Witness

Being a "good witness" involves both nonverbal and verbal behaviors. As in any interview situation, you will be judged in part by your dress, posture, attending behaviors, and speech. Some behaviors that make you a skilled interviewer will assist you in court. Sitting erect, listening attentively to the person speaking to you, avoiding the temptation to look around the courtroom, and looking at the attorney or judge to whom your answer is directed are important, as are speaking slowly and enunciating clearly. Rehearsing or role-playing a trial situation may be especially useful to get a sense of what it is like to give direct testimony and to be cross-examined.

Direct and Cross-examination

The attorney who is representing you or your agency or for whom you are testifying as an expert conducts direct examination. Opposing counsel conducts the cross-examination. Preparation for direct examination will consist of a review of questions that you will be asked or a review of the topics that you will be asked to address, as well as the answers you will give. In preparing you for cross-examination, the attorney will suggest the kinds of questions that you might be expected to answer.

Before taking the witness stand, you should review your testimony, including relevant documents. For example, if you gave a deposition before trial, you should review it. Memorizing your testimony is not advised because your responses may appear stilted and you will not have the flexibility that you need to answer questions that you will be asked on cross-examination. You are allowed to take notes to the stand and to consult your notes before answering a question, but you should not answer questions by reading from your notes. Impressions are important, and reading from your notes will make you appear less knowledgeable than if you answer questions without reference to documents.

Testifying as an Expert

In direct examination you may be asked to describe your observations, to give an opinion about what your observations mean, and to state the basis for your opinion.

Assume that you have reviewed the case records of a number of children in foster care. Your review was guided by a series of questions that you, as an expert, formulated. Your objective in this review was to see whether agency practices conform to professional standards. The following exchange illustrates questions that might be asked in direct examination:

Q: Have you reviewed any records of children in state custody?

A: Yes.

Q: Can you describe what you learned about parental visiting of children in foster care?

A: My review of the records showed that fifty percent of the children in care for more than eighteen months have a plan of return home but have not been visited by a parent in the six months prior to my review of records.

Q: Is this important information?

A: Yes.

Q: Please tell the court why you consider this information to be important.

A: Research has shown that parental visiting of children in care is a significant predictor of whether parents will resume full-time care of their children. In order to plan for a child it is important to monitor parental visiting. Parents' failure to visit their children may signal the importance of considering other kinds of plans, such as adoption.

Q: In your opinion what importance would you assign to the information that you acquired about parental visiting?

A: Because the children had been in care more than eighteen months and had not been visited in the six months before my review of records, and because the plan was to return these children to the home, I would conclude that information available to workers was not being used to assure that permanent homes were found for the children whose records I reviewed.

Q: If available information were being used, what would you expect to find in the records?

A: I would expect to find evidence that other plans were being considered for these children, or I would expect to find information describing why a plan of return home was being maintained despite the lack of visits.

The attorney who is cross-examining you will try to undermine your testimony. It is that lawyer's job to do so. If you are testifying as a fact witness, one of your greatest areas of vulnerability will be your case records if they do not support your testimony. Vulnerability for experts comes from different sources. If your testimony is based on a review of agency records, you may be vulnerable if your methodology for selecting records was weak. For instance, if you failed to review a random sample of records, the defendant's attorney will try to show that you were biased, choosing only those records likely to reflect bad practices within the agency. Here are some guidelines for testifying.

Do Not Respond Defensively. The verbal style that some lawyers use for cross-examination suggests by tone of voice and inflection that you are less than competent. If this occurs, it is easy to take cross-examination as a personal attack and to respond defensively. This is a disservice to yourself and to those counting on your testimony. The best defense is to remind yourself that it is merely a style and that it is not personal.

One of the first tacks likely to be taken by a cross-examiner will be to establish that you are "selling" your testimony. You will be asked how much money you are earning—in a manner that suggests that the only unbiased testimony is free testimony. Do not be intimidated by such a question. Receiving a fee for your services is perfectly acceptable.

Regardless of the attorney's style, you may feel defensive if you feel trapped. In the sample testimony about parent-child visits, assume that in your review of records you failed to take into account reasons why some parents have not visited their children. For example, a parent may have been hospitalized, or the court may have suspended visits for a period of time. The attorney conducting the cross-examination may uncover your failure to account for these facts. The effect of failing to take this information into account may reduce from 50 percent to 40 percent the number of children without visits in the six months before your record review. Although the 40 percent figure may still be damaging to the defendants, the attorney will imply that your failure to take into account legitimate reasons for not visiting throws doubt on your entire testimony. If this occurs, acknowledge your error. You may point out that 40 percent of children whose plan is return home and who have not been visited by their parents is also an unacceptably high figure by professional standards.

The attorney for whom you are testifying will have the opportunity on redirect examination, which follows cross-examination, to ask questions to clarify aspects of your testimony that the lawyer thinks need to be expanded. The significance of the 40 percent figure may be brought out at this time.

Limit your testimony to what you can support. As an expert, you are responsible for drawing the line between the opinions that you can and cannot support. Avoid the temptation to please an attorney by making statements that you cannot accurately support. Social science knowledge, which will inform your testimony, is rarely equivocal. Avoid the use of adverbs such as *always* and *never.* Do not draw conclusions that your data do not support. For example, the data about parental visiting of children in foster care describes a general relationship that cannot be interpreted to predict whether any individual child will or will not go home. Your answer must be interpreted to mean that, in general, children not visited by their parents tend not to be reunited with them.

Be familiar with the professional literature that bears on your testimony. As an expert, you should be prepared to support your opinions with reference to empirical studies and the professional literature in which standards for practice are set forth. Your familiarity with the professional literature should not be limited to opinions and data that support your position. Be knowledgeable of the limits of the research to which you refer, and be prepared to say why, despite limitations, it is important. For example, written case plans provide an important framework for decision making to achieve the objective of returning to the home children who are in foster care or planning for adoption for those who cannot return home. While the relationship between written case plans, decision making, and finding permanent homes for children is not a perfect one, it is of sufficient importance to have become a requirement in federal law.

Stay within your area of expertise. Some witnesses become defensive because they think that they should be able to answer any question that relates to their work. For example, you may be qualified as an expert in the area of child protective service investigations and have a working knowledge, but not expertise, in the area of child development. If you are asked a question about child development and you have not been qualified as an expert in this area, say that this is outside your expertise.

Likewise, even within your area of expertise, if you are not certain about the answer to a question, say so. If you are generally knowledgeable, your inability to answer any single question will not diminish your credibility as an expert.

Never try to bluff your way through an answer. The attorney who is examining you can follow up on the first question with a series of increasingly more specific questions that can highlight your lack of knowledge in a certain area.

Pay careful attention to the wording of questions. In direct examination you may have described a parent's behavior by reporting that he did not answer directly the questions that you asked. You may have described the difficulties that he had in trying to stand up, and you may have reported that he bumped into furniture when walking across a room. In giving testimony, you avoided drawing the conclusion he was under the influence of alcohol or drugs, although you may have believed this to be so. The attorney who is cross-examining you may ask a leading question in an effort to have you draw conclusions that you cannot support. For example, she may say, "You said that Mister Reynolds was drunk when you interviewed him on April tenth." If you respond affirmatively, you may then be asked how you know this to be true. That you cannot support the inference of drunkenness will be used to undermine your credibility as a witness.

Answer the question that is asked. If you do not understand a question, ask the lawyer to repeat it. Be especially careful not to respond to double questions. If an attorney says, "Isn't it true that you picked the child up on September fifth for a visit with her mother, and didn't the child tell you that she was excited about going to see her mother?" respond by saying, "You have asked me two questions." If both parts of the question are true, say so. If one statement is correct and the other inaccurate, respond separately to each question.

When you are asked to respond by saying yes or no to a question that you think cannot be answered in this way, say, "I cannot provide a sufficient answer by simply stating yes or no." The judge may instruct you to respond to the question by saying yes or no, but she may allow you to answer in a manner that you consider appropriate. During redirect examination the attorney for whom you are testifying should give you the opportunity to clarify your answer by providing additional information.

Ask to see documents. On cross-examination opposing counsel may ask you questions based on documents, such as a deposition that you gave before trial, an affidavit that you wrote, or an article that you published in a professional journal. You have the right to ask to see the document to which the attorney is referring, and you should make this request if you have reason to believe that you are being misquoted or quoted out of context.

SUMMARY

This chapter has focused on issues that concern the actions of professional social workers in a legal environment. Forensic social work requires that the practitioner apply professional principles and practices to the purpose of law. The worker engaged in forensic activities undertakes a task with knowledge of the legal framework that surrounds social work practice, including (a) legislative matters, (b) legal processes, (c) system operations, (d) the roles played by the various parties in a court proceeding, and (e) an understanding of what evidence is admissible in court.

Practice in a legal environment requires also that you have a basic understanding of what constitutes legally admissible evidence. Such knowledge will influence the process of gathering facts, preparing reports, and preparing to testify in court. Evidence is classified into categories, among them, (1) direct evidence based on firsthand knowledge of events; (2) real evidence, such as documents and photographs; (3) circumstantial evidence, which is a series of factors that, standing alone, are not sufficient to prove a case but that when woven together suggest that the person charged with misbehavior should be held accountable; and (4) hearsay evidence. The last refers to certain circumstances when courts allow information compiled out of court to be entered into a legal proceeding, even though the person with firsthand knowledge of the evidence is not available to be cross-examined.

Any social worker may be called upon to testify in court as a fact witness, and some will be qualified as expert witnesses. Although case records are hearsay, they are admissible in court under what is called the "business records exception," meaning that the record was created in the regular course of business. Because witnesses rely on case records as a basis for testifying in court, the information recorded must be descriptive, comprehensive, and jargon free.

Testifying as an expert, you may base your evidence on your experience or on a theory of human behavior. Regardless of the basis for your testimony, it (1) must be relevant to the matter before the court; (2) must assist the judge or jury by providing information that is beyond the experience of the average person; (3) cannot be construed as an opinion regarding the veracity of the victim; and (4) may, regardless of its relevance, be excluded if a judge determines that it is unduly prejudicial.

When evidence rests on theoretical propositions, various factors enter into a judicial determination of whether your evidence is admissible, including (1) whether the theory or technique in question been tested; (b) whether it has been subjected to peer review and publication; (c) what is known of its error rate; (d) whether the procedure has been accepted within a relevant scientific community; and (e) whether the methodology was correctly applied, meaning that the standards that you used meet standards within your profession.

The material in the final section of this chapter reviewed the topic of privileged communication and provided some guidance for testifying in court. The main points alerted you to the importance of (1) listening attentively to the attorney who is questioning you; (2) reviewing your testimony before trial; (3) not allowing yourself to take personally and respond defensively to an attorney whose questions suggest that you are not competent; (4) candidly acknowledging errors if the attorney who cross-examines you uncovers any; (5) limiting your testimony to matters within your expertise; (6) becoming familiar with the professional literature that pertains to your testimony; (7) never bluffing your way through an answer; (8) asking to see documents to which a questioner refers if you are uncertain that you are being correctly quoted or paraphrased.

7

Professional Liability

THE FOCUS IN this chapter will be the vulnerability of professional social workers to being sued.[1] A variety of conditions render social workers, their supervisors, and/or the agencies that employ them vulnerable to suit, including (1) an increase in the number of states that license social workers and the provisions in licensing law for disciplining those whose practices do not conform to statutory mandates; (2) ethical codes and standards of practice that provide yardsticks against which behavior can be measured and judged as suitable or lacking; (3) laws that mandate reporting of child abuse and neglect and that provide penalties for failure to report; (4) laws that require a professional to warn a third party whose health or safety is threatened by a client and that provide a basis for suits that allege a "failure to warn"; (5) an increase in the number of states that have waived their sovereign immunity, thereby eliminating a shield that barred suits against state employees; (6) the litigious nature of our society and the conviction of some that a legal remedy exists for all injuries, real and imagined, coupled with an increase in the number of social workers going into private practice, which increases the visibility of social work as a profession; (7) the application of unconventional therapeutic techniques that, when scrutinized, raise questions about the competence of the professional who chose to use untested methods; and (8) the trend of providing Internet-based services, which raises new issues in regard to maintaining confidentiality and ensuring that those who seek help reside in the state in which the social worker is licensed to practice.[2]

When a lawsuit is filed, the plaintiff cites one or more "causes of action." A cause of action (1) refers to a legal theory such as malpractice or breach of contract, and (2) contains facts that the plaintiff contends support his or her right to sue. The majority of suits involving social workers are brought in civil court (chapter 3), but you should know that a social worker may be charged under a state's criminal law. For example, some states provide criminal penalties for mandated reporters who fail to report child abuse or neglect, and suits against social workers can be brought in state or federal court and may allege violations of state or federal law. It has been alleged that a worker (1) inappropriately treated a client, contributing to his suicide[3]; (2) fraudulently induced (a) parents to sign agreements in which they surrendered their child for adoption[4]; (b) fraudulently induced clients to adopt a child by misrepresenting as healthy a child known to suffer from mental health problems[5]; and (c) fraudulently induced a client to sell his house to the worker without telling him that the proceeds of the sale would cause him to lose his eligibility for Supplemental Security Income and Medicaid[6]; (3) conspired to prosecute a parent as a sex offender and to convict him of sexually abusing his daughter[7]; (4) implanted false memories during treatment, causing the client's mental illness[8]; (5) breached a contract (a) when a couple's expectation that they would be allowed to adopt a child failed to come to pass[9]; and (b) by failing to provide counseling services in a competent manner when the counselor engaged in a sexual relationship with the client's husband[10]; (6) claimed that the social worker breached professional ethics by having sexual relations with a client[11] or a spouse, or claimed that the partner of a client[12] (7) coerced a client to have a tubal ligation as a condition for having her children returned from foster care[13]; (8) interfered with a mother's constitutionally protected right to the companionship of her daughter by placing the youngster in a shelter without the mother's permission[14]; (9) libeled a client by distributing a report that contained allegations of sexual abuse[15]; (10) invaded a client's privacy by disclosing confidential information to a client's wife[16]; and (11) maliciously prosecuted a person charged with sexually abusing a child.[17]

This chapter has three parts. The first part reviews several legal theories that are used to support litigation against social workers. The second part covers the ways in which professionals respond to litigation, and the third part discusses remedies available to an injured party.

Before we begin, I want to make a point. Some reasons that clients cite as a basis for suit lack foundation or appear to be frivolous, and indeed some are. For example, a parent who sued a social worker alleged that a hospital and its employees were engaged in a conspiracy and argued that a physical examination of her daughter had been conducted without parental consent. The suit was without a foundation, because the law under which it was brought does not allow allegations of conspiracy when all the actors are employed by the same agency, as were the social workers and other hospital employees. The attorney who filed this suit should have known there was no foundation for the conspiracy claim.[18] In another case a parent's argument that placement of an abused child in foster care constituted false imprisonment was frivolous because the social worker was acting within the authority conferred on her by the state.[19] Suits that fail to state a cause of action or that contain frivolous allegations will likely be dismissed by the courts at an early stage of litigation. However, any lawsuit must be defended, and while the dollar costs of litigation may be borne by an agency, its insurance carrier, or the private practitioner's insurance carrier, the personal costs with reference to time and the damage to one's professional reputation may be high.

PART 1—THEORIES OF LEGAL LIABILITY

Malpractice

Malpractice refers to professional misconduct or practices that demonstrate an "unreasonable lack of skill."[20] Malpractice is a form of negligence that is defined as a failure to do something that a reasonable person would do (nonfeasance) or the doing of something that a reasonable person would not do (malfeasance or misfeasance). Whether practices are reasonable is judged by comparing those employed by the charged practitioner to those employed by others with similar education, experience, and skills practicing under similar circumstances. Allegations of malpractice involve civil law. You will recall from the discussion in chapter 3 that civil law involves implied contracts or torts. The latter refer to losses or harms that a person sustains by the acts of another.

Malpractice law developed from suits brought against physicians. It has been applied to other groups, including psychotherapists, social workers, attorneys, and teachers. Malpractice suits proceed on the assumption that the behavior of any practitioner can be evaluated and found adequate or deficient when compared to professional standards of conduct. Malpractice law, especially as applied to suits against mental health personnel, is tied to social theory. For example, I may sue my therapist, claiming misdiagnosis and subsequent emotional damage. The viability of my claim rests in part on my ability to establish that I experienced mental suffering. This claim gains credibility to the extent that mental health professionals who may testify as experts or laypersons who serve on a jury accept that mental suffering is a possible consequence of inadequate treatment. In earlier periods of history such a claim may not have been considered.

The Elements of a Malpractice Action

When a person sues a professional for malpractice, the plaintiff must establish that(1) she or he was owed a duty of care; (2) that the professional breached the duty; and (3) that the breach was the cause of the injury suffered.

Duty of Care Professionals owe a duty of care to those with whom they enter into professional relationships, once the professional provides service for an agreed-upon purpose. The duty owed is to conduct one's practice in a reasonable manner where, as noted, *reasonable* is defined with reference to how others with similar education and experience would conduct their practice under similar circumstances.

Duty is linked to providing an agreed-upon professional service, and courts will have little difficulty in finding that a social worker who is providing counseling services or who agrees to conduct a mental health evaluation owes a duty of care to the person who engaged those services.

It is doubtful that a professional relationship is created during an intake interview, if the focus is limited to an exchange of information sufficient for the professional to determine whether she or he can be of help and for the client to determine whether to hire the professional. When a third party hires a professional, for example, when a court engages a social worker to conduct a mental health evaluation, the social worker does not owe a duty to the person evaluated because the court is the client.[21]

In some situations a practitioner does owe a duty of care to a person who is not a client, and there are situations where the duty of care falls on a unit of government. The *Tarasoff* case, discussed in chapter 5, is an example of a situation in which a duty is owed to a third party. Analogous to the *Tarasoff* case are divorce or child-visitation cases where a parent hires a mental health professional to evaluate a child whom the parent believes has been abused by the child's other parent or another family member. Responding to the question, "Does the evaluator owe a duty of care to the person charged with misconduct?" some courts have responded in the affirmative, while others have not.[22]

Courts also have grappled with the question, "Does a unit of government owe a duty of care to a child known to have been abused or neglected?" We shall revisit the subject of government liability later in this chapter. Consider the following for the purposes of illustration. In 1989 the U.S. Supreme Court was asked whether the state owed a duty of care to a child who was severely beaten by his father. The question was brought to a trial court by the mother of Joshua DeShaney when she sued Wisconsin for failing to protect her son.[23] Joshua was known to the state, whose social workers had investigated reports alleging abuse by the boy's father, with whom he lived. The boy's being in the custody of his father, not the state, was the critical factor in the Supreme Court's ultimate ruling. The Court reasoned that the state did not owe a duty to Joshua. Because he was living with his father, Joshua was a member of the "public at large," and the state does not owe a duty of care to the general public.

Once the state assumes custody of a person, be it a prisoner, a person confined to a mental health facility, or a child placed in foster care, the placed individual has a liberty interest that is rooted in the Fourteenth Amendment to the U.S. Constitution and must be protected. Thus the state may be found liable for failing to take measures to ensure a reasonable degree of safety.[24] The question is how far the state's duty of protection extends, or, stated another way, what harms must the government must protect against?

Consider a suit filed in 1997 by Andrea, a fourteen-year-old who claimed that a county child welfare agency and its social workers failed in their duty to protect her from the pregnancy that resulted after she engaged in consensual sex with the teenage son of her foster parents. Andrea claimed that the state had a duty to place her in an "appropriate placement [and that she had a right] to reasonable safety."[25] The court agreed that the county agency owed Andrea such a duty; had her pregnancy been the result of "coercive, abusive or unwanted" sex, her claim would have been substantial. However, this was not the case, and it was not clear in what way the state had breached its duty to protect Andrea from her own consensual acts. The lesson to be learned from Andrea's case is that the courts will not extend the state's duty to protect beyond requirements that the person in custody be cared for in a reasonable and safe manner. What is reasonable and safe may vary according to age and the physical or mental abilities of the person in custody, but the standard for determining whether the state had a duty to protect from a particular harm will be answered on the basis of reasonable practice. The state's duty will be to provide the minimum care necessary to ensure safety.

Breach If duty is defined as an obligation to act with reasonable care, then breach is a failure to act in a reasonable and cautious manner, judged in relation to how others with similar experience and education would act in similar circumstances. Breach of a duty does not make an actor liable; it merely subjects the actor to liability. Whether one is liable depends on whether the breach results in an injury, whether the resulting injury was foreseeable, and whether a duty was owed to the injured party.[26]

A critical issue in any malpractice litigation is to find a standard against which practitioner behavior can be measured. An expert witness may review the case files of a social worker or physician who is charged with malpractice and testify that in his or her opinion the practices described in the record are not what would be expected. In addition, standards are set by national organizations, such as the National Association of Social Workers or the Child Welfare League of America. Standards can also be found in statutes, regulations, and agency policy.

The following abstract illustrates how one court addressed an allegation of breach of duty. Dr. Dan Dallas was a state-certified social worker whose patient tried to commit suicide.[27] The patient later sued the therapist. She argued that he had breached his duty of care by failing to consult with her previous therapist. Presumably, consultation would have revealed the risk that the patient would attempt suicide and Dallas would then have taken steps to reduce the risk. Dallas acknowledged his failure to consult with the therapist but defended his inaction in an affidavit prepared for the court. He reported that the patient had told him that her previous therapist had not been helpful and that he knew from the patient's written history that she had previously attempted suicide. For these reasons, the court found, the social worker's decision not to contact the previous therapist was reasonable and did not constitute a breach of duty.

Causation A professional cannot be held liable for injury to another unless the professional's behavior was causally related to the injury suffered. Cause as a legal concept has two meanings. "Cause-in-fact" directs attention to actions taken or failures to act when there is a duty to do so. Here the argument is that the harm alleged would not have occurred but for the action or omission. Used in this way, the legal concept of cause is analogous to the way in which social scientists talk about cause and effect. Thus if a social worker licensed a foster home without first checking to see whether the applicant had ever been convicted of a crime against children, and if a child was placed in the home and soon thereafter was injured, a court could find that the worker's actions caused the injury in the sense that, "but for the worker's failure to do a background check," the home would not have been licensed. Similarly, a social worker's failure to comply with agency rules requiring routine monitoring of a foster home was found to be cause-in-fact of the child's death at the hands of his foster mother because regular visits would have uncovered a routine practice of beating the boy.[28]

The second reference to causation is to "proximate cause," sometimes called the "legal cause," of an event. Questions concerning proximate cause take into account that a series of events may intervene between the breach of a duty and the resulting harm. When a court addresses the question of proximate cause, it is asking, "How far down the chain of causal events does a practitioner's responsibility extend?" Stated in another way, "Was the ultimate event that caused the injury foreseeable, such that the practitioner should be held accountable?" Posed in this fashion, proximate cause questions are less concerned with scientific notions of cause and effect than they are with public policy. The latter takes into account the consequences to the public good of extending liability to a point where the practice of certain professions becomes so costly that people elect not to enter into professional practice. If this happens, society loses the benefits that accrue from having available the services of social workers, other mental health professionals, attorneys, and physicians. An example will be helpful in considering how courts decide how far to extend the chain of responsibility.

Ellen was a social worker who participated in the decision to place Sharon, who had been diagnosed as mentally ill, in a unlocked board-and-care home.[29] One week after her placement Sharon left the facility. Several days later she was found sleeping outdoors. Finding a new placement for Sharon was not easy, but approximately three weeks after she walked away from her first placement, she was placed in another unlocked facility. Ellen did not inform the facility operator that Sharon had walked away from her previous placement.

Within the first ten days of her placement, Sharon walked away from the facility on two occasions. On her third departure she wandered onto a highway, where she was struck by an automobile and gravely injured. Sharon's attorney sued various parties, including Ellen. The court, for the sake of argument, assumed that Ellen had a duty of care to Sharon and that this duty had been breached. The question that concerned the court was whether the breach was the proximate cause of Sharon's injuries. Stated otherwise, can Ellen's failure to inform the operator of the board-and-care home that Sharon had walked away from her earlier placement be considered a proximate cause of her injuries? The answer is no. No one can say whether full disclosure at the time of placement would have affected the decision to accept Sharon as a resident, and it was not clear that if that facility rejected Sharon, she would not have been injured when she walked away from another facility. What was clear was that when Sharon walked away from the facility on two occasions before she was injured, the facility operator was put on notice that Sharon had a tendency to wander.

Breach of Contract and Fraud

An agency that places a child for adoption is not a guarantor of the child's future health, but an agency must strive to provide adoptive parents with complete and accurate information concerning a child's health and family background.[30] Failure to provide such information or providing information known to be false has led adoptive parents to sue adoption agencies, claiming that the agencies were in breach of contract and had perpetrated fraud in intentionally misrepresenting as healthy children with physical or emotional problems. Cases involving breach of contract and fraud, in the adoption context, are known as wrongful adoption torts.

In 1986 the Ohio Supreme Court was the first to recognize the tort of wrongful adoption. The Burrs, who were seeking to adopt an infant, contacted the county adoption agency and within a few days were informed that Patrick, a seventeen-month-old boy, was available for adoption.[31] The caseworker told the family that the boy's mother was eighteen and not able to care for her child. Russell Burr would testify that he and his wife were told that Patrick was a "nice big, healthy, baby boy." Patrick became a member of the Burr family. In the years that followed, the child developed a series of physical and mental problems. When he entered primary school, he was classified as mentally retarded. By the time he entered high school, Patrick was experiencing hallucinations and was diagnosed with Huntington's Disease, a genetic disease that destroys the central nervous system. The Burrs obtained a court order to open the sealed records that contained information about Patrick's background.

They quickly learned that they had been lied to. For example, Patrick's mother was a thirty-one-year-old mental patient, not an eighteen-year-old unable to provide for her baby. The baby was delivered at a state mental hospital where the mother lived. The identity of the boy's father was not known, but it was assumed that he was also a mental patient. All the information that the Burrs had been given about Patrick, save for his age and sex, was false. Patrick should have been classified as a "special needs" child (chapter 10) because his background suggested the likelihood that he would become dependent upon public funds to defray the costs associated with caring for him.

The court ruled that in order to prevail, the Burrs had to prove the elements of fraud, which include proof that the charged party (1) withheld or misrepresented information that there was a duty to disclose and that was material to the issue at hand, in this case, to the question of Patrick's physical and mental health; (2) knew that the information provided was false or that it was imparted with no regard for its truth or falsity; (3) intended to mislead the person to whom the information was given; and (4) that the person receiving the information relied on it in making the decision to go forward. As a rule, the party bringing a wrongful adoption suit is seeking monetary damages to defray the costs of caring for a child with physical or mental health problems[32] and/or the emotional distress caused by the agency's fraudulent behavior.[33] The Burrs were awarded $125,000 to cover medical expenses.

Courts are not likely to hold agencies accountable when the injuries later sustained by a child were not foreseeable at the time of the adoption. For example, whether premature birth will lead to health problems is hypothetical. A California court ruled that an adoption agency could not be charged with a failure to warn adoptive parents of an event with no certainty of occurrence.[34] Nor was an agency liable for breach of contract based on a claim by parents that they had been promised no "entanglements" in the adoption process. A Georgia appellate court found no evidence of such a promise and reasoned that such a promise would be unreasonable to make and impossible to keep.[35]

Action Taken by a State Licensing Board

Statutes that govern the issuance of professional licenses provide that a licensee who engages in conduct that violates a standard of professional practice places that license at risk. A typical social work–licensing statute provides that the state licensing board "may refuse to issue, refuse to renew, suspend, or revoke any license, or may place on probation, censure, reprimand, or take other disciplinary action deemed appropriate [including] . . . the imposition of fines . . . for each violation."[36] This statute lists the following bases as ground for disciplinary action: (1) falsifying information provided to an insurance company concerning a claim; (2) being convicted of a felony or misdemeanor that involves dishonesty; (3) engaging in dishonorable, unethical, or unprofessional conduct that is likely to deceive, defraud, or harm the public; (4) using to excess any controlled substance that impairs one's judgment or skill; (5) suffering disciplinary action by another jurisdiction; (6) continuing misbehavior while on probation; (7) abandoning a client without cause; (8) failing to report known or suspected child abuse or neglect; and (9) failing to file and pay income tax.[37] Social workers have had their licenses suspended, lost their privilege to practice, or had a license denied for (1) engaging in Medicaid fraud by falsifying records[38]; (2) falsifying educational information to obtain a license to practice[39]; (3) violating the Code of Ethics of the National Association of Social Workers[40]; and (4) practicing without a license.[41]

The penalties levied by licensing boards may take the form of a slap on the wrist, since board actions are meant to protect the public, not to punish the offender. For example, in the mid-1990s a social worker practicing in Maryland had her license suspended for six months by the Board of Social Work Examiners. An administrative court convened by the state's licensing board determined that the social worker had engaged in fraud. She had billed the government for services rendered to Medicaid patients who were in fact never served, and she engaged in "collateral billing," which occurs where service is rendered to a relative of a patient who is not covered by insurance. On appeal the sentence was reduced to one month.[42] You should note that the action taken by a licensing board has no bearing on action that the government may take to recoup its losses, nor does it bear on the question of whether criminal charges could be filed against the worker for fraud.

Federal Claims: Civil Rights and Constitutional Violations

In reading case law, you are likely to come upon the phrase "plaintiff brought a 1983 action against social workers" or words to that effect. Section 1983 is part of the *United States Code* bearing the title "Civil Action for Deprivation of Rights."[43] This section of the *Code* provides a mechanism for any U.S. citizen to sue another who is acting "under color of state law" for depriving the aggrieved party of a constitutional or statutory right.

People act under color of state law when they exercise power that they have as a result of state law and only because they are clothed in the authority of state law. Thus a social worker (1) employed by a unit of government, a private agency, or in private practice; (2) charged with carrying out a public function; and (3) whose work is supported by public funds may be deemed to be a state actor and therefore vulnerable to suit based on a claim that the social worker deprived another of a constitutional or civil right if, for example, the alleged misconduct occurred in the context of performing a job function. Thus a social worker in private practice who, under contract to Utah, conducted statutorily required psychological assessments of applicants for the position of state trooper was a state actor and could be held liable for gross negligence in the conduct of evaluations.[44]

In addition to establishing that the offending conduct was undertaken by a state actor performing duties under color of state law, the client who files a Section 1983 action must show that the actions resulted in the deprivation of a federally secured right.[45] A federally secured right is any right (1) under the Constitution, such as the right to a hearing before benefits are terminated, which is rooted in the due process clause of the Fourteenth Amendment; (2) under a civil rights statute, such as the right under the Americans with Disabilities Act (ADA) to be judged on one's ability, not on the basis of one's disability; or (3) rights granted under certain statutes, such as the right conferred on children in foster care to a written case plan as described in the Adoption Assistance and Child Welfare Act. Recall the earlier discussion of Andrea, who sued a county agency for failing to protect her from the pregnancy that resulted after she engaged in consensual sex with the teenage son of her foster parents. Andrea brought her suit under Section 1983. In determining that she did not have a claim against the county, the court noted that while the Constitution may offer protection from severe physical injury for those in government custody, no one has a federally secured right to be protected from consensual sex.

Federal rights said to have been restricted by social workers, social work supervisors, agency administrators, or state officials include Fourteenth Amendment due process rights where clients have alleged that they have been (a) denied a right to decide to procreate after being coerced into having a tubal ligation[46]; (b) placed at risk of physical injury because of a failure to supervise a foster home placement and to provide care in a manner consistent with competent professional judgment[47]; (c) falsely imprisoned based on an allegation that a child was abducted[48]; (d) denied the right to raise a child free from state interference when a social worker threatened to remove a child from parental custody if parents were not cooperative[49]; (e) deprived of a privacy right when forced to see a psychiatrist and to divulge private matters[50]; (f) deprived of treatment and visitation opportunities available under departmental policy because of a person's sexual orientation.[51] Federal rights said to have been restricted by social workers, social work supervisors, agency administrators, or state officials also include First Amendment rights, where it was alleged that

(a) grandparents were restricted in their constitutional right to petition a court because a social worker unreasonably delayed initiating court proceedings on their behalf in a state whose law prevented the grandparents from initiating proceedings on their own[52]; and (b) grandparents were denied their constitutional right to familial association because the state sought temporary custody of a minor. Federal rights include those found in the Adoption Assistance and Child Welfare Act, the Child Abuse Prevention and Treatment Act (both are discussed in detail in chapter 10), and the Individuals with Disabilities in Education Act (chapter 9), and suits have been brought where children have claimed a right to (a) case plans; (b) case reviews; (c) placement in the least restrictive setting; (d) timely and thorough protective service investigations; (e) protection from harm; (f) the right to be placed for adoption without regard to race, color, or national origin; and (g) the right to privacy in their educational records.[53]

Civil rights statutes protect us from discrimination based on a characteristic such as race, color, national origin, sex, disability, age and, in some instances, sexual orientation and from workplace harassment. Civil rights statutes provide an added basis for suit. Included here are the Civil Rights Act of 1964, the Vocational Rehabilitation Act of 1973 (VRA), the Americans with Disabilities Act of 1990 (ADA) (the VRA and ADA are reviewed in chapters 9, 13, and 14), Title IX of the Education Amendments of 1972 (chapter 11), and the Fair Housing Act of 1968 (chapter 9.).

The following briefly illustrates one type of coverage provided by the VRA and the ADA and how disability rights statutes have been used in lawsuits against providers of social services. The VRA and the ADA protect people from disability-based discrimination, but the VRA applies to entities that receive federal funds, while the ADA applies as well to individuals in private practice, private and public employers, and social service agencies, regardless of whether they receive federal funds. Subsequent chapters will explore the definition of *disabilities* in greater detail, but it may be helpful to know that disabled people are those with a physical or mental impairment that limits significantly their ability to undertake a major life activity that the average person can perform with little or no difficulty, such as "caring for ones-self, performing manual tasks, walking, seeing, hearing, speaking, breathing, learning and working."[54]

Title II of the ADA states that qualified individuals with disabilities should not be excluded because of their disability from "services, programs or activities of a public entity," such as units of state or local government.[55] Title III offers the same protection from discrimination by private entities, for example, hotels, places of entertainment, shops, and private providers of social, mental health and medical services. A qualified individual is one who meets the eligibility criteria for the service or program that person is seeking. For example, a child in foster care cannot be excluded from an adoption program solely because of a disability, nor can a private provider, be it a physician or social worker in private practice, deny service to a disabled person solely on the basis of a disability.

Referring to the public service provisions of the ADA, a federal district court ruled that New York City violated the rights of people with HIV/AIDS by denying them "meaningful access to public assistance programs." Access, the court ruled, should take into account the debilitating nature of the disease and the inability of people with HIV/AIDS to negotiate the complicated social service system without the aid of a case manager.[56] In another case the U.S. Court of Appeals for the Second Circuit found that New York City violated the rights of children with HIV/AIDS by failing to ensure that they had meaningful access to the child welfare system, for example, by failing to assess one child's need for the medical staff to monitor his condition and another child's need for services to address his neurological problems.[57] In Ohio a parent with a hearing impairment had a cause of action against the state court system for failing to provide him with adequate hearing assistance during a prolonged child custody dispute, thus preventing him from participating in a public service.[58] Institutionalized patients with a mental disability prevailed in their claim that they had a right to community-based placement when the individual responsible for their treatment determines that such placement is appropriate.[59]

PART 2—RESPONSES TO LITIGATION

Once a suit is filed, a defendant may respond in various ways. Shortly after the suit is filed, the defendant may file a motion asking that the court dismiss the suit, arguing that (1) the plaintiff has failed to cite as a cause of action a legal theory recognized by law; (2) the facts stated in the complaint do not support the plaintiff's claim; or (3) the social worker who is being sued may claim (a) that there was never a professional relationship with the plaintiff, so no duty was owed; or (b) that the social worker is immune from suit. After discovery (see chapter 3) either party may file a motion for summary judgment, moving that no factual issue exists for a judge or jury to decide. If the court denies a motion to dismiss or a motion for summary judgment, an appeal may follow in which the losing party asks that the ruling of the trial court be overturned. Once trial commences, the charged party is most likely to defend his or her practices by presenting expert testimony to show that the practices said to have caused harm met professional standards of conduct.

Immunity defenses are often raised by a government entity or an individual who is acting on behalf of a government entity. We will consider these at length, then examine defenses based on a statute of limitations.

Eleventh Amendment and Sovereign Immunity

State government and state agencies are immune from suit in federal court under the doctrine of sovereign immunity. The doctrine is given expression in the Eleventh Amendment to the Constitution,[60] which states that individuals cannot bring suit against the states in a federal court unless a state waives its immunity or there is a valid congressional waiver of state immunity.[61] For example, Congress has declared that states cannot claim Eleventh Amendment immunity when they accept federal funding under a program such as the Individuals with Disabilities in Education Act or the Adoption Assistance and Child Welfare Act,[62] and Congress may waive a state's immunity when with sufficient data Congress demonstrates a pervasive pattern of civil rights violations.[63] In addition, the immunity conferred by the Eleventh Amendment is generally not applicable in suits seeking injunctive relief,[64] nor is there a bar to bringing suit against local levels of government and their agencies since they are not "states."

Fearing that immunity would lead to irresponsible behavior by their agents, some states abrogated their immunity in certain circumstances by drawing a distinction between acts of a policy-making nature, thus exempting the legislature and the judiciary from suit, and acts through which policy is administered. Thus the state legislature cannot be sued for failing to increase financial or medical benefits beyond those required by federal law, but state agencies may be sued for failing to administer entitlements in accordance with federal or state law.

Social Worker Liability and the Immunity from Suit

Immunity from suit is a common defense offered by social workers and their supervisors. The standard for determining whether a social worker can be held liable for professional misconduct is different from that used in an action brought under Section 1983 or in a claim of negligence under a state's malpractice rules. We begin with 1983.

A plaintiff in a Section 1983 action will not prevail unless she or he can establish that the social worker's allegedly wrongful conduct violated a clearly established statutory or constitutional right and that the worker knew or should have known that a right was being violated.[65] Courts strive to balance client rights against the public good that social workers seek to achieve when their actions restrict client rights, such as when people are involuntarily committed or children removed from the care of their parents.

For example, parents have a right, rooted in the Constitution, to the care, custody, and control of their children; this right is well established. Consequently, a social worker practicing in the field of child welfare should know that when a child is removed from parental care, removal could be construed as violating a constitutional right. Such a claim was made in the spring of 2000, when parents brought a Section 1983 action against social workers and New Hampshire after their child was placed in foster care. The state moved for summary judgment and prevailed. In reaching its decision, the court balanced the parental rights at issue against the child's right to safety and found that the social worker was entitled to qualified immunity because his suspicion that the child was abused was reasonable, as was his suspicion that the child was in danger if left in the home. However, in another case six social workers employed by a public department of social services were not entitled to qualified immunity where they failed to investigate adequately a home in which a child was placed and failed to supervise the home after the children were placed.[66] The court reasoned that the state's obligation to safeguard children that it had placed in care was firmly established at the time the social workers acted and that they either knew or should have known that their actions had the potential to violate the client's rights.

When a supervisor is charged with negligent supervision, the standard for liability may be formulated as either of two questions: "Did the supervisor know of, or should the supervisor have known of, the alleged misconduct of the supervisee?" or "Can it be shown that the supervisor was deliberately indifferent to or tacitly approved of the practices that resulted in an injury to a client?" Either formulation creates a burden of proof that is difficult to meet.[67] For example, in one case supervisors could not be held liable where a social worker was accused of sexually assaulting a child. There was no indication that any supervisor was aware of the abuse until after allegations arose. The social worker had been accused of abuse ten years earlier and one supervisor was aware of this, but neither circumstance created liability, since no finding of abuse was lodged at the conclusion of an investigation of the old complaint.[68] But in another case negligent supervision was found after the client showed that the medical center charged with negligence knew that an employee had a history of abusing patients and did not act on its knowledge.[69]

When a client brings a malpractice action under state law, an immunity defense may be raised, citing provisions in state law that grant immunity to "classes" of social workers, for example, social workers involved in child protection. In addition to social workers, other public employees, public officials, and private-sector employees working under a contract with the public sector may be immune from suit as long as their actions were taken in good faith. Immunity may be absolute or qualified. Absolute immunity, which is extended to judges and prosecutors, acts as a complete bar to suit for actions that a person takes in her or his official capacity. Some courts have extended absolute immunity to social workers, but this is the exception.[70] The general rule is that the immunity enjoyed by social workers is qualified, meaning that they cannot be sued for actions taken in an official capacity when they were motivated by a good faith belief.

Knowledge that one is immune from suit serves a public good because it encourages social workers and others to use the discretion that their jobs require, and it may increase the chances that qualified people will not turn away from public service out of a fear of lawsuits. As noted, immunity exists for actions taken in good faith; the standard used to determine whether actions were taken in good faith seeks to strike a balance between protecting the public employee's exercise of discretion while allowing for compensation for those whose rights are violated.[71] Thus when a social worker, acting at the direction of the court, prepared a report describing the results of a mental health evaluation, she was immune from a libel suit arising from any false statements in the report because she was fulfilling her quasi-judicial duties.[72] However, while child abuse–reporting laws afford immunity to those who report in good faith, liability may be found where the actions of officials violate a statute that governs reporting and investigation of child abuse. In *K.B. v. Mills* a state trooper and a social worker who were investigating a report of child abuse took the child to a hospital to be examined by a physician. The child's guardian sued, charging the state trooper and the social worker with battery, stemming from a gynecological examination to which the child was subjected. The court ruled that neither the police officer nor the social worker was entitled to immunity because both failed to seek a court order before authorizing the exam, and in so doing, they violated a state law that provides for a medical examination without a court order only if the reporter is a physician or if the child's health is seriously endangered and a court order cannot be obtained.[73]

The qualified immunity enjoyed by social workers in public employment may extend to practitioners in private agencies who are performing a public function. Recall the discussion in chapter 5 of *Richardson v. McKnight.* In that case the U.S. Supreme Court ruled that prison guards who were employed by a private corporation were not entitled to claim immunity from suit. In 1998 in *Bartell v. Lohiser*[74] a federal judge ruled that social workers in the employ of a nonprofit social service agency who were working under contract with a public agency were entitled to qualified immunity. The court referred to the reasoning of the U.S. Supreme Court in distinguishing *Bartell* from *Richardson.* In *Richardson,* even though the prison guards were performing a public function, they were employed by a private firm with no direct and ongoing supervision by the state. Moreover, private firms that wish to have their contracts renewed have an incentive to hire and retain the most qualified personnel, do not operate under the constraints of a civil service system, and thus can readily discharge unsatisfactory staff and provide fiscal incentives to those who perform well.

Finally, private firms are shielded by the insurance that they are statutorily required to carry.

The *Bartell* court said that the private nonprofit agency employed its workers to perform a public service task at the express direction and under the close supervision of government officials. Moreover, the public agency purchased the service only when it was not able to meet the particular needs of an individual child. As such, the private agency was serving as an adjunct to the state agency in performing an essential government activity of protecting wards of the state. The court was concerned that without immunity workers in the private agency would not undertake to make the difficult decisions that their jobs required, in this case, recommending whether a parent was fit to resume care of a child. Faced with liability, nonprofit firms were not likely to enter into contracts with state agencies. If the nonprofit organization refused to contract with the public sector, this would only increase the pressure on a system whose resources were already strained.[75]

It is important to emphasize that a court will generally go out of its way to find that a social worker's actions were taken in good faith, thereby finding that the worker is immune from suit. However, workers may lose sight of their responsibilities and engage in overzealous advocacy, as the case in figure 7.1 illustrates.

When a client believes that the actions of a social worker are harmful, she or he will specify the basis for this claim. These are reported in the "Summary of Action" section in figure 7.1, where we learn that Steve Poulos, the plaintiff, claimed that the worker intentionally and maliciously falsified information about him. The "Procedural History" section makes clear that Poulos prevailed at trial and that the case comes before the court on an appeal raised by the state. The state claimed, as reported in the "Issue" section, that the social worker had immunity and that Poulos had failed to prove the elements of his case, so the appellate court should reverse the jury's decision.

The following items in the "Facts" section are key to understanding why the appellate court supported the jury's decision: (1) the social worker prejudged Poulos, as is clear from her statement that her work with the family would proceed on the assumption that he was guilty; (2) although Poulos's employer was aware of the sex abuse allegations, the worker felt compelled to report them once again; and (3) the social worker misled the school by failing to report (a) that the results of a test for a sexually transmitted disease were incorrect, (b) that the boy who accused Poulos had severe mental problems, (c) that the boy recanted his allegations, and (d) that his brother denied the allegations entirely. Next, the applicable law is set forth. There was no denying that the worker's actions placed Poulos in a false light, meaning the information provided was not true, and that the information was provided "before the public,"

FIGURE 7.1

Litigation Against a Social Worker

Poulos v. Lutheran Social Services of Illinois, Inc.,
312 Ill. App. 3d 731, 728 N.E.2d 547 (Ill. Ct. App. 1st Dist., March 24, 2000)

Summary of Action:
In 1993, plaintiff, Steve Poulos, sued a social worker and her employer, a nonprofit social service agency, alleging that the social worker: (1) intentionally falsified information she provided to plaintiff's employer, and (2) acted with malice in that she knew the provided information to be false.[1] Held: Social worker was not immune from suit. The evidence showed that she acted with actual malice which cannot coexist with the good faith requirement for a claim of immunity.

Procedural History:
The jury awarded compensatory damages of $219,000 for lost wages. Both parties appealed. [The bases for these appeals appear in the "Issue" section].

Issue:
Defendant asks the appellate court to overturn the jury's decision. It argues that (1) the trial court erred by failing to "direct a verdict" for defendant [meaning that the court should have ordered the jury to return a verdict for defendant] because the social worker was qualifiedly immune; and (2) plaintiff failed to establish all of the elements for false light [see section on the law]. Plaintiff appealed because the trial court did not instruct the jury that he was entitled to punitive damages.

Facts:
In 1985, Katherine and Steve Poulos became the foster parents of three boys, R.F., J.F., and Daniel whom they later adopted. In 1988, R.F. and J.F. were moved to another foster home because they were exhibiting behavioral problems that posed a danger to Daniel.

Approximately 9 months later R.F. accused Steve of sexual abuse. The Department of Children and Family Service investigated. Following their attorney's advice, the Poulos' had Daniel examined by a physician. The examination indicated the presence of gonorrhea but on re-examination these results were shown to be a false positive. Nevertheless, Daniel was temporarily placed in foster care and the state petitioned the court to declare Daniel a ward of the state.

In January 1989, Katherine and Steve met with defendant Nancy Golden, a social worker employed by defendant Lutheran Social Services. Golden had been assigned to monitor Daniel's placement in foster care and to provide counseling and related services to Katherine and Steve. At the trial, Katherine testified that Golden told them they had to proceed under the assumption that Steve was guilty if they hoped to regain custody of Daniel and that Golden told her to divorce her husband if she ever wanted to see her son again.

Steve was a physical education teacher at a secondary school. The school had been informed of the sex abuse allegations but chose to retain Steve in his position. Approximately two weeks after a February 1989 meeting between Golden and the

Pouloses, Steve was asked to take a paid leave of absence from his teaching position and he did so. He was fired in July of 1989.

In December of 1989 the child abuse proceedings were dismissed. Daniel was returned to his parents. Steve refused an offered from the school because the contract required that he be evaluated during the school year.

Testimony by Nancy Golden and school officials revealed that Golden called the school in early 1989, although she knew that they had been informed of the charges against Steve. Golden spoke with an official and informed him of the allegations against Steve. She told him that Daniel had tested positive for gonorrhea but failed to inform him that retesting confirmed an error in the first test. She did not reveal that Steve's accuser had severe mental problems, that he had recanted his allegations, nor that his brother denied the allegations in their entirety.

Law:

Plaintiff's claim was based on the tort of "false light" which requires that he establish that (1) that defendant placed him in a false light before the public, (2) that the false light in which he was placed would be highly offensive to a reasonable person, and (3) that defendant acted with actual malice.

A claim of immunity rests on actions taken in good faith.

An award of punitive damages is possible where actions convey actual malice, or where a defendant's actions demonstrate negligence that is so gross as to indicate a wanton disregard of the rights of others.

Decision & Reasoning:

"Before the public" in an action for false light means that false and highly offensive information was disclosed to a person with whom a plaintiff has a special relationship. It was established at trial that Golden spoke with a school official about plaintiff and that the official, whose responsibilities included hiring . . . and overseeing a variety of school matters, had a special relationship with the plaintiff.

Malice is defined as knowledge that the statements made were false or that they were made with reckless disregard as to their truth or falsity. At trial it was established that Golden knew, before she telephoned the school, that the second examination of Daniel showed that he was not infected with gonorrhea. It was also established Golden knew that plaintiff had been examined and was free of gonorrhea before she telephoned the school.

Based upon the evidence, the jury finding that Golden's actions placed plaintiff in a false light is reasonable. Golden acted with malice when she telephoned the school and misrepresented the results of the test for gonorrhea. The social worker was neither conditionally nor qualifiedly privileged to act as she did.

The jury should have been allowed to consider plaintiff's request for punitive damages and the case is remanded for consideration of this matter.

---

1. An additional allegation on which plaintiff was successful was that the worker intentionally caused of breach of contract between plaintiff and his employer where, relying on the information provided by the worker, plaintiff lost his job.

Source: Excerpted from Illinois Appellate Court decisions. Edited by the author.

meaning before a person or people with whom the plaintiff had a "special relationship," here, his employer. That the provided information would be found offensive by a reasonable person cannot be disputed, and most significant for overcoming the claim to immunity was the complete absence of good faith on the worker's part and the actual showing of malice. As the court reports, malice is knowledge that the statements made to a party with whom the plaintiff had a special relationship were false. Alternatively, malice could be shown by demonstrating that the statements were made with "reckless disregard" for their truth or falsity. Under the facts presented, the social worker acted with malice when she telephoned the school and misrepresented information and in so doing waived any claim to immunity.

Statute of Limitations

A statute of limitations sets an outside time limit beyond which a suit is barred. Time limits vary by state, but a one- or two-year limit for actions alleging negligence or malpractice is common. Longer time periods may be set for actions that proceed on other legal theories, such as fraud or breach of contract.

It is helpful to know what time limits are set in the state where you practice, but it is equally important to know what action or actions trigger the time limits. Two issues are important. The first is the "continuing treatment doctrine," which holds that the statute of limitations is triggered by the termination of the relationship of client and professional with respect to the issue for which treatment was provided. This doctrine was developed and has been applied almost exclusively in the context of medical malpractice where, for example, following a surgical procedure, a patient's course of treatment may continue with respect to the after-effects of the surgery. Once a therapist formally terminates treatment with a client, it may be difficult to apply the doctrine to subsequent contacts. For example, an Illinois appellate court ruled that letters and telephone conversations between a therapist and client did not constitute treatment for the purposes of applying the doctrine to extend the statute of limitations for a claim of negligent practice.[76]

The second issue is concerned with what are called "discovery rules," where the statute of limitations is triggered when the client discovers or reasonably should have discovered the injury. Two examples will illustrate this important issue.

In 1984 Martha Hall began treatment with Darrell Miller, a licensed clinical social worker, and continued in individual treatment until 1993 but remained in group therapy for an additional year.[77] In the course of individual therapy Hall became convinced that she was the victim of "satanic ritual abuse" perpetrated by her parents and friends. One year after terminating treatment she came to doubt that she had been victimized. In 1995 she came across a magazine article that discussed "false memories." She consequently attended a meeting of the False Memory Syndrome Foundation, where she learned that Miller had a reputation for "advocating the existence of Satanic cults and the fallacies of Satanic Ritual Abuse Therapy."[78] In 1996, almost three years after terminating individual treatment, Hall sued Miller. The statute of limitations provided that suit had to be filed within two years. The trigger for calculating the time was (1) the action that caused the alleged injury, which here would have been the treatment itself, or (2) the time when the injury became reasonably ascertainable. Because Hall filed suit more than two years after terminating treatment, the court had to decide when her condition became "reasonably ascertainable." Given Hall's "fragile mental state," the court ruled that it was not reasonable to expect that she could have become aware before 1995 that Miller caused her injury; that was when she learned of "false memory syndrome." Thus her suit could go forward under the "reasonably ascertainable" prong of the statute.

Another case began in 1969 when a couple adopted their first child. Almost twenty years later they sued the adoption agency for fraud, arguing that the agency had represented as healthy a newborn whom it knew was not healthy at birth and who was at risk for both physical health and mental health problems. The statute of limitations provided that an action for fraud had to be brought within four years of the time that the cause for action accrued. The cause accrued, the court ruled, in 1982 when the parents obtained a court order that allowed them to review their son's sealed medical records, not in 1969 when the fraudulent actions took place.[79]

PART 3—REMEDIES

A variety of remedies may be available to the client who brings suit, including agreed-upon remedies that parties may reach before a verdict is rendered. Some remedies take the form of damage awards that seek to compensate the injured party for the value of the injury, for example, for lost wages or medical expenses incurred. This was illustrated in figure 7.1; in this case Steve Poulos was awarded compensatory damages to make up for lost wages after it was demonstrated that a social worker had falsified information. Punitive damages may be awarded when the defendant's conduct involves malice or fraud or is, in some other way, "wicked" and the injury to the plaintiff is serious enough to warrant inflicting the punishment that is the purpose of awarding punitive damages. Recall from the Poulos case that the court remanded the case so that the trial court could consider an award of punitive damages because the offending conduct showed evidence of malicious intent.

Negotiated remedies are attractive to defendants because they rarely involve admissions of guilt and because some provide that plaintiffs not disclose the settlement terms, thereby, it is hoped, discouraging others from suing in expectation of a substantial award. From the plaintiff's viewpoint a settlement may be attractive because the compensation or other remedy will be promptly forthcoming, whereas any significant judicial or jury award may be appealed, causing a plaintiff to wait many years before compensation is received or other remedies put in place.

Some parties seek a "declaratory judgment," which is a judicial ruling that clarifies and settles the rights at issue in a legal action. A declaration of rights by a court provides relief from the uncertainty that follows when rights are ambiguous. For example, a group of New York City residents with HIV/AIDS brought a class action against the city. A class action is a suit brought by a small number of named individuals, half a dozen, for example, on behalf of a class of people with a common characteristic(s) or common legal problem(s). The class may number in the thousands. In a class action it is assumed the problem advanced by the class can be settled with a common remedy or remedies. In their suit six plaintiffs alleged that the city violated the ADA and the VRA by failing to provide "meaningful access to public assistance programs, benefits, and services," meaning that it failed to take into account the extreme difficulties that people with AIDS confront in gaining access to benefits without the assistance of a case manager to negotiate the system on their behalf. Plaintiffs sought and received a declaration of their rights and a ruling that the city was in violation of the ADA and VRA.[80] People who bring suit usually want more than a declaration of rights. The request that a court issue a declaration may be accompanied by a request for an injunction, which is a court order that directs a defendant to perform a certain action or to stop doing what limits or infringes upon the rights of others. The class of people with HIV/AIDS asked the court to issue an injunction ordering the city to comply with applicable statutes and regulations requiring meaningful access to public assistance programs.

Attorneys who bring suit on behalf of children in foster care, prisoners, and adults who are institutionalized for mental illness may seek a complete overhaul of the system or of an institution that serves clients. Such litigation, which is often called "institutional reform litigation," may be resolved by a negotiated remedy that produces a "consent decree." A consent decree is a contract between plaintiffs and defendants that seeks to resolve the problems identified at trial. The decree must be approved by the court; once approved, it binds the parties. Consent decrees may be entered into before trial or once trial commences. When decrees are entered into in the early stages of litigation, the parties save the time and expense associated with lengthy trials and conserve judicial resources. Defendants may find decrees attractive for the reasons noted in the earlier discussion of settlements. Decrees may be attractive to plaintiffs who are able to achieve a measure of comprehensive reform that goes beyond what a judge would order. For example, in 1989, the Connecticut Civil Liberties Union and the American Civil Liberties Union sued Connecticut on behalf of neglected and abused children. The lawsuit was settled in 1990 without going to trial. The terms of the settlement were outlined in a consent decree and described in detail in twelve manuals developed to guide implementation of the decree. The consent decree and manuals, adopted as orders of the court in 1992, sought to reform (1) administrative practices such as budgeting, policy development, contracting, and resource allocation; (2) program operation by requiring new procedures to govern protective services, foster care, and adoption, and by creating new programs and services; and (3) day-to-day practices by affecting the hiring and training of social workers, caseload size, and access to consultants.[81]

Consent decrees have been used to modify mental health systems,[82] the prison systems in at least thirty states,[83] and the child welfare systems in at least twenty states and the District of Columbia.[84]

SUMMARY

Different legal theories provide a basis for suing social workers, social work supervisors, and their private and public employing agencies. These include malpractice, breach of contract, and fraud. Although precise figures are not available, malpractice, which is a form of negligence, is probably the most common basis for suit.

The malpractice plaintiff must demonstrate that she or he had a professional relationship with the practitioner being sued, that there was a breach of a duty of care, and that the breach was the cause of the injury suffered. Although there are situations where a professional has a duty of care to a person who is not a client, for example, to a child who has been victimized by a family member or to a person whose health or safety is threatened by the client, the general rule is that duty flows to the client with whom a professional relationship was established for the purpose of providing services for an agreed-upon purpose. The duty owed is to conduct one's practice in a reasonable manner. *Reasonable* is defined with reference to how others with similar education and experience would conduct their practice under circumstances similar to those that gave rise to the lawsuit.

Action against a social worker may also be taken by a state licensing board if a worker engages in conduct that violates a standard of professional practice. Workers are most vulnerable to disciplinary action when they engage in behavior that is dishonorable, unethical, or unprofessional and so creates a risk of harm to the public or when they engage in behavior that is dishonest, for example, falsifying information for the purpose of monetary gain. Additional factors that create a foundation for disciplinary action include violating the Code of Ethics of the National Association of Social Workers and practicing without a license.

Section 1983 of the *United States Code* provides a framework for a private party to sue a professional whose salary is paid from public funds, if in the performance of her or his job functions the professional violates a client's constitutional or statutory rights. For a Section 1983 litigant to be successful, it must be shown that the professional knew of or should have been aware of the possibility that her or his actions violated a client's rights.

The professional or organization being sued may respond in a number of ways. The defendant may file motions asking the court to dismiss the suit before it goes to trial because the plaintiff has failed to state a cause of action, because a reasonable person could not find that the facts alleged support a claim for damages, or because the suit was filed after the statute of limitations expired.

Immunity defenses are commonly offered by the state when it claims that the doctrine of sovereign immunity bars suit or by individual workers who claim that they acted in good faith in the performance of their state-supported job and that they should not be held liable for harms suffered by the plaintiff. When courts consider immunity defenses, they strive to balance the public good that social workers seek to achieve and client rights. Thus a court may sanction restrictions placed on a client, for example, the restricted freedom that results from involuntary commitment to a mental institution, if the person poses a danger to the public whose right to safety overrides the committed person's right to freedom. However, courts will not sanction irresponsible conduct when social workers deliberately ignore statutory rules, thus endangering clients, or when a professional's conduct evidences a malicious intent to cause harm.

A variety of remedies are available to the successful litigant. These include compensatory and punitive damages, declaratory judgments, and injunctions that compel or prevent action by the party being sued. Lawsuits often result in negotiated remedies where the parties enter into a mutually acceptable settlement before a verdict is returned by a judge or jury. When class-action suits are brought on behalf of children in foster care, prisoners, and adults who are institutionalized for mental illness, a common remedy is the complete overhaul of the system or of the institution that serves clients. Such litigation may result in a consent decree, which is a negotiated remedy that spells out in detail the actions that a defendant must take to reform the offending system. Consent decrees may be sweeping in their breadth, affecting all aspects of an institution or state system in an effort to reform administrative practices, policy development, and program operation.

PART 3

This part of the text consists of nine chapters. Chapters 8 through 13 focus on "family law" issues that are of concern to social workers. After looking at traditional and alternative family forms, and discussing matters concerning child custody and visitation when parents divorce or separate (chapter 8), we will turn our attention to legal issues in the education of children (chapter 9), the state's role in investigating allegations of child abuse and neglect, its role in providing for the protection and care of maltreated children (chapter 10), and family formation through adoption (chapter 11). Chapter 12 discusses domestic violence between adult members of a household, including violence perpetrated against the elderly. In the two concluding chapters we shift our attention to focus on legal issues involving the provision of health care services (chapter 13) and mental health services (chapter 14).

As will be clear throughout the chapters that follow, social workers play a key role in family law matters, just as they do in the provision of health and mental health services. Among other tasks, social workers (1) investigate reports of child or elder abuse; (2) prepare reports for use in court; (3) initiate petitions for court action on behalf of a child or adult client; (4) support with affidavits petitions initiated by others; and (5) work with attorneys and judicial officers as a consultant or independent contractor and (a) prepare social studies, (b) interpret studies prepared by others, and (c) testify as fact or expert witnesses.

8

Families and the Law

SOCIAL WORKERS play a key role in providing services to families. These roles may be categorized by (1) population served, such as the family, the elderly family member, or the child; (2) the practice setting, such as family services agency, child welfare agency, hospital, or school; and (3) by task performed, such as preparation of social studies, interpretation of studies prepared by others, and investigation following a report of child abuse or neglect. Therefore, knowledge of family law is critical to a significant number of practitioners.

Typically, family law is concerned with marriage and divorce, family violence, child custody, visitation and support, adoption, ownership of property, and inheritance rights. But other topics may be included because they affect family members, including benefits available through government-funded programs such as income assistance, housing and food assistance, and health care.

This chapter has two parts. Part 1 discusses family formation and begins by asking, "What is a family?" Then we turn our attention to marriage and then to alternative family forms, such as cohabiting couples, including domestic partnerships. Child custody, visitation, and child suppport are the focus of part 2, which reviews standards and rules that courts follow in awarding custody when parents divorce or separate.

PART 1—WHAT IS A FAMILY?

Society has an interest in supporting stable families to ensure that adults provide for their children, and to establish havens of mutual support, thus relieving government of an obligation to act as family surrogate. Because government provides financial support to some families, it has an interest in controlling the definition of *family* in order to limit the number eligible to receive public funds. The federal government and all states recognize as family those united by marriage, birth, and adoption. Those so united may be eligible for income tax benefits and for financial assistance through programs operated by government at the federal and state levels. In addition, individuals who are members of families created by marriage, birth, and adoption have rights, including those (a) of inheritance, (b) of visiting a critically ill family member who is hospitalized, and (c) of suing for the wrongful death of a loved one. In addition, employment benefits such as health insurance are often available to one's legally married spouse and dependents.

To some people the concept of family evokes images of an "ideal" of a wage-earning husband, his stay-at-home wife, and their one or more biological children.[1] Whether this notion of family life is "ideal" for those who have lived it, whether it existed for many, and, if it existed, whether it was normative or reflected an historical anachronism are matters of debate.[2] Regardless, the United States in the twenty-first century is made up of a diversity of family forms, including married couples, single-parent heads of household, blended families of married adults and their children from earlier marriages, and unmarried opposite-sex and same-sex couples. In addition, despite a recent decline in the divorce rate, nearly 50 percent of marriages are dissolved, meaning that a significant number of adults and children will spend part of their lives in a variety of family forms. The U.S. Census Bureau reports that households comprised of a family that is defined by marriage, birth, or adoption decreased from 81 percent of households in 1970 to 69 percent in 2000, with an increase in "nonfamily" households, which the Census Bureau defines as including people who live alone and those who share their homes with others.[3] While marriage has declined, cohabitation has increased, and 40 percent of cohabiting couples are parents living with children.[4]

These data describing family diversity suggest to some that the family is "under siege" from forces ranging from no-fault divorce laws that ease family breakup to cultural norms that encourage out-of-wedlock births and support never-married families.[5] Concerned with the survival of the "ideal family," some members of Congress have proposed a constitutional amendment to define marriage as a union of a man and a woman,[6] the Bush administration is pursuing funds for marriage initiatives, and some states have enacted laws that provide for "covenant marriages" as a return to "fault-based" divorce.

Although the legal definition of *family* embraces units formed by marriage, birth, or adoption, legal definitions of family are not unambiguous. In fact, close scrutiny of statutory law and court rulings reflects the changing nature of families in the United States and the ambivalence of government in defining *family*. Consider some examples:

- Massachusetts argued that only a married person should qualify for unemployment benefits when a claim was based on voluntary separation from work to relocate with a partner. The state Supreme Court disagreed. A woman's status as unmarried was not relevant to her eligibility for benefits, even though she voluntarily left her job to relocate with her domestic partner of thirteen years.[7]
- The unit of eligibility for food stamps is the "household." Parents, children, and siblings living together are generally treated as a single household, whereas unrelated individuals who live together may be treated as separate households unless they routinely purchase food and prepare meals together.[8] Thus the value of food stamps available to unrelated individuals who share living space may be greater than what is available to a family unit.
- In 1988 an appellate court in Missouri awarded child custody to a biological father and limited a mother's visitation because she was an "openly practicing homosexual."[9] In 1995 a court in the same state, reflecting changes in the concept of family, ruled that homosexuals are not unfit parents per se. It awarded visitation to a lesbian coparent who had formed a family unit with the child she had helped to raise. The court so ruled because it was clear that the child would suffer if the court were to sever the bond that had been created.[10]
- Although New York State does not recognize same-sex unions, after the World Trade Center attack Gov. George Pataki issued an executive order that extended spousal benefits to gay partners under New York's State Crime Victims Act.[11]
- Laws that define family as people related by marriage, birth, or adoption do not consider cohabiting couples as families. Nevertheless, jurisdictions across the United States have modified their laws to provide to those in domestic partnerships benefits that were previously available only to legally defined families. Vermont grants to those who enter into civil unions the same rights and responsibilities under state law as couples who marry.
- Members of Congress are on the record as opposing same-sex marriage. Nevertheless, benefits for domestic partners are available to some federal employees, including those working for the House of Representatives. In addition, Congress passed and President George W. Bush signed legislation allowing federal funds to pay for health care benefits for domestic partners of government employees in the District of Columbia, and lesbian and gay partners of fire fighters and police officers who die in the line of duty are eligible for federal death benefits.[12]
- New York City's rent control regulations provided that a property owner could not evict the surviving spouse of a deceased tenant or another family member who was living with the tenant. However, the law did not contain a

definition of family. After his life partner died, Miguel Braschi, claiming family status, sued for the right to remain in the apartment that he had shared with his partner. Ruling in Braschi's favor, New York's high court opined that family, as used in the rent control laws, "should not be rigidly restricted" to those with a marriage certificate or adoption order. The protection offered by the law should not rest on "fictitious legal distinctions or genetic history, but . . . in the reality of family life."[13]

- The law does not routinely recognize any right on the part of an adult not legally related to a child to interfere with the constitutionally protected relationship between parent and child. Nevertheless, the California Supreme Court awarded custody of a boy to his mother's boyfriend, who had acted as the child's father, even though he was not biologically related to the boy, by taking the child into his home, supporting him emotionally and financially, and by treating him as his son.[14]

Marriage

Marriage is a contractual union between a man and a woman. The relationship is controlled mainly by state law, and the state's authority to regulate marriage is extensive.[15] Although marriage begins with the voluntary consent of the parties, it cannot be terminated by mutual consent alone. The termination of a marriage requires state approval, and the terms of dissolution are controlled by state law. Even no-fault divorce, which minimizes state control, exists only through state action. Moreover, the statutes that permit no-fault divorce can be modified to require proof of fault. In New York, where a couple must live apart for one year pursuant to a written separation agreement, a no-fault divorce is encumbered with stringent requirements.[16]

The U.S. Constitution places certain restraints on the states. The U.S. Supreme Court has ruled that a state cannot prevent the marriage of (1) interracial couples[17]; (2) individuals with a support obligation to children from a previous marriage unless the parents prove that their children will not become dependent on public assistance[18]; or (3) prisoners, except those sentenced to life in prison (who cannot be expected to carry out the duties of marriage).[19] And federal law can limit a state's ability to set ground rules for who can marry. Thus Utah could not prevent individuals with AIDS from marrying without violating provisions in the Vocational Rehabilitation Act (VRA) and the Americans with Disabilities Act (ADA) that preclude discrimination against qualified individuals with a disability.[20]

The rules that govern marriage are similar in kind across the states, although the rules of any state may vary. For example, the age at which one may marry without parental consent may differ by state. The discussion that follows highlights the common rules.

Basic Conditions for Entering into a Marriage Contract

The law refers to marriages that are "void" and "voidable." Void marriages are those the state will not recognize and therefore are void from their inception. Such is the case when one party is married to another person or when the parties bear a certain relationship to each other. Marriages are void between (a) parent and child, (b) grandparent and grandchild, (c) brother and sister, (d) uncle and niece or aunt and nephew, and, (e) in some states, between first cousins.[21]

A voidable marriage is subject to being annulled but is valid until a request is made to end the union. For example, if one party to a marriage is under the age of consent, a court may annul the marriage if asked to do so. In addition, a marriage may be voidable if (a) either party is not capable of consenting, meaning that she or he lacks the mental capacity to understand that marrying means entering into a contractual relationship; (b) either party lacks the physical capacity to enter into sexual relations; or (c) the marriage was the result of force or duress applied to a party.

Licenses and Solemnization All states require the issuance of a marriage license. A waiting period after applying for the license may be required to allow the parties to reconsider their decision before solemnizing their marriage. The licensing procedure affords the state an opportunity to check that basic conditions have been met, for example, to verify birth certificates or divorce papers. Some states require that the parties have a blood test to detect the presence of sexually transmitted diseases (STDs),[22] and some require that the parties provide an affidavit identifying themselves by name, age, address, and Social Security number. A state may require the affidavit to include a statement of the parties' understanding that they may learn about STDs from a health department and that STDs can be transmitted in utero.[23] If the official who is issuing the license has reason to question the competence of either party who is entering into a marriage contract, the official may be authorized to require the appearance of witnesses to testify under oath to matters of concern.[24] Additionally, licensing allows a state to create a public record of all marriages. Finally, marriages must be solemnized by a civil official, such as a judge, town justice, or other official designated by law, or by a member of the clergy.

Annulment and Separation A marriage may be terminated by annulment or a married couple may live apart with or without a written separation agreement. A marriage may be annulled by a judicial officer or an ecclesiastical declaration, either of which is a pronouncement that the marriage never existed.[25] Grounds for an annulment include (a) lack of consent, (b) failure to consummate, and (c) being under age.

A married couple that chooses to live apart but does not wish to divorce may voluntarily enter into a written separation agreement that provides for (a) the disposition of property; (b) spousal support; (c) child support and visitation; and (d) other matters, such as provisions for one party to maintain health and life insurance for the benefit of the other and/or for children. Should the couple later divorce, the terms of the settlement agreement may be incorporated into the divorce decree.

Divorce

The state's interest in overseeing marriage plays itself out in requirements for licensing and solemnization and in establishing procedures for dissolving a marriage. Because the state is interested in sustaining the institution of marriage, it seeks to make the dissolution of marriage difficult and to regulate divorce to ensure fairness (1) in the distribution of marital property, (2) in providing financial support for children, and (3) in some cases in providing financial support of an adult party to the marriage.

State Rules

All states have rules conferring subject-matter jurisdiction (see chapter 3) on a state court to grant a divorce, resolve property matters, and adjudicate disputes about child support, child custody, and child visitation. In addition, state laws (1) require that those seeking a divorce have lived in the state for a specified time period; (2) set forth the grounds for obtaining a divorce; and (3) allow for temporary as well as permanent separations for those who choose to live apart but do not wish to divorce.

Grounds for divorce can be categorized as "fault" or "no fault" and include "conversion" divorce. The latter is a form of no-fault divorce where the status of living separately may be "converted" into a divorce based on the assumption that having lived apart for a statutorily specified period of time, the parties do not intend to resume their marital relationship.[26]

Common grounds for a "fault" divorce include (a) abandonment for a specified time period such as one year; (b) cruel and inhuman treatment where the conduct of the offending party endangers the physical or mental well-being of the other party; (c) imprisonment of a party for a statutorily specified period of time; and (d) adultery. "Proof of fault" requirements can be unfortunate if their fulfillment requires the parties to conspire to lie to justify their divorce. This may exacerbate an already difficult situation for adults, and it provides a poor example for children. For such reasons no-fault divorce has become available in a majority of states. No-fault laws allow a divorce on the basis of "irreconcilable differences" or the "irretrievable breakdown" of a marriage.

Mediation

When parties look to the courts to resolve their conflicts, they enter into an adversarial contest where (1) "winning" may become primary; (2) one's ability to influence the outcome is significantly diminished relative to nonadversarial approaches to conflict resolution; and (3) the emotional costs are high, especially when the process involves children. Moreover, judicial proceedings are time consuming and costly. For these reasons mediation, a form of alternative dispute resolution (see chapter 3) is gaining favor for resolving the myriad issues that may arise in a divorce action, from property settlements to child custody disputes.[27]

In mediation an impartial third party, the mediator, facilitates the resolution of a dispute by promoting the participants' voluntary agreement.[28] Thirty-eight states have legislation to regulate mediation in family matters.[29] Client self-determination is a fundamental principle of family mediation. Participation is voluntary, participants are expected to make informed decisions, and either party may withdraw if he or she thinks the process is not beneficial.

The values expressed in mediation are familiar to social workers. However, the voluntary nature of mediation may be undermined when courts mandate participation and because the parties know that their withdrawal from the process will require that they turn problem solving over to a court. Professional standards of confidentiality apply to mediation, but as with other professional matters, there are limits. For example, depending upon state law, confidentiality may be waived if a participant threatens suicide or violence against another or if child abuse or neglect comes to light.

In some states the person appointed as a mediator must have completed a course of "mediation training." Louisiana, for instance, provides that the person must have a college degree and, unless licensed by the state as an attorney, psychologist, social worker, or family counselor, must complete forty hours of general mediation training and twenty hours of specialized training.[30] Idaho requires that mediators be members of the Academy of Family Mediators and licensed or certified to practice in the state.[31] In other states a mediator may be anyone found suitable by the court.[32] Statutes vary in their specificity. California requires (a) a master's degree in psychology, social work, or related disciplines; (b) two or more years of experience as a counselor; and (c) knowledge of (i) the California court system, (ii) resources to which the client can be referred, and (iii) child development, child abuse, the effects of divorce on children, and domestic violence.[33] Other states list acceptable disciplines, including certified or licensed social workers.[34]

The freedom of the court to order participation in mediation is limited in some states by statutes that preclude court-ordered mediation when an order of protection has been issued (see chapter 12) or if a party objects because the relationship involved domestic violence. Depending upon state law, an agreement reached by the parties in mediation may be subject to judicial review and approval.

Fees and Counsel

Obtaining a divorce means incurring costs. These may be minimal, consisting of a filing fee required by the state, but many people require legal advice and therefore the money to retain an attorney. A state cannot deny access to its courts to obtain a divorce because of an inability to pay fees because doing so would violate the Fourteenth Amendment to the U.S. Constitution.[35] However, the state is not obliged to provide legal representation,[36] although some states do so.[37] A judicial officer has the authority to order that one spouse pay the other's attorney fees.[38]

Marital Property

Marital property is property acquired during a marriage and is distinct from property to which either party held title before the marriage. However, marital property includes increases in the value of premarital property if the increase is attributable to the use of marital property or work performed by either party during the marriage. Property includes savings, retirement accounts, tangible property such as real estate, and an interest in a person's future earnings if, for example, one or both parties acquired a professional license during the marriage. In addition to distributing property, a court may order one spouse to provide health insurance for another, place a child in custody of either or both parents, and/or order child support and alimony, including "rehabilitative alimony," which is provided to encourage a dependent spouse to become self-supporting.[39]

A couple may enter into a prenuptial or antenuptial agreement, either of which is a contract specifying how property will be divided in the event of death or divorce.[40] An agreement may contain provisions for spousal maintenance in the event of divorce. Courts generally enforce pre- or postmarital agreements that reflect the voluntary choices of the parties. Some courts frown on such agreements if they are developed in contemplation of divorce, because they are against the public policy that supports marriage.[41]

Absent a written agreement, courts apply statutorily derived rules to determine property distribution. Most state courts apply principles of equitable distribution,[42] whereby a marriage is viewed as an "economic partnership" and the contributions of the parties, whether as wage earners or homemakers, are taken into account.[43] Before states provided for equitable distribution, title to property usually remained with the person in whose name it was taken. This created a hardship for the "nontitled" spouse, usually the wife, when a husband accumulated property during marriage and held title in his name. If a couple divorced, ownership went to the title-holding spouse without regard to the contributions made by the nontitled spouse.[44] In states where equitable distribution is the rule, courts take the following factors into account in distributing property: (1) the parties' predivorce standard of living; (2) the ability of each spouse to earn a livelihood; (3) the income and property of each when married and when the action for divorce began; (4) the duration of the marriage and the age and health of the parties; and (5) the need of a custodial parent to remain in the marital residence and to use or own its household effects.[45]

Interstate Recognition of Marriage

Earlier I said that the states have authority to regulate marriage as long as established rules do not violate constitutional principles. Many rules governing marriage are similar across the states, but there are differences. The question addressed in this section is, "Will a marriage valid in one state be recognized in another that would not have allowed the marriage in the first place?"

The answer to this question begins with consideration of the full faith and credit clause of the U.S. Constitution. Article 4, section 1 provides: "Full Faith and Credit shall be given in each State to the public Acts, Records, and judicial Proceedings of every other State."[46] "Public acts" include statutes and constitutions. The laws that govern marriage are public acts. "Records" commonly refers to documents describing "judicial proceedings,"[47] such as those governing awards of child custody, property distribution, or financial support, and these will ordinarily be recognized by other states.

The purpose of the full faith and credit clause is to ensure that the states, although independent "sovereigns" in many respects, do not ignore obligations created in and officially recognized by other states. Stated in another way, in certain matters the states must act as integral parts of a single nation.[48] However, states need not extend full faith and credit when the action of another state offends the public policy of the state being asked to accept the other's judgment.[49]

Consider the following: Common-law marriage is recognized in some but not all states. The prerequisites of marriage, such as licensing and solemnization, are not found in common-law marriage, which comes into being when a couple voluntarily cohabitates and holds themselves out as husband and wife. In 1991 in Florida a man filed for divorce from his common-law wife. He had established a relationship with her in Georgia, which, at the time the union was formed, recognized common-law marriages.[50] The trial court ruled that the "marriage" was not valid because Florida does not recognize such unions. Overruling the trial court, an appellate court held that the validity of a marriage is determined by the law of the place where the marriage was entered into and that a valid common-law marriage had been established under Georgia law. The couple was entitled to a Florida divorce.[51] However, Missouri refused to grant full faith and credit to a common-law marriage on public policy grounds because the state had a strong interest in requiring solemnization to ensure that a marriage of a couple living in Missouri is a "real" marriage.[52]

Defending Marriage

On May 1, 1991, three same-sex couplesfiled suit against the Hawaii after being denied a marriage license. The couples argued that denying them a license violated the state constitution.[53] Acknowledging the power of the state to regulate marriage, the Hawaii Supreme Court ruled that the state's power to regulate marriage was limited by provisions in the state constitution that banned gender-based discrimination. Denying a marriage license to same-sex couples was gender-based discrimination, thus subject to strict scrutiny by the court. This placed a burden on the state to demonstrate that its rule limiting marriage to opposite-sex couples served a compelling state interest and that the law was narrowly tailored to achieve that interest (see chapter 2 for a discussion of compelling state interest).

The court was not persuaded by the state's argument that (1) the institution of marriage needed protection; (2) the community derived benefits from the institution that would be adversely affected by issuing marriage licenses to same-sex couples; (3) fostering procreation was an essential justification for limiting licenses to opposite-sex couples; and (4) issuing marriage licenses to same-sex couples would adversely effect the state treasury. The gender-based classification violated the constitutional requirement for equal protection, and the court enjoined the state from denying an application for a marriage license solely because the applicants were of the same sex. The court's decision was rendered moot in late 1998 when the Hawaii electorate voted to amend the state constitution to restrict marriage to opposite-sex couples.

Two other cases raising similar questions came before state courts in the 1990s. A trial court in Alaska, using language similar to the Hawaii court's, ruled in favor of two men who had been denied a marriage license and who argued that same-sex couples have a fundamental right to choose a life partner.[54] The court ruled that the choice of a life partner is a fundamental right and that the state could deny the marriage license only if it had a compelling interest. Before hearings could be held to determine whether the state could establish a compelling interest, Alaska voters followed Hawaii's lead and amended their constitution to limit marriage to a union between a man and a woman.

The outcome in *Baker v. Vermont* was very different.[55] Three same-sex couples had applied for and were denied marriage licenses. The question addressed by the Vermont Supreme Court was, "May the State . . . exclude same-sex couples from the benefits and protections that its laws provide to opposite-sex married couples?" The court ruled that the state constitution prevented such discrimination.[56] Rather than enjoining the state from denying licenses to same-sex couples, the court suspended its decision to give the legislature the opportunity to enact legislation that would uphold the constitutional rights of lesbians and gay men. Vermont's Civil Unions Law, enacted by the state legislature and signed into law in 2000, was the result. Civil unions are an option only for same-sex couples who obtain from the state a "certificate of civil union." Couples who enter into civil unions have the same rights and responsibilities under state law as those who marry, but it is important to note that federal benefits are not conferred on those who enter into civil unions.

In 1996, when the Hawaii courts were considering the issue of same-sex marriage, the Defense of Marriage Act (DOMA) was introduced in Congress. President Bill Clinton signed it into law later that year.[57] The impetus for the act was a concern that if Hawaii legalized same-sex marriages, the full faith and credit clause would force other states to recognize these marriages.

DOMA does not prohibit marriages between same-sex couples, nor does it prohibit any state from legalizing same-sex marriage; rather, it does two things. First, it prohibits federal recognition of same-sex marriages. For purposes of federal law DOMA defines *marriage* as a union between one man and one woman, and it defines *spouse* as a person of the opposite sex. This latter definition is important because federal law makes certain benefits available to a "spouse"; thus passage of DOMA closed the door to federal benefits for the spouse of a lesbian or gay person. The act also provides that no state will be required to give full faith and credit to another state's recognition of same-sex marriage.[58] As this book went to press, thirty-five states had passed their own versions of the Defense of Marriage Act.

The discussion and passage of DOMA provided a medium for members of Congress to express their disapproval of same-sex marriage, but it did not establish clear and necessary legal guidelines. For example, the full faith and credit clause does not require the states to recognize any marriage that is against the public policy of the state, for example, Missouri's refusal to recognize a common-law marriage formed in another state. Moreover, DOMA may violate the equal protection clause, because it singles out lesbians and gays for unfavorable treatment.

Put in a temporal context, DOMA was more than a reaction to the possibility that Hawaii would legalize same-sex marriage and the implications of this for other states. Some saw same-sex marriage as simply another "attack" on the institution of marriage, which, as earlier noted, some constituencies already saw as under siege from various sources, including the availability of no-fault divorce and "a sex-saturated culture."

Thus it should not come as a surprise that in addition to defending opposite-sex marriage through federal and state legislation, federal and state governments took other steps to encourage and strengthen the institution. Some examples follow.

- One goal of Temporary Assistance to Needy Families (see chapter 10), the program that provides financial support to children and their caretakers, is to "encourage the formation and maintenance of two-parent families."[59] In 2002 President Bush proposed to allocate $100 to $300 million in matching grant funds for research and demonstration projects focused on activities that foster the formation of healthy marriages and families.[60]
- A number of states have undertaken "marriage initiatives." These include (1) appointing commissions to recommend ways to strengthen marriage and to review state laws to ensure that laws such as those concerning income tax and child care do not discourage marriage; (2) implementing support and education programs for opposite-sex couples; and (3) implementing "fatherhood initiatives," which provide employment and education services to very young fathers, including parenting classes and education regarding responsible fatherhood.[61]
- Louisiana and Arizona have codified "covenant marriage."[62] Such a covenant is an agreement by a betrothed couple that they will stay married for life, effectively renouncing the possibility of no-fault divorce.

Alternative Family Forms

American families come in many forms, including more than 55 million married couples, 16 million households headed by single mothers and single fathers, approximately 4 million unmarried opposite-sex partnerships, and more than 1.6 million same-sex partnerships.[63]

Alternative families are formed in a variety of ways. We have considered common-law marriages and civil unions, and we will soon consider domestic partnerships. Unions formed under common-law principles, through statutory grants as with civil unions, and under rules that provide for recognition of domestic partnerships differ from marriages in three important ways. First, marriage is available to opposite-sex couples in all states, but common-law unions are possible in only ten plus the District of Columbia; civil unions are legal only in Vermont; and domestic partnerships are legal in some segments of the private sector and by law in a handful of states and a number of cities and towns. A second difference is that the principles of full faith and credit require that all states recognize a marriage licensed and solemnized in another state. As discussed earlier, a common-law marriage may or may not be recognized by another state, and to date no couple united by a civil union or whose relationship is recognized by a domestic partner statute has asked to have their union acknowledged after moving to a new state. A couple who moves to a place that does not recognize their union operates at a disadvantage. The couple cannot ask a court in the new state to dissolve their union and divide their property. If they have children, but one party is not legally related to the child, that party may not have standing, meaning a right to petition a court for custody or visitation if the union is dissolved. Finally, when the state has an interest in supporting stable marriages—as expressed through laws requiring licensing and solemnization, precluding common-law unions, and governing how a divorce is obtained—the state has no interest in maintaining common-law marriages, civil unions, or domestic partnerships. This lack of interest is evidenced by the little or no state interference when these alternative family forms are created or dissolved. Consequently, such unions cannot legally be considered the equivalent of marriage.

Other family forms escape simple categorization and may be little studied, because the parties do not claim legal recognition or, as a family unit, public benefits. Some families are formed by unrelated individuals who choose to live in a communal manner; others consist of extended families whose members may or may not be related. The public becomes aware of some families of choice when they separate and ask a court to resolve a property dispute. A court may do so if the parties have a written agreement governing property distribution and/or financial support, and some courts will find an implied contract and distribute property acquired during the relationship, while others will not recognize implied agreements.[64]

In some situations legal recognition of an alternative family form is limited to a specific context or is supported by the unique facts of a case presented to a court. The former is exemplified by the decision, noted earlier, of New York's highest court when it ruled that a man had the right to remain in the apartment that he had shared with his life partner after it determined that the term and concept of *family*, as used in the rent control laws, should not be rigidly restricted to those with a marriage certificate or adoption order. And the Supreme Court of Rhode Island ruled that a written agreement between two lesbians concerning visitation with their child was enforceable. The court's conclusion was based on the following facts: (1) the child was conceived through artificial insemination, based on a joint decision between the women to raise a child together; (2) the nonbiological mother bore primary responsibility for the costs associated with artificial insemination; (3) the women lived together and raised the child together for four years before they separated; (4) the child's name on the birth certificate was a compound name created from the last names of both women; and (5) the women held the child out as theirs.[65]

In later chapters we will consider families that are formed when a single person elects to foster or adopt a child, as well as families that simultaneously occupy different statuses. For example, a legally recognized single- or two-parent family with biological or adoptive children may elect to foster a child. Should this occur, some family members will have all the rights and responsibilities that society provides to parents and biological or adoptive children, while others will occupy a different status defined by the state and applicable only to adults and the children whom they foster (see chapter 10).

Domestic Partnerships

Prevented from marrying but wanting legal and social recognition of their relationships, including access to benefits provided to legally recognized families, lesbians and gays have pressed the public sector to enact legislation acknowledging domestic partnerships. And they have lobbied both the private and public sectors to extend to employees in committed relationships the same employment benefits offered to married couples.

In 1982 the *Village Voice,* a New York City newspaper, became the first private business to provide for its employees' domestic partners, and in 1984 Berkeley, California, enacted the first municipal statute recognizing domestic partnerships. At the time of this writing, eight states, the District of Columbia, and more than three dozen cities and towns have legislation that recognizes domestic partnerships, as do 5 units of the federal government, more than 2,000 corporations, 80 academic institutions, and 31 labor unions.[66] In addition, foreign countries from Brazil to Canada and across Western Europe grant special status to same-sex couples,[67] and in Denmark, Sweden, and the Netherlands same-sex couples are on an equal footing with married couples.[68] At the time of this writing, legislation was being drafted that would legalize same-sex marriage in Canada; it is already legal in Ontario and British Columbia. The legislation was expected to pass the Canadian House of Commons.[69]

Domestic Partnerships Defined

There is no single definition of *domestic partner.* Elements commonly found in statutes require that domestic partners (1) be eighteen or older; (2) in an intimate and committed relationship based on mutual caring; (3) share a principal residence; (4) agree to be responsible for each other's basic living expenses; and (5) not be related by blood, in another domestic partnership, or married.[70] Some jurisdictions provide for the parties to make a formal declaration of their relationship by submitting an affidavit to a state or municipal official or by registering with a unit of government.[71] For example, California provides that domestic partners may file a "declaration of domestic partnership" with the secretary of state, who will register the declaration.[72] In some jurisdictions a domestic partnership is closed to opposite-sex couples because they are free to marry, while in others the provisions apply equally to heterosexual and homosexual couples.

Why Domestic Partnerships Are Recognized

Just as society has an interest in supporting marriage, so it can gain by supporting domestic partnerships, although the gains may vary for government compared to the private sector. To some units of government, offering benefits to domestic partners is a matter of fairness, while others offer the benefits to compensate for the unwillingness of other governments to support same-sex marriage. For example, I reported that voters in Hawaii amended their constitution to define marriage as a union between a man and a woman. As the constitutional amendment was being developed, a bill was working its way through the Hawaii legislature[73] that amended the state's *Code of Family Law* to provide for reciprocal beneficiaries, Hawaii's name for domestic partners.[74] The preamble to the measure(1) says that the people of Hawaii wish to "preserve the tradition of marriage . . . for one man and one woman"; (2) refers to the multiplicity of benefits available to married couples; (3) acknowledges alternative family forms based on committed relationships between parties prevented by law from marrying; and (4) states that certain rights and benefits attendant to marriage should be available to those in committed relationships who are unable to marry. Hawaii's statute, as well as California's domestic partner statute, limit this status to people who cannot marry,[75] except that in California Social Security recipients aged sixty-two and older may register as domestic partners if they find marriage financially disadvantageous.[76]

Private employers may offer domestic partner benefits because it seems fair to treat all employees in committed relationships in the same way, and offering benefits to domestic partners may be good public relations and provide an incentive that helps business recruit and retain employees.

Benefits Available

There is considerable variation in the benefits available to domestic partners. It may be useful to think of benefits in the following way. A private business may offer or withhold whatever benefits it chooses, and it is likely that benefits available to domestic partners will be the same as those offered to married couples. To do otherwise would defeat the purpose of using benefits as an incentive to recruit and retain employees and of improving a public image of fairness.

Unlike the private sector, where the benefits offered are concrete, such as life insurance or health insurance, a unit of government may provide concrete benefits to its employees as well as less tangible but equally important benefits to all domestic partners. Some examples of the latter are (1) the right to claim unemployment benefits to relocate with a domestic partner; (2) an exemption from state income tax for health benefits provided to a partner, although an employee may be liable to pay federal tax[77]; (3) the right to petition the court to adopt a partner's child; (2) the right to sue in the event of a partner's wrongful death; (3) the right to make medical decisions for an incapacitated partner; and (4) the right to visit in the hospital and in a correctional facility.

Legal Challenges to Domestic Partner Statutes

The courts have seen legal challenges to domestic partner statutes. The University of Oregon denied insurance benefits to domestic partners who were not considered family members. Lesbian employees sued the university and prevailed after a state appellate court ruled that the institution's denial of insurance benefits to employees' domestic partners violated the state constitution.[78] Citizens have challenged some domestic partner ordinances, arguing that a unit of government exceeded its authority in enacting domestic partner legislation. In *Slattery v. City of New York,* the plaintiffs argued that the domestic partner statute in New York City effectively legalized common-law marriage, which the state does not recognize.[79] The plaintiffs argued that the city had usurped the prerogative of the state legislature. The trial court denied the plaintiffs' claim, holding that the city had a right to enact the legislation. Domestic partnerships differ in many respects from marriage, the court opined. Marriage has more stringent requirements before it can be formalized and imposes certain rights and responsibilities upon spouses after formalization that are not found in the legal rules governing domestic relationships. Responding to a similar challenge, an appellate court in Illinois held that domestic partnerships did not create a new "marital status."[80] However, a case in Boston produced a different result. Plaintiffs in *Connors v. City of Boston*[81] were successful in having an executive order issued by the mayor overtured. The states highest court found that the mayor exceeded his authority by extending health care benefits to registered domestic partners of city employees and their dependents. The mayor lacked the authority to expand the definition of *dependents,* which could be changed only by an act of the legislature.

Termination of Domestic Partnerships

If two conditions for entering into a legally recognized domestic partnership are registration and that one cannot be in another domestic partnership, the law must provide procedures for terminating partnerships. Hawaii provides that either party may terminate the relationship by filing a signed and notarized declaration that the relationship has been terminated. Also, a marriage license issued after registration of a domestic partnership automatically terminates the partnership.[82] California provides for termination of a domestic partnership when (1) one partner notifies the secretary of state in writing, transmitted by certified mail, that he or she is terminating the partnership; (2) a partner dies; (3) a partner marries; or (4) the partners no longer share a common residence.[83] If the action to terminate the union is unilateral, the partner who is dissolving the relationship must notify the other of the decision. The American Law Institute recommends that courts preside over the demise of domestic partnerships as they do divorces and that states provide for a division of property and alimony as they would in a divorce.[84] Same-sex couples who reside in Vermont and enter into a civil union are subject to the same state laws that affect married couples who divorce.

PART 2—CUSTODY AND VISITATION

When married parents divorce or unmarried parents elect to live apart, decisions must be made concerning child custody, visitation, and child support. Social workers play a key role in the decision-making process when they assist judges and attorneys by (1) evaluating parents to determine fitness for custody and visitation; (2) interpreting evaluations conducted by others; (3) testifying as lay and expert witnesses concerning parental fitness and child well-being; (4) helping to arrange for orders of child support; and (5) locating parents who avoid their support obligations. In addition, social workers play a key role when the state intervenes in the parent-child relationship following a report of abuse or neglect or if foster parents act to prevent the state from removing from their custody a child for whom they have provided care for many years. Our concern here is with child custody and visitation when parents separate or divorce. Chapter 10 discusses child abuse and neglect and issues concerning foster parents. Before we begin, note that divorcing parents may resolve issues concerning custody, visitation, and financial support and submit their resolution to the court for approval.

Parents' Rights to Custody and Visitation

The parental right to the care, custody, and control of their children is rooted in the liberty clause of the Fourteenth Amendment,[85] and courts will support a parent's rights unless she or he is unfit.[86] The marital status of parents alone is not a relevant factor when courts award custody or grant visitation, although some courts show a distinct bias against lesbian and gay parents.[87] The laws of many states admonish courts to take domestic violence into account in an award of child custody (chapter 12). Courts will consider the wishes of children old enough to express their desire to live with one or another parent, but a child's wishes will not control a custody decision.[88]

Types of Custody

Custody may be legal or physical, and it may be vested in either parent. A child's legal custodian has the right to make major decisions such as those involving medical care and education. A child's physical custodian has responsibility for day-to-day care. A court may determine that a child's best interests are served if both parents retain legal custody, with physical custody granted to one parent and visitation to another. In some cases physical custody may be split between a child's parents.

Standard for Custody

All states have statutes dealing with child custody and visitation. When there is a custody dispute between a child's biological parents, laws admonish the courts to focus their decision making on the best interests of the child.[89] Although the best-interests standard applies also to decisions modifying an order concerning both custody and visitation, neither will, as a rule, be modified solely because it is in the best interests of the child, without evidence that there has been a material change in the circumstances in which the child is being reared.

Some states specify factors to be considered in applying the best-interests standard, and states vary in the extent to which they seek to constrain judicial decision making. One extreme is Alabama's statute, which has vague language requiring only that the court consider the "moral character and prudence of the parents."[90] At the other extreme is Minnesota's statute, which is based on but goes beyond the Uniform Marriage and Divorce Act and limits judicial discretion by (1) delineating factors to be considered in custody decisions; (2) precluding consideration of parental conduct that does not affect a child's well-being; (3) requiring detailed fact finding regarding each factor identified in the statute; and (4) requiring that judges explain the relationship between the factors and the conclusions reached.[91]

Presumptions

The best-interests-of-the-child standard reflects the value that societies place on children. However, this standard is subjective, its application is not likely to produce consistent results, and it is unlikely to be a useful guide for the decision maker in a custody battle between two parents when all things are equal. When this situation occurs, courts typically use as "tie breakers" presumptions such as the "tender years doctrine," which assumes that mothers are more important than fathers in the early years of a child's development, and the maternal preference rule. Both rules create a rebuttable presumption in favor of maternal custody.[92]

The search for gender-neutral rules has resulted in statutes permitting joint custody and in a reliance on the primary caretaker rule, by which custody is awarded to the parent who has provided continuity in care and met the child's physical and psychological needs.[93] An award made under this rule is presumptively in the child's best interests. Because most primary caretakers are women, the result of applying the primary caretaker rule is probably no different from applying the tender years doctrine or the maternal preference rule. Despite this similarity, the primary caretaker rule does provide a framework for gender-neutral decision making.[94]

Fathers' Rights

Legal tradition held that children whose parents were not married were exclusively in the custody of their biological mother, who is the natural guardian of her children. By contrast, men not married to but living with a child's mother when a child is born must establish their paternity in a court to protect their rights. Until the last quarter of the twentieth century, unmarried fathers were assumed to be unfit custodians. This assumption was challenged in the early 1970s by Peter Stanley, whose three children were declared wards of Illinois for purposes of adoption after their biological mother died.[95] Stanley had lived with the mother on and off for eighteen years. When the state tried to terminate his rights, he argued that he had never been judged unfit and that the state, in taking custody of his children, violated his due process rights. The U.S. Supreme Court agreed. The state could not assume that Stanley's status as an unmarried father supported the assumption that he was an unfit parent. The case was remanded for a hearing on the father's fitness. Stanley eventually was declared unfit, and his children were placed in the permanent custody of the state.

In 1978 the Supreme Court had the opportunity to clarify its earlier ruling when it accepted for review a second challenge on behalf of nonmarital fathers. Leon Quilloin challenged a Georgia law that vested control of nonmarital children in the biological mother unless the father and mother married or he acknowledged his paternity by filing a petition to legitimatize the child.[96] The *Quilloin* case differed from the *Stanley* case in several ways. In *Quilloin* the nonmarital father had not lived with his child or the child's mother since the child's birth thirteen years earlier; the mother had married, and her husband of nine years was petitioning to adopt the boy; and the nonmarital father had never asserted any rights until after the adoption petition was filed. For these reasons, the U.S. Supreme Court ruled, Quilloin's rights could be terminated without a showing that he was unfit because the decision was in the child's best interests.

If Quilloin had lived with his child or had otherwise established a relationship with him, the court ruling might have been different, but here "the unwed father [never] sought . . . custody . . . [and] the proposed adoption . . . [would grant] full recognition to a family unit already in existence."[97]

What of the unmarried father whose child is born to a married woman living with her husband at the time of the birth? The U.S. Supreme Court had reason to rule on such a case in 1989 after a man sought to establish his paternity. The Court affirmed a long-standing presumption that a child born to married woman living with her husband is a child of the marriage. The man claiming biological parenthood had no constitutional right to demonstrate his paternity, nor did the child have a due process right to a paternal relationship with the man claiming to be her father. To grant the request of the putative father would be too disruptive of family harmony.[98]

The "Thwarted" Father

In the 1990s professional social workers became aware of the "thwarted father," who is a man "prevented from meeting his parenting responsibilities because the mother did not tell him of the pregnancy or birth, lied about her plans for the child, [or] disappeared after the child's birth."[99] The following case illustrates the difficulties that may result when adults conspire to conceal a child's birth from the biological father.

In 1995, four years after "Baby Richard" was placed for adoption, the Illinois Supreme Court ordered that he be returned to his father, whose rights had been terminated.[100] The facts are these. In March 1991 Baby Richard's birth mother placed him in a preadoptive home. She would not disclose the father's identity, and she told the father that the child was born dead. Not believing her, he sought evidence that his child was alive, including "peering" into the birth mother's car at 3 *a.m.* to see whether there was an infant car seat in it, calling hospitals to learn about the birth of his child, and sifting through the birth mother's garbage in search of diapers. The trial court found these efforts insufficient to meet the statutory requirement that a father demonstrate a reasonable degree of interest, concern, or responsibility for his child within thirty days of birth. The case went to the Illinois Supreme Court after an appellate court affirmed the lower court ruling. The Illinois Supreme Court ruled that the lower courts had improperly terminated the father's rights, because they focused on what was in Baby Richard's best interests and thereby missed the key issue, which was whether the father was fit, willing, or able to care for his child. In seeking to terminate parental rights in favor of a third party, a finding of parental unfitness is a necessary predicate to addressing what is in a child's best interests.

In its ruling the Illinois Supreme Court took pains to point out that Baby Richard's adoptive parents knew of the biological mother's deception. They went along with the birth mother's plot to the point of helping to select a hospital for the birth in the hope of keeping the father ignorant. They knew that he would not consent to the adoption. Less than three months after Baby Richard's birth, the mother confessed to the child's father what she had done, and he instituted proceedings to gain custody of his son. At this point, the court stated, the preadoptive parents "had both a legal and moral duty to surrender Richard to the custody of his father." Richard was then less than three months old. Instead, the adoptive family "selfishly clung to the custody of Richard. They have prolonged these painful proceedings to the child's fourth birthday and have denied the father access to his own son."[101]

Expedited Appeals and Putative Father Registries

The case of *Baby Richard* and similar cases, such as that of *Baby Jessica,*[102] create a conflict between (1) the generally accepted rule that parental rights cannot be terminated in favor of a third party based solely on the child's best interests, and (2) the desire to protect children from the trauma assumed to occur when they are removed from stable environments.

The problem is created in part by legal procedures that permit multiple appeals by each party that delay the resolution of custody disputes. Four years elapsed between Baby Richard's placement and the final ruling of the Illinois Supreme Court. If stability in placement were decisive in determining custody, the law would reward that party who is able to hold on to the child, thus encouraging the nonparent who has physical custody to prolong the litigation.

Some states prioritize cases involving child custody for expedited appeals.[103] An expedited appeals procedure (1) limits the time within which an appeal can be filed, (2) requires hearings be conducted promptly, and (3) requires courts to render their decisions expeditiously.

Putative father registries seek to address the problem of the thwarted father who knows or has reason to believe that he has fathered a child. Registries allow a man to document his knowledge or belief regarding his paternity, and they impose on the state an obligation to notify a registered father of a pending adoption procedure. States may require registration within a predetermined time period before or after the birth of the child.[104]

Judicial Discretion

Society has vested judges with a great deal of discretion in reaching decisions that affect the welfare of children, although states differ in the discretion granted. Some states limit judicial discretion when they impose a "nexus test," which instructs the court to ascertain how parental behaviors or conditions of concern affect a child's well-being.[105] Application of a nexus test focuses attention on the child. Its use limits discrimination by a judge who, in the guise of objective decision making, denies custody to a parent based solely on a personal characteristic, such as a physical disability or sexual orientation, without regard to how the child is affected. Because judicial discretion plays a large role in custody and visitation decisions, social work practitioners must review case law to identify the factors that courts consider relevant and how they weigh these factors. Two examples follow.

Disability

In 1979 the California Supreme Court addressed the extent to which a parent's disability will affect his or her ability to provide child care when it ruled on a biological mother's request for custody of her two children; her husband had cared for the children for five years, during which time she had not contributed to their support or had personal contact with them.[106]

The father was a quadriplegic. Despite expert testimony that supported his continued custody and discounted the care provided the children by the woman with whom the father lived, the trial court ordered a change in custody. Focusing its attention on the father's disability, the trial judge found that

> It would be detrimental to the boys to grow up until age 18 in the custody of their father. It wouldn't be a normal relationship between father and boys. [The father] can't do anything for the boys . . . except maybe talk to them and teach them, be a tutor, which is good, but it's not enough. I feel that it's in the best interests of the two boys to be with the mother even though she hasn't had them for five years.[107]

Criticizing the trial court for its gender stereotypes, evocation of "Norman Rockwell covers on the *Saturday Evening Post*,"[108] and its perception that the father "as a person [was] deemed forever unable to be a good parent simply because he is physically handicapped,"[109] the court found that the trial court had abused its discretion and reversed its ruling.

Stigma

Stigma may attach to people based on a medical condition, for example, AIDS; on behavior, as is the case with an intravenous drug user; or on the basis of status, as with gays and lesbians. It may be impossible to separate the stigma that attaches to a person's medical condition from that which attaches to sexual orientation or status as an intravenous drug user. The Supreme Court of New York County recognized this problem.[110] After noting that stigma attaches to AIDS, this trial court highlighted the responsibility of courts to act as a "bulwark against discrimination,"[111] which, where AIDS is concerned, is compounded by "possible racism and homophobia,"[112] and cautioned against misuse of court procedures in child custody and visitation cases to further discriminatory ends.

The law concerning stigma and its relationship to child custody decisions was settled by the U.S. Supreme Court in 1984. The case concerned Linda Palmore, who was awarded custody of her three-year-old daughter when the mother divorced Anthony Sidoti. He subsequently petitioned the court for custody because his ex-wife, who was caucasian, was living with an African American man whom she later married. The trial court acknowledged that both parents were devoted to the child, that the home was adequate, and that both parents had remarried "respectable" spouses. Nevertheless, the court awarded custody to the father because the child's mother had chosen a lifestyle that was "unacceptable to the father and to society [and that] the [school age] child . . . will be . . . subject to environmental pressures not of choice."[113] A Florida appellate court affirmed the ruling and an appeal was taken to the U.S. Supreme Court. The High Court, recognizing that stigma may attach to a child because of the situation in which she or he lives, held that this concern was not a permissible consideration in a custody decision. The Court said:

> The question . . . is whether the reality of private biases and the possible injury they might inflict are permissible considerations for removal of an infant child from the custody of its natural mother. We have little difficulty concluding that they are not. The Constitution cannot control such prejudices but neither can it tolerate them. Private biases may be outside the reach of the law, but the law cannot, directly or indirectly, give them effect. Public officials sworn to uphold the Constitution may not avoid a constitutional duty by bowing to the hypothetical effects of private racial prejudice that they assume to be both widely and deeply held.[114]

Modifying Custody Orders

A court order concerning child custody or visitation is subject to modification, and it is not unusual for parents who are displeased with an original ruling to return to court to seek modification. To prevent parents from using the courts as a tool to carry on their disputes, state laws make it difficult to modify a custody order. Orders are to be modified only if the circumstances that existed when the original decree was awarded have changed in a way that jeopardizes a child's physical or emotional well-being. In deciding whether to modify a custody order, a court may consider an array of factors, including (1) the duration of the current arrangement, (2) the parental guidance furnished, (3) the quality of the respective home environments, (4) each parent's past performance, and

(5) each parent's ability to provide for and guide the child's emotional and intellectual development.[115]

Interstate Custody Disputes and Uniform Laws

Some custody disputes involve the courts of two or more states, when, after an initial award of custody, (1) the custodial parent relocates to a new state and later requires court intervention to resolve a custody or visitation dispute; (2) a noncustodial parent kidnaps the child, crosses state borders, and asks a court in the new state to grant full custody; or (3) a child is sent to live temporarily with relatives, who conclude that the child would be better off living with them, so they ask a court in their state to grant them custody.

Interstate custody disputes pose unique problems, because orders affecting child custody and visitation are not "final" judgments, meaning that they are subject to modification. The U.S. Supreme Court has not determined whether the full faith and credit clause applies to such interim orders. To resolve this matter the National Conference of Commissioners on Uniform State Laws (NCCUSL), a group of more than three hundred lawyers, judges, and law professors appointed by the states to draft model state laws,[116] developed the Uniform Child Custody Jurisdiction Act in 1968. All states have adopted the UCCJA. Before I discuss this law, a brief digression is in order to consider the rationale behind the development of model laws.

I have reported that laws vary by state. Differences in state laws may cause significant problems (1) for the practitioner whose ability to place a child may be thwarted by differences in state law; (2) for parents seeking custody or visits with a child while they await the decisions of courts in different states; and (3) for children whose custody may be "jockeyed" back and forth as courts in different states, operating under different laws, decide which jurisdiction has the authority to make the difficult decision regarding custody. Recall the earlier discussion of standards for custody that contrasted the focus in Alabama law on the moral character of parents and Minnesota's version of the Uniform Marriage and Divorce Act (UMDA). It is not difficult to imagine that the same facts presented to courts in Alabama and Minnesota might produce very different results.

Model laws are developed to reduce differences in state law, thereby providing consistent guidelines for the practitioner and certainty for parents. Note that the NCCUSL has no official authority to compel states to adopt model laws. Unlike the UCCJA, which all states have adopted, only a handful of states have adopted some model laws, thus failing to achieve the uniformity that is the model law's objective. In addition, states that adopt model laws may alter some terms and conditions in the model, resulting in continuing, albeit fewer, differences between states.

Uniform Acts Affecting Custody in Interstate Disputes

The UCCJA is best understood in the context of an example.[117] Assume the following: (a) When Sandra and Miguel were divorced in Florida, a court gave physical custody of their son Michael to Sandra and a grant of visitation to Miguel; (b) one year after the divorce Sandra moved to Illinois where she resided for two years, during which time she and Miguel engaged in ongoing disagreements concerning Miguel's access to their son; and (c) Miguel subsequently kidnaped Michael and relocated in New Mexico, where he asked a court to award him custody.

When courts of different states are asked to resolve a dispute, the first question that must be answered is which state has jurisdiction to resolve the custody dispute. If the full faith and credit clause applied to child custody matters, Sandra would be advised to take her Florida order, present it to a New Mexico court, and petition the court to enforce the order by returning her son. However, absent any rule concerning interstate comity, a court in New Mexico is free to rule for either parent. Since courts seek to protect state residents, a court could award custody to Miguel, even though he obtained custody of his son by kidnaping him. However, the situation is not as bleak as it sounds. The issues raised by this hypothetical may be resolved with reference to one of three sources of authority.

The UCCJA is the first. Because it has been adopted by all states, the law provides the framework for resolving interstate custody disputes when there is no existing court decree regarding custody nor a pending a court proceeding on this matter. The UCCJA outlines four principles that courts are to weigh and balance in determining where custody lies. Framed as questions, the principles ask: (1) "Where is the child's home state?" which is defined as the state where the child lived for at least six consecutive months at the time a custody proceeding began[118]; (2) "What is in the child's best interests?" which focuses attention on whether substantial evidence concerning the child's care and relationships is found in one of the states involved such that judicial economy requires holding hearings in that state; (3) "Is there an emergency?"—does abuse or neglect of a child, for example, warrant a court's taking emergency jurisdiction? and (4) "Have other states declined to exercise jurisdiction?" which permits the court deciding the issue to assume jurisdiction.

The second source of authority is federal. If a child has been kidnapped, and there is an existing custody decree or custody proceedings are underway in another state, the Parental Kidnaping Prevention Act of 1981 (PKPA) is controlling.[119] When Congress enacted the PKPA, it provided that states give full faith and credit to the custody decrees of other states.[120] When questions of jurisdiction must be resolved, the act gives priority to home-state jurisdiction.

In 1997 the NCCUSL modified the UCCJA when it promulgated the Uniform Child Custody Jurisdiction and Enforcement Act, a third source of authority for resolving interstate custody disputes. By 2002 the new custody jurisdiction act had been adopted by twenty-three states. The most important change is that, taking its lead from the PKPA, the home-state rule determines which state has custody.

Parents and Third Parties

A rule in family law has been that parents' rights vis à vis their children include the right to day-to-day companionship and the right to make decisions affecting a child's well-being. This rule is fundamental, and the rights to which it refers are safeguarded by the U.S. Constitution. The Supreme Court has interpreted the Constitution to hold that the relationship between parent and child will not be disturbed unless a parent is first deemed unfit by reason of abandonment, neglect, or abuse.[121] The Court affirmed these rights throughout the twentieth century and into the twenty-first. In 2000 the High Court ruled that a Washington statute that allowed any person to petition a court for visitation with a child, and that allowed a court to order visitation if it determined that it was in the child's best interests, was an unconstitutional infringement of the rights of a fit parent to control such decisions.[122] Notwithstanding this basic rule, state courts have sought to carve out exceptions since the 1970s.

Extraordinary Circumstances In 1976 New York's highest court ruled that when a court finds "extraordinary circumstances," the state may permanently sever the ties between parent and child even when the parent has never been found unfit.[123] The case from which this ruling arose involved the relinquishment of an infant by her biological mother eight years before the New York Court of Appeals issued its ruling. The child had grown up in the continuous care of her adoptive parents. The court found that the procedure resulting in the child's relinquishment (chapter 11) was flawed and that, as a result, there had never been a legal relinquishment or any finding that the mother was unfit. Nevertheless, the court ruled that the child should remain with her adoptive parents due to extraordinary circumstances. The relevant circumstances were the length of time that the mother and child had been separated, the bond that had formed between the child and her adoptive parents, the mother's failure to establish a household on her own, and her unmarried state.

In 1995 the Pennsylvania Supreme Court also questioned the presumption that a parent who has never been found unfit has an absolute right to custody as against a third party.[124] In that case the court applied a rule that would require courts to weigh parenthood as a strong factor but not dispositive one. The determination of what affiliation will be best for a child would consider additional factors, including the child's physical, emotional, intellectual, moral, and spiritual well-being. However, in 2000 the Pennsylvania court, reflecting the ambivalence found in the scholarly literature concerning state interference in parent-child relationships, retreated from its earlier position. The court held that the earlier case had not commanded a majority vote and was thus not binding as precedent. The presumption that parents should prevail against third parties should remain in effect, the court ruled. The "main idea," according to this court, is that parents are to receive special consideration and that special weight and deference should be accorded the parent-child relationship.[125]

Uniform Marriage and Divorce Act The rules that require proof that a parent is not fit as a predicate to intervening in the parent-child relationship are found in state laws generally denominated as a "Children's Code," "Family Code," or the like.

Some states have statutes that provide an alternative set of rules that grant "standing," meaning the right to petition a court to do a thing, to a nonparent, who is allowed to request custody based solely on the best interests of the child.[126] For example, in Colorado a nonparent who has had physical custody of a child for six months has standing to petition a court for permanent custody, and a party may prevail without proving parental unfitness.[127] A single Colorado woman chose to place her son for adoption and signed a form releasing custody the day after his birth. The infant was placed with an adoptive couple, in whose custody he remained. Six months after relinquishing her son, the birth mother attempted to revoke her consent. The court rejected her effort, holding that the child's best interests were to remain with his adoptive parents.[128]

Equitable Parents and Psychological Parenthood Both equitable and psychological parenthood are concepts that appear in case law. Both refer to the bonds that may develop between a child and caretaker based on day-to-day interaction. Both views of parenthood rest on the notion that biology alone does not create a parent-child relationship and that a child will bond with a caretaker who nurtures the child on a daily basis and who provides emotional support.

The U.S. Supreme Court acknowledged that familial expectations may arise from the "intimacy of daily association" and the emotional attachments that result, not simply from the fact of biology. Such relationships might, the Court ruled, enjoy due process guarantees even if the relationship is not sanctioned by state law.[129]

The law defines an *equitable parent* as an individual who has "provided for the physical, emotional, and social needs of a child" after having physical custody of the child for an extended period, and it defines a *psychological parent* as a person to whom a child forms an attachment based on day-to-day interaction, companionship, and shared experience.[130]

Based on notions of equitable parenthood, a court in Missouri ruled that a lesbian coparent was an equitable parent who had provided care out of a sincere concern for the child. The relationship between the child and the adult seeking equitable parent status had begun with the legal parent's consent, the court found. The court granted the request of the nonbiological mother for continued contact with the child and set rules that provided for both women to participate in making major decisions affecting the child.[131] And in 2002 the Supreme Court of California ruled in favor of a nonbiological father who was the former boyfriend of the mother of a six-year old. He had taken the boy into his home, held him out to be his biological son, and provided a loving home for the boy. The court found that under these circumstances, the former boyfriend is presumed to be the child's father, even if he later acknowledges that he is not the biological father. The court's decision supported a trial court's ruling that the child could be placed with his presumed father.[132]

Child Support

Parents are obligated to support their children financially, and government at the federal and state level will search for a noncustodial parent and petition a court for an order of financial support.[133] For this to happen the parent must be located and paternity established. In the discussion that follows I refer to "fathers" and "paternity" because the noncustodial parent with a child-support obligation is far more likely to be a man than a woman: Women are 4.5 times more likely than men to head single-parent families.[134]

Locating Noncustodial Parents

The first step in trying to locate a noncustodial parent is to ask the custodial parent to provide information, including his name, address, place of employment, Social Security number, and the names of friends and relatives who may know his whereabouts. If the parent is not found, the staff of a state child support enforcement program will search records, including (1) telephone directories, (2) motor vehicle registries, (3) tax files, and (4) employment and unemployment records. If these methods are not productive, the state may ask for help from the Federal Parent Locator Service, which has access to data from various agencies, including the Social Security Administration, the Internal Revenue Service, the Selective Service System, and the Department of Defense.

Establishing Paternity

The noncustodial parent's paternity must be established to obtain an award of child support. Paternity establishes a child's legal claim to a father's income, regardless of whether the parents were married, ever lived together, or the duration of their relationship. Provisions in the Child Support and Establishment of

Paternity Act, Title IV-D of the Social Security Act,[135] states that mothers who apply for public assistance must cooperate in establishing paternity as a condition for receiving financial aid, unless the claimant establishes a "good cause" exception. States define *good cause,* but most exempt families if pursuing a child's father could result in physical or emotional harm to the child or caretaker, if the child was conceived as a result of incest or rape, or if legal procedures are underway for the child's adoption.

Once located, the father will be asked to acknowledge his paternity in writing. If he refuses, he may be brought before a judicial officer for a determination of paternity. The court may order genetic testing and may call witnesses to testify about the relationship between the mother and putative father. If the testing and testimony support a mother's claim, the state will ask the court to issue a declaration of paternity and an order of support, which will stipulate the amount and frequency of payment.[136] To ensure that child support awards are based on objective criteria, federal law requires each state, as a condition for receiving federal financial support for its child support enforcement efforts, to establish guidelines for determining the amount of an award. Application of the guidelines creates a "rebuttable presumption" that the amount of the award is correct.[137]

Collecting Support Payments

State courts issue orders of support and seek to enforce their orders if a noncustodial parent fails to meet his obligation. Wage withholding is the most common method used, but other means include placing (1) liens on property; (2) attaching unemployment benefits; (3) seizing state or federal income tax refunds; and (4) revoking licenses, including driver's licenses and business or occupational licenses, to force compliance.

Interstate Enforcement

Earlier I said that orders affecting custody and visitation are not "final" judgments, meaning that they are subject to modification, and that the full faith and credit clause has no effect on the enforcement of interim orders. Orders of child support are also interim orders, subject to modification if circumstances change.

The interim status of child support orders was an obstacle to their enforcement if a noncustodial parent moved across state lines. In 1986 and again in 1996 Congress enacted legislation requiring the states to grant full faith and credit to the child support orders of other states.[138]

Federal Criminal Penalties

Provisions in the Deadbeat Parents Punishment Act make it a federal crime, punishable by a two-year term of imprisonment, for a parent (1) to willfully fail to make support payments to a child living in another state if the obligation is greater than $5,000 or has remained unpaid for more than one year; or (2) to travel across state or national boundaries for the purpose of evading a support obligation, if the obligation has remained unpaid for more than a year or is greater than $5,000.[139]

SUMMARY

This chapter has focused on families and their formation through marriage and through alternative arrangements. Marriage is a contractual union between a man and a woman. Its formation and dissolution are controlled mainly by state law within limits set by the U.S. Supreme Court. States determine (1) who may marry, including stipulating minimum age requirements and that the parties must be competent to enter voluntarily into a marriage contract; (2) the prerequisites for marriage, such as waiting periods, blood tests, state licensing, and solemnization; (3) the conditions to be met for divorce; and (4) how marital property is to be divided unless a court-approved prenuptial or antenuptial agreement addresses this matter.

Other states honor marriages licensed and solemnized by any state, in keeping with the full faith and credit clause of the U.S. Constitution, which seeks to ensure that in certain matters the states act as integral parts of a single nation. Therefore, a couple who establishes residency in a new state after marrying will have access to the courts of their new home state to dissolve their marriage, to distribute marital property, and to resolve disputes about child custody. States need not extend full faith and credit to a marriage that offends its public policy; thus a state need not recognize a common-law marriage if it is seen as undermining the state's objectives in requiring licenses and solemnization to form a marriage.

Other than families formed by marriage, birth, and adoption, which are recognized as legal in all states, a variety of family forms exist in the United States. These include common-law marriages, the civil unions for lesbian and gay couples available in Vermont, and domestic partnerships, which are recognized by some segments of the private sector and by law in some states, cities, and towns.

The states demonstrate their interest in marriage by denying to alternative families many benefits accorded to a married couple; to the extent that federal benefits are contingent on marital status, federal laws reserve benefits to marriages defined as unions between one man and one woman. Key differences between marriage and other unions is that common-law marriages, domestic partnerships, and civil unions are not available in every state, and the Defense of Marriage Act provides that states need not accord full faith and credit to marriages between same-sex partners, should any state elect to legalize such marriages. Whereas state laws govern the means for dissolving a marriage, alternative family forms may, for the most part, be dissolved at the will of the parties.

When married parents divorce or unmarried parents elect to live apart, decisions must be made concerning child custody, visitation, and child support. A court may award legal and physical custody to either parent, or it may determine that a child's best interests are served if both parents retain legal custody, with physical custody granted to one parent and visitation to the other. The noncustodial parent, regardless of marital status, has an obligation to suppport her or his children, and the federal government as well as state government will search for the missing parent and seek a court order of support.

In resolving custody disputes between a child's biological parents, courts are admonished to focus their decision making on the best interests of the child. This standard for decision making is vague, however, allowing a judicial officer to render decisions based on animus toward one or another parent or on personal biases regarding child rearing. To lend uniformity to these decisions, some states have developed criteria to guide the decision maker. These guidelines require, for instance, that parental conduct not be a factor unless it affects a child's well-being and that the court explain the relationship between the factors and the conclusions reached.

Some parents who are dissatisfied with a custody ruling express their dissatisfaction by kidnaping a child, establishing residency in a new state, and then asking a court to grant them custody. The inapplicability of the full faith and credit clause to custody orders has provided an incentive for parents to misbehave in this fashion. To remedy this situation states modified their statutes by adopting principles from the Uniform Child Custody Jurisdiction Act and the Uniform Child Custody Jurisdiction Enforcement Act, which, together with the Parental Kidnaping and Prevention Act, provide uniform rules for resolving interstate custody disputes.

The definition of *family* is changing to embrace a variety of forms, and the law is recognizing these changes in ways discussed in this chapter. As the legal definition of *family* is modified, some states and some courts are modifying their statutes and rulings to reflect new notions of parenthood and child custody. These changes are diverse and include recognizing that (1) when a couple separates, their status as never married is not decisive in an award of child custody; (2) an unmarried man who provides emotional and financial support for his children is not an unfit father per se; (3) an award of custody may be made to a man who is prevented from meeting his parenting responsibilities because the mother did not tell him of the pregnancy or birth, even though the child has lived for several years in an adoptive home; (4) when extraordinary circumstances exist, a mother may be deprived of custody of her child even though she has never been declared unit; (5) when a state has adopted a version of the Uniform Marriage and Divorce Act, an award of custody may be made to a nonparent based solely on the best interests of the child if the nonparent has had physical custody of a child for six months; (6) some courts are granting awards of custody based on notions of equitable parenthood and psychological parenthood, both of which stress the importance of bonds that develop between a child and the person who provides day-to-day care. Thus a lesbian coparent was recognized as an equitable parent because she had provided ongoing care for the child, and a mother's former boyfriend was awarded custody of her son, although he and the man were not blood relations, because the former boyfriend had taken the boy into his home and provided a loving home and a father-son relationship.

9

Education

IN SEVERAL PLACES in this text I have said that parents have a right to the care, custody, and control of their children. Authority for this proposition is found in the U.S. Constitution, which protects family privacy and which the U.S. Supreme Court has said limits the situations in which the state may interfere with parental authority.[1] However, a family's right to privacy is not absolute. Parents have an obligation to provide for their children and to protect them from harm. If parents fail in their social contract, the law authorizes the state to act in loco parentis, meaning in the place of the parent. But the state does not passively wait for parents to fail before asserting its authority. The state requires that children (1) receive an education; (2) be vaccinated against certain diseases; and (3) not work, except as provided in child labor laws. In addition, many states allow a young person to receive certain medical services without parental consent or knowledge, such as service to terminate a pregnancy and services to treat sexually transmitted diseases, as well as mental health services.

This chapter considers primary and secondary education. Other topics involving the care and protection of children are addressed in chapters 10 and 11. Social workers fill an important role in educational settings where, according to the School Social Work Association of America, they

> provide a vital link among the school, home and community . . . provid[e] services to all students [including] direct services to students and their families, including casework, group work and classroom presentations as well as providing crisis intervention and consultation and making referrals to community agencies. School Social Workers are part of the assessment process for special education students [and] . . . often provid[e] direct and indirect services to those students. School Social Workers consult with teachers and administrators and frequently participate on teams within the schools.[2]

We shall begin with a brief summary of state and federal roles in education and then review decisions by the U.S. Supreme Court that affect education. Next, there will be an overview of federal laws that affect primary and secondary education and an in-depth discussion of disability-related educational laws. The chapter concludes with a discussion of the education rights of homeless children.

THE STATE AND FEDERAL ROLES IN EDUCATION

The content and methods of instruction used in primary and secondary schools are controlled by state and local law, and the daily operation of school systems is under state and local control. More than 90 percent of the money spent on education each year is provided by state and local government.[3] The federal government is prohibited by law from interfering with educational curricula; federal agencies do not have the authority to direct, supervise, or control the curriculum or program of instruction of an educational institution.[4]

Nevertheless, the federal government has a significant presence in education. It exercises its authority by (1) funding programs for children who are disadvantaged as a result of poverty, disability, and limited English proficiency; (2) supporting financially programs to educate native American native Alaskan, and native Hawaiian children[5]; (3) establishing national rules that govern access to a child's school records[6]; (4) enforcing civil rights legislation that prohibits (a) discriminatory denial of educational opportunities based on race, color, and national origin[7]; (b) educational institutions from denying equal access to federally funded programs because of gender[8]; and (c) sexual harassment of schoolchildren.[9]

THE U.S. SUPREME COURT AND EDUCATION

The educational rules set by government and the constitutional right of parents to control the education of their children foster tension between state or local government on the one hand and parents on the other. One of the earliest Supreme Court decisions addressing parents' rights and state control was issued in 1923, in *Meyer v. Nebraska,* when the Court struck down as an infringement of parent's rights a statute that criminalized the teaching of subject matter in a language other than English.[10] And in *Pierce v. Society of Sisters* (1929), the Supreme Court ruled that an Oregon statute requiring children to attend public school was not constitutional. The Court recognized the authority of the states to regulate schools and compel attendance. However, the requirement that the school be a public school rather than a parochial school "interfered with the liberty of parents and guardians to direct the upbringing and education of children under their control."[11]

If the importance of a High Court decision is related to public impact, then the most significant education decisions were issued in the midtwentieth century when the Court ended race-based discrimination in public schools. In 1954 and again in 1955, in *Brown v. Board of Education,* the High Court ruled that schools were to be desegregated and then that they were to be integrated.[12] Because some states and local school districts did not comply with rulings of federal district courts, the Supreme Court sanctioned district court orders that required (1) reassignment of teachers to achieve faculty desegregation; (2) the use of white to nonwhite ratios as a starting point for setting integration goals; (3) altering school attendance zones; and (4) busing to achieve integration.[13]

Some decisions of the Supreme Court deal directly with young people and ask, "When, if ever, can a young person's rights 'trump' the authority of school officials to set rules to control student behavior?" Two cases that addressed this topic were referred to in chapter 3, where we learned that the High Court sanctioned random drug testing in schools and a warrantless search of a student's personal belongings. The Court agreed with the schools' argument that these actions were essential to ensure student safety and to maintain order. However, the Court has limited school authority when the actions taken affect First Amendment rights involving speech or religious freedom. Such was the case in 1943 when the High Court found unconstitutional a West Virginia statute requiring all students to salute the flag. This mandate violated the First Amendment rights of students who were Jehovah's Witnesses, because the pledge elevated nation over God.[14] In 1969 the Court reiterated the rule that the First Amendment protects young people's freedom of expression. This case raised the question of whether students had a right to wear to school armbands protesting the Vietnam War, and the Court ruled they did, because the armbands were a form of political speech protected by the First Amendment.[15] Schools may not become "enclaves of totalitarianism," the Court opined, where students are seen as "closed-circuit recipients" of what the state chooses to communicate. This ruling does not mean that the free speech rights of students are unbridled. For example, a school district was within its right to discipline a student for giving a speech on school grounds that contained "offensively lewd and indecent speech."[16] Also, a school principal had the authority to censor a student newspaper because an article on pregnancy contained enough information for the pregnant students to be identified and because the article's discussion of sexual activity and birth control was deemed inappropriate for younger students. When the High Court limits freedom of speech in school settings, it does so based on the uniqueness of the school environment and the necessity to balance student rights against the responsibility of school officials to maintain order and to ensure safety.[17]

The Supreme Court has also addressed public school funding. In general, funds for primary and secondary education are provided by the states and supplemented at the local level by property-tax revenues. An unfortunate aspect of this funding scheme is that it disadvantages children who live in poor communities because these jurisdictions are limited in their ability to raise funds. In 1973 in *San Antonio v. Rodriguez,* the High Court was asked whether such funding practices violated the equal protection clause of the Fourteenth Amendment.[18] The Court found no violation because education is not a fundamental right. Thus the state could justify its funding scheme if it was rationally related to achieving a legitimate government interest (see chapter 2). That interest, the Court ruled, lies in the state's need to control spending. Note that the Court's position on education is similar to its position on welfare benefits (see chapter 2). As with education, there is no fundamental right to welfare benefits. Whether considering education or welfare, the Court is concerned that a different ruling would open the door to a host of claims seeking to gain constitutional protection for diverse federal and state benefits.

In 1992 the Supreme Court was asked whether a state could deny educational opportunities to children not legally in the United States. The Court expressed its concern for children when it ruled that a state could not do so.[19] The case of *Plyler v. Doe* involved children of Mexican descent. Texas refused to provide money to local school districts if that money was used to educate children not legally in the United States, and the state authorized local school districts to deny enrollment to these children. As in the *San Antonio* case, the state justified its action by saying it needed to constrain fiscal costs. Referring to the equal protection clause and its provision that no state shall "deny to any person within its jurisdiction the equal protection of the laws," the Court found that someone not legally in the United States is a "person" protected by the Fourteenth Amendment. Reiterating that education is not a fundamental right and that resident aliens are not a protected class, the Court found that the law in question

> impose[d] a lifetime hardship on a discrete class of children not accountable for their disabling status. These children can neither affect their parents' conduct nor their own undocumented status. The deprivation of public education is not like the deprivation of some other governmental benefit. Public education has a pivotal role in maintaining the fabric of our society and in sustaining our political and cultural heritage: the deprivation of education takes an inestimable toll on the social, economic, intellectual, and psychological well-being of the individual, and poses an obstacle to individual achievement. In determining the rationality of the Texas statute, its costs to the Nation and to the innocent children may properly be considered.[20]

At the dawn of the twenty-first century the Supreme Court agreed to hear a challenge to a school voucher program in Cleveland, Ohio. The program provided vouchers that allowed parents to choose the school that their child would attend.[21] The challenge arose because parents used vouchers to send children to parochial schools, and in the 1999–2000 school year more than 80 percent of the private schools involved in the Cleveland program had a religious affiliation. There were no public schools participating.

The suit was brought by a group of taxpayers who sought to stop the program because public funds were being used to support religious institutions, which, they argued, violated the establishment clause of the First Amendment. A further concern was that programs such as this would drain off funds from public schools, resulting in their further deterioration. The Court ruled against the taxpayers, finding that the program did not violate the constitutional requirement for separation of church and state. The program was neutral with respect to religion, the Court ruled. Program assistance was made available to a broad class of citizens who chose to direct the educational benefit to religious schools. The outcome, the Court concluded, is the product of independent choice; that the money assists religious institutions cannot be attributed to a choice of government and is thus constitutionally permissible.

FEDERAL STATUTES AFFECTING EDUCATION

The Elementary and Secondary Education Act of 1965

This law, reauthorized in 2001 as the No Child Left Behind Act (NCLB), allows the federal government to financially support primary and secondary education.[22] Congress has authorized the use of federal funds to help the states increase educational opportunities for economically disadvantaged students and for students who lack English-language proficiency.

The goals of the NCLB are ambitious and include (1) developing and implementing uniform testing procedures to assess annually student achievements in reading and math; (2) informing parents, the general public, educators, and policy makers about school performance using data from annual assessments; (3) reporting achievement data by race, gender, and other criteria to demonstrate student achievement and progress in closing the achievement gap between disadvantaged students and others; (4) allowing parents with children in "failing schools" to transfer their child to a better-performing public or charter school[23] once a school is identified as failing; (5) using federal funds to provide supplemental educational services such as tutoring, after school services, and summer school programs, for children in failing schools; (6) expanding federal support for charter schools by giving parents, educators, and interested community leaders greater opportunities to create new charter schools; (7) facilitating recruitment and retention of excellent teachers, including the use of federal funds to hire new teachers, increase teacher pay, and improve teacher training; and (8) consolidating programs for bilingual education and the education of immigrant children.[24]

The Family Educational Rights and Privacy Act

The Family Educational Rights and Privacy Act (FERPA) of 1974 requires educational institutions that receive federal funds to provide parents with access to the education records of their children. FERPA also prohibits educational institutions from disclosing records without a student's prior consent, except in limited circumstances, such as when information is (1) required for a federal audit; (2) requested by the juvenile justice system; (3) requested under a subpoena; or (4) needed in an emergency "to protect a child's health or safety or the health or safety of others."[25]

When a statute prevents disclosure of information in the control of an institution, it is important to know what information is protected. FERPA's protection is limited to an educational record, which is defined as a "record, file, document [or] other material which contains information directly related to a student . . . maintained by [the] educational institution or agency or by a person acting for [the] institution or agency."[26] Not covered are (1) records in the possession of a teacher or other instructional personnel that cannot be accessed by others; (2) grades assigned by students at a teacher's direction[27]; or (3) information contained in a school record if it is known to others from observing a later-recorded incident.[28]

The Equal Access Act

In 1984 Congress passed the Equal Access Act (EAA), which relates to student speech. The EAA was enacted to ensure that public high schools that receive federal funds do not deny student-initiated religious groups access to school facilities that are available to nonreligious student-initiated groups, although the protections offered by the act extend to any excluded group. The EAA provides that if a school has set aside space for students to use for meetings, it cannot deny a group access because the school disapproves of the message that the group seeks to convey, whether the message is spirited by "religious, political, or philosophical" content.[29] The protection afforded by the EAA falls squarely within the First Amendment's guarantee of free speech.

A group qualifies for protection under the EAA (1) if it is voluntary, student initiated, and student controlled and if nonschool personnel are not in regular attendance; (2) if it is not sponsored by the school, a unit of government, or government employee; (3) if it is religious in nature and not officiated by a school employee or government official; and (4) if its actions do not materially and substantially interfere with the orderly conduct of educational activities within the school.[30]

For example, in 1999 a group of high school students wanted to form a "gay-straight alliance." The school board denied the group's application, and the students sued. After determining that the EAA applied to the school because it made meeting space available to other student groups, the court ruled that the board violated the act by denying access. The school board's animus toward the group was clear in its requirement that eligibility to use school space was contingent on the group's deleting any reference to a "gay-straight alliance" from its name and changing its mission statement to proscribe discussion of sexual activities at club meetings. Other groups were not required to conform in this manner, and the board's actions violated the EAA.[31]

Title IX of the Education Amendment of 1972

Title IX prohibits educational programs that receive federal financial assistance from discriminating on the basis of sex.[32] The protections offered extend to employment and funding for women's athletic programs, and they provide a remedy for victims of sexual harassment, which is a form of discrimination.[33] Harassment includes the behavior of teachers, colleagues, and peers.[34] Educational institutions include public or private preschools, elementary or secondary schools, trade schools, professional schools, and colleges and universities. Educational institutions run by religious organizations are exempt if the provisions of Title IX are inconsistent with the institutions' religious principles.

Reviewing a case may facilitate understanding of Title IX. In 1994 LaShonda's parents filed suit on her behalf, alleging that the fifth grader had been the victim of a prolonged pattern of sexual harassment by a male classmate that included offensive touching, offensive verbal behavior, and acts mimicking sexual contact.[35] Other students complained of being the targets of offensive conduct by the same student, and the incidents were allegedly reported to school officials. According to the complaint, (1) the school principal was not willing to talk with the student victims; (2) disciplinary action was not taken; (3) the school board had no guidelines or express policy to direct officials in their response to allegations of sexual harassment; and (4) several months would pass after LaShonda first reported the harassment and before the school allowed her to change her classroom seat so that she no longer sat next to her harasser.

The U.S. Supreme Court ruled that the school board could be found liable under Title IX if its actions amounted to deliberate indifference to student-on-student sexual harassment that took place during school hours on school grounds. When the misconduct occurs on school property during school hours, it occurs in circumstances where the school exercises significant control over the harasser.

The Court cautioned lower courts that in cases such as LaShonda's, they must determine that the misbehavior prevented the victim from accessing the educational benefits offered by the school. Also, whether the conduct in question is actionable "harassment" depends on the circumstances, expectations, and relationships of those involved, including their ages and the number of individuals involved. In addition, the justices admonished lower courts to take into account that children may act in a manner that would be unacceptable among adults. A plaintiff will not prevail when the behaviors in question are no more than teasing and name calling. Finally, harassment must be because of sex. Thus in a case where a male high school student was assaulted by his football teammates, who then taped him to a towel bar, taped his genitals, and brought in a girl he had dated to view him, the U.S. Court of Appeals for the Tenth Circuit ruled that he was not harassed because of sex. None of the facts alleged involved unwelcome sexual advances, nor was sex used to contribute to a hostile environment. The court further observed that the student alleged that similar "hazing" occurred with women and that it was similarly ignored by school officials.[36]

Laws Affecting Children with Disabilities

Three federal statutes protect children with disabilities from discrimination: the Vocational Rehabilitation Act (VRA) of 1973, the Americans with Disabilities Act (ADA) of 1990, and the Individuals with Disabilities in Education Act (IDEA, formerly the Education for All Handicapped Childrens Act of 1975). The VRA and the ADA prohibit public entities from discriminating against qualified individuals with a disability by excluding them from any services, programs, or activities because of their disability.[37]

Public entities include state or local government, government agencies and departments, "instrumentalities" of government, for example, a state university, and the National Railroad Passenger Corporation.[38] A qualified individual is a person with a disability who "with or without reasonable modifications to rules, policies, or practices, the removal of architectural, communication, or transportation barriers, or the provision of auxiliary aids and services, meets the essential eligibility requirements for the receipt of services or the participation in programs or activities provided by a public entity."[39] Taken together, the VRA, ADA, and IDEA guarantee to children with disabilities the same right to a free public education as nondisabled children, although, as we shall see, which statute applies to any child depends upon the child's disability. In addition to protecting children with disabilities from discriminatory denial of educational opportunities, the VRA and ADA provide that children with disabilities will have full and equal access to the services and programs operated by entities such as social service agencies and hospitals, and the ADA ensures equal access to the services offered by individuals in private practice, such as physicians and mental health professionals. We shall begin with a review of the provisions in the IDEA that secure to eligible children with disabilities the right to a free public education. The VRA and the ADA will be discussed subsequently.[40]

THE INDIVIDUALS WITH DISABILITIES IN EDUCATION ACT

Despite the socially recognized importance of education, the exclusion of "uneducable and untrainable" children from public schools and segregation of children with disabilities in separate classrooms have been normative practices in the United States.[41] To ameliorate this problem, Congress enacted the Education for All Handicapped Children Act in 1975, renamed the Individuals with Disabilities in Education Act in 1990. The act created an entitlement for all eligible children to receive a free appropriate public education. In 2001 the U.S. General Accounting Office reported that approximately six million children and youth aged three through twenty-one were qualified to receive educational services under the IDEA, and the federal government provided $6 billion to the state and local governments to provide services.[42]

Each state is free to participate or not in the IDEA. If a state elects to receive federal funds, it must submit a plan to the secretary of the U.S. Department of Education describing the procedures that it will use to ensure that each eligible child receives a "free appropriate public education." A free appropriate public education for disabled children is one that addresses the child's special education needs by providing special education classes and related services, such as transportation, counseling, and physical therapy, at public expense. Although states submit a plan and comply with requirements, it is important to note that the act does not impose national standards for educating disabled children. Each state is free to decide the content and methods to be used in its educational programs.

Definition of *Disability*

The IDEA covers children with severe disabilities, who are defined to include children who are mentally retarded, are hearing impaired, or experience speech, language, or visual impairments. Children who are seriously emotionally disturbed are protected, as are those who have orthopedic impairments, suffer from traumatic brain injury, and have specific learning disabilities requiring special education and related services because of their disability.[43]

The Requirement for a Free Appropriate Public Education and the Individualized Education Plan

Each eligible child is entitled to an individualized education plan (IEP), which is the foundation for her or his educational entitlement. The IEP is a written statement that describes (1) the specific instructional program that will be put in place to meet the unique educational needs of the child for whom it is developed and (2) any related services that will be provided.

In 1982 the U.S. Supreme Court addressed the question, "What does the entitlement referred to by the phrase 'Free Appropriate Public Education' entail?" In the case under consideration the parents of Amy Rawley, who had a severe hearing impairment, asked the school district to provide her with a sign-language interpreter to aid her in class. The Court found that the law did not mandate the assignment of a sign-language interpreter. Amy was entitled to an educational program that was "reasonably calculated to enable [her] to achieve passing marks and advance from grade to grade."[44] However, the law does not oblige the school district to maximize a child's potential or to guarantee any particular educational outcome. Amy's performance was better than average and she was advancing from grade to grade. The Court conceded that her full potential was not realized because of her hearing impairment but found that the statute did not obligate the school district to ensure that she maximize her potential.

In 1983 the U.S. Court of Appeals for the Sixth Circuit elaborated on a school's obligation under the IDEA. A free public education for an autistic child is appropriate, the court ruled, if the plan provides a reasonable opportunity for the child to acquire skills that would permit him or her to function in a noninstitutional setting. However, this ruling does not mean that a school must provide any and all services that might benefit the child.[45]

Procedural Safeguards

Parents have the right to participate in the development of their child's IEP and the right to review all records (1) concerning their child, which includes a right to review the evaluations that contributed to a decision that a child required special education; (2) that contain information regarding the selection of a child's educational placement; and (3) that describe the way in which the school district would provide a free appropriate public education. A child's parents have a right to obtain an independent educational evaluation of their child if they so choose.

School districts are required to have procedures to protect the rights of any child whose parents are not known or whose parents are not available, including procedures to protect the rights of children who are wards of the state. Under any of these circumstances a person who is not an employee of any state or local educational agency involved in the education or care of the child is to be assigned to act as a parental surrogate.

The adult who is acting for the child, whether parent, guardian, or surrogate, must receive written notice in the adult's native language, unless it is clearly not possible to do so, before any change is made to a child's IEP, including any change in the child's physical placement. The adult must have the opportunity to register any objections that he or she may have regarding proposed changes, and he or she is entitled to a hearing and the right to appeal an adverse decision. The latter right includes the right to bring in an attorney and others who have special knowledge or training in the area of childhood disabilities. At a hearing the child's representative has the right to present evidence, to confront and cross-examine witnesses, and the right to compel the attendance of witnesses. In addition, the adult who is representing the child's interests is entitled to a verbatim transcript of the proceedings and the right to have the final decision, including the facts that supported the final decision, put in writing.

Related Services

Related services are to be provided when necessary for a disabled child to attain the benefits of her or his educational plan. Related services may include transportation, speech pathology, audiology, occupational therapy, recreational services, medical services for diagnosis and evaluation, and social work services, which are defined to include (1) preparing a social or developmental history for a child; (2) group and individual counseling with the child and family; (3) working with parents and others on problems in a child's living situation that affect the child's school adjustment; (4) mobilizing school and community resources to enable the child to learn effectively; and (5) assisting in developing behavioral intervention strategies.[46]

Related services may be costly to a school district, and fiscal concerns have caused districts to deny parental requests for services. For this reason the litigation has been extensive, with courts asked to determine whether a particular service or service array is necessary to enable a child to benefit from school.[47] The person arguing for the necessity of a service must show that a child will not benefit from an educational program if the service is not provided. However, the necessity of a service to educational attainment is not always clear cut, and reasonable professionals will disagree as to whether a service is essential to a child's education or is necessary, regardless of an educational objective. When this kind of disagreement occurs, court rulings may be influenced as much by the testimony of a persuasive expert as by the objective facts of the case. It is important to bear this kind of influence in mind in reviewing the case examples that follow, because you may see little difference between the facts of any two cases with opposite outcomes.

In 1999, in *Cedar Rapids v. Garret,* the U.S. Supreme Court was asked to resolve a dispute between the parents of a quadriplegic student, who argued that their son could not benefit from an educational program without continuous nursing services, and the boy's school district, which took the position that the service was a medical service not required by the IDEA.[48] The Court agreed with the boy's parents. In their ruling the justices said that to determine whether a requested service is a related service, it is necessary to ask first whether the service is "required to assist a child with a disability to benefit from special education," as opposed to a service that the child needs in the ordinary course of treatment.[49] If the child will not benefit from an educational program without the service, it is necessary to decide whether the service is a medical service, the provision of which goes beyond the diagnostic and evaluative medical services permitted by law. The medical service exclusion, the Court ruled, referred only to services provided by a physician. Since the service in question was provided by a nurse during the school day, the district had to provide the service that allowed the disabled child to remain in school and provided him with "the meaningful access to education that Congress envisioned."[50]

Contrast the *Cedar Rapids* case with that of Andrea Butler, whose parents sought reimbursement from the child's school district for the cost of maintaining her in a psychiatric hospital. Andrea's parents argued that the hospitalization was necessary because the school district delayed in finding a residential placement for their daughter. In arguing their case, her parents cited the U.S. Supreme Court's ruling in *Cedar Rapids v. Garret* and urged the appellate court to find Andrea's situation analogous to that of the youngster in *Cedar Rapids.* The court did not agree. It distinguished between the two cases, noting that the hospitalization experienced by Andrea was not comparable to the in-school nursing assistance provided in *Cedar Rapids.* Andrea's inpatient medical care was necessary "in itself and was not a special accommodation . . . to allow her to attend school or receive education."[51] By implication the nursing services provided to the quadriplegic youth in *Cedar Rapids* were not necessary, except that they facilitated the youth's access to an educational program. In Andrea's case educational attainment was not the reason why she was hospitalized, and the hospitalization was not meant to give her access to a meaningful public education.

Education in Public, Private, and Residential Settings

Another area of dispute between parents and school officials concerns placement of children in residential settings. As was the case with related services, courts ask whether the services provided in a residential setting are essential to the child's education or are a response to other, unrelated matters.

In *Burlington v. Department of Education*, the U.S. Court of Appeals for the First Circuit ruled that if a school district's choice of placement is found by a judicial officer to be inappropriate, the district is obligated to reimburse parents for their decision to replace their child in an appropriate educational setting.[52] And in *Vander Malle v. Ambach* a court found that a child's placement in a residential setting providing intensive psychiatric treatment was appropriate because earlier efforts to educate the child without psychiatric services failed.[53] The school district was obligated to reimburse the parents for the expenses that they incurred while their child was placed at a residential center. Considering a school district's obligation to reimburse parents for the costs of privately educating a child, the U.S. Supreme Court, in *Carter v. Florence County School District Four*, held that school districts can avoid such costs if they provide the child with a free appropriate public education in a public setting or place the child in an appropriate private setting chosen by the state.[54]

Where residential placement is found to be in response to medical or social problems that can be separated from matters related to a child's education, the school district is not required to pay for the noneducational services.[55] Thus when a child was diagnosed with an emotional disorder that caused "unpredictable and at sometimes violent behavior," residential placement was not required because it was shown that the child was deriving educational benefits despite these problems.[56]

Mainstreaming

The IDEA stresses but does not mandate "mainstreaming" of children with disabilities, which means educating them in the least restrictive environment.[57] Segregated placements should occur only when the nature or severity of a child's disability prevents him or her from participating in regular classes, even with the use of supplementary aids and services. The IDEA requires school districts to have in place a continuum of alternative placements in a variety of settings that would include "regular classes, special classes, special schools, home instruction, and instruction in hospitals and institutions."[58]

Mainstreaming may produce social as well as academic gains, and courts have sought to balance the concern that a child be educated in an integrated setting with the need to ensure that the child benefits educationally as well as socially from the educational experience. Courts agree that a child's educational goals may be achieved by integrating children for some but not all of the school day or for some but not all academic subjects.[59] But a program fails to meet the requirements of the law if it simply fills the time of a child with a disability by engaging her or him in activities that have no educational purpose and that limit the child's contacts with other students without disabilities.[60] Even though a private residential placement may maximize a child's educational opportunities, such a placement is not required when mainstreaming the child satisfies the statutory mandate.[61] However, mainstreaming does not require that a child be integrated into a regular classroom if doing so would be at the expense of the child's educational needs.[62] For example, mainstreaming is not necessary nor is it appropriate if the result is failure for the child who would succeed if taught in a segregated classroom.[63]

Some parents do not wish to have their children integrated into regular classroom settings because they think that a child's educational needs can be met only in special, segregated settings; they have sued school districts for integrating their children into regular classrooms.[64] If a child is performing well in a regular classroom, her parents cannot remove her to a private residential center and ask the state to reimburse them for the costs of educating the child.[65]

Discipline

Disciplining children for disability-related misbehavior presents unique problems if the disciplinary procedures interfere with a child's right to an education. Problems do not occur when school officials use routine disciplinary methods, such as "time-outs," detention, or restriction of privileges, that do not overly disrupt a child's education.[66] However, schools must follow procedural rules if the disciplinary measure results in a change in the child's educational placement.

Procedural Safeguards—Suspension Less Than Ten Days

IDEA regulations allow a school district to remove a child from her or his current placement if the reason for removal would apply to children who are not disabled and if the period of removal is no more than ten consecutive school days in the same school year. Additional removals of equal duration for separate incidents of misbehavior are allowed, but the school district must provide services to the child who is removed for more than ten school days in any one year.[67] An exception is suspension of a child for as long as forty-five days for carrying a weapon to school or to a school function or for using, selling, or soliciting the use of illegal drugs at school or a school function. During such a suspension the child must be placed in an interim alternative educational setting.[68]

The law also permits a suspension not to exceed forty-five days if a child's behavior is deemed likely to result in injury to the child or to others. However, whereas a school may unilaterally institute a suspension of this duration for carrying a weapon or engaging in behavior involving illegal drugs, it cannot suspend a student based on physical dangerousness without the sanction of a hearing officer.[69]

The Stay-Put Rule

Any change in a child's educational placement must be preceded by written notice to the child's parents, who have the right to a hearing.[70] Unless parents agree to a change in placement, a school district must permit a child to "stay put" in her or his classroom while a hearing to contest the school's removal decision is conducted.[71] If a child poses an immediate threat to the safety of others, school officials may request an expedited hearing to facilitate re-placing the child.

The Vocational Rehabilitation Act and the Americans with Disabilities Act

The Vocational Rehabilitation Act (VRA) and the Americans with Disabilities Act (ADA) are civil rights statutes that seek to protect from discrimination children and adults with disabilities. These acts prohibit institutions and individuals from denying access to programs, services, and employment opportunities based on a person's disability.[72] Prohibitions against discrimination offer protection to disabled children and youth in receipt of education, in employment, and in access to public transportation, public accommodations, and health and social services. We shall begin with a comparison of the provisions in the VRA and ADA and continue with a brief discussion of a decision of the U.S. Supreme Court that may limit individual rights under the ADA. The chapter also includes a comparision of the VRA, ADA, and IDEA, followed by a description of how the VRA and ADA operate to protect children from disability-based discrimination.

The VRA Compared to the ADA The VRA prohibits discrimination against people with disabilities by entities that receive federal funds, including hospitals, public and voluntary social service agencies, and schools and institutions of higher education. Such entities must provide to the disabled person equal access to programs and services. The ADA goes further by prohibiting discrimination by organizations and individuals, regardless of whether they receive federal funds. Thus the ADA prohibits a physician, social worker, or mental health professional in private practice from refusing to provide services to a disabled person on the basis of the person's disability.

When Congress passed the ADA, it expressed its intent that the statute be construed to apply at least the same standard of protection that had been applied under the VRA or its regulations.[73] Thus in considering the rights of children with disabilities, the protections afforded by the VRA and the ADA are distinguishable only in the applicability of the ADA to private practitioners. For the sake of simplicity, I shall use the acronym ADA/VRA unless the subject under discussion requires that a distinction be drawn.

Disability Statutes, the Eleventh Amendment, and State Immunity from Suit

Recall the discussion in chapter 7 about the immunity of state government and state agencies from suit under the doctrine of sovereign immunity, which is expressed in the Eleventh Amendment to the U.S. Constitution. The doctrine provides that individuals cannot sue the states in a federal court unless a state waives its immunity or Congress has provided a valid waiver of state immunity.

In 2001 the U.S. Supreme Court reiterated this position when it ruled that Congress had failed to demonstrate the pattern of irrational discrimination necessary for Congress to abrogate a state's sovereign immunity when it authorized individual suits under the ADA. In regard only to the employment provisions of Title I, the result of the High Court ruling is that individuals cannot sue a state in federal court for employment discrimination.[74]

However, states may be unable to claim Eleventh Amendment immunity when they accept federal funding, because Congress has the authority to require states to waive their Eleventh Amendment immunity as a condition for receiving federal funds. This requirement does not pose a conflict between federal and state law since states can elect to forgo federal funding. The VRA contains such a requirement, and a suit not permissible under the ADA may proceed under the VRA. A case did so proceed when an HIV-positive mother sued the New Jersey Division of Youth and Family Services.[75] Jane Doe, as she was identified in court papers, alleged that she was treated differently from HIV-negative mothers only because of her HIV status. She claimed that she was denied the right to make decisions concerning the medical treatment received by her newborn. Doe claimed protection under Title II of the ADA and under section 504 of the VRA, both of which prohibit public entities from discriminating against qualified individuals with a disability on account of the individual's disability.

The federal district court in which Doe filed suit considered the U.S. Supreme Court ruling concerning Title I. The district court opined that although the High Court decision did not involve Title II, the conclusion would have been the same had it done so. Thus the district court held that the mother could not bring suit under the ADA. However, her claim under the VRA was viable since the agency was a recipient of federal funds. (See chapter 14 for a U.S. Supreme Court ruling on Title II of the ADA.).

The VRA and ADA Compared to the IDEA

The protections afforded by the VRA and the ADA are broader in some ways and narrower in other ways than those offered by the IDEA. The VRA and the ADA are broader in that both prevent discrimination in matters that go beyond education, and the definition of *disability* in the VRA and the ADA is broader than that in the IDEA, thus protecting a greater number of people. For example, to be eligible for services under the IDEA, a child's disability must adversely affect her or his educational performance in a manner that necessitates special education.[76] The act does not protect the child or youth who is denied access to an institution's regular educational programs, unless denial is based on a demonstrable disability. However, protection from discrimination for those not demonstrably disabled is provided by the VRA and the ADA. Neither statute requires the child who is seeking protection to have special educational needs, although, as discussed later, the VRA and the ADA both provide for access to educational opportunities for children with mild and moderate disabilities. For example, children who are HIV positive have experienced extensive discrimination in educational settings.[77] The child who is HIV positive but asymptomatic does not, by definition, have special educational needs as a result of her or his HIV status. This child needs only protection against discriminatory exclusion from educational settings. The child with a severe disability who needs special education will seek assistance under the IDEA, while the child who needs protection from discrimination will seek assistance from either the VRA or the ADA.

Benefits Provided

All social policy confers some type of benefit. The conferred benefit is often concrete, as it is with the related services available under the IDEA, or, as with other policies, the benefit is cash, food, or payment for medical services. Civil rights policies are different. Their benefits are less tangible but of critical importance, since their goal is to eliminate discrimination in education, employment, and housing by providing avenues of legal redress for people who are subject to discrimination. These policies or statutes confer "status," because their goal is to place all members of society on an equal footing by eliminating discrimination based on stereotypes where a person's physical condition, gender, or race underpins decisions denying equal access.

Eligibility for protection under the IDEA is based on the results of a medical or mental health evaluation, while eligibility for the protections offered by the VRA/ADA is more complicated. To understand how eligibility is determined, it is necessary to understand the definition of *disability* common to both statutes; define a series of statutory terms, including (a) *otherwise qualified,* (b) *reasonable accommodation,* and (d) *undue burden;* and finally to illustrate the application of these terms.

Definition of Disability

The definition of *disability* in the VRA/ADA is much broader than in the IDEA. The VRA/ADA defines as disabled a person with a physical or mental impairment that limits significantly his or her ability to undertake a major life activity that the average person can perform with little or no difficulty, such as "caring for ones-self, performing manual tasks, walking, seeing, hearing, speaking, breathing, learning and working."[78]

The definition also includes those who have a "record" of an impairment. A record may be found when an individual has a history of an impairment or has been misclassified as having a mental or physical impairment that substantially limits one or more major life activities.[79] Covered also are people who are "regarded" as having an impairment.[80] The latter category covers those (1) who have physical disabilities that do not substantially limit a major life activity but who are treated as though they are so limited; (2) who have physical or mental disabilities that substantially limit a major life activity only because of others' attitudes toward the disability; or (3) who have no impairments but who are treated as having a substantially limiting impairment.

The Otherwise Qualified Child, Reasonable Accommodation, and Undue Burden

The VRA and ADA prohibit discrimination against the otherwise qualified person. Both statutes require schools and other covered entities to make reasonable accommodation to the needs of the otherwise qualified person, unless doing so would create an undue burden on the covered entity or unless the child poses a direct threat to the health or safety of others and the threat cannot be remedied by reasonable accommodation. An otherwise qualified claimant is one who meets the basic requirements for admission to the educational program or for the medical or social services that he or she is seeking. The procedure for assessing whether a person is otherwise qualified; which reasonable accommodation, if any, must be made; and whether the required accommodation creates an undue burden or would pose a risk to the health or safety of others is determined on a case-by-case basis and can be illustrated as follows.

In 1979 in *Southeastern Community College v. Davis,* the U.S. Supreme Court considered a claim that a woman with a severe hearing disability had been discriminated against in violation of the VRA when she was denied admission to a nursing program.[81] The position taken by the college to which Frances Davis had applied was that her hearing disability would prevent her from successfully completing the clinical component of the nursing program. Assistance from a person able to sign or otherwise provide aid to deal with any complications created by Davis's hearing difficulty, which might represent a reasonable accommodation in a classroom setting, were not seen as reasonable in the hectic world of hospital-based clinical practice.

The Court ruled that the VRA does not compel educational institutions to disregard the disabilities of the handicapped, nor does it require programs to make substantial modifications, such as eliminating the clinical requirement that Davis had requested, so that a disabled person is able to participate in the program. The law requires only that otherwise qualified people not be excluded from participation solely by reason of their handicap, meaning that mere possession of a handicap is not a permissible ground for assuming an inability to function.

The Supreme Court's decision in *Southeastern Community College* rests, in part, on the fact that Davis would not, if admitted to the nursing program, have been able to derive the benefit that the program was meant to confer. It follows that a refusal to modify a program could be unreasonable if the recipient was able to attain the program's ultimate benefit.[82]

Whether a requirement is reasonable may be judged by whether the person to be accommodated poses a threat to the health or safety of others. A number of cases involving the educational rights of children who are HIV infected have raised the issue of whether allowing a child with HIV to attend public school poses such a threat.[83]

In the early years of the HIV epidemic, schools provided for HIV-positive children through a series of accommodations because of a fear that children with the HIV posed a threat to the health of other children. These accommodations included consigning them to receive instruction through home study,[84] via telephone,[85] in the schoolhouse but segregated in a modular classroom that ruled out visual or auditory contact with other children,[86] or (in one case) in a separate classroom,[87] including a separate classroom constructed within the regular classroom with a window and sound system.[88] Over time the Centers for Disease Control and the American Academy of Pediatrics have made recommendations to reduce the risk of HIV infection in school, preschool, and foster care settings. The recommendations include providing access to regular classrooms for children who are HIV positive and whose presence in regular classrooms has never been shown to have resulted in the transmission of HIV.[89]

Homeless Children and the McKinney-Vento Act

Without special assistance, school attendance and school success for homeless children may be impossible. The problems confronting homeless parents in sending their children to school, and the problems confronting homeless children in obtaining an education, are numerous. They include (1) rules that limit the length of shelter stays, causing families to move frequently and perhaps put a child in another school district; (2) difficulties in locating a school and arranging transportation with each move to a new shelter; (3) the barriers to school enrollment when state and local law contain residency requirements and require a child's birth, medical, and school records as a condition for school enrollment; and (4) the endless difficulties that must exist for the child who tries to study in a shelter and the debilitating effect of having one's learning continually interrupted. Estimates of the percentage of homeless children not attending school vary from a high of 50 percent to a low of 14 percent.[90]

The McKinney-Vento Homeless Assistance Act requires that states guarantee equal access to public education for children of homeless families, and the act confers on homeless children a legally enforceable right to an education.[91] Under the act, grants to local educational agencies are available to facilitate the enrollment, attendance, and success in school of homeless children and youth.

To receive money allocated under McKinney-Vento, state educational agencies submit a plan to the U.S. Department of Education describing the assistance that will be provided to homeless children and youth. States are expected to revise laws and practices, for example, by eliminating residency requirements for homeless children and youth, so that they will have the same free appropriate public education as other children.

States are to establish the Office of Coordinator of Education of Homeless Children and Youth to compile data and submit reports to the secretary of education describing (1) the number of homeless children and youth and the number served with money under the act, (2) the problems confronting homeless children and youth in gaining access to education, (3) the special needs of homeless children and youth, (4) progress made by state and local education agencies in addressing problems identified, and (5) whether programs funded with act monies are successful in allowing homeless children and youth to enroll in, attend, and succeed in school. In addition, the coordinator is to facilitate cooperation between (1) the state educational agency, (2) the state social services agency, and (3) other agencies providing services to homeless children and youth and to develop and coordinate relationships with (a) other education, child development, or preschool programs; (b) providers of services to homeless children and their families; and (c) runaway and homeless youth centers.

McKinney-Vento grants may be used to assist homeless youngsters in different ways, including (1) providing tutoring and other forms of supplemental instruction; (2) expediting evaluations to identify educational strengths and needs and eligibility for special programs, for example, those serving gifted students, disabled students, and students with limited English proficiency; and (3) assessing the need for any service available under Title I of the Elementary and Secondary Education Act and through school-based nutrition programs; (4) referring homeless youngsters for medical, dental, health, and mental health services; (5) providing financial assistance to defray excess transportation costs; (6) providing early childhood education not available through other programs; (7) providing before and after school mentoring, and summer programs; and

(8) paying the cost of locating, obtaining, and transferring any records needed to enroll a child in school; (9) educating and training parents about the rights of and resources available to their children; (10) providing school supplies; and (11) providing other assistance to reduce or eliminate extraordinary or emergency situations that hinder school attendance.

Local education agencies are to select a school in accordance with parental choice to the extent possible and consistent with the best interests of the child or youth. The preference is for continuing children in the school they attended before becoming homeless or enrolling them in the school district in which they are temporarily living.[92]

SUMMARY

This chapter focused on the federal role in primary and secondary education. Although the states, acting with local school districts, control the content of educational curricula and the manner of instruction and provide the lion's share of education funds, the federal government plays a significant role in this area. The federal government (1) supplements state funds to provide educational opportunities for children disadvantaged by poverty, disability, and limited English-language proficiency; (2) supports financially programs to educate native American, native Hawaiian, and native Alaskan children and children who are homeless; (3) sets rules governing access to information contained in school records; (4) seeks to prevent educational entities from discriminating against children based on race, color, national origin, gender, and disability; and (5) seeks to prevent sexual harassment of children in school settings.

The U.S. Supreme Court has played a significant role in the education of primary and secondary school children. Rulings support the right of children to equal educational access regardless of race and support the right of parents to control certain aspects of their child's education, including their right to provide education in languages other than English and to send children to parochial schools, even when education is funded with public monies. In addition, acknowledging that the uniqueness of the school environment allows school officials to limit children's rights, the Court has recognized that there are limits to permissible state restrictions on a young person's First Amendment right to free speech.

Education is not a fundamental right, meaning that states may set rules for educational funding as long as the rules are rationally related to a legitimate state interest, such as controlling public spending, but here as well there are limits. Thus the Supreme Court has ruled that the children of illegal immigrants have a right to primary and secondary education.

Educational opportunities for children with disabilities have been a main focus of this chapter. Three federal laws, the Individuals with Disabilities in Education Act (IDEA), the Vocational Rehabilitation Act (VRA), and the Americans with Disabilities Act (ADA), taken together, guarantee to children with disabilities the same right to a free public education as nondisabled children. The laws can be distinguished in the following way: The VRA and the ADA are civil rights statutes that seek to protect from discrimination children with disabilities by prohibiting institutions from denying them access to programs and services based on their disability. The protections afforded by the VRA and the ADA are broader than those found in the IDEA, because the definition of *disability* in civil rights law is far reaching compared to the education law's definition of *disability,* which requires that a child's disability must adversely affect her or his educational performance in a manner that necessitates special education. The IDEA does not protect the child or youth who is denied access to an institution's regular educational programs, unless denial is based on a demonstrable disability. However, neither the VRA nor the ADA requires the child who is seeking protection to have special educational needs. Whereas the IDEA supports the provision of services that a child needs to obtain his or her educational entitlement, civil rights statutes are different. Their benefits are less tangible but of critical importance. Given that their goal is to eliminate discrimination in education and other matters, these policies or statutes confer "status" because their goal is to place all members of society on an equal footing by eliminating discrimination.

10

Care and Protection of Children

THIS CHAPTER will continue the theme introduced in chapters 8 and 9 concerning families. Parents have a right to the care, custody, and control of their children, a responsibility to provide for their children, and a duty to protect them from harm. If parents fail to meet their responsibilities, the state, under the doctrine of *parens patriae*—meaning the state as parent or protector—has the authority to intervene in family life to protect children from harm. A state establishes its *parens patriae* authority in its family code or children's code (chapter 8) and gives its juvenile courts the jurisdiction to hear cases involving three groups of children: (1) those who have suffered abuse or neglect; (2) those who have engaged in status offenses, which are acts that society finds troublesome because of the actor's youth; and (3) those who commit crimes.

This chapter considers each of these groups. I shall begin with an overview of statutory rules that govern receiving and investigating reports of abuse and neglect. Next, I will address the role played by the juvenile court. I also will discuss, for each group of children, the procedural, statutory, and constitutional rules that govern juvenile court proceedings as well as the issue of trying as adults youths who have committed crimes.

CHILD ABUSE AND NEGLECT AND PLACEMENT OF CHILDREN IN FOSTER CARE

Between 1963 and 1967 all the states enacted statutes mandating that professionals who come into contact with children report known or suspected child abuse and neglect. In addition, all states have laws that provide for placing children in foster care if their parents cannot or will not provide day-to-day care. States find support for their child protective work in two federal statutes, the Child Abuse Prevention and Treatment Act of 1974 (CAPTA)[1] and the Adoption Assistance and Child Welfare Act of 1980 (AACWA).[2] We begin with a discussion of CAPTA.

CAPTA authorizes the use of federal funds to assist the states in their child protective work, if they (1) accept and investigate reports of child abuse and neglect; (2) are able to provide a safe haven for injured and at-risk children; (3) maintain the confidentiality of case records; (4) appoint a guardian *ad litem* or court-appointed special advocate to represent children; (5) educate the public concerning child abuse and neglect; and (6) immunize from suit people who report in good faith.[3] Provisions that govern the acceptance and investigation of reports of child abuse and neglect in most states are listed in table 10.1.

Receiving Reports

Those mandated to report include professionals who come into contact with children and in some states nonprofessionals, such as school bus drivers and teacher aides. Some states accept reports from the lay public. Knowledge that a child has been abused or neglected or information that supports a reasonable belief that a child is at risk should trigger a report. Such information or belief obligates the reporter to inform a designated state or local agency, to provide enough information to establish the reported incident as one covered by state law, and to locate the child. Reporters are immune from suit for reports made in good faith; it follows that confidentiality is waived in regard to the information reported. Failure to report may subject the mandated reporter to a fine or criminal penalty.

The definition of abuse and neglect in figure 10.1 comes from federal law. At a minimum state laws must conform to this definition, which focuses on four issues: a child's injury, a caretaker's behavior, acts recently committed, and serious injuries. A number of states include prenatal exposure to drugs or alcohol in their definition of child abuse and neglect, and some include exposure to domestic violence.[4] When a newborn tests positive for drugs or is born with a birth defect suggestive of maternal alcohol use, such as congenital heart disease, cleft lip and palate, or low birthweight, the medical professionals are required to make a report.

The federal definition shown in figure 10.1 applies to child abuse but not necessarily to neglect, for example, to a lack of supervision or parental failure to send a child to school. Neglect is defined in state law. For example, in Pennsylvania child abuse includes "serious physical neglect [such as] prolonged or repeated lack of supervision or the failure to provide the essentials of life, including adequate medical care, which endangers a child's life or development

TABLE 10.1 Common Elements of Child Abuse and Neglect Reporting Laws

ACCEPTING REPORTS	
Who reports.	Those mandated to report include professionals who come into contact with children (e.g., social workers, medical and mental health workers, teachers and law enforcement personnel, and nonprofessionals such as school bus drivers and teacher aides).
Reporting trigger.	Knowledge of or reasonable cause to believe a child is being neglected or physically or sexually abused.
Who receives reports.	Social services and/or the police or a central hotline.
Contents of report.	Information to establish that the report concerns abuse or neglect of a child and sufficient information to locate the reported child.
Immunity.	States provide immunity from liability for reports made in good faith.
Penalty for failure to report.	Criminal and civil penalties may be levied for failure to make a report.
Definition of abuse and neglect.	A recent act or failure to act on the part of a parent or caretaker, including foster parents, which results in death, serious physical or emotional harm, sexual abuse or exploitation, or an act or failure to act that presents an imminent risk of serious harm. State laws will specify the age of people covered, usually someone younger than eighteen (42 U.S.C.A. 5106g [West 2002]).
INVESTIGATING REPORTS	
Interagency reporting.	Some states require that cases involving serious harm be reported to a district attorney for possible criminal prosecution and/or that social workers may contact a law enforce ment agency and request assistance with the investigation.
Conduct of the investigation	Statutes specify when the investigation is to begin (e.g., within twenty-four hours of receipt of a report), and who conducts the investigation (e.g., child protective service and/or law enforcement personnel). Procedural require ments may be specified (e.g., a mandatory evaluation of the child's environment and a determination of risk to a children if they continue to remain in the home).
Protective custody.	Specifies who is allowed to take a child into custody without parental consent and the conditions that justify such action. States limit the amount of time that a child may be held in

	protective custody (e.g., twenty-four to forty-eight hours, for instance) before a petition must be filed with the court.
X-rays, photographs, emergency medical care.	Permits taking x-rays and/or photographs of a child with and without parental consent when needed for emergency medical treatment.
Definition of abuse and neglect.	See definition under "Accepting reports."

or impairs the child's functioning."[5] In Georgia neglect means "harm to a child's health or welfare . . . which occurs through negligent treatment, including the failure to provide adequate food, clothing, shelter, and medical care."[6]

Interagency Reporting

Interagency reporting is a process of exchanging reports between a department of social services and law enforcement officials. Laws that permit or require interagency reporting are governed by state statute. Alaska, for example, requires reporting to law enforcement if abuse or neglect results in the need for medical treatment.[7] Colorado requires reporting to law enforcement of any report of abuse or neglect,[8] and Massachusetts requires reporting to a district attorney if abuse or neglect results in death, serious physical injury, or sexual assault.[9]

Investigating Reports

Instructions to guide the investigation are detailed in state statutes, regulations, and procedural manuals. Time frames for commencing and completing an investigation routinely require that the investigation begin within twenty-four or forty-eight hours of receiving a report and be completed within thirty or sixty days.

Coordinating Investigations

When abuse or neglect has been reported to both a department of social services and a law enforcement agency, parallel investigations may take place, each with a different objective. Police compile data to aid in criminal prosecution, while social workers, unless they are working under the direction of a prosecutor, are concerned with family preservation or reunification. Some states mandate that dual investigations always be coordinated, while others require coordination if a case is categorized as one involving serious injury, sexual assault, or death of a child.[10] If a report suggests serious injury, a prosecutor may elect to oversee the investigation to ensure that warrants are acquired before conducting searches (chapter 3) and to ensure that investigative techniques do not result in the contamination of evidence, as occurred in the McMartin Pre-School case and the Margaret Kelly Michaels case (see chapter 6).

Taking Children into Protective Custody

Some situations warrant immediate removal of a child who is at risk of injury, whose already-sustained injuries are apparent, or whose parent appears unable to care for her or him. Emergency removal may be accomplished with or without a court order. However, if there is no court order, state law will specify who has the authority to remove a child, usually social workers or the police, and the circumstances that warrant emergency removal. If a child is removed under emergency circumstances, a court hearing will take place shortly after the removal (see the section on emergency removal hearings in this chapter and figure 10.1). The general rule that parental consent is required before a child receives medical attention is waived in a medical emergency.

Decisions Made in Conjunction with an Investigation

In addition to making decisions concerning emergency removal, social workers must decide whether (1) there is evidence to sustain an allegation of neglect or abuse; (2) a child will be safe if left at home; (3) the family requires any services; and (4) to refer a case to court.

The law is not concerned with injuries per se but with those intentionally inflicted by a child's caretaker or with caretaker indifference to the child's needs. However, determining parental intention may be difficult. The key to decisions that result in removing a child from the home or to sustaining an allegation of abuse or neglect may be a parent's willingness to follow through with treatment recommendations made by a social worker who determines that a child requires professional assistance.

LEGAL LIABILITY AND CHILD ABUSE AND NEGLECT INVESTIGATIONS

A social worker and social service agency are vulnerable to lawsuits for actions taken or not taken during an investigation. The general rule is that social workers are immune from suit for actions taken in good faith (chapter 7). Judicial officers recognize the difficulties that confront social workers who do child protection work, and they usually will go out of their way to find good faith. However, workers may lose sight of their responsibilities and engage in overzealous advocacy. That is what occurred in the case reviewed in chapter 7 where a worker was found to have acted in bad faith and with malicious intent after she failed to report accurate and complete information concerning a schoolteacher who was charged with sexual abuse.

Social workers and their employing agencies have been sued under the Child Abuse Prevention and Treatment Act of 1974 by clients who allege that a worker's actions did not conform to professional standards. For example, suits have alleged failure to initiate prompt investigations or to provide necessary services. The federal appellate courts in two circuits have considered this matter and ruled that plaintiffs cannot prevail in a suit filed under CAPTA because it is not specific and detailed enough to sustain a claim that a client is owed a specific duty or that a social worker's actions were deficient.[11] A federal judge in New York City reached an opposite conclusion when he ruled that children had a right to sue the city for its failure to conduct the prompt investigations and to take the immediate steps to protect at-risk children required by CAPTA.[12]

Failure to protect a child from injury has provided another basis for suit. Consider the following case resolved by the U.S. Supreme Court. In early 1989 the mother of a child who suffered severe brain damage after being beaten by his father sued social workers and agency officials. The case of Joshua DeShaney had first come to the attention of protective services in 1982 when a complaint was filed on behalf of this three-year-old.[13] Joshua was living with his father, who denied that he abused his son. No action was taken. The boy was hospitalized in early 1983, and doctors suspected that his injuries were not the result of accidents. Joshua remained in the hospital under court order, but the case was dismissed after social workers, medical personnel, and others determined that the evidence was not sufficient to continue custody. A second hospitalization occurred one month later. There was no court action, but a caseworker visited the child's home monthly for six months. The worker observed injuries to Joshua that she recorded along with her suspicion that he was being abused. In late 1983 the child was admitted to the hospital for a third time. Once again, suspected abuse was noted, but the boy was returned home. The worker continued to visit the DeShaney home but was not allowed to see the boy. No further action was taken by the department of social services. The severe beating that caused brain damage occurred in March 1984.

Ms. DeShaney sued social workers and agency administrators and argued that the due process clause of the Fourteenth Amendment imposed an obligation on the state to protect children known to be abused or neglected. A majority of the U.S. Supreme Court disagreed with her claim. The Court ruled that the Fourteenth Amendment serves to protect people from the state, not from each other, and that therefore the state had no legal duty to protect Joshua from the abuse he suffered at his father's hands. However, the Court left open the possibility that it might have ruled differently had Joshua been in state custody.

Had the state by affirmative exercise of its power removed Joshua from free society and placed him in a foster home operated by its agents, we might have a situation sufficiently analogous to incarceration or institutionalization to give rise to an affirmative duty to protect.[14]

JUVENILE AND FAMILY COURTS

A case that goes to court may proceed through the criminal justice system if the evidence is sufficient to prove the elements of the crime charged (chapter 3) and the goal is punishment. If the evidence is not sufficient to sustain a criminal charge or if the goal is to rehabilitate the offender and preserve the family, the case will proceed through the civil justice system.

Topics reviewed in earlier chapters that are relevant to this discussion include (1) the overview of the civil and criminal justice process and burdens of proof in chapter 3); (2) the discussion of evidence in chapter 6; (3) the role of the social worker as fact witness or forensic expert in chapter 6; and (4) the review of due process rights, including the right to notice and counsel in this chapter. Civil cases involving abuse or neglect of children are heard in juvenile court, family court, or in courts of general jurisdiction in some states. As discussed in chapter 3, a case may be heard in a specialized court such as a family treatment court or domestic violence court. For the sake of simplicity I shall refer throughout to "the juvenile court."

Juvenile courts play a significant role in the day-to-day operation of the child welfare system. Courts determine (1) whether the evidence presented by a department of social services is sufficient to sustain an allegation of child abuse or neglect; (2) where a child will live; and (3) whether the agency has made reasonable efforts, where warranted, to preserve the family unit or to return to the home a child who had been placed in foster care. In addition, judicial approval of a child's foster care placement is a condition for a state to claim federal financial support to defray the costs of maintaining a child in foster care. Also, a court or administrative body that is not under the supervision or direction of the state agency must review each child's case plan and either sanction its continuance or order a change.[15]

In parallel investigations the state may proceed simultaneously against a parent with civil and criminal actions. The implications of such action go beyond the possibility of incarceration to include the chance that a criminal conviction may result in termination of parental rights. Congress provided for this in 1996 when it amended CAPTA and again in 1997 when it passed the Adoption and Safe Families Act (ASFA), which amends the Adoption Assistance and Child Welfare Act of 1980 (AACWA).

Congress enacted ASFA in response to several concerns, including an increase in the number of children in foster care and the many children who drift from foster home to foster home rather than being placed in permanent homes. Key to its enactment was concern about how the "reasonable efforts" requirement of the AACWA had been implemented. Since 1980, when the AACWA was passed, states have been required to make reasonable efforts to prevent removal of children from their own homes and to reunite those in foster care with their families of origin. Some members of Congress believed that the reasonable efforts requirement was incorrectly interpreted, such that social workers were making unreasonable or extraordinary efforts to prevent placement and to reunite children with their families, often without regard to a child's safety.[16] ASFA modified the earlier law. Federal law no longer requires reasonable efforts if a parent is convicted of committing a felony assault that resulted in serious bodily injury to his or her child or of the murder or voluntary manslaughter of another child in the family. Such a conviction provides grounds for a state to terminate the rights of the convicted parent, although states have the discretion not to take such action.[17]

Jurisdiction, Notice, and the Petition

In chapter 3, I referred to jurisdiction, which consists of subject-matter jurisdiction and personal jurisdiction. The subject-matter jurisdiction of juvenile courts is spelled out in a state's family or children's code. Jurisdiction generally extends to abused and neglected children, status offenders, and juvenile delinquents. Courts have personal jurisdiction over people living in the state where the court is located.

A civil proceeding, whether involving neglect, abuse, a status offense, or delinquent behavior, is initiated when a petition, sometimes called a complaint, is filed with the appropriate court. The state obtains personal jurisdiction over a child's caretaker first by serving a summons and complaint on the person involved; when the allegation is a status offense or delinquent act, the youth is served as well. The summons informs the person served that she or he must appear in court; it also specifies the time, date, and place of appearance. The complaint lists the reasons why the action was brought. The reasons are known as "cause(s) of action," for example, an allegation that a parent neglected or abused a child or that a youth charged as a delinquent has committed a specified crime. The injury is identified, as is the remedy sought, for example, that the court sanction the state's placement of a child in foster care or the youth's placement in a treatment or detention facility.

Notice and a copy of the petition containing the charges or issue must be provided to (1) parents; (2) a legal guardian, if the child's custody has been transferred from the parent(s); (3) the agency or organization having legal custody of the child; (4) foster parents, although whether notice is required may depend on the length of time the child has been in a foster home; (5) attorneys; and (6) any other parties the court deems necessary.

The law prefers personal service on a party, although this is not possible when the identity and/or whereabouts of a party are not known.[18] If the latter occurs, notice by publication satisfies due process even though providing notice in this manner is "probably futile," the Supreme Court has acknowledged.[19] When publication is used, the notice (1) appears in a newspaper a specified number of days before trial; (2) reports the date and time of the court proceeding; and (3) is addressed to "All Concerned Parties." The notice reports that a hearing will take place that concerns a child who is identified by the name of one parent. If the identity of both parents is not known, another identifier is used to direct attention to the child.

A copy of a petition appears in figure 10.1. The information at the top of the first page is the case caption. From reviewing this material, we learn that the case (1) was filed in family court; (2) concerned the neglect of David James Lee by Noreen Lee, his mother; and (3) that the court has jurisdiction over David because he was younger than eighteen and his parent was accused of neglecting him. As I noted in chapter 3, the party who files an abuse or neglect petition is referred to as the petitioner, rather than identifying the unit of government, and the party charged with misbehavior is the respondent, not the defendant.

The first paragraph notifies parents of the possibility that their parental rights may be terminated if their child remains in foster care for fifteen of twenty-two months, a federal requirement imposed by ASFA. This notice alerts parents to the chance that they will lose permanent custody of their child if they fail to actively participate in programs to improve the conditions that led to placement.

In the paragraphs that follow in figure 10.1, the county that filed the petition is identified by name and address (paragraph 1); the child on whose behalf the petition was filed is named and date of birth reported (paragraph 2); the child's residence is reported, as is the name of the person with whom he was living (paragraph 3); the names and addresses of his parents as reported (paragraph 4).

Paragraph 5 contains the allegation of neglect couched in the language of the state's statute, with a notation that specifics applying to this case appear in an appendix (exhibit A). The phrase "information and belief" is commonly used at the early stages of a court proceeding since all the proof on which the case will rest is not available. The phrase also is used because some evidence will be secondhand, meaning that the person signing the petition will not necessarily be the person to testify to all the evidence at the subsequent fact-finding hearing. Nevertheless, the petitioner avers that the allegations are true to the best of

FIGURE 10.1

Neglect Petition

STATE OF NEW YORK
FAMILY COURT: COUNTY OF CROSS[1]

In the Matter of	Docket # N-3687-00C
DAVID JAMES LEE,	PETITION
A Child Under Eighteen Years of Age Alleged to Be Neglected by	(Neglect)
NOREEN LEE,	Respondent.

PLEASE TAKE NOTICE OF THE FOLLOWING

THAT IF A CHILD IS IN FOSTER CARE FOR FIFTEEN OF THE MOST RECENT TWENTY-TWO MONTHS, THE CROSS COUNTY DEPARTMENT OF SOCIAL SERVICES MAY BE REQUIRED BY LAW TO FILE A PETITION TO TERMINATE THE PARENTAL RIGHTS OF THE PARENTS

TO THE FAMILY COURT OF CROSS COUNTY:

The undersigned Petitioner respectfully alleges that:
1. The Petitioner, the Cross County Department of Social Services, is a duly authorized agency having its office and place of business at 2626 Phillips Ave., Medford, New York 16987.
2. The child who is the subject of this proceeding is:

Name	Sex	Date of Birth
David James Lee	Male	May 2, 1998

3. Upon information and belief, the child resides with Noreen Lee at 1867 Edwards Ave., Medford, New York 16987.
4. Upon information and belief, the names of parents or other persons legally responsible for the care of the child, the persons with whom the child resides, and any Respondent, and their respective residential addresses are:

Name	Address	Relationship
Noreen Lee	1867 Edwards Ave. Medford, New York 16987	Mother
Roger Lee	Address unknown	Father.

5. Upon information and belief, as more specifically alleged in Exhibit A annexed hereto, the child is a neglected child in that the child's physical, mental, or emotional

condition has been impaired or is in imminent danger of becoming impaired as a result of the failure of the Respondent to exercise a minimum degree of care in supplying the child with adequate food, clothing, shelter, or education in accordance with the provisions [the state statute is cited], though financially able to do so or offered financial or other reasonable means to do so;

6. Upon information and belief, Noreen Lee, a parent who is legally responsible for the care of the child, is the person who is responsible for the neglect of the child.

7. Upon information and belief, the child is not subject to the Indian Child Welfare Act.

WHEREFORE, the Petitioner prays that an order be made determining the child to be a neglected child and otherwise dealing with the child in accordance with the provisions of Article 10 of the Family Court Act.

Dated:

Jonathan Washington

Cross County Department of Social Services
Supervisor—CPS/Preventive Services

EXHIBIT A

1) until approximately February 16, 2001, the Respondent and the child had been living on Edwards Ave., Medford, New York. The Respondent's residence was regularly in an unsanitary and dangerous condition;

2) as a result of the condition of the residence, a fire hazard existed. On February 16, 2001, a fire started in the child's bedroom;

3) the child has dental problems. The Respondent has failed to follow through with treatment for the problems;

4) the child's speech development is delayed. The Respondent has failed to pursue services to address the problem.

VERIFICATION

STATE OF NEW YORK
COUNTY OF CROSS

Jonathan Washington, being duly sworn, deposes and says:

1) I am the supervisor of CPS/Preventive Services of the Cross County Department of Social Services, the Petitioner herein;

2) I am familiar with the facts and circumstances of the above-entitled proceeding;

3) I have read the foregoing petition and know the contents thereof;

4) The contents of the petition are true to my own knowledge, except as to those matters therein stated to be alleged upon information and belief, and, as to those matters, I believe them to be true.

Jonathan Washington

(The verification is notarized)

Note: All place and person names are fictitious.

his or her knowledge, which informs the court that the petitioner is acting in good faith.

David's mother is the party charged with neglect (paragraph 6), followed by the notation (paragraph 7) that David is not a native American child. If he were, jurisdiction to hear this case might be deferred to a tribal council, under provisions in the Indian Child Welfare Act, which I discuss later in this chapter.

Exhibit A contains the allegations to be proved in court. The petitioner may seek permission from the court to amend the petition before the fact-finding hearing if new allegations come to light or if the petitioner learns that some of allegations listed cannot be sustained.

The last part of the petition is a "verification" by a child protective services supervisor whose unit handles David's case. A verification attests to the truth of the information in the petition. Since other people supplied some information on which the social worker relied in framing the allegations, she has noted that in addition to statements known by her to be true, the petition rests on statements "believed" to be true. This reference is to information not in the social worker's direct experience.

HEARINGS

Table 10.2 lists all the hearings that may occur from the time that a petition is filed through adoption.

The Emergency Removal Hearing

The emergency removal hearing is also called a probable cause hearing, shelter care hearing, or preliminary protective hearing. This hearing occurs if a child was removed from the family home on an emergency basis or if the petitioner wants the court to sanction removal. The court must determine whether the available evidence supports removal and, if so, where the child should live. If the evidence is deficient, the child who has already been removed will be returned home and the case will be dismissed, with or without a recommendation for services. This hearing routinely takes place twenty-four to seventy-two hours after the child's removal. The judge will make an initial judicial determination concerning reasonable efforts.

If it is a parent's first court appearance on the matter covered by the petition, the court will advise the parent of (1) the allegations; (2) the right to counsel, and if provided by state law, the right to court-appointed counsel; and (3) the right to request an adjournment to allow time to confer with counsel. If there is no emergency hearing, the judge will explain these rights to a parent at a later proceeding.

TABLE 10.2 Court Hearings

EMERGENCY HEARING
Questions Addressed: (1) Is there probable cause to believe that a child has been abused or neglect? If so, should the child be removed from her or his own home? (2) Should the removed child be retained in care or returned home? (3) If reasonable efforts are required, have they been made?
ADJUDICATION HEARING
Question Addressed: Has the state presented evidence sufficient to sustain the allegation of abuse or neglect?
DISPOSITION HEARING
Questions Addressed: (1) Where will the child live? (2) Who will have legal custody of the child? (3) If reasonable efforts are required, have they been made? (4) Are services required? (5) What arrangement should be made for parent child visits?
REVIEW HEARINGS
Questions Addressed: (1) Is progress being made toward the goal in the child's case plan? (2) If not, should the plan be changed? (3) If reasonable efforts are required, have they been made?
PERMANENCY PLANNING HEARING
Question Addressed: Should the child be returned home, her or his placement extended, or an alternative plan ordered by the court?
TERMINATION OF PARENTAL RIGHTS HEARING
Question Addressed: Has the state presented clear and convincing evidence to support its request that parental rights be terminated?
BEST INTERESTS HEARING
Question Addressed: Assuming that the evidence is sufficient to terminate parental rights, is it in the child's best interests to do so?

In addition to representation for a parent, CAPTA requires the states to appoint a representative for the child for every judicial proceeding.[20] The representative may be a guardian *ad litem*, a court-appointed special advocate (CASA), or an attorney.[21] A guardian *ad litem* may be an attorney or a layperson, and a CASA is a layperson. The role assigned to a guardian *ad litem* or CASA is to conduct an investigation of the child's situation and to make a recommendation to the court as to what, in the guardian or CASA's opinion, is in the child's best interests. Unlike guardians, who offer their own opinion to the court, attorneys acting in the traditional role of counsel represent the express wishes of their client.

A conference may take place before an adjudicatory hearing. A conference provides the opportunity for the parties to develop a settlement proposal for court approval and to avoid a formal hearing. The child's case plan may be developed at this time.

The Adjudicatory Hearing

The adjudicatory hearing, or fact-finding hearing, as it is called in some states, is akin to a trial in criminal court. At this proceeding the petitioner must prove each element of its case by a preponderance of the evidence. Recall that this standard requires that the evidence offered in support of an allegation be greater or more convincing than the evidence offered in opposition to it. The elements to be proved in an abuse or neglect proceeding may include proof (1) that the adult charged is the child's parent or guardian; (2) that the adult charged harmed or allowed another to harm the child or to place the child at risk of injury; and (3) that the harm was not accidental.

Prosecutors present their case by using any of the forms of evidence reviewed in chapter 6, including (1) "real evidence," such as photographs showing the location of a child's injuries or school attendance records that support an allegation of truancy; (2) the testimony of fact witnesses, including a child's social worker, foster parents, and schoolteachers; and (3) the testimony of experts, including social workers, physicians, psychologists, and psychiatrists.

The rules of evidence that apply at a civil proceeding are not as restrictive as they are at a criminal proceeding, because the law views the loss of custody that may result from a civil proceeding as less onerous than the loss of liberty that may result if one is convicted of a crime. The rules of evidence are also relaxed because a child is often the only witness to an act of abuse, and the wish to prosecute an offender must be balanced against the wish to protect a child from the burden of testifying. To strike a balance between these competing goals, courts and legislatures have created exceptions to the rules regarding the admission of hearsay evidence (see chapter 6, especially the discussion of *State v. Sorenson*). In chapter 6, I said that a judge may make an exception to the hearsay rule if the nature and circumstances under which a statement was made offer strong assurances of its accuracy and if the witness is not available to testify. In *Sorenson* five factors influenced the court's decision to allow a social worker to present hearsay evidence concerning what the child had told her. To determine whether the statements were reliable, the court considered (1) attributes of the child, such as age, ability to communicate, and ability to know the difference between truth and falsehood; (2) the relationship of the victim to the person told and the motivation of that person to falsify or distort contents; (3) the circumstances of the disclosure; (4) the content of the statement (i.e., does it allude to knowledge of sexual matters not ordinarily known by children of the victim's age?); and (5) other corroborative evidence such as physical evidence.

Before I illustrate how one court determined whether the state presented evidence sufficient to sustain an allegation of abuse, we will digress to consider two matters: (1) the legal standard for determining custody, and (2) child testimony in criminal trials.

THE LEGAL STANDARD FOR DETERMINING CHILD CUSTODY

In chapter 8, where I discussed the legal standard for determining child custody, I said that when the court seeks to resolve a dispute between divorcing parents, the standard is the best interests of the child. With few exceptions the state cannot intervene in an intact family solely because the intervention is in the child's best interests. As we know from the earlier discussion, the reason is that parents have a constitutionally protected right to the care, custody, and control of their children, and the state may not intrude in family life unless it first demonstrates that a parent is not a fit custodian. Only then can the state act in the child's best interests.

In chapter 8, I said that society has vested judges with a great deal of discretion for making decisions that affect the welfare of children, although some states limit judicial discretion by imposing a "nexus test." This test requires that the court ascertain how the parental behaviors or conditions of concern affect a child's well-being. Application of a nexus test limits judicial discrimination by making it difficult for a judge to deny custody to a parent based solely on a personal characteristic, such as a physical disability or sexual orientation, without regard to how the child is affected. In chapter 8 two case examples illustrate judicial decision making; one involves a parent with a disability and the other includes interracial marriage.

Custody may be legal or physical. If a parent is found to have abused or neglected a child, the court may remove the child from parental care and award temporary physical and legal custody to a department of social services or to a responsible adult, a relative, for example. As an option, the court may leave the child in the physical custody of the parent but grant legal custody to the department of social services, which can readily intervene if a parent misbehaves.

TESTIMONY OF CHILDREN

When the state prosecutes a case under a criminal statute, the rules regarding hearsay evidence are stricter than for a civil case because criminal prosecution implicates a person's constitutional rights under the Sixth Amendment (chapter 3). Nevertheless, criminal prosecution of child abuse is often hindered by (1) lack of medical evidence; (2) lack of eyewitnesses; and (3) weak investigatory methods that compromise data, precluding its use in court. Because corroborating evidence in the form of medical reports and eyewitness accounts is difficult to obtain, a child's testimony may be critical to successful prosecution, and a child may be called upon to testify despite concern about further victimizing the young person by having her or him testify and subjecting the child to cross-examination. Issues that may arise include (1) whether the child is competent to testify; (2) whether admissible evidence corroborates the testimony of a child who is not available to testify; and (3) how to protect a child from being traumatized while giving testimony and being cross-examined yet preserve the constitutional rights of the adult defendant.

Competency

People are competent to testify if they are intelligent enough to make their testimony worthwhile and if they recognize the need to testify truthfully. Most states assume that children are competent to testify unless their incompetency is established.

If a child's competency is in question, a judge may ask questions to determine whether the child (1) is capable of observing and recalling facts; (2) is able to relate facts to the judge or jury; and (3) has a moral sense of obligation to tell the truth.[22]

Protective Devices

Policy makers have struggled with protecting children who must testify from the possible trauma of cross-examination while maintaining the presumption of the accused's innocence and protecting that person's Sixth Amendment right to confront and cross-examine witnesses. Efforts to resolve this dilemma have led to the use of such protective devices as closed-circuit television and videotaped testimony, which are allowed in a majority of states. The U.S. Supreme Court has ruled twice on the use of protective devices.

In 1988 the Court heard a case that involved the use of a screen placed between a defendant and two child witnesses that blocked the defendant from the view of the children.[23] The defendant objected to the use of the screen on two grounds: that the screen violated his Sixth Amendment right to face-to-face confrontation because the screen prevented the witnesses from seeing him during their testimony; and that use of the screen would make him appear guilty to a jury. The judge had instructed the jury to draw no inference from use of the screen.

Attorneys for the state argued that the screen was necessary to protect the child from trauma during court proceedings. The U.S. Supreme Court rejected this argument because the justices found that the presumption of trauma was too generalized. Use of the screen violated the defendant's rights under the confrontation clause. Justice Sandra Day O'Connor, concurring with the majority, wrote a separate opinion in which she left the door open for use of other procedural devices to protect children. She recognized the "disturbing proportions of [child abuse] in today's society" and acknowledged the difficulty of detecting and prosecuting abuse because witnesses often are not available. According to O'Connor, the right to face-to-face confrontation is not absolute. The confrontation clause reflects a preference that may be overcome if "close examination of competing interests warrants."[24] Thus, while agreeing that the assumption that a child witness will suffer trauma from testifying was too general, she suggested that case-by-case determinations of the necessity for protective devices may suffice.

In *Maryland v. Craig* the U.S. Supreme Court again considered the use of protective devices. Here the question was whether a child witness could testify via closed-circuit television rather than in the courtroom with the defendant. The Court ruled that the use of closed-circuit television did not violate the defendant's Sixth Amendment rights, if the decision that the child might suffer trauma from testifying in the presence of the defendant was made on a case-by-case basis. Moreover, the procedures followed in Maryland contained safeguards to protect the defendant's constitutional rights. The child's competency to testify had to be determined, and the child testified under oath. The defendant had the opportunity for contemporaneous cross-examination, and the video monitor allowed the fact finder and the defendant to view the demeanor and body language of the witness giving testimony.[25]

THE DECISION AT THE CLOSE OF AN ADJUDICATORY HEARING

At the close of an adjudicatory hearing the judge must weigh all the evidence presented and determine whether the petitioner has met its burden of proof to demonstrate that the child was abused or neglected as defined in state law. Consider an example of how one court fulfilled this task.

C.F. left her ten-month-old child on a bunk bed for fifteen minutes while she prepared a bottle of milk.[26] The infant suffocated after getting caught in the side of the bed. The social worker who conducted the investigation determined that the mother had abused the child by leaving him unattended, but the death was subsequently ruled accidental. Nevertheless, the social worker's finding was recorded in state records, which C.F. sought to have expunged.

The statute defining abuse and neglect was the starting point for the court to determine whether C.F.'s actions constituted abuse. The statute stated, among other things, that *abuse* means (1) a recent act or failure to act that causes nonaccidental serious physical injury; or (2) serious physical neglect that constitutes prolonged or repeated lack of supervision or the failure to provide the essentials of life.

C.F. argued that she did not abuse her son under the first definition because his death was accidental. But the law did not define *accidental,* and the court faced the task of distinguishing abuse or deliberate injury from accidental injury. To determine whether an injury is nonaccidental the court turned to the criminal law and to the standard used to define criminal negligence. Criminal negligence exists when a person should be aware of the existence of a substantial and unjustifiable risk or one that may result from the conduct of the person charged. The risk must be such that failure to perceive it involves a gross deviation from the standard of care that a reasonable person would observe in the actor's situation.

The court found that C.F. could not have foreseen that her son would die when she left him on the bunk bed for fifteen minutes, and her failure to perceive such a risk did not involve a "gross deviation" from the care expected of a reasonable person in her situation. This conclusion was supported by the medical examiner's ruling that the infant's death was an accident. Note, however, that the decision that C.F.'s conduct was not a "gross deviation" from expected care was a judgment call, and another court might have ruled differently. The court also agreed with C.F.'s argument that leaving the infant on the bed for fifteen minutes was not serious physical neglect. The latter is defined as a physical condition caused by an action or by a failure to act that "endangers a child's life or development or impairs the child's functioning [as a result of] prolonged or repeated lack of supervision."[27]

The law did not define *prolonged* or *repeated*. The court opined that where a term is not defined, "[w]ords and phrases shall be construed according to rules of grammar and according to their common and approved usage."[28] Thus the court looked to the dictionary, which defines "to prolong" as "to lengthen in duration, scope or extent" and "to repeat" as a thing "said, done, or occurring again and again." Since the infant was left alone only once, the act was not a "repeated" act. The remaining question, then, is whether the period of time the infant was left alone was long enough to constitute a "prolonged" lack of supervision.

The court could not find any cases where "prolonged" was defined in the context of child abuse. Under such circumstances the court looked for definitions in other areas of the law. The court considered the concept of "prolonged" in the context of police interrogations and found that an interrogation that lasts no more than one hour is not "prolonged" but one that continues for more than five hours, throughout the night or day, or for five days is prolonged.

In light of these definitions, the fifteen minutes during which C.F. left her infant son alone on a bunk bed was not prolonged. But the court also considered the social worker's report, which referred to the home as "clean and neat," to C.F.'s family as "supportive," and to the absence of indications that C.F. neglected her son. He was not underweight and had not, according to the medical examiner, suffered trauma. Considering the cumulative effect of these circumstances, the court concluded that the infant was not a victim of "prolonged or repeated lack of supervision," nor had C.F. committed "serious neglect." The court hastened to note that in some situations, such as leaving an infant near a swimming pool or alone in an automobile on a hot day, fifteen minutes could be considered a prolonged lack of supervision.

THE DISPOSITIONAL HEARING

A dispositional hearing is held if the petitioner proves its case by a preponderance of the evidence or other applicable standard; otherwise, the case is dismissed. At the dispositional hearing the court will decide and order (1) where the child will live; (2) who will have legal custody; (3) what obligations, if any, it will place on the parent and department of social services; and, (4) when appropriate, a schedule for parent-child visitation. The dispositional hearing may be a continuation of the adjudicatory hearing or there may be a delay, if the court requires additional information, for example, a report concerning the child's home or schooling, the availability of relatives to care for the child, or services needed to assist the parent and/or child.

Dispositional options include (1) suspending judgment for a period of time and dismissing the case, if the department of social services receives no further reports; (2) releasing a child to a parent and placing the family under the supervision of social services; (3) placing a child in the custody of a relative or other suitable person or in the custody of social services for placement in a foster home or residential treatment setting; or (4) issuing an order of protection to prevent a person charged with abuse from coming near the child or the child's home. Legal custody may remain with a parent or be vested in a department of social services or its representative. The latter is most likely to occur if a child enters foster care but legal custody may be awarded to social services even if the child returns home, in order to impress the parents with the severity of their conduct and to enhance the likelihood of parental participation in social service programs.

Courts will grant parent-child visitation unless there is a compelling reason to curtail contact, such as when a petition to terminate parental rights has been or is to be filed or when a child's injuries were so serious as to suggest that continued contact could result in further harm to a child. Courts may limit the time, place, and duration of visits; if questions about child safety arise, the court may order supervised visitation. Note that several courts have found that prisoners have a right to visits with their children,[29] but this right may be limited if prison officials show that restrictions are necessary to maintain prison security.[30]

If a child is placed in foster care, the federal Adoption Assistance and Child Welfare Act (AACWA) and state statutes that incorporate its provisions provide the framework for subsequent judicial proceedings. This federal law also authorizes the disbursement of federal funds to provide services to children and their families and to defray the costs of maintaining children in foster care. We shall digress to review the major provisions of this law before I address review hearings.

Congress enacted the adoption assistance law in 1980. Its objectives were twofold: (1) to prevent the removal of children from their own homes, and (2) to facilitate the placement of these children in permanent family homes, either by reuniting them with their families of origin or through placement in adoptive homes.

The Indian Child Welfare Act addresses prevention, foster care placement, and adoption of native American children. The objective of this law is to protect the best interests of native American children within their tribal culture. Whether the concern is with placement in a substitute care setting or an adoptive setting, preference is given to placing native American children with extended family members, tribal members, or another Indian home or institution rather than a non-Indian home. Tribal courts, not a state's juvenile court, have decision-making authority, and when a tribal court exercises jurisdiction, it may hold hearings concerning placement in foster care, placement in a preadoptive home, and termination of parental rights.[31]

Title IV-E of the AACWA authorizes the use of federal matching funds to defray the costs that states incur in maintaining children in foster care. Title IV-E monies may support the placements of abused and neglected children, or status offenders, and of juvenile delinquents if (1) a judge determines that the state made reasonable efforts as required by the law; (2) they meet the procedural requirements, such as written case plans and case review; and (3) the child is placed in a licensed foster home, group home, or child-caring institution. Title IV-E funds may not be used to support placement in a detention facility. The likelihood that states will make the reasonable efforts required, develop case plans, and place children in a suitable setting is greatest for children adjudicated as neglected and abused and for some status offenders. But the state is less likely to try to prevent placement of delinquent youth if the youth are likely to be placed in a detention facility where the activities and services required by Title IV-E are difficult to provide.[32]

Title IV-B of the AACWA authorizes the expenditure of federal funds to enable the states to provide services for children and their families. In addition, each child in foster care must have a written case plan. Case plans must conform to federal law, which states that a case plan must (1) be in writing; (2) be developed no later than sixty days after the child was removed from the home; (3) include a discussion of (a) how the plan is designed to achieve a safe placement in the least restrictive, most family-like setting near the home of the parent(s), if the goal is reunification with the parents; and (b) how the placement is consistent with the best interests and special needs of the child. The plan must also (4) include a description of the services offered and provided to prevent removal of the child from the home and to reunify the family; and (5) must document the steps to finalize a placement when the case plan goal is or becomes adoption or placement in another permanent home. When the goal is adoption, the documentation must describe the child-specific recruitment efforts to find an adoptive home.[33] If the agency responsible for locating a foster home elects to place a child out of state, with a relative, for example, the state is likely to enter into a compact with the state in which the child will live. The Interstate Compact on the Placement of Children provides a framework for authorities in the state where the child will live (the receiving state) to evaluate the appropriateness of the selected placement and to provide information to the state seeking to place the child (the sending state). A plan will be developed between the two states concerning ongoing supervision of the child, and the compact will describe arrangements for financial support and medical care for the child. Now let us return to the subject of hearings.

Review Hearings

Federal law requires review hearings. They provide a forum for review of case plans, which must occur at least once every six months. At this hearing, relying on reports submitted by social workers and, where necessary, on testimony, the court determines whether progress is being made in attaining the goals of a case plan. If it is not, the court may consider a request for a change of plan, or it may order the child's social worker to explore alternative plans and to report to the court. The court will consider also whether reasonable efforts required have been made.

Review may be conducted by a juvenile court, other state court, a tribal court, or by an administrative panel. If the panel is chosen, it must include a member not responsible for the case management or delivery of services to either the child or family being reviewed.

A Permanency Planning Hearing

A permanency planning hearing must be held no later than twelve months after the child enters custody. The purpose of this review is to decide the permanency plan for the child, including whether the child should be returned home, placed for adoption, or continued in care for a specified period of time or on a permanent or long-term basis. If adoption is the plan, AACWA encourages the states to petition for termination of parental rights, to support a petition filed by another, or to file for legal guardianship for a child.[34] Evidence may be presented to the court in any of the ways identified in the discussion of review hearings.

A Termination of Parental Rights Hearing

A hearing to terminate parental rights will occur if the state has decided to petition the court to sever the ties between parent and child. ASFA encourages the state to file a petition to terminate parental rights or to support a petition filed by another party for children (1) who have been in foster care for fifteen of the most recent twenty-two months; (2) found by a court to have been abandoned; and (3) whose parent(s) murdered another of their children or caused serious bodily harm to another of their children. The exceptions include when (a) a child is in the care of a relative; (b) terminating parental rights is not in the child's best interests and the child-caring agency has documented a compelling reason to justify its decision not to pursue adoption; (c) the agency has determined that adoption is not appropriate; (d) there are no grounds for terminating parental rights; or (e) the child protective agency has failed to make the reasonable efforts required by the law. At a termination hearing the state must prove its case by clear and convincing evidence, a higher burden than the preponderance of the evidence standard used at the adjudicatory hearing.

A Best Interests Hearing

The court holds a best interests hearing because the state should not terminate parental rights unless a court has determined that termination of parental rights and adoption is in the best interests of the child. This hearing may be a continuation of the termination hearing or it may be held at a later date.

STATUS OFFENDERS AND JUVENILE DELINQUENTS

In addition to dependent children, juvenile courts have jurisdiction over status offenders and juvenile delinquents. Social workers and others involved in the juvenile justice system use a variety of terms to refer to status offenders: juveniles, minors, and children or persons "in need of supervision." And they may use a variety of acronyms to refer to children in the last category: JINS, MINS, CHINS, and PINS: juveniles/minors/children/persons in need of supervision. They are distinguished from juvenile delinquents, who are young people who have committed a crime, in that the behaviors that cause children in the first group to run afoul of the law would not be illegal if committed by an adult.

Status Offenders

What status offenders have in common with abused and neglected children is that the goal of the state is rehabilitation. Status offenses include truancy, running away, breaking curfew, "incorrigibility," or "ungovernability." It has been argued that terms such as *incorrigibility* or *ungovernability* violate due process, because they are so vague as to not inform the ordinary person of the behaviors that violate the law. Courts have rejected this argument, ruling that the conduct is easily understood and not unconstitutionally vague.[35]

Family courts may be ill equipped to deal with status offenders who fall between the cracks in a system designed to serve young children in foster homes and delinquents in secure facilities. Finding foster parents willing to care for teenagers is difficult, and youth who are said to be ungovernable or incorrigible may be ill suited to family life; this may be inferred because the majority of status offenders are referred by their parents. School personnel who report truancy run a close second in filing status offense petitions. According to the National Center for Juvenile Justice, law enforcement agencies report less than half of all cases that are formally processed (meaning that they are not diverted for services or dismissed). However, delinquency cases that involve law enforcement account for 86 percent of referrals.[36]

Foster home placements are hard to find, and alternative placements, such as group homes, are in short supply, as are services to assist the youth charged with a status offense.[37] Status offenders cannot be committed to secure detention facilities,[38] unless the youths violate a court order.[39] The federal Office of Juvenile Justice and Delinquency Prevention reports that some states hold status offenders in secure detention between referral and case disposition.[40]

Juvenile courts also have few options for dealing with youth who disobey court orders. Some states permit placement in a secure facility for a determinate period of time if a youth is found in contempt of court[41]; other states do not sanction such court action.[42] In New York, for example, a court can do no more to a youth who disobeys a court's order than it could do when the youth was first adjudicated. This limitation of the courts may result in the "recycling" of the young person through a system that has not been able to cope with him or her in the first place.[43]

Recall the hearing process outlined in table 10.2. When a youth is charged with a status offense, the process is both similar and different. Like dependency cases, action is initiated by filing a petition that must be served on appropriate parties. A petition may be filed by the state, by a youth's parent or guardian, and in some states by anyone who has been injured by the youth's behavior. If the youth was detained, the state will hold a preliminary hearing; if the youth is charged, she or he will appear for an adjudicatory hearing, followed by a dispositional hearing, if the court assumes jurisdiction over the young person. At the adjudicatory hearing the rules regarding admissible evidence and standard of proof are the same as those for abused or neglected children. If the youth is placed in a foster home or facility that is not a detention facility, the state may claim Title IV-E funds from the federal government, which entitles the youth to case plans, permanency planning, and review hearings. Status offender cases are distinguished from dependency cases in the efforts made to divert them from the juvenile justice system.

In 1996, the latest year for which data are available, approximately 48 percent of petitioned status offenders were not adjudicated.[44] Some cases are screened out at intake, when the case may be (1) dismissed, (2) diverted to a social service agency or community treatment program, or (3) resolved by subjecting the offender to a fine. If the intake worker is unsure what the correct disposition should be, the intaker may refer the case to a social worker or other professional employed by the probation department for an assessment and determination of whether mediation or referrals for service might resolve the difficulties. If a petition is filed, a prosecutor may request a waiver hearing to determine whether the youth should be tried as an adult (see the discussion later in this chapter) or adjudicated before a juvenile court judge.

If the courts adjudicate the juvenile as a status offender, they have a range of dispositional options. Relying on a predispositional report filed by a probation department, a court may (1) suspend judgment for a period of time; (2) commit the youth to a residential treatment facility or other institution for mental health services; (3) impose a fine, community service, or require restitution to the injured party; (3) order participation in a nonresidential counseling or treatment program; or (5) order that the youth be supervised by placing the youth in a group home, foster home, or other residential facility or on probation.

Juvenile Delinquents

The statutes that define delinquency are found mainly at the state level, although proceedings against a juvenile may be brought under the federal Juvenile Delinquency Act of 1948.[45] Under federal law a juvenile is a youth younger than eighteen who has violated a federal law, for example, by transporting stolen goods across state lines or destroying federal property.

State Law Definitions

States establish a maximum age for charging a person as a delinquent, and some states establish a minimum age below which a charge of delinquency cannot be lodged. For example, in New York a juvenile delinquent is a person older than seven and younger than sixteen who commits an act that would constitute a crime if committed by an adult but who is not held criminally responsible because of young age. This means that the youth's case will be heard in juvenile court.[46]

Procedural and Constitutional Rights

In the discussion in chapter 3 of the Fifth and Fourteenth Amendments to the U.S. Constitution, I said that due process in civil proceedings is less stringent than in criminal proceedings, because the former rarely results in loss of liberty. From the founding of the first juvenile court in 1899, informality has characterized juvenile court proceedings. Based on the assumption that all parties were acting in the best interests of the child, coupled with the courts' focus on rehabilitation rather than punishment, due process safeguards were not seen as necessary.

Whether the assumed benevolence of the court and its rehabilitative focus were sufficient to justify the lack of due process was addressed by the U.S. Supreme Court on behalf of Gerald Gault, who was arrested and accused of making obscene telephone calls to a neighbor.[47] Gault was adjudicated as a delinquent and committed to a state institution for the period of his minority. Because he was fifteen when adjudicated, his sentence could have lasted six years. If he had been an adult when he was arrested, the maximum penalty would have been a fine of $5 to $50 or imprisonment for as long as two months.

In 1967 the High Court ruled in favor of Gault. Its opinion challenged some basic premises of the juvenile court, particularly the claim that the courts' rehabilitative focus justified the lack of due process. Citing social science research, especially the finding that "a high percentage of youths [who come] before the juvenile court [were] two-time offenders," the justices questioned the success of the courts' rehabilitative mission. The Court stated that "the absence of substantive standards has not necessarily meant that children receive careful, compassionate, individualized treatment. The absence of procedural rules based upon constitutional principle has not always produced fair, efficient and effective procedures. Departures from established principles of due process have frequently resulted not in enlightened procedure, but in arbitrariness."[48] After handing down the *Gault* ruling, the Court extended some, but not all, due process protections to juveniles at the adjudicatory stage of delinquency proceedings. Juveniles would have the right to (1) be notified in writing of the specific charges; (2) consult a lawyer, including the right to be represented by a court-appointed counsel; (3) cross-examine complaining witnesses; (4) exercise their Fifth Amendment right not to testify; (5) have the state prove its case beyond a reasonable doubt[49]; and (6) be protected against double jeopardy.[50] However, juveniles charged with a crime and tried in juvenile court do not have a right to a jury trial.[51]

Waiving Juveniles to Adult Court

Between 1988 and 1994 juvenile arrests for violent crimes, such as murder, aggravated assault, robbery, and rape, increased 62 percent. The arrest rate declined thereafter, but in 1997 it was 25 percent higher than in 1988.[52] These data, troublesome in and of themselves, take on a new dimension when the media attend to the most sensational cases, for example, when two brothers aged thirteen and fourteen are charged with murdering their father and setting fire to the family home to hide their crime; when a youth is convicted of murdering a man whom he thinks stole his cell phone; or when a high school student is raped by a classmate. Media attention fuels public outrage and leads to a demand for stricter penalties for young people.[53] Throughout the 1990s states responded by enacting legislation to ease the process of transferring a juvenile to adult court,[54] and federal law allows a juvenile to be tried as an adult.[55]

Some states specify a minimum age for transfer to adult court, twelve or fourteen, for example, while in others the transfer may occur at any age. The youthful offender may be transferred based on (1) a judicial decision, (2) prosecutorial discretion, or (3) a statute that excludes certain juvenile offenders, based on age and offense, from the jurisdiction of the juvenile court.[56] Transfer is most likely if the youth (1) committed a serious offense, such as murder, aggravated assault, robbery, a violent sex offense, illegal drug use, or a property crime, such as robbery; (2) committed a series of offenses; or (3) has been found by a court to be unreceptive to treatment. For example, a juvenile was charged with armed carjacking in which a person was murdered; since carjacking is a federal crime, federal jurisdiction was warranted. Justification for transferring the case to adult court was found in a combination of factors, including that the juvenile (1) would have been tried as an adult in state court for the crime committed; (2) was an active participant in the crime that led to the murder; (3) had a previous record, first established when he was thirteen; (4) encouraged his peers to violence during a recent period of detention at a diagnostic center; and (5) had no effective treatment available to him as juvenile.[57]

Arrest

A youth may be taken into custody by a police officer. The rules reviewed in chapter 3 concerning warrants, custodial interviews, right to counsel, and Miranda warnings apply. As with status offenders, a young person may go through "intake" and be released, with or without a requirement for later appearance, or the youth may be detained. In some jurisdictions the youth may be remanded to a specialized court (see chapter 3) at this or a later stage, including postadjudication.

Appearances

The pretrial hearing process discussed in chapter 3 is generally applicable to youth charged with a crime, except that youth do not have a constitutional right to have a court consider bail. With some state-by-state variations, the following can be said: If a young person was detained before a petition was filed, a detention hearing will take place and a probable cause determination made. If a petition has been filed, the initial appearance will be the first hearing. At the youth's first appearance, whether at a detention hearing or an initial appearance, the young person will be informed of the charges, of his or her right to remain silent, and of the right to be represented by counsel, and that counsel will be appointed for the unrepresented youth.[58]

If the court determines that the evidence presented is not sufficient to bind the youth over for an adjudicatory hearing, the case may be dismissed and the youngster released to the custody of a parent or other legally responsible adult. Even if an adjudicatory hearing is scheduled, the youth should be released unless the court finds it is highly likely that she or he will not return to court when expected or if release creates a serious risk that a crime will be committed. The court may set terms and conditions for release, such as reporting to probation or involvement in a treatment program. If an adjudicatory hearing is scheduled, plea negotiations may take place.

A youth charged as an adult will be subject to the criminal trial procedure described in chapter 3. If the youth is tried as a juvenile, the procedure is similar in many respects, but the youth does not have a right to a jury trial, and juvenile proceedings may be closed to public scrutiny and records sealed.

Dispositional Options

If the state proves its case beyond a reasonable doubt, the court will assume jurisdiction over the young person and schedule a dispositional hearing. The court may order a predispositional report to help it decide the best alternative. Depending upon state law, a youth may be (1) conditionally discharged, meaning that she or he need not report to probation but must follow any order issued by the court. Such orders could include orders to (a) attend school, (b) obey parents, (c) refrain from designated activities or from going to designated places, or (d) cooperate with mental health or social service personnel. The court could also (2) place the juvenile under the supervision of the probation department and issue any of the orders listed; (3) release the juvenile to the care of a parent, relative, or other suitable adult, including the department of social services for placement in a foster home or treatment facility; or (4) place the juvenile in a secure detention facility.

If the young person was tried as an adult, she or he may be confined for a term of years. In twenty-two states, if the youth is found guilty of a capital crime committed when she or he was at least sixteen, the death penalty may be imposed.[59]

Legal Liability and Placement of Children in State Custody

In the earlier discussion of the case of Joshua DeShaney, I reported that the U.S. Supreme Court found no liability on the part of the state for failure to protect Joshua from the injuries he suffered at his father's hands. At the same time, the Court suggested that the result might have been different if Joshua been in state custody, which the Court likened to incarceration or institutionalization that gives rise to an affirmative duty of protection. The analogy rested on two cases. In 1976 a prisoner filed suit in which he argued that he had been denied necessary medical care and that the denial violated the Eighth Amendment's prohibition against cruel and unusual punishment.[60] The Court reasoned that the prisoner, unable to arrange for his own medical care, relied on the state. If the state failed to provide care and its failure amounted to "deliberate indifference," such failure would constitute cruel and unusual punishment in violation of the Eighth Amendment. In 1982 the High Court revisited the question of the state's obligation to those in its care when it reviewed a suit filed by the mother of a mentally retarded boy, who was involuntarily incarcerated in a state institution. She argued that her son, who had suffered injuries in the institution, was entitled to be confined under safe conditions, to be free from bodily restraint, and to receive training.[61] The Court agreed, finding that the liberty clause of the Fourteenth Amendment gave rise to a claim that confinement should be under "reasonably safe conditions . . . [that the boy was entitled to] freedom from unreasonable bodily restraints, and such minimally adequate training as reasonably might be required by these interests."[62] These cases have two commonalities: first, that the parties were involuntarily confined, and, second, that they were dependent on the state for their care and protection.

Since 1981 federal circuits have addressed the question, "Does the liberty clause of the Fourteenth Amendment confer on children in state custody, and who have been placed in foster homes, a right to be protected from harm?" The courts for seven circuits have held that children involuntarily placed in state custody have a right to be protected from harm[63]; three ruled that no such right exists, but in two cases the child's placement was voluntary.[64] In the remaining circuit the appellate court did not address the question of a child's right to safety, because it ruled that social workers were performing a prosecutorial function and thus had absolute immunity from suit (chapter 7).[65]

All eleven cases rest on constitutional claims. The question is whether the concept of liberty in the Fourteenth Amendment imposes on the state a duty to protect from harm those it has involuntarily taken into custody. Claims resting on statutory law form another basis for litigation. I referred to this in discussing legal liability in child abuse investigations where I reported that two federal circuits have ruled that plaintiffs could not prevail in a suit filed under CAPTA, because the federal law is not specific and detailed enough to sustain a client's claim that she or he is owed any particular benefit. Plaintiffs filing suit under the AACWA have argued that the statute is specific, imposing certain obligations on the state, for example, to develop and implement case plans and to conduct periodic review hearings.[66]

Until 1992 a number of courts had acknowledged the right of individuals to sue states under the AACWA.[67] In 1992 the U.S. Supreme Court ruled that individuals could not bring such suits, because it had concluded that (1) Congress, in passing the AACWA, had not intended to confer on individuals a right to sue states to enforce the provisions of the act, and (2) the measure's "reasonable efforts" requirement was too vague to be enforced.[68] In 1994 Congress amended the AACWA to confer on children and their parents the right to sue states to enforce all provisions in the law except the reasonable efforts provision.[69] Since 1994 federal courts have disagreed about whether children may bring suit against the state under the AACWA, although a majority has supported a child's right to sue.[70]

SUMMARY

This chapter discussed the legal framework for the state to intervene in family life on behalf of abused and neglected children and to assert its authority over status offenders and juvenile delinquents, as well as the procedures that state courts follow when allegations are brought against parents and youth.

Each state has vested jurisdiction in a court, usually the juvenile or family court, to hear cases that involve children and youth. The judicial process is initiated when a petition, sometimes called a complaint, is filed with a court; jurisdiction is obtained by serving the petition on a child's legal custodian or on the youth charged when a status offense or delinquency is the matter at hand. If the judicial process begins with the arrest of a young person, law enforcement must apprise the youth of her or his Miranda rights and the rights afforded to an adult arrestee, including protection against unreasonable search and seizure and the right to counsel.

Whether the court seeks jurisdiction because of abuse or neglect, a status offense, or delinquent act, the judicial hearings are similar in type and progression. Whenever the state places a child in foster care or arrests and detains a young person, the state must justify its action before a court. Preliminary hearings—whether denominated as emergency hearings, shelter hearings, probable cause hearings, detention hearings, or pretrial hearings—are convened for this purpose. An initial hearing also provides an opportunity for the court to apprise the charged party of the allegations and of the party's right to counsel.

A conference may take place and a settlement may be reached before an adjudicatory hearing is held, thereby avoiding a formal finding. When a youth is charged with a status offense or a crime, the state may make an effort to divert the young person from the judicial system by requiring the youthful offender to participate in counseling or another form of treatment.

At the adjudicatory hearing the petitioner must prove each element of its case by a preponderance of the evidence or, when the charge is delinquency, beyond a reasonable doubt. If the petitioner fails to meet its burden of proof, the case will be dismissed. Otherwise, the court will enter an order of disposition and (1) suspend judgment; (2) release a child to a parent and place the family under the supervision of social services; (3) place a child with a relative, other suitable person, or the department of social services for out-of-home placement; or (4) issue an order of protection to prevent a person charged with abuse from coming near the child or the child's home. If the youth is adjudicated as a status offender or delinquent, the court may (1) impose a fine, period of community service, or require restitution to the injured party; (2) order participation in a counseling program; or (3) place the offender on probation. Youth convicted of a crime may be incarcerated in a secure detention facility.

Review hearings at six-month intervals and a permanency planning hearing twelve months after placement will be held for those placed in foster care. The purpose of both hearings is to ensure that progress is being made in attaining the goal of a child's case plan. If the state moves to terminate parental rights, a special hearing will be convened, including a hearing to determine whether termination of parental rights is in the best interests of the child.

The case of a young person charged with a crime may be transferred to adult court. Transfer is most likely when the youth (1) committed a serious offense such as murder or aggravated assault; (2) committed a series of offenses; or (3) has been found by a court to be unreceptive to treatment. If charged as an adult, the youth will be subject to criminal, not civil, procedures. If tried as a juvenile, the procedures followed are similar to those afforded an adult, except that young people do not have a right to a jury trial in juvenile court and juvenile court proceedings are routinely closed to public.

Children and their parents have sued social workers and their employing agencies. The courts in two federal circuits have ruled that individuals cannot bring suit under the Child Abuse Prevention and Treatment Act because the law is neither specific nor detailed enough to sustain a claim that any particular benefit is owed; and the U.S. Supreme Court has ruled that the state does not have a duty to protect a child from injuries suffered at the hands of his father with whom he lived, even though the family had been reported to child protective services. When children are in state custody, courts for seven of eleven federal circuits have held that the liberty clause of the Fourteenth Amendment confers on children in state custody a right to be protected from harm, and a majority of federal courts, considering whether children have a right to sue a state for benefits conferred by the Adoption Assistance and Child Welfare Act, have ruled in favor of the children.

11

Adoption

THIS CHAPTER is about adoption, which, as I said in chapter 8, is one of the ways in which legally recognized families are created. The exact number of children adopted each year is not known. The National Adoption Information Clearinghouse estimated the figure at 120,000 children each year throughout the 1990s, including children adopted through public agencies as well as those adopted privately.[1]

Social workers are significant actors in all phases of the adoption process. Involvement begins when a social worker (1) meets an individual or couple who wishes to adopt, (2) comes into contact with a child in need of a permanent family, or (3) is asked by a court, an attorney, or a social service agency (a) to prepare a preadoption home study, (b) consult on any of the myriad issues that arise in a pending adoption, or (c) testify on matters before the court.

This chapter is divided into two parts. Part 1 presents an overview of adoption law, and the second part reviews current issues in adoption law. Before beginning, I wish to make several points about terminology. Single people as well as couples adopt children. I use the plural *parents* in referring to those who adopt, unless a particular example calls for the singular. The term *legal parent* refers to biological parents and to adoptive parents who have already completed the adoption process. Finally, public and voluntary agencies arrange for adoptions. Public agencies include those operated directly by a unit of government as well as voluntary agencies that have a contract to provide services to children for whom the public sector is responsible. However, voluntary agencies also arrange private adoptions that do not involve the children that these agencies are under contract to assist.

PART 1—ADOPTION LAW

The purpose of adoption is to provide a family for children whose parents (1) have died, (2) voluntarily relinquished their rights, or (3) had their rights terminated. When a child is adopted, all rights and responsibilities that existed between the child and its biological parents are transferred to the adoptive parents. The legal relationship is then similar to that between a child and its biological parents.

As with other family law matters, adoption is controlled mainly by state law, and only state courts and Indian tribal courts can finalize adoptions. Nevertheless, as we saw in chapter 8, the rights of a biological father are affected by decisions of the U.S. Supreme Court in its rulings concerning involuntary termination of parental rights. In addition, Supreme Court decisions affect (1) a parent's right to legal counsel, including court-appointed counsel; (2) a parent's right to receive notice before the state intervenes in family life; (3) the burden of proof that the state must meet to sever parental ties; and (4) the circumstances that grant to tribal courts jurisdiction over native American children. Also, federal statutes (1) control the adoption of children from foreign countries; (2) make it a violation of the Civil Rights Act of 1964 to consider race as a factor in adoption; and (3) allow government funds to be used (a) to subsidize the adoption of children with special needs[2] and (b) to reward states that increase the number of children adopted.[3]

Types of Adoption

Adoption is classified as regular, private or independent, and black market. Black market adoptions involve baby selling, which is illegal in all states.

Regular Adoptions

Regular adoptions are those arranged by public or voluntary social service agencies. Regular adoptions are characterized by the provision of services (1) to help biological parents decide whether to relinquish a child, (2) to help adoptive parents find an appropriate child and complete the adoption process, and (3) to place a child in an adoptive home most suitable to her or his needs. Postadoption services may be offered to assist adoptive parents and children through the process of adjustment. In a regular adoption the child may be relinquished to the agency, rather than to the adopting parents, and the child may spend some time in foster care before placement in an adoptive home.

Private Adoptions

Private adoptions, also called independent or direct placement adoptions, are arranged (1) directly by a birth mother and prospective adoptive parents or (2) indirectly through an intermediary, such as an attorney, physician, clergy, or adoption agency. In some states agencies that arrange private adoptions must be licensed, but otherwise state involvement is limited to the judicial process through which an adoption is finalized. In contrast to regular adoptions, children privately adopted are relinquished directly to adoptive parents.

Birth parents and those wishing to adopt may prefer private adoptions because (1) all may participate in the selection process, in contrast to agency adoption where birth and adoptive parents may never meet; (2) the newborn goes directly to an adoptive home rather than into foster care; (3) birth parents have the option to select the adoptive parents and to negotiate ongoing contact with their child; and (4) the adoptive parents have the chance to learn about their child's social and medical history directly from the birth parents. A disadvantage of private adoptions is that the birth mother may change her mind, causing emotional distress to the couple hoping to adopt and the loss of any sums paid for pregnancy- and birth-related expenses.

Private adoptions are costly and thus limited to a narrow segment of the population. Costs are estimated to run between $8,000 and $30,000,[4] compared to $2,500 for an agency adoption, and the state may subsidize an agency adoption when the child has been in foster care. Costs for private adoptions are reduced when (1) the birth mother has health insurance, (2) her medical expenses during pregnancy and at birth are ordinary, and (3) the adoptive parents and birth mother live in the same state, eliminating travel. Costs may escalate when an intermediary charges a high fee.

To eliminate the notion that private adoptions are a form of baby selling, most states regulate through statute the expenses and fees that may be paid. Some states require that an accounting be presented to the court overseeing the adoption, and the court subsequently may not allow certain costs. Consider the following case.

Katherine and Timothy petitioned a New York court to adopt an eight-month-old whose parents consented to the adoption.[5] The adoptive parents paid for counseling to help the biological mother cope with the emotional impact of releasing her child; they also paid for her travel costs, certain living expenses, medical costs, and attorney fees. Katherine and Timothy submitted the required affidavit itemizing sums paid to the birth mother. In its ruling the court began with reference to the state's public policy that does not allow an adopting couple to pay costs not related to pregnancy. Thus the costs associated with prenatal care, physician and nurse fees, and hospital expenses associated with birth were permitted if payment was made directly to the professional or institution.[6]

The affidavit that Katherine and Timothy submitted showed that their payments to the biological mother covered some living expenses, including rent and utilities, and other costs associated with maintaining a household. The sums covered a period when the birth mother lived with her husband and children. Because the husband benefited, the court disallowed expenses not related to the pregnancy. The judge also disallowed monies advanced to the mother to cover living expenses for five weeks after delivery, sums paid to her for the costs of raising her one-year-old, and the down payment for an automobile. The court did not find persuasive the birth mother's claim that she was in "dire financial need" and that the allowance was essential to her health and safety. To remedy the violation the attorney for the adoptive parents was ordered to have the disallowed amounts returned to his clients.

Standing to Petition a Court to Terminate Parental Rights

Standing refers to the right to petition a court and ask for something the court has the power to grant. Those seeking to adopt must ensure that a child is available to be adopted; a child who is not an orphan is not available unless the rights of biological parents are terminated. However, efforts to terminate parental rights involuntarily are viewed as an attack on the sanctity of family life, and courts will protect against this intrusion by limiting the categories of people with standing to pursue this outcome. Those with standing to petition a court to terminate parental rights include

- A unit of government responsible for caring for neglected and abused children or a private agency in whose care a child has been placed.
- Foster parents who are or recently were providing care for the child, when a statute confers this right, or when a court sanctions such action. Courts are not likely to do so unless foster parents are seeking to adopt the child.
- A parent or stepparent.
- In some states a person acting in loco parentis, meaning one who acts as a child's temporary guardian, or any interested party.

Who May Adopt?

At one time agency policies regarding who was eligible to adopt reflected what the Child Welfare League of America called a search for the ideal parents. Requirements were often rigid, restricting adoption to relatively young and affluent couples who were not able to conceive a child. The search for the ideal changed in the last quarter of the twentieth century. The availability of abortion on demand and the social acceptance of single parenthood decreased significantly the number of newborns and infants available for adoption. The result was that the universe of children available for adoption through public and many voluntary agencies became synonymous with children in foster care, who tended to be older and seen by many as less desirable than a newborn. This decrease in the number of available newborns led to an increase in private adoptions, including intercountry adoptions, which in turn caused the public sector to rethink its standards concerning who could adopt. State statutes reflect these changes. Connecticut's Termination of Parental Rights and Adoption Statute captures the current thinking of many legislators and professionals in the adoption field. The statute reinforces the rule that the best interests of the child should drive the search for adoptive parents. It states that a child's best interests are promoted (1) by having people in the child's life who manifest a deep concern for the child's growth and development; (2) by having as many people loving and caring for the child as possible; and (3) by making the child a part of a loving, supportive, and stable family, whether that family is a nuclear, extended, split, blended, single-parent, adoptive, or foster family.[7]

The general rule across the nation is that any single adult or married couple, both of whom wish to adopt, may do so.[8] A stepparent may adopt a stepchild with the consent of the parent's spouse, so long as the rights of the noncustodial parent have been terminated; in a handful of states a cohabiting partner may petition a court to adopt the partner's child even though the adults are not married.[9] In some states a married person who is legally separated is eligible to adopt without the consent of her or his spouse. In Florida a homosexual may not adopt,[10] although homosexuals may become foster parents.[11] Some states require that the petitioner be a resident of the state for a statutorily specified period of time before petitioning a court to adopt a child.

The federal Adoption and Safe Families Act requires that states conduct criminal record checks of prospective adoptive parents, creating an exception to the general rule that any adult may adopt. Unless expressly exempted by state law, federal law provides that an adult convicted of felony child abuse or neglect, spousal abuse, rape, sexual assault, or homicide cannot become an adoptive parent of a child whose adoption will be subsidized with federal funds (see the discussion of adoption subsidies later in this chapter).[12]

Cohabiting Couples

Cohabiting couples seek to adopt in two situations. First, a couple may wish to adopt a child that is not legally the child of either party. Second, one person may seek to adopt the child of her or his partner. The latter are called "second-parent adoptions," and they are analogous to adoptions by a stepparent. Whether adoption is possible under either set of circumstances depends upon state law. For example, Utah does not allow adoption by a cohabiting couple whose relationship is not a legally binding marriage,[13] and Mississippi does not allow couples of the same gender to adopt.[14] However, a majority of states have no express prohibition against adoption by unmarried couples.

If there is no statutory rule on adoption by cohabiting couples, a court's approach to interpreting a state's adoption statute is key to understanding the outcome of a couple's quest. For example, an appellate court in Louisiana denied the adoption petition of an unmarried couple. The state's adoption statute allows a single person or a married couple to adopt a child, and the court reasoned that the couple was neither a "single person" nor a married couple.[15] This court took a literal approach to statutory interpretation. Using such an approach, a court may reason that had the legislature meant to sanction adoption by unmarried couples, it would have included the required language in the statute. Although the court may think that adoption is a good result for the child, it may also think that it is not within its authority to grant the petition.

A literal approach to statutory interpretation stands in contrast to a public policy approach by which a court may determine that it has the power to achieve the result sought by the statute even if the course that it takes goes beyond the express language in the statute. A New York court did just that. Noting that the state's adoption law did not expressly preclude adoption by a cohabiting couple, but stressing that the purpose of the statute was to act in the best interests of the child, the court approved the adoption of a child who had lived with two men since her birth. The court noted that the cohabitants had lived together for twenty-four years, that the child was very attached to both, as well as to members of their extended families, and that each male cohabitant acted as father to the child and the child saw him as his father.[16]

Second-Parent Adoptions

The phrase "second-parent adoption," or "stepparent adoption," refers to an adoption by a spouse or partner of a child's legal parent. When the couple involved is married, the general rule is that the spouse may adopt with the written consent of the legal parent, if the other biological parent is deceased or had her or his rights terminated. If the couple is not married, the outcome of an effort to adopt a partner's child will depend upon the court's approach to statutory analysis. Some courts approach this task with a literal interpretation of the terms in a statute, while others will interpret terms with reference to the goals that the statute seeks to achieve. Two examples will help to illustrate these different approaches.

In 1992 Annette petitioned a Wisconsin court to adopt Angel Lace, the daughter of Annette's partner, Georgina. The women had lived together, coparenting Angel Lace for approximately two years. The barrier that the women confronted was that under Wisconsin law a child is not eligible for adoption unless the rights of both parents have been terminated, except when the person seeking to adopt is the spouse of the child's parent.[17] Although the court found that the adoption would be in the best interests of the child, it ruled that it could not authorize the adoption. Annette was not Georgina's spouse under Wisconsin law, and Angel Lace would be available for adoption only if Annette's rights were terminated. This ruling speaks only to the conditions that would have to exist for the child to become available. Whether the court would have sanctioned the adoption had Angel Lace been available cannot be known. Confronted with similar facts, courts in other states have reached the same conclusion as the Wisconsin court's.[18]

However, a Massachusetts court reached the opposite conclusion. As with Annette and Georgina, Helen and Susan had a long-standing relationship. They had coparented Tammy, and the court found that the adoption would be in the child's best interests.

The Massachusetts statute allowed adoption by a "person," and the Court asked whether the singular could be read in the plural. It could, the court ruled, unless doing so would result in a ruling that was inconsistent with legislative intent. Since the goal of the adoption statue was to further the best interests of the child, and since adoption, whether the individuals were married or not, furthers attainment of that goal, construing the term in the plural enhances, rather than defeats, the intent of the legislature.[19]

Children Who Are Available for Adoption

As I noted earlier in this chapter, children are available for adoption (1) upon the death of their parents, (2) after their parents voluntarily relinquish their custodial rights, or (3) when a court involuntarily terminates parental rights based on a finding that the parent is not a fit custodian and that adoption is in the child's best interests. I shall begin with a discussion of voluntary relinquishment. Then, in the context of a case example, I will discuss and illustrate involuntary termination of parental rights.

Voluntary Relinquishment

Parents may consent to the adoption of their child, and they may set conditions for their consent, such as naming the person or couple who will adopt.[20] Consent is not an issue if the court finds that the parents (1) are incompetent, (2) have abandoned their child, or (3) have engaged in certain behaviors described in state law that allow a court to involuntarily terminate parental rights (see the discussion later in this chapter). In some states a father's consent may be given before or immediately after birth, but most states will not take a mother's prebirth relinquishment. In addition, states generally impose a post-birth waiting period of several days before a woman may relinquish her rights, as well as a statutorily defined period of time in which a woman who has agreed to the adoption of her child may change her mind. In some states, however, a relinquishment given in front of a judicial officer is irrevocable. If the child is in the custody of an agency, or if the court has appointed a guardian of the child, state law requires consent of the agency or guardian. Many states require the consent of the children if they have attained a certain age, twelve or fourteen, for example, although state law may confer on a judge the authority to override a young person's objection. We shall begin with a case example.

Voluntary Termination of a Father's Rights: An Example Amelia was four years old in the spring of 1999 when the Norfolk County Department of Social Services filed a petition charging her mother, Ellen, with neglect (I have changed all names and other identifying characteristics). The infant was placed in foster care, and the court determined that Ellen had neglected her daughter. The court ordered the county to provide Ellen with services that would enable her to regain custody of Amelia. As we shall see later, the county eventually would proceed to terminate Ellen's rights. Here we are concerned with Amelia's father, Thomas, who voluntarily relinquished his rights in the spring of 2000.

As I suggested earlier, the point at which a surrender of parental rights becomes final and irrevocable depends upon where it is given. When a surrender is given in New York in front of a judge, it is final and irrevocable when given by the parent and signed by the court (see paragraph 1, fig. 11.1). If a surrender is "extrajudicial," meaning that it is given outside court, it is not final for forty-five days, during which time a parent may revoke consent.

As I have discussed in several places in this text, the Constitution protects parent-and-child rights, and it is imperative that a parent understand the consequences of surrendering her or his rights. Five paragraphs in figure 11.1 address these important issues. Paragraph 2 refers to a parent's right to consult with a lawyer and the right in New York—but not all states—to have a lawyer appointed if a parent is poor; paragraph 7 refers to the right to make the decision to give up or retain parental rights without force or threat of adverse legal consequences.

Paragraph 8 is especially important. Here the court avers that it has fulfilled its obligation to inform the parent of his rights and of the consequences of his behavior. This judicial affirmation assures all who are concerned that the parent's consent was informed, and it protects the child and adoptive parents,

FIGURE 11.1

Judicial Surrender

In the Matter of the Surrender for Adoption of a Child Whose Name Is

Amelia Cairnes JUDICIAL SURRENDER

(1) THIS SURRENDER BECOMES FINAL AND IRREVOCABLE IMMEDIATELY UPON EXECUTION AND ACKNOWLEDGMENT BY THE PARENT, AND THE PARENT CANNOT BRING A CASE IN COURT TO REVOKE THE SURRENDER OR TO REGAIN CUSTODY OF THE CHILD.

(2) Before signing the surrender, the parent has the right to speak to a lawyer . . . and any other person she or he wishes. The parent has the right to have [a] lawyer . . . present . . . at the time of the signing of the surrender. . . . The parent has the right to ask the court to appoint a lawyer free of charge if the parent cannot afford to hire one; also, the parent has the right to have support counseling;

(3) Upon execution and acknowledgment of this surrender, the parent is giving up all rights to have custody, visit with, speak with, write to or learn about the child, forever,

(4) unless the parent and . . . agency have agreed to different terms . . . written in this surrender, or, if the parent registers with the adoption information register . . . [indicating] that the parent may be contacted at any time after the child reaches the age of eighteen years . . . if . . . the parent and the adult child choose;

(5) The child will be adopted without the parent's consent and without further notice to the parent, and will be adopted by any person that the agency chooses, (6) unless this surrender paper contains the name of the person or persons who will be adopting the child; and

(7) The parent cannot be forced to sign this surrender . . . and cannot be punished . . . for refusing to sign. . . .

I, Thomes Cairnes, residing in New York, New York, and having my place of business in . . . am the father of Amelia Cairnes, do hereby voluntarily surrender guardianship and custody of my daughter, to the Norfolk County Department of Social Services, a duly authorized agency.

Dated:

STATE OF NEW YORK
COUNTY OF Norfolk

(8) On this 21ST day of March, 2000, before me personally came Thomas Cairnes, the person described in and who executed the foregoing instrument, and he acknowl-

edged that he executed the same. I have informed such person of the consequences of the act of execution and acknowledgment . . . including that the parent is giving up all the rights to have custody, visit with, speak with, write or learn about the child, forever, unless the parent and the authorized agency agree to different terms . . . or if the parent and the adult child register with the adoption information register. I have informed the parent that the surrender becomes final and irrevocable immediately upon its execution and acknowledgment. I have informed him of the right to be represented by legal counsel of his own choosing; of the right to obtain supportive counseling and of any rights to assigned counsel. . . . I have given him a copy of this surrender upon execution thereof.

____

Hon. Sandra Creemor
Family Court Judge

should the parent try to rescind his revocation by claiming that he was ignorant of the consequences of his actions. Paragraphs 3 and 5, which appear above the parent's signature, further ensure that the parent has read, or has had read to him or her, the text describing the consequences of surrendering parental rights with reference to future contact with a child (paragraph 3), and to the right of the agency to place the child for adoption with a family of its choice (paragraph 5).

Withdrawal of Consent State laws vary regarding the withdrawal of consent. Pennsylvania, whose law allows a parent to revoke an extrajudicial consent at any time before a final adoption decree is entered, represents one extreme.[21] New York, as I noted earlier, allows a parent the opportunity to revoke within forty-five days but not at all if the parent gave consent before a judge.[22]

Involuntary Termination of Parental Rights

Involuntary termination of parental rights is the most extreme form of state intervention in family life. In reviewing the voluntary relinquishment by Amelia's father in figure 11.1, I discussed the consequences of having one's rights terminated. This section begins with a discussion of the procedural rights retained by parents when action is taken to terminate their rights without consent. Next I will discuss the evidentiary burden that must be met by the organization or individual who has asked the courts to terminate parental rights.

Then I review grounds for terminating parental rights that appear in the statutes of most states.

Involuntary Termination and Procedural Rights

In chapter 3, I referred to procedural rules that come into play when acts of government threaten to deprive an individual of life, liberty, or property, and chapter 8 says that parents have a constitutionally protected liberty interest in their relationship with their child. It follows that when the state seeks to terminate parental rights, it must ensure that certain due process rights of biological parents are not violated.[23] Among these are (1) the right to receive notice of the charges levied by the state, (2) the right to prepare and respond to charges, and (3) the right to be represented by counsel.

Notice As I noted in chapter 10, the parties to a judicial proceeding are to receive notice. The U.S. Supreme Court carved out an exception in 1983. In the case of *Lehr v. Robertson* the Court found an exception to the requirement for notice in termination of parental rights cases. The case before the Court involved the parental rights of a putative father who never established a relationship with his child. His rights were terminated without notice.[24] The High Court sanctioned the move because the father chose not to register his paternity with the state's putative father registry, which was necessary if he wanted to protect his rights.

However, in 1988 the Missouri Supreme Court ruled that a mother should have been notified when the state proved that she abandoned her child and terminated her rights.[25] Unlike the facts before the U.S. Supreme Court in *Lehr*, Missouri did not have a registry to which the mother could have submitted her name, and notice was required as a condition for terminating her rights.

Right to Counsel Parents have a right to be represented by counsel but no constitutional right to court-appointed counsel. Some states provide counsel for indigent parents by statute, and in others a court may decide that counsel is required. In ruling that there is no constitutional right to court-appointed counsel, the justices of the U.S. Supreme Court justified their ruling by referring to the different outcomes of criminal and civil procedures. Unlike a criminal proceeding, civil proceedings do not entail a loss of liberty, so no Sixth Amendment right to state-financed counsel applies (see chapter 3). The High Court admonished lower courts to weigh the following factors when rendering decisions regarding appointed counsel: (1) the private interest affected by the official action (here the permanent severing of ties between parent and child); (2) the risk that the procedures used will result in an erroneous deprivation of the interests involved and whether additional safeguards will be of value; and

(3) the government's interest, including the fiscal and administrative burdens that the additional or substitute procedures would entail.[26]

It is not difficult to imagine that a parent who is not represented by counsel will be at a disadvantage during a trial. Advocating for oneself by presenting evidence, challenging evidence presented by others, cross-examining witnesses, and carrying out these tasks in a manner prescribed by law necessitates skills not generally found in the repertoire of laypersons. Nevertheless, courts have denied parents' requests for appointed counsel when the parents failed to (1) make the request in a timely manner; (2) appear at a hearing; (3) participate with previous counsel; (4) establish poverty; (5) raise a first objection to the child's adoption on appeal; or (6) demonstrate an ability to participate without counsel, for example, by testifying on their own behalf and cross-examining witnesses.[27]

Involuntary Termination of Parental Rights—Evidentiary Nurden

In chapter 3, I said that to obtain a conviction at a criminal trial the state must produce evidence of all the statutory elements of a crime. The same is true in a civil trial. For example, when the state seeks to terminate parental rights. it must prove all the elements contained in the statute that it cites in support of its position that parent-child ties must be severed. But in a criminal case the state must prove the statutory elements beyond a reasonable doubt. In contrast, the state's burden in a civil proceeding to terminate parental rights is to prove its case by clear and convincing evidence, meaning that the evidence it offers is sufficient to establish with reasonable certainty that the facts asserted are true.

Permanent neglect is one basis for terminating parental rights in New York, and other states have statutes with similar elements. To prove permanent neglect the state must show that (1) reasonable or "diligent efforts" were made to strengthen the parent-child relationship, unless a judicial ruling dispenses with this requirement, and (2) that a parent failed to plan for the future of the child although physically and financially able to do so.[28]

But the evidence presented in court to establish that a parent neglected a child may not be sufficient to terminate parental rights for two reasons. First, in a neglect proceeding the state meets its burden of proof if the evidence that it offers in support of an allegation is greater or more convincing than the evidence offered in opposition to it. This "preponderance of the evidence standard" (chapter 3) is the lowest standard of proof and is justified because the state's objective in a neglect proceeding is temporary, not permanent, interference in a parent's relationship with the child. And this low evidentiary burden provides the court with maximum flexibility to protect children. Because efforts to terminate parental rights involve constitutionally protected rights (chapter 8), the burden of proof is greater, and a court may not find the evidence introduced at a neglect hearing sufficient.

Second, to establish the elements of permanent neglect, unless dispensed with by the court, the state must present evidence describing both the services provided by the state as well as the parent's response to the state's efforts to reunite the family. Some of this evidence may be available when the neglect charge is heard because of the interval between the child's placement and the date of the hearing on the neglect charge. However, the available evidence may not be sufficient to satisfy the court that the state did all that was expected of it, and the documentation may not be sufficient to satisfy the higher burden of proof for which it is offered.

Grounds for Involuntary Termination of Parental Rights

Abandonment

Abandonment is defined as desertion for a statutorily specified time period. Six months to one year is common, but a court may use a shorter period for a younger child, for example, sixty days for a child younger than six months.[29] The party seeking to terminate parental rights based on abandonment may be required to show that the parent intended to sever ties with the child.[30] Intent may be inferred from such conduct as failure to maintain contact with a child when able to do so or failure to provide financial support to a child, which will suffice to show a conscious decision to abandon.[31]

Parent-child contact may not defeat an effort to prove abandonment.[32] Thus a trial court's decision to terminate a mother's parental rights was upheld on appeal. Even though she visited with her daughter five to seven times when the child was hospitalized, she had initiated only three visits in the seven years before the hospitalization.

Confinement as a Form of Abandonment *Confinement* refers to conditions that limit a parent's ability to interact with a child and includes incarceration in prisons and mental hospitals and limitations on parental freedom that result from being on probation or parole. In many cases where a state cites confinement to justify a state's efforts to terminate parental rights, the state argues that the confined parent has abandoned the child.

In deciding whether termination is a proper course of action, courts usually consider factors other than confinement, such as (1) the relationship between parent and child before confinement; (2) whether a parent financially supported a child before confinement[33]; (3) whether a parent made an effort to maintain contact while confined; (4) whether the length of confinement will prevent a parent from assuming a parenting role; and (5) the likelihood of parole if the parent is incarcerated.[34] For example, the Florida Supreme Court ruled that a statute governing parental abandonment could not be applied to terminate the rights of an imprisoned father whose numerous requests to visit with his children had been denied.[35] However, when incarceration is for life, parental rights may be terminated because the parent cannot be expected to resume full-time child care.[36]

Abandonment may be found when a parent on parole fails to visit a child.[37] But a court may not involuntarily terminate a parent's rights without first determining whether the parent's failure to make contact was due to the parent's conduct or was affected by the terms of parole.[38]

Child in Foster Care More Than Twelve Months

A court may terminate parental rights if a parent does not make reasonable progress in remedying the conditions that led to removal of a child. For example, an appellate court in North Carolina terminated a mother's rights based on evidence presented by (1) a psychiatrist, who testified that the mother suffered from mental illness and was unable to interact with her child; (2) a social worker, who testified that the mother was aggressive and whose interactions with her child were not positive; and (3) the child's guardian *ad litem*, who testified to a lack of affection between mother and child.[39]

Murder or Serious Bodily Harm

The Adoption and Safe Families Act, which I discussed in chapter 10 and will be consider in greater detail here, requires the state or social service agency caring for the child to petition a court to terminate parental rights. It also requires a state to support a petition filed by another party in the case of children whose parents (1) have murdered or caused serious bodily harm to another of their children; (2) are criminally responsible for the death of another of their children; or (3) have had their rights concerning a another child involuntarily terminated.[40] States have amended their statutes concerning termination of parental rights to permit severing parental ties when facts such as these are proved.

Also, severe physical or sexual abuse of one's child may constitute grounds for terminating parental rights (see discussion of Amelia's mother in this chapter.). Other grounds for termination may include a parent's failure to protect a child by allowing another to sexually abuse the child when that parent knew or should have known the child was being victimized.[41]

Incompetency or Mental Illness

A person may not be competent to care for a child because of either mental retardation or mental illness. However, a parent's mental state is relevant in terminating parental rights only if the parent's ability to care for a child is affected. In one case a mentally retarded parent's rights could be terminated because she was not able to care for her special needs child, but the state could not terminate her rights to her other children, who did not have special needs.[42] In another case a court-appointed psychiatrist testified that a mother suffered from paranoid schizophrenia. Because her illness was long term, her symptoms severe, and her noncompliance with treatment ongoing, the expert testified that her child would be at risk of neglect if returned to the mother.[43]

Parent's Use of Illegal Drugs

As I noted in chapter 10, substance abuse has been cited as one cause of the increase in the numbers of children in foster care. In all states a parent's use of illegal drugs is ground for terminating parental rights, but a parent is ordinarily given an opportunity to participate in drug counseling or rehabilitation before a court acts to permanently sever parental ties.[44]

Nevertheless, parental rights have been terminated even while the parent was participating in a drug rehabilitation program, because (1) the likelihood of a success was "too speculative"; (2) the mother's history of failed attempts at rehabilitation did not provide reason for optimism; (3) the anticipated duration of treatment was too long, and the court had no assurance that the mother would be able to protect her child; and (4) there was no obvious connection between a mother's recent interest in church activities and her reduced drug abuse.[45]

Freeing a Child for Adoption

The Petition—Amelia Continued

Previously, I said that Amelia was placed in foster care, and a court determined that Ellen, her mother, had been neglectful. The court ordered services to reunite mother and daughter. As we know, Amelia's father voluntarily relinquished his rights.

In March 2002 the county amended its original neglect petition and filed new charges in which it alleged that Ellen had sexually abused Amelia. The county asked the court to terminate Ellen's parental rights (see fig. 11.2).

The information at the top of figure 11.2 is the case caption. From reviewing this material we learn that the case was filed in family court and concerned guardianship and custody of Amelia, who is younger than eighteen, meaning that the court has jurisdiction to hear this matter. Additional information in the caption informs us that this case involves allegations of "severe or repeated abuse," seeks termination of Ellen's parental rights, and was brought under New York's Social Services Law.

The first three paragraphs identify by name and county the agency that filed the petition (paragraph 1), the child on whose behalf the petition was filed

FIGURE 11.2

Petition: Termination of Parental Rights

FAMILY COURT OF THE STATE OF NEW YORK

In the Matter of the Commitment of
Guardianship and Custody pursuant to

384-b of the Social Services Law PETITION SEVERE OR REPEATED ABUSE & TERMINATION OF PARENTAL RIGHTS AMELIA "KK"

A Child under the Age of Eighteen Years,
alleged to be a Severely & Repeatedly
Abused Child

TO THE FAMILY COURT:
The undersigned Petitioner respectfully alleges that:

1. Petitioner, Norfolk County Department of Social Services (CCDSS), is an authorized agency having its office and place of business in the State of New York.

2. Amelia "KK" (D.O.B. 6/24/95) is a female child under the age of eighteen years who now resides at a foster home certified by the CCDSS.

3. (Here the names and address of the parties to receive notice are set forth.)

4. The subject child is not a Native American child subject to the Indian Child Welfare Act of 1978 (25 U.S.C. 1901–1963).

5. Amelia Cairnes was removed from the home of Ellen Cairnes in June of 1999 pursuant to an order of the Norfolk County Family Court. Child was placed with CCDSS for a period of one year pursuant to an Order of Fact-finding and Disposition rendered in August of 1999 after a hearing held in June of 1999 which found that the Respondent neglected the child. Pursuant to an abuse petition filed by this agency, the Court extended placement for a period of 12 months, terminating on 9/14/01.

6. The authorized agency has not made diligent efforts to encourage and strengthen the parental relationship because a judicial order that reasonable efforts are not required was rendered in January of 2001.

7. Upon information and belief the Respondent mother has severely abused the above-named child, in that: On at least one occasion, Respondent did subject her child, Amelia, to sexual contact in that Respondent did touch the vagina of Amelia Cairnes with her hand and did cause Amelia to touch the Respondent's breasts, vagina and buttocks, for the purpose of sexual gratification.

8. Upon information and belief, the following prior child abuse findings support the allegations in this case: Decision rendered by Hon. Sandra Creemor dated August 10, 1999, in which the Court found by clear and convincing evidence that Respondent severely abused said child.

9. The best interests of the child will be promoted by commitment of the guardianship and custody of the child to CCDSS, an authorized agency for the following reason: The child will be adopted into a safe and secure home by a certified foster/adoptive parent.

WHEREFORE, Petitioner requests an order determining that the above-named child is a severely abused child, and committing the guardianship and custody of the child to CCDSS, an authorized agency, and for such other and further relief as in the best interests of the child may be granted.

Dated: March 18, 2002

Anna Rodriguez
Family & Children's Services Social Worker

VERIFICATION

Anna Rodriguez, being duly sworn, says that she is the Petitioner in the above-named proceeding and that the foregoing Petition is true to her own knowledge, except as to matters therein stated to be alleged on information and belief and as to those matters she believes it to be true.

[Document is signed by Rodriguez and notarized.]

His opinion was that mother and daughter "bonded together . . . in an appropriate manner."

(paragraph 2), and the parties to be notified (paragraph 3), although figure 11.2 does not repeat their names. Recall the discussion of the Indian Child Welfare Act in chapter 10, and the reference to it earlier in this chapter, when I said that this federal law confers standing on a tribal council to participate in judicial proceedings that affect the custody of native American children. The statement in paragraph 4 informs all concerned that officials have determined that this law does not apply to Amelia.

Paragraphs 5, 7, and 8 report a brief history of the case. Paragraph 5 tells us that Amelia entered foster care in 1999 and that the court determined that she was neglected. She was placed in a foster home for a period not to exceed one year, at which time the permanency planning review discussed in chapter 10 would have taken place. The last sentence tells us that the court had extended Amelia's placement for one year. The information in paragraph 5 is updated in paragraph 7, where the new allegations involving sex abuse are reported. Paragraph 8 repeats the court's earlier determination that Amelia had been severely abused. It contains the important information that this determination was made by clear and convincing evidence, which we know is the evidentiary standard that the state must meet when it moves to terminate parental rights.

Recall that in chapter 10, I said that the reasonable efforts requirement has two parts. First, reasonable efforts are to be made to prevent family breakup and to reunite children in care with their families of origin. However, the Adoption and Safe Families Act altered the first requirement (see chapter 10). Reasonable efforts to preserve family life are not required if a judge determines that a parent has subjected a child to aggravated circumstances, as defined in state law, which may include abandonment, torture, and extreme forms of physical or sexual abuse. The second reasonable efforts requirement is necessary unless a judge orders otherwise. In termination cases courts will evaluate agency reunification efforts in determining whether to terminate parental rights. Earlier I said that in proving its case, the state must show that reasonable or diligent efforts were made. The information in paragraph 6 of figure 11.2 addresses this matter; it tells us that the court had ruled that such efforts were not required. Paragraph 7 reports in detail the allegations of severe abuse.

The statement in paragraph 9 regarding Amelia's best interests is important. The law in New York and other states provides that a court should not terminate parental rights simply because it has grounds to do so. Stated otherwise, a court that is considering a petition to terminate parental rights should in most circumstances hold a dispositional, or "best interests," hearing to address the question, "Is it in the child's best interests to terminate parental rights?" Only if the answer is affirmative should the court act on the termination petition. As a rule, a court will want to know whether there is an adoptive home for the child, lest the consequences of termination be that the child becomes a legal orphan.

The last part of the petition is a verification by Amelia's social worker that the information in the petition is true. Since others provided some information that the social worker relied on in framing the allegations, she has noted that in addition to statements known by her to be true, the petition rests on statements "believed" to be true, which refers to information not in the social worker's direct experience.

The Trial

A trial, or fact-finding hearing, as it is sometimes called, took place to determine whether the county could prove its case by clear and convincing evidence. Recall that the basis for the petition to terminate Ellen's parental rights was that Amelia had been subjected to severe or repeated abuse (see fig. 11.2). The court had relieved the department of social services from providing services under the "diligent efforts" requirement; such relief eliminated the need to introduce the testimony of the worker who had been assigned to work with Ellen and Amelia. To meet its burden of proof the county relied on three witnesses, who were identified from a review of the case record.

A pediatrician testified first. She reported that she had examined Amelia. In her opinion the child had been sexually abused at some indeterminate point in time. Amelia's foster mother testified that the child exhibited behavior that was "sexual in nature" and that these behaviors began when unsupervised visits between mother and daughter began. The latter testimony was bolstered by one of Amelia's teachers, who reported that she exhibited "sexual behavior" in class.

A school social worker presented conflicting testimony, telling the court that she had observed Amelia display sexual behavior several months before the first unsupervised visit with her mother. This worker testified that, in her opinion, the behaviors that she observed were consistent with those displayed by a child who had been sexually abused.

Two social workers testified on Ellen's behalf. The first reported that she observed mother and daughter "cuddling, hugging, and reading stories together and playing with puzzles." The second testified that Ellen successfully completed parenting classes and that his observations of mother and daughter indicated an affectionate relationship. His opinion was that mother and daughter had "bonded together in an appropriate manner."

The Court Ruling The court ordered that Ellen's parental rights be terminated and that Amelia's custody be transferred to the department of social services. The court authorized the department to consent to Amelia's adoption, subject to approval by a court.

Contradictory evidence was presented at trial, which is not unusual. One of the tasks that a judge must perform is to sift through the evidence and determine which is most credible. At times a judge may discount testimony. Based on a witness's demeanor and method of expressing himself or herself, a judge may conclude that the witness was not candid. At other times, as in this case, all the evidence presented may reflect accurately the assessment of those who testified. The task that confronts the judge is to determine the weight to assign to each person's testimony and to integrate the evidence into a persuasive argument to support the judge's ruling. When judges fail to specify the facts that support their conclusion, an appellate court may overrule the trial court.

The first task that confronts the trial court is to determine whether the evidence is sufficient to sustain the allegation of severe or repeated abuse. If it is, the court must then determine whether the evidence was sufficient to show that Ellen was the perpetrator. There is little doubt as to the first point, because a physician testified that Amelia had been sexually abused. The testimony linking Amelia's acting-out to visits with her mother, although contradictory, was sufficient for the court to find that Ellen was the perpetrator. Bear in mind that when such a serious allegation is made, judges are not prone to risk taking and therefore are not likely to rule against the county, unless the parent has brought very strong evidence to undermine the allegation of the identity of the perpetrator. Because of the latitude that judges have to weigh and balance evidence based on their observations of those who testify, winning a case on an appeal on the merits is quite difficult (see chapter 3).

The Dispositional Hearing

The dispositional, or "best interests," hearing, as it is sometimes called, takes place only after a court has determined that the charges against the parent are accurate. Social workers play a key role at this phase of court proceedings, since the central question before the court—"Is it in the child's best interests to terminate parental rights?"—is answered from "social facts," which are concerned with what a child needs emotionally, educationally, and so on and address the best situation for meeting these needs.

A court has several dispositional options: (1) to terminate parental rights, thereby freeing the child to be adopted; (2) suspend judgment for a period of time, if the court has reason to think that a parent's behaviors may be modified and the child returned home, or if the court determines that termination is not in the child's best interests; or (3) dismiss the petition and (a) keep the child in foster care or (b) reunite parent and child.

Dispositional hearings are not required under New York law if (1) termination proceeds on the basis of mental retardation or mental illness when reuniting parent and child is not possible; or (2) the parent abandoned a child, since the parent is not available as a resource to the court.

Finalizing an Adoption

Once the court terminated Ellen's rights, it could appoint a person to act as guardian *ad litem* (see chapter 10). With her mother's rights terminated, Amelia is available for adoption. Anyone eligible to adopt could petition a court to become Amelia's legal parent, although, as often occurs with children in foster care, Amelia's foster parents adopted her.

In regular as well as private adoptions, the person wishing to adopt must undergo a home study, although this requirement may be waived if the petitioner is related to the child or has been the child's foster parent. For the adoptive applicant the home study process is critical. The suitability of the applicant will be judged from information compiled through (1) interviewing the applicant and other permanent household members; (2) observing the interaction of household members; and (3) gathering information from health care providers. The agency will verify income and compile references. In addition, it will conduct criminal background checks as well as "registry checks" to determine whether the adoptive applicant or other household member is listed on a state's child-abuse or sex-offender registry. The agency also will ensure that fingerprint-based criminal background checks are conducted. All the information compiled goes into a written report that is submitted to the court. After a period of time, if the court determines that the adoption is in the best interests of the child, it will sign an order of adoption and issue a new birth certificate for the adopted child.

PART 2—ISSUES IN ADOPTION

Many laws governing adoption are undergoing change. To increase the numbers of children who are adopted from foster care, Congress has amended federal laws and enacted new ones. State laws are changing as well. Some issues addressed are old, such as amending statutes to provide access to sealed adoption records. Other issues are new, including cooperative adoptions, the law governing the enforceability of cooperative adoption agreements, and questions concerning the legality of surrogacy contracts.

Federal Initiatives

Concerned with finding permanent homes for children in foster care, Congress amended the Adoption Assistance and Child Welfare Act (AACWA) by passing the Adoption and Safe Families Act (see chapter 10.). The latter's goals are to be accomplished through four provisions that modified existing law. One provision, discussed in chapter 10, modified the reasonable efforts requirement of the law. Amelia's case illustrates a situation where the requirement was eliminated (see fig. 11.2). Another provision required a judicial hearing, the permanency planning hearing, which takes place twelve months after the first judicial finding of abuse or neglect. Third, the federal government has made fiscal incentives available, ranging from $2,000 to $4,000 per child, for states that have increased the number of adoptions relative to previous years.

The fourth provision may have the greatest impact on the day-to-day practice of social work in a legal environment. With some exceptions (see chapter 10) the Adoption and Safe Families Act requires that a child care agency file a petition to terminate parental rights, or support a petition filed by another, (1) for children in foster care for fifteen of the most recent twenty-two months; (2) for those found by a court to have been abandoned; and (3) for children whose parents murdered or caused serious bodily harm to another of their children.[46] Implementation of this provision could (1) increase significantly the workload of social workers who supervise foster care caseloads; (2) increase judicial oversight of record-keeping practices; and (3) increase the demand for accurate and detailed recording, which is often required to sustain a termination petition.

Special Needs Children and Interstate Adoptions

Some children in foster care have special needs that make it difficult to find them adoptive homes. Special needs may exist because of the child's "ethnic background, age, or membership in a minority or sibling group, or [because of a child's] . . . medical . . . physical, mental, or emotional handicaps."[47]

To facilitate the adoption of special needs children, all states operate adoption subsidy programs supported by federal funds. Federal funds may be used only to subsidize the adoption of children who were receiving federally supported financial aid before their adoption. Federal subsidies are not available to children who are adopted privately.[48] To expand the universe of special needs children for whom subsidies are available, all the states operate and pay for their own programs to benefit special needs children who are ineligible for federal support. In addition, twenty-three states subsidize guardianship of children with special needs.[49]

Historically, families that adopted special needs children lacked assurance that a subsidy would continue if they moved across state lines. Thirty-five states have resolved this issue by adopting the Interstate Compact on Adoption and Medical Assistance. The compact ensures that children supported by Title IV-E funds (see chapter 9) will continue to receive health insurance and other necessary services if they move to a new state.

Transracial Adoption

In a transracial adoption the race of the child and adoptive parents differs. Although any racial combination would meet the definition of *transracial*, most domestic transracial adoptions have been of black children by white parents.

The practice of placing black children with white families peaked in the 1960s. In 1972 the National Association of Black Social Workers (NABSW) stated its opposition to this practice. Subsequently, states enacted statutes favoring same-race placements. Social service agencies amended their policies to reflect this preference, and courts endorsed practices that took race into account in selecting an adoptive home.[50]

Conventional wisdom holds that the number of transracial adoptions decreased significantly after 1972, but data on this subject are sparse and were last reported in 1975. In 1987, fifteen years after the NABSW staked out its position, transracial adoptions accounted for 8 percent of domestic adoptions; most were adoptions of black children by white women. Changes in the law contributed to an increase in transracial adoptions, which accounted for 15 percent of all adoptions in 1998.[51]

In 1994, finding that tens of thousands of children in foster care were awaiting adoption, Congress passed the Multiethnic Placement Act.[52] This law allows states to consider race and ethnicity in choosing adoptive homes but prohibits states from denying or delaying a child's placement solely on the basis of race or ethnicity. In 1996 Congress found that the 1994 act had not facilitated the adoption of minority children. This failure was partly the result of the confusion created by language that permitted states to consider race but precluded the use of race as a decisive factor. In 1996 Congress passed the Adoption Promotion and Stability Act, which applies to any agency receiving federal funds.[53] Henceforth, any consideration of race, color, or national origin in placing a child for adoption could be considered illegal discrimination under the 1964 Civil Rights Act. Rather than assuming that same-race placements are always in a child's best interests, the 1996 amendments require that an adoption decision that takes race into account be justified by showing why a specific child's placement demands a same-race placement.

The Indian Child Welfare Act

I discussed this federal law in chapter 10 and referred to it in discussing Amelia's case. There I said that Congress enacted this measure to protect the best interests of Indian children within their tribal culture.[54]

In 1989 the U.S. Supreme Court affirmed the intent of this law when the Court overturned the adoption of a native American child that has been granted by a civil court without the sanction of the tribal council. The case concerned twins born to a native American couple who voluntarily relinquished their rights. The twins were placed in an adoptive home, and an adoption decree was entered.

The birth parents were enrolled members of the Choctaw tribe who had lived on the reservation before the birth of their children. Based on the Indian Child Welfare Act (ICWA), the tribe moved to vacate the adoption. The case turned on whether tribes have exclusive jurisdiction over child custody proceedings involving Indian children domiciled on the tribe's reservation. In this case the parents took pains to ensure that the birth of their twins would take place off the reservation so that the tribal council would not have jurisdiction to place their children. The U.S. Supreme Court noted first that a child's domicile is that of the parents. Since the domicile of the parents was the reservation, that the twins were never on the reservation had no bearing on tribal jurisdiction. The Court overturned the adoption decree entered by the civil court and awarded custody of the children to the tribe.[55]

Sealed Records

Since 1917, when Minnesota passed the first law on adoption records, these records have been sealed, meaning that information concerning the adopted child's birth family could not be acquired without a court order.[56] Subsequently, all states enacted statutes sealing adoption records. This practice was supported by a wish to protect the anonymity of the birth mother whose child was likely "born out of wedlock [and to ensure] that her indiscretion [would] not be divulged." In addition, sealed records were seen as necessary to protect the child, whose "illegitimacy" would remain secret, and to guarantee the privacy of adoptive parents.[57]

In the last quarter of the twentieth century, spurred by the increased social acceptance of unwed motherhood and by a grassroots movement of adoptees who wished to learn about their families of origin, states began to modify their laws. All states allow records to be opened if ordered by a court after the party requesting access has demonstrated a compelling need, such as medical necessity.[58] Most states allow the adopted child and adoptive parents access to nonidentifying information describing the medical, genetic, and social history of birth parents; Alaska and Kansas allow adopted people to have unlimited access to their adoption records.[59] Some states allows access to records but permit the adopted child or birth parent to veto disclosure; Oregon allows adoptees older than twenty-one to obtain copies of their original birth certificate.[60]

Two other approaches to acquiring confidential information are (1) hiring an intermediary, who searches for the unknown party whose permission to unseal records is needed, and (2) using "mutual consent registries," which exist in a number of states to allow birth parents and adoptees to register their interest in making contact.[61]

Cooperative Adoption

Cooperative adoption, referred to also as open adoption, involves an agreement for ongoing contact between birth parents who voluntarily relinquish their child and the adoptive family. Contact may be limited to an exchange of information between the parties or it may include telephonic, mail, or in-person contact.

From the standpoint of traditional adoption law, cooperative adoption is a radical concept, since it undermines the notion that permanently severing the ties between a child and its birth family is essential if a new family is to be created. The acceptance of cooperative adoption can be linked to the availability through public agencies of many older children with ties to their biological families, which may be more receptive to relinquishing their rights if ongoing contact is possible. The law in New York and Nebraska limits cooperative adoptions to children in foster care, and in Nebraska the agreements are renewable every two years.[62]

Typically, the agreement that frames a cooperative adoption must be (1) in writing, (2) court approved, (3) in the best interests of the child,[63] and (4) acceptable to the child if she or he is older than twelve.[64] If the child has an attorney or guardian *ad litem*, that person's approval may be required.[65]

Enforceability of Cooperative Adoption Agreements

If birth parents sue to enforce a postadoption agreement, they may ask the court to return their child to them or they may seek "specific performance," meaning that they are asking the court to enforce the contact provisions in their agreement. Courts are not likely to disrupt an adoption unless deceit was used to obtain consent, as in the case of Baby Richard (chapter 8); the remedy of specific performance is problematic because court-ordered visitation may disrupt the adoptive family. For this reason an appellate court in Louisiana would not enforce a written visitation agreement, because it was contrary to the public policy goal of stability in a child's placement.[66] However, when a parent surrenders a child conditioned on continued contact and the agency to whom the child was surrendered fails to inform the adoptive family of this condition, the birth parent may petition the court to enforce the agreement. Thus a New York court opined that the adoptive parents had an obligation to review the surrender agreement. Had they done so, they would have learned of the conditions imposed on the adoption. The court gave the adoptive parents the choice of accepting the conditions for visitation or invalidating the adoption.[67]

Where visitation agreements are permitted by statute or case law, the central concern of a court asked to enforce an agreement is whether this would be in the best interests of the child. Thus the Supreme Court of Connecticut ruled that postadoption visitation agreements do not violate the public policy of the state so long as visitation is in the child's best interests, and an appellate court in Maryland reached the same conclusion.[68]

Intercountry Adoption

In discussing who may adopt, I said that efforts to place children with the "ideal parent" changed as public interest in adopting children from foster care waned. This situation was the result of the unavailability of infants, which in turn was linked to the availability of abortion on demand and the social acceptance of single parenthood. These changes gave rise to the practice of adopting children from foreign countries, which is the main alternative to infertility treatment, donor insemination, and surrogacy.[69]

Intercountry adoption is a political issue considered by some to be the "taking by the powerful and rich the children of the poor and powerless," while others consider it a humane solution to the problem of orphaned and often homeless children growing up in orphanages in different parts of the world.[70] Since some children are adopted by different-race parents, intercountry adoption raises many of the same issues that were raised in domestic transracial adoptions.

In 1998, the last year for which data are available, the United States had nearly fifteen thousand intercountry adoptions. Half the children were born in Asia, approximately 37 percent in Europe, 10 percent in South and Central America, and 1 percent or less in Africa, Mexico, and the Caribbean.[71]

The individual or couple wishing to adopt a child from another country must seek approval from the Immigration and Naturalization Service (INS), which is part of the U.S. Department of Justice, because the child must have a visa to enter the United States. Under current law children eligible to be adopted from foreign countries by U.S. citizens are "orphans," defined for immigration purposes as a child

> whose parents have died or disappeared, or who has been abandoned or otherwise separated from both parents . . . [or] a child whose sole or surviving parent is incapable of providing . . . proper care and who has, in writing, irrevocably released the child for emigration and adoption. . . . To enter the U.S., an orphan must have been adopted abroad by a U.S. citizen (and spouse, if married) or be coming to the United States for adoption by a citizen.[72]

Qualified children who are adopted by a U.S. citizen and who reside permanently in the United States acquire citizenship automatically under the Child Citizenship Act of 2001.[73]

In an effort to standardize procedures for the adoption of children from foreign countries, sixty-six countries, including the United States, have ratified the Hague Convention on the Protection of Children and Cooperation in Respect to Intercountry Adoptions (1993).[74] However, the convention will not take effect in the United States until the federal government publishes final regulations, which are not expected before the fall of 2004.[75]

A key objective of the convention is to prevent the abduction, sale, or trafficking of children or any other practices that involve using children for financial gain. The convention requires that each signatory country establish a "central authority" to oversee intercountry adoptions. In the United States the State Department will be the central authority for purposes of implementing the convention. The agency will coordinate adoption matters between the federal government and the central authorities of other countries. To ensure that children adopted by U.S. citizens have not been "snatched" from their families, the adoption of a foreign-born child will require certification by the State Department that the central authority of the child's country of origin has notified it of that country's finalization of the adoption by a U.S. citizen or that the person or couple seeking to adopt has been granted custody of the child for purposes of emigration and adoption.

Once the child enters the United States, assuming that the adoption has been completed outside the country, twenty-five states and one U.S. territory will grant full faith and credit (see chapter 8) to the foreign decree, and six states will allow "readoption" of the child by a state court. The remaining states and territories have no statutory laws on this matter.[76]

Surrogacy

Surrogacy is a type of assisted reproductive technology whereby one woman, the surrogate mother, agrees to bear a child for another. The popularity of surrogacy, as with private adoptions and intercountry adoptions, is tied to the wish to parent a newborn, with the added benefit, for some, of having a child who is genetically related. The number of children born through surrogacy arrangements is not known, but the high cost, $35,000 to $50,000, suggests it will be low.[77]

Surrogacy has given rise to new concepts of parenthood and to new legal issues. For example, while laboratory testing may be required to resolve questions of paternity, until very recently no one ever had a question regarding the identity of a child's mother unless a woman abandoned her child at birth. In the past, distinctions between genetic and biological parenting would have made little sense. But consider the following as one example of the complexity of untangling concepts of modern parenthood. A couple wishing to adopt may be (1) genetically related to the child, if all the genetic material was contributed by the couple or members of their family for implantation in the surrogate; (2) genetically related to the surrogate mother, who contributed the female gestational and genetic components of reproduction and who was artificially inseminated with the sperm of the intended father or the sperm of a family member of the intended mother; or (3) not genetically related to the intended parents or the surrogate mother because all the reproductive material was contributed by others who were not family members. Court rulings may refer to the woman who gives birth to a child as the "gestational mother" or the "biological mother," and the person or people who wish to raise the child as the "genetic parents" or the "intended parents."

Surrogacy to some is a form of economic exploitation that finds a poor woman offering her reproductive capabilities for a fee, thus creating a class of "breeders," and it is seen by some as a form of baby selling, because children are the subject of contracts whose terms require the surrender of a newborn in exchange for money. To others surrogacy provides an opportunity for a woman to assist another who wishes to have a child and to offer to the intended parents a chance to raise a child who is genetically related to them. In addition, the decision to become a surrogate mother is seen as one of choice.[78]

The Law on Surrogacy

Nineteen states and the District of Columbia have statutes addressing some aspect of surrogacy.[79] Surrogacy contracts may be prohibited, permitted, or voidable. Surrogacy is a complex subject, and a discussion of all the legal, moral, and ethical questions to which it gives rise is beyond the scope of this text.[80] Some legal issues that arise are highlighted in the context of the cases reviewed next.

Surrogacy came to public attention in 1988 in the case of *Baby M.*, when the New Jersey Supreme Court ruled that a surrogacy agreement was void and thus unenforceable.[81] The *Baby M.* case involved (1) William and Elizabeth Stern, who wished to have a child but could not conceive; (2) Mary Beth Whitehead, who agreed to be a surrogate, to being artificially inseminated with William Stern's sperm, and to relinquishing her rights after birth; Richard Whitehead, who agreed to do all that was required of him to rebutt the presumption that he was the child's father; and Elizabeth Stern, who wished to adopt the newborn. After the baby was born, Mary Beth Whitehead changed her mind about relinquishing the infant, and the issue came before the New Jersey courts.

The New Jersey Supreme Court ruled that the surrogacy contract was void. Some of the court's reasons for voiding the contract should be familiar to you from material presented earlier in this chapter. For example, we know that a parent's right may not be terminated without a finding of unfitness; that a woman's prebirth relinquishment of her child is void in most states; that a woman has a statutorily defined postbirth period when she may rescind her relinquishment; and that a court must find that it is in the child's best interests to be adopted and that the person seeking to adopt is a suitable custodian. It should not be surprising that the court found violations of state law in (1) the provisions for terminating Mary Beth Whitehead's rights so that Elizabeth Stern could adopt without the required judicial determination of parental unfitness; (2) the absence of a provision allowing Mary Beth Whitehead to rescind her consent; (3) the provision for surrendering a child before birth; and (4) the exchange of money, because that constitutes baby selling and is repugnant and contrary to the best interests of a child, who is sold without regard to whether the "purchasers" are suitable parents.

The court resolved the issue of custody by granting physical custody to William Stern and visitation rights granted to Mary Beth Whitehead, effectively creating the conditions for ongoing contact that neither family may have chosen for itself.

The ruling reached by a California court is the opposite of that rendered in New Jersey. The facts of *Johnson v. Calvert* differ from *Baby M.* in that the child was genetically related to the parents, who contributed all the reproductive material.[82] The question addressed by the court can be stated as follows: "When, pursuant to a surrogacy agreement, a fertilized egg is implanted in the uterus of another woman, who carries the fetus to term and gives birth to a child not genetically related to her, who is the child's 'natural mother' under California law?"

The California Supreme Court, in reaching its decision, was the first to use of the concept of "intended parent." The court ruled:

> Mark and Crispina [Calvert] . . . desired to have a child of their own genetic stock but are physically unable to do so without the help of reproductive technology. They affirmatively intended the birth of the child, and took the steps necessary to effect in vitro fertilization. But for their acted-on intention, the child would not exist. Anna [Johnson] agreed to facilitate the procreation of Mark's and Crispina's child. The parties' aim was to bring Mark's and Crispina's child into the world, not for Mark and Crispina to donate a zygote to Anna. Crispina from the outset intended to be the child's mother. Although the gestative function Anna performed was necessary to bring about the child's birth, it is safe to say that Anna would not have been given the opportunity to gestate or deliver the child had she, prior to implantation of the zygote, manifested her own intent to be the child's mother. No reason appears why Anna's later change of heart should vitiate the determination that Crispina is the child's natural mother.[83]

The Court ruled that the surrogacy agreement was enforceable against Anna.

A California appellate court extended the analytic framework articulated in *Johnson.* The court was asked to rule on whether an intended father could be ordered to pay child support when he was not genetically related to the child, who was not born when he filed divorce papers.[84] The child was conceived from reproductive material contributed by anonymous sperm and egg donors. Before the child's birth the intended father filed for divorce. The trial court concluded that because the infant had no lawful parents, no one was obligated to provide for the child. The surrogate mother was not the "mother," the trial court concluded, nor was her husband the father. Since the intended parents had not contributed genetic material, neither could be the child's parent.

Finding this reasoning extraordinary, the appellate court ruled that the husband had intended to become a father when he agreed to the surrogacy arrangement, and by causing conception of the child, he had a support obligation.

A New York appellate court agreed with the intent test developed in California. The New York case involved a woman who gave birth to a child from a donated egg fertilized by her husband. Intent, the court ruled, was determinative in reaching the conclusion that the woman who gave birth was the "natural mother" of the child for purposes of a custody dispute between her and her husband.[85] An Ohio court refused to determine parentage with reference to intent, because it is too difficult to prove, the court ruled, even with a written agreement, since the parties may later disagree concerning this important matter. Moreover, a decision based on the existence of a written agreement would subvert public policy. Among other things, the financial aspects of surrogacy could place undue pressure on a woman to relinquish her child, and the custody of the child would be transferred without a best interests ruling by a court.[86]

SUMMARY

In this chapter I presented an overview of adoption law and reviewed issues that affect adoption law. Adoption is controlled mainly by state law within a framework established by (1) the U.S. Supreme Court to ensure that parents' constitutional rights are protected and (2) by federal statutes that (a) govern the adoption of children from foreign countries; (b) address the right of tribal councils to oversee the adoption of native American children; and (c) sanction the use of federal funds to increase adoption opportunities for children in foster care in need of permanent homes. When a child is adopted, a new family is formed, and the legal relationship is then similar to that between a child and its biological parents.

With few exceptions, all states will consider a petition to adopt a child from (1) single people; (2) married people when both wish to adopt; (3) the spouse of a child's biological parent, if the rights of the other parent have been terminated; and (4) in some states, cohabiting couples. Those seeking to adopt may use the services of public and voluntary agencies that serve mainly children in foster care, or they may adopt privately. In private adoptions the prospective parents make direct contact with a pregnant woman who wishes to relinquish her child, or an intermediary makes the contact.Private adoptions include intercountry adoptions, which have grown in popularity because many people wish to adopt an infant and few infants are available for adoption. The paucity of infants also has led to an increase in surrogacy arrangements, where one woman agrees to carry a child for another person or couple and to relinquish the child after birth.

Children whose parents have died are available for adoption, as are those whose parents voluntarily relinquish their custodial rights or whose parents' rights have been involuntarily terminated by a court. Some adoptions are cooperative, meaning that they proceed according to an agreement for ongoing contact between a child and biological parents, but the general rule is that adoption is an irrevocable separation and all records that concern the adoption are sealed to protect the anonymity of all parties and to support the view that a new family has been formed.

Because the Constitution protects ties between parent and child, safeguards exist to ensure that revoking parental rights is a step not lightly taken. In general, a mother cannot relinquish her child before it is born, although a father may and a mother may rescind her decision to relinquish within a statutorily set time period. However, relinquishment is irrevocable if given before a judicial officer, who strives to ensure that a parent understands the consequences of her or his action.

All states have laws that permit a court to terminate parental rights against the wish of the parent, based on a judicial determination that the parent is not a fit custodian and that termination is in the best interests of the child. Parental rights may be involuntarily terminated for diverse reasons, including parental (1) abandonment; (2) failure to make progress in resolving the problems that led to removal of a child more than twelve months before the state acts to terminate rights; (3) incompetency or mental illness; and (4) acts that cause serious physical harm to a child or that constitute sex abuse.

Because the Constitution protects parental rights, parents retain their procedural rights under the Fourteenth Amendment, including the right to (1) receive notice that an action has been filed against them; (2) respond at a hearing to the allegations that they are not a fit custodian; (3) be represented by a lawyer but not always the right to court-appointed counsel; and (4) hold the state to a higher burden of proof than in a neglect proceeding by requiring the state to prove by clear and convincing evidence that parental rights should be terminated. After the state has shown that a parent is not fit, courts routinely conduct dispositional, or best interests, hearings, at which time the court will hear evidence that termination is in the child's best interests.

12

Domestic Violence

THE CONCEPT of domestic violence brings to mind an altercation between two adults in an intimate relationship, and this is the definition used by the U.S. Department of Justice, which defines domestic violence as criminal acts occurring between individuals with an existing or formerly close relationship. However, in some states the term *family violence* has replaced *domestic violence*, and this concept embraces child abuse and elder abuse as well as violence between intimate partners.[1]

In the pages that follow, I shall use the term *domestic violence* as it is used by the Justice Department and *elder abuse* to refer to mistreatment of the elderly. Child abuse was the subject of chapter 10 and is considered here only to the extent that it may be imputed to an adult or adults whose relationship is violent.

Because of the disproportionate rate of victimization reported by women, I shall use female pronouns throughout, although the law is written in gender-neutral terms. As with other subjects we have reviewed, the laws governing domestic violence and elder abuse are found mainly at the state level. There are significant differences between states, a discussion that is beyond the scope of this text. For purposes of illustration I rely heavily on New York law.

The chapter is divided into two parts. The topic of part 1 is violence between partners in intimate relationships. After reviewing data describing the incidence of domestic violence, we shall consider how this social problem is addressed in federal law, then consider in detail the state response, including police action, filing a complaint in court, and orders of protection. The topic of child custody will be addressed next. First, we shall consider how the judiciary takes domestic violence into account when making child custody decisions when parents separate or divorce; then we shall turn our attention to the impact of domestic violence on reports to child protective services. Whether domestic violence may be considered a hate crime will be the last topic reviewed in part 1.

In part 2 we shall turn our attention to elder abuse. As with part 1, this part will begin by considering data describing the incidence of this social problem. Then our attention will turn to consider the way that elder abuse is addressed in federal and state law. The rights accorded by federal and state law to nursing home patients will be our next topic; in that discussion I will address the role of ombudsmen, who are advocates for nursing home patients. Guardianship is the last topic in this chapter.

PART 1—VIOLENCE BETWEEN PARTNERS IN AN INTIMATE RELATIONSHIP

Scope of the Problem

State laws govern the investigation and prosecution of domestic violence, and there is state-by-state variation in how this crime is treated by the police and the courts. Some states limit the definition to actions that occur between spouses, or between unmarried adults with a child, thus denying protection to childless women abused by their cohabiting partners. Some states do include acts between "boyfriends and girlfriends," and some include acts involving same-sex partners.[2] The behaviors of concern include "hitting, pushing, kicking, sexually assaulting, using a weapon, and threatening violence, [and use of] verbal or psychological abuse, stalking, or enforced social isolation."[3]

Accurate data describing the incidence of domestic violence are limited. Data collection is hampered by poor definitions of the crime and lack of training of police to determine what should be classified as domestic violence. In addition, some counts are based on reports made. Since there may be multiple reports for any one victim, this approach to counting may result in overestimates, if the number of reports is considered synonymous with the number of victims. The problem of data collection is compounded when those states whose laws address family violence group together child as well as adult victims. Problems arise also where states gather data from different state "systems," for example, from child welfare, health care, law enforcement, and victim assistance services, likely yielding an overestimate, unless reports include names so that double counting can be avoided. Given these issues, it should not come as a surprise that the number of victims of domestic violence is said to vary from one million to four million.[4]

From the results of a survey of more than 293,000 households containing 574,000 individuals aged twelve and older, and from homicide data obtained from the Federal Bureau of Investigation, the Justice Department reports that there were about one million crimes committed against individuals by their current or former spouses and boyfriends or girlfriends, including same-sex and opposite-sex couples. Eighty-five percent of crimes were directed against women.[5] These data are limited in that they do not include the homeless and people living in shelters.

Federal Response to Domestic Violence

The earliest federal response to domestic violence occurred in the 1980s when Congress enacted the Family Violence Prevention and Services Act[6] and the Victim Compensation and Assistance Fund.[7] The former provides grants to the states to combat child abuse and neglect, to increase public awareness of domestic violence, to train law enforcement, judicial, health, and social service personnel in matters concerning domestic violence, and to provide shelter and related services to victims of domestic violence. The Victims Compensation Fund, as the name suggests, provides monetary compensation to victims as well as funds to improve services that benefit victims of domestic violence who appear in federal court.

In 1994 Congress passed the Violence Against Women Act (VAWA).[8] VAWA's chief objective is to combat the problem of violence against women by making grants to (1) improve the legal system by increasing the effectiveness of a state's law enforcement and judicial response; (2) provide victim services, including shelters for battered women and a nationwide toll-free domestic violence hot line; (3) criminalize interstate acts of domestic violence, including interstate violations of protective orders[9]; and (4) educate the public in order to prevent future violence. The VAWA requires the states to give full faith and credit (chapter 8) to orders of protection issued by courts in other states, including orders issued by tribal courts.[10]

To increase the availability and effectiveness of legal assistance for victims of domestic violence, the federal Violence Against Women Office provides grants under the Victims' Civil Legal Assistance Discretionary Grant Program. Funds may be used to support programs that reach battered women on a broad range of issues, including the provision of legal services to aid in resolving civil matters that are an outgrowth of domestic violence, for example, (1) to obtain, modify, or enforce orders of protection; (2) to assist in obtaining a divorce or legal separation; (3) to obtain and enforce an order of spousal and child support; (4) to deal with matters concerning child custody and/or visitation; and (5) to facilitate access to benefits, such as income support and housing.

When VAWA was enacted, it contained a civil rights provision in Title III that allowed a victim of domestic violence to sue her attacker in federal court.[11]

In 2000 the U.S. Supreme Court ruled that this title was unconstitutional. The Court concluded that Congress exceeded its authority under the commerce clause and the Fourteenth Amendment (see chapter 2) in enacting this civil rights provision, and Title III was struck from the law.[12]

State Response to Domestic Violence

Until the 1970s a number of states treated domestic violence as a private matter and not as a real crime. The failure of police to investigate complaints was tolerated and to some extent encouraged.[13] For example, in 1962 New York decriminalized domestic violence. Cases were transferred from criminal court to family court to enhance the likelihood of rehabilitating the perpetrator rather than punishing him. The practice of treating domestic violence solely as a civil matter, combined with "the benign attitude of various police departments in refusing to make arrests in the face of actual ongoing assaults by abusing spouses"[14] and the "marital rape exemption," whereby marriage to the victim was a defense against a charge of rape,[15] all could be construed as "giving an abusing spouse a practical license to continue assaults."[16]

In response to the women's movement of the 1960s and the 1970s, states undertook statutory reform and created an array of legal remedies for victims of domestic violence. Today victims in all states may obtain an order of protection that limits or proscribes contact between the offender and victim. A majority of states have done away with the "marital privilege" laws that prevented spouses from providing adverse testimony against each other, so that a victim may sue her abusing spouse for monetary damages, and criminal charges may be filed against the offender.[17] Courts in many states have the authority to order the abuser into treatment, and a number of states are training law enforcement personnel in how to handle reports and investigations of domestic violence.

Lodging a Complaint with the Police

When the New York victim of domestic violence lodges a complaint with the police, the officer who responds must arrest the perpetrator, regardless of the victim's point of view, if a felony has been committed. Arrest is mandatory as well when the crime is a misdemeanor, but in that case police will not make an arrest if the woman asks them not to.

A felony, as we learned in chapter 3, is a crime punishable by death or a term of imprisonment exceeding one year. Thus when domestic violence involves an assault with the elements of intent and serious injury to another, the perpetrator may be charged with a felony and must be arrested. Crimes not classified as felonies are misdemeanors, which are usually punishable by a fine and/or short periods of incarceration. Harassment, defined as intentionally and repeatedly following another in or near a public place or committing acts that place another in reasonable fear of physical injury, is a misdemeanor.[18]

When an officer responds to a domestic dispute and each party accuses the other of misbehavior, New York law requires that the officer

> identify and arrest the primary physical aggressor . . . [by] . . . considering: (I) the . . . extent of any injuries inflicted by and between the parties; (ii) whether one person . . . is [or has] threatened . . . future harm against another party or another family or household member; (iii) whether [one party] has a . . . history of domestic violence that the officer can reasonably ascertain; and (iv) whether [one party] acted defensively to protect himself or herself from injury.[19]

The police are not to ask the victim whether she wants them to make an arrest, nor are they to threaten the arrest of any person for the purpose of discouraging requests for police intervention.[20] When an officer is presented with a copy of an order of protection, she or he has the authority to arrest the person charged with violating the order. The order of protection should encourage police involvement, since it provides evidence of what the court has ordered and clarifies the authority of the police and their responsibilities in family matters.[21]

However, victims of domestic violence are not likely to be successful in suing the police for failing to protect them. When sued, defendants typically file a motion asking for summary judgment (chapter 3), based on the general rule that the duty owed by police is to protect the general public, not any particular individual. Citing the *DeShaney* case (chapters 7 and 10) as precedent, defendants argue that the special relationship that gives rise to a duty to protect an individual does not exist when injuries are suffered at the hands of a private party. To survive the motion for summary judgment, a plaintiff must establish that the lesser protection afforded female victims of domestic violence is (1) based on a policy or custom of the police department; (2) motivated by animus toward women; and (3) causal to an injury suffered by the plaintiff as a result of the policy or custom.[22]

Arresting Officer's Responsibility to Provide Information to a Victim

The law enforcement official who investigates a family offense is required under New York law to advise the victim of the availability of shelter or other services and to provide her with information concerning her legal rights and the legal remedies available. The required notice includes the right of the victim to ask the officer to assist her (1) by telling her how to obtain a temporary order of protection; (2) in obtaining essential personal effects, if she chooses to leave the family home; (3) by locating and taking her, or assisting her in making arrangements to take her and her children, to a safe place, such as a shelter or the residence of a family member or friend; (4) in obtaining medical treatment for herself and her children; (5) by providing her with a copy of an incident report; (6) by informing her of her right to seek legal counsel and, if she proceeds in family court, her right to a court-appointed attorney if she is indigent.

Lodging a Complaint in Court

When the victim is a married woman who is filing a petition against her husband in a New York court, her journey may begin at the intake unit of the probation department, which offers conciliation services.[23] Personnel in the probation department will review the case and determine with the petitioner whether to invite her spouse to participate in conciliation rather than proceeding to court adjudication. Conciliation services may be offered by staff in the probation department or after referral to a community agency. If the petitioner's spouse fails to appear for a conciliation conference, the court may order his participation.

Court Process

As with any civil proceeding, the court process is initiated with the filing of a petition. If the case is to proceed in criminal court, an "accusatory instrument" is filed. The New York petitioner may file her complaint in family court, criminal court, or both.[24] The decision how best to proceed will depend on whether she is interested in services to effect rehabilitation or whether her goal is to punish the offender. The jurisdiction of the New York Family Court in matters involving family offenses, New York's generic term for domestic violence, ranges from relatively minor infractions, such as disorderly conduct, which involves intentionally causing a public disturbance, to offenses where a perpetrator intentionally causes serious injury.[25] The most serious crimes—attempted murder, murder, and assault with a deadly weapon—must be prosecuted in criminal court.

When criminal prosecution is not mandatory, a family court judge, with permission of the victim and notice to a district attorney, may transfer the case to criminal court.[26] However, a prosecutor may decline to proceed with criminal charges. The woman who is proceeding in family court may withdraw her petition, but if a child is involved, the court may decline her request to withdraw, given the state's interest in protecting children.[27]

The woman who proceeds in family court has the right to have her petition and request for an order of protection heard on the day that she first appears in court or the next day that court is in session. If the perpetrator was arrested, then released at his initial appearance, a criminal court may issue an order of protection.

The petition filed in family court must allege misconduct over which the court has jurisdiction. The petition will name the parties and their relationship to each other, the names of children in the household and their relationship to both the petitioner and the respondent, a request for an order of protection or for conciliation services, and report whether there is a criminal action pending concerning the acts alleged in the petition.[28]

At the first court appearance the petitioner is told that she may (1) proceed in criminal court, (2) in family court, or (3) concurrently in both.[29] A decision by the petitioner to proceed in family court does not divest the criminal court of jurisdiction to hear a family offense, meaning that a county attorney could proceed against the abuser.[30]

Orders of Protection

A request for an order of protection may be filed as an independent action or in conjunction with a proceeding for divorce or child support, or in an abuse and neglect proceeding. If the petitioner files ex parte, meaning with only one side present, she may receive a temporary order of protection (TOP). TOPs are effective as soon as they are issued, but it is necessary to serve the accused with a copy of the petition.

A TOP is not a finding of wrongdoing, and by definition it is of short duration.[31] However, the New York statute does not specify a maximum period of time, and a judge may extend the term of a temporary order.[32] Time limits may be inferred because an order of protection issued after a hearing cannot exceed one year, unless special circumstances justify issuing an order for a "reasonable period" of time.[33] If the petitioner wants a permanent order of protection, she must proceed to a formal hearing at which she bears the burden of proving her case by a preponderance of the evidence. A hearing will also occur if the respondent denies the allegations, and he may defend his actions by arguing self-defense or lack of capacity (chapter 3).

A TOP, and an order of protection issued after fact-finding and dispositional hearings, may direct that the perpetrator (1) stay away from any designated place, such as the home, school, or business of the other party, or from any children involved, if the court finds these provisions necessary to protect the party on whose behalf the order is issued; (2) be allowed to visit with a child under supervised conditions; (3) pay child support and continue medical insurance; (4) be allowed to enter the family home during a set time period to remove personal belongings; (5) participate in a treatment program that teaches alternatives to violent behavior or in a drug or alcohol counseling program; and (6) observe any other conditions deemed necessary to further the purposes of protection.[34] Failure to obey the terms of an order of protection may result in (1) review and modification of the original order; (2) the filing of a new offense, for which criminal penalties may apply[35]; or (3) a finding of contempt of court and a term of imprisonment not to exceed six months.[36]

Enforcement

An order of protection is analogous to an arrest warrant and provides authority for a police officer to take custody of the person charged with violating the order.[37] In addition, if the order is violated, the petitioner may request that the prosecutor bring criminal charges against the offender[38]; if the victim files a petition alleging a violation of the order, the family court judge may transfer the case to criminal court. Alternatively, the family court may convene a contempt proceeding to hear the allegations concerning violations of an order of protection. If a violation is found, the court may (1) issue a new order; (2) modify an existing order; (3) revoke or order the forfeiture of bail; (4) order the respondent to pay the petitioner's counsel fees; (5) commit the respondent to jail for a term not to exceed six months; and/or (6) revoke the respondent's firearms license.[39]

Domestic Violence and Child Custody

Some states have enacted legislation directing their courts to take domestic violence into account when deciding child custody following a divorce or separation, and in some states domestic violence is considered by child protective services during an investigation.

Domestic Violence in Custody Awards When Parents Divorce or Separate

In some states evidence of domestic violence creates a rebuttable presumption against an award of child custody to the perpetrator. A rebuttable presumption is an inference that rests on certain facts that at first glance support a predetermined conclusion, in this case that the perpetrator of domestic violence is not a fit custodian. A rebuttable presumption may be overcome by the introduction of contrary evidence,[40] for example, when a parent presents evidence that he successfully completed a treatment program or no longer uses alcohol or illegal drugs, that the actions of concern occurred in the distant past, or that the child never witnessed the violent acts cited.[41]

When both parents are violent, the presumption may "cease to exist."[42] For example, in *Krank v. Krank* joint legal custody was awarded to Bruce and Annette with sole physical custody to Bruce. The Supreme Court of North Dakota reversed the trial court and remanded the case for further consideration. The record showed that Bruce and Annette hurled accusations at each other. Annette claimed to have been raped by Bruce, and Bruce claimed to have been shot by Annette. Each party alleged additional acts of violence, agreeing only that the violence ended more than five years earlier, before their son was born. North Dakota's high court reasoned that when there is credible evidence that both parents were violent, the amount and extent of domestic violence inflicted by each should have been measured. If the violence inflicted by one parent was significantly greater than that inflicted by the other, the presumption against awarding custody to the perpetrator applies only to the parent who has inflicted the greater violence. But if the amount and extent of the violence is roughly the same and both parents are otherwise fit, the presumption against awarding custody to either parent ceases to exist.

The court cautioned that the fact that the domestic violence occurred more than five years earlier and before their child was born did not, by itself, overcome the presumption against an award of physical custody to Bruce. It could not be assumed, the court said, that the chance of future violence was overcome by the age of the earlier incident. It would have been more persuasive had Bruce introduced evidence that he had "participated in treatment or counseling related to domestic violence."[43]

A difficulty confronting North Dakota's high court lay in the failure of the trial court to make findings of fact. The record was not clear regarding which of the claims made by either party was considered by the trial court to be true. In its ruling the state supreme court noted that it did not mean to suggest that a slap in the face was roughly proportional to rapes and physical beatings; in fact, the trial court found that those incidents did occur. However, an unjustified shooting, if that had happened, might be considered roughly proportional to those acts of domestic violence. These, the court held, were factual determinations that must be made by the trial court in order to resolve the custody dispute appropriately in this case. On remand the trial court ruled that Bruce had perpetrated "disproportional violence" and awarded custody to Annette. The award was sustained on appeal.[44]

Some courts have ruled that a statutory presumption against an award of custody assumes a "history of violence" or evidence that violence is "typical behavior." Thus the presumption is not triggered by a single act of violence since one act does not constitute the required history,[45] nor, for that matter, will two assaults within a twenty-year marriage be construed as evidence of typical behavior.[46] However, Louisiana statutes admonish courts that a history of family violence may be found where the court finds that one incident has resulted in serious bodily injury.[47] In its Model Code on Domestic Violence, the National Council of Juvenile and Family Court Judges takes the position that a judicial determination that domestic or family violence has occurred gives rise to a rebuttable presumption that it is in the best interests of the child to reside with the parent who is not a perpetrator of domestic or family violence in the location of that parent's choice within or outside the state.[48]

Totality of the Circumstances

Whereas a rebuttable presumption presumes a parent unfit and places on her or him the burden of overcoming the presumption with evidence to suggest that future violence is unlikely, some courts consider violence as only one factor to be considered in an award of custody. Other matters of concern include the quality of the home environment, the existence of siblings, the parent's financial status, the quality of parental guidance, and the ability of each parent to provide for the child's emotional and intellectual functioning.[49] Thus a New York court, in ruling that it was in the child's best interests that custody be awarded to the mother, took into account that the father (1) abused alcohol; (2) operated an automobile without a valid driver's license; and (3) engaged in verbal, economic, sexual, and physical abuse of the mother.[50]

In *Carstens v. Carstens* the Alaska Supreme Court considered a wife's claim that the trial court failed to address her husband's history of domestic violence when it awarded custody of their daughter to him.[51] The state supreme court disagreed with the appellant, finding that the trial court had considered violence by both parents and determined that there was no evidence that the child had been affected, was currently affected, or would in the future be affected significantly. Likewise, in *Canty v. Canty* a mother contested a trial court ruling granting custody to the children's father.[52] She argued that the trial court failed to take into account previous domestic violence. The Arizona appellate court opined that the trial court had found that any violence that occurred had taken place so long ago as to be no longer relevant and that its relevance to the best interests of the children was never shown at trial.

Domestic Violence and Child Protective Services

In some states a child's exposure to domestic violence is to be reported to child protective services,[53] and state statutes may direct protective services staff to consider the presence of domestic violence when an investigation is conducted, even if the violence is not a reportable condition.[54] The neglect statutes of most states are broad enough to support a finding of abuse or neglect on the assumption that a child has suffered or will suffer from exposure to domestic violence. Minnesota statutes, for example, provide that "child neglect includes a failure to protect a child from conditions . . . that seriously endanger the child's . . . mental health."[55] In Utah and Georgia it is criminal child abuse for one household member to abuse another in the presence of a child.[56]

But the connection between acts of domestic violence and child abuse is complicated. Summing up expert testimony on this matter, a federal district judge in New York opined that

> Expert consensus was that children may be—but are not necessarily—negatively affected by witnessing domestic violence. The experts agreed that children who witness domestic violence exhibit a range of responses . . . from none to serious. . . . Three [recent] studies concluded that at least half of the child participants who witnessed domestic violence had "few or no problems evident" when compared with children who were not experiencing domestic violence. . . . There was "a great deal of variability in children's experiences and the impact of those experiences." . . . The evidence was equally mixed as to the question of whether children suffer long-term effects from domestic violence. On the question of the relationship between the presence of domestic violence in a household and direct maltreatment of children, the experts generally agreed that there is some correlation between the two [but it is slight,] with the results of 30 studies showing a 40 percent median co-occurrence.[57]

Courts have removed children from the care of a nonoffending parent and charged her with failing to protect her child.[58] To stop this practice a group of women filed a class-action suit in April 2000 against New York City. The women alleged that their children were removed from their care solely because they were victims of domestic violence.[59]

Finding for the women, the U.S. District judge ruled that the city's policy and practice of removing children from their mothers who were victims of domestic violence was both unnecessary and cruel and motivated mainly by the goal of protecting the city's Administration for Children's Services from criticism, rather than safeguarding children.[60] The city's practice violated the equal protection clause of the Fourteenth Amendment, since the parental rights of women not involved in domestic violence were not interfered with. The court issued a preliminary injunction ordering the city to stop removing children based solely on evidence that a mother was battered.

Is Domestic Violence a Hate Crime?

Hate crimes are defined either by the perpetrator's speech during the crime that reflects animus toward a victim based on her or his membership in a group or by the use of symbols such as swastikas or written derogatory language posted on property.[61] The paradigmatic hate crime involves an individual who is assaulted by one or more people, where the conclusion that the victim was chosen because of a characteristic is inescapable, for example, when a black man is beaten, then tied to a truck driven by three white supremacists, who drag the man behind their truck for three miles until he dies, or when a young gay man is kidnapped, tied to a fence, and left to die.[62] Hate crimes statutes provide for extending the sentence of a convicted person.

Federal law deals with hate crimes in two ways. First, a perpetrator of a crime motivated by the race, color, religion, or national origin of the victim may be prosecuted under federal law.[63] In addition, the Hate Crime Statistics Act authorizes the attorney general to compile yearly data about hate crimes, defined broadly to include acts that manifest prejudice based on race, religion, disability, sexual orientation, or ethnicity.[64] In 2001 the Senate proposed an amendment to the law that added gender to the characteristics covered, but the amendment did not pass.[65]

Those who support statutes that penalize hate crimes argue that such laws are a logical extension of civil rights laws enacted in the late nineteenth century when Congress acted to punish those who committed violent acts based on a victim's race, religion, or national origin.[66] Proponents argue further that hate crimes laws are necessary to send a clear message to perpetrators and to ensure enhanced penalties for bias-motivated crimes.

Those opposed argue that hate crimes laws punish thoughts and speech, thus violating a person's First Amendment rights. In addition, judges already have the power to enhance penalties for crimes that are especially egregious. The U.S. Supreme Court disagreed with the proposition that hate crimes laws implicate the First Amendment. In June 1993 it ruled that a Wisconsin hate crimes statute that provided for sentence enhancement for bias crimes was constitutional and that evidence regarding animus could be entered at sentencing.[67] A physical assault is not expressive conduct that is protected by the First Amendment, the Court ruled, even though the person committing the assault intends to express an idea.

Hate Crimes and Gender

In 2002 fifty-four jurisdictions had hate crimes laws, thirty-four of which included gender-based violence.[68] When gender-based violence is included in hate crimes legislation, it is clear that violent crimes committed by a stranger could be considered hate crimes. However, it does not follow that domestic violence would viewed be in this manner because the intimate relationship between the perpetrator and victim makes it difficult to prove that the crime was motivated by gender bias rather than any of the myriad factors that might exist in a relationship between intimates.

Those who argue for inclusion of domestic violence point out that it is important to recognize domestic violence for the hate-motivated crime that it is, that its inclusion sends an important message to the community at large about the government's position on this matter, and that enhanced penalties can act as an important deterrent. Those opposed refer to many of the arguments advanced by proponents and take the position that (1) there are adequate laws to deal with domestic violence; (2) the judiciary would be overwhelmed by the number of cases generated by the inclusion of domestic violence in hate crimes statutes; (3) treating domestic violence as a hate crime militates against rehabilitation; and (4) if the police have problems determining what is and is not domestic violence, how could they be expected to determine whether a crime is motivated by hate?[69] Stated otherwise, if only some of these crimes reflect discriminatory bias, how can we discern the ones that do from the ones that don't?[70]

Thus proving that a victim was selected because of gender may be difficult. In California, for example, it must be shown that the crime was committed "because of" bias toward the group of which the victim is a member, meaning that the bias factor must be the "cause in fact" of the attack, even if other causes exist (chapter 7).[71] In New York the victim must be "intentionally selected in whole or substantial part" because of the person's gender.[72] Thus the difficulty in a domestic violence context is untangling a variety of motives and establishing that the assault was based on gender.

In its report on gender-motivated violence, the Senate Committee on the Judiciary opined that whether an assault is gender motivated could be determined from the "totality of the circumstances" surrounding an event, including, when the parties involved are of the opposite sex, evidence that (1) the victim was female; (2) the attacker was male; (3) the attacker did not typically assault men but has a history of assaulting women or a history of making discriminatory statements about women; and (4) that the attacker shouted gender-based epithets during the assault.[73] Taken together, these elements may demonstrate that an attack was motivated by gender.

Following the line of thinking advocated by the Senate Judiciary Committee, a federal district judge in Washington state, commenting on the "many causes of violence within a marital relationship," found that the facts alleged by a victim could support an inference that gender motivated the violence within the marital relationship.[74] The relevant evidence included (1) sex abuse within the marital relationship; (2) the use of gender-specific epithets such as calling the plaintiff a "dumb-ass woman" and saying, "You're a woman, what do you know?" (3) acts that perpetuate a stereotype of women in a submissive role, for example, the defendant controlled all of the family's finances, held plaintiff's passport, and did not disclose family finances to her; (4) "severe and excessive" attacks on plaintiff, especially during her pregnancy; and (5) violence without provocation and in response to the plaintiff's assertion of her independence.

PART 2—ELDER ABUSE

The problem of elder abuse came to public attention in the late 1970s, following public awareness of and statutory reform that addressed child abuse and domestic violence between adults in intimate relationships.[75] State laws governing adult protective services (APS) define as vulnerable adults aged sixty or sixty-five and in some states anyone older than eighteen who is vulnerable because a disability prevents the individual from acting on his or her own behalf.[76] Abuse of a vulnerable adult may be prosecuted as a civil or criminal matter and may be treated as domestic violence if the parties are husband and wife or, depending upon state law, cohabitants. Criminal charges may be brought if the abuse involves a felony assault or financial exploitation.

The Scope of the Problem

The National Elder Abuse Incidence Study compiled data from a nationally representative sample of twenty counties in fifteen states. The data came from APS records and from "sentinels," individuals with frequent contact with the elderly who were trained by the researchers to recognize signs and symptoms of abuse or neglect. From their report we learn that in 1996 approximately 450,000 adults were abused or neglected or were the victims of financial exploitation, with an additional 100,000 adults suffering from self-neglect. In 90 percent of cases where the perpetrator was identified, she or he was a family member, and two-thirds of this group were adult children or spouses.[77] No more than 21 percent of cases were reported to APS; the remaining reports were made by sentinels. According to the study authors, the number of unreported incidents is four to five times greater than what is reported,[78] a conclusion supported in a report issued by the Committee on Aging of the U.S. House of Representatives, based on its survey of APS in fifty states. Committee members expressed their surprise at the estimate of unreported cases, since reporting of elder abuse is mandated in forty-two states and the District of Columbia.[79]

What Actions Constitute Elder Abuse?

Federal and state laws categorize elder abuse, neglect, and exploitation as mistreatment that includes

- Abuse, defined as "the willful infliction of injury, unreasonable confinement, intimidation, or cruel punishment . . . resulting [in] physical harm, pain, or mental anguish; or the deprivation by [another] . . . of goods or services that are necessary to avoid physical harm, mental anguish, or mental illness."

- Neglect, defined as "the failure to provide needed medical care, food, abandonment and withholding medical devices such as hearing aids, canes, [and] walkers and may include 'self neglect,' which results from an adult's inability, due to physical and/or mental impairments, to perform tasks essential to caring for oneself, including but not limited to, providing essential food, clothing, shelter and medical care, obtaining goods and services necessary to maintain physical health, mental health, emotional well-being and general safety; or managing financial affairs."
- Exploitation, defined as "the illegal or improper act or process of an individual, including a caregiver, using the resources of an older individual for monetary or personal benefit, profit, or gain."[80]

A caregiver is an individual who voluntarily, by contract, or by accepting a fee assumes responsibility for the care of an older person.[81]

Federal Role in Elder Abuse

The Older Americans Act (OAA) of 1965 is the only federal law specifically targeting the problem of elder abuse. Title VII of the OAA authorizes grants to the states to carry out activities to protect vulnerable elders.[82] Funds may be used for (1) an ombudsman program; (2) programs to prevent abuse, neglect, and exploitation, including outreach, counseling, mental health services, and shelter; and (3) legal assistance programs.[83] In addition, a victim of elder abuse whose situation fits a state's definition of domestic violence may benefit from services funded under the Violence Against Women Act, and some states use a portion of their Title XX funds to support APS.[84]

To qualify for OAA funds states must have (1) laws that provide immunity for those who report elder abuse; (2) laws that provide for prompt investigation of reports; and (3) the means to protect victims.[85]

State Role in Elder Abuse—Adult Protective Services

Adult protective services is a unit or department located in a social service agency. APS workers undertake preventive and remedial activities on behalf of adults who are vulnerable due to age or disability and who cannot protect themselves from maltreatment, defined to include abuse, neglect, and financial exploitation at the hands of another, or self-inflicted harm that results from "ignorance, illiteracy, incompetency, mental limitation, substance abuse, or poor health."[86]

Reporting

In forty-two states reporting known or suspected maltreatment of vulnerable adults is mandatory, and in others it is permitted. The list of mandated reporters includes some professionals mandated to report child abuse, such as social workers, health care professionals, and law enforcement personnel, and may include physical and occupational therapists, clergy, and staff in residential facilities and adult day-care centers. As with child abuse laws, reporters are immune from suit for reports made in good faith; state laws provide for the confidentiality of information and anonymity for the reporter. Some states maintain a central registry of reports. Depending upon the degree of injury and inferences of intent, elder abuse will be classified as a misdemeanor or a felony.

Investigations are typically carried out by social workers or by the police when the matter at hand may give rise to criminal charges. Tasks routinely assigned to the social worker who investigates a report include (1) conducting an assessment to determine the needs of the person on whose behalf the investigation is being conducted, including whether the person is safe if he or she is living alone; (2) arranging for needed services; (3) arranging for evaluations to determine competency; (4) initiating where appropriate a petition for guardianship; (5) referring for services; and (6) providing assistance for obtaining an order of protection.[87]

Nursing Homes

Long-term nursing home care may be provided under the Medicaid program, and time-limited care in a skilled nursing home may be provided under the Medicare program.[88] The majority of nursing homes participate in the Medicaid and Medicare programs. These programs support only state-licensed care facilities, in which an estimated 1.5 million elderly and disabled residents reside.[89] Some facilities are not certified for Medicaid or Medicare reimbursement but house disabled individuals who are recipients of Supplemental Security Income (SSI). Standards for care in facilities not certified by Medicare or Medicaid where SSI beneficiaries reside are governed by the "Keys amendment,"[90] which limits the use of SSI funds to support substandard facilities.

Rules established by the Centers for Medicaid and Medicare Services[91] in the U.S. Department of Health and Human Services provide that nursing home residents have a series of rights and impose on the care facility the obligation to inform residents of their rights, including the right to (1) choose an attending physician; (2) be fully informed about planned care and to participate in developing a plan for care, including any changes in a plan for care and treatment; (3) be free from physical or mental abuse, corporal punishment, involuntary seclusion, and the use of physical or chemical restraints imposed for disciplinary purposes or for staff convenience and not required to treat the resident's medical symptoms.[92]

Investigations and Complaints of Maltreatment in Nursing Homes Complaints of inadequate care may be made by residents, family members, staff, and ombudsmen, and a variety of federal, state, and local agencies play a part in the investigative process. Depending on state law, investigations may be undertaken by a state agency, such as a state department of health, or by a state's Medicaid fraud unit, APS, or law enforcement when it is necessary to conduct a criminal investigation.

Ombudsman Program Each state that receives federal funds must establish an office of the state long-term care ombudsman, whose task is to protect residents of nursing homes and other long-term care facilities by identifying, investigating, and resolving complaints made by, or on behalf of, residents and that relate to action, inaction, or decisions that may adversely affect the health, safety, welfare, or rights of the residents.[93]

An ombudsman may (1) represent the interests of residents as they seek administrative and legal remedies to protect themselves; (2) recommend changes in laws and regulations pertaining to the health, safety, welfare, and rights of residents and facilitate public comment on these issues; (3) educate consumers and the general public regarding issues related to long-term care; (4) promote the development of citizen organizations to participate in the programs; and (5) provide technical support for the development of resident and family councils to protect the well-being and rights of residents.

Guardianship

When a person is not able to act on his or her own behalf, a guardian or conservator may be appointed (1) as a "guardian of property" to manage the estate of a person, referred to as a "ward," who is unable to manage his or her own affairs; or (2) as a "guardian of the person," who acts as a substitute decision maker, for example, by making medical decisions that the ward is not able to make; or (3) as both. To maintain the autonomy of the individual, guardianship may be limited to certain matters,[94] such as making judicially defined medical decisions or managing only the day-to-day finances of a ward but not major financial decisions, such as those concerning real estate or investments.

New York's APS law permits a department of social services to petition the court for appointment of a person to act as a "community guardian."[95] As the name implies, the community guardian is charged with maintaining her or his ward outside hospitals and residential treatment facilities through the provision of community-based services. A person is eligible for the appointment of a community guardian, if she or he is (1) eligible for or a current recipient of adult protective services; (2) without a friend or relative able and willing to serve; and (3) not living in a hospital or residential facility or, if living in either, has a plan to return to the community.[96]

Who May Be Appointed Guardian?

In some states any competent person may be appointed guardian,[97] but a court may take into account the wishes of the incapacitated person that are expressed in a will or the wishes of the person's spouse. The Uniform Guardianship and Protective Proceedings Act lists a hierarchy of those qualified to serve, including (1) anyone currently acting for the incapacitated person; (2) anyone nominated by the incapacitated person when she or he had the capacity to make a reasonably intelligent choice; or the incapacitated person's (3) spouse; (4) adult child; (4) parent; or (5) adult friend or relative with whom the person lived for more than six months before a petition for guardianship was filed.[98]

Petitioning the Court

Guardianship may be voluntary, as when an elderly person appoints a relative or friend to manage his or her affairs, but it is necessary to petition the court for involuntary guardianship. The framework that governs the legal process is by now familiar to us because of previous discussions. The process is initiated when a petition is filed: In an emergency situation a guardian may be appointed following an ex parte hearing, but a formal hearing to determine competency must occur. The petition must be served on the incapacitated person, regardless of her or his state of mind, and on affected parties such as family members, a person with whom the allegedly incapacitated person lives, and creditors.

Depending upon state law, the presence of a seriously incapacitated person may not be mandated at a formal hearing, but concern with including the person on whose behalf action is taken is such that hearings may be held at the home of incapacitated people, at a nursing home, or at a hospital. States differ on whether an attorney or guardian *ad litem* is appointed to represent the interests of a vulnerable adult.

Competency or Incapacity

The law presumes that people are competent, thus capable of managing their own affairs. The party that petitions the court for appointment of a guardian must present evidence that the person on whose behalf action is being taken lacks the capacity to make her or his own decisions. In New York the proof must go to the "decisional or functional" ability of the person, meaning that a guardian should not be appointed based solely on a label that refers to mental illness or physical disability. The court must address the individual's ability to manage the "activities of daily living," such as preparing food, housekeeping, shopping, "money management, banking, driving or using public transportation, and other activities related to personal needs and to property management."[99]

The Court Evaluator When a petition is filed, unless the respondent has an attorney or the court deems it necessary to appoint an attorney, the court will appoint a court evaluator, who may be a social worker, other mental health professional, nurse, or physician.[100] The evaluator is charged with conducting an independent investigation to assist the court in determining whether the person on whose behalf the petition was filed has the capacity to act on her or his own behalf. The evaluator will interview the petitioner, the person alleged to be incapacitated, and others with information that contributes to the investigation and recommendations. The evaluator must report to the court her or his "personal observations" concerning the person on whose behalf the guardianship petition was filed.

The general rule is that any competent person may be appointed as a guardian, but there are variations by state. Possible choices include a social service agency and, in states with a public guardian program, a person from that office. Guardianship terminates on the death of a ward and should be terminated if the ward regains competence to act on his or her behalf. Two options, in addition to guardianship, include standby guardianship and power of attorney. (See the discussion of substitute decision making in chapter 13.)

Alternatives to Guardianship

While still competent, a person may foresee the need to have a substitute decision maker to act on his or her behalf. Two options, in addition to guardianship, include standby guardianship and power of attorney. (See the discussion of substitute decision making in chapter 13.)

In some states a person may appoint another as a standby guardian, who is authorized to step in, should a court-appointed guardian be unable to act, or a person may appoint another to step in, should she or he become incapacitated due to physical illness or mental incapacity.[101]

Any competent adult may create a power of attorney by appointing another to act in her or his place. For example, a person who enters the hospital for major surgery may appoint another to manage his or her financial affairs during the term of the hospitalization, or to act in his or her stead to complete a transaction such as the sale of property.

Whereas a power of attorney becomes void when a court appoints a guardian after a finding of incompetency, a durable power of attorney remains in effect. Thus people who want to ensure that their elected representative will retain authority should they become incapacitated will execute a durable power of attorney.

Representative Payee

A representative payee may be appointed by a federal agency responsible for paying cash benefits such as Social Security retirement benefits or Supplemental Security Income, when the agency determines that "representative payment is in the interest of a beneficiary . . . even if the beneficiary is a legally competent individual." The federal agency may designate a family member, friend, or public or private institution as the representative payee based on a determination that the beneficiary is not able to manage her or his own affairs, but the latter is not equivalent to a judicial determination of incompetency.[102] A representative payee must be appointed for an individual for whom drug addiction or alcoholism is a contributing factor material to the determination of disability.[103] The representative payee assumes responsibility for disbursing funds for food, clothing, shelter, and the like.

SUMMARY

In this chapter we have reviewed two types of family violence: domestic violence and elder abuse. The former is a crime perpetrated primarily against women by their spouses or partners, whereas the latter is concerned with acts of violence against vulnerable adults perpetrated by family members and caretakers but also includes self-neglect.

The federal government responds to these forms of violence through grant-in-aid programs that support state efforts to provide shelter and victims' services and to improve through training the ways in which state officials respond to these crimes. The federal government also regulates the care of vulnerable adults in nursing homes.

The laws of New York illustrate how one state responds to domestic violence. We learned that the police must arrest the perpetrator and must provide information and immediate assistance to the victim, who may pursue a legal remedy in civil or criminal court. The victim interested in salvaging her relationship will elect a civil remedy where the possibility exists for rehabilitative services, in contrast to seeking to criminally punish the perpetrator who, if convicted, may be imprisoned. When domestic violence involves attempted murder, murder, and assault with a deadly weapon, the state is free to pursue criminal charges regardless of the victim's choice.

A court may issue an order of protection after a petition is filed. An order of protection may direct the perpetrator to stay away from the victim, limit or preclude visitation with children, and provide for child support and medical insurance. Since an order of protection is analogous to an arrest warrant, a violation is grounds for arrest, and, following a court hearing, forfeiture of bail and a jail sentence are possible.

Domestic violence may have an impact on child custody in two ways. First, in some states, when parents are having a custody battle, evidence of domestic violence may create a rebuttable presumption against an award of child custody to the perpetrator, unless the presumption is rebutted with evidence of rehabilitation. In other states domestic violence is viewed as one factor among many to be considered by a court, which also considers such factors as the quality of the home environment and the parent's ability to provide for a child's emotional and intellectual functioning. The second way that domestic violence may affect child custody occurs in those states that view a child's exposure to such violence as a condition to be reported to child protective services and where statutes direct protective services staff to consider the presence of domestic violence when an investigation is conducted.

Scholars and advocates debate whether domestic violence is a hate crime. Both sides present a range of arguments. Proponents often take the position that including domestic violence in hate crimes statutes is important because it recognizes domestic violence for the hate-motivated crime that it is and that enhanced penalties can act an important deterrent. Opponents often note that laws that punish hate crime punish thoughts and speech and that judges already have the authority to enhance penalties for crimes that are especially egregious. A key difficulty in including domestic violence as a hate crime lies in the intimate relationship between the perpetrator and victim, which makes it difficult to prove that the crime was motivated by gender bias rather than any of the myriad factors that might exist in a relationship between intimates.

Depending upon the relationship between the perpetrator and victim, elder abuse may be classified as domestic violence and treated in the ways just discussed, or it may be classified as abuse or neglect. When classified as abuse or neglect, forty-two states have mandated reporting of abuse or neglect of a vulnerable adult to adult protective services, whose staff will investigate the allegation.

When the adult who is the subject of a report lives in a nursing home, federal, state, and local agencies play a part in the investigative process. For example, an investigation may be undertaken by a state agency such as a department of health or by a state's Medicaid fraud unit, APS, or the police. In addition, each state that receives federal funds must establish an office of the state long-term care ombudsman. Staff are charged with protecting residents of nursing homes and other long-term care facilities by identifying, investigating, and resolving complaints that, if left unresolved, may adversely affect the health, safety, welfare, or rights of the residents.

An adult may decide to appoint another to act on her or his behalf, should she or he become incapacitated. Available options include power of attorney, standby guardianship, and guardianship. For the adult who has not appointed another and who subsequently becomes unable to act on his or her own behalf, a guardian or conservator may be appointed to manage the individual's property and/or to act as a substitute decision maker. However, when the request for a guardian is made by a third party, a court may not appoint a guardian unless it conducts a hearing to determine the competency of the vulnerable adult. Since the law presumes that people are competent, thus capable of managing their own affairs, the party that petitions the court for appointment of a guardian must present evidence that the person on whose behalf action is being taken lacks the capacity to make her or his own decisions.

13

Legal Issues in Health Care

THE FOCUS of this chapter will be on legal issues in health care that affect social practice and the clients that social workers serve. Health care services are provided by the public and private sectors. The work of social workers is affected by publicly funded programs, such as Medicare, Medicaid, the State Children's Health Insurance Program, programs operated by the Indian Health Service and the Veterans Administration, as well as by private insurance schemes. Regardless of the funding source or treatment setting, social workers play a significant role in the health care field by (1) providing direct services to patients and their families; (2) planning for a patient's aftercare needs, including arranging for and coordinating aftercare services; (3) helping patients understand their rights, for example, to participate in making medical decisions; (4) participating in the evaluation of adults whose competency to make medical decisions is challenged; and (5) advocating for patients.

Despite the existence of publicly funded health care, most Americans derive their health insurance from their employment. Approximately 64 percent of the population with medical coverage at any point in time is covered by employment-based insurance. An additional 13.5 percent is covered through the Medicare program, eligibility for which is linked to employment history. In 2001 the U.S. Census Bureau estimated that 41.2 million Americans lacked health insurance for the entire year, but the number of uninsured people during the year varied with periods of economic recession and growth, as it did when eligibility rules for public programs changed.[1]

I referred to issues related to health care in earlier chapters. In chapter 2, I reported that a competent adult has the right to elect an appropriate course of treatment as well as the right to refuse treatment; and in chapters 2 and 5, I reported that the U.S. Supreme Court has held that people have a right to privacy in their medical records. Chapter 5 included a discussion of confidentiality of medical records and addressed disclosure of confidential information, including confidentiality provisions in the Americans with Disabilities Act (ADA) that protect from disclosure medical information discovered in the course of a pre-employment interview.

This chapter will begin with a general discussion of patients' bills of rights. Next we will focus on specific topics, including (1) the right to treatment; (2) informed consent; (3) the right to refuse treatment; (4) surrogate decision making; and (5) the state's interest in compelling treatment. Next our attention will turn to medical issues concerning children and will cover the following topics: (1) lodging civil charges against parents for withholding medical care; (2) lodging criminal charges against parents for withholding medical care; and (3) a minor's right to consent to medical treatment.

PATIENT RIGHTS—BILLS OF RIGHTS

Patient rights may be expressed in bills of rights, which include such guarantees as patients' involvement in making decisions affecting their care, patients' privacy, and patients' right to voice grievances regarding medical care without fear of retaliation. Efforts to codify bills of rights have taken place at the federal level as well as in the states, with the greatest success at the state level.

Federal efforts to codify bills of rights are an outgrowth of the consumer concern that traditional "fee-for-service" arrangements—where the insured person selects his or her care provider, who is reimbursed at a rate set by the insurer—are giving way to managed care plans, most of which are health maintenance organizations (HMOs). In an HMO (1) the insurer is often the provider; (2) access to health care is often controlled by a physician-gatekeeper, generally a primary care physician who determines whether the patient may see specialists; and (3) members may be served on a capitated basis, which means that the insurer pays a fixed sum to a provider to cover medical costs for each plan member. If the cost of care exceeds the capitated sum, the provider absorbs the extra fees. If costs are less than the capitated sum, the provider keeps the difference.

Consumers' concerns regarding HMOs stem from the possibility that their insurance carrier will compel them to join a managed care program and, if this happens, the possibility that (1) a change of primary care provider will be necessary if their physician of choice does not participate in an HMO; (2) access to specialists will be curtailed by gatekeepers; (3) decisions concerning access to services will be made in an arbitrary fashion by faceless decision makers working for a managed care plan; and (4) those to whom one appeals an adverse decision will act as arbitrarily as the person who denied the care requested.[2] Given these concerns, it should not come as a surprise that federal legislation addressing patients' rights has focused on managed care issues. For example, in 2001 legislation was introduced in the House and Senate that guaranteed a patient's right to grieve adverse health care decisions and to receive certain specialized care. Both versions prohibited payment schemes that encouraged physicians to deny care, and both held plans accountable for medical decisions that resulted in injury or death.[3] Congress adjourned without enacting any legislation.

Patient advocates have had greater success at the state level, where patients' bills of rights have been enacted, with most focusing on the mentally ill and nursing home residents. Statutory protections include a patient's right to (1) have the information necessary to decide whether to accept the care offered; (2) voice grievances concerning treatment by facility staff and the care received; (3) personal privacy, and for those in institutional settings, to communicate by telephone and uncensored mail with the outside world as well as to receive visitors; and (4) confidentiality of records.[4]

For a bill of rights to be more than a statement of principle, those covered must have a right to bring suit to enforce the provisions in a bill of rights, and there must be mechanisms for pursuing a grievance that go beyond administrative procedures conducted by the institution against which the grievance is lodged. For example, such mechanisms would allow procedures that allow a petitioner to pursue a claim in a court of law.

An appellate court in Minnesota found that a patient had a right to sue when it ruled that the state's patient bill of rights precluded a hospital from arbitrarily discharging or transferring a patient based on her refusal to accept a particular course of treatment. The hospital should have conducted a comprehensive assessment and developed a care plan that included an exploration of alternative treatments, the court ruled.[5] Likewise, a trial court in Connecticut determined that a woman who had been forced to disrobe in front of a male hospital attendant, under threat that she would be forcibly disrobed if she did not comply, could pursue under the state's bill of rights a claim that she had not received "humane and dignified" treatment.[6] In 2000 California amended its patient bill of rights to include a provision allowing an individual in a managed care plan who is infected with HIV or who has AIDS to have an enforceable right to a "standing referral" to a specialist in treating either condition.[7]

RIGHT TO TREATMENT

There is no federal constitutional right to receive medical care,[8] although an individual's right to receive emergency medical care and to receive care without regard to disability are protected by statute. In addition, those eligible for medical coverage under the Medicaid or Medicare programs have an enforceable right to receive care.[9]

Provisions for emergency care are found in the Emergency Medical Treatment and Active Labor Act, which requires hospitals with emergency departments that receive federal funds to provide medical screenings and stabilizing treatments to any individual requesting assistance, regardless of ability to pay.[10] Once stabilized, patients may be transferred to another hospital if the care required is not provided by the hospital at which the patient sought help, but a hospital may not delay screening or providing needed treatment to inquire about the individual's ability to pay. Service must be provided even if the hospital knows that the patient's insurance will not pay because preauthorization was not obtained.

Care without regard to disability is provided for in the Vocational Rehabilitation Act (VRA) and the Americans with Disabilities Act (ADA). In chapter 9, I said that these civil rights statutes protect from discrimination children and adults with disabilities. Both statutes require institutions and individuals to provide to qualified people with disabilities the same access to programs and services provided to people who are not disabled. A qualified person is one who is in all respects but for her or his disability eligible to receive the service sought. Thus the U.S. Supreme Court found that a dentist violated the ADA by requiring that a woman who was HIV positive and needed routine dental care be treated in a hospital, where she would have to absorb additional costs.[11]

Medicare, Title XVIII of the Social Security Act, and Medicaid, Title XIX of the Social Security Act, are entitlement programs.[12] Operating nationwide, Medicare provides health insurance for almost all people who are older than sixty-five and for some younger people with disabilities who receive Supplemental Security Disability Income. Health care coverage under the Medicaid program is available for people who are categorically eligible because of age, disability, or membership in a family with dependent children, and to pregnant women. All must meet the program's financial need standard. In addition, a majority of states extend Medicaid coverage to the "medically needy," who are categorically eligible but whose income is too high to qualify for coverage. In 2001 Medicaid provided health care coverage to approximately 11 percent of the population, excluding those in institutions, and close to 40.5 percent of people with incomes below the poverty level.[13] Medicaid is the major source for health coverage for individuals who depend on publicly supported health care.

While both Medicare and Medicaid provide coverage for health care, neither contains a guarantee that any particular treatment will be available.[14] Both programs require health care providers, including hospitals that serve Medicare and Medicaid patients, to provide services that are "medically necessary."[15] A medically necessary service is a

> medical, surgical, or other service required for the prevention, diagnosis, cure, or treatment of a health- related condition including services necessary to prevent a decremental change in either medical or mental health status. Medically necessary services must be provided in the most cost effective and appropriate setting and shall not be provided solely for the convenience of the member or service provider.[16]

However, although a service may be deemed medically necessary, a patient does not necessarily have a right to receive treatment.[17] For example, a physician may determine that a mammogram or prostate cancer test is medically necessary, but Medicare pays for the former only if a woman is older than thirty-five and for the latter only for men older than fifty. Moreover, the cost of providing either test will not be covered if performed more frequently than allowed by statute.[18]

In addition to these limits, Congress may decide that federal monies cannot be used to provide a particular service. This kind of decision was made in 1976, when Congress enacted the Hyde Amendment, which precludes the use of federal funds to pay for abortions, except in cases of incest or rape or when the woman's life would be threatened unless an abortion were performed.[19] The U.S. Supreme Court upheld the right of Congress to enact this limit on the use of federal monies.[20]

Medical Care for Noncitizens

When Congress enacted the Personal Responsibility and Work Opportunity Reconciliation Act of 1996 (PRWORA; see chapter 1),[21] it limited the eligibility of noncitizens to receive federally funded public assistance, including health benefits, under the Medicaid program. Under PRWORA, aliens are deemed qualified or not qualified for Medicaid coverage.[22] Exceptions allow the provision of medical services to people who are not eligible for federal aid, including the receipt of (1) emergency medical treatment; (2) medical treatment for battered spouses and their children, whose injuries stemmed from the battering; (3) immunizations; and (4) treatment for communicable diseases.[23]

Litigation on Behalf of Noncitizens

Medicaid is funded by a combination of federal and state contributions. When Congress enacted PRWORA, it provided that federal funds not be used to support unqualified aliens. Each state is free to use state funds to provide medical care for aliens. Some states, including New Jersey, Connecticut, Pennsylvania, California, and Massachusetts, decided to provide Medicaid benefits to those not eligible under federal law, while other states, including New York, Texas, and Florida, declined to do so.[24] In 2001 New York's highest court heard an appeal filed by twelve noncitizens lawfully residing in New York state who sued the state for denying them health care benefits.[25] Plaintiffs asked whether the denial of state-funded Medicaid benefits to legal aliens is a violation of the equal protection clause of the U.S. Constitution and Article 17 of the New York Constitution. The latter provides that "the aid, care and support of the needy are public concerns and shall be provided by the state and by such of its subdivisions, and in such manner and by such means, as the legislature from time to time may determine." The court agreed with the plaintiffs' claim that denying Medicaid benefits violated the state and federal constitutions and ruled that New York state could not deny Medicaid benefits to legal aliens.

In another case a class action was filed on behalf of women not legally residing in the United States who claimed a right to prenatal care; the suit also was brought on behalf of their American-born children, who, they claimed, should be eligible for Medicaid.[26] As to the argument for prenatal care, the women claimed that denying prenatal care affected their unborn children, who would be American citizens if born in the United States, thus denying them equal protection of the law. The court rejected this argument since "unborn children" are not "persons" under the Constitution and could not, therefore, claim any constitutional rights. However, whether newborns who were citizens at birth were eligible for Medicaid was not determined by the status of their mothers as illegal aliens.

INFORMED CONSENT

The U.S. Supreme Court has said that an individual has a right at common law to self-determination, which refers to a person's right not to be touched by another person without legal justification or permission from the person touched.[27] The doctrine of informed consent developed from this precept. A medical provider cannot treat a patient without the consent of the person to be treated except (1) in an emergency when a person is not able to give consent, or (2) under a court order, for example, when the patient is a child or not legally competent to give consent.

The purpose of informed consent is to enable a person to make a "knowing and willful" decision without coercion to proceed with a plan of treatment.[28] Coercion may be overt or subtle. For example, a provider may strive to sway a decision by the choice and use of words and phrases, by selecting what information to provide and to withhold, and by body language that conveys a predisposition to one or another treatment option.

A decision cannot be knowing and willful unless a person has all the information that a reasonable person would consider relevant to the decision to be made. Statutes governing informed consent may require that consent to be in writing, signed by the person to be treated, and to report that she or he has been told (1) that treatment is voluntary; (2) that consent may be withdrawn; (3) the objective sought by providing treatment; (4) the likely benefits and risks; (5) the procedures to be followed; and (6) the alternative treatments available, including those the physician is not able to provide.[29]

When a patient sues a medical provider alleging a failure of informed consent, courts judge the claim by applying one of two standards. The first is an objective standard, where the question to be answered is, "What information would a reasonable practitioner in the same or similar medical community have provided to the patient?" The second standard is a subjective test that asks, "What did the patient need to know to make an intelligent decision?" Regardless of the standard applied, a physician need not disclose all risks attendant to a procedure, only those that are of a "serious nature."[30]

RIGHT TO REFUSE TREATMENT

A corollary to the doctrine of informed consent is the right of an individual to refuse treatment, which may be exercised for different reasons, including (1) religious conviction; (2) certainty that the gains do not offset the risks; and (3) the wish not to prolong needless suffering when death seems inevitable. In 1985 the Supreme Court of New Jersey opined that self-determination allows a competent person to refuse medical treatment, even if death is a likely result.[31] However, the right to refuse treatment extends to adults who are competent, and this right may in certain circumstances be weighed against certain state interests. These matters, along with the subject of treating a person without the person's consent, will be considered next.

Competency and the Right to Refuse Treatment

The ability to participate in decisions regarding a course of medical treatment requires that the affected person be competent. In chapter 12 we learned that the law presumes that a person is competent unless it is proved otherwise. Thus the person seeking to have a guardian appointed to make medical decisions for another must show by clear and convincing evidence that the person over whom guardianship is sought is not able to decide for himself or herself.

Courts are most likely to appoint a guardian for a minor, for an adult who is comatose, or for a person whose mental faculties are so limited as to preclude her or his ability to render a reasoned decision. However, because the appointment of a guardian results in a deprivation of liberty, courts are reluctant to order an appointment solely to override a disfavored decision. For example, a court in Pennsylvania declined to appoint a guardian because a person's decisions simply seemed "unwise, foolish or ridiculous," even though the person was a patient in a mental hospital.[32] Likewise, an appellate court in Oregon ruled that to justify appointment of a guardian, the person seeking guardianship had to prove that the person to be protected had severely "impaired perception or communication skills causing life-threatening disability." The court then refused to appoint a guardian for an eighty-six-year-old woman when the only evidence presented was that she had mildly impaired cognitive skills, occasional mental confusion, and memory lapses.[33]

Consider another case, where an appellate court in Massachusetts was confronted with a petition filed by the daughter of a seventy-seven-year-old woman who was seeking guardianship over her mother, Mrs. C.[34] Mrs. C. had gangrene in her foot but refused to have it amputated even though death was the probable result of her decision. Her daughter argued that a reasonable person would not make such a choice, therefore, it followed that her mother was not competent.

Two psychiatrists testified. One opined that Mrs. C. was not rational, but the court discounted his testimony after deciding that it was a conclusion drawn from Mrs. C.'s unwillingness to discuss the matter with him rather than an opinion based on direct evidence of irrationality. In addition, the psychiatrist characterized "an unwilling[ness], for whatever reason, to consent to life saving treatment . . . as suicidal." The second psychiatrist concluded that Mrs. C. was rational and opined that he and the other psychiatrist who testified had a difference in opinion stemming from their philosophies about choices that people have a right to make. Mrs. C.'s social worker also testified that in her opinion Mrs. C. was rational but did have a tendency to "tune out" when someone tried to tell her something that she did not want to hear.

The court considered the reasons offered by Mrs. C., including that she (1) had been unhappy since her husband's death; (2) did not wish to be a burden to her children; (3) did not believe that the operation would cure her, since previous operations had not arrested the advance of the gangrene; (4) did not wish to live as an invalid or in a nursing home; and (5) did not fear death but welcomed it. She told the judge that she would prefer to get well but stated also that she was resigned to death and was adamantly opposed to the operation. The court concluded that there was no "indication in any of the testimony that [Mrs. C.'s] choice was made without a full appreciation of the consequences. The most that is shown is that the decision involves strong, emotional factors [and] that she does not choose to discuss the decision with certain persons."[35]

State's Interest in Compelling Treatment

An individual's right to refuse treatment is balanced against the state's interest in (1) prolonging life; (2) protecting third parties, for example, children who may encounter emotional and financial problems following a parent's death; (3) preventing suicide; and (4) maintaining the ethical integrity of the medical profession and allowing hospitals the opportunity to care for people in their custody and control.[36]

The state expresses its interest in safeguarding the health of its citizens in various ways. For example, state laws (1) provide for appointment of a guardian to protect the interests of an incompetent person; (2) require parents to have their children vaccinated as a condition for admission to public school; (3) require medical providers and medical laboratories to report certain contagious and communicable diseases to public health officials; (4) require, in certain circumstances, that public health officials notify a person who has been exposed to a contagious or communicable disease; and (5) provide for quarantine of people with contagious diseases.

The state's interest is greatest when there is a threat from outside, for example, when a person with a contagious or communicable disease threatens the health of others, or when the person in need of care is not able to care for himself or herself.[37] For example, the general rule is that parents have a right to determine what medical care their children receive, but this parental right may be limited by statute or judicial ruling when the public good would be better served by overruling parental choice. Therefore, a state's public health law may require that children be immunized against childhood diseases, including polio, mumps, measles, and hepatitis B, and that admission to public school may hinge on a parent's presenting to school officials a certificate of vaccination. An exception may be made when a parent's decision not to have a child vaccinated is based on "genuine and sincere religious belief."[38] Otherwise, parental failure to comply with an immunization law may result in a court's declaring a child neglected if noncompliance rests on a knowing failure to act and where objections to vaccination, while sincere, rest on "medical and scientific concerns rather than religious convictions."[39]

Treatment Without Consent

The state's interest in protecting the health of its citizens does not mean that the state can always order treatment over an individual's objections. There are limited circumstances, such as those just discussed, or medical emergencies when a person is not able to make a decision, when there is not enough time to contact a person authorized to do so, or when an accident victim may be treated without consent. The latter rests on the presumption that most people would consent to be treated under emergency circumstances.[40]

The person treated without consent may sue the individual or institution that authorized treatment by alleging violation of his or her Fourteenth Amendment right to privacy or by bringing a suit for assault or battery. A corollary to the proposition that a person may not be treated without consent is that informed consent is needed before a person may be tested for the presence of drugs or a sexually transmitted disease. For example, courts have held that a patient's Fourth Amendment rights have been violated when urine is tested for the presence of drugs or when blood is drawn or tested for HIV without patient consent.[41]

The most common "treatment without consent" cases involve patients who refuse treatment on religious grounds, but there are cases where physicians seek to administer treatment that individuals and family members do not wish for. The state's interest in preserving life and a medical professional's obligation to seek this end may be pitted against the wish of a family member not to provide treatment or to stop treatment. When this kind of disagreement occurs, either the state must seek a court order to sanction involuntary care or the person wishing to stop treatment must seek a court order preventing the state from acting. The latter happened after Nancy Cruzan sustained severe injuries when her car went off the road.[42] Cruzan never regained consciousness, and her doctors determined that she was in a persistent vegetative state, which is defined as a condition in which, despite the presence of motor reflexes, there is no evidence of significant cognitive function. Cruzan was placed on artificial nutrition and hydration, which kept her alive; her parents sought to terminate these procedures when it became clear there was no reasonable chance that she would regain consciousness. The Cruzans brought suit to enjoin the hospital from treating their daughter, and the case wound its way through the court system and reached the U.S. Supreme Court in late 1989. The next year the High Court denied the parents' request. There was no proof, the Court opined, that Nancy Cruzan would have chosen to terminate the life-support systems had she been able to voice her opinion. Moreover, the state was not under an obligation to accept her parents' wishes as a substitute, and the hospital could continue to treat Cruzan although there was no likelihood that she would regain her faculties. We shall return later to the topic of medical decision making for people unable to choose for themselves.

The majority of cases involving refusal of treatment on religious grounds involve Jehovah's Witnesses, whose religious convictions cause them to refuse blood transfusions. Most courts support the right of the competent patient to refuse transfusions, but when the patient is pregnant or a parent, judges have ordered transfusions based on the state's claim that it had a right to act to preserve the parent's life for the sake of the child or, acting *in parens patriae,* to intervene and order transfusions for the sake of the child.[43]

However, a court may decline to intervene. For example, in 1990 New York's highest court was asked to decide whether a competent adult who was a parent could refuse blood transfusions that the hospital argued were necessary to save her life.[44] The court noted that courts in other states, as well as lower courts in New York, had allowed transfusions when the patient was a parent. The court also referred to the "one-parent" and "two-parent" rule that says the state's interest is greater when the patient at risk is the child's only parent and whose death would leave the child an orphan. However, the court stated as a general proposition that the law does not restrict people from engaging in dangerous activities because they are parents, nor are parents required to take special precautions, the state's concern with children notwithstanding. Moreover, when the legislature codified the common-law rule sanctioning the individual's right to refuse treatment, it had not restricted this right to two-parent families or to individuals without children.

SURROGATE DECISION MAKING

A surrogate is a person who stands in the place of another and speaks for the person he or she represents. In medical situations the concept of surrogate decision maker arises in two contexts. In the first, a person competent to select a spokesperson designates another as surrogate. In the second situation the person spoken for did not designate a surrogate. A court is asked to appoint a guardian to make medical decisions for an incompetent person or a person who is already appointed guardian asks the court's permission to withdraw life support from an incompetent patient whose condition is terminal. Guardianship was discussed in chapter 12, where I said that when a person is not able to act on her or his own behalf, a court may appoint another to act as a substitute decision maker. The court process, including the burden of establishing that a person is not competent, was also discussed in chapter 12.

Surrogate decision making has became an issue because of advances in medical technology that can keep alive a person who is in a persistent vegetative state. In the typical case the surrogate asserts the patient's right to die a natural death by withdrawing life support. One of the first cases to address this matter was filed in 1976 when the father of Karen Quinlan asked a New Jersey court to appoint him as surrogate for his twenty-two-year-old daughter, who had been in a persistent vegetative state for one year. Quinlan's request to the court was twofold: that (1) he be appointed his daughter's guardian; and (2) the court authorize the removal of a respirator that had been sustaining her life.[45] The court acknowledged that had she been competent, she would have had the right to refuse treatment, stemming from her common-law rights to self-determination and privacy. Since her condition made it impossible for her to act for herself, the court concluded that her father should be allowed to express her intent, provided that the decision he made was reasonable. The court dismissed the state's argument that it had a compelling interest in sustaining Karen Quinlan in her condition. It found that her interest in resisting the bodily intrusion required to sustain her life, coupled with no possibility of recovery, made her interests superior to any that the state could advance.

Having acknowledged that Karen Quinlan and others in similar circumstances have the same right as a competent person to refuse medical treatment, the court had to determine how to ascertain the wishes of a person who was not able to speak for herself or himself and who had not left written instructions before becoming ill. In the *Quinlan* case the court stated the dilemma this way: "[We affirm] Karen's . . . right of choice . . . [which] would ordinarily be based upon her competency to assert it. The sad truth . . . is that she is grossly incompetent and we cannot discern her supposed choice."[46]

The court rejected testimony that Karen Quinlan had told friends that she would not choose to be sustained on life-support equipment should she become incompetent. The testimony was without sufficient probative weight, the court ruled, meaning that it could not be relied upon to establish the point that it was offered to prove. Nevertheless, the court sanctioned the withdrawal of life support (1) upon agreement between Karen Quinlan's family, her physicians, and the hospital's ethics committee that this was the correct course of action; and (2) after a finding by medical professionals that there was no reasonable chance that she would ever regain consciousness.

Earlier in this chapter the case of Nancy Cruzan was briefly reviewed. The *Cruzan* case came before the U.S. Supreme Court in 1989, twelve years after the New Jersey court ruled on the request of Karen Quinlan's father to have life support withdrawn from his daughter. There are similarities between these cases. In both, the hospitalized patient was a young woman who had not left any written directive regarding future health care; and in both, the evidence offered at trial to establish the treatment preferred by the young women consisted of statements made to friends or housemates.

Both the New Jersey Supreme Court and the U.S. Supreme Court had to address the same question: "What evidence should a court require concerning the preferred treatment of a person not currently competent to express their wishes?" The U.S. Supreme Court, like the New Jersey Supreme Court, rejected statements made to friends as not reliable indicators of the intent of Nancy Cruzan. Rather than providing examples of situations or statements that would be deemed reliable, the U.S. Supreme Court ruled that trial courts could weigh available evidence by using a clear and convincing standard to determine whether the evidence presented reflected the patient's intent.

In 1985 in *In re* Conroy, the New Jersey Supreme Court had cause to revisit the issue of what evidence was probative of a person's intent concerning medical care when the person was not able to speak for herself or himself. This case was different than the situations presented in *Quinlan* and *Cruzan,* because it focused on an elderly nursing home patient. The patient was formerly competent and was presently awake and conscious, but her mental functioning was severely and permanently impaired and her life expectancy was short.[47] The court held that life-sustaining treatment "could be withheld or withdrawn from an incompetent patient when it is clear that the patient would have refused the treatment under the circumstances involved."[48]

Again, addressing the question of what evidence would be probative, the court rejected its reasoning in *Quinlan* concerning acceptable evidence of a person's wishes and concluded that a person might express intent in (1) a "living will" or other document expressing a preference or empowering another to act on one's behalf; (2) an oral directive to a family member, friend, or health care provider; or (3) reactions expressed by the patient to others regarding medical treatment administered. Thus, when there is no clear evidence concerning a person's wishes, a best interests analysis involving deductions that could highlight a person's position could serve as a substitute. A person's position might be deduced from her or his religious beliefs or from the patient's consistent pattern of conduct with respect to previous decisions about her or his own medical care.

The *Conroy* court opined that the decision-making rule that it had applied in *Quinlan,* requiring the concurrence by family, guardian, physicians, and hospital's ethics committee, was not necessarily applicable to nursing home patients because of differences between nursing home patients and patients in a hospital. Among the differences were that (1) most of the former will die in nursing homes, their deaths consistent with age and infirmity, thus negating any compelling state interest in preserving life; (2) many have no family to act as substitute decision makers; and (3) many have no personal physicians familiar with their personalities and preferences.[49] The court sanctioned removal of the feeding tube because of (1) the medical opinion that Conroy, even with the life-sustaining measures, would soon die; (2) evidence presented by her nephew regarding her view of medical care; and (2) the fact that her nephew had nothing to gain from her death.

Courts distinguish between suicide and a decision to withhold medical treatment or to withdraw life-sustaining equipment. Suicide involves self-inflicted injury, with the intent to cause death, and/or physician-assisted suicide; both are illegal in all states. When a person chooses to decline medical intervention, the decision allows a disease to take its natural course. If death occurs, "it is the result primarily of the underlying disease and not the result of a self-inflicted injury," as would be the case with suicide.[50] The state justifies its prohibition on suicide with reference to the state's interest in (1) preventing intentional killing; (2) maintaining the ethical integrity of the medical profession; and (3) preserving life. The latter includes the state's concern in (1) protecting vulnerable people from indifference, prejudice, psychological pressure, and financial pressure to end their lives; and (2) avoiding a possible social practice and acceptance of euthanasia.[51]

Anticipating that cases such as *Quinlan, Cruzan,* and *Conroy* would increase as medical technology advanced, states enacted statutes that provide for the appointment of a surrogate decision maker for a person judged incompetent to make decisions on his or her own who did not provide any written directive concerning his or her health care. These statutes deal with two questions: (1) Who will be allowed to speak for an incompetent person? and (2) what evidence will be required for a court to sanction the abandonment of life-sustaining measures?

As to the first issue, a statute usually lists decision makers in order of preference, for example, (1) a guardian; (2) spouse; (3) adult child; (4) a parent; (5) adult sibling; or (6) close friend.[52] A state may qualify the latter by requiring that there is evidence that the close friend has had regular contact with the patient sufficient to be familiar with the patient's activities, health, and personal beliefs.[53]

As to the second point, the surrogate's decision should be based on the patient's wishes. However, if these are not known, the patient's best interests may be used as a guide. Factors to be considered include (1) current diagnosis and prognosis; (2) religious and moral beliefs and personal values; (3) prior acts and expressed attitudes concerning medical treatment in general; (4) how the patient has reacted to the provision, withholding, or withdrawal of treatment for another; and (5) opinions expressed regarding the effect on the patient's family or intimate friends if a treatment were provided, withheld, or withdrawn.[54]

Providing Advance Health Care Instructions

All states have laws that allow an individual to express her or his wishes regarding future medical care should they become incapacitated, and states will require that one or more physicians certify that a patient is in a terminal condition or a persistent vegetative state before sanctioning the withholding or withdrawal of life support equipment. In the pages that follow, the various ways in which people may express their wishes regarding future medical care will be reviewed.

Advance Directives

An advance directive is a written instruction in which a person outlines the health or mental health services that may be provided to him or her in the event that he or she becomes incompetent. Advance directives include living wills with instructions regarding the use of specific medical treatments and procedures, as well as health care proxies and durable powers of attorney, in which a person appoints another person to decide about such treatment and procedures.[55] An advance directive may include a person's decision not to be resuscitated in the event of cardiac arrest, or an order not to resuscitate a person may be entered by a physician who received instructions on this matter from a patient's surrogate.

Providing advance directives for patients served by Medicare and Medicaid providers was the intent of Congress in 1990 when the Patient Self-Determination Act was passed. The act requires health care providers who participate in either of these health insurance programs to tell all competent patients about state laws concerning advance directives.[56]

As with other areas of the law, there are significant state-by-state variations in the form in which a person may express her or his wishes regarding medical care and medical providers, and state courts may not honor an advance directive that is not statutorily mandated within their state. For example, New York does not recognize living wills, but it will honor a health care proxy. Thus a New York physician and hospital refused to remove a patient from a respirator even when ordered to do so by the patient's sister, who presented a living will to medical providers. The patient made a partial recovery, following which she and her sister sued the hospital, alleging that it had violated the patient's rights by refusing to honor the living will. The court dismissed the complaint, holding that the decision to remove a patient from a respirator requires (1) a valid health care proxy; (2) an order not to resuscitate signed by the patient or surrogate; or (3) a court order.[57]

Because states have different rules concerning the proper form of an advance directive, and in view of the possibility that a person might become incapacitated while traveling and not have the proper type of directive required by the state in which he or she is traveling, the commissioners on uniform state laws promulgated the Uniform Health-Care Decisions Act, which has been adopted by six states. The act seeks to replace state laws that authorize living wills, powers of attorney, and other forms of substitute decision making with a uniform law that acknowledges the right of a competent individual to make health care decisions, including the right to decline care or to direct that care be discontinued even if the result is death. The act authorizes the individual to appoint an agent, be it a family member or close friend, to act as substitute decision maker, whose choices are guided by instructions provided by the person making the appointment or by knowledge of the individual's wishes. If these wishes are not known, the decision should be made in accordance with the best interests of the individual in a manner that is consistent with the individual's known values. The act directs a health care provider or institution to comply with an instruction of the patient's surrogate but recognizes that disagreement might result in court action.[58]

Durable Power of Attorney

As discussed in chapter 12, a competent adult may create a power of attorney by appointing another to act in his or her place. Thus before a person enters the hospital, she or he may appoint another to make medical decisions should the patient be unable to act. Whereas a power of attorney becomes void when a court appoints a guardian after a finding of incompetency, a durable power of attorney remains in effect. Thus a person who wants to ensure that her or his elected representative will retain authority, should she or he become incapacitated, may execute such a document.

Health Care Proxies and Living Wills

A health care proxy empowers another person to make medical decisions when a person is no longer competent to act on her or his own behalf. This is in contrast to a living will in which a person sets forth instructions to be followed in the event of incapacity. A living will may specify the type of medical care desired and whether, if at all, to use life-sustaining treatment, but it does not empower another to act in one's stead.

New York law sanctions the development of health care proxies in which an individual appoints a "health care agent," who is an adult to whom one delegates the authority to make any health care decision that the person making the appointment, "the principal," could make were she or he able to do so.[59] The agent has a right to receive medical information, including medical records, necessary to make an informed decision. Other states provide the means for a person to appoint a surrogate decision maker. The law in Alabama, Maine, and Oklahoma refers to health care proxies,[60] whereas Illinois uses the term *health care power of attorney*, which has the same effect as a health care proxy.[61]

In addition to identifying the principal and agent and stating that the principal intends the agent to have authority to make health care decisions on the principal's behalf, a health care proxy may (1) include specific instructions of the principal; (2) set limits on the agent's authority; and (3) specify that the proxy terminates on a specific date or on the occurrence of a specific event. An alternative agent may be appointed in the event that the person appointed is not available.

New York law sets forth a decision-making standard that requires the health care agent to consult with a licensed physician, registered nurse, licensed clinical psychologist, or certified social worker regarding the decision, which is to be made (1) in accordance with the principal's wishes, including the principal's religious and moral beliefs; or (2) in accordance with the principal's best interests if the principal's wishes are not reasonably known and cannot with reasonable diligence be ascertained.

Neither a hospital nor a physician need honor the health care decision if it is contrary to a policy formally adopted by the hospital and that the competent patient was told of before admission, or if the action requested runs counter to the moral convictions of the hospital or physician asked to act. The hospital not willing to execute the agent's decision is responsible for promptly transferring the patient to another hospital that is accessible and willing to honor the agent's decision. If transfer is not possible, the hospital must honor the decision or seek a court order to sustain its unwillingness to act. In the event that the decision not to honor the agent's decision is that of the individual physician but not the hospital, the hospital is to transfer responsibility for the patient to another individual health care provider who is willing to honor the agent's decision.

MEDICAL DECISION MAKING FOR CHILDREN

Parents have the authority to make decisions concerning the medical treatment that their children will receive. However, if a parent fails to provide care and the failure is likely to jeopardize a child's health or safety, a petition may be filed by a department of social services, a hospital, a child's attorney, or a child's guardian to ask the court to exercise its *parens patriae* authority and order medical treatment.[62]

When a court is asked to overrule parental choice, it may appoint a guardian *ad litem* to represent the child's interests; before ruling, a court will hear evidence describing the effects and outcome of treatment as well as the consequences for the child who is not treated. For example, a Massachusetts court ordered that a child receive treatment for leukemia over his parent's objections, despite the possibility of serious side-effects, because death was likely if the child was not treated and the risks of treatment were minimal.[63]

LODGING CIVIL CHARGES AGAINST A PARENT FOR WITHHOLDING MEDICAL CARE

State laws that govern the reporting of child abuse and neglect (chapter 10) provide for (1) receiving reports of medical neglect; (2) investigating reports received; (3) lodging civil charges against a parent for failing to provide needed care and asking the court to order medical treatment; and (4) court appointment of a guardian *ad litem* to represent the child's interests. Failure to provide medical care may be due to (1) parents' religious convictions; (2) sincere belief by the parents that the side-effects of treatment are severe and will reduce the quality of life for a child for whom a prognosis is not positive; (3) poverty; or (4) indifference to a child's needs.

In deciding an appropriate course of action, courts weigh a number of factors, including (1) whether the recommended procedure is necessary to save a child's life; (2) the child's chances of survival without the procedure; (3) the risks to the child of submitting to the procedure; (4) the likelihood that the procedure will be successful; (5) the wishes of the child old enough to state a position regarding the recommended course of treatment; and (6) parents' rights to make medical decisions concerning their children.

When a parent's decision not to provide medical care has jeopardized a child's health or safety, various courts have ordered treatment, placed a child in foster care because parents did not comply with a court order to provide treatment, or terminated parental rights.[64] If a child enters foster care and legal custody is transferred to the state, the state assumes an obligation to provide medical care and has the duty to make medical decisions (chapter 10), including decisions that allow a child's participation in experimental drug trials if an institutional review board determines that the research is suitable for children. However, a state's authority may be circumscribed. For example, the law in Florida, Pennsylvania, and New Hampshire limits the decision-making authority of the person with legal custody to making "ordinary medical decisions"[65] but not necessarily sanctioning treatment that requires surgery,[66] in contrast to the law in Georgia and Michigan, where "any person temporarily standing *in loco parentis*" may consent to medical treatment for a child.[67]

A court may reject a state request that it order medical treatment when evidence concerning the effectiveness of treatment is equivocal. Thus the Supreme Court of Maine upheld a mother's decision to delay an aggressive course of drug therapy for her son who was HIV positive. The court found that the mother's decision did not constitute serious neglect because the state did not produce evidence of a clear benefit from drug treatment, nor did it produce evidence of the possible long-term side-effects of the treatment, which was experimental.[68] Conversely, an Alabama appellate court ordered treatment for an HIV-infected child over the objections of the child's mother, who did not believe that her child was infected with HIV. The court reasoned that the mother's objection to treatment suggested that she was not able to make a "well-reasoned, rational decision regarding best interests of her child."[69]

In the 1980s the U.S. Department of Health and Human Services (HHS) issued regulations that would have made it a violation of the Vocational Rehabilitation Act (VRA) to withhold medical treatment from newborns with severe physical or emotional impairments. HHS cited as authority for its regulation the provision in the VRA that states that a person with a disability who is qualified to receive the benefits offered by a program supported by federal funds cannot be denied access to program benefits based solely on the person's disability.[70]

The regulations were issued in the spring of 1982 after the parents of an infant born with Down's syndrome and other handicaps would not consent to surgery. The hospital petitioned for a court order to override the parents' decision, but the court turned down their request, and child protective services agreed with the court ruling. The infant died shortly thereafter. The regulations included requiring (1) health care providers to post notices that withholding medical treatment from infants with disabilities might violate the VRA; (2) child protective services agencies to establish procedures to prevent unlawful medical neglect of disabled infants and, if necessary, to act to protect the disabled infant's life or health. The U.S. Supreme Court ruled that the regulations were not valid because HHS lacked the authority to investigate or regulate treatment decisions concerning infants with disabilities.[71] Subsequently, Congress amended the Child Abuse Prevention and Treatment Act to require the states to have the means to respond to reports of medical neglect, defined to include instances of withholding medically indicated treatment from disabled infants with life-threatening conditions.[72]

LODGING CRIMINAL CHARGES AGAINST A PARENT FOR WITHHOLDING MEDICAL CARE

Failure to provide medical care for a child may result in criminal charges being lodged against a parent or other person responsible for the child's care. To sustain a conviction the state must establish each element of the crime beyond a reasonable doubt, including that the defendant had the requisite state of mind and that the defendant's actions caused the harm with which she or he is charged (chapter 3). This burden of proof is more difficult to meet than the lesser burden that applies in a civil matter, where the state must prove by a preponderance of the evidence that (1) the adult charged is the child's parent or guardian, (2) the adult charged harmed the child or placed the child at risk of injury; and (3) the harm was not accidental.

Consider several cases. Elaine Craig died from pneumonia, and her parents were charged with gross negligence for failing to provide medical care.[73] The Craigs were convicted, but their conviction was overturned by an appellate court after it ruled that the evidence did not support a finding that the parents' failure to obtain medical help was the cause of the child's death. The court opined that parents have a reasonable degree of discretion in deciding when to call for medical help for an ill child. The behavior of parents may, in the opinion of others, be negligent, but simple negligence will not sustain a criminal charge because such a charge requires that the behavior rise to the level of "gross negligence" or "criminal negligence," either of which implies a reckless disregard for human life, and the disregard shown must be the cause of the child's death. The court concluded that the state did not provide evidence that the parents were aware of how serious their daughter's illness was until the days immediately preceding her death when, medical testimony established, administering antibiotics would not likely have saved the child's life.

The result may be different, however, when a parent has knowledge that a child's condition is serious enough to warrant medical attention. A Ms. Eversley took her son to a clinic to obtain formula. After observing that the boy was having difficulty breathing, a nurse and a physician told her to take the boy to the hospital, because the clinic did not have the equipment needed to determine whether the child had pneumonia. Eversley went to the hospital but left because she would have to wait for her son to be seen. The boy continued to have difficulty breathing, but his mother did not seek medical help and her son died. As with the case of Elaine Craig, whether the parent's failure to act caused the child's death was a key issue at trial. Eversley's position was that pneumonia, not her failure to act, caused her son's death; the state argued that the boy might have survived had the mother heeded medical advice and waited to see a physician. Eversley's argument was rejected and she was found guilty of causing her son's death.[74]

Parental Objection Based on Religion

In 1944 and again in 1972 the U.S. Supreme Court held that parents have the right to control the medical care received by their children, but this right is not absolute, the court found, even when a decision rests on religious grounds. A court's *parens patriae* authority is sufficient to justify state intervention when the choice made by a parent jeopardizes a child's health,[75] but the party who petitions the court must establish by clear and convincing evidence that the decision not to provide treatment is likely to have this effect. Parental objections may be to any form of medical intervention or to a specific procedure such as transfusing blood. Consider several cases.

A minor was injured in an automobile accident and his parents, Jehovah's Witnesses, authorized surgery but not blood transfusions. A petition was filed by an unknown party, and a state court judge entered an order allowing surgeons to transfuse the boy if necessary.[76] In response, a class-action suit was filed on behalf of all Jehovah's Witnesses in the state of Washington. Arguing that the court order violated their rights under the U.S. Constitution, plaintiffs asked the court to enjoin defendants' future efforts to administer blood transfusions to members of the plaintiff class. The court dismissed the request, reasoning that the constitutional right to practice religion does not include the right to expose a child to disease, ill health, or death. However, courts will weigh the likelihood of a successful intervention against the intrusiveness of the procedure and the pain and discomfort that the procedure may cause. Thus in *Newmark v. Williams*[77] the Supreme Court of Delaware refused to order "radical chemotherapy" for a three-year-old whose parents refused treatment based on their convictions as Christian Scientists that medical care be rejected in favor of spiritual aid.[78] Medical testimony claimed the treatment's chances for success were less than 50 percent and that it was invasive, painful, and had negative side-effects.

MINOR'S RIGHT TO CONSENT TO MEDICAL TREATMENT

All states specify an age, generally eighteen, at which a minor is emancipated and has many of the rights conferred on adults, including the right to make medical decisions. However, there are exceptions to the general rule that a physician may not treat a minor without parental consent. The exceptions are based on a minor's (1) constitutional rights, (2) status, (3) conditions or disease,[79] and (4) common-law rights.

Constitutional Exceptions

A minor has a constitutionally protected right to terminate a pregnancy, although this right may be restricted by laws requiring parental notification, parental consent, or judicial bypass.[80] The last requires that the young woman demonstrate either that she is mature enough to make the decision to terminate her pregnancy or that it is in her best interests to do so.[81]

Status-Based Exceptions

Emancipation generally occurs at age eighteen, when a young person is freed from parental control and parents are relieved of the legal obligation to support their children. However, a young person may be emancipated early. Depending upon state law, this change of status is possible when a young person (1) marries, (2) becomes pregnant, (3) enlists in the military, (3) is judged by a judicial officer competent to manage her or his own affairs, or (4) voluntarily leaves the home of her or his parents. It is also possible when (5) parents divorce and the noncustodial parent is relieved of an obligation toward the child who is "rude, disrespectful, and disobedient" or who refuses to visit with a parent.[82]

Another status exception rests on a judicial determination that a youngster is a "mature minor," meaning that she or he is old enough to understand the consequences of making a decision regarding a given medical procedure. Whereas an emancipated minor assumes all responsibility for herself or himself, a declaration that a young person is a mature minor frees the young person from parental control only for the purpose of making a specific medical decision. Authority for this status, rarely conferred on a person younger than fourteen, may be found in statute or common law, providing that a young person may consent to certain medical treatment without parental consent.[83]

Condition-Based Exceptions

As with adults, a physician may treat a minor in a medical emergency without parental consent on the assumption that the parents would, if available, give their approval. Other situations in which treatment may proceed without parental consent are (1) when it is assumed to be in society's best interests that a young person receive care, and (2) when it is judged to be detrimental to the course of treatment to seek parental consent. Condition-based exceptions allow a minor to receive treatment (1) for a sexually transmitted disease; (2) if pregnant, or (3) if seeking mental health or substance abuse treatment.[84] However, when a minor's decision may negatively affect others with whom the young person comes into contact, a court may intervene for the public good. Such intervention happened in the case of J.J., who refused to be treated for a sexually transmitted disease based on a religious belief in faith healing. After hearing J.J.'s admission that he was sexually active and after establishing the risk that this created for the community at large if he went untreated, the court declared him a dependent for the purposes of ordering medical care.[85]

Common-Law Rights

I said in the preceding discussion that competent adults have a right to refuse medical treatment. The common law provides a source of authority for this rule. An appellate court in Michigan extended this right to minors when it ruled that a young person has a right to decline life-saving treatments. If the minor is not able to speak for herself or himself, a surrogate may express the minor's wishes.

The case before the court involved Joelle Rosebush, sixteen, who was involved in a traffic accident. She suffered severe injuries that left her in a persistent vegetative state. Medical evidence that she would not regain consciousness or be able to breathe on her own was not disputed. The court ruled that Rosebush had a right to refuse treatment and that her parents could speak for her as surrogate decision makers and order the withdrawal of life-support equipment. According to the court, surrogate decision makers speaking for incompetent patients, whether adults or children, should approximate the patient's wishes as closely as possible by making use of available evidence or, in lieu of such, the surrogate should make decisions based on the best interests of the patient.[86]

SUMMARY

The focus of this chapter has been on (1) legal issues affecting the rights of health care consumers; (2) the obligation of parents to provide health care for their children; (3) the obligation of the state to ensure that parents do so; and (4) a minor's right to consent to medical treatment.

The law provides the person seeking medical care with a right to (1) receive emergency care, regardless of ability to pay, at a hospital with an emergency room, if the hospital receives federal funds, and (2) receive care without regard to disability. In addition, with few exceptions a medical provider cannot treat a competent patient without the person's informed consent, which obliges the care provider to give to the patient all the information that a reasonable person would consider relevant to the decision to be made.

Implicit in the doctrine of informed consent is the right to refuse medical care. A court may circumscribe this right when the person who declines care is not competent, or if the person's choice is outweighed by a state interest, for example, in preserving life. The latter may result in a court order to treat an unwilling patient, such as a pregnant woman who declines on religious grounds a blood transfusion considered medically necessary to ensure a safe delivery.

Advances in medical technology have made it possible to sustain life through artificial means. This has resulted in requests that a court allow a surrogate to speak for a patient unable to express his or her wishes. The law prefers the certainty of knowing what the patient would have wanted, thus the preference that people express in writing their wishes for future medical care. All states allow for such expression with different means, including (1) advance directives, which are written instructions in which a person outlines the health services that may be provided to them in the event that they become incompetent; (2) durable power of attorney, where a competent adult appoints another to act in his or her place should he or she be unable to act for themselves; and (3) health care proxies and living wills, the former referring to a document that empowers another to make medical decisions when a person is no longer competent, and the latter referring to a document in which a person sets forth instructions to be followed in the event of incapacity. However, there are situations when a person has not provided in advance for a surrogate decision maker and a court is asked to appoint one. States have enacted statutes that provide for this by authorizing a person such as a guardian, spouse, adult child, or close friend to make medical choices.

Parents have an obligation to provide medical care for their children, and failure to do so may result in a report of child neglect or in criminal charges if a child dies or becomes severely disabled as a result of parental neglect. When a parent will not authorize medical care and the likely result is serious injury to a child, a court may exercise its *parens patriae* authority and order medical treatment, even when the parental objection rests on religious grounds. The constitutional right to practice religion does not include the right to expose a child to disease, ill health, or death.

Despite the law's respect for parental authority, there are situations where a minor may consent to medical treatment without involving her or his parents. In addition to a minor's constitutional right to terminate a pregnancy without parental consent, there are situations where treatment may proceed based solely on the minor's wishes because it is assumed to be in society's best interests that a young person receive care, and where it is considered detrimental to the course of treatment to seek parental consent. These exceptions allow a minor to receive treatment (1) for a sexually transmitted disease; (2) if pregnant, or (3) if seeking mental health or substance abuse treatment.

14

Mental Health and the Law

THIS CHAPTER will be about mental health and mental illness. The latter refers to "mental disorders [which] are health conditions . . . characterized by alterations in thinking, mood, or behavior . . . associated with distress and/or impaired functioning."[1] As with health care services (chapter 13), mental health services are provided by the public and private sectors, and social workers practice in both. Social work practice is affected by publicly funded programs such as Medicare and Medicaid, by the Mental Health Block Grant, which provides funds to support community-based treatment services, and by programs operated by the Indian Health Service and the Veterans Administration, as well as by private insurance schemes. Regardless of funding source or treatment setting, social workers play a significant role in the field of mental health by (1) providing direct services; (2) evaluating individuals and families; (3) preparing reports and treatment plans; (4) interpreting reports for nonprofessionals; (5) initiating commitment proceedings; and (6) advocating for the rights of the mentally ill.

In the United States the cost of mental health services is paid for with public and private funds, 53 percent and 47 percent, respectively. However, because of the concern that "long-term and intensive psychotherapy" and prolonged hospital stays will drive up insurance costs for employers and the government, insurance coverage is more restrictive for mental health than physical health services. Deductibles and copayments are generally higher, and insurance coverage may limit the number of therapeutic sessions allowed and/or the length of a hospital stay.[2] Moreover, employers need not provide insurance coverage for mental health, but when they do, the Mental Health Parity Act (MHPA) provides that a group plan may not impose different standards for receipt of mental health and physical health services.[3] Annual limitations or aggregate lifetime benefits must apply equally to both. The MHPA does not apply to benefits for the treatment of substance abuse or chemical dependency problems.

Mental health has been referred to throughout this book, including references in chapter 1 to the tasks that social workers perform for the courts; in chapter 2 to the common-law right to refuse medical treatment, which applies to those whose care involves mental illness; in chapter 3 to mental health courts, to the fact that an arrest warrant is not required when a person is believed by the police to be mentally ill and a danger to himself or others, and to the role that social workers play in decisions to commit a person to a mental health facility; in chapter 5 to the congressional directive that states review and revise laws to protect the confidentiality of patient records, to ensure patient access to their records, and to the duty that some states impose on social workers and others to warn third parties who are threatened by patients. In chapter 7, I discussed the state's obligation to protect from harm those incarcerated in mental health facilities matters concerning mental illness and malpractice, and the rights of people with disabilities. The references to mental health include, in chapter 9, reference to the education of children with disabilities; in chapter 11, to mental illness as a basis for terminating parental rights; and in chapter 13, to patient bills of rights, advance directives, appointment of guardians, and a minor's right to receive mental health services without parental permission.

Before we begin, two caveats are in order. The focus of this chapter will be on the rights of the involuntarily committed mentally ill adult, except for a brief discussion addressing the voluntary commitment of children. Adults who seek inpatient services on a voluntary basis may have rights, such as a right to treatment that is conferred by a state statute, but because voluntary patients are assumed able to leave a hospital at will, courts are less sympathetic to a claim for constitutional protections than they are with involuntary patients.[4] Second, we are concerned with the mentally ill although there is some reference in the following material to the rights of the mentally retarded or developmentally delayed.

This chapter begins with a review of the law governing civil commitment of the mentally ill adult and a discussion of civil commitment of children. Patient rights are reviewed next, including a discussion of protection from harm, right to treatment, informed consent, and placement in the least restrictive setting. Then we shall turn our attention to outpatient commitment and the process that may result when a court orders participation in an outpatient treatment program. Mental illness and the criminal law will be the final topic, which will include a review of (1) competency to stand trial; (3) the insanity defense; and (3) other defenses suggesting that a person is not responsible for committing the crime with which she or he is charged.

THE LAW OF CIVIL COMMITMENT

Civil commitment refers to procedures used to confine a person who is "ill, incompetent, drug-addicted, or the like."[5] Civil commitment can be contrasted with confinement of a person who has committed a crime (chapter 3) or the commitment of a person to an outpatient treatment program (discussed later in this chapter). The process of involuntary commitment to a state institution is controlled by state law, and there may be considerable differences among the states with regard to (1) the mental conditions and behaviors that justify commitment; (2) the professional groups sanctioned to initiate commitment procedures; and (3) the role played by the courts or administrative bodies charged with overseeing commitment procedures.

All states provide for emergency detention of limited duration, forty-eight to seventy-two hours, for example, when a person's behavior poses a danger to self or others.[6] The detained person will be released at the end of the statutory time period, unless the commitment is extended by court order or by the voluntary and informed consent of the person involved. To retain a person in custody the law may require that a psychiatrist or psychologist certify in writing the reason and need for detention. In addition to providing for emergency detention, state law may allow a person to be detained for several days if a court orders a mental health evaluation.[7]

From our study of physical health in chapter 13, we know that the law presumes a person to be competent. The person seeking to have another declared incompetent for the purpose of civil commitment must overcome this presumption with clear and convincing evidence that the person whose freedom will be limited is not able to control his or her behavior. Since civil commitment implicates a person's Fourteenth Amendment rights, when the actor seeking to restrict another's liberty is the state, it must establish that the loss to the individual is outweighed by a gain to public health or safety. According to the U.S. Supreme Court, commitment is acceptable when the person to be confined (1) presents a danger or threat of danger to self or others as a result of mental illness; (2) is likely to benefit from treatment; and (3) is confined in the least restrictive setting and is receiving the least restrictive method of treatment available.[8]

You should know that before the 1970s, a mentally ill person confronting involuntary commitment had few due process rights; the commitment process was, by and large, controlled by the judgment of medical professionals.[9] Change came with the civil rights movement of the 1950s and 1960s. In a series of decisions federal courts extended to people confronting involuntary incarceration the right to notice[10] and to a hearing[11] and required that the public official or private party seeking commitment prove by clear and convincing evidence that commitment was required[12] (see chapter 3 for a discussion of burdens of proof).

State statutes generally confer a right to counsel, including court-appointed counsel for the indigent. In addition, state law may require (1) that one or more mental health professionals assert in writing that they have examined the person who is the subject of the petition or (2) that the person refuses to submit to an examination; and (3) that the professional's opinion is that inpatient treatment is required. Depending on state law, the person whose commitment is sought may be entitled to a jury trial.

The procedures that the state must follow when seeking to confine a mentally ill person began to change in 1971 when Kenneth Donaldson sued Florida. Donaldson was civilly committed to a state hospital, where he remained in custody against his will for fifteen years. He repeatedly asked that he be released, claiming that he was neither dangerous nor mentally ill, and said that he was not receiving any treatment at the hospital. His plea was ignored.

In ordering Donaldson's release the U.S. Supreme Court was no doubt swayed by testimony that his confinement consisted solely of custodial care with no service to ameliorate or cure his illness. He was said to be receiving "milieu" therapy, but it was conceded at trial that this was a "euphemism for confinement in the 'milieu' of a mental hospital" where he was confined in a large room housing sixty patients.[13] His request for grounds privileges, occupational training, and an opportunity to discuss his case with staff were repeatedly denied. The High Court held that the state cannot justify indefinite detention of a person solely due to mental illness. To do so violated the individual's Fourteenth Amendment right to liberty. The state must justify detaining a person in an appropriate proceeding, and the person must be released when the reasons that justified detention no longer exist.

States justify the involuntary detention of a person judged to be mentally ill by referring either to the state's police power or its *parens patriae* authority. The doctrine of police power grants to the states the authority to enforce laws to protect the safety, health, morals, and general welfare of the public. Thus the state may remove from the community a person whose behavior poses a serious threat of harm to others.[14] The state's obligation to the person said to be mentally ill stems from the doctrine of *parens patriae* (discussed in chapter 10), which focuses attention on the state as parent or protector of those unable to care for themselves.

We know from the review of criminal and civil procedure in chapter 3 that the due process rights extended in a civil proceeding are less than the rights granted to a person in a criminal proceeding. Commenting on this disparity when either proceeding results in the loss of liberty, a federal district judge said:

> The power of the state to deprive a person of the fundamental liberty to go unimpeded . . . must rest on a consideration that society has a compelling

> interest in such deprivation. In criminal cases, this authority is derived from the [state's] police power [which is] tempered with stringent procedural safeguards designed to protect the rights of one accused of crime. . . . In civil commitment proceedings the same fundamental liberties are at stake. State commitment procedures have not . . . traditionally assured the due process safeguards against unjustified deprivation of liberty . . . accorded [to] those accused of crime. This [is] . . . justified on the premise that the state [must] protect society from the potentially dangerous acts of [a] person . . . likely to act irrationally. [But] were a sociologist [to] predict that a person was eighty per cent likely to commit a felonious act, no law would permit his confinement, but under the same circumstances a psychiatrist's recommendation of commitment is likely to be accepted [and] justified on the basis of potential benefit to the one confined in a mental institution.[15]

Despite the loss of liberty that involuntary commitment entails, the U.S. Supreme Court has not extended to the civilly committed the same due process protections afforded people who are charged with a crime. The Court has ruled that to determine the amount of process due, lower courts are to apply a three-part test that takes account of (1) the private interest affected by the official action; (2) the risk that the procedures used will result in an erroneous deprivation of the interest involved and whether additional safeguards will be of value; and (3) the government's interest, including the fiscal and administrative burdens that additional or substitute procedures would entail (see chapter 11 for a discussion of this test in the context of adoption).[16]

The private interest affected is clearly the right of an individual to live freely in the community as well as the individual's right not to be stigmatized by being labeled mentally ill. The procedures that might result in either consequence must be balanced against the interest of the government in exercising its police power to protect the public while asserting its *parens patriae* authority to help those not able to help themselves.

Consider these matters in relation to three standards of proof (chapter 3). In 1979 the U.S. Supreme Court, in *Addington v. Texas,* ruled that a standard of proof requiring a preponderance of the evidence created too great a risk that individual liberty would be restricted (which has to do with the private interest in the test set forth by the Supreme Court). However, a standard requiring proof beyond a reasonable doubt placed too great a burden on the state, given the "uncertainties of psychiatric diagnosis,"[17] (which has to do with the government's interest, part 3 of the test). This standard might create a barrier to providing necessary medical treatment, thus undermining the state's efforts to further its legitimate interests as well as those of the patient. A standard that is intermediate to the two requires clear and convincing evidence. Use of this standard provides a needed safeguard for the rights of the mentally ill (which has to do with parts 1 and 2 of the test) while also serving the state's interest (part 3 of the test). The Court found that a proper balance between the rights of the individual and the obligation of the state could be met if the state were required to prove its case by clear and convincing evidence.

The government's interest in limiting fiscal and administrative burdens may take into account whether to (1) allow hearsay evidence, which is less costly and time consuming than requiring live witness testimony[18]; (2) allow hearings to take place at a treatment facility, because it is "less disruptive for patients . . . makes the process seem less criminal in nature [and] reduces the amount of time the commitment process takes away from physicians' clinical duties"[19]; (3) require hearings before a court or allow a less costly administrative procedure; (4) limit the number of appeals that may be filed[20]; and (5) require the patient's attendance or excuse it if waived by his or her counsel as being in the patient's best interest. Confinement is generally time limited, six months, for example, before the case must be reviewed by an administrative or judicial body.[21]

Civil Commitment of Children

In 1979 the U.S. Supreme Court addressed the question, "What procedural safeguards, if any, are required for children whose parents voluntarily commit them to a state institution?" The case before the Court was filed as a class action on behalf of children incarcerated in a state mental hospital in Georgia. Advocates for the children argued that a hearing with due process safeguards was a necessary predicate to detention, challenging the traditional notion that parents represent the best interests of their children.

The High Court acknowledged that children have a Fourteenth Amendment liberty interest in not being unnecessarily (1) confined; (2) physically restrained; and (3) erroneously labeled as mentally ill. These interests are to be balanced, the Court ruled, against the responsibility of parents for raising their children and the right of parents to do so without state interference, unless parents have abused or neglected their children.

On balance, the Court found that the child's rights and the nature of the commitment decision are such that parental discretion to institutionalize a child is not absolute: A parent's authority to seek mental health services for a children is subject to an independent medical judgment. While parents need not submit their decision to a formal due process hearing, the margin for error in mental health commitments is sufficient to warrant an investigation by a "neutral fact-finder to determine whether statutory admissions criteria are satisfied."[22] The investigator, who may be a social worker, must review the child's background and conduct interviews with the child, the child's parents, and personnel in schools and other agencies who may have knowledge that would inform the decision as to whether the commitment is necessary. Admission may be refused if medical standards are not met. The ongoing need for commitment must be reviewed using similar procedures.

The High Court ruling did not allow for a disagreement between a parent and a child who views the commitment as involuntary. Provisions in state law may allow for balancing the interests of both parties. For example, in California a youngster who is fourteen or older is entitled to a hearing if she or he disagrees with a parent's commitment decision, and the young person has a right to counsel if the hospital is public.[23]

PATIENT RIGHTS

The restrictions that confinement places on an individual who has not committed a crime are balanced by granting certain rights to the confined person. Bills of rights were discussed in chapter 13, where I said that patient advocates at the state level have succeeded in having bills passed to benefit the mentally ill and nursing home residents, with protections that include the right to (1) have the information necessary to decide whether to accept or reject the care offered; (2) voice grievances concerning treatment by facility staff and the care received; (3) personal privacy, including the right to communicate by telephone, to receive uncensored mail, and to receive visitors; and (4) confidentiality of records. Additional rights will be reviewed next.

Protection from Harm

In chapter 7, I said that when the state assumes custody of a person, be it a prisoner, a child placed in foster care, or a person confined to a mental health facility, the person whose liberty has been constrained has a right, rooted in the Fourteenth Amendment to the U.S. Constitution, to be protected from harm.[24]

Harm may come from different sources, including (1) the aggression of other patients; (2) self-abuse; (3) failure of authorities to provide the care necessary to prevent physical deterioration of people with disabilities; and (4) unsanitary and unsafe facility conditions such as broken windows and exposed electrical wiring. Confined patients have argued successfully that the Eighth and Fourteenth Amendments to the U.S. Constitution guarantee a right to "freedom from harm" that is violated by unsafe conditions; federal courts finding evidence to support these claims have closed institutions and ordered that residents be placed in community settings.[25]

Right to Treatment

In statute and case law the concept of treatment may refer to whether (1) the day-to-day treatment of an incarcerated person is humane; (2) a person is being treated in the least restrictive environment possible; (3) habilitation or training services are being provided for the mentally retarded; or (4) problem-solving interventions are being provided to reduce or eliminate the problems causal to or arising from mental illness.

In reading the case that follows, note the similarities in the reasoning of the U.S. Supreme Court to cases that we have already reviewed and that reflect the Court's position that (1) any obligation the state has to an individual arises only when the person is taken into custody (*DeShaney v. Winnebago County*, chapter 10); (2) where an obligation is found, the state's duty is to ensure minimum levels of care, not to maximize the potential of the person served (*Board of Education v. Rawley*, chapter 9); and (3) the U.S. Constitution does not confer any right to services (*Dandridge v. Williams*; see chapter 2).

In *Youngberg v. Romeo* the U.S. Supreme Court ruled that a person who has been involuntarily committed is entitled to "more considerate treatment and conditions of confinement than criminals whose conditions of confinement are designed to punish,"[26] and the Court addressed training or "habilitation," a reference to programs that provide training to the mentally retarded in basic self-help skills such as dressing and personal hygiene.

The *Youngberg* case was filed by the mother of Nicholas Romeo, a mentally retarded man who was involuntarily confined at a state institution. Nicholas suffered numerous injuries at his own hands and at the hands of others. Ms. Romeo's objections to her son's care went unanswered, and she filed suit on his behalf. She argued that he had a right to be confined in safe conditions, to be free of bodily restraints, and to receive minimal training for developing basic skills. The High Court ruled that in general a state does not have a constitutional obligation to provide services. However, when a person is institutionalized and wholly dependent on the state, it has a duty to provide certain services but with "considerable discretion in determining the nature and scope of its responsibilities."[27] A state need not decide whether to address every aspect of a problem or to not address the problem at all. Thus the Court accepted Nicholas's claims, finding that he had a constitutional right to minimally adequate or reasonable training. The Court also ruled that the proper standard for evaluating whether the state adequately protected the rights of an individual involuntarily committed in a state institution for the mentally retarded is whether professional judgment was exercised (chapter 5).

The U.S. Supreme Court has never ruled on the right to treatment of the involuntarily incarcerated mentally ill as distinguished from the duty owed by the state to provide minimum habilitation services to the mentally retarded.[28]

The absence of the Court's involvement may be due to the uncertainties of psychiatric treatment, for example, whether there is treatment for all forms of mental illness and whether existing treatments are efficacious. However, while never finding a right to treatment, in 1999 the Court made it clear that treatment is not essential when the state seeks to confine a person for preventive reasons. Considering the constitutionality of commitment procedures for people labeled sexual predators (chapter 3), the Court found that an act allowing the state to confine a sexual predator for preventive reasons was not necessarily punitive because the state failed to offer treatment where treatment for a specific condition was not possible or when treatment was possible but merely an ancillary, rather than an overriding, state concern. The latter suggests that the Court might find that an involuntarily committed person has a right to treatment that could supersede the rights of the state.

Notwithstanding these matters, funding for treatment of the hospitalized mentally ill is available through the Medicaid program and provided for in the statutes of some states.[29] Clarifying the scope of a patient's right to treatment, two state supreme courts ruled that treatment must be "adequate and appropriate"[30] so as to provide the civilly committed person with a "reasonable opportunity to be rehabilitated . . . or to improve his mental condition."[31] Some states require that the treatment to be provided be described in a written plan that includes the goals of service and procedures to be used to realize goals.[32]

The U.S. Court of Appeals for the District of Columbia was the first federal appellate court to consider whether there was a right to treatment. In *Rouse v. Cameron* the court ruled that the district's statutes created a right to psychiatric treatment for a person involuntarily incarcerated for mental illness. It would violate due process, the court ruled, to incarcerate against her or his will a person who was not guilty of a crime and in need of treatment and then not to provide treatment.[33]

Another case was decided in 1971 by a U.S. District Court in Alabama. *Wyatt v. Stickney* was a class-action suit filed on behalf of patients at a state mental hospital in Alabama. Unlike the District of Columbia case, which concerned a local statute, the Alabama plaintiffs argued that the right to treatment was supported by the U.S. Constitution. The trial court agreed, going well beyond the ruling of the appellate court in the District of Columbia, which had found that the right to treatment required a bona fide effort to treat but did not find that this right embraced a right to be "cured or even to improve."[34] The federal court in Alabama ruled that involuntarily committed mental patients have a "constitutional right to receive such individual treatment as will give each of them a realistic opportunity to be cured or to improve his or her mental condition."[35]

In 1975 the U.S. Supreme Court rejected such an expansive a view of patient rights. Chief Justice Warren Burger wrote: "Given the present state of medical knowledge regarding abnormal human behavior and its treatment, few things would be more fraught with peril than to irrevocably condition a State's power to protect the mentally ill upon the providing of such treatment as will give [them] a realistic opportunity to be cured."[36]

Informed Consent

In chapter 13 we learned that with few exceptions people cannot be treated by a medical provider without their informed consent. The federal patients' bill of rights concerning care of the mentally ill states that mental illness alone does not prevent a person from making an informed decision to refuse a course of treatment.[37] Factors that courts consider in deciding whether medication should be administered include whether (1) there may be side-effects; (2) there are less restrictive ways to treat a patient; and (3) the treatment is necessary to protect the patient or others.[38] But a person cannot make the "knowing and willful" decision that is the hallmark of informed consent unless she or he is competent, thus able to understand and apply to her or his situation the information provided.

Next I will review five cases, each addressing informed consent in a different context. First, the case of Daniel Burch asks, "Can a person's consent to treatment be voluntary when mental health professionals acknowledge that the patient is delusional?" The second question, taken up in the next four cases, asks, "Can the state medicate a person against her or his will?" This question will be addressed first for a patient who is a prisoner, next (in two cases) for defendants awaiting trial, and last, for a patient involuntarily committed to a state mental hospital. For the first question, we turn to the case of Daniel Burch.[39]

> On December 7, 1981, Daniel Burch was found wandering along a Florida highway, appearing to be hurt and disoriented. He was taken to . . . a private mental health . . . facility designated by the State to receive patients suffering from mental illness. . . . [Facility] staff [noted] that . . . Burch was hallucinating, confused and psychotic and believed he was "in heaven." . . . Burch . . . sign[ed] forms giving his consent to admission and treatment. He remained at [the facility] for three days. . . . The facility's staff diagnosed his condition as paranoid schizophrenia and gave him psychotropic medication. [Finding] that Burch was in need of longer-term stabilization, . . . [he was] referred . . . to [Florida State Hospital (FSH)], . . . a public hospital owned and operated by the State as a mental health treatment facility. . . . Burch signed forms requesting admission and authorizing treatment. . . . One form . . . recited that the patient requests admission for observation, diagnosis, care and treatment of [my] mental condition, and that the patient, if admitted, agrees to accept such treatment as may be prescribed by members

of the medical and psychiatric staff in accordance with the provisions of expressed and informed consent.

[Later in the month of December] Burch [would reauthorize treatment by signing a] form . . . stat[ing] that . . . the professional staff . . . [could] administer treatment . . . that he had been informed of the purpose of treatment [and] . . . side effects . . . alternative treatment modalities; approximate length of care; and of his power to revoke consent to treatment.

[At the time of Burch's admission] Doctor Zinermon wrote a progress note indicating that Burch was "refusing to cooperate," would not answer questions, "appears distressed and confused, and related that medication has been helpful." A nursing assessment form dated December 11 stated that Burch was confused and unable to state the reason for his hospitalization and still believed that "this is heaven." Zinermon on December 29 made a further report on Burch's condition, stating that, on admission, Burch had been "disoriented, semi-mute, confused and bizarre in appearance and thought, not cooperative to the initial interview, [and] extremely psychotic, appeared to be paranoid and hallucinating." The doctor's report also stated that Burch remained disoriented, delusional, and psychotic.

Burch remained at FSH until May 7, 1982, five months after his initial admission. . . . During that time, no hearing was held regarding his hospitalization and treatment.

After his release, Burch complained that he had been admitted inappropriately . . . and did not remember signing a voluntary admission form. His complaint reached [a state] Human Rights Advocacy Committee. . . . The Committee investigated and [wrote] to Burch [stating that he] . . . had signed a voluntary admission form, but that there was documentation that you were heavily medicated and disoriented on admission and . . . you were probably not competent to be signing legal documents. The letter also stated that . . . hospital administration was made aware that they were very likely asking medicated clients to make decisions at a time when they were not mentally competent.[40]

In February 1985 Burch filed a complaint in federal court. He claimed that he had been deprived of liberty in violation of the Fourteenth Amendment. He argued that hospital staff knew that he was heavily medicated, disoriented, and apparently suffering from a psychotic disorder and that those admitting him should have known that he was not competent to give informed consent. He argued that he should have been afforded due process safeguards before the commitment. The U.S. Supreme Court found that "Florida chose to delegate to petitioners a broad power to admit patients to FSH, i.e., to effect what, in the absence of informed consent, is a substantial deprivation of liberty. Because petitioners had state authority to deprive persons of liberty, the Constitution imposed on them the State's concomitant duty to see that no deprivation occur without adequate procedural protections."[41]

The next case that concerns us was decided in 1990 by the U.S. Supreme Court. Walter Harper was a prisoner in the Washington state penal system; he had been treated with antipsychotic drugs both in and out of prison. When he stopped taking his medication, his behavior turned violent. He was transferred from prison to a program serving convicted felons with serious mental problems, was diagnosed with a manic depressive disorder, and was put on medication.[42] The program did not seek a court order before administering drugs to Harper, who later challenged in federal court the policy that allowed him to be treated without his consent and without a court hearing.

The Supreme Court agreed with Harper that he had a liberty interest, protected by the Fourteenth Amendment, to be free from the arbitrary administration of medication. However, the Court disagreed with Harper's contention that before the state could administer antipsychotic drug treatment there had to be a judicial finding that he was not competent. The Court ruled that Harper's position failed to take into account the state's legitimate interest in treating him, when medically appropriate, for the purpose of reducing the danger that he posed. The Court ruled that the Fourteenth Amendment allows the state to treat against their will those with a serious mental illness who are dangerous to themselves or others, if the treatment is deemed to be in the patient's best interests. For the same reason the Court rejected Harper's claim that he was entitled to a court hearing before medication was administered. Thus in *Washington v. Harper* the Court ruled that he could be treated against his will without a finding of incompetence, but this ruling may be limited in its application because Harper was a prisoner.

The question posed in *Harper* was rephrased in *Riggins v. Nevada*.[43] A pretrial detainee claimed a right not to be medicated at his murder trial so that the jury could see him in the state he claimed to have been in when he committed his crime. The U.S. Supreme Court agreed and overturned *Riggins* verdict. The High Court found that the protections offered by the Fourteenth Amendment apply to those the government has detained for trial, as it does to convicted inmates. Pretrial detainees have a liberty interest in being free from unwanted psychotropic medication.

In part, the Court's support of Riggins's right to forgo medication at trial stemmed from the known side-effects of psychotropic medications, specifically, that they could dull Riggins's ability to testify, to communicate with counsel, and to comprehend the proceedings, thus prejudicing his rights and violating the constitutional requirement for a fair trial. The Court did not close the door on the possibility that different circumstances could support forcible medication at trial. However, the Court held that a prisoner could not be forced to take medication unless a court found that there was an overriding state justification for taking such action, accompanied by a determination that it is medically appropriate.

In 2003 the U.S. Supreme Court revisited the question of whether a person can be forcibly medicated to make him competent to stand trial. Thomas Sells was charged with Medicaid fraud and conspiracy to commit murder. The Court ruled that the United States could not forcibly medicate Sells. Unlike the defendant in *Harper,* Sells was not dangerous, and comparisons with *Riggins* were unwarranted because the lower courts had failed to focus sufficiently on trial competence and what effects medication might have on Sells. Moreover, he was confined in a treatment center where he was likely to stay if he continued to refuse medication, and his confinement mitigated the state's concern that he might commit another crime.[44]

None of these cases has dealt with a patient committed to a mental hospital on an involuntary basis, and the U.S. Supreme Court has not addressed informed consent in this context. Consider a case decided by the New York Court of Appeals in 1986.

In *Rivers v. Katz* New York's highest court addressed the question, "Could a person hospitalized for mental illness refuse treatment?" In a general proclamation the court ruled that the right of a patient to decide whether to accept or refuse medical treatment extends to the mentally ill, who are "not to be treated as persons of lesser status or dignity because of their illness."[45] However, as with the *Harper* case, New York's high court found that the right of an involuntarily committed patient to refuse antipsychotic medication is not absolute; where a patient presents a danger to self or others, "or engages in dangerous or potentially disruptive conduct within the institution,"[46] the state may exercise its police power to protect others, act in *parens patriae,* and order treatment over a patient's objections. Absent an argument that the state's police power justifies treating a patient against her or his will, the state must seek a judicial order that the patient lacks the capacity to make an informed decision regarding treatment before drugs may be administered pursuant to the state's *parens patriae* power. The state's interest may override a patient's objections where the patient was presently dangerous and the most appropriate way to reduce risk was by administering drugs.[47]

PLACEMENT IN THE LEAST RESTRICTIVE ENVIRONMENT

In 1972 a federal judge in Wisconsin had the following to say about placement in restrictive settings:

> Perhaps the most basic and fundamental right is the right to be free from unwanted restraint. It seems clear . . . that persons suffering from the con-

> dition of being mentally ill, but who are not alleged to have committed any crime, cannot be totally deprived of their liberty if there are less drastic means for achieving the same basic goal. . . . The person recommending full-time involuntary hospitalization must bear the burden of proving (1) what alternatives are available; (2) what alternatives were investigated; and (3) why the investigated alternatives were not deemed suitable. These alternatives include voluntary or court-ordered out-patient treatment, day treatment in a hospital, night treatment in a hospital, placement in the custody of a friend or relative, placement in a nursing home, referral to a community mental health clinic, and home health aide services.[48]

The availability of psychotropic medications made it possible to control the symptoms of mental illness and was key to the movement to deinstitutionalize the mentally ill and to place previously hospitalized patients in less restrictive settings. Congress supported this endeavor by making Medicaid funds available to support care in nursing homes. The nursing home population of psychiatric patients older than sixty-five increased from 188,000 in 1963 to 368,000 in 1969, while the population in large congregate institutions fell from 153,000 in 1962 to 78,000 in 1972. Congress provided funds for the construction of community mental health centers (CMHCs), which were to provide inpatient, outpatient, partial hospitalization, emergency services, and consultation education services.[49] But federal regulations did not require that those discharged from state hospitals be directed to CMHCs or that CMHCs and state hospitals coordinate their efforts on behalf of the mentally ill.[50] Moreover, the money saved when an institution is downsized is not necessarily directed toward community care. As a consequence, some of those who were discharged from congregate care settings were left to their own devices without any help from the state.[51]

Even when community placements are available, it does not follow that there is a constitutional right to such care. In *Pennhurst v. Halderman*[52] the U.S. Supreme Court ruled that federal judges cannot impose on state officials the obligation to consider less restrictive alternatives.[53] However, state laws may contain provisions for placement in the least restrictive setting, although many statutes use qualifying language, providing for placement in the least restrictive placement "available," thus providing a loophole for a state that is financially strapped and unable to develop enough placements in the community.[54]

The position of the U.S. Supreme Court regarding community placement changed in 1999 when the Court ruled that the Americans with Disabilities Act (ADA) required the states to place people with disabilities in the least restrictive environment. We shall turn first to consider the relevant sections of the ADA and then to the *Olmstead* case, in which the Court changed its position on this subject.

The Americans with Disabilities Act

The Americans with Disabilities Act (ADA) was discussed in chapter 9. The ADA prohibits public entities such as state or local government from discriminating against qualified individuals who are disabled. Specifically, Title II proscribes discrimination in the provision of public services and specifies that no qualified individual with a disability shall "by reason of such disability" be excluded from participation in or be denied the benefits of a public entity's services, programs, or activities.[55] Mental illness is a disability.

In 1990, when Congress passed the ADA, it referred to the isolation and segregation of individuals with disabilities, calling such treatment a serious and pervasive form of discrimination.[56] Pursuant to an instruction from Congress, the U.S. Department of Justice issued regulations to guide the implementation of the ADA.[57] Two regulations are of concern to us. The first, the "integration regulation," requires a "public entity [to] administer . . . programs . . . in the most integrated setting appropriate to the needs of qualified individuals with disabilities"[58]; and the second requires public entities to make reasonable modifications to avoid "discrimination on the basis of disability."[59]

Olmstead v. Zimring

Relying on the regulations issued by Justice, L.C. and E.W., two women diagnosed as mentally retarded and mentally ill, sued Georgia in the 1990s.[60] According to court papers:

> Both women had a history of treatment in institutional settings. In May 1992, L. C. was voluntarily admitted to Georgia Regional Hospital at Atlanta (GRH), where she was confined for treatment in a psychiatric unit. By May 1993, her psychiatric condition had stabilized, and L. C.'s treatment team . . . agreed that her needs could be met appropriately in one of the community-based programs the State supported. Despite this evaluation, L. C. remained institutionalized until February 1996, when the State placed her in a community-based treatment program.
>
> E. W. was voluntarily admitted to GRH in February 1995; like L. C., E. W. was confined for treatment in a psychiatric unit. In March 1995, GRH sought to discharge E. W. to a homeless shelter but abandoned that plan after her attorney filed an administrative complaint. By 1996, E. W.'s treating psychiatrist concluded that she could be treated appropriately in a community-based setting. She nonetheless remained institutionalized until . . . 1997.[61]

Seeking placement in community care, L.C. and E.W. brought a Section 1983 action against Georgia officials that claimed discrimination under Title II of the

ADA. You will recall from reading chapter 7 that Section 1983 provides a mechanism for a citizen to sue another who is acting "under color of state law" for depriving the aggrieved party of a constitutional or statutory right. A person acts under color of state law when he or she exercises power possessed by virtue of state law and made possible only because the actor is clothed with authority of state law. Thus Olmstead, the commissioner of the Georgia Department of Human Resources, was vulnerable to suit since he was charged with implementing state law governing commitment of the mentally ill. The client who files a Section 1983 action, in addition to establishing that the offending conduct was undertaken by a state actor performing duties under color of state law, must show that the actions resulted in the deprivation of a federally secured right, which includes any right conferred by statute such as the ADA.

> L. C. [and E. W.] alleged that the State violated Title II [by] failing to place [them] . . . in a community-based program once . . . treating professionals determined that such placement was appropriate. The District Court . . . order[ed] placement [of the women] in an appropriate community-based treatment program. The court rejected the State's argument that inadequate funding, not discrimination against L. C. and E. W. by reason of [their] disabilit[ies], accounted for their retention at GRH. Under Title II, the court concluded, unnecessary institutional segregation constitutes discrimination . . . which cannot be justified by a lack of funding.[62]

In rendering its decision, the U.S. Supreme Court said that the case required the Court to determine how to construe the antidiscrimination provision contained in Title II of the ADA. Specifically, the Court said that the following question must be answered: "Whether the proscription of discrimination may require placement of persons with mental disabilities in community settings rather than in institutions."[63] The Court responded with what it called "a qualified yes." Community placement is in order when (1) treatment professionals employed by the state determine that community placement is appropriate; (2) the person to be transferred from an institutional setting to a less restrictive setting is not opposed to the transfer; and (3) the placement is reasonable, taking into account resources available to the state and the "needs of others with mental disabilities."[64]

In reaching its conclusion, the Court relied on the regulations promulgated by the Justice Department. The court reasoned that:

> Undue institutionalization qualifies as discrimination by reason of . . . disability. The [Justice Department] has consistently advocated that it does.

> Because the Department [was] directed by Congress to issue Title II regulations, its views warrant respect. . . . The well-reasoned views of the agencies implementing a statute constitute a body of experience and informed judgment to which courts and litigants may properly resort for guidance. [The Justice Department has written that] . . . a public entity shall administer services, programs, and activities in the most integrated setting appropriate to the needs of qualified individuals with disabilities. The preamble to the Attorney General's Title II regulations defines the most integrated setting appropriate to the needs of qualified individuals with disabilities to mean a setting that enables individuals with disabilities to interact with nondisabled persons to the fullest extent possible.
>
> According to the State, L. C. and E. W. encountered no discrimination by reason of their disabilities because they were not denied community placement on account of those disabilities. . . . In rejecting th[is] position . . . the Court [opines that] the ADA . . . requires all public entities to refrain from discrimination . . . and specifically identifies unjustified segregation of persons with disabilities as a form of discrimination. . . . The identification of unjustified segregation as discrimination reflects two evident judgments: Institutional placement of persons who can handle and benefit from community settings perpetuates unwarranted assumptions that persons so isolated are incapable or unworthy of participating in community life . . . and institutional confinement severely diminishes individuals' everyday life activities. . . . This Court emphasizes that nothing in the ADA or its implementing regulations condones termination of institutional settings for persons unable to handle or benefit from community settings. Nor is there any federal requirement that community-based treatment be imposed on patients who do not desire it. In this case, however, it is not genuinely disputed that L. C. and E. W. are individuals qualified for noninstitutional care: The State's own professionals determined that community-based treatment would be appropriate for . . . [both] woman [neither of whom] opposed such treatment.[65]

Lest the Court's ruling be read as a mandate to further deinstitutionalize patients in mental hospitals, the Court made clear what obligations it was imposing on the state:

> The State's responsibility, once it provides community-based treatment to qualified persons with disabilities, is not boundless. The [ADA] speaks of reasonable modifications to avoid discrimination. . . . The ADA is not reasonably read to impel States to phase out institutions, placing patients in

> need of close care at risk. Nor is it the ADA's mission to drive States to move institutionalized patients into an inappropriate setting, such as a homeless shelter. . . . If . . . the State were to demonstrate that it had a comprehensive, effectively working plan for placing qualified persons with mental disabilities in less restrictive settings, and a waiting list that moved at a reasonable pace not controlled by the State's endeavors to keep its institutions fully populated, the reasonable-modifications standard would be met. In such circumstances, a court would have no warrant effectively to order displacement of persons at the top of the community-based treatment waiting list by individuals lower down who commenced civil actions.
>
> Consistent with these provisions, the State generally may rely on the reasonable assessments of its own professionals in determining whether an individual meets the essential eligibility requirements for habilitation in a community-based program. Absent such qualification, it would be inappropriate to remove a patient from the more restrictive setting.[66]

In June 2001, two years after the Supreme Court decision in the *Olmstead* case, President George W. Bush issued an executive order in which he addressed the High Court's ruling. The president stated that the federal government was committed to fostering the independence of the mentally ill by placing qualified individuals in community settings, and he noted his agreement with the High Court's ruling when he said that unnecessary institutionalization was a form of disability-based discrimination. The president ordered federal agencies—Health and Human Services, and the Departments of Labor and Housing and Urban Development, for example—to assist the states in implementing the *Olmstead* decision by providing technical assistance to those states that were developing plans to provide community-based services, and by revising where necessary federal regulations to facilitate implementation of *Olmstead*. He instructed the Justice Department to enforce Title II of the ADA on behalf of individuals who claim that they have been unjustly institutionalized.[67]

OUTPATIENT CIVIL COMMITMENT

There is no way to guarantee that one who is released from a congregate setting to live in the community at large will continue to take prescribed medication; statutes that provide for outpatient civil commitment are a way of trying to deal with the difficulties that arise for the patient and for others in the community when a person elects to stop taking medication.

In 1966 the U.S. Court of Appeals for the District of Columbia articulated a rationale for helping to avoid rehospitalization. The case concerned a woman in her midsixties who had been found wandering the streets of the District of Columbia. She was taken into custody, diagnosed as mentally ill, and committed to St. Elizabeth's Hospital. She later petitioned for her release. The court opined that the options for treating a person who was mentally ill were not limited to returning her to a hospital or unconditionally releasing her to the community. "We have the option," the court determined, "to order any . . . course of treatment . . . [we] . . . believe will be in the best interests of the person or of the public." Citing an opinion of the U.S. Department of Health, Education and Welfare (now HHS), the court opined that "the entire spectrum of services should be made available, including outpatient treatment, foster care, halfway houses, day hospitals, nursing homes, etc." Thus, the court concluded, it had a duty to explore alternatives, and the state had an obligation to make an earnest effort to review and exhaust available resources of the community in order to provide care reasonably suited to the woman's needs.[68] In the late 1990s a series of tragedies occurred in New York City that focused the media spotlight on the mentally ill living in community settings. On January 3, 1999, a young woman named Kendra Webdale was tragically pushed to her death in front of an oncoming Manhattan subway train by twenty-nine-year-old Andrew Goldstein, a diagnosed schizophrenic with a history of violence who failed to take his prescribed medication. Other similarly tragic incidents occurred that year, including the April 6 police shooting of Charles Stevens, a man with a history of mental illness who swung a sword at passengers on the Long Island Railroad. In another instance, on April 28, 1999, Edgar Rivera's legs were severed after Julio Perez, an untreated schizophrenic, shoved him into the path of an oncoming subway train. Stories such as these led to a demand for mandatory outpatient treatment under certain circumstances.

Shortly thereafter, evoking its police power and the authority found in the doctrine of *parens patriae,* the New York legislature enacted the Assisted Outpatient Treatment Act (AOTA).[69] The legislature articulated the philosophy underpinning the act as follows:

> There are mentally ill persons . . . capable of living in the community with the help of family, friends and mental health professionals, but who, without routine care and treatment, may relapse and become violent or suicidal, or require hospitalization [and] there are mentally ill persons who can function well and safely in the community with supervision and treatment, but who without such assistance, will relapse and require long periods of hospitalization.
>
> Effective [assistance requires] the establishment of assisted outpatient treatment as a mode of treatment; improved coordination of care for men-

> tally ill persons living in the community; the expansion of the use of conditional release in psychiatric hospitals; and the improved dissemination of information between and among mental health providers and general hospital emergency rooms.
>
> ... If ... court-ordered treatment is to achieve its goals, it must be linked to a system of comprehensive care, in which state and local authorities work together to ensure that outpatients receive case management and have access to treatment services.... Assisted outpatient treatment ... is compassionate, not punitive, will restore patients' dignity, and will enable mentally ill persons to lead more productive and satisfying lives.[70]

At the time of this writing, forty states and the District of Columbia have laws that provide for outpatient commitment for people suffering from mental illness. Unlike involuntary commitment, where the criteria for court-ordered incarceration require evidence that a person be suffering from mental illness and be a danger to self or others, an order for outpatient commitment may be made without the latter finding. In Arizona an order may be entered by a court for a person who suffers from a "mental disorder [who] is persistently or acutely disabled or gravely disabled and in need of treatment, and is either unwilling or unable to accept voluntary treatment"[71]; and Alabama provides for outpatient commitment for a person who suffers from mental illness, is likely to "deteriorate" due to untreated mental illness, and whose ability to function independently will be compromised and who cannot make a rational and informed decision as to whether or not treatment for mental illness would be desirable.[72] In New York a court order may be obtained for the patient who is at least eighteen who (1) suffers from a mental illness; (2) is unlikely to voluntarily participate in treatment; (3) has been deemed unlikely to survive safely in the community without supervision; (4) has failed in the past to comply with treatment for mental illness that has contributed significantly to at least two hospitalizations or periods of incarceration in the last thirty-six months, or resulted in one or more acts or threats or, or attempts at serious violent behavior toward self or others within the last forty-eight months; (5) based on history and current behavior is in need of assisted outpatient treatment to prevent a relapse or deterioration that would likely result in serious harm to self or others; and (6) is likely to benefit from assisted outpatient treatment.[73]

Assisted outpatient treatment consists of court-ordered services, where a case manager or community treatment team provider coordinates care. Treatment may include a variety of interventions, such as medication, counseling, including counseling and treatment for substance abuse, day or partial day programming, and educational and vocational services.

The Process of Effecting Outpatient Civil Commitment

In New York the petition that initiates the outpatient commitment process may be filed by (1) an adult roommate of the person on whose behalf commitment is sought; (2) a member of that person's family; (3) a psychiatrist; or (4) an official, such as the director of a hospital serving the patient, the director of a mental health agency, or a parole or probation officer.[74]

As with inpatient commitment, a physician must support the request, but with outpatient care the physician must be willing and able to testify at a hearing and present evidence that this commitment is the least restrictive form of treatment.[75] The person who is the subject of the petition may present evidence, call witnesses, and cross-examine those who testify in support of the petition.

The required written treatment plan must provide for services to coordinate patient care and may include other services, such as medication, individual or group therapy, programming activities, educational and/or vocational activities, alcohol or substance abuse treatment and counseling, and other appropriate services. If the treatment plan recommends medication, it may also include periodic blood tests or urinalysis to determine compliance with prescribed medications.

Failure to comply with an order for assisted outpatient treatment is not, in and of itself, grounds for involuntary civil commitment, but an individual's refusal to take prescribed medication may be considered by a physician in deciding whether to pursue involuntary admission. Continued oversight is done through mandatory immediate and quarterly reports that are to be developed and submitted to the Office of Mental Health program coordinator by the assisted outpatient treatment program.[76]

Legal Challenges to Outpatient Commitment

In 2000 the first legal challenge to the constitutionality of New York's assisted outpatient treatment statute was made. Plaintiffs argued that their constitutional right to due process was violated since the statute denied them the right to elect their own course of medical treatment; they also argued that the law violated their right to equal protection of the law because the law created three classes of people who could be deprived of their right to direct the course of their own treatment, while equal protection requires that the law treat the groups alike. The three groups were those (1) subject to guardianship proceedings; (2) involuntarily committed to an institution; and (3) outpatients. Plaintiffs argued that outpatients were treated unfairly compared to other groups since the law did not extend to them the requirement that they not be treated without their consent unless a court found them incompetent.[77]

Regardless of the basis for their constitutional claim, plaintiffs' concern was that they were denied the right to direct their own course of treatment. They rested their argument on *Rivers v. Katz,* where the New York Court of Appeals ruled that the right of a patient to decide whether to accept or refuse medical treatment extends to the involuntarily committed mentally ill patient.

The New York court disagreed with the plaintiffs, finding that New York's assisted outpatient treatment statute did not unconstitutionally violate the patient's fundamental right to choose the course of her or his medical treatment. The court distinguished the case from *Rivers* as follows: Unlike the involuntarily committed patients whose rights were the subject of that case, plaintiffs subject to assisted outpatient treatment have been discharged from the hospital, and there is no question of forcing medication. The patient has the protection of the treatment plan in whose development she or he, or an elected representative, is an active participant. If a court considering whether to order the treatment plan hears evidence that the patient and/or the patient's representative was denied the opportunity to participate in plan development, the plan of treatment should not be approved.

The court also rejected plaintiffs' argument that compliance with the treatment plan was coercive because failure to comply with the requirements in the plan subjected them to arrest. The court pointed out that the law expressly precludes involuntary civil commitment or a finding of contempt of court for failure to comply. The rule of law, by which people cannot be treated without their consent unless found mentally ill and dangerous to self or others, applies to those involved in assisted outpatient treatment.

MENTAL ILLNESS AND CRIMINAL LAW

In the introduction to this chapter I said that mental illness is a condition characterized by alterations in thinking, mood, or behavior associated with distress and/or impaired functioning. Mental illness is not synonymous with *insanity,* which is a legal term that refers to the ability to form the intent that is an element of a crime (chapter 3) or to comprehend the consequences of an act. The subject of insanity arises when questions are posed regarding a person's (1) competency to stand trial; (2) state of mind at the time the crime was committed; (3) release from prison; and (4) treatment while in care.

Competence to Stand Trial

Criminal defendants have a constitutionally protected right not to be tried for a crime unless they are legally competent. To do otherwise would violate due process.[78] The person claiming to be incompetent must establish by a preponderance of the evidence that she or he is "suffering from a mental disease or defect and is not able to understand the nature and consequences of the proceedings or assist properly in his or her defense."[79]

Under federal law competency is determined at a hearing where evidence, including court-ordered mental health evaluations, is presented. The defendant who is found incompetent may be hospitalized for as long as four months to determine whether there is a substantial likelihood that the person will attain competency in the near future so that a trial may proceed. If four months is not sufficient time, a defendant may be hospitalized for an "additional reasonable time" if a court finds a "substantial probability" that competency will be regained. The defendant who remains incompetent may be committed for dangerousness.[80] A defendant who is not dangerous cannot be held longer than the maximum length of the sentence for the crime charged.[81]

Insanity Defense

Whereas a claim of incompetency to stand trial concerns the defendant's present state of mind, an insanity defense concerns a defendant's state of mind at the time a crime was committed. A person may be found competent to stand trial but not guilty by reason of insanity in the crime charged.

A plea of not guilty by reason of insanity is an affirmative defense. As we learned in chapter 3, the defendant who asserts an affirmative defense acknowledges wrongdoing but argues either justification, as in the battered woman defense, or that she or he should not be held criminally accountable because of a severe mental disease or defect. The likelihood that an insanity defense will be successful is slim. Depending upon the state, the likelihood of success ranges from less than 1 percent to 8.5 percent.[82]

Over time, the courts have employed different tests to determine sanity, focusing on whether a defendant (1) knew or understood the consequences that could result from the action taken; (2) knew or understood that the act or actions were wrong; and (3) was suffering from a form of mental illness.[83] Under federal law the defendant who asserts an insanity defense must establish by clear and convincing evidence that when the act or acts were committed, the actor suffered from severe mental illness and that she or he did not appreciate the wrongfulness of that behavior.[84] Voluntary alcohol or drug abuse cannot be taken into account.[85]

Insanity is established by expert testimony. Consider the following case. James Carbullido was charged with setting a series of fires and was found not guilty by reason of insanity. He admitted to burning and vandalizing churches because he believed that members of the congregation had planted an electrical device in his brain that projected voices into his head in an attempt to control his mind and body. The vandalism and fires were explained as an attempt to stop this assault. Experts testified that Carbullido lacked the cognitive ability to understand that his acts were wrong and that he suffered from paranoid schizophrenia. His medical records indicated that he had been suffering from severe mental illness for approximately ten years, that he believed his efforts were necessary to combat the voices in his mind, and that the church congregation conspired to control his life.

An expert for the state agreed with Carbullido's expert on the question of the severity of his mental illness and his inability to appreciate the consequences of his crime, but the state's expert judged Carbullido competent to stand trial because he was able "to assist counsel, to aid in his own defense, to recall evidence reliably, and to give responsible testimony if called upon to do so."[86] This expert reported that he was confident in believing Carbullido was suffering from a mental illness of psychotic proportions to the extent that he did not know he was doing a wrongful act and should therefore be considered insane at the time of the commission of the acts charged against him.

However, a defendant may provide expert testimony that he is mentally ill but fail to establish that he is legally insane. For example, David Hiebert was charged with distributing marijuana and possession of a firearm. At trial he offered expert testimony to the effect that he was delusional and that he believed that the judge and jury were conspiring against him. The court agreed with Hiebert's contention that he was seriously mentally ill but nevertheless found him legally sane because he had made efforts to conceal his criminal conduct. The court interpreted this behavior as proof that Hiebert appreciated that his behavior violated the law.[87]

Guilty but Mentally Ill

In 1982 John W. Hinckley Jr. attempted to assassinate President Ronald Reagan. The jury's finding that Hinckley was not guilty by reason of insanity focused public attention on the insanity defense and is reported to be causal to changes in state law.[88] The goal of statutory reform was to broaden the range of choices available to a jury beyond finding a defendant guilty, when there were concerns about a defendant's mental health, or not guilty by reason of insanity when the evidence indicated that the mentally ill defendant appreciated that his or her behavior was criminal.[89]

When a jury is not convinced by the evidence presented at trial that a person is legally insane, it may find the defendant "guilty but mentally ill" rather than "not guilty by reason of insanity" if the jury concludes (1) that the defendant is guilty beyond a reasonable doubt in the offense charged and (2) that the defendant, while mentally ill, was not legally insane at the time of the commission of the offense charged.[90] Such a verdict means that the defendant is legally responsible for criminal conduct but in need of treatment while incarcerated.[91]

Diminished Capacity

Unlike the insanity defense, where a defendant claims justification (chapter 3), the defendant asserting diminished capacity is legally sane and admits liability for the charged crime. However, the defendant seeks a lower sentence by offering evidence that his or her mental condition prevented forming the intent that the law requires for a guilty verdict. Diminished capacity may be the result of mental retardation, antisocial personality, or a lobotomy.[92]

Disposition

Federal law provides a range of dispositional alternatives for a person who suffers from a mental condition or mental disease. These include the following. When a person is found not guilty by reason of insanity, she or he is committed to a suitable facility and remains there until it is determined that the person does not pose a danger to another person or to property.[93] Release may be conditional upon compliance with a plan of care or treatment.

Another scenario envisions a person who has been found guilty but who alleges before being sentenced to prison that she or he is suffering from a mental disease or defect. Here the convicted party offers evidence of mental illness or defect and pleads for commitment to a facility for care and treatment in lieu of a prison sentence. After recovery the person may at the discretion of the court be released or sentenced to complete a term in prison.

In some cases people who are already imprisoned argue successfully that they suffer from a mental disease or defect and should therefore be transferred to an appropriate facility for care or treatment until the need for care and treatment has passed or the term of the original sentence has passed, whichever comes first.

SUMMARY

My objective in this chapter has been to familiarize you with a number of legal issues that affect social work practice in mental health. We began with a discussion of the law of civil commitment, which refers to procedures used to confine a person who is "ill, incompetent, drug-addicted, or the like." Civil commitment is controlled mainly by state law and sanctioned by a state's police power, which refers to actions taken by the state to protect public health and safety, and/or the *parens patriae* authority, which refers to the state's commitment to help those not able to help themselves.

Involuntary confinement restricts a person's freedom, which is protected by constitutional law. In seeking to restrict personal freedom, the state must justify its actions by showing that the loss to the individual is outweighed by a gain to public health or safety. The law sanctions civil commitment when the person to be confined (1) presents a danger or threat of danger to self or others as a result of the mental illness; (2) is likely to benefit from treatment; and (3) is confined in the least restrictive setting and is receiving the least restrictive method of treatment available.

The person the state seeks to commit has certain due process rights, including the right to notice and to a hearing and to require that the party seeking commitment prove by clear and convincing evidence that commitment is required. Some states confer a right to counsel, including court-appointed counsel for the indigent, and state law may require that one or more mental health professionals assert in writing that commitment is necessary.

The restrictions of civil confinement are balanced by granting certain rights that are authorized by state statute or inferred from constitutional analysis. The rights include (1) the right to be free from harm; (2) the right of the mentally retarded to habilitation; and (3) the right to have treatment provided to reduce or eliminate the mental health problems that necessitated confinement.

Mental illness does not by definition mean that a person is in all ways incompetent, nor does it necessarily rob a person of the ability to make informed choices regarding treatment. A confined person has a Fourteenth Amendment liberty interest in refusing the arbitrary administration of medication, but a court is likely to allow the state to administer psychotropic medication if it can show that the person to be treated poses a danger to self or others and that treatment is necessary to reduce the danger.

Confined mentally ill people have argued that they have a right to be placed in the least restrictive setting, but the U.S. Supreme Court has ruled that there is no constitutional authority to support this claim. However, in 1999 the Court, relying on provisions in the Americans with Disabilities Act, ruled that it was illegal discrimination to exclude the qualified mentally ill from publicly funded programs because of their disability. Community placement is required for the person not opposed to living in the community when state-employed treatment professionals determine that it is appropriate and when such placement is reasonable, taking into account resources available to the state.

As a rule, community placement means that the previously confined person will not be regularly supervised. Lacking supervision, she or he may stop taking medication, experience again the symptoms that initially led to hospitalization, and pose a danger to self and others through violent acts. States have responded by sanctioning outpatient civil commitment, which provides the option of retaining the person in the community with services, including counseling, housing assistance, case management to coordinate service delivery, and service to ensure that a person takes her or his medication. Outpatient commitment is distinguished from inpatient commitment because it may be permissible as a preventive measure and a court order does not require evidence that a person is suffering from mental illness and is currently a danger to self or others.

The law precludes trying for a crime a person not competent to participate in her or his own defense. When a person is not able to stand trial, the law provides that the suspect may be confined in a hospital for the mentally ill until competent to stand trial or until the time spent in an institution is equal to the maximum sentence for the charged crime. Incompetency to stand trial concerns a defendant's present state of mind, whereas an insanity defense concerns a defendant's state of mind at the time a crime was committed. A person may be competent to stand trial but not guilty of the crime charged by reason of insanity, which is a legal term. The federal defendant who mounts an insanity defense must establish through expert testimony that at the time the crime was committed, she or he suffered from severe mental illness and could not appreciate the wrongfulness of her or his behavior.

The law allows other mental state defenses, including "guilty but mentally ill," whereby a judge or jury concludes that the defendant is guilty but mentally ill and not legally insane. Thus the defendant is legally responsible for criminal conduct but in need of treatment while incarcerated. An alternative is the claim of diminished capacity, when a defendant argues that although he or she was legally sane and liable for the crime charged, he or she is nevertheless unable, as a result of his or her mental condition (such as mental retardation or antisocial personality), to form the intent that the law requires for a guilty verdict and therefore seeks a lower sentence.

Notes

PREFACE

1. Heather A. Wydra, "Keeping Secrets Within the Team: Maintaining Client Confidentiality While Offering Interdisciplinary Services to the Elderly Client," *Fordham Law Review* 62 (1994): 1517–45.
2. Louise G. Trubek and Jennifer J. Farnham, "Social Justice Collaboratives: Multidisciplinary Practices for People," *Clinical Law Review* 7 (2000): 227–72.

1. INTRODUCTION

1. For an in-depth discussion of Settlement House workers, the law, and the connection to social work, See: Theodore J. Stein, *Social Policy and Policymaking by the Branches of Government and the Public-at-Large* (New York: Columbia University Press, 2001).
2. Administrative Procedures Act, 5 U.S.C.A. § 553(c) (West 2002).
3. Personal Responsibility and Work Opportunity Reconciliation Act, Pub. L. No. 104–193, 110 U.S. Stat. 2105 (1996).
4. General provisions for Temporary Assistance for Needy Families (TANF), 45 C.F.R. § 260.31 (1999).
5. *Aliessa v. Novello,* 96 N.Y.2d 418, 754 N.E.2d 1085 (N.Y. 2001).
6. Barbara A. Babb and Judith D. Moran, "Substance Abuse, Families, and Unified Family Courts: The Creation of a Caring Justice System," *Journal of Health Care Law and Policy* 3 (1999): 1–16.
7. Allen F. Davis, *Spearheads for Reform: The Social Settlements and the Progressive Movement, 1890–1914* (New York: Oxford University Press, 1967), 266 n21; Lela B. Costin, *Two Sisters for Social Justice: A Biography of Grace and Edith Abbott* (Chicago: University of Illinois Press, 1983), 45.
8. Leigh Goodmark, "Can Poverty Lawyers Play Well with Others? Including Legal Services in Integrated, School-Based Service Delivery Programs," *Georgetown Journal on Fighting Poverty* 4 (1997): 243–67.

9. Ibid.; see also Jacqueline St. Joan, "Building Bridges, Building Walls: Collaboration Between Lawyers and Social Workers in a Domestic Violence Clinic and Issues of Client Confidentiality," *Clinical Law Review* 7 (2001): 403–67; Christina T. Pierce, Patricia Gleason-Wynn, and Marilyn G. Miller, "Social Work and Law: A Model for Implementing Social Services in a Law Office," *NAELA (National Association of Elder Law Attorneys) Quarterly* 13 (2000): 3–7; Paula Galowitz, "Collaboration Between Lawyers and Social Workers: Re-Examining the Nature and Potential of the Relationship," *Fordham Law Review* 67 (1999): 2123–54.
10. Family Court Act, § 249, Appointment of a Law Guardian (McKinney 2000). When a case involves abuse or neglect, delinquency, or a child who was in foster care, the New York statute requires the judge to appoint a law guardian. The law guardian acts as counsel for a child by representing the child's interests as expressed by the child and should not be confused with a guardian ad litem, who may be appointed by a court to represent the child's interests as the guardian ad litem sees those interests. See chapter 10.
11. St. Joan, "Building Bridges, Building Walls," 420–21; Pierce, Gleason-Wynn, and Miller, "Social Work and Law."
12. Gary Solomon, "Child Abuse, Neglect and the Foster Care System 2002: Effective Social Work and the Legal System; The Attorney's Role and Responsibilities," *Practicing Law Institute: Litigation and Administrative Practice Course Handbook Series* 189 (2002): 303–56.
13. American Bar Association, *Model Rules of Professional Conduct,* rule 1.3 (2000), and *Model Code of Professional Responsibility,* DR 7–101(A)(1) (2000).
14. *In re* William D. Robinson, Esq., 639 A.2d 1384 (Vt. 1994).
15. Joshua Cook, "Good Lawyering and Bad Role Models: The Role of Respondent's Counsel in a Civil Commitment Hearing," *Georgetown Journal of Ethics* 14 (2000): 179–95; Martin Guggenheim, "A Paradigm for Determining the Role of Counsel for Children," *Fordham Law Review* 64 (1996): 1399–1433.
16. National Association of Social Workers, "Social Workers' Ethical Responsibility to Clients," rule 1.02, Self-Determination, *Code of Ethics* (2000), http://www.nasw.org.
17. Practicing Law Institute, *City Attorney Ethical Issues* 188 (2001): 38–39.
18. NASW, *Code of Ethics,* rule 1.06(d).
19. R. A. Russel, "Role Perceptions of Attorneys and Caseworkers in Child Abuse Cases in Juvenile Court," *Child Welfare* 67 (1988): 205–16.
20. Michael Weil, "Research on Issues in Collaboration Between Social Workers and Lawyers," *Social Service Review* 56 (1982): 393–405.

2. SOURCES OF LAW

1. Louis Blom-Cooper, "Article 6 and Modes of Criminal Trial," *European Human Rights Law Review* 1 (2001): 1–14.
2. U.S. Constitution, Art. 6, Sec. 2.
3. Article 5 provides that a constitutional convention may be convened if the legislatures of two-thirds of the states support such an action.
4. *Romer v. Evans,* 517 U.S. 620 (1996). In *Equality Foundation of Greater Cincinnati v. City of Cincinnati,* 128 F.3d 289 (6th Cir. 1997), *cert. denied,* 525 U.S. 943 (1998), the

city of Cincinnati's charter was amended to remove homosexuals, lesbians, and bisexuals from any protection contained in municipal antidiscrimination ordinances. The amendment precluded restoring protected status. The U.S. Court of Appeals for the Sixth Circuit found that the amendment did not violate the Constitution and distinguished *Cincinnati* from the *Romer* decision on two grounds: The amendment did not disenfranchise any group or citizen from gaining special protection at all levels of state government but affected only municipally enacted protections; and the charter amendment eliminated only "special class status" and "preferential treatment for gays as gays," leaving untouched the application, to gay citizens, of any and all legal rights generally accorded by the municipal government to all persons as persons. In denying review, Chief Justice William Rehnquist took pains to note that a denial of certiori (the term used to refer to a request that the Supreme Court review a case) was not a ruling on the merits of the case, thus quieting any suggestion that the Court had turned its back on its *Romer* decision.

5. *Barron v. City of Baltimore,* 32 U.S. 243 (1833).
6. William J. Brennan, "The Bill of Rights and the States: The Revival of State Constitutions as Guardians of Individual Rights," *New York University Law Review* 61 (1986): 535.
7. U.S. Constitution, Art. 14, Sec. 1.
8. Brennan, "The Bill of Rights and the States."
9. *Brown v. Board of Education,* 347 U.S. 483 (1954) (*Brown* I); *Brown v. Board of Education,* 349 U.S. 294 (1955) (*Brown* II).
10. *Baker v. Carr,* 369 U.S. 186 (1962).
11. *Shapiro v. Thompson,* 394 U.S. 618 (1969).
12. *Griswold v. Connecticut,* 381 U.S. 479 (1965).
13. *Robinson v. California,* 380 U.S. 400 (1965).
14. *Gideon v. Wainwright,* 372 U.S. 335 (1963).
15. *Parker v. Gladden,* 385 U.S. 363 (1966); *Klopfer v. North Carolina,* 386 U.S. 213 (1967).
16. *Immigration and Naturalization Service v. Chadha,* 462 U.S. 919 (1983).
17. On discrimination in renting motel rooms, see *Heart of Atlanta Motel, Inc. v. United States,* 379 U.S. 241 (1964); on New York City and voting rights, see *Katzenbach v. Morgan,* 384 U.S. 641 (1966); on possession of handguns in a school zone, see *United States v. Lopez,* 514 U.S. 549 (1995); and on violence against women, see *United States v. Morrison,* 529 U.S. 598 (2000).
18. Section 5 of the Fourteenth Amendment, in what is referred to as the enforcement clause, provides another source of authority. Section 5 grants to Congress the authority "to enforce by appropriate legislation" the provisions of the Fourteenth Amendment. The Supreme Court has sanctioned congressional legislation under Section 5 when the legislation seeks to prevent state government from depriving an individual of an existing right or when the legislation seeks to remedy government action that has deprived a citizen of an existing right. For example, the Supreme Court supported Congress when it enacted the Voting Rights Act of 1965 for the purpose of eliminating barriers that had been erected to keep African Americans from exercising their Fifteenth Amendment right to vote (*Katzenbach,* 384 U.S. at 646). However, the Court has not shown a willingness to sanction Congress's use of the enforcement clause when the result is to create new rights (*City of Boerne v. Flores,* 521 U.S. 507 [1997]).

19. *Perez v. United States,* 402 U.S. 146 (1971).
20. *Hammer v. Dagenhart,* 247 U.S. 251 (1918); *Bailey v. Drexel,* 259 U.S. 20 (1922).
21. *United States v. Butler,* 297 U.S. 1 (1936).
22. *Steward v. Davis,* 301 U.S. 548 (1937).
23. *United States v. Darby,* 312 U.S. 100 (1941).
24. On civil rights in general, see Theodore J. Stein, *Social Policy and Policymaking by the Branches of Government and by the Public-at-Large* (New York: Columbia University Press, 2001). chap. 13. On child support see, for example, *United States v. Mussari,* 95 F.3d 787 (9th Cir. 1996); *United States v. Bailey,* 115 F.3d 1222 (5th Cir. 1997).
25. Judith S. Kaye, "Brennan Lecture: State Courts at the Dawn of a New Century: Common Law Courts Reading Statutes and Constitutions," *New York University Law Review* 70 (1995): 1–35.
26. *Plessy v. Ferguson,* 163 U.S. 537 (1896).
27. *Brown v. Board of Education,* 347 U.S. 483, 493 (1954).
28. *Planned Parenthood of Southeastern Pennsylvania v. Casey,* 505 U.S. 833, 862–64 (1992).
29. *United States v. Lopez,* 514 U.S. 549 (1995).
30. *Kimel v. Florida Bd. of Regents,* 528 U.S. 62 (2000).
31. *Printz v. United States,* 521 U.S. 898 (1997).
32. *United States v. Morrison,* 529 U.S. 598 (2000). See also *City of Boerne v. Flores,* 521 U.S. 507 (1997), in which the Court ruled that Congress overstepped its authority in enacting the Religious Freedom Restoration Act, which made substantive changes to the First Amendment's provisions governing freedom of religion; *Seminole Tribe v. Florida,* 517 U.S. 44 (1996), in which the Court found that Congress acted wrongly when it abrogated a state's sovereign immunity by authorizing native tribes to sue states; and *New York v. United States,* 505 U.S. 144 (1992), in which the Supreme Court determined that Congress lacked the authority to order a state legislature to implement a federal policy that governed the disposal of radioactive waste.
33. *Harris v. McRae,* 448 U.S. 297 (1980).
34. *Women of the State of Minnesota v. Gomez,* 542 N.W.2d 17 (Minn. 1995).
35. See note in "Discrimination Against the Poor and the Fourteenth Amendment," *Harvard Law Review* 81 (1967): 435–452.
36. *Helvering v. Davis,* 301 U.S. 619 (1937).
37. *Fullilove v. Klutznick,* 448 U.S. 448 (1980). In 1995 the Supreme Court ruled that the constitutionality of the type of race-based policy involved in *Fullilove* would be subject to the strictest standard of review (*Adarand v. Pena,* 515 U.S. 200 [1995]). See the discussion in this chapter of the standards of review that the Supreme Court uses.
38. *Dandridge v. Williams,* 397 U.S. 471 (1970).
39. *Wyman v. James,* 400 U.S. 309, 345 (1971).
40. *Shapiro v. Thompson,* 394 U.S. 618 (1969).
41. Because the District of Columbia is not a state, the Fourteenth Amendment protections against state action do not apply to residents of the District. Thus, although the Fifth Amendment does not contain an equal protection clause, the

Court has found that that amendment's guarantee of due process is sufficient to ensure equal protection.

42. In 1992 California enacted a statute that limited the maximum welfare benefit available to newly arrived residents to the amount that they had received in the state in which they previously lived. In *Saenz v. Roe,* 526 U.S. 489 (1999), the Supreme Court found this provision unconstitutional even though Congress authorized the practice in 1996 when it enacted the Personal Responsibility and Work Opportunity Act to shield high-paying welfare states from an influx of people from low-paying states (Personal Responsibility and Work Opportunity Act, 42 U.S.C.A. §604[c] [West 2001]).
43. *Goldberg v. Kelly,* 397 U.S. 254 (1970).
44. *Dandridge v. Williams,* 397 U.S. 471 (1970).
45. Ibid., 472.
46. *Lindsey v. Normet,* 405 U.S. 56 (1972).
47. *San Antonio Independent School Dist. v. Rodriguez,* 411 U.S. 1 (1973).
48. *Harris v. McRae,* 448 U.S. 297 (1980).
49. Alabama Constitution, Art.4, Sec. 88.
50. Kansas Constitution, Art. 7, Sec. 4.
51. New York Constitution, Art. 17, Sec. 1.
52. Montana Constitution, Art. 12, Sec. 3(3).
53. *Tucker v. Toia,* 43 N.Y.2d 1, 7 (N.Y. 1977), 371 N.E.2d 449 (N.Y. 1977).
54. James E. Anderson, *Public Policymaking,* 3d ed. (New York: Houghton Mifflin, 1997), 158.
55. *Yakus v. United States,* 321 U.S. 414, 426 (1944).
56. Administrative Procedures Act of 1946, 5 U.S.C.A. § 551 *et seq.* (West 2001).
57. Under the APA an agency may avoid publication after a finding of good cause that notice is "impracticable, unnecessary, or contrary to the public interest" (5 U.S.C.A. § 553[b][B]) [West 2001]). When final rules are issued, a brief statement of the reasons for not publishing the rule is required.
58. APA, 5 U.S.C.A. § 553(c) (West 2001).
59. Ibid., § 553(c), § 556, and § 557 (West 2001).
60. In its 1974 report on the use of executive orders, a Senate committee concluded that it was not possible to distinguish situations where an executive order was preferable to a presidential proclamation (or vice versa), noting that President Dwight Eisenhower issued an executive order to facilitate integration of schools in the South, whereas John F. Kennedy issued a proclamation to accomplish the same goal. See U.S. Senate Committee on National Emergencies and Delegated Emergency Powers, *Executive Orders in Times of War and National Emergency,* 93d Cong., 2d sess. S. Rept. 93–1280, October 1974, 4.
61. Federal Register and Code of Federal Regulations, 44 U.S.C.A. § 1505 (West 2001).
62. The number of executive orders issued since the founding of the country cannot be determined because they were never systematically recorded until 1935, when the *Federal Register* was first published. Since that time all such orders have been numbered consecutively and published in the *Register* (U.S. Senate Committee on the Judiciary, *Separation of Powers Annual Report,* 93d Cong., 2d sess., S. Rept. 93–1195, September 1974.

63. Senate Committee on National Emergencies, *Executive Orders*, 38.
64. *Youngstown Sheet and Tube v. Sawyer*, 343 U.S. 579 (1952).
65. "United Nations Millennium Declaration," *U.N. Chronicle* 37, no. 3 (January 1, 2000), 2000 WL 25574373 (2002). The United Nations has a number of committees that work on human rights issues such as the Committee on the Rights of the Child, the Committee to Eliminate Discrimination Against Women, and the Committee to Eliminate Racial Discrimination. Information about the objectives of these committees may be found at www.un.org/Depts/dhl/resguide/spechr.htm (March 4, 2003).
66. The Universal Declaration of Human Rights (U.N. General Assembly Res. 217 A [III], December 1948) is part of the International Bill of Human Rights, which also contains the International Covenant on Economic, Social and Cultural Rights, and the International Covenant on Civil and Political Rights. See Ann Taylor, "Globalization and Biotechnology: UNESCO and an International Strategy to Advance Human Rights and Public Health," *American Journal of Law and Medicine* 25 (1999): 479–541.
67. Russell G. Donaldson, "United Nations Resolution as Judicially Enforceable in United States Domestic Courts," *American Law Reports* 42 (2000 Supplement): 578.
68. *Sei Fujii v. State*, 242 P.2d 617 (1952).
69. Ibid.
70. *Doe v. Plyler*, 628 F.2d 448 (5th Cir. 1980), *renamed Plyler v. Doe*, 457 U.S. 202 (1982).
71. Ellen Ash Peters, "Common Law Judging in a Statutory World," *University of Pittsburgh Law Review* 42 (1982): 995–1011.
72. Stein, *Social Policy and Policymaking*, chap. 6.
73. Kaye, "Brennan Lecture."
74. Federal courts were created after the Republic was formed and do not have the inherited common-law tradition of state courts. Scholars debate whether there is any such thing as federal common law. See Martha A. Field, "Sources of Law: The Scope of Federal Common Law," *Harvard Law Review* 99 (1986): 883–984.
75. *Fosmire v. Nicoleau*, 551 N.E.2d 77 (N.Y. 1990).
76. Ibid.
77. *Planned Parenthood of Southeastern Pennsylvania v. Casey*, 505 U.S. 833, 854 (1992).
78. The Court has upheld a ban on the use of federal funds to pay for abortions for poor women (*Harris v. McRae*, 448 U.S. 297 [1980]); upheld a state ban on the performance of abortions by public employees in public hospitals (*Webster v. Reproductive Health Services*, 492 U.S. 490 [1989]); found that a state may require a judge to approve the decision of a minor who wishes to terminate her pregnancy and who does not have the consent of her parents (*Hodgson v. Minnesota*, 497 U.S. 417 [1990]); and ruled that a state may require a woman to wait twenty-four hours before having her pregnancy terminated and that physicians must provide certain information to a woman seeking an abortion (*City of Akron v. Akron Center for Reproductive Health*, 462 U.S. 416 [1983]).
79. *Planned Parenthood*, 505 U.S. at 855–56.
80. *Griswold v. Connecticut*, 381 U.S. 479 (1965).
81. *Roe v. Wade*, 410 U.S. 113 (1973).
82. *Whalen v. Roe*, 429 U.S. 589 (1977).

83. *Pierce v. Society of Sisters,* 268 U.S. 510 (1925).
84. *Loving v. Virginia,* 338 U.S. 1 (1967).
85. For the right to procreate see *Skinner v. Oklahoma,* 316 U.S. 535 (1942); for the right to obtain contraceptives see *Griswold;* and for the right to terminate a pregnancy see *Roe.*
86. For discussions of original intent see Erwin Chemerinsky, "The Supreme Court, 1988 Term: Foreword: The Vanishing Constitution," *Harvard Law Review* 103 (1989): 43–104.
87. Ronald Dworkin, *A Matter of Principle* (Cambridge, Mass.: Harvard University Press, 1985), chap. 1.
88. R. Randall Kelso and Charles D. Kelso, "How the Supreme Court Is Dealing with Precedents in Constitutional Cases," *Brooklyn Law Review* 62 (1996): 973–1038.
89. *Cabell v. Markham,* 148 F.2d 737, 739 (2d Cir. 1945).
90. Kaye, "Brennan Lecture," 26.
91. Americans with Disabilities Act of 1990, 42 U.S.C.A. § 12201(a) (West 2001).
92. *Public Citizen v. United States,* 491 U.S. 440, 454 (1989).
93. *Blanchard v. Bergeron,* 489 U.S. 87, 98 (1989).
94. Kaye, "Brennan Lecture," 26.
95. *Braschi v. Stahl,* 74 N.Y.2d 201, 543 N.E.2d 49 (N.Y. 1989).
96. Ibid., 788.
97. U.S. Constitution, Amend. 14, Sec. 1.
98. *Plyler v. Doe,* 457 U.S. 202 (1982).
99. Ibid., 218 n. 14.
100. *Koramatsu v. United States,* 323 U.S. 214 (1944).
101. *United States v. Paradise,* 480 U.S. 149, 237 (1987), cited in *Adarand Constructors, Inc. v. Pena,* 515 U.S. 200 (1995).
102. *Weinberger v. Wiesenfeld,* 420 U.S. 636, 645 (1975).
103. *Michael M. v. Superior Court of Sonoma County,* 450 U.S. 464 (1981).
104. *FCC v. Beach Communications, Inc.,* 508 U.S. 307, 315 (1993), quoting *Lehnhausen v. Lake Shore Auto Parts Co.,* 410 U.S. 356, 364 (1973).
105. *Kimel v. Florida Bd. of Regents,* 528 U.S. 62, 82 (2000).

3. THE JUSTICE SYSTEM AND AN INTRODUCTION TO CRIMINAL AND CIVIL LAW

1. Jurisdiction is not to be confused with venue. The question inherent in venue is, of those courts with subject-matter and personal jurisdiction, which may hear the suit in question? Generally, venue resides in that court where a person lives, where business was transacted, or where an injury was sustained.
2. The circuit courts and their geographic reach are as follows: First Circuit: Massachusetts, Maine, New Hampshire, Rhode Island, and Puerto Rico; Second Circuit: New York, Connecticut, and Vermont; Third Circuit: Pennsylvania, New Jersey, Delaware, and the Virgin Islands; Fourth Circuit: Virginia, Maryland, West Virginia, North Carolina, and South Carolina; Fifth Circuit: Texas, Louisiana, and Mississippi; Sixth Circuit: Ohio, Kentucky, Michigan, and Tennessee; Seventh Cir-

cuit: Illinois, Indiana, and Wisconsin; Eighth Circuit: Arkansas, Nebraska, Missouri, Minnesota, North Dakota, Iowa, and South Dakota; Ninth Circuit: California, Montana, Alaska, Arizona, Hawaii, Nevada, Oregon, Washington, Idaho, Northern Mariana Islands, and Guam; Tenth Circuit: Oklahoma, New Mexico, Colorado, Utah, Wyoming, and Kansas; Eleventh Circuit: Florida, Alabama, and Georgia; and the Court of Appeals for the District of Columbia.

3. *Bragdon v. Abbott,* 524 U.S. 624 (1998).
4. *Hudgens v. United States,* 424 U.S. 507 (1976).
5. *New Jersey Coalition Against War in the Middle East v. J.M.B. Realty,* 138 N.J. 326 (1994).
6. Justice System Improvement: Mental Health Courts, 42 U.S.C.A. § 3796ii (West 2001).
7. U.S. General Accounting Office, *Drug Courts: Overview of Growth, Characteristics, and Results,* GAO/GGD 97–106 (Washington, D.C.: General Accounting Office, 1997).
8. Justice System Improvement: Mental Health Courts, 42 U.S.C.A. § 3796ii (West 2001). Funds may also be used to train law enforcement and judicial personnel to identify and address the unique needs of a mentally ill or mentally retarded offender.
9. *Goldberg v. Kelly,* 397 U.S. 254 (1970).
10. Wayne R. LaFave and Austin W. Scott, *Substantive Criminal Law* (St. Paul, Minn.: West, 1986), chap. 2.
11. In the early part of the twentieth century, the U.S. Supreme Court sanctioned Congress's assertion of jurisdiction over narcotics and gambling under its Article 1, Section 8 taxing power (*Nigro v. United States,* 276 U.S. 332 [1928]). In the 1960s the Court would suggest that Congress could regulate such activities under its commerce clause authority (*Minor v. United States,* 396 U.S. 87 [1969]).
12. Child Support Recovery Act, 18 U.S.C.A. § 228(b) (West 2002).
13. *Miranda v. Arizona,* 384 U.S. 436 (1966).
14. *Melton v. State,* 790 S.W.2d 322 (Tex. Crim. App. 1990).
15. *Miranda.*
16. *Doe v. Bagan,* 41 F.3d 571 (10th Cir. 1994); *State v. P.Z.,* 703 A.2d 901 (N.J. 1997).
17. See Timothy L. Perrin, "Expert Witnesses Under Rules 703 and 803(4) of the Federal Rules of Evidence: Separating the Wheat from the Chaff," *Indiana Law Journal* 72 (1997): 939–1014; Brian D. Gallagher, " 'The Right of the People . . .': The Exclusionary Rule in Child Abuse Litigation," *Thomas M. Cooley Journal of Practical and Clinical Law* 4 (2000): 1–26.
18. *State v. P.Z.*
19. *Argersinger v. Hamlin,* 407 U.S. 25 (1972).
20. *Kirby v. Illinois,* 406 U.S. 682, 683 (1972).
21. *Parham v. J.R.,* 442 U.S. 584 (1979).
22. Judiciary and Judicial Procedure: Fees and Costs, 28 U.S.C. § 1915(e) (West 2001).
23. *Hill v. Michigan,* 2001 WL 857200 (6th Cir. 2001).
24. U.S. Constitution, Amend. 4; Uniting and Strengthening America by Providing Appropriate Tools Required to Intercept and Obstruct Terrorism Act of 2001 (USA Patriot Act), Pub. L. No. 107–56, 115 Stat. 272, amending 31 U.S.C. § 5318(h).

25. *Johnson v. United States,* 333 U.S. 10 (1948).
26. *Illinois v. Gates,* 462 U.S. 213 (1983).
27. Seanna M. Beck, "Overview of the Fourth Amendment," *Georgetown Law Journal* 89 (2001): 1055.
28. *Katz v. United States,* 389 U.S. 347 (1967).
29. *Bond v. United States,* 120 S. Ct. 1462 (2000).
30. *Doe v. Broderick,* 225 F.3d 440 (4th Cir. 2000).
31. *United States v. Taylor,* 90 F.3d 903 (4th Cir. 1996).
32. *United States v. Cardoza-Hinojosa,* 140 F.3d 610 (5th Cir. 1998).
33. *Mapp v. Ohio,* 367 U.S. 643 (1961).
34. Beck, "Overview of the Fourth Amendment," 1055.
35. *New Jersey v. T.L.O.,* 469 U.S. 325 (1985).
36. *O'Connor v. Ortega,* 480 U.S. 709 (1987).
37. *Board of Education v. Earls,* 2002 WL 1378649 (U.S. 2002).
38. *Skinner v. Railway Labor Executives' Association,* 489 U.S. 602 (1989).
39. *Maag v. Wessler,* 960 F.2d 773 (9th Cir. 1991).
40. *Ferguson v. City of Charleston,* 532 U.S. 67 (2001).
41. *Darryl H. v. Coler,* 801 F.2d 893 (7th Cir. 1986).
42. *Good v. Dauphin County,* 891 F.2d 1087 (3d Cir. 1989).
43. *Calabretta v. Floyd,* 189 F.2d 808 (9th Cir. 1999).
44. *Franz v. Lytle,* 997 F.22d 784 (10th Cir. 1993).
45. *Wayte v. United States,* 470 U.S. 598 (1985).
46. A grand jury has investigative powers, for example, it may issue subpoenas to compel testimony. However, the main function of a grand jury is to determine whether there is probable cause to believe that the person accused of a crime committed the crime and, if so, to issue an indictment. See "Grand Jury," *United States' Attorney Manual.* Washington, D.C.: U.S. Department of Justice, 2001, §§ 9–11.000.
47. Ibid.
48. *Duke v. United States,* 301 U.S. 492 (1937).
49. *Federal Rules of Criminal Procedure* 16(a)(2) (West 2002).
50. *Brady v. Maryland,* 373 U.S. 83 (1963).
51. *United States v. Agurs,* 427 U.S. 97 (1976).
52. *United States v. Bagley,* 473 U.S. 667 (1985).
53. *Federal Rules of Criminal Procedure* 26(b)(1) (West 2002).
54. On the discoverability of e-mail see *Boone v. Federal Express Corp.,* 59 F.3d 84 (8th Cir. 1995); *United States v. Microsoft Corp.,* No. Civ. 98–1232 (D.D.C., filed May 18, 1998); *Playboy Enterprises v. Welles,* 60 F. Supp. 2d. 1050, 1053 (S.D. Cal. 1999); *Proctor & Gamble Co. v. Haugen,* 179 F.R.D. 622 (C.D. Utah 1998), *rev'd in part on other grounds,* 222 F.3d 1262 (10th Cir. 2000).
55. *Gerstein v. Pugh,* 420 U.S. 103 (1975).
56. *Riverside v. McLaughlin,* 500 U.S. 44 (1991).
57. *Federal Rules of Criminal Procedure* 11 (Pleas) (West 2002).
58. Rule 12.2(a) of the *Federal Rules of Criminal Procedure* (West 2002) provides that notice of intention to use the insanity defense be given within the time allowed for pretrial motions. In New York notice must be provided with thirty days of entering a plea (McKinney's Criminal Procedure Law § 250.10 [West 2002]). California

provides for such a plea to be made at the arraignment but provides that the court may for good cause allow a defendant who enters a plea before trial to raise an insanity defense (*California Penal Code* § 1016 (West 2002).

59. *Santobello v. New York,* 404 U.S. 257 (1971).
60. H. D. Warren, "Court's Duty to Advise or Admonish Accused as to Consequences of Plea of Guilty, or to Determine That He Is Advised Thereof," *American Law Reports* 97 (1964): 549–83.
61. The Eighth Amendment requires that a person be released on a bail no greater than the minimum amount necessary to assure that person's appearance in court, unless special circumstances justify detention. Thus there is no right to bail, but a statutory provision that allows for pretrial detention must serve a compelling state interest (*United States v. Salerno,* 481 U.S. 739 [1987]).
62. Crimes and Criminal Procedure: Release and Detention Pending Judicial Proceedings, 18 U.S.C.A. § 3142 (West 2002).
63. *Ballew v. Georgia,* 435 U.S. 223 (1978).
64. *United States v. Chavez,* 204 F.3d 1305 (11th Cir. 2000).
65. Sarah Jane Cole, "Speedy Trial," *Georgetown Law Journal* 89 (2001): 1377.
66. *Globe Newspaper Co. v. Superior Court for Norfolk County,* 457 U.S. 596 (1982).
67. *Addington v. Texas,* 441 U.S. 418 (1979).
68. U.S. Sentencing Commission, 28 U.S.C.A. § 991(a) (West 2002).
69. A defendant is a career offender if (1) she or he was at least eighteen years old when the offense was committed; (2) the offense is a crime of violence that constitutes a felony or a controlled substance offense; and (3) the defendant has at least two previous felony convictions involving a crime of violence or a controlled substance offense. See Devaleena Das and Stephen Bradford Ballas, "Sentencing Guidelines," *Georgetown Law Journal* 89 (2001): 1655.
70. Ibid.
71. *Federal Rules of Civil Procedure* 32.
72. *Payne v. Tennessee,* 501 U.S. 808 (1991).
73. *Federal Rules of Civil Procedure* 32(i)(4)(B) (West 2002).
74. Margaret Hoefner Martin, "Restitution," *Georgetown Law Journal* 89 (2001): 1731.
75. Crime and Criminal Procedure: Sentences, 18 U.S.C.A. § 3563(a)(4) (West 2002).
76. Criminal Procedure: Sentences, 18 U.S.C.A. §§ 3551–3673; U.S. Sentencing Commission, 28 U.S.C.A. §§ 991–98 (West 2002).
77. In developing this section, I have relied heavily on Stephen S. Sypherd and Gary M. Ronan, "Substantive Rights Retained by Prisoners," *Georgetown Law Journal* 89 (2001): 1898–1938.
78. *Greenholtz v. Inmates of Nebraska Penal* and *Correctional Complex* 442 U.S. 1 (1979); *Board of Pardons v. Allen,* 482 U.S. 369 (1987).
79. *Morrissey v. Brewer,* 408 U.S. 471 (1972).
80. Paul H. Robinson, "Punishing Dangerousness: Cloaking Preventive Detention as Criminal Justice," *Harvard Law Review* 114 (2001): 1429–56.
81. *Kansas v. Crane,* 534 U.S. 407 (2002).
82. The Jacob Wetterling Crimes Against Children and Sexually Violent Offender Registration Act was passed as Title XVII of the Violent Crime Control and Law Enforcement Act, Pub. L. No. 103–322, 108 Stat. 1796, 103d Cong., 2d sess. (1994), codified at 42 U.S.C.A. § 14071.

83. Megan's Law, Pub. L. No. 104–145, 104th Cong., 2d sess., H. Rept. no. 104–155 (May 1996), 42 U.S.C.A. § 14071(d) (West 2002).
84. Pam Lynchner Sex Offender Tracking System, Pub. L. No. 104–236, 110 Stat. 3903, 104th Cong., 2d sess., October 1996.
85. Richard J. Broughton, "On Horror's Head Horrors Accumulate: A Reflective Comment on Capital Child Rape Legislation," *Duquesne Law Review* 39 (2000): 1–42.
86. The federal government supports financially the development of sex-offender registration programs. See Jacob Wetterling Crimes Against Children and Sexually Violent Offender Registration Act, 42 U.S.C.A. § 14071 (West 2001).
87. *Smith v. Doe,* 123 S. Ct. 1140 (2003); *Connecticut Department of Public Safety v. Doe,* 123 S. Ct. 1160 (2003), 2003 WL 728779 (2003); *E.B. v. Verniero,* 119 F.3d 1077 (3d Cir. 1997) *cert. denied,* 522 U.S. 1110 (1998).
88. The Alternative Dispute Resolution Act of 1998, Pub. L. No. 105–315, 112 Stat. 2993, 28 U.S.C.A. §§ 651–58 (West 2002).
89. Alternative Dispute Resolution Act, 28 U.S.C.A. §§ 652(b), 654 (West 2002).
90. *McKeiver v. Pennsylvania,* 403 U.S. 528 (1971).
91. *In re* Winship, 397 U.S. 358 (1970).
92. *Sherfey v. Sherfey,* 2002 WL 63800 (Ky. 2002).
93. *Kromm v. Literal,* 2002 WL 59608 (Wash. 2002).
94. Henry C. Black, *Black's Law Dictionary,* 7th ed. (St. Paul, Minn.: West, 1999), http://www. westlaw.com.

4. LEGAL RESEARCH

1. *Black's Law Dictionary,* 7th ed. (St. Paul, Minn.: West, 1999), http://www. westlaw. com.
2. Mitchell J. Waldman and Joseph E. Conley, "§53. Social Workers and Similar Workers," in *American Jurisprudence: Cumulative Supplement* (St. Paul, Minn.: West, 2002).
3. *Black's Law Dictionary.*

5. THE ORGANIZATION OF SOCIAL SERVICES AND THE REGULATION OF THE PROFESSION

1. Margaret Gibelman and Philip H. Schervish, *Who We Are: A Second Look* (Washington, D.C.: The National Association of Social Workers, 1997).
2. N.Y. Executive Law, ch. 18, art. 21. (McKinney 2002).
3. Matther Diller, "The Revolution in Welfare Administration: Rules, Discretion, and Entrepreneurial Government," *New York University Law Review* 75 (2000): 1121–1220.
4. *Reynolds v. Giuliani, New York Law Journal* 224, no. 20 (2000): 35.
5. Carol J. DeVita, "Nonprofits and Devolution: What Do We Know?" in Elizabeth T. Boris and C. Eugene Steuerle, eds., *Nonprofits and Government: Collaboration and Conflict* (Washington, D.C.: Urban Institute, 1999), 219.

6. Personal Responsibility and Work Opportunity Reconciliation Act, 42 U.S.C.A. § 604a (West 2002). As of March 2002, the charitable choice provisions apply only to programs created under several block grant programs: (a) TANF; (b) Community Service Block Grant; (c) Substance Abuse Prevention and Treatment Block Grant; and (d) Projects for Assistance in Transition from Homelessness. See Center for Faith-Based and Community Initiatives, *What Is Charitable Choice?* (Washington, D.C.: U.S. Department of Health and Human Services, 2002).
7. Exec. Order No. 13199, 66 FR 8499 and Exec. Order No. 13198, 66 FR 8497. Both were signed on January 29, 2001.
8. *Arneth v. Gross*, 699 F. Supp. 450 (S.D.N.Y. 1988).
9. See, for example, "Private Sector Survey on Cost Control." 1982. Exec. Order No. 12369 (charged with studying how the federal government could reduce costs); President's Commission on Housing, Exec. Order No. 12310 (1982) (governmental functions should be transferred to the private sector); President's Commission on Indian Reservation Economies. (1984). Exec. Order No. 12401 (charged with studying, and providing advise to the president, on ways to reduce the dependence of tribes on federal government and on how to strengthen private-sector investments on the reservations); President's Commission on Privatization. (1988). Exec. Order No. 12607 (review the current activities of the federal government and identify those functions that are not properly the responsibility of the federal government and should be divested or transferred to the private sector).
10. Personal Responsibility and Work Opportunity Reconciliation Act, 42 U.S.C.A. § 604a (1998).
11. The Federal Activities Inventory Reform Act of 1998 originally was introduced as the "Freedom from Government Competition Act." See 143 Cong. Rec. S7664–01, 7667.
12. Federal Activities Inventory Reform Act of 1998, 105th Cong., 1st sess., Pub. L. No. 105–270.
13. *Richardson v. McKnight*, 521 U.S. 399 (June 1997).
14. CO-ST-ANN § 12–43–405 (West 2001); ALA-ST-ANN § 34–30–3 (West 2001).
15. *Dunn v. Catholic Home Bureau*, 142 Misc. 2d 316 (N.Y. Sup. Ct. 1989).
16. National Association of Social Workers, *Code of Ethics*, (Washington, D.C.: NASW, 1999), standard 1.07, "Privacy and Confidentiality."
17. *Jaffee v. Redmond*, 518 U.S. 1 (1996).
18. Ellen Alderman and Caroline Kennedy, *The Right to Privacy* (New York: Alfred A. Knopf, 1995), 176.
19. *Whalen v. Roe*, 429 U.S. 589, 599 (1977).
20. "Standards for Privacy of Individually Identifiable Health Information," *Federal Register* 65, no. 250 (December 28, 2000): 13711, and 45 C.F.R. Parts §§ 160–64.
21. "Standards for Privacy."
22. See § 165.3 *et seq.* in *American Jurisprudence*, 2d ed. (St. Paul, Minn.: West, 2002), vol. 61. The National Conference of Commissioners on Uniform State Laws is a group of attorneys, judges, law professors, and legislators who are appointed by their governors to propose uniform state laws. Adoption of uniform laws helps to overcome problems that are created by variations in state laws, for example, regarding control of and access to confidential information. The conference has no legislative authority and cannot impose its recommendations.

23. *Urbaniak v. Newton*, 277 Cal. Rptr. 354 (Cal. App. 1st Dist. 1991).
24. *Hillman v. Columbia County*, 474 N.W.2d 913 (1991), *review granted*, 482 N.W.2d 105 (Wis. 1992).
25. Ryan White Comprehensive AIDS Resources Emergency Act, 42 U.S.C.A. § 300ff (West 2002).
26. Americans with Disabilities Act, 42 U.S.C.S. § 12112(d)(3)(B) (West 2002).
27. Public Health Service Regulations, 42 C.F.R. § 2.31 (West 2002).
28. Restatement of Bill of Rights for Mental Health Patients, 42 U.S.C.A. § 10841(H)(I)(i) (West 2002).
29. Ibid.
30. Administrative Procedures Act, 5 U.S.C.A. § 552a(b) (West 2002).
31. Ibid., § 552a (West 2002).
32. Paul M. Schwartz, "The Protection of Privacy in Health Care Reform," *Vanderbilt Law Review* 48 (1996): 295–347.
33. Administrative Procedures Act, 5 U.S.C.A. § 552 (West 2002).
34. See, for example, *Baldridge v. Shapiro*, 455 U.S. 345 (1982); *United States v. Provenzano*, 469 U.S. 14 (1984); *Church of Scientology v. Internal Revenue Service*, 484 U.S. 9 (1987); *United States v. Julian*, 486 U.S. 1 (1988).
35. In addition to the privacy issues identified here, HIPAA addresses an individual's right to maintain health insurance after changing jobs, despite the existence of a preexisting medical condition. See Health Insurance Portability and Accountability Act, § 262. 104th Cong., 2d sess., Pub. L. No. 104–191, 110 Stat. 1936 (August 21, 1996).
36. See Public Welfare—General Administrative Procedures, 45 C.F.R. §§ 160–64, for a discussion of already issued rules and those to be issued.
37. "Health: Lawmaker Asks Thompson to End Work on Administrative Simplification Mandate," editorial, *BNA's Health Care Daily Report*, May 16, 2001.
38. National Academy of Sciences, National Research Council, Committee on Maintaining Privacy and Security in Health Care Applications, *For the Record: Protecting Electronic Health Information* (Washington, D.C.: National Academy of Sciences Press, 1997).
39. Medical clearinghouses collect medical information regarding individuals and provide information to subscribers for a fee. Insurance companies give the data to clearinghouses, which compile data from third-party treatment records and their own investigations of individuals. The subscribers to clearinghouses have virtually instantaneous access to this information. The system "operates in the shadows. Its integrity is untested and the accuracy or security of the accumulated data is seldom questioned and poses a risk to everyone who applies for health or life insurance, or who joins an Health Maintenance Organization. Individuals with grievances against clearinghouses may look to the federal Consumer Credit Protection Act that grants to individuals the right to inspect and challenge the data collected and to seek sanctions for abusive practices" (Robert J. Conroy and Mark D. Brylski, "Access to Medical Records Versus Patient's Privacy Interests, *New Jersey Lawyer* 173 [1995]: 25).
40. National Academy of Sciences, 278.
41. Ibid.
42. "Quest for Health Information Privacy Law Likely to Be Long and Full of Pitfalls," editorial, *Health Legislation* and *Regulation* 23, no. 24 (1997): 6, 1997 WL 8740348 (1997).

43. *Tarasoff v. Regents of the University of California*, 526 P.2d 553 (Cal. 1974).
44. *Tarasoff v. Regents of the University of California*, 551 P.2d 334 (Cal. 1976).
45. *Thompson v. Alameda County*, 614 P.2d 728 (Cal. 1980).
46. See, for example, NJ-ST-ANN § 2A:62A-16 (West 2001); LS-ST-ANN § 9:2800.2 (West 2001).
47. See CO-ST-ANN § 13–21–117 (West 2002); IN. CODE ANN. §§ 34–30–16–1 *et seq.* (West 2001); KY-ST-ANN § 202A.400 (West 2001); LA-ST-ANN § 9:2800.2 (West 2002); MI-ST-ANN § 330.1946 (West 2002); MT-ST-ANN §§ 27–1-1101, *et seq.* (West 2001); NB-ST-ANN § 71–1,206.30 (West 2001); NH-ST-ANN § 329:31 (West 2001); NJ-ST-ANN § 2A:62A-16 (West 2002); UT-ST-ANN § 78–14a-102 (West 2001); WA-ST-ANN § 71.05.120 (West 2001).
48. *Kerrville State Hospital v. Clark*, 900 S.W.2d 425 (Tex. Ct. App. 3d Dist. 1995), *rev'd for other reasons*, 923 S.W.2d 582 (Tex. 1996); *Schuster v. Altenberg*, 424 N.W.2d 159 (Wis. 1988).
49. *Ellis v. Peter* 211 A.D.2d 353 (N.Y.A.D. Dept. 2d 1995); *Santa Cruz v. Northwest Dade Community Health Center*, 590 So. 2d 444 (Fla. App. 3d Dist. 1991), review denied, 599 So. 2d 238 (Fla. 1992); *Nasser v. Parker*, 455 S.E.2d 502 (Va. 1995); *Boulanger v. Pol*, 900 P.2d 823 (Kan. 1995).
50. *Tenuto v. Lederle Laboratories and Bishop*, 90 N.Y.2d 606, 687 N.E.2d 1300 (N.Y. 1997).
51. *Ellis v. Peter*.
52. *Pike v. Honsinger*, 49 N.E. 760 (N.Y. 1898).
53. *Oelsner v. New York*, 66 N.Y. 2d 636 (N.Y. 1985).
54. *Schrempf v. New York*, 66 N.Y.2d 289 (N.Y. 1985); *Topel v. Long Island Jewish Medical Center*, 55 N.Y.2d 682 (N.Y.A.D. 1981); *McDonnell v. County. of Nassau*, N.Y. Sup. Ct., Nassau County. No. 11152/73, unreported (1986).
55. *Yula v. State*, 127 N.Y.S.2d 147 (N.Y.A.D. 2d Dept. 1954); *Centeno v. New York*, 40 N.Y.2d 932 (N.Y. 1976); *Fiederlein v. New York Health & Hospitals Corp.*, 56 N.Y.2d 573 (N.Y. 1982).
56. See *O'Shea v. United States*, 623 F. Supp. 380 (E.D.N.Y. 1985).
57. *Homere v. State*, 361 N.Y.S.2d 820 (N.Y. Ct. Cl. 1974); *Bell v. New York City Health & Hospitals Corp.*, 456 N.Y.S.2d 787 (N.Y.A.D. 2d Dept. 1982); *Huntley v. New York*, 62 N.Y.2d 134 (N.Y. 1984).
58. *Cohen v. New York*, 51 A.D.2d 494 (N.Y.A.D. 3d Dept. 1976), *aff'd*, (1977), 41 N.Y.2d 1086 (N.Y. 1977).

6. SOCIAL WORKERS AND THE COURTS

1. Henry C. Black, "Forensic," *Black's Law Dictionary*, 7th ed. (St. Paul, Minn: West, 1999), http://www. westlaw.com.
2. Information concerning the National Organization of Forensic Social Workers may be found at http://www.nofsw.org (March 4, 2003).
3. Robert R. Rugani, "The Gradual Decline of a Hearsay Exception: The Misapplication of Federal Rule of Evidence 803(4), The Medical Diagnosis Hearsay Excep-

tion," *Santa Clara Law Review* 38 (1999): 867–904; *State v. Michaels,* 625 A.2d 489 (N.J.A.D. 1993), *aff'd,* 642 A.2d 1372 (N.J. 1994).

4. D. J. Besharov, "Protecting the Innocent: The McMartin Preschool Case," *National Review* 42 (1990): 17–26.
5. *State v. Michaels,* 625 A.2d at 517.
6. *In re* Scott County Master Docket, 618 F. Supp. 1534 (D. Minn. 1985), *rev'd* by *Myers v. Morris,* 810 F.2d 1437 (8th Cir. 1987).
7. See Stephen J. Ceci and Maggie Bruck, "Suggestibility of the Child Witness: A Historical Review and Synthesis," *Psychological Bulletin* 113, no. 3 (1993): 403–39; Stephen J. Ceci and Richard, D. Friedman, "The Suggestibility of Children: Scientific Research and Legal Implications," *Cornell Law Review* 86 (2000): 33–108; Maggie Bruck and Stephen J. Ceci, "Amicus Brief for the Case of *State of New Jersey v. Michaels* Presented by Committee of Concerned Social Scientists," *Psychology, Public Policy, and Law* 1 (1995): 272–322.
8. See Ceci and Friedman, "Suggestibility of the Child Witness," 403 n. 7; Thomas D. Lyon, "False Allegations and False Denials in Child Sexual Abuse," *Psychology, Public Policy, and Law* 1 (1995): 429–37; John E. B. Myers, "New Era of Skepticism Regarding Children's Credibility," *Psychology, Public Policy, and Law* 1 (1995): 387–98; John E. B. Myers, Karen J. Saywitz, and Gail S. Goodman, "Psychological Research on Children as Witnesses: Practical Implications for Forensic Interviews and Courtroom Testimony," *Pacific Law Journal* 28 (1996): 3–91.
9. See Bruck and Ceci, "Amicus Brief," 403 n. 7.
10. See Nancy E. Walker, "Forensic Interviews of Children: The Components of Scientific Validity and Legal Admissibility," *Law and Contemporary Problems* 65 (2002): 149–78.
11. Ibid., 180 n. 10.
12. American Academy of Child and Adolescent Psychiatry, "Guidelines for the Clinical Evaluation of Child and Adolescent Sexual Abuse," *Journal of the American Academy of Child and Adolescent Psychiatry* 27 (1988): 655; American Psychological Association, "Guidelines for Child Custody Evaluations in Divorce Proceedings," *American Psychologist* 49 (1994): 677.
13. Nancy E. Walker and Matthew Nguyen, "Interviewing the Child Witness: The Do's and the Don't's, the How's and the Why's," *Creighton Law Review* 29 (1996): 1587–1606.
14. California Rules of Court, Special Rules for Trial Courts, Rule 1257.3 *et seq.* (West 2002).
15. J. Doris, R. Mazur, and M. Thomas, "Training in Child Protective Services: A Commentary on the Amicus Brief of Bruck and Ceci," *Psychology, Public Policy, and Law* 1 (1995): 479–91.
16. Sarah H. Ramsey, "The Wingspread Report and Action Plan: High-Conflict Custody Cases—Reforming the System for Children," *Family Court Review* 39 (2001): 146–56.
17. Theodore J. Stein, *Child Welfare and the Law* (Washington, D.C.: Child Welfare League of America, 1998), 275.
18. *Humphrey v. State,* 2002 WL 321941 (Ala. Crim. App. 2002).

19. *State v. Fortin,* 109 Wash. App. 1064 (Wash. App. Div. 1 2001) 2001 WL 1664012, unpublished.
20. *Hunt v. State,* 904 S.W.2d 813 (Tex. App. 1995).
21. *Glover v. State,* WL 192009 (Tex. App. 2002), *opinion withdrawn,* 102 S.W.3d 754 (Tex App. 2003).
22. *State v. Ashford,* 2001 WL 137595 (Ohio App. 2001).
23. *Cassidy v. State,* 74 Md. App. 1, 536 A2d 666 (Md. App. 1988), *superseded by rule, Walker v. State,* 107 Md. App. 502, 668 A.2d 990 (Md. App. 1995).
24. *Ohio v. Roberts,* 448 U.S. 56 (1980).
25. *White v. Illinois,* 502 U.S. 346 (1992).
26. *State v. Sorenson,* 143 Wis. 2d 226, 421 N.W.2d 77 (Wis. 1988).
27. *Idaho v. Wright,* 497 U.S. 805 (1990).
28. *In re* Linda K., 521 N.Y.S.2d 705 (N.Y.A.D. 2d Dept. 1987), *appeal denied,* 526 N.Y.S.2d 437 (1988); *In re* Dutchess County Department of Social Services, 522 N.Y.S.2d 210 (N.Y. App. 2d Dept. 1987), *appeal denied,* 532 N.Y.S.2d 368 (1988); *In re* Meggan C., *New York Law Journal,* December 17, 1987: 27; *In re* E.M., 137 Misc. 2d 197 (N.Y. Fam. Ct. 1987).
29. This section, including the subheadings of assessment, referrals, acceptability, coordination, and monitoring, is taken from Stein, *Child Welfare and the Law.*
30. Federal Rules of Evidence, Rule 702.
31. *In re* J.L.H. and P.L.L.H., 316 N.W.2d 650 (S.D. 1982).
32. *Commonwealth v. Seese,* 512 Pa. 439, 517 A2d 920 (Pa. 1986).
33. *Commonwealth v. Davis,* 541 A.2d 315 (Pa. 1988).
34. *United States v. Bighead,* 128 F.3d 1329 (9th Cir. 1997).
35. *People v. Petitt,* 613 N.E.2d 1358 (Ill. App. 2d Dist. 1993).
36. *In re* Adoption of M.T.S., 489 N.W.2d 285 (Minn. 1992).
37. *State v. Vega,* 788 A.2d 1221 (Conn. 2002).
38. *Perkins v. General Motors,* 129 F.R.D. 655, (W.D. Mo. 1990); *aff'd,* 965 F.2d 597 (8th Cir. 1992), *cert. denied,* 113 S. Ct. 654 (1992).
39. *Johnson v. State,* 58 S.W.3d 496 (Mo. 2001).
40. *LaShawn A. v. Dixon,* 762 F. Supp. 959 (D.D.C. 1991).
41. Federal Rules of Evidence, Rules 401.
42. *Sims v. Medical Center of Baton Rouge,* 1997 WL 527330 (E.D. La. 1997).
43. Federal Rules of Evidence, Rule 403.
44. In 1993 the U.S. Supreme Court ruled that trial judges must ensure that scientific testimony is relevant and reliable (*Daubert v. Merrell Dow Pharmaceuticals, Inc.,* 509 U.S. 579). The Court extended this requirement in 1999 to any expert testimony that rests on "technical" or "other specialized" knowledge, which included an engineer's visual and tactile inspection of the tires of an automobile that had been involved in an accident (*Kumho Tire Company v. Carmichael,* 526 U.S. 137).
45. In class actions expert testimony may be based on evidence gathered from a random sample of cases representative of the universe on whose behalf the suit was brought. The sampling methodology, the procedures used to compile data regarding the sample, and the statistical methods used throughout the research are subject to a *Daubert* type of inquiry. See Stein, *Child Welfare and the Law.*
46. *Daubert v. Merrell Dow; Kumho Tire v. Carmichael.*

47. *Frye v. United States,* 293 F. 1013 (App. Div. D.C. 1923).
48. *State v. Ortiz,* 831 P.2d 1060 (Wash. 1992); *State v. Sanders,* 832 P.2d 1326 (Wash. Ct. App. 1992).
49. Ann W. Burgess and Lynda L. Holmstrom, "Rape Trauma Syndrome," *American Journal of Psychiatry* 131 (1974): 981–96.
50. On "false memory syndrome," see *State v. Carol M.D. and Mark A.D.,* 948 P.2d 837 (Wash. App. Div. 1997); *Hall v. Miller,* 36 P.3d 328 (Kan. App. 2001), and *State v. Plaskett,* 27 P.3d 890 (Kan. 2001). On "urban survival syndrome," see Wally Owens, "*State v. Osby,* The Urban Survival Defense," *American Journal of Criminal Law* 22 (1995): 809–21. On "Vietnam veteran syndrome," see *State v. Sharp,* 418 So. 2d 1344 (La. 1982); *Gahagan v. Tennessee,* 1985 WL 4113 (Tenn. Crim. App. 1985), unpublished; and *Carter v. State,* 1991 WL 168432 (Ark. App. 1991). On "battered parent syndrome" see *People v. Colberg,* 701 N.Y.S.2d 608 (N.Y. Cty. Ct. 1999); *People v. Christel,* 537 N.W.2d 194 (Mich. 1995), and *State v. Williams,* 525 N.W.2d 538 (Minn. 1995). On "parental alienation syndrome," see *People v. Fortin,* 289 A.D.2d 590 (N.Y.A.D. 2d Dept. 2001); *Bates v. Bates,* 2001 WL 1560915 (Ohio. App. 11th Dist. 2001).
51. David McCord, "Syndromes, Profiles and Other Mental Exotica: A New Approach to the Admissibility of Nontraditional Psychological Evidence in Criminal Cases," *Oregon Law Review* 66 (1986): 19–108.
52. See the *Diagnostic and Statistical Manual of Mental Disorders,* 4th ed. (Washington, D.C.: American Psychiatric Association, 1994), 366. For a discussion of the origins of the phrase "battered woman syndrome," see Lenore E. A. Walker, "Battered Women Syndrome and Self-Defense," *Notre Dame Journal of Law, Ethics, and Public Policy* 6 (1992): 321–34.
53. *State v. Riker,* 869 P.2d 43 (Wash. 1994).
54. *Soutiere v. Soutiere,* 657 A.2d 206 (Conn. 1995).
55. *Knock v. Knock,* 621 A.2d 267 (Conn. 1993).
56. Erin M. Masson, "Admissibility of Expert or Opinion Evidence of Battered-Woman Syndrome on Issue of Self-Defense," *American Law Reports—Fifth* 58 (1998): 749–782.
57. *Johnson v. State,* 469 S.E.2d 152 (Ga. 1996).
58. A court may consider syndrome evidence at the sentencing phase of a trial (*United States v. Johnson,* 956 F.2d 894 [9th Cir. 1992]).
59. See, for example, *People v. Bledsoe,* 681 P.2d 291 (Cal. 1984). See also *State v. Jaquez,* 2000 WL 241260 (Wash. App. 2000); *People v. McAuliffe,* 632 N.Y.S.2d 253 (N.Y. App. 3 Dept. 1995); *People v. Beckley,* 456 N.W.2d 391 (Mich. 1990); *People v. Emerick,* 2002 WL 384489 (Cal. App. 3d Dist. 2002).
60. *State v. Saldana,* 324 N.W.2d 227 (Minn. 1982), and *State v. Danielski,* 350 N.W.2d 395 (Minn. 1984).
61. *State v. Black,* 745 P.2d 12 (Wash. 1987).
62. *People v. Erickson,* 67 Cal. Rptr. 2d 740 (Cal. App. 5th Dist. 1998).
63. Ibid. See also *State v. Taylor,* 552 N.Y.S.2d 883 (N.Y. 1990).
64. See *State v. McQuillen,* 689 P.2d 822 (Kan. 1984); *State v. McCoy,* 366 S.E.2d 731 (W. Va. 1988); *State v. Marks,* 647 P.2d 1292 (Kan. 1982); *State v. Liddell,* 685 P.2d 918 (Mont. 1984); *State v. Huey,* 699 P.2d 1290 (Ariz. 1985).

65. *People v. Jackson,* 18 Cal. App. 3 Dept. (1971).
66. *State v. James,* 850 P.2d 495 (Wash. 1993).
67. Ibid., 496.
68. *In re* Sara M., 239 Cal. Rptr. 605 (Cal. App. 3d Dist. 1987); *Sacramento County v. Christine I.,* 239 Cal. Rptr. 605 (Cal. App. 3d Dist. 1987).
69. *People v. Jeff,* 251 Cal. Rptr. 135 (Cal. App. 5th Dist. 1988).
70. Testimony based on the use of anatomically correct dolls has been rejected in these cases: *In re* Amber B., 236 Cal. Rptr. 623 (Cal. App. 1st Dist. 1987); *In re* Christine C., 236 Cal. Rptr. 630 (Cal. App. 5th Div. 1987); *United States v. Gillespie,* 852 F.2d 475 (1988); *U.S. v. Bonnet,* 882 F.2d 1360 (8th Cir. 1989), *rev'd for other reasons,* 110 S. Ct. 3267 (1990); *State v. Waddell,* 527 S.E.2d 644 (N.C. 2000). But testimony based on the use of anatomically correct dolls has been accepted in the following cases: *United States v. Ellis,* 935 F.2d 385 (1st Cir. 1991); *Smallwood v. State,* 716 So. 2d 684 (Ala. Civ. App. 1998); *Linda P. v. Thomas,* 659 N.Y.S.2d 55 (A.D. 2 Dept. 1998); *Perez v. State,* 925 S.W.2d 324 (Tex. App. 1996).
71. *State v. Lawrence,* 541 A.2d 1291 (Me. 1988).
72. *People v. Nelson,* 561 N.E.2d 439 (Ill. App. 5th Dist. 1990); *State v. J.Q.,* 599 A.2d 172 (N.J.A.D. 1991), *aff'd,* 617 A.2d 1196 (N.J. 1993); *State v. Doan,* 498 N.W.2d 804 (Neb. Ct. App. 1993); *State v. Jones,* 393 S.E.2d 585 (N.C. Ct. App. 1990); *Frenzel v. State,* 849 P.2d 741 (Wyo. 1993); *State v. Michaels,* 642 A.2d 1372 (N.J. 1994).
73. *Commonwealth v. Dunkle,* 602 A.2d 830 (Pa. 1992) ; *Gier v. Education Service Unit,* 845 F. Supp. 1342 (D. Neb. 1994); *Newkirk v. Commonwealth,* 937 S.W.2d 690 (Ky. 1996); *State v. Cressey,* 628 A.2d 696 (N.H. 1993), *State v. Chamberlain,* 628 A.2d 704 (N.H. 1993).
74. *Commonwealth v. Dunkle; Newkirk v. Commonwealth; State v. Foret,* 628 So. 2d 1116 (La. 1993); *Hadden v. State,* 690 So. 2d 573 (Fla. 1997); *State v. Dickerson,* 789 S.W.2d 566 (Tenn. Crim. App. 1990); *People v. Bowker,* 249 Cal. Rptr. 886 (Cal. App. 4th Dist. 1988); *People v. Jeff,* 251 Cal. Rptr. 135 (Cal. App. 5th Dist. 1988).
75. The material in this concluding section is taken from Stein, *Child Welfare and the Law.*

7. PROFESSIONAL LIABILITY

1. Suits often name social workers and their employing agencies as defendants. For the sake of simplicity, I refer to the individual unless the charges against the agency are the subject of the discussion.
2. For a discussion of issues involved in Internet-based counseling, see Brett R. Harris, "Counseling Clients on the Internet," *Practicing Law Institute* 685 (2001): 135–225 (although concerned with legal practice, the issues discussed are interdisciplinary). On an increase in Internet-based counseling, see K. Humphreys and E. Klaw, "Can Targeting Nondependent Problem Drinkers and Providing Internet-Based Services Expand Access to Assistance for Alcohol Problems?" *Journal of Studies on Alcohol* 62, no. 4 (2001): 528–32; A. Meier, "Offering Social Support via the Internet: A Case Study of an Online Support Group for Social Workers," *Journal of Technology in the Human Services* 17, no. 2/3 (2000): 237–66; J. Levine, "Internet: A

Framework for Analyzing Online Human Service Practices," *Journal of Technology in the Human Services* 17, no. 2/3 (2000): 173–92; M. Banach and F. P. Bernat, "Liability and the Internet: Risks and Recommendations for Social Work Practice," *Journal of Technology in the Human Services* 17, no. 2/3 (2000): 153–71.

3. *Tanous v. United Behavioral Health Care,* 2002 WL 378508 (D. Neb. 2002).
4. *Hector M. v. Commission of Social Services,* 425 N.Y.S.2d 199 (N.Y. Fam. Ct.1980).
5. *Roe v. Catholic Charities of the Diocese of Springfield, Illinois,* 588 N.E.2d 354 (Ill. App. 5th Dist. 1992), *appeal denied,* 602 N.E.2d 475 (Ill. 1992).
6. *Werdein v. Johnson,* 633 N.Y.S.2d 908 (N.Y. App. 4th Dept. 1995).
7. *Rowe v. City,* 279 F.3d 1271 (11th Cir. 2002).
8. *Hall v. Miller,* 36 P.3d 328 (Kan. Ct. App. 2001).
9. *Brown Eyes v. South Dakota Department of Social Services,* 630 N.W.2d 501 (S.D. 2001).
10. *Martino v. Family Service Agency of Adams County,* 445 N.E.2d 6 (Ill. Appl. 4th Dist. 1983).
11. *Horak v Biris,* 474 N.E.2d 13 (Ill. App. 2d Dist. 1985).
12. *Rowe v Bennett,* 514 A.2d 802 (Me. 1986).
13. *Vaughn v. Ruoff,* 253 F.3d 1124 (8th Cir. 2001).
14. *Kubik v. State,* 664 N.Y.S.2d 365 (N.Y. App. 3 Dept. 1997).
15. *Dunajewski v. School District,* 526 N.Y.S.2d 139 (N.Y. App. 2 Dept. 1988).
16. *Ledbetter v. Ross,* 725 N.E.2d 120 (Ind. Ct. App. 2000).
17. *United States v. Houston,* 215 F.2d 1172 (10th Cir. 2000); *Miller v. City of Philadelphia,* 954 F. Supp. 1056 (E.D. Pa. 1997).
18. *Armstrong v. Brookdale University Hospital and Medical Center,* 2002 WL 13222 (E.D.N.Y. 2002).
19. *Jenkins v. County of Orange,* 212 Cal. App. 3d 278 (Cal. App. 1989).
20. Henry C. Black, *Black's Law Dictionary,* 7th ed. (St. Paul, Minn.: West, 1999), http://www. westlaw.com.
21. *Felton v. Schaeffer,* 279 Cal. Rptr. 713 (Cal. App. 4th Dist. 1991).
22. Heather J. Rhoades, "*Zamstein v. Marvasti:* Is a Duty Owed to Alleged Child Sexual Abusers?" *Connecticut Law Review* 30 (1998): 1411–43.
23. *DeShaney v. Winnebago County Department of Social Services,* 489 U.S. 189 (1989).
24. See *Estelle v. Gamble,* 429 U.S. 97 (1976) (prisoners have an Eighth Amendment right to adequate medical care); *Youngberg v. Romeo,* 457 U.S. 307 (1982) (the state owes a duty of care to those it places in mental health facilities); *Andrea L. v. Children and Youth Services of Lawrence County,* 987 F. Supp. 418 (W.D. Pa. 1997) (when the state places a child in foster care, it assumes certain duties of protection). On children in foster care see *K.H.* ex *rel. Murphy v. Morgan,* 914 F.2d 846 (7th Cir. 1990); *Doe v. New York City Department of Social Services, 649 F.2d 134 (2d Cir. 1981);* Walker v. Ledbetter, *818 F.2d 791 (11th Cir. 1987).*
25. *Andrea L. v. Children and Youth Services,* 987 F. Supp. at 423.
26. Restatement of the Law Second, Torts § 4. The American Law Institute (2002).
27. *Wogelius v. Dallas,* 504 N.E.2d 791 (Ill. App. 1st Dist. 1987).
28. *Vonner v. State,* 273 So. 2d 252 (La. 1973).
29. *Brookhouser v. State,* 13 Cal. Rptr. 2d 658 (Cal. App. 6th Dist. 1992).
30. Harriet Dinegar Milks, "Wrongful Adoption Causes of Action Against Adoption

Agencies Where Children Have or Develop Mental or Physical Problems That Are Misrepresented or Not Disclosed to Adoptive Parents," *American Law Reports—Fifth* 74 (1999): 1–33.

31. *Burr v. Board of County Commissioners,* 491 N.E.2d 1101 (Ohio 1986).
32. Ibid., 1103.
33. *Michael J. v. Los Angeles County,* 247 Cal. Rptr. 504 (Cal. App. 2d Dist. 1988). See also *Mohr v. Commonwealth,* 653 N.E.2d 1104 (Mass. 1995), where an adoptive couple was awarded $200,000 because the agency falsified information concerning the birth mother's mental health.
34. *Richard P. v. Vista Del Mar,* 165 Cal. Rptr. 370 (Cal. App. 2d Dist. 1980).
35. *Moore v. Department of Human Resources,* 469 S.E.2d 511 (Ga. Ct. App. 1996).
36. Smith-Hurd Illinois Statutes, 225 L 20/19 (1) (West 2002). See also California Bus. Code § 499203 (West 2002); Colo. Rev. Stat. § 12–43–101 (West 2002); Conn.Gen.Stat.§ 20–195p (West 2002); Delaware Code of Professions and Occupations § 3915 (West 2001); Kansas Statutes, Social Workers, § 65–6311 (West 2000); Mississippi Code, Professions and Vocations, § 73–53–21 (West 2002); North Carolina, Social Worker Certification and Licensure Act, § 90B-11 (West 2002).
37. These provisions were abstracted from Smith-Hurd Illinois Statutes, 225 ILCS 20/19 (West 2002).
38. *Maryland State Board of Social Work Examiners v. Chertkov,* 710 A.2d 391 (Md. App. 1997).
39. *Gersch v. Illinois Department of Professional Regulation,* 720 N.E.2d 672 (Ill. App. 1999).
40. *Prinz v. State of Ohio Counselor and Social Worker Board,* 2000 WL 43707 (Ohio Ct. App. 2000).
41. *In re* Eliot Levin, 625 So. 2d 756 (La. Ct. App. 1993).
42. *Maryland v. Chertkov.*
43. Civil Rights Act, 42 U.S.C. § 1983.
44. *Schaefer v. Wilcock,* 676 F. Supp. 1092 (D. Utah 1987).
45. *Monell v. Department of Social Services,* 436 U.S. 658 (1978).
46. *Vaughn v. Ruoff,* 253 F.3d 1124 (8th Cir. 2001).
47. *LaShawn A. v. Dixon,* 762 F. Supp. 959 (D.D.C. 1991).
48. *Anthony v. White,* 376 F.Supp. 567 (D. Del. 1974).
49. *King v. Olmstead County,* 117 F.3d 1065 (8th Cir. 1997).
50. *Rinderer v. Delaware County,* 703 F. Supp. 358 (E.D.Pa. 1987).
51. *Zavatsky v. Anderson,* 130 F. Supp. 349 (D. Conn. 2001).
52. *Whisman v. Rinehart,* 119 F.3d 1303 (8th Cir. 1997).
53. See, for example, *B.H. v. Johnson,* 715 F. Supp. 1387 (N.D. Ill. 1989); *Juan F. v. Weicker,* 37 F.3d 874 (2d Cir. 1994), *cert. denied,* 515 U.S. 1142 (1995); *Marisol v. Giuliani,* 929 F. Supp. 662 (S.D.N.Y. 1996); *Charlie H. and Nadine H. v. Whitman,* 83 F. Supp. 2d 476 (D.N.J. 2000); *Sean R. by Dwight R. v. Board of Education of Woodbridge,* 794 F. Supp. 467 (D. Conn. 1992).
54. Americans with Disabilities Act, 42 U.S.C.A. § 12102(2) (West 2002).
55. Ibid., § 12132 (West 2002).
56. *Henrietta v. Giuliani,* 119 F. Supp. 2d 181 (E.D.N.Y. 2000).

57. *Marisol A. v. Giuliani*, 929 F. Supp. 662 (S.D.N.Y. 1996), *cert. denied*, 520 U.S. 1211 (1997), aff'd, 126 F.3d 372 (1997).
58. *Popovich v. Cuyahoga County Court of Common Pleas*, 276 F.3d 808 (6th Cir. 2002).
59. *Olmstead v. Zimring*, 527 U.S. 581 (1999).
60. The Eleventh Amendment states that "the Judicial power of the United States shall not be construed to extend to any suit in law or equity, commenced or prosecuted against one of the United States by Citizens of another State, or by Citizens or Subjects of any Foreign State."
61. *Seminole Tribe of Florida v. Florida*, 517 U.S. 44 (1996); *Idaho v. Coeur d'Alene Tribe of Idaho*, 521 U.S. 261 (1997).
62. *Stanley v. Litscher*, 217 F.3d 340 (7th Cir. 2000); *Bradley v. Arkansas Department of Education*, 189 F.3d 745 (8th Cir. 1999), *cert. denied*, 533 U.S. 949 (2001).
63. On a state's pervasive pattern, see *Board of Trustees of the University of Alabama v. Garrett*, 531 U.S. 356 (2001), *on remand to Garrett v. University of Alabama*, 261 F.3d 1242 (11th Cir. 2001); *aff'd in part, vacated in part*, 276 F.3d 1227 (11th Cir. 2001).
64. *Idaho v. Coeur d'Alene.*
65. *Harlow v. Fitzgerald*, 457 U.S. 800 (1982).
66. *Burton v. Richmond*, 276 F.3d 973 (8th Cir. 2002).
67. Concerning either formulation, see *McNeal v. Harper*, 816 F. Supp. 421 (E.D. Va. 1993); *Doe v. Garcia*, 961 P.2d 1181 (Idaho 1998).
68. *M.R. v. Cox*, 881 P.2d 108 (Ok. App. 1st Div. 1994), *cert. denied*, 514 U.S. 1019 (1995).
69. *Sparks Regional Medical Center v. Smith*, 976 S.W.2d 396 (Ark. App. 2d Div. 1998).
70. Eric P. Gifford, "42 U.S.C. § 1983 and Social Worker Immunity: A Cause of Action Denied," *Texas Tech Law Review* 26 (1995): 1013–40. See also *Coverdall v. Department of Social and Health Services*, 834 F.2d 758 (9th Cir. 1987).
71. Ibid.
72. *Finkelstein v. Bodek*, 516 N.Y.S.2d 464 (N.Y. App. 1st Dept. 1987).
73. *K.B. v. Mills*, 639 N.W.2d 261 (Mich. Ct. App. 2002).
74. *Bartell v. Lohiser*, 12 F. Supp. 2d 640 (E.D. Mich. 1998).
75. *Sherman v. Four County Counseling Center*, 987 F.2d 397 (7th Cir. 1993). See also *Frazier v. Bailey*, 957 F.2d 920 (1st Cir. 1991) (social workers under contract to perform statutorily mandated government duties were entitled to raise qualified immunity as they functioned as government employees).
76. *Pavlik v. Kornhaber*, 761 N.E.2d 175 (Ill. App. 1st Dist. 2001).
77. *Hall v. Miller*, 36 P.3d 328 (Kan. Ct. App. 2001).
78. Ibid., 330.
79. *Burr v. Board of County Commissioners*, 491 N.E.2d 1101 (Ohio 1986).
80. *Henrietta v. Giuliani*, 119 F. Supp. 2d 181, 183 (E.D.N.Y. 2000).
81. *Juan F. v. Weicker*, 37 F.3d 874 (2d Cir. 1994).
82. Steven J. Schwartz, "Damage Actions as a Strategy for Enhancing the Quality of Care of Persons with Mental Disabilities," *New York University Review of Law and Social Change* 17 (1990): 651–87.
83. Gregory C. Keating, "Settling Through Consent Decree in Prison Reform Litigation: Exploring the Effects of *Rufo v. Inmates of Suffolk County Jail*," *Boston College Law Review* 34 (1992): 163–201.

84. Christina A. Zawisza, "Child Welfare Managed Care in Florida: Will It Be Innovation or Abdication?" *Nova Law Review* 25 (2001): 619–39.

8. FAMILIES AND THE LAW

1. Heidi Stirrup, testimony before the Senate Committee on Finance, Federal Document Clearing House, 1996 WL 90840 (1996); R. W. Apple Jr., "Politics: The Issues—Interview with Newt Gingrich," *New York Times,* June 25, 1996, p. 18A.
2. Arlene Skolnick, *Embattled Paradise: The American Family in the Age of Uncertainty* (New York: Basic Books, 1991).
3. Jason Fields and Lynne M. Casper, "America's Families and Living Arrangements: Population Characteristics—2000," *Current Population Reports* (Washington, D.C.: U.S. Census Bureau, 2001).
4. Tamara Halle, "Charting Parenthood: A Statistical Portrait of Fathers and Mothers in America," 2002, http://www.childtrendsdatabank.org (March 6, 2003).
5. Gary L. Bauer, testimony before the Senate Judiciary Committee, 1996 WL 387291 (1996).
6. *Congressional Record,* 148, H2511–01, 2002 WL 991791 (May 15, 2002).
7. *Reep v. Commissioner,* 593 N.E.2d 1297 (Mass. 1992). But see *Davis v. Employment Security Department,* 737 P.2d 1262 (Wash. 1987). A woman who voluntarily left her job to be with her long-term partner was not entitled to unemployment compensation.
8. *Lyng v. Castillo,* 477 U.S. 635 (1986).
9. *S.E.G. v. R.A.G.,* 735 S.W.2d 164, 166 (Mo. Ct. App. 1987).
10. *In re* T.L., 1996 WL 393521 (Mo. Cir. 1996), unpublished.
11. See"World Trade Center Relief Fund Distribution to Begin" and "Governor Pataki Joins WTC Families to Announce 'Family Rally," press releases of November 15, 2001, and January 10, 2002, http://www.nystate.gov (March 4, 2003).
12. On domestic partner benefits to federal employees and in the District of Columbia, see Lambda Legal Defense and Education Fund, "Domestic Partnership 08/01/02." http://www.lambdalegal.org/cgi-bin/iowa/documents/record?record&equals (March 4, 2003). On federal benefits to the same-sex partners of fire fighters and police who die in the line of duty, see Mychal Judge Police and Fire Chaplains Public Safety Officers Benefit Act of 2002, *Congressional Record,* 148, E1030–01, 2002 WL 1300185 (2002).
13. *Braschi v. Stahl,* 74 N.Y.2d 201, 543 N.E.2d 49, 53 (N.Y. 1989).
14. *In re* Nicholas H., 46 P.3d 932 (Cal. 2002).
15. *Boddie v. Connecticut,* 401 U.S. 371 (1971).
16. McKinney's Domestic Relations Law of New York, § 170(6) (West 2002).
17. *Loving v. Virginia,* 388 U.S. 1 (1967).
18. *Zablocki v. Redhail,* 434 U.S. 374 (1978).
19. *Turner v. Safley,* 482 U.S. 78 (1987).
20. *T.E.P. v. Leavitt,* 840 F. Supp. 110 (D. Utah 1993).
21. See, for example, California's law on incestuous marriages, Cal. Family Code, § 2200 (West 2002); McKinney Domestic Relations Law of New York, § 5 Incestuous and Void Marriages (West 2001); Georgia's statute on who can contract marriage,

GA-ST-ANN § 19–3-2 2 (West 2001). But see *Leszinske v. Poole,* 798 P.2d 1049 (N.M. Ct. App. 1990), *cert. denied,* 797 P.2d 983 (N.M. 1990). In that case an uncle married his niece in Costa Rica, where the marriage was legal. The marriage would be recognized as legal in New Mexico and California, where the couple planned to reside.

22. See McKinney's Domestic Relations Law of New York, § 13-aa (West 2002); D.C. Domestic Relations Law, Marriage, § 46–417—Blood Tests (2001); § Code of Georgia, Title 19, art. 2, and Domestic Relations, Art 2. License and Ceremony, § 19–3-40—Blood Tests (2002).
23. AZ-ST-ANN § 25–121 (West 2002); McKinney's Domestic Relations Law of New York § 6 Void marriages (2002); OR-REV-ST-ANN § 106.050 (West 2001); WA ST § 6.04.210 Affidavits required for issuance of license (West 2002).
24. OK-ST-ANN Marriage and Family, § 10 Evidence Before Issuance of a License (West 2001).
25. Henry C. Black, *Black's Law Dictionary,* 7th ed. (St. Paul, Minn.: West, 1999), http://www.westlaw.com.
26. Roger Adams et al., "§ 25 General Matters," in *American Jurisprudence,* 2d ed. (St. Paul, Minn.: West, 2002).
27. Mediation and alternative dispute resolution have been referred to as forms of "therapeutic jurisprudence," which is concerned with the emotional effect of legal proceedings on the parties involved. See Andrea Kupfer Schneider, "The Intersection of Therapeutic Jurisprudence, Preventive Law, and Alternative Dispute Resolution," *Psychology, Public Policy and Law* 5 (1999): 1084–1102.
28. See the note in "Model Standards of Practice for Family and Divorce Mediation." *Family and Conciliation Courts Review* 39 (2001): 121–34.
29. Carrie-Anne Tondo, Rinarisa Coronel, and Bethany Brucker, "Mediation Trends," *Family Court Review* 39 (2001): 431–45.
30. LA-ST-ANN Part III. Child Custody, Subpart A. Evaluation and Mediation. § 9:334. Mediator Qualifications. (West 2002).
31. *Idaho Rules of Civil Procedure,* rule 16(j) (West 1999).
32. AK-ST-ANN § 25.24.060 (West 2001).
33. Cal. Fam. Code, §§ 3164, Qualifications of Mediators (West 2002), and § 1815, Supervising and Associate Counselors. California also provides that members of the staff of the probation department of mental health may act as mediators.
34. Michie's Idaho Court Rules. Rule 16(j). Mediation of child custody and visitation disputes. (West 1999).
35. *Boddie v. Connecticut,* 401 U.S. 371 (1971).
36. Joel E. Smith, "Appointment of Counsel for Indigent Husband or Wife in Action for Divorce or Separation," *American Law Reports—Third* 85 (1978): 983–92.
37. *Harris v. Harris,* 424 F.2d 806 (D.C. Cir. 1970); *Puissegur v. Puissegur,* 220 So. 2d 547 (La. Ct. App. 1969); *Bartlett v. Kitchin,* 352 N.Y.S.2d 110 (N.Y. Sup. 1973).
38. *Glover v. Torrence,* 723 N.E.2d 924 (Ind. Ct. App. 2000); *Murray v. Murray,* 598 So. 2d 921 (Ala. Civ. App. 1992); *Lothman v. Lothman,* 464 P.2d 1006 (Ariz. Ct. App. 1970); Cal. Fam. Code, § 272 (West 2001).
39. *Butcher v. Butcher,* 357 S.E.2d 226 (W. Va. 1987).
40. Robert Roy, "Modern Status of Views as to Validity of Premarital Agreements Contemplating Divorce or Separation," *American Law Reports—Fourth* 53 (1987): 22–126. The information is current through 1997.

41. Ibid.
42. McKinney's Domestic Relations Law of New York § 236 (West 2002).
43. Alan D. Scheinkman, "Introduction to the Practice Commentaries," McKinney's New York Adoption Law—Private Adoption § 115-c. (St. Paul, Minn.: West, 2002).
44. Ibid.
45. McKinney's Domestic Relations Law of New York, § 236 (West 2002); *Hartog v. Hartog,* 623 N.Y.S.2d 537 (N.Y. 1995).
46. U.S. Constitution, Art. 4, Sec. 1.
47. Procedure: Evidence, 28 U.S.C.A. § 1738 (West 2002).
48. *Milwaukee County v. White,* 296 U.S. 268 (1935).
49. *Restatement of the Law, Conflicts of Law,* § 283(2) Validity of Marriage (West 2002). See *City of Philadelphia v. Cohen,* 184 N.E.2d 167 (N.Y. 1962), *cert. denied,* 371 U.S. 934 (1962).
50. Georgia banned common-law marriages after 1997. See GA-ST-ANN § 19–3-1.1 (West 2001).
51. *Anderson v. Anderson,* 577 So. 2d 658 (Fla. Dist. Ct. App. 1991).
52. *Enlow v. Fire Protection Systems, Inc.,* 803 S.W.2d 148 (Mo. Ct. App. 1991).
53. *Baehr v. Lewin,* 852 P.2d 44 (Haw. 1993), rehearing granted in part, 875 P.2d 225 (Haw. 1993), on remand to *Baehr v. Miike,* 1996 WL 694235 (Haw. Ct. App. 1996), *aff'd,* 950 P.2d 1234 (Haw. 1997).
54. *Brause v. Bureau of Vital Statistics,* 1998 WL 88743 (Alaska Super. 1998).
55. *Baker v. Vermont,* 744 A.2d 864 (Vt. 1999).
56. Both the Hawaii and Alaska cases were decided on the basis of equal protection, where the courts determined that lesbian and gay couples were denied the equal protection of the law when denied the right to marry. The Vermont case was decided on the basis of the common benefits clause of the state constitution, which provides that "government is, or ought to be, instituted for the common benefit, protection, and security of the people, nation, or community, and not for the particular emolument or advantage of any single person, family, or set of persons, who are a part only of that community" Vt Const, Chap I, Art 7).
57. Defense of Marriage Act of 1996, 28 U.S.C.A. § 1738c (West 2002).
58. Defense of Marriage Act, 142 Cong. Rec. S10100–02, 104th Cong., 2d sess., September 10, 1996.
59. Temporary Assistance to Needy Families, 42 U.S.C.A. § 601(a)(4) (West 2002).
60. Tommy G. Thompson, secretary of Health and Human Services, testimony before the Senate Finance Committee, 2002 WL 384664 (March 12, 2002), concerning welfare reform. Different sources report other sums; see "Bush Proposal Includes $300 Million," *Newsday*, March 31, 2002, Queens ed., p. B06, and Laura Meckler, "Marriage Promotion Invites Unease in U.S., State Officials Uncertain How to Push $300m Plan," *Boston Globe,* April 16, 2002.
61. Rebecca Wood, *A Summary of States' Activities in Support of Marriage and Promoting and Maintaining Health Intact Families* (Albany: New York Office of Temporary and Disability Assistance, n.d.)
62. See LA-ST-ANN, § 9:272 (West 2002); AZ-ST-ANN § 25–901 (West 2002).
63. Fields and Casper, "America's Families." On same-sex couples see "Unpublished Tables—Marital Status and Living Arrangements—1998 Update," *U.S. Census*

Bureau, http://www.census.gov/prod/99pubs (March 4, 2003). Most data are from the 2000 census; the exception is the data regarding same-sex couples, which are-from 1998, the latest year for which these data were available.

64. On relationships with no contract, see *Connell v. Francisco,* 898 P.2d 831 (Wash. 1995)—at the termination of a meretricious relationship, courts will equitably distribute property acquired during the relationship. Compare *Connell* with the finding in *Friedman v. Friedman,* 24 Cal. Rprt. 2d 892 (Cal. App. 1st Dist. 1993), where the court ruled that, although the couple had been living together for twenty-five years, the evidence was not sufficient to find a implied agreement of spousal support. On those with a contract, see *Posik v. Layton,* 695 So. 2d 759 (Fla. App. 1997), where the court found that a cohabitation agreement between unmarried homosexual adults was enforceable. In general, see Georgle L. Blum, "Property Rights Arising from Relationship of Couple Cohabiting Without Marriage," *American Law Reports—Fifth* 69 (1999): 219–96.
65. *Rubano v. DiCenzo,* 759 A.2d 959 (R.I. 2000).
66. These dates are found the website of the Lambda Legal Defense and Education Fund, http://www.lambdalegal.org (March 4, 2003). The number of private and public sector entities offering domestic partner benefits may increase or decrease over time.
67. William C. Duncan, "Domestic Partnership Laws in the United States: A Review and Critique," *Brigham Young University Law Review* (2001): 961–92.
68. Mark Bell, "Mainstreaming Equality Norms into European Union Asylum Law," *European Law Review* 26, no. 1 (2001): 20–34.
69. Clifford Krauss, "Canadian Leaders Agree to Propose Gay Marriage Law," *New York Times,* June 18, 2003, p. 1A.
70. See, for example, Cal. Fam. Code, § 297 (West 2002); HI-ST-ANN § 572C-4 (West 2000); DC CODE § 32–701 (West 2001).
71. 1998 WL 855396 (IRS PLR 1998) Internal Revenue Service, Private Letter Ruling December 11, 1998.
72. Cal. Fam. Code § 298(b)(2), 298.5(a)(b) (West 2002).
73. David Oregon Coolidge, "The Hawaii Marriage Amendment: Its Origins, Meaning and Fate," *University of Hawaii Law Review* 22 (2000): 19–118.
74. HRS § 572C-1 *et seq.* (West 2002).
75. Ibid. CCP-FAM S 20:111. See also *Tanner v. Oregon Health Sciences University,* 971 P.2d 435 (Or. Ct. App. 1998), where the court found that domestic partners are those who would be married to each other if Oregon law permitted it.
76. Cal. Fam. Code, § 297 (West 2002).
77. The federal government does not tax benefits provided to a worker's dependent children or spouse. However, after the passage of the Defense of Marriage Act, the definition of *spouse* in federal law was limited to a man or woman in a marital relationship. Thus an employer's contributions for health insurance for domestic partners are subject to tax. See P.L.R. 96–03–011 (Oct. 18, 1995); P.L.R. 92–42–012 (July 20, 1992); P.L.R. 92–31–062 (May 7, 1992); P.L.R. 91–09–060 (Dec. 6, 1990); P.L.R. 90–34–048 (May 29, 1990).
78. *Tanner v. Oregon Health Sciences University.*
79. *Slattery v. City of New York,* 686 N.Y.S.2d 683 (N.Y. Sup. Ct. 1999).

80. *Crawford v. City of Chicago,* 710 N.E.2d 91, 93 (Ill. App. Ct. 1999).
81. *Connors v. City of Boston,* 714 N.E.2d 335 (Mass. 1999).
82. HRS § 572C-7 (West 2001).
83. CCP-FAM § 299. Termination of Domestic Partnership. (West 2002).
84. The American Law Institute, *Principles of the Law of Family Dissolution: Analysis and Recommendations* (Washington, D.C.: American Law Institute, 2002). The membership of the ALI consists of judges, lawyers, and professors dedicated to studying the law and recommending change.
85. *Meyer v. Nebraska,* 262 U.S. 390 (1923).
86. *Stanley v. Illinois,* 405 U.S. 645 (1969).
87. Theodore J. Stein, "Child Custody and Visitation: The Rights of Lesbian and Gay Parents," *Social Service Review* 70, no. 3 (1996): 586–602.
88. *Ebert v. Ebert,* 346 N.E.2d 240 (N.Y. 1976); § *Vogel v. Vogel,* 637 N.W.2d 611 (Neb. 2002); *In re* Marriage of Hunt, 476 N.W.2d 99 (Iowa Ct. App. 1991); *In re* Custody of Peal, 290 S.E.2d 664 (N.C. 1982).
89. *Palmore v. Sidoti,* 466 U.S. 429, 104 S. Ct. 1879 (1984). When the dispute is between a biological parent and the state, a court must determine whether a parent is fit before determining whether an action is in the best interests of the child.
90. Alabama's statute provides that the court may grant custody "to either father or mother, as may seem right and proper, having regard to the moral character and prudence of the parents and the age and sex of the children" (AL-ST-ANN, Marital and Domestic Relations, § 30–3-1 (West 2001).
91. MN-ST-ANN, § 257.025 Custody Disputes, (West 2001).

    If two or more parties seek custody of a child the court shall consider and evaluate all relevant factors in determining the child's best interests, including: (1) the wishes of the parties as to custody; (2) the older child's preference; (3) the child's primary caretaker; (4) the intimacy of the relationship between each party and the child; (5) the interaction and interrelationship of the parties with the child including siblings, and others who may significantly affect the child's best interests; (6) the child's adjustment to home, school, and community; (7) the length of time the child has lived in a stable, satisfactory environment and the desirability of maintaining continuity; (8) the permanence, as a family unit, of the existing or proposed custodial home; (9) the mental and physical health of all individuals involved; except that a disability . . . of a proposed custodian or the child shall not be determinative of the custody of the child, unless the proposed custodial arrangement is not in the best interest of the child; (10) the capacity and disposition of the parties to give the child love, affection, and guidance, and to continue educating and raising the child in the child's culture, religion, or creed, if any; (11) the child's cultural background; and (12) the effect on the child of the actions of an abuser, if related to domestic abuse that occurred between the parents or the parties. The court may not use one factor to the exclusion of all others. The fact that the child's parents were not married to each other shall not be decisive and a court shall not consider conduct of a proposed custodian that does not affect the custodian's relationship to the child.

92. For a discussion of how these doctrines have been applied, see, Ira Mark Ellman, Paul M. Kurtz, and Katharine T. Bartlett, *Family Law: Cases, Text, Problems,* 2d ed., Contemporary Legal Education Series (Charlottesville, Va.: Michie, 1991), chap. 6.

93. For a discussion of issues and cases involving joint custody, see Vitauts M. Gulbis, "Annotation: Propriety of Awarding Joint Custody of Children," *American Law Reports—Fourth* 17 (1993): 1013–72.
94. For a discussion of issues and cases involving the primary caretaker rule, see Andrea G. Nadel, "Annotation: Primary Caretaker Role of Respective Parents as a Factor in Awarding Custody of Child," *American Law Reports—Fourth* 41 (1993): 1129—82.
95. *Stanley v. Illinois,* 405 U.S. 645 (1969).
96. *Quilloin v. Wolcott,* 434 U.S. 246 (1978).
97. Ibid., 255.
98. *Michael H. v. Gerald D.,* 491 U.S. 110 (1989).
99. Uniform Adoption Act of 1994, Uniform Laws Annotated. Art. 2 Adoption of Minors. Consent to and Relinquishment for Adoption (1994). 1999 Commentary to Main Volume (West 2002).
100. *In re* Petition of Doe, 638 N.E.2d 181 (Ill. 1994), *sub nom. In re* Petition of Kirchner, 649 N.E.2d 324 (Ill. 1995).
101. *In re* Petition of Kirchner, 649 N.E.2d at 327.
102. Deception also played a role in the case of Baby Jessica, *In re* Baby Girl Clausen, 502 N.W.2d 649 (Mich. 1993). As with Baby Richard, Baby Jessica's adoptive parents knew soon after obtaining physical custody of the newborn that their petition to adopt would be contested. Court papers reveal that within nine days of taking physical custody and less then one month after the child's birth, her preadoptive parents knew that (1) the birth mother had lied in naming the child's father, whose rights had never been terminated; (2) she intended to contest the termination of her rights; and (3) that their attorney had taken her relinquishment under unlawful conditions because the birth mother had been denied the seventy-two-hour hour waiting period required by law. In December 1991, a little more than nine months after the petition to adopt was filed, the trial court found that the biological father had not abandoned his child and he was not shown to be unfit. Thus the placement decision based on a best interests analysis was not appropriate. On December 3, 1992, the trial court terminated the adoptive parents' rights, finding that they had no legal claim to the baby Jessica.
103. Mich. Ct. Rules, rule 7.213; Ind. App. Rules, rule 21(A); Mass. Gen. Laws, ch. 211A, Appellate Courts, rule 2.3.4.
104. On putative father registries see: *In re* Baby Girl P., 2002 WL 1343814 (N.H. 2002); *Smith v. Solgon,* 561 S.E.2d 850 (Ga. Ct. App. 2002); *In re* Adoption of Coppersmith, 761 N.E.2d 1163 (Ohio Ct. App. 2001); Il-ST-ANN, Ch. 750, § 50/7(C)(b) (West 2001); N.Y. Soc. Serv. Law, § 372-c. Putative Father Registry.
105. See Stein, "Child Custody and Visitation."
106. *Carney v. Carney,* 598 P.2d 36 (Cal. 1979).
107. Ibid., 735.
108. Ibid., 736–37.
109. Ibid.
110. *Doe v. Roe,* 526 N.Y.S.2d 718 (N.Y. Supr. Ct. New York County 1988).
111. Ibid., 220.
112. Ibid.
113. *Palmore v. Sidoti,* 466 U.S. 429, 431 (1984).

114. Ibid., 433.
115. *Friederwitzer v. Friederwitzer,* 432 N.E.2d 765 (N.Y. 1982); *Ex parte* McLendon, 455 So. 2d 863 (Ala. 1984); Tex. Fam. Code Ann., § 153.131(a) (West 2002).
116. The address of the website for the National Conference of Commissioners on Uniform State Laws is http://www.nccusl.org (March 3, 2003).
117. Matters of child custody affecting native American children are covered by the Indian Child Welfare Act (see chapter 9), which requires that full faith and credit be given to tribal custody orders. See 25 U.S.C.A. § 1911(d) (West 2002).
118. If a child is less than six months old, "home state" means the state in which the child has resided for a majority of the time since birth. A person acting as parent is one with physical custody of a child who has a court order awarding custody or one who claims a right to custody, for example, based on the length of time the child has been in her or his care.
119. The Parental Kidnaping Prevention Act of 1981, 28 U.S.C.A. § 1738-A (West 2002).
120. Ibid., § 1738A(a,c,g).
121. *Stanley v. Illinois,* 405 U.S. 645 (1969).
122. *Troxel v. Granville,* 535 U.S. 57 (2000).
123. *Bennett v. Jeffreys,* 40 N.Y.2d 543 (N.Y. 1976).
124. *Rowles v. Rowles,* 668 A.2d 126 (Pa. 1995).
125. *B.A. v. E.E. ex rel. C.E.,* 741 A.2d 1227 (Pa. 1999).
126. The states are Arizona, Colorado, Illinois, Kentucky, Missouri, Montana, and Washington. See Lawrence Schlam, "Children Not in the Physical Custody of One of [Their] Parents: The Superior Rights Doctrine and Third-Party Standing Under the Uniform Marriage and Dissolution of Marriage Act," *Southern Illinois University Law Journal* 24 (2000): 405–52.
127. Colorado adopted this law in 1972 and retitled it the "Uniform Dissolution of Marriage Act," Colo. Rev. Stat., §§ 14–10–101 (<year pls>).
128. See also IL-ST-CH 750 § 5/601 and *In re* Custody of Peterson, 491 N.E.2d 1150 (Ill. 1986). In that case the court found that when a nonparent demonstrates that the child is not in the physical custody of a parent, the nonparent will be considered for legal custody under a "best interests of the child" standard with no necessity to demonstrate unfitness of the biological parent or parents.
129. *Smith v. O.F.F.E.R.,* 431 U.S. 816 (1977).
130. J. Goldstein, A. Freud, and A. J. Solnit, *Beyond the Best Interests of the Child* (New York: Free Press, 1973); J. Goldstein, A. Freud, and A. J. Solnit, *Before the Best Interests of the Child* (New York: Free Press, 1979); J. Goldstein, A. Freud, A. J. Solnit, and S. Goldstein, *In the Best Interests of the Child* (New York: Free Press, 1986).
131. *In re* T.L., 1996 WL 393521 (Mo. Cir. Ct. 1996).
132. *In re* Nicholas H., 46 P.3d 932 (Cal. 2002).
133. Financial support is available for dependent children, and in some cases for their caretaker, through Temporary Assistance to Needy Families (42 U.S.C.A. § 601 *et seq.* [West 2002]) and for children with disabilities through Supplemental Security Income (42 U.S.C.A. § 1382 *et seq.* [West 2002]).
134. In 1998, the last year for which data are available, the United States had 9.8 million female-headed, single-parent families compared to 2.1 such families headed by men. See U.S. Census Bureau, Economics and Statistics Administration, "Growth

in Single Fathers Outpaces Growth in Single Mothers," 1998, http://www.cb.gov/Press-Release/cb98–228.html (July 11, 2003).

135. Child Support and Establishment of Paternity Act, 42 U.S.C.A. § 651 *et seq.* (West 2002).
136. U.S. General Accounting Office, *Child Support: Need to Improve Efforts to Identify Fathers and Obtain Orders of Support.* Report GAO/HRD-87–37 (Washington, D.C.: U.S. General Accounting Office, 1997).
137. Child Support and Establishment of Paternity Act, 42 U.S.C.A. § 664(b) (West 2002).
138. Full Faith and Credit in Child Support, 28 U.S.C.A. § 1738B (West 2002), amended by the Balanced Budget Act of 1997, Pub. L. No. 105–33, 111 Stat. 251 (1997). In 1996, as a condition for receiving federal aid under the Personal Responsibility and Work Opportunity Reconciliation Act (42 U.S.C.A. § 601 *et seq.* [West 2002]), Congress mandated that states adopt the Uniform Interstate Family Support Act (formerly the Uniform Reciprocal Enforcement of Support Act). The act describes rules for courts to obtain jurisdiction over nonresidents in order to limitto one the number of support orders issued, and for enforcement and modification of existing orders.
139. The Deadbeat Parents Punishment Act, 18 U.S.C.A. § 228 (West 2002), supersedes the Child Support Recovery Act of 1992.

9. EDUCATION

1. *Pierce v. Society of Sisters,* 268 U.S. 510 (1925); *Meyer v. Nebraska,* 262 U.S. 390 (1923); *Prince v. Massachussetts,* 321 U.S. 158 (1944); *Skinner v. Oklahoma,* 316 U.S. 535 (1942); *Wisconsin v. Yoder,* 406 U.S. 205 (1972).
2. Information about the School Social Work Association of America may be found at http://www.sswaa.org (March 7, 2003).
3. U.S. Census Bureau, "Summary of Public School Finances for Elementary-Secondary Education by State: 1999–2000," *Statistical Abstract of the United States: 2000* (Washington, D.C.: U.S. Government Printing Office, 2001), secs. 4 and 9. The country spent $373,961,479 on education in the 1999–2000 school year. Federal funds amounted to $26,672,296, or approximately 7 percent of total spending.
4. Education: General Provisions Concerning Education, 20 U.S.C.A. § 1232A (West 2002).
5. Funding for children disadvantaged by poverty is authorized under the Strengthening and Improvement of Elementary and Secondary Schools Act, 20 U.S.C.A. § 7801 *et seq.* (West 2002). Authorization to fund programs for native American children is found in the Indian Self-determination and Education Assistance Act, 25 U.S.C.A. § 450 *et seq.* (West 2002), with funding for native Hawaiian and native Alaskan children specified in the Native Hawaiian Education Act, 20 U.S.C.A. § 7511 *et seq.* (West 2002).
6. The Family Educational and Privacy Rights Act of 1974, codified at 20 U.S.C.A. § 1232g (West 1999).
7. Civil Rights Act, 42 U.S.C.A. § 2000a *et seq.* (West 2002).

8. Title IX of the Education Amendments of 1972, 20 U.S.C.A. § 1681 *et seq.* (West 2002).
9. Ibid.
10. *Meyer v. Nebraska,* 262 U.S. 390 (1923).
11. *Pierce v. Society of Sisters,* 268 U.S. 510, 534 (1925).
12. *Brown v. Board of Education,* 347 U.S. 483 (1954) (Brown I); *Brown v. Board of Education,* 349 U.S. 294 (1955) (Brown II).
13. *Swann v. Charlotte-Mecklenburg,* 402 U.S. 1 (1971).
14. *West Virginia Board of Education v. Barnette,* 319 U.S. 624 (1943).
15. *Tinker v. Des Moines Independent School District,* 393 U.S. 503 (1969).
16. *Bethel School District v. Fraser,* 478 U.S. 675, 685 (1986).
17. *Hazelwood School District v. Kuhlmeier,* 484 U.S. 260 (1988).
18. *San Antonio v. Rodriguez,* 411 U.S. 1 (1973).
19. *Plyler v. Doe,* 457 U.S. 202 (1982).
20. Ibid.
21. *Zelman v. Simmons-Harris,* 536 U.S. 639 (2002).
22. No Child Left Behind Act, Pub. L. No. 107–110, 115 Stat. 1425 (2002). In 1994 the Elementary and Secondary Education Act of 1965 was reauthorized as the Improving America's Schools Act, Pub. L. No. 103–382, 108 Stat. 3518, which was repealed by the 2001 reauthorization.
23. A charter school is a public school whose development and operation are authorized by a public entity such as a state department of education. Charter schools may operate with greater flexibility than a traditional public school, allowing experimentation in approaches to education.
24. Family Educational and Privacy Rights Act of 1974, 20 U.S.C.A. § 1232g (West 2002).
25. Ibid., § 1232g(b)(1)(l).
26. Ibid., § 1232g(a)(4)(A) (West 2002).
27. *Owasso Independent School District v. Falvo,* 534 U.S. 426 (2002).
28. *Daniel S. v. Board of Education,* 152 F. Supp. 2d 949 (N.D. Ill. 2001).
29. Equal Access Act, 20 U.S.C.A. § 4071 *et seq.* (West 2002).
30. Ibid.
31. *Colin v. Orange Unified School District,* 83 F. Supp. 2d 1135 (C.D. Cal. 2000).
32. Education—Discrimination Based on Sex or Blindness, 20 U.S.C.A. § 1681 (West 2002).
33. *Davis v. Monroe,* 526 U.S. 629 (1999).
34. *Franklin v. Gwinett County Public Schools,* 503 U.S. 60 (1992).
35. *LaShonda D. v. Monroe County Board of Education,* 526 U.S. 629 (1999).
36. *Seamons v. Snow,* 84 F.3d 1226 (10th Cir. 1996).
37. Americans with Disabilities Act, 42 U.S.C.A. § 12132 (West 2002).
38. Ibid., § 12131(1).
39. Ibid.
40. Sections of the discussion of the IDEA, VRA, and ADA taken with permission from Theodore J. Stein, *Child Welfare and the Law* (Washington, D.C.: Child Welfare League of America, 1998).
41. *Pennsylvania Association for Retarded Children v. Commonwealth of Pennsylvania,* 334 F. Supp. 279 (E.D. Pa. 1972).

42. U.S. General Accounting Office, *Student Discipline: Individuals with Disabilities in Education Act.* Report No. GAO-01–210 (Washington, D.C.: U.S. General Accounting Office, 2001).
43. Individuals with Disabilities in Education Act, 20 U.S.C.A. § 1401 *et seq.* (West 2002). "Children with specific learning disabilities" are those with a disorder that implicates the psychological processes involved in understanding or in using spoken or written language. The child's difficulties may be observed in an "imperfect ability to listen, think, speak, read, write, spell, or do mathematical calculations . . . perceptual disabilities, brain injury, minimal brain dysfunction, dyslexia, and developmental aphasia," among other manifestations.
44. *Board of Education v. Rowley,* 458 U.S. 176, 177 (1982).
45. *Rettig v. Kent City School District,* 720 F.2d 463 (6th Cir. 1983), *cert. denied,* 467 U.S. 1201 (1984), *rehearing denied,* 467 U.S. 1257 (1984).
46. Assistance to States for the Education of Children with Disabilities, 34 C.F.R. § 300.24 (West 2002).
47. Ann K. Wooster, "What Constitutes Services That Must be Provided by Federally Assisted Schools Under the Individuals with Disabilities Education Act?" *American Law Reports—Federal* 161 (2000): 1–110.
48. *Cedar Rapids Community School District v. Garret,* 526 U.S. 66 (1999).
49. Ibid., 67, citing Assistance to States for the Education of Children with Disabilities, 20 U.S.C.A. § 1401(a)(17).
50. *Cedar Rapids,* quoting *Irving Independent School District v. Tatro,* 468 U.S. 883, 891 (1984).
51. *Butler v. Evans,* 225 F.3d 887, 894 (7th Cir. 2000).
52. *Burlington v. Department of Education,* 736 F.2d 773 (1st Cir. 1984), *aff'd,* 471 U.S. 359 (1985).
53. *Vander Malle v. Ambach,* 667 F. Supp. 1015 (S.D.N.Y. 1987).
54. *Carter v. Florence County School District Four,* 950 F.2d 156 (4th Cir. 1991), *aff'd sub nom., Florence County School District Four v. Carter,* 510 U.S. 7 (1993).
55. *McKenzie v. Smith,* 771 F.2d 1527 (D.C. Cir. 1985); *King v. Pine Plains Central School District,* 918 F. Supp. 772 (S.D.N.Y. 1996).
56. *Ciresoli v. Maine School Administrative District,* 901 F. Supp. 378, 382 (D.C. Me. 1995).
57. Individuals with Disabilities in Education Act, 20 U.S.C.A. § 1412(5)(B) (West 2002).
58. Regulations—Assistance to the Statrs for the Education of Children with Disabilities, 34 C.F.R. § 300.551.
59. *Daniel R. R.,* 874 F.2d 1036 (5th Cir. 1989); *Liscio v. Woodland Hills School District,* 734 F. Supp. 689 (W.D. Pa. 1989), *aff'd,* 902 F.2d 1561 (3d Cir. 1990).
60. *Campbell v. Talladega County Board of Education,* 518 F. Supp. 47 (N.D. Ala. 1981).
61. *Roland M. v. Concord School Committee,* 910 F.2d 983 (1st Cir. 1990), *cert. denied,* 489 U.S. 912 (1991).
62. *Board of Education v. Illinois State Board of Education,* 41 F.3d 1162 (7th Cir. 1994).
63. *Capistrano Unified School District v. Wartenberg,* 59 F.3d 884 (9th Cir. 1995); *St. Louis Developmental Disabilities Treatment Center Parents Association v. Mallory,* 591 F. Supp. 1416 (W.D. Mo. 1984), *aff'd,* 767 F.2d 518 (8th Cir. 1985).

64. *Learning Disabilities Association of Maryland, Inc. v. Board of Education of Baltimore County,* 837 F. Supp. 717 (D. Md. 1993); *Farrell v. Carol Stream School District No. 25,* 1996 WL 364743 (N.D. Ill. 1996).
65. *Hall v. Shawnee Mission School District,* 856 F. Supp. 1521 (D.C. Kan. 1994).
66. *Honig v. Doe,* 484 U.S. 305 (1988).
67. Individuals with Disabilities in Education Act, 34 C.F.R. § 300.520 (West 2002).
68. Ibid.
69. Individuals with Disabilities in Education Act, 20 U.S.C.A. § 1415(k)(1)(A) (West 2002).
70. Ibid., § 1415.
71. *Honig v. Doe.*
72. The Americans with Disabilities Act is found at 42 U.S.C.A. § 12101 *et seq.* (West 2002) and the Vocational Rehabilitation Act at 29 U.S.C.A. § 701 *et seq.* (West 2002).
73. Americans with Disabilities Act, 42 U.S.C.A. § 12201(a) (West 2002).
74. *Board of Trustees of University of Alabama v. Garrett,* 531 U.S. 356 (2001).
75. *Doe v. Division of Youth and Family Services,* 148 F. Supp. 2d 462 (D.N.J. 2001).
76. Individuals with Disabilities in Education Act, 20 U.S.C.A. § 1401(a)(1) (West 2002).
77. *Doe v. Belleville Public Schools District,* 672 F. Supp. 342 (S.D. Ill. 1987); *Doe v. Dolton Elementary School District No. 148,* 694 F. Supp. 440 (N.D. Ill. 1988); *District 27 Community School Board v. Board of Education,* 130 Misc. 2d 398 (N.Y. Sup. Ct. 1986); *Martinez v. School Board of Hillsborough County,* 675 F. Supp. 1574 (M.D. Fla. 1987), 692 F. Supp. 1293 (M.D. Fla. 1988), *vacated,* 861 F.2d 1502 (11th Cir. 1988), *on remand,* 711 F. Supp. 1066 (M.D. Fla. 1989); *Phipps v. Saddleback Valley Unified School District,* 204 Cal. App. 3d 1110 (Cal. App. 4th Dist. 1988); *Ray v. School District of DeSoto County,* 666 F. Supp. 1524 (M.D. Fla. 1987).
78. The definition of *disability* in the ADA appears at 29 C.F.R. § 1630.2(a)(3)(ii). For the VRA see 29 U.S.C.A. § 706(8)(b). Congress declined to create a definitive list of the conditions, diseases, or infections that might constitute physical or mental impairments, but guidance can be found in federal regulations that identify a variety of conditions, diseases, and disorders covered by the law. The regulation at 29 C.F.R. § 1630.2 (h)(1) & (2) defines physical or mental impairment as "(1) Any physiological disorder, or condition, cosmetic disfigurement, or anatomical loss affecting one or more of the following body systems: neurological, musculoskeletal, special sense organs, respiratory (including speech organs), cardiovascular, reproductive, digestive, genito-urinary, hemic and lymphatic, skin, and endocrine; or (2) Any mental or psychological disorder, such as mental retardation, organic brain syndrome, emotional or mental illness, and specific learning disabilities."
79. Nondiscrimination on the Basis of Handicap in Programs and Activities Receiving Federal Financial Assistance, 45 C.F.R. § 84.3(j)(2)(iii) (West 2002).
80. Regulations to Implement the Equal Employment Provisions of the Americans with Disabilities Act, 29 C.F.R. 1630.2(1)-(3) (West 2002).
81. *Southeastern Community College v. Davis,* 442 U.S. 397 (1979).
82. *Alexander v. Choate,* 469 U.S. 287 (1985).
83. See note 77.
84. *Phipps v. Saddleback Valley,* 204 Cal. App. 3d 1110 (Cal. App. 4th Dist. 1983).

85. *White v. Western School Corp.*, IP 85–1192-C, *slip op*. (S.D. Ind. 1985).
86. *Robertson v. Granite City Unified School District,* 684 F. Supp. 1002 (S.D. Ill. 1988).
87. *Ray v. School District of DeSoto County,* 666 F. Supp. 1524 (M.D. Fla. 1987).
88. *Martinez v. School Board of Hillsborough County,* 675 F. Supp. 1574 (M.D. Fla. 1987), 692 F. Supp. 1293 (M.D. Fla. 1988), *vacated,* 861 F.2d 1502 (11th Cir. 1988), *on remand,* 711 F. Supp. 1066 (M.D. Fla. 1989).
89. Task Force on Pediatric AIDS, American Academy of Pediatrics, "Pediatric Guidelines for Infection Control of Human Immunodeficiency Virus (Acquired Immunodeficiency Virus) in Hospitals, Medical Offices, Schools, and Other Settings," *Pediatrics* 82 (1988): 18–24; Task Force on Pediatric AIDS, American Academy of Pediatrics, "Guidelines for Human Immunodeficiency Virus (HIV)-Infected Children and Their Foster Families," *Pediatrics* 89 (1992): 36–44; U.S. Centers for Disease Control, "1995 Revised Guidelines for Prophylaxis Against Pneumocystis *carinii* Pneumonia for Children Infected with or Perinatally Exposed to the Human Immunodeficiency Virus," *Morbidity and Mortality Weekly Report* 44 (1995): 21–29.
90. Leslie Slaughter, testimony before the House of Representatives Education Subcommittee, Federal Document Clearing House, 1998 WL 210930 (1998).
91. Previously, the Stewart B. McKinney Homeless Assistance Act, renamed in 2000. See Pub. L. No. 106–400, 106th Cong., 2d sess., 114 Stat. 1675, codified at 42 U.S.C.A. § 11431 *et seq*. (West 2002).
92. Ibid., 42 U.S.C.A. § 11432(g)(3)(A)(B) (West 2002).

10. CARE AND PROTECTION OF CHILDREN

1. Child Abuse Prevention and Treatment Act, 42 U.S.C.A. § 5101 *et seq*. (West 2002).
2. Adoption Assistance and Child Welfare Act, Pub. L. No. 96–272, 94 Stat. 500, codified in various sections of Title 42 of the *United States Code.*
3. Child Abuse Prevention and Treatment Act, 42 U.S.C.A. § 5101 *et seq.* (West 2002).
4. Lois A. Weithorn, "Protecting Children from Exposure to Domestic Violence: The Use and Abuse of Child Maltreatment," *Hastings Law Journal* 53 (2001): 1–152.
5. Domestic Relations: Chap. 63—Child Protective Services, 23 Pa. C.S. § 6303(b)(i)–(iv) (West 2002). The quote is from § 6303 (b)(1)(iv).
6. Georgia Domestic Relations Code: Chap. 14—Child Abuse and Neglect Prevention, § 19–14–2 (West 2002). The Georgia statute has a repeal date of 2010. The quote appears in § 19–14–2(4).
7. AK-ST-ANN, § 47.17.020 (West 2001).
8. CO-ST-ANN § 19–3–307 (West 2002).
9. MA-ST-ANN Ch. 119 § 51B(4) (West 2002).
10. Marcia Sprague and Mark Hardin, "Coordination of Juvenile and Criminal Court Child Abuse and Neglect Proceedings," *University of Louisville Journal of Family Law* 35 (1996–97): 239–324.
11. *Doe v. District of Columbia,* 93 F.3d 861 (D.C. Cir. 1996); *Tony L. By and Through Simpson v. Childer,* 71 F.3d 1182 (6th Cir. 1995). See also *Jeanine B. by Blondis v. Thompson,* 967 F. Supp. 1104 (E.D. Wis. 1997).

12. *Marisol v. Giuliani*, 929 F. Supp. 662 (S.D.N.Y. 1996); *cert. denied*, 520 U.S. 1211 (1997), *aff'd*, 126 F.3d 372 (1997). But see *Charlie H. and Nadine H. v. Whitman*, 83 F. Supp. 2d 476 (D.N.J. 2000), which found that protections in CAPTA are too vague and beyond the realm of judicial enforcement.
13. *DeShaney v. Winnebago County Department of Social Services*, 489 U.S. 189 (1989).
14. Ibid., 200.
15. Regulations Relating to Public Welfare, C.F.R. § 1355.20(a) (2002).
16. Theodore J. Stein, "The Adoption and Safe Families Act: Creating a False Dichotomy Between Parents' Rights and Childrens' Rights," *Families in Society* 81, no. 6 (2000): 586–92.
17. The amendments are found in the Child Abuse Prevention and Treatment Act, 42 U.S.C.A. § 5106a(b)(2)(A)(xii),(xiii) (West 2002); and the Adoption Assistance and Child Welfare Act amendment commonly known as the Adoption and Safe Families Act, Pub. L. No. 105–89, codified at 3 Stat. 2115 (Nov. 19, 1997).
18. *Mullane v. Central Hanover Bank and Trust Co.*, 339 U.S. 306 (1950).
19. Ibid.
20. Child Abuse Prevention and Treatment Act, 42 U.S.C.A. § 5106a (West 2002).
21. Forty states appoint counsel for children. Thirty appoint an "attorney–guardian *ad litem*," who undertakes both to represent the child's wishes and to express what the attorney thinks is in the best interests of the child. Ten states appoint counsel and a guardian *ad litem*, allowing the attorney to perform the single role of representing the child's wishes. In the remaining ten states an attorney is not routinely appointed, but nine of the ten appoint a guardian *ad litem* (Donald N. Duquette, "Legal Representation for Children in Protection Proceedings: Two Distinct Lawyer Roles Are Required," *Family Law Quarterly* 34 [2000]: 441–66). Duquette reports the results of a 1998 survey conducted by the National Council of Juvenile and Family Court Judges.
22. *Griffin v. State*, 526 So. 2d 752 (Fla. Dist. Ct. App. 1988).
23. *Coy v. Iowa*, 487 U.S. 1012 (1988).
24. Ibid., 1022.
25. *Maryland v. Craig*, 497 U.S. 836 (1990).
26. *C.F. v. Pennsylvania Department of Public Welfare*, 804 A.2d 755 (Pa. Commw. Ct. 2002).
27. Ibid., 758.
28. Ibid., 759.
29. *Hamilton v. Saxbe*, 428 F. Supp. 1101 (N.D. Ga. 1976), *aff'd*, 551 F.2d 1056 (5th Cir. 1977); *Barnes v. Virgin Islands*, 415 F. Supp. 1218 (D.C.V.I. 1976); *White v. Keller*, 438 F. Supp. 110 (D.C. Md. 1977), *aff'd*, 588 F.2d 913 (4th Cir. 1978).
30. *Feeley v. Sampson*, 570 F.2d 364 (1st Cir. 1978); *In re* Smith, 112 Cal. App. 3d 956 (Cal. Ct. App. 1980).
31. Cases interpreting application of the Indian Child Welfare Act are reported in Carol Schultz Vento, "Construction and Application of Indian Child Welfare Act of 1978 (ICWA) 25 U.S.C.A. § § 1901 *et seq*. Upon Child Custody Determinations," *American Law Reports—Fifth* 89 (2001): 195–235.
32. A detention facility includes "forestry camps, training schools, or any other facility operated primarily for the detention of children determined to be delinquent." The

test for determining whether a facility is a detention facility asks whether it is (1) physically restricting and and (2) it would exist without a population of adjudicated delinquents. See U.S. General Accounting Office, *Foster Care: HHS Should Ensure that Juvenile Justice Placements Are Reviewed,* Report GAO/HEHS-00–42 (Washington, D.C.: U.S. General Accounting Office, 2000), 7–8.

33. Requirements Applicable to Title IV, 45 C.F.R. § 1356.21 (West 2002).
34. Adoption Assistance and Child Welfare Act of 1980, 42 U.S.C.A. § 675(5)(C) (West 2002).
35. *A. v. City of New York,* 31 N.Y.2d 83, 335 N.Y.S.2d 33 (1972); *In re* Napier, 532 P.2d 423 (Okla. 1975); *District of Columbia v. B.J.R.,* 332 A.2d 58 (D.C. 1975); *Blondheim v. State,* 529 P.2d 1096 (Wash. 1975); *In re People in Interest of K.*, 514 P.2d 1131 (Colo. 1973). Statutes may be declared "void for vagueness" when they forbid or require conduct "in terms so vague that men of common intelligence must necessarily guess at [the] meaning [of the terms]" (*Champlin Refining Co. v. Corporation Com'n of State of Oklahoma,* 286 U.S. 210 [1932]).
36. The percentage of cases referred by parents and schools is not reported. See Howard Snyder and Melissa Sickmund, "Juvenile Courts and Juvenile Crime," in *Juvenile Offenders and Victims: 1999 National Report* (Washington, D.C.: National Center for Juvenile Justice, Office of Juvenile Justice and Delinquency Prevention, 1999), 142–43.
37. Michael White, Edward J. Loughran, Donna Wulkan, and Jerome G. Miller, "Systematic Critique and Transformation," *District of Columbia Law Review* 3 (1995): 403; Byron Oedekoven, "Youth Violence Programs," congressional testimony, Federal Document Clearing House. 1996 WL 7137245 (1996); Kenneth E. Watson, 1996. "Juvenile Justice and Delinquency." Federal Document Clearing House. 1996 WL 10163920 (1996); Joseph A. Myers, testimony before the Senate Committee on Indian Affairs, Federal Document Clearing House, 1996 WL 50663 (1996); Leslie Kaufman, "Burden Grows on Services for Teenagers," *New York Times,* October 28, 2002.
38. The Juvenile Justice and Delinquency Prevention Act of 1974 provides that states receiving federal funds not place status offenders in detention facilities (42 U.S.C.A. § 5601 *et seq.* [West 2002]).
39. Juvenile Justice and Delinquency Prevention Act, 42 U.S.C.A. § 5633(12)(A) (West 2002). The juvenile justice act, through its Runaway and Homeless Youth provisions (42 U.S.C.A. § 5701 [West 2002]), funds services for at-risk and runaway youth. In addition, the law funds (1) training for professionals and volunteers who work in the juvenile justice system; (2) technical assistance to programs that serve status offenders and delinquent youth, including juvenile courts; (3) state and local efforts to deinstitutionalize youth incarcerated in jails and prisons; and (4) research on the problems of delinquency and at-risk youth, including dissemination of information.
40. Office of Juvenile Justice and Delinquency Prevention, "Offenders in Juvenile Court," *Juvenile Justice Bulletin* (2000), http://www.ncjrs.org/html/ojjdp/jjbul2000_10_3/contents.html (July 13, 2003).
41. *In re* Catrice S., 470 S.E.2d 856 (S.C. Ct. App. 1996); *In re* M.B., 3 P.3d 780 (Wash. App. Div. 1 2000); *A.D. v. State,* 736 N.E.2d 1274 (Ind. Ct. App. 2000); *In re* Francisco

S., 26 P.3d 562 (Cal. App. 2d Dist. 2000); *B.P. v. Commonwealth,* 568 S.E.2d 412 (Va. Ct. App. 2002).

42. *Commonwealth v. Florence F.,* 429 Mass. 523, 709 N.E.2d 418 (Mass. 1999); *In re* Naquan J., 727 N.Y.S.2d 124 (N.Y. App. Div. 2d Dept. 2001).
43. *In re* Naquan J., 727 N.Y.S.2d 124 (N.Y. App. Div. 2d Dept. 2001).
44. Snyder and Sickmund, *Juvenile Offenders and Victims,* 169.
45. Juvenile Delinquency Act, 18 U.S.C.A. § 5031 *et seq.* (West 2002).
46. McKinney's Family Court Act, Art. 3, § 301.2(1) (West 2002).
47. *In re* Gault, 387 U.S. 1 (1967).
48. Ibid., 18.
49. *In re* Winship, 397 U.S. 358 (1970).
50. *Breed v. Jones,* 421 U.S. 519 (1975).
51. *McKeiver v. Pennsylvania,* 403 U.S. 528 (1971).
52. Snyder and Sickmund, *Juvenile Offenders and Victims,* 120.
53. See Dana Canedy, October 6, 2002. "Boys' Case Is Used in Bid to Limit Trials of Minors as Adults," *New York Times,* October 6, 2002; Barry Adams and Beth Williams, "Student Raped at West High During School," *Wisconsin State Journal,* September 19, 2002; Kevin Blocker, "Teen Sentenced to 22 Years in Prison; Boy Killed Man in Mistaken Belief That He Had Stolen His Cell Phone," *Spokesman (Spokane, Wash.) Review,* September 10, 2002.
54. Christine Chamberlin, "Not Kids Anymore: A Need for Punishment and Deterrence in the Juvenile Justice System," *Boston College Law Review* 42 (2001): 391–419.
55. Correction of Youthful Offenders—Juvenile Delinquency—Delinquency Proceedings, 18 U.S.C.A. § 5032 (West 2002).
56. Snyder and Sickmund, *Juvenile Offenders and Victims,* 101–10.
57. *United States v. Juvenile Male No. 1,* 86 F.3d 1314 (4th Cir. 1996).
58. McKinney's Family Court Act, Art. 3, § § 301.2(1), 320.3, 341.2 and 320.5 (West 2002).
59. *Stanford v. Kentucky,* 492 U.S. 361 (1989).
60. *Estelle v. Gamble,* 429 U.S. 97 (1976).
61. *Youngberg v. Romeo,* 457 U.S. 307 (1982).
62. Ibid., 307.
63. The seven cases are *Doe v. New York City Dept. of Social Services,* 649 F.2d 134 (2d Cir. 1981); *Nicini v. Morra,* 212 F.3d 798 (3d Cir. 2000); *Meador v. Cabinet for Human Resources,* 902 F.2d 474 (6th Cir. 1990); *K.H. ex rel.. Murphy v. Morgan,* 914 F.2d 846 (7th Cir. 1990); *Norfleet v. Arkansas Dept. of Human Services,* 989 F.2d 289 (8th Cir. 1993); *Yvonne L. v. New Mexico Dept of Human Services,* 959 F.2d 883 (10th Cir.); and *Taylor ex rel. Walker v. Ledbetter,* 818 F.2d 791 (11th Cir. 1987).
64. *Milburn v. Anne Arundel County D.S.S.,* 871 F.2d 474 (4th Cir. 1989); *Walton v. Alexander,* 44 F.3d 1297 (5th Cir. 1995). *Walton* involved placement in a state-operated school for deaf children.
65. *Babcock v. Tyler,* 884 F.2d 497 (9th Cir. 1989).
66. Case plans must be in writing and a discrete part of the case record. The statute is specific about plan content, which, among other things, must include "a description of the . . . home or institution [where] the child is to be placed, including a discussion of the appropriateness of the placement. . . . The plan must ensure that the child receives proper care and that services are provided to the parents, child,

and foster parents in order to improve the conditions in the parents' home, facilitate return of the child to his or her own home, or the permanent placement of the child, and addresses the needs of the child while in foster care, including a discussion of the appropriateness of the services that have been provided to the child under the plan" (Adoption Assistance and Child Welfare Act, 42 U.S.C.A. § 675[1] [West 2002]).

67. *Lynch v. Dukakis*, 719 F.2d 504 (1st Cir. 1983); *B.H. v. Johnson*, 715 F. Supp. 1387 (N.D. Ill. 1989); *LaShawn v. Dixon*, 762 F. Supp. 959 (D.D.C. 1991), *aff'd with remand*, 990 F.2d 1319 (1993), *cert. denied*, 510 U.S. 1044 (1994); *Joseph A. v. New Mexico Department of Human Services*, 575 F. Supp. 346 (1983).
68. *Suter v. Artist*, 503 U.S. 347 (1992).
69. Social Security Act Amendments of 1994, Pub. L. No. 103–432, codified at 108 Stat. 4398, 103d Cong., 2d sess., 1994.
70. A right to sue has been supported by courts in *Timothy S. v. Stumbo*, 916 F.2d 312 (6th Cir. 1990); *Brian A. v. Sundquist*, 149 F. Supp. 2d 941 (M.D. Tenn. 2000); § *Marisol A. v. Giuliani*, 929 F. Supp. 662 (S.D.N.Y. 1996); *Norman v. McDonald*, 930 F. Supp. 1219 (N.D. Ill. 1996); *Jeanine B. v. Thompson*, 877 F. Supp. 1268 (E.D. Wis. 1995). The right to sue has not been supported in *Charlie H. and Nadine H. v. Whitman*, 83 F. Supp. 2d 476 (D.N.J. 2000) and *Eric L. v. Bird*, 848 F. Supp. 303 (D.N.H. 1994).

11. ADOPTION

1. Melinda Lucas, "Adoption: Distinguishing Between Gray Market and Black Market Activities," *Family Law Quarterly* 34 (2000): 553–64.
2. Federal Payments for Foster Care and Adoption Assistance, 42 U.S.C.A. § 673(c)(2) (West 2002).
3. Ibid., § § 671(a)(15)(F), 675(5)(C).
4. "Cost of Adopting," *National Adoption Information Clearinghouse*, 2000, http://www.calib.com/naic/pubs (July 14, 2003).
5. *In re* Adoption of Stephen, a Minor, 645 N.Y.S.2d 1012 (N.Y. Fam. Ct. 1996).
6. McKinney's Social Service Law of New York, § 374(6) (West 2002).
7. CT-ST-ANN, Ch. 803. § 45a-727a.
8. See, for example, AL-ST-ANN § 26–10A-5 (West 2001); AZ-ST-ANN § 58–103 (West 2001); CA-ST-ANN § 19–5-202 (West 2002); CT-ST-ANN § 45a-727a (West 2002); DE-ST-ANN§ 903 (West 2001); DC-ST-ANN § 16–302 (West 2002); HI-ST-ANN § 578–1 (West 2001); ID-ST-ANN § 16–1501 (West 2001); ILL-ST-ANN § 50/2 (West 2002); KY-ST-ANN § 199.470 (West 2001); MA-ST-ANN 210 1 (West 2002); MD-ST-ANN § 5–309 (West 2002); MS-ST-ANN § 93–17–3 (West 2001); N.H. § 170-B:4 9West 2002); UT-ST-ANN § 78–30–1 (West 2001).
9. Appellate courts in six states and the District of Columbia have approved adoptions by cohabiting same-sex partners. See *In re* Adoption of Tammy, 416 Mass. 205 (Mass. 1993); *In re* M.M.D. & B.H.M., 662 A.2d 837 (D.C. 1995); *In re* Adoptions of B.L.V.B. and E.L.V.B., 628 A.2d 1271 (Vt. 1993); *In re* Jacob, 636 N.Y.S.2d 716 (N.Y. 1995); *In re* Adoption of Two Children by H.N.R., 666 A.2d 535 (N.J. Super. 1995);

In re Petition of K.M. & D.M., 653 N.E.2d 888 (Ill. App. 1st Dist. 1995). In some states, including Alabama, Alaska, California, Indiana, Iowa, Maryland, Michigan, Minnesota, Nevada, New Mexico, Ohio, Oregon, Rhode Island, Texas, and Washington, such adoptions have been approved at the trial level. Since trial court rulings have no precedential value, an adoption by a cohabiting partner may not be approved by another trial court in the same state.

10. FL-ST-ANN § 63.042(3) (West 2002). The Florida statute is being challenged as unconstitutional. See *Lofton v. Kearney,* 157 F. Supp.2d 1372 (S.D. Fla. 2001).
11. *Matthews v. Weinberg,* 645 So. 2d 487 (Fla. Dist. Ct. App. 1994).
12. Adoption and Safe Families Act, codified in scattered sections of 42 U.S.C. 670 *et seq.* (West 2003). This restriction also applies to those who apply to become foster parents.
13. UT-ST-ANN § 78–30–1 (West 2001).
14. MI-ST-ANN § 93–17–3(2) (West 2001).
15. *In re* Adoption of Meaux, 417 So. 2d 522 (La. App. 3d Cir).
16. *In re* Adoption of Carl, 184 Misc. 2d 646, 709 N.Y.S.2d 905 (N.Y. Fam. Ct. 2000).
17. *In re* Angel Lace M., 516 N.W.2d 678 (Wis. 1994).
18. See *In re* Adoption of C.C.G., 726 A.2d 724 (Pa. Super. Ct. 2000); *In re* Adoption of Baby Z., 724 A.2d 1035 (Conn. 1999); *In re* Adoption of T.K.J. and K.A.K., 931 P.2d 488 (Colo. 1996); *In re* Adoption of Luke, 640 N.W.2d 374 (Neb. 2002).
19. *In re* Adoption of Tammy, 416 Mass. 205 (Mass. 1993).
20. *In re* Christopher F., 701 N.Y.S.2d 171 (N.Y. App. 3d Dept. 1999).
21. PA-ST-ANN § 2711(d)(1) (West 2002).
22. McKinney's Domestic Relations Law of New York, § 115-b(3) (West 2002).
23. *Prince v. Massachusetts,* 321 U.S. 158 (1944); *Pierce v. Society of Sisters,* 268 U.S. 510 (1925); *Meyer v. Nebraska,* 262 U.S. 390 (1923).
24. *Lehr v. Robertson,* 463 U.S. 248 (1983).
25. *Loveheart v. Long,* 762 S.W.2d 32 (Mo. 1988).
26. *Lassiter v. Department of Social Services,* 452 U.S. 18 (1981); *Mathews v. Eldridge,* 424 U.S. 319 (1976).
27. Patricia C. Kussmann, "Right of Indigent Parent to Appointed Counsel in Proceeding for Involuntary Termination of Parental Rights," *American Law Reports—Fifth* 92 (2000): 379–418.
28. McKinney's Social Services Law of New York, § 384-b (West 2002).
29. Mo. Ann. Stat. § 453.040 (West 2002).
30. Mitchell Waldman, "Adoption. § 80. What Constitutes Abandonment, Desertion, or Neglect, Generally," in *American Jurisprudence* (St. Paul, Minn.: West, 2002), 2:1–6.
31. *In re* Adoption of Amy S. S., 486 N.Y.S.2d 912 (N.Y. 1985).
32. *In re* Shandra C. C., 672 N.Y.S.2d 490 (N.Y. App. 3d Dept. 1998).
33. *In re* the Adoption of Dobbs, 531 P.2d 303 (Wash. Ct. App. 1975).
34. *In re* Michael M., 614 A.2d 832 (Conn. App. Ct. 1992); *In re* R.P., 498 N.W.2d 364 (S.D. 1993); *William v. Townsend,* 629 N.E.2d 252 (Ind. App. 5th Dist. 1994).
35. *In re* B.W., 498 So. 2d 946 (Fla. 1986).
36. *Hutson v. Haggard,* 475 S.W.2d 330 (Tex. App. 1971); *In re* Adoption of M.J.H., 501 A.2d 648 (Pa. Super. Ct. 1985), *appeal denied,* 522 A.2d 1105 (Pa. 1987), *appeal dismissed,* 108 S. Ct. 49 (1987).

37. *In re* Adoption of M.D.L., 682 S.W.2d 886 (Mo. Ct. App. 1984).
38. *In re* J.J.J., 718 P.2d 948 (Alaska 1986).
39. *In re* Fletcher, 558 S.E.2d 498 (N.C. Ct. App. 2002).
40. Adoption and Safe Families Act, codified in scattered sections of 42 U.S.C. 670 *et seq.* (West 2003).
41. Elizabeth Trainor, "Sufficiency of Evidence to Establish Parent's Knowledge or Allowance of Child's Sexual Abuse by Another Under Statute Permitting Termination of Parental Rights for 'Allowing' or 'Knowingly Allowing' Such Abuse to Occur," *American Law Reports—Fifth* 53 (1997): 499–529.
42. Waldman, "Adoption," 1–3, § 75.
43. *In re* Erica D., 742 N.Y.S.2d 112 (N.Y. App. 2d Dept. 2002).
44. *Fitzgerald v. Montgomery County Dept. of Social Services,* 2002 WL 17514213 (Va. App. 2002); *In re* S.M.H., 2002 WL 1374508 (Mich. App. 2002); *In re* Aleese W., 2002 WL 1492166 (Conn. Super. 2002); *In re* Shammo, 2002 WL 1173623 (Ohio App. 5th Dist. 2002); *In re* Brianna D., 798 A.2d 413 (R.I. 2002); *State of Tenn. Dept. of Children's Svcs. v. T.S.W.,* 2002 WL 863289 (Tenn. Ct. App. 2002); *In re* I.B., 2002 WL 531924 (Iowa App. 2002); *Francisco G. v. Superior Court,* 110 Cal. Rptr. 2d 679 (Cal. App. 6th Dist. 2001); *C.W. v. State,* 23 P.3d 52 (Alaska 2001); *Wilkins v. Arkansas Dept. of Human Services,* 2001 WL 419201 (Ark. App. 2001); *J.B. v. State,* 2001 WL 311172 (Utah App. 2001).
45. Mary E. Taylor, "Parent's Use of Drugs as Factor in Award of Custody of Children, Visitation Rights, or Termination of Parental Rights," *American Law Reports—Fifth* (1994): 534–701.
46. Adoption and Safe Families Act, codified in scattered sections of 42 U.S.C. §670 *et seq.* (West 2003). (West 2002). The reasons for not filing a termination petition must be case specific. The pursuit of adoption is not mandated (1) for children who are in the care of a relative, (2) for children for whom the state can justify in writing why it is not in the child's best interests to pursue adoption, (3) for children on whose behalf the state has not made the required reasonable efforts to reunite the family, (4) where the state has no grounds to file a termination petition, or (5) where the minor's status in the United States is affected by immigration law or international law (45 C.F.R. § 1356.21 (2003). In addition, a court may order (6) a plan of emancipation when requested by an older teen, (7) an alternative plan for a child who has a significant bond to a parent who is not able to care for the child because of an emotional or physical disability, (8) a plan of long-term care where a foster parent is willing to raise the child and facilitate visitation with the parent; or (9) an alternative plan where a tribe has identified an alternative for a native child (45 C.F.R. § 1356.21 [2003]).
47. U.S. Department of Health and Human Services, Administration for Children, Youth and Families, "Final Rule—Title IV-E Adoption Assistance Program; Nonrecurring Expenses," 1988.
48. Adoption Opportunities Act, 42 U.S.C.A. § 5111 (West 2002), as amended by the Keeping Children and Families Safe Act, Pub. L. No. 108–36, 117 Stat. 800, 108th Cong., 1st sess., 2003. Eligible children were receiving Aid to Families with Dependent Children in July 1996, or are current recipients of Supplemental Security Income, or are in foster care and supported financially by the Title IV-E program (see chapter 9).

49. Jeanette W. Bower and Rita Laws, *Support for Families of Children with Special Needs: A Policy Analysis of Adoption Subsidy Programs in the United States* (St. Paul, Minn.: North American Council on Adoptable Children, 2002).
50. *Drummond v. Fulton County Department of Family and Children's Services,* 563 F.2d 1200 (5th Cir. 1977), *cert. denied,* 437 U.S. 910 (1977); Suzanne B. Campbell, "Taking Race Out of the Equation: Transracial Adoption in 2000," *Southern Methodist University Law Review* 53 (2000): 1599–1626.
51. "Transracial Adoption," *National Adoption Information Clearinghouse,* 2002, http://www.calib.com/naic/pubs (July 14, 2003).
52. Multiethnic Placement Act, Pub. L. No. 103–382, 108 Stat. 4056 (1994).
53. Adoption Promotion and Stability Act, 42 U.S.C.A. § 671 (West 2002).
54. Indian Child Welfare Act, 25 U.S.C.A. § 1914 (West 2002).
55. *Mississippi Band of Choctaw Indians v. Holyfield,* 490 U.S. 30 (1989).
56. Burton Z. Sokoloff, "Antecedents of American Adoption," *Future of Children* 3, no. 1 (1993): 21, citing J. H. Hollinger, ed., "Aftermath of Adoption: Legal and Social Consequences," in *Adoption Law and Practice* (New York: Mathew Bender, 1991), 13.
57. *People v. Doe,* 138 N.Y.S.2d 307, 309 (N.Y. County Ct. 1955).
58. Kristine C. Karnezis, "Restricting Access to Judicial Records of Concluded Adoption Proceedings," *American Law Reports* 83 (2000): 468–78.
59. AK-ST-ANN § 18.50.500 (West 2001); KS-ST-ANN § 59–2122 (West 2001).
60. Heidi Hildebrand, "Because They Want to Know: An Examination of the Legal Rights of Adoptees and Their Parents," *Southern Illinois University Law Journal* 24 (2000): 515–40.
61. National Adoption Information Clearinghouse, "Adoption Laws: Confidentiality," http://www.calib.com/naic/pubs (July 14, 2003).
62. McKinney's Social Service Law of New York, § 383-c (West 2002); NE-ST-ANN § 43–155 *et seq*. (2001).
63. See, for example, WA-ST-ANN § 26.33.295 (West 2002); OR-ST-ANN § 109.308 (West 2001); CA-ST-ANN § 8714.7 (West 2002); Conn. Gen. Stat. Ann. § 17a-112 (West 2002).
64. CA-ST-ANN § 8714.7 (West 2002).
65. WA-ST-ANN § 26.33.295 (West 2002).
66. *Hill v. Moorman,* 525 So. 2d 681 (La. App. 1st Cir. 1988).
67. *In re* Ronald D., 673 N.Y.S.2d 559 (N.Y. Fam. Ct. 1998).
68. *Michaud v. Wawruck,* 551 A.2d 738 (Conn. 1988); *Weinschel v. Srople,* 466 A.2d 1301 (Md. Ct. Spec. App. 1983).
69. Elizabeth Bartholet, "International Adoption: Current Status and Future Prospects," *Future of Children* 3, no. 1 (1993): 89–103.
70. Ibid., 96.
71. U.S. Department of Justice. *Statistical Yearbook of the Immigration and Naturalization Service* (Washington, D.C.: U.S. Government Printing Office, 1999), table 15.
72. Aliens and Nationality Act, 8 U.S.C.A. § 1101 *et seq*. (West 2002).
73. Nationality Through Naturalization Act, 8 U.S.C.A. § 1431 (West 2002).
74. Hague Convention on the Protection of Children and Cooperation in Respect to Intercountry Adoptions, 32 I.L.M. 1211 (1993).
75. U.S. Immigration and Naturalization Service, "Information Sheet Regarding the Intercountry Adoption Act of 2000," http://www.bcis.gov/graphics/index.htm (July 14, 2003).

76. National Adoption Information Clearinghouse. 2001. Summary of Laws Regarding International Adoptions Finalized Abroad 50 States and 6 United States Territories. available at www.calib.com/naic/pubs (July 14, 2003).
77. See Surrogate Parenting Services, Inc., "Estimated Cost of Surrogacy," 2002, http://www.surrogateparenting.com (March 10, 2003); Surrogate Mothers International, "Surrogacy Solutions," 2002, http://www.surrogate-solutions.com (March 10, 2003).
78. Angie G. McEwen, "So You're Having Another Woman's Baby: Economics and Exploitation in Gestational Surrogacy," *Vanderbilt Journal of Transnational Law* 32 (1999): 271–304; Christin E. Kerian, "Surrogacy: A Last Resort Alternative for Infertile Women or a Commodification of Women's Bodies and Children?" *Wisconsin Women's Law Journal* 12 (1997): 113–66.
79. Ala. Code § 26–10A-34(c) (West 2000); Ariz. Rev. Stat. Ann. § 25–218 (West 2000); Ark. Code Ann. § 9–10–201 (West 1999); D.C. Code Ann. § 16–402 (Michie 1998); Fla. Stat. Ann. §§ 742.15, 742.16 (West 2000); Ill. Stat. Ann. § 45/6 (West 2000); Ind. Code Ann. §§ 31–20–1-1 to 20–3 (West 2000); Iowa Code § 710.11 (West 2000); Ky. Rev. Stat. Ann. § 199.590(4) (West 2000); La. Rev. Stat. Ann. § 9:2713 (West 2000); Mich. Comp. Laws Ann. § 722.855 (West 2000); Neb. Rev. Stat. § 25–21, 200 (West 2000); Nev. Rev. Stat. Ann. § 126.045 (West 2000); N.H. Rev. Stat. Ann. § 168-B: 16 (West 2000); N.Y. Dom. Rel. Law §§ 122, 123 (McKinney 1999); N.D. Cent. Code § 14–18–05 (West 1999); Utah Code Ann. § 76–7-204 (West 2000); Va. Code Ann. § 20–159 (West 2000); Wash. Rev. Code Ann. §§ 26.26.230 *et seq*. (West 2000); W. Va. Code § 48–4-16 (West 2000).
80. See Task Force on Life and the Law, *Assisted Reproductive Technologies: Analysis and Recommendations for Public Policy* (Albany: New York State Department of Health, 1998); Ardis L. Campbell, "Determination of Status as Legal or Natural Parents in Contested Surrogacy Births," *American Law Reports—Fifth* 77 (2000): 567.
81. *In re* Baby M., 537 A.2d 1227 (N.J. 1988). The court noted that a surrogacy arrangement would be acceptable if a woman entered into it voluntarily and without payment. However, the law could not bind her to surrender her child.
82. *Johnson v. Calvert,* 5 Cal. 4th 84, 851 P.2d 776 (Cal. 1993), *cert. denied,* 510 U.S. 874 (1995).
83. Ibid., 851 P.2d at 782.
84. *In re* Marriage of Buzzanca, 72 Cal. Rptr. 2d 280 (Cal. App. 4th Dist. 1998).
85. *McDonald v. McDonald* 608 N.Y.S.2d 477 (A.D.2 Dept. 1994).
86. *Belsito v. Clark,* 644 N.E.2d 760 (Ohio Ct. Com. Pl. 1994).

12. DOMESTIC VIOLENCE

1. Justice Research and Statistics Association, *Domestic and Sexual Violence Data Collection: A Report to Congress Under the Violence Against Women Act* (Washington, D.C.: National Institute of Justice, Bureau of Justice Statistics, 1996), 9–10.
2. Ibid.
3. U.S. General Accounting Office, *Violence Against Women: Data on Pregnant Victims and Effectiveness of Prevention Strategies Are Limited.* Report GAO-02–530 (Washington, D.C.: U.S. General Accounting Office), 4.

4. The lower figure was reported by Carey Goldberg, citing Department of Justice statistics, in "Spouse Abuse Crackdown, Surprisingly, Nets Many Women," *New York Times,* November 23, 1999, pp. 16A. The figure of four million is found in Maurice Goldman, "The Violence Against Women Act: Meeting Its Goal in Protecting Battered Women," *Family and Conciliation Courts Review* (1999): 375–85.
5. Callie Marie Rennison and Sarah Welchans, *Intimate Partner Violence* (Washington, D.C.: U.S. Department of Justice, Bureau of Justice Statistics, 2000).
6. Family Violence Prevention and Services Act, 42 U.S.C.A. § 10401 *et seq.* (West 2002), as amended by Pub. L. No. 108–36, 108th Cong., 1st sess., June 2003.
7. Codified at 42 U.S.C.A. § 10601 *et seq.* (West 2002).
8. The VAWA was enacted as Title IV of the Violent Crime Control and Law Enforcement Act of 1994, Pub. L. No. 103–322, 103d Cong., 2d sess., 108 Stat. 1796, and reauthorized in 2000.
9. Codified at 18 U.S.C.A. § 2261 (West 2002).
10. Ibid., §§ 2265, 2266.
11. *Kuhn v. Kuhn,* 1998 WL 673629 (N.D. Ill. 1998), *aff'd,* 1999 WL 519326 (N.D. Ill. 1999).
12. *United States v. Morrison,* 529 U.S. 598 (2000).
13. Darold W. Killmer and Mari Newman, "VAWA: A Civil Rights Tool for Victims of Gender-Motivated Violence," *Colorado Lawyer* 28 (1999): 77–81.
14. *State v. Daniel T.,* 95 Misc. 2d 639, 641 (N.Y. Crim. Ct., Kings County 1978).
15. In 1984 the New York Court of Appeals, the state's highest court, became the first court in the nation to eliminate the marital rape exemption. See *People v. Liberta,* 485 N.Y.S.2d 207 (1984), *cert. denied, Liberta v. New York,* 471 U.S. 1020 (1985).
16. *State v. Daniel T.,* 95 Misc. 2d at 641.
17. Catherine F. Klein and Leslye E. Orloff, "Providing Legal Protection for Battered Women: An Analysis of State Statutes and Case Law," *Hofstra Law Review* 21 (1993): 801–1189.
18. Assault and harassment are defined in McKinney's New York Penal Law, with the former at § 120.05 and the latter at § 240.25. Provisions for mandatory arrest are found in the McKinney's New York Criminal Procedure Law, § 140.10.
19. McKinney's New York Criminal Procedure Law, § 140.10.
20. Ibid., § 140.10(4).
21. Douglas J. Besharov, 1998. "Practice Commentary," McKinney's New York's Family Court Act § 168 (West 2002).
22. *Brown v. Grabowski et al.,* 922 F.2d 1097 (3d Cir. 1991), *cert. denied,* 501 U.S. 1218 (1991). See also *Thurman v. City of Torrington,* 595 F. Supp. 1521 (D.C. Conn. 1984). In this case a wife established a violation of the equal protection clause of the U.S. Constitution. She alleged that the city and its police officers classified domestic violence differently than similar crimes perpetrated by strangers, resulting in full protection to women abused by strangers but less protection when the woman was abused by her spouse or boyfriend.
23. Conciliation services are required by McKinney's New York Family Court Act, FCA § 915 *et seq.* (West 2002).
24. McKinney's New York Criminal Procedure § 530.11 (West 2002).
25. Disorderly conduct is defined in McKinney's New York Penal Law at § 240.20 and assault at McKinney's New York Penal Law § 120.05.

26. McKinney's New York Family Court Act § 821 (West 2002).
27. *Houck v. Garroway,* 293 A.D.2d 782 (N.Y. App. 3d Dept. 2002).
28. McKinney's New York Family Court Act § 821 (West 2002).
29. McKinney's New York Family Court Act, § 821-a(5)(a) (West 2002).
30. McKinney's New York Criminal Procedure Law § 530.11 (West 2002).
31. McKinney's New York Family Court Act § 828(2) West 2002.
32. McKinney's New York Family Court Act § 828(3) (West 2002).
33. McKinney's New York Family Court Act § 841, 842 (West 2002).
34. McKinney's New York Family Court Act § 842 (West 2002).
35. McKinney's New York Family Court Act § 847 (West 2002).
36. McKinney's New York Family Court Act § 846 (West 2002).
37. McKinney's New York Family Court Act § 155(1), 168(1) (West 2002).
38. McKinney's New York Family Court Act § 847 (West 2002).
39. McKinney's New York Family Court Act § 846, 846-a (West 2002).
40. Henry C. Black, *Black's Law Dictionary,* 7th ed. (St. Paul, Minn.: West, 1999), http://www.westlaw.com.
41. *Krank v. Krank,* 529 N.W.2d 844 (N.D. 1995).
42. Ibid.
43. Ibid., 849.
44. Ibid.
45. *Simmons v. Simmons,* 649 So. 2d 799 (La. App. 2 Cir. 1995).
46. *Hamilton v. Hamilton,* 866 S.W.2d 711 (Mo. App. W.D. 1994).
47. Louisiana Revised Statutes, § 9:364 Child Custody, Visitation. (West 2002).
48. Advisory Committee, *Model Code on Domestic and Family Violence—Sec. 403. Presumption Concerning Residence of Child* (Reno, Nev.: National Council of Juvenile and Family Court Judges, 1994).
49. *J.D. v. N.D.,* 170 Misc. 2d 877, 652 N.Y.S.2d 468 (N.Y. Fam. Ct. Westchester County 1996).
50. Ibid.
51. *Carstens v. Carstens,* 867 P.2d 805 (Alaska 1994).
52. *Canty v. Canty,* 874 P.2d 1000 (Ariz. App. Div. 1 1994).
53. Lois A. Weithorn, "Protecting Children from Exposure to Domestic Violence: The Use and Abuse of Child Maltreatment," *Hastings Law Journal* 53 (2001): 1–153.
54. See, for example: AK-ST-ANN § 47.17.035 (West 2002); CT-ST-ANN § 17a-106b (West 2002); CA-ST-ANN § 1037.3. (West 2002).
55. MN-ST-ANN § 626.556 (West 2002).
56. Weithorn, "Protecting Children from Exposure."
57. *Nicholson v. Williams,* 203 F. Supp. 2d 153, 196 (E.D.N.Y. 2002).
58. *In re* Doe, 2002 WL 31513378 (Haw. 2002); *In re* G.S., 2002 WL 31491370 (Mont. 2002); *In re* S.O., 126 Cal. Rptr. 2d 554 (Cal. App. 4th Dist. 2002); *State ex rel. C.J.K.,* 774 So. 2d 107 (La. 2000); *Nicholson v. Williams.*
59. *Nicholson v Williams.*
60. Ibid., 205.
61. Statistics compiled by the FBI show that in 2000, the majority of hate crimes involved racial bias (more than 4 million), with crimes directed against blacks numbering more than 2.8 million, compared to crimes involving religious bias (more than 1.4 million); sexual-orientation bias (1.3 million); and ethnicity bias

(911,000). See "FBI Overview," Anti-Defamation League, http://www.adl.org/seach/query.asp (March 10, 2003).

62. Dan Hasenstab, "Is Hate a Form of Commerce? The Questionable Constitutionality of Federal 'Hate Crime' Legislation," *St. Louis University Law Journal* 45 (2001): 973–1017.
63. Crimes and Criminal Procedure—Civil Rights, 18 U.S.C.A. § 245 (West 2002).
64. Hate Crimes Statistics Act, —42 U.S.C.A. § 14503 *et seq.* (West 2003).
65. The Local Law Enforcement Enhancement Act (LLEEA) (a.k.a. the Hate Crimes Prevention Act) amended federal law to include gender-motivated crime as a bias crime and sanctioned federal prosecution for bias crimes based on gender, sexual orientation, and disability. See 148 Cong. Rec. S11308–01, 2002 WL 31548659 (2002), Proceedings and Debates of the 107th Cong., 2d sess., November 18, 2002. Earlier versions include the Hate Crimes Prevention Act of 2000, S2783 106th Cong., 2d sess., June 2000, and HR 2670, 106th Cong., 1st sess., 1999.
66. The Violence Against Women Act of 1993, 103d Cong., 1st sess., S. Rept. 138, 1993 WL 355167 (1993).
67. *Wisconsin v. Mitchell,* 508 U.S. 476 (1993).
68. Hate crimes laws may be applicable statewide or confined to a local unit of government. State-by-state information is available from the Anti-Defamation League at http://www.adl.org/seach/query.asp (July 15, 2003)
69. Marguerite Angelari, "Hate Crime Statutes: A Promising Tool for Fighting Violence Against Women," *American University Journal of Gender and the Law* 2 (1994): 63–105.
70. Julie Goldscheid, "Gender-Motivated Violence: Developing a Meaningful Paradigm for Civil Rights Enforcement," *Harvard Women's Law Journal* 22 (1999): 123–41; Julie Goldscheid and Risa E. Kaufman, "Seeking Redress for Gender-Based Bias Crimes—Charting New Ground in Familiar Legal Territory," *Michigan Journal of Race and Law* 6 (2001): 265–83.
71. CA-ST-ANN § 422.75(I)(1) (West 2002).
72. McKinney's Penal Law of New York, § 485.05 (West 2002).
73. "Violence Against Women Act." S. Rept. 103–138, 103d Cong. 1st sess., September 1993, 1993 WL 355617 (1993).
74. *Ziegler v. Ziegler,* 28 F. Supp. 2d 601, 607 (E.D. Wash. 1998). *Ziegler* was decided under Title III of the Violence Against Women Act, which, as noted, has been ruled unconstitutional by the U.S. Supreme Court. Nevertheless, the analytic approach taken by the Court is illustrative of how a court determined whether gender motivated domestic violence.
75. Seymour Moskowitz, "Saving Granny from the Wolf: Elder Abuse and Neglect—The Legal Framework," *Connecticut Law Review* 31 (1998): 77–164.
76. See, for example, FL-ST-ANN § 415.102(1) and (26) (West 2002). "Vulnerable adults" are people aged eighteen and older who are disabled to a degree that prevents them from performing the normal activities of daily living or from providing for their own care or protection due to a mental, emotional, physical, or developmental disability or dysfunction, or brain damage, or the infirmities of aging. For a further example, see McKinney's Social Service Law of New York, § 473 (West 2001).

77. Toshio Tatara et al., *The National Elder Abuse Incidence Study* (Washington, D.C.: American Public Human Services Association and Westat, 1998), 1–20.
78. The U.S. General Accounting Office has conducted several studies that address the issue of abuse in nursing homes. See the following reports from the U.S. General Accounting Office: *Nursing Homes: More Can Be Done to Protect Residents from Abuse*. Report GAO-02–312 (Washington, D.C.: U.S. General Accounting Office, 2002); *Nursing Homes: Sustained Efforts Are Essential to Realize Potential of the Quality Initiatives.* GAO/HEHS-00–197 (Washington, D.C.: U.S. General Accounting Office, 2000); *Nursing Homes: Complaint Investigation Processes Often Inadequate to Protect Residents.* GAO/HEHS-99–80 (Washington, D.C.: U.S. General Accounting Office, 1999); *Nursing Homes: Additional Steps Needed to Strengthen Enforcement of Federal Quality Standards.* GAO/HEHS-99–46 (Washington, D.C.: U.S. General Accounting Office, 1999).
79. Activities of the House Select Committee on Aging, H.R. Rep. No. 997, 101st Cong., 2d sess., 1990, 1990 WL 252123 (1990).
80. Definitions are found in the Older Americans Act, 42 U.S.C.A. § 3002 (2003), with abuse defined at 3002(13)(A)(B); neglect at 3002(34)(A)(B); and exploitation at 3002(24). For state definitions see Moskowitz, "Saving Granny from The Wolf."
81. Older Americans Act, 42 U.S.C.A. § 3002(20) (West 2002).
82. Ibid., 42 U.S.C.A. § 3058 *et seq.*
83. Ibid., 42 U.S.C.A. § 3003 *et seq.*
84. Title XX—Block Grants to the States for Social Services, 42 U.S.C.A. § 1397a(a)(2)(A) (West 2002).
85. Older Americans Act, 42 U.S.C.A. § 3058i.
86. CA-ST-ANN § 15610.10 (West 2002).
87. New York Code of Rules and Regulations, § 457.6 (West 2002).
88. Federal law regulates the operation of nursing homes that receive Medicare and Medicaid funding under the Nursing Home Reform Act of 1987, enacted as part of the Omnibus Budget Reconciliation Act of that year. Regulations are found at 42 C.F.R. § 483.5 *et seq.* (West 2002).
89. U.S. General Accounting Office, *Nursing Homes: More Can Be Done.*
90. Supplemental Security Income, 42 U.S.C.A. § 1382e (West 2002). Regarding regulations, see 48 FR 54184–01 (November 30, 1983) and 1995 WL 293977 (1995).
91. Formerly, the Health Care Financing Administration.
92. Other rights include the right to (1) privacy with regard to accommodations, medical treatment, written and telephonic communications, visits, and meetings of family and of resident groups; (2) confidentiality of personal and clinical records and access to clinical records; and (3) voice grievances with respect to treatment or care without discrimination or reprisal for voicing the grievances and the right to prompt efforts by the facility to resolve grievances that concern the behavior of other residents. See Administration on Aging, http://www.aoa.dhhs.gov/factsheets/ombudsman.htm (March 10, 2003).
93. Older Americans Act, 42 U.S.C.A. § 3058g.
94. See, for example, WA-ST-ANN § 11.88.005 (West 2002); WI-ST-ANN § 880.33 (West 2002); IL-ST-ANN, CH 755 § 5/11a-12 (West 2002).
95. McKinney's Social Service Law of New York State, § 473-d(a) (West 2002).

96. Ibid., § 473-d(2)(a)-(c) (West 2002).
97. See, for example: AR-ST-ANN 28–65–204 (West 2002); IN-ST-ANN 29–3-5–4 (West 2002); NH-ST-ANN 464-A:10 (West 2002); MO-ST-ANN 475.055 (West 2002).
98. National Conference of Commissioners on Uniform State Laws, Uniform Guardianship and Protective Proceedings Act, 1997, http://www.nccusl.org (January 12, 2003).
99. McKinney's Laws of New York State. Mental Hygiene Law, § 81.03. (West 2002).
100. Ibid., § 81.09–81.10. (West 2002).
101. Ibid., Art. 81. Proceedings for Appointment of a Guardian (West 2002).
102. Rules regarding retirement benefits are found at 20 C.F.R. § 404.2001 (2002), and those regarding SSI are found at 20 C.F.R. § 416.601 (2002).
103. Ibid.

13. LEGAL ISSUES IN HEALTH CARE

1. U.S. Census Bureau, "Health Insurance Coverage—2001." *Current Population Survey: Annual Demographic Supplements*. Washington, D.C.: U.S. Government Printing Office, 2002.
2. Theodore J. Stein, *Social Policy and Policymaking by the Branches of Government and the Public-at-Large* (New York: Columbia University Press, 2001), chap. 12.
3. The legislation includes (1) the Ganske-Dingell Bill, H.R. 526; (2) the McCain-Edwards Bill, S.B. 1052; (3) the Ganske-Dingell-Norwood-Berry Bill, H.R. 2563; and (4) the House GOP Bill, H.R. 2315.
4. Robin Cheryl Miller, "Construction and Application of State Patient Bill of Rights Statutes," *American Law Reports—Fifth* 87 (2001): 277–326. The rights of a person who is mentally ill may be limited when a physician determines that harm may result from the exercise of a particular right. See Texas Administrative Code, § 404.151 *et seq.* (West 2002).
5. *In re* Involuntary Discharge or Transfer of J.S., 512 N.W.2d 604 (Minn. Ct. App. 1994).
6. *Scherer v. Waterbury*, 2002 WL 254535 (Conn. Super. Ct. 2000), unpublished.
7. Cal. Health and Safety Code, § 1374.16 (West 2002).
8. *Maher v. Roe*, 432 U.S. 464 (1977); *Harris v. McRae*, 448 U.S. 297 (1980).
9. *Westside Mothers v. Haveman*, 2002 WL 987291 (6th Cir. 2002).
10. Emergency Medical Treatment and Active Labor Act, 42 U.S.C.A. § 1395dd (West 2002).
11. *Bragdon v. Abbott*, 524 U.S. 624 (1998).
12. Medicare is found at 42 U.S.C.A. §§ 1395 *et seq.* (West 2002) and Medicaid at 42 U.S.C.A. § 1396 *et seq.* (West 2002).
13. U.S. Census Bureau, "Health Insurance Coverage."
14. *Harris v. McRae*, 448 U.S. 297 (1980).
15. Social Security—General Provisions, Peer Review, and Administrative Simplification, 42 U.S.C.A. § 1320c-5 (West 2002) and Medicaid, 42 U.S.C.A. § 1396b (West 2002).

16. U.S. Department of Health & Human Services, "Medically Necessary Services," 2003, http://www.ahrq.gov/chip/text/content/workshop_materials/leddy6OHD/tsld011.htm (July 17, 2003).
17. Medicare, 42 U.S.C.A. § 1395y (West 2002).
18. Regarding mammograms, see Medicare, 42 U.S.C.A. § 1395m(c)(2) (West 2002) and for prostate cancer tests see 42 U.S.C.A. § 1395x(oo) (West 2002).
19. Omnibus Consolidated and Emergency Supplemental Appropriations Act of 1999, Pub. L. No. 105–277, §§ 508(a), 509(a), 112 Stat. 2681 (1998).
20. *Harris v. McRae.*
21. Personal Responsibility and Work Opportunity Reconciliation Act of 1996, Pub. L. No. 104–193, 110 Stat. 2105 (1996, codified in scattered sections of Titles 8 and 42 of the U.S. Code).
22. Qualified aliens include those (a) lawfully admitted for permanent residence (holders of green cards), (b) granted political asylum, (c) certain refugees, and (d) victims who were battered or who suffered extreme cruelty at the hands of family members and who entered the United States before August 22, 1996. Those entering on or after this date, except for refugees, asylum seekers, veterans, and active military personnel and certain of their family members, are not eligible until five years after entry.
23. Aliens and Nationality—Restricting Welfare and Public Benefits for Aliens, 8 U.S.C.A. §§ 1611(b)(1)(A) and (C), 1641(c) (West 2002).
24. John Caher, "Legal Resident Aliens Win Medicaid Dispute; Statute Violated Federal and State Constitutions," *New York Law Journal* 225, no. 108 (June 6, 2001): 1.
25. *Aliessa v. Novello,* 96 N.Y.2d 418, 754 N.E.2d 1085 (N.Y. 2000).
26. *Lewis v. Thompson,* 252 F.3d 567 (2d Cir. 2001). This suit was filed in 1979 after the Department of Health, Education, and Welfare (predecessor to Health and Human Services) issued regulations denying Medicaid to any alien not a permanent resident. In 1987 the U.S. Court of Appeals for the Second Circuit enjoined the state of New York from denying benefits to certain legally admitted aliens. The action was amended after PRWORA was passed to encompass plaintiffs' claim under the new law.
27. *Cruzan v. Director, Missouri Dept. of Health,* 497 U.S. 261, 268 (1990).
28. *Zinermon v. Burch,* 494 U.S. 113 (1990).
29. John H. Derrick, "Medical Malpractice: Liability for Failure of Physician to Inform Patient of Alternative Modes of Diagnosis or Treatment," *American Law Reports—Fourth* 38 (1885): 900–24.
30. *Adams v. Richland Clinic, Inc., P.S.,* 37 Wash. App. 650, 681 P.2d 1305 (Wash. Ct. App. 1984).
31. *In re* Claire C. Conroy, 98 N.J. 321, 486 A.2d 1209 (N.J. 1985).
32. *In re* Yetter, 62 Pa. D. & C.2d 619, 620 (Pa. Com. Pl. 1973).
33. *Schaefer v. Schaefer,* 183 Or. App. 513, 517, 52 P.3d 1125 (Or. Ct. App. 2002).
34. *Lane v. Candura,* 6 Mass. App. Ct. 377 (Mass. App. Ct. 1978), 376 N.E.2d 1232 (Mass. App. Ct. 1978).
35. *Lane v. Candura,* 6 Mass. App. Ct. 377, 382 (Mass. App. Ct. 1978).
36. *Superintendent of Belchertown State School v. Saikewicz,* 373 Mass. 728, 370 N.E.2d 417 (Mass. 1977).

37. *Fosmire v. Nicoleau,* 75 N.Y.2d 218, 551 N.E.2d 77 (N.Y. 1990).
38. McKinney's Public Health Law of New York, § 2164(9) (West 2002).
39. *In re* Christine M., 157 Misc. 2d 4, 595 N.Y.S.2d 606 (N.Y. Fam. Ct. 1992).
40. *Fosmire v. Nicoleau.*
41. Robin Cheryl Miller, "Damage Action for HIV Testing Without Consent of Person Tested," *American Law Reports* 77 (2000): 541–68.
42. *Cruzan v. Director, Missouri Dept. of Health,* 497 U.S. 261 (1990).
43. Kristine C. Karnezis, "Patient's Right to Refuse Treatment Allegedly Necessary to Sustain Life," *American Law Reports—Third* 93 (1979): 67–101.
44. *Fosmire v. Nicoleau.*
45. *In re* Karen Quinlan, 70 N.J. 10, 355 A.2d 647 (N.J. 1976), *cert. denied, sub nom., Garger v. New Jersey,* 429 U.S. 922 (1976), *overruled for other reasons, In re* Claire C. Conroy, *98 N.J. 321, 486 A.2d 1209 (N.J. 1985).*
46. *In re* Quinlan, 70 N.J. at 13.
47. *In re* Conroy.
48. Ibid., 486 A.2d at 1229.
49. Ibid., 1238.
50. Ibid., 1224.
51. *Vacco v. Quill,* 521 U.S. 793 (1997). See also *Washington v. Glucksberg,* 521 U.S. 702 (1997).
52. See, for example, 755 ILCS 40/25 (West 2002).
53. MD-ST-ANN § 5–605 (West 2002).
54. Ibid.
55. See, for example, Medicare, 42 U.S.C.A. § 1395cc(f)(3) (West 2002); MD-ST-ANN § 5–602 (West 2002); NM-ST-ANN § 24–7A-1 (West 2002).
56. Medicare provisions are found in 42 U.S.C.A. § 1395cc(f)(1)(A)–(E) (West 2002) and Medicaid provisions in 42 U.S.C.A. § 1396a(w)(1)(A)–(E) (West 2002).
57. Steven M. Ratner, 2001. "Revisiting Health Care Proxies and Living Wills," *New York Law Journal* 226, no. 117 (December 18, 2001): 6–7.
58. The National Conference of Commissioners on Uniform State Laws, Uniform Health Care Decisions Act, http://www.nccusl.org (January 10, 2003).
59. McKinney's Public Health Law of New York. Health Care Proxy Law. § 2980 *et seq.* (West 2002).
60. AL-ST-ANN § 22–8A-2 West 2002; ME-ST-ANN, Part II, Title II, Ch. 201D (West 2002); OKL-ST-ANN. § 3101.2 (West 2002).
61. David A. Berek, "The Nuts and Bolts of the Health Care Power of Attorney," *Chicago Bar Association Record* § 14 (2000): 28.
62. *Prince v. Massachusetts,* 321 U.S. 158 (1944).
63. *In re* Custody of a Minor, 375 Mass. 733, 379 N.E.2d 1053 (Mass. 1978).
64. Angela R. Holder, "Circumstances Warranting Court-Ordered Medical Treatment of Minors," in *American Jurisprudence* (St. Paul, Minn.: West, 2002), 24:169.
65. FL-ST-ANN § 39.01(29) (West 2002); 42 Pa. C.S.A. § 6357 (West 2002); NH-ST-ANN § 169-C:3 (West 2002).
66. *Department of Children and Family Services v. G.M.,* 816 So. 2d 830 (Fl. Dist. Ct. App. 2002).
67. GA-ST-ANN § 31–9-2 (West 2002); MI-ST-ANN § 400.66h (West 2002).

68. *In re* Nicholas E., 720 A.2d 562, 1998 Me. 243 (Me. 1998).
69. *A.D.H. v. State Department of Human Resources,* 640 So. 2d 969, 971 (Ala. Civ. App. 1994).
70. Vocational Rehabilitation Act, 29 U.S.C.A. § 794 (West 2002).
71. *Bowen v. American Hospital Ass'n,* 476 U.S. 610, 647 (1986).
72. Child Abuse Prevention and Treatment Act, 42 U.S.C.A. §§ 5106a, 5106g (West 2002), and Child Abuse and Neglect Prevention and Treatment, 45 C.F.R. Pt. 1340, App. (West 2002)
73. *Craig v. State,* 220 Md. 590, 155 A.2d 684 (Md. Ct. Spec. App. 1959).
74. *Eversley v. State,* 748 So. 2d 963 (Fla. 1999).
75. *Prince v. Massachusetts,* 321 U.S. 158 (1944); *Wisconsin v. Yoder,* 406 U.S. 205 (1972).
76. *Jehovah's Witnesses of Washington v. King County Hospital,* 278 F. Supp. 488 (W.D. Wash. 1968), *aff'd,* 390 U.S. 598 (1968).
77. *Newmark v. Williams,* 588 A.2d 1108 (Del. 1991).
78. Ibid., 1110.
79. Jennifer L. Rosato, "Let's Get Real: Quilting a Principled Approach to Adolescent Empowerment in Health Care Decision Making," *DePaul Law Review* 51 (2002): 769–803.
80. *Bellotti v. Baird,* 443 U.S. 622 (1979); *Hodgson v. Minnesota,* 497 U.S. 417 (1990); *Planned Parenthood of Southeastern Pennsylvania v. Casey,* 505 U.S. 833 (1992).
81. *Ex parte* Anonymous, 803 So. 2d 542 (Ala. 2002).
82. Alice M. Wright, "What Voluntary Acts of Child, Other Than Marriage or Entry into Military Service, Terminate Parent's Obligation to Support?" *American Law Reports* 55 (1998): 557–89.
83. Carolyn O. O'Connor, "Illinois Adolescents' Rights to Confidential Health Care," *Illinois Bar Journal* 82 (1994): 24.
84. McKinney's Mental Hygiene Law of New York, § 22.11 Treatment of Minors. (West 2002).
85. *In re* J.J., 64 Ohio App. 3d 806, 582 N.E.2d 1138 (Ohio Ct. App. 1990).
86. *Rosebush v. Oakland County Prosecutor,* 195 Mich. App. 675, 491 N.W.2d 633 (Mich. Ct. App. 1992).

14. MENTAL HEALTH AND THE LAW

1. Surgeon General of the United States, "Mental Health," 2000, http://www.surgeongeneral.gov (January 28, 2003).
2. Ibid., 419.
3. Employee Retirement Income Security Program, 29 U.S.C.A. § 1185a (West 2002); Health Insurance Portability and Accountability Act, 42 U.S.C.A. § 300gg-5 (West 2002). See U.S. General Accounting Office, *Mental Health Parity Act: Despite New Federal Standards, Mental Health Benefits Remain Limited.* Report GAO/HEHS-00–95 (Washington, D.C.: U.S. General Accounting Office, 2000).
4. For a discussion of the constitutional protections for voluntary patients, see Michelle M. Hughes, "Rights of Mentally Impaired Persons," in *American Jurisprudence* (St. Paul, Minn.: West, 2003), 53:93–98, sec. 93.

5. Henry C. Black, *Black's Law Dictionary*, 7th ed. (St. Paul, Minn.: West, 1999), http://www. westlaw.com.
6. See, for example, CO-ST-ANN § 27–10–105 (West 2002); DC-ST-ANN § 21–523 (West 2002); FL-ST-ANN § 394.463(1) (West 2002); HI-ST-ANN § 334–59 (West 2002); MA-ST-ANN § 123.12 (West 2002); McKinney's New York Mental Hygiene Law, § 9.31 (West 2002).
7. FL-ST-ANN § 394.463(2)(a) (West 2002).
8. *Heller v. Doe*, 509 U.S. 312 (1993).
9. Joshua Cook, "Good Lawyering and Bad Role Models: The Role of Respondent's Counsel in a Civil Commitment Hearing," *Georgetown Journal of Legal Ethics* 14 (2000): 179–95.
10. *Lessard v. Schmidt*, 349 F. Supp. 1078 (E.D. Wis. 1972), *judgment vacated by* 414 U.S. 473 (1974), *on remand*, 413 F. Supp. 1318 (1976).
11. *O'Connor v. Donaldson*, 422 U.S. 563 (1975).
12. Ibid.
13. Ibid., 569.
14. *Addington v. Texas*, 441 U.S. 418 (1979).
15. *Lessard v. Schmidt*, 349 F. Supp. at 414. (E.D. Wis. 1972), *judgment vacated and remanded*, 414 U.S. 473 (1974).
16. *Lassiter v. Department of Social Services*, 452 U.S. 18 (1981); *Mathews v. Eldridge*, 424 U.S. 319 (1976).
17. *Addington v. Texas*, 441 U.S. at 432.
18. *People v. Munoz*, 2001 WL 1397287 (Cal. App. 4th Dist. 2001), unpublished; overruled for other reasons.
19. *New Mexico Department of Health v. Compton*, 131 N.M. 204, 34 P.3d 593, 602 (N.M. 2001).
20. *In re* Richard A., 146 N.H. 295, 771 A.2d 572 (N.H. 2001).
21. FL-ST-ANN § 394.467 (West 2002).
22. *Parham v. J.R.*, 442 U.S. 584, 585 (1979).
23. Miye A. Goishi, "Unlocking the Closet Door: Protecting Children from Involuntary Civil Commitment Because of Their Sexual Orientation," *Hastings Law Journal* 48 (1997): 1137–82.
24. See *Estelle v. Gamble*, 429 U.S. 97 (1976); *Youngberg v. Romeo*, 457 U.S. 307 (1982).
25. *Pennhurst State School and Hospital v. Halderman*, 451 U.S. 1 (1981); *New York State Ass'n for Retarded Children, Inc. v. Rockefeller*, 357 F. Supp. 752 (D.C.N.Y. 1973).
26. *Youngberg v. Romeo*, 486 A.2d at 322.
27. Ibid., 317.
28. *Pennhurst v. Halderman.*
29. Medicaid, 42 U.S.C.A. § 1396d(h) (West 2002). For state rules see AK-ST-ANN § 47.30.915 (West 2002); AZ-ST-ANN § 36–501 (West 2003); AR-ST-ANN § 16–93–1202 (West 2002); CA-ST-ANN § 5349.1 (West 2002); MN-ST-ANN § 144.651 (West 2002); MT-ST-ANN § 33–22–702 (West 2002). See also Hughes, "Rights of Mentally Impaired Persons."
30. *In re* R.A., 146 Vt. 289, 501 A.2d 743 (Vt. 1985).
31. *In re* Burton, 11 Ohio St. 3d 147, 464 N.E.2d 530, 532 (Ohio 1984).

32. See, for example, AR-ST-ANN § 20–47–202 (West 2002); DC-ST-ANN § 7–1131.02 (West 2002); GA-ST-ANN § 17–7–131 (West 2002); ILL-ST-ANN § 5/2–107.1 (West 2002); N.Y.C.R.R. Title 14 § 27.3 (West 2002).
33. *Rouse v. Cameron,* 373 F.2d 451 (D.C. Cir. 1967). See also *Covington v. Harris,* 419 F.2d 617 (D.C. Cir. 1969); *United States v. Ecker,* 543 F.2d 178 (D.C. Cir. 1976).
34. *Rouse v. Cameron,* 373 F.2d at 456.
35. *Wyatt v. Stickney,* 325 F. Supp. 781, 784 (M.D. Ala. 1971), *aff'd,* 503 F.2d 1305 (5th Cir. 1974).
36. *O'Connor v. Donaldson,* 422 U.S. 563, 570 (1975).
37. Mental Health Bill of Rights, 42 U.S.C.A. § 9501 (West 2002).
38. Hughes, "Rights of the Mentally Impaired Persons," sec. 121.
39. *Zinermon v. Burch,* 494 U.S. 113 (1990).
40. Ibid., 118–120.
41. Ibid., 135.
42. *Washington v. Harper,* 494 U.S. 210 (1990).
43. *Riggins v. Nevada,* 504 U.S. 127 (1992).
44. *Sells v. United States, 539 U.S.* 166, 123 S. Ct. 2174 (2003).
45. *Rivers v. Katz,* 67 N.Y.2d 485, 493, 495 N.E.2d 337 (N.Y. 1986).
46. Ibid., 67 N.Y.2d at 486.
47. *Kulak v. City of New York,* 88 F.3d 63 (2d Cir. 1996).
48. *Lessard v. Schmidt,* 349 F. Supp. at 1095.
49. John Petrila, "Ethics, Money, and the Problem of Coercion in Managed Behavioral Health Care," *St. Louis University Law Journal* 40 (1996): 359–404, citing Gerald N. Grob, "Government and Mental Health Policy: A Structural Analysis," *Milbank Quarterly* 72 (1994): 491–92; Joseph T. Carney, "American's Mentally Ill: Tormented Without Treatment," *George Mason University Civil Rights Law Journal* 3 (1992): 181–202.
50. Carney, "American's Mentally Ill."
51. Hughes, "Rights of Mentally Impaired Persons," sec. 92.
52. *Pennhurst v. Halderman.*
53. See also *Society for Good Will to Retarded Children, Inc. v. Cuomo,* 737 F.2d 1239 (2d Cir. 1984), *rev'd on other grounds,* 902 F.2d 1085 (2d Cir. 1990), *on remand,* 745 F. Supp 879 (E.D.N.Y. 1990).
54. See, for example, AL-ST-ANN § 22–52–10.1 (West 2002); CT-ST-ANN § 17a-77 (West 2003); GA-ST-ANN § 37–3–83 (West 2002); ID-ST-ANN § 66–329 (West 2002); MN-ST-ANN § 253B.065 (West 2002).
55. Americans with Disabilities Act, 42 U.S.C.A. § 12132 (West 2002).
56. Americans with Disabilities Act, 42 U.S.C. § § 12101(a)(2), (5) (West 2002).
57. Americans with Disabilities Act, 42 U.S.C.A. § 12134(a) (West 2002).
58. Nondiscrimination on the Basis of Disability in State and Local Government Services, 28 C.F.R. § 35.130(d) (West 2003).
59. Ibid., § 35.130(b)(7).
60. *Olmstead v. Zimring,* 527 U.S. 581 (1999). The quoted portions of the case that follow were taken from the official publication issued by the federal government. Internal citations were omitted.

61. Ibid., 593.
62. Ibid., 581.
63. Ibid., 587.
64. Ibid., 590.
65. Ibid., 583. The regulations discussed by the Court are found in Nondiscrimination on the Basis of Disability in State and Local Government Services, 28 C.F.R. § 35.130(d) (West 2003), and 28 C.F.R. pt. 35, App. A, p. 450 (West 2003).
66. *Olmstead v. Zimring,* 527 U.S. at 591.
67. George W. Bush, "Community-Based Alternatives for the Mentally Ill," Exec. Order No. 13217, *Federal Register* 66 (June 18, 2001): 33155.
68. *Lake v. Cameron,* 364 F.2d 657, 659 (D.C. Cir. 1966).
69. McKinney's Mental Hygiene Law of New York. § 9.60 *et seq* (West 2003).
70. McKinney's Mental Hygiene Law of New York. 1999. Historical and Statutory Notes. § 9.60 (West 2003).
71. AZ-ST-ANN § 36-540 (West 2002).
72. AL-ST-ANN § 22-52-10.2 (West 2002).
73. McKinney's Mental Hygiene Law of New York, § 9.60(c) (West 2002).
74. New York State Office of Mental Health, "Kendra's Law: The Process for Obtaining Assisted Outpatient Treatment," 2002, http://www.omh.state.ny.us/omhweb/omhq/q1299/ kendras_law_the_process.htm (February 12, 2003).
75. McKinney's Mental Hygiene Law of New York, § 9.60(e)(3) (West 2002).
76. New York State Office of Mental Health, "Kendra's Law."
77. *In re* Urcuyo, 185 Misc. 2d 836, 714 N.Y.S.2d 862 (N.Y. Super. 2000).
78. *Cooper v. Oklahoma,* 517 U.S. 348 (1996); for the reference to violation of due process, see *Medina v. California,* 505 U.S. 437 (1992).
79. Prisons and Prisoners—Offenders with Mental Disease or Defect, 18 U.S.C.A. § 4241 (West 2002).
80. *United States v. Ecker,* 78 F.3d 726 (1st Cir. 1996).
81. *Greenwood v. United States,* 350 U.S. 366 (1956).
82. Ira Mickenberg, "A Pleasant Surprise: The Guilty but Mentally Ill Verdict Has Both Succeeded in Its Own Right and Successfully Preserved the Traditional Role of the Insanity Defense," *University of Cincinnati Law Review* 55 (1987): 943—96.
83. See *M'Naghten's Case,* 8 Eng. Rep. 718, 722 (1843); and The American Law Institute, Model Penal Code, § 4.01 (1985).
84. Insanity Defense Reform Act, 18 U.S.C.A. § 17a (West 2002).
85. *United States v. Henderson,* 680 F.2d 659 (9th Cir. 1982); *United States v. Garcia,* 94 F.3d 57 (2d Cir. 1996); *United States v. Knott,* 894 F.2d 1119 (9th Cir. 1990), *cert. denied,* 498 U.S. 873 (1990).
86. *United States v. Carbullido,* 307 F.3d 957, 959 (9th Cir. 2002).
87. *United States v. Hiebert,* 30 F.3d 1005 (8th Cir. 1994), *cert. denied,* 513 U.S. 1029 (1994).
88. *Daniels v. State,* 538 A.2d 1104 (Del. 1988); Lisa Callahan, Connie Mayer, and Henry J. Steadman, "Insanity Defense Reform in the United States–Post-Hinckley," *Mental and Physical Disability Law Reporter* 11 (1987): 54–59.
89. *Daniels v. State.*
90. *United States v. Lane,* 815 F.2d 1106 (7th Cir. 1987).

91. Debra T. Landis, " 'Guilty but Mentally Ill' Statutes: Validity and Construction," *American Law Reports—Fourth* 71 (2000): 702–53.
92. *State v. Bales,* 2002 WL 31814849 (Tenn. Crim. App. 2002), unpublished, on mental retardation; *Com. v. Walzack,* 468 Pa. 210, 360 A.2d 914 (Pa. 1976), on lobotomy; Ex parte Loggins, 771 So. 2d 1093 (Ala. 2000), on antisocial personality.
93. Prisons and Prisoners—Offenders with Mental Disease or Defect, 18 U.S.C.A. § 4243 *et seq.*

Cases

A. v. City of New York, 31 N.Y.2d 83, 335 N.Y.S.2d 33 (1972).
A.D. v. State, 736 N.E.2d 1274 (Ind. Ct. App. 2000).
A.D.H. v. State Department of Human Resources, 640 So. 2d 969 (Ala. Civ. App. 1994).
Adams v. Richland Clinic, Inc., P.S., 37 Wash. App. 650, 681 P.2d 1305 (Wash. Ct. App. 1984).
Adarand v. Pena, 515 U.S. 200 (1995).
Addington v. Texas, 441 U.S. 418 (1979).
Alexander v. Choate, 469 U.S. 287 (1985).
Aliessa v. Novello, 96 N.Y.2d 418, 754 N.E.2d 1085 (N.Y. 2001).
Anderson v. Anderson, 577 So. 2d 658 (Fla. Dist. Ct. App. 1991).
Andrea L. v. Children and Youth Services of Lawrence County, 987 F. Supp. 418 (W.D. Pa. 1997).
Anthony v. White, 376 F. Supp. 567 (D. Del. 1974).
Argersinger v. Hamlin, 407 U.S. 25 (1972).
Armstrong v. Brookdale Univesity Hospital and Medical Center, 2002 WL 13222 (E.D.N.Y. 2002).
Arneth v. Gross, 699 F. Supp. 450 (S.D.N.Y. 1988).
B.A. v. E.E. ex rel. C.E., 741 A.2d 1227 (Pa. 1999).
B.H. v. Johnson, 715 F. Supp. 1387 (N.D. Ill. 1989).
B.P. v. Commonwealth, 568 S.E.2d 412 (Va. Ct. App. 2002).
Babcock v. Tyler, 884 F.2d 497 (9th Cir. 1989).
Baehr v. Lewin, 852 P.2d 44 (Haw. 1993), *review granted in part*, 875 P.2d 225 (Haw. 1993), *on remand* to *Baehr v. Miike*, 1996 WL 694235 (Haw. Ct. App. 1996), *aff'd*, 950 P.2d 1234 (Haw. 1997).
Bailey v. Drexel, 259 U.S. 20 (1922).
Baker v. Carr, 369 U.S. 186 (1962).
Baker v. Vermont, 744 A.2d 864 (Vt. 1999).
Baldridge v. Shapiro, 455 U.S. 345 (1982).
Ballew v. Georgia, 435 U.S. 223 (1978).
Barnes v. Virgin Islands, 415 F. Supp. 1218 (D.C.V.I. 1976).

Barron v. City of Baltimore, 32 U.S. 243 (1833).
Bartell v. Lohiser, 12 F. Supp. 2d 640 (E.D. Mich. 1998).
Bartlett v. Kitchin, 352 N.Y.S.2d 110 (N.Y. Sup. 1973).
Bates v. Bates, 2001 WL 1560915 (Ohio. Ct. App. 2001).
Bell v. New York City Health & Hospitals Corp., 456 N.Y.S.2d 787 (N.Y.A.D. 2d Dept. 1982).
Bellotti v. Baird, 443 U.S. 622 (1979).
Belsito v. Clark, 644 N.E.2d 760 (Ohio Ct. Com. Pl. 1994).
Bennett v. Jeffreys, 40 N.Y.2d 543 (N.Y. 1976).
Bethel School District v. Fraser, 478 U.S. 675 (1986).
Blanchard v. Bergeron, 489 U.S. 87 (1989).
Blondheim v. State, 529 P.2d 1096 (Wash. 1975).
Board of Education v. Earls, 2002 WL 1378649 (U.S. 2002).
Board of Education v. Illinois State Board of Education, 41 F.3d 1162 (7th Cir. 1994).
Board of Education v. Rowley, 458 U.S. 176 (1982).
Board of Pardons v. Allen, 482 U.S. 369 (1987).
Board of Trustees of University of Alabama v. Garrett, 531 U.S. 356 (2001), *on remand* to *Garrett v. University of Alabama,* 261 F.3d 1242 (11th Cir. 2001), *aff'd in part, vacated in part,* 276 F.3d 1227 (11th Cir. 2001).
Boddie v. Connecticut, 401 U.S. 371 (1971).
Bond v. United States, 120 S. Ct. 1462 (2000).
Boone v. Federal Express Corp., 59 F.3d 84 (8th Cir. 1995).
Boulanger v. Pol, 900 P.2d 823 (Kan. 1995).
Bowen v. American Hospital Ass'n, 476 U.S. 610 (1986).
Bradley v. Arkansas Department of Education, 189 F.3d 745 (8th Cir. 1999), *cert. denied,* 533 U.S. 949 (2001).
Brady v. Maryland, 373 U.S. 83 (1963).
Bragdon v. Abbott, 524 U.S. 624 (1998).
Braschi v. Stahl, 74 N.Y.2d 201, 543 N.E.2d 49 (N.Y. 1989).
Brause v. Bureau of Vital Statistics, 1998 WL 88743 (Alaska Super. 1998).
Breed v. Jones, 421 U.S. 519 (1975).
Brian A. v. Sundquist, 149 F. Supp. 2d 941 (M.D. Tenn. 2000).
Brookhouser v. State, 13 Cal. Rptr. 2d 658 (Cal. App. 6th Dist. 1992).
Brown Eyes v. South Dakota Department of Social Services, 630 N.W.2d 501 (S.D. 2001).
Brown v. Board of Education, 347 U.S. 483 (1954) (*Brown I).*
Brown v. Board of Education, 349 U.S. 294 (1955) (*Brown II).*
Brown v. Grabowski et al., 922 F.2d 1097 (3d Cir. 1991), *cert. denied,* 501 U.S. 1218 (1991).
Burlington v. Department of Education, 736 F.2d 773 (1st Cir. 1984), *aff'd,* 471 U.S. 359 (1985).
Burr v. Board of County Commissioners, 491 N.E.2d 1101 (Ohio 1986)
Burton v. Richmond, 276 F.3d 973 (8th Cir. 2002).
Butcher v. Butcher, 357 S.E.2d 226 (W. Va. 1987).
Butler v. Evans, 225 F.3d 887 (7th Cir. 2000).
C.F. v. Pennsylvania Depart of Public Welfare, 804 A.2d 755 (Pa. Commw. Ct. 2002).
C.W. v. State, 23 P.3d 52 (Alaska 2001).
Cabell v. Markham, 148 F.2d 737 (2d Cir. 1945).
Calabretta v. Floyd, 189 F.2d 808 (9th Cir. 1999).

Campbell v. Talladega County Board of Education, 518 F. Supp. 47 (N.D. Ala. 1981).
Canty v. Canty, 874 P.2d 1000 (Ariz. App. Div. 1 1994).
Capistrano Unified School District v. Wartenberg, 59 F.3d 884 (9th Cir. 1995).
Carney v. Carney, 598 P.2d 36 (Cal. 1979).
Carstens v. Carstens, 867 P.2d 805 (Alaska 1994).
Carter v. Florence County School District Four, 950 F.2d 156 (4th Cir. 1991), *aff'd sub nom., Florence County School District Four v. Carter*, 510 U.S. 7 (1993).
Carter v. State, 1991 WL 168432 (Ark. Ct. App. 1991).
Cedar Rapids Community School District v. Garret, 526 U.S. 66 (1999).
Centeno v. New York, 40 N.Y.2d 932 (N.Y. 1976).
Champlin Refining Co. v. Corporation Com'n of State of Oklahoma, 286 U.S. 210 (1932).
Charlie H. and Nadine H. v. Whitman, 83 F. Supp. 2d 476 (D.N.J. 2000).
Church of Scientology v. Internal Revenue Service, 484 U.S. 9 (1987).
Ciresoli v. Maine School Administrative District, 901 F. Supp. 378 (D.C. Me. 1995).
City of Akron v. Akron Center for Reproductive Health, 462 U.S. 416 (1983).
City of Boerne v. Flores, 521 U.S. 507 (1997).
City of Philadelphia v. Cohen, 184 N.E.2d 167 (N.Y. 1962), *cert. denied*, 371 U.S. 934 (1962).
Cohen v. New York, 51 A.D.2d 494 (N.Y.A.D. 3d Dept. 1976), *aff'd*, 41 N.Y.2d 1086 (N.Y. 1977).
Colin v. Orange Unified School District, 83 F. Supp. 2d 1135 (C.D. Cal. 2000).
Com. v. Walzack, 468 Pa. 210, 360 A.2d 914 (Pa. 1976).
Commmonwealth v. Seese, 512 Pa. 439, 517 A.2d 920 (Pa. 1986).
Commonwealth v. Davis, 541 A.2d 315 (Pa. 1988).
Commonwealth v. Dunkle, 602 A.2d 830 (Pa. 1992).
Commonwealth v. Florence F., 429 Mass. 523, 709 N.E.2d 418 (Mass. 1999).
Connecticut Department of Public Safety v. Doe, 123 S. Ct. 1160 (2003), 2003 WL 728779 (2003).
Connell v. Francisco, 898 P.2d 831 (Wash. 1995).
Connors v. City of Boston, 714 N.E.2d 335 (Mass. 1999).
Cooper v. Oklahoma, 517 U.S. 348 (1996).
Coverdall v. Department of Social and Health Services, 834 F.2d 758 (9th Cir. 1987).
Covington v. Harris, 419 F.2d 617 (D.C. Cir. 1969).
Coy v. Iowa, 487 U.S. 1012 (1988).
Craig v. State, 220 Md. 590, 155 A.2d 684 (Md. Ct. Spec. App. 1959).
Crawford v. City of Chicago, 710 N.E.2d 91, 93 (Ill. App. Ct. 1999).
Cruzan v. Director, Missouri Dept. of Health, 497 U.S. 261 (1990).
Custody of a Minor, 375 Mass. 733, 379 N.E.2d 1053 (Mass. 1978).
Dandridge v. Williams, 397 U.S. 471 (1970).
Daniel S. v. Board of Education, 152 F. Supp. 2d 949 (N.D. Ill. 2001).
Daniels v. State, 538 A.2d 1104 (Del. 1988).
Darryl H. v. Coler, 801 F.2d 893 (7th Cir. 1986).
Daubert v. Merrell Dow Pharmaceuticals, Inc., 509 U.S. 579 (1993).
Davis v. Employment Security Department, 737 P.2d 1262 (Wash. 1987).
Davis v. Monroe, 526 U.S. 629 (1999).
Department of Children and Family Services v. G.M., 816 So. 2d 830 (Fl. Dist. Ct. App. 2002).

DeShaney v. Winnebago County Department of Social Services, 489 U.S. 189 (1989).
District of Columbia v. B.J.R., 332 A.2d 58 (D.C. 1975).
District 27 Community School Board v. Board of Education, 130 Misc. 2d 398 (N.Y. Sup. Ct. 1986).
Doe v. Bagan, 41 F.3d 571 (10th Cir. 1994).
Doe v. Belleville Public Schools District, 672 F. Supp. 342 (S.D. Ill. 1987).
Doe v. Broderick, 225 F.3d 440 (4th Cir. 2000).
Doe v. District of Columbia, 93 F.3d 861 (D.C. Cir. 1996).
Doe v. Division of Youth and Family Services, 148 F. Supp. 2d 462 (D.N.J. 2001).
Doe v. Dolton Elementary School District No. 148, 694 F. Supp. 440 (N.D. Ill. 1988).
Doe v. Garcia, 961 P.2d 1181 (Idaho 1998).
Doe v. New York City Department of Social Services, 649 F.2d 134 (2d Cir. 1981).
Doe v. Plyler, 628 F.2d 448 (5th Cir. 1980), renamed *Plyler v. Doe,* 457 U.S. 202 (1982).
Doe v. Roe, 526 N.Y.S.2d 718 (N.Y. Sup. Ct. 1988).
Drummond v. Fulton County Department of Family & Children's Services, 563 F.2d 1200 (5th Cir. 1977), *cert. denied,* 437 U.S. 910 (1977).
Duke v. United States, 301 U.S. 492 (1937).
Dunajewski v. School District, 526 N.Y.S.2d 139 (N.Y. App. 2 Dept. 1988).
Dunn v. Catholic Home Bureau, 142 Misc. 2d 316 (N.Y. Sup. Ct. 1989).
E.B. v. Verniero, 119 F.3d 1077 (3d Cir. 1997), *cert denied,* 522 U.S. 1110 (1998).
Ebert v. Ebert, 346 N.E.2d 240 (N.Y. 1976).
Ellis v. Peter, 211 A.D.2d 353 (N.Y.A.D. 2d Dept. 1995).
Enlow v. Fire Protection Systems, Inc., 803 S.W.2d 148 (Mo. Ct. App. 1991).
Equality Foundation of Greater Cincinnati v. City of Cincinnati, 128 F.3d 289 (6th Cir. 1997), *cert. denied,* 525 U.S. 943 (1998).
Eric L. v. Bird, 848 F. Supp. 303 (D.N.H. 1994).
Estelle v. Gamble, 429 U.S. 97 (1976).
Eversley v. State, 748 So. 2d 963 (Fla. 1999).
Ex parte Anonymous, 803 So. 2d 542 (Ala. 2002).
Ex parte Loggins, 771 So. 2d 1093 (Ala. 2000).
Ex parte McLendon, 455 So. 2d 863 (Ala. 1984).
Farrell v. Carol Stream School District No. 25, 1996 WL 364743 (N.D. Ill. 1996).
FCC v. Beach Communications, Inc., 508 U.S. 307 (1993).
Feeley v. Sampson, 570 F.2d 364 (1st Cir. 1978).
Felton v. Schaeffer, 279 Cal. Rptr. 713 (Cal. App. 4th Dist. 1991).
Ferguson v. City of Charleston 532 U.S. 67 (2001).
Fiederlein v. New York Health & Hospitals Corp., 56 N.Y.2d 573 (N.Y. 1982).
Finkelstein v. Bodek, 516 N.Y.S.2d 464 (N.Y. App. 1st Dept. 1987).
Fitzgerald v. Montgomery County Dept. of Social Services 2002 WL 17514213 (Va. App. 2002).
Fosmire v. Nicoleau, 75 N.Y.2d 218, 551 N.E.2d 77 (New York 1990).
Foster Care and Adoption Data Collection, 45 C.F.R. 1355.40.
Francisco G. v. Superior Court, 110 Cal. Rptr. 2d 679 (Cal. App. 6th Dist. 2001).
Franklin v. Gwinett County Public Schools, 503 U.S. 60 (1992).
Franz v. Lytle, 997 F.22d 784 (10th Cir. 1993).
Frazier v. Bailey, 957 F.2d 920 (1st Cir. 1991).

Frenzel v. State, 849 P.2d 741 (Wyo. 1993).
Friederwitzer v. Friederwitzer, 432 N.E.2d 765 (N.Y. 1982).
Friedman v. Friedman, 24 Cal. Rprt. 2d 892 (Cal. App. 1st Dist. 1993).
Frye v. United States, 293 F. 1013 (C.A.D.C. 1923).
Fullilove v. Klutznick, 448 U.S. 448 (1980).
Gahagan v. Tennessee, 1985 WL 4113 (Tenn. Crim. App. 1985), unpublished.
Gersch v. Illinois Department of Professional Regulation, 720 N.E.2d 672 (Ill. App. Ct. 1999).
Gerstein v. Pugh, 420 U.S. 103 (1975).
Gideon v. Wainwright, 372 U.S. 335 (1963).
Gier v. Education Service Unit, 845 F.Supp. 1342 (D. Neb. 1994).
Globe Newspaper Co. v. Superior Court for Norfolk County, 457 U.S. 596 (1982).
Glover v. State, 2002 WL 192009 (Tex. App. 2002), *opinion withdrawn*, 102 S.W.3d 754 (Tex App. 2003).
Glover v. Torrence, 723 N.E.2d 924 (Ind. Ct. App. 2000).
Goldberg v. Kelly, 397 U.S. 254 (1970).
Good v. Dauphin County, 891 F.2d 1087 (3d Cir. 1989).
Greenholtz v. Inmates of Nebraska Penal & Correctional Complex 442 U.S. 1 (1979).
Greenwood v. United States, 350 U.S. 366 (1956).
Griffin v. State, 526 So. 2d 752 (Fla. Dist. Ct. App. 1988).
Griswold v. Connecticut, 381 U.S. 479 (1965).
Hadden v. State, 690 So. 2d 573 (Fla. 1997).
Hall v. Miller, 36 P.3d 328 (Kan. Ct. App. 2001).
Hall v. Shawnee Mission School District, 856 F. Supp 1521 (D.C. Kan. 1994).
Hamilton v. Hamilton, 866 S.W.2d 711 (Mo. App. W.D. 1994).
Hamilton v. Saxbe, 428 F. Supp. 1101 (N.D. Ga. 1976), *aff'd*, 551 F.2d 1056 (5th Cir. 1977).
Hammer v. Dagenhart, 247 U.S. 251 (1918).
Harlow v. Fitzgerald, 457 U.S. 800 (1982).
Harris v. Harris, 424 F.2d 806 (D.C. Cir. 1970).
Harris v. McRae, 448 U.S. 297 (1980).
Hartog v. Hartog, 623 N.Y.S.2d 537 (N.Y. 1995).
Hazelwood School District v. Kuhlmeier, 484 U.S. 260 (1988).
Heart of Atlanta Motel, Inc. v. United States, 379 U.S. 241 (1964).
Hector M. v. Commission of Social Services, 425 N.Y.S.2d 199 (N.Y. Fam. Ct. 1980).
Heller v. Doe, 509 U.S. 312 (1993).
Helvering v. Davis, 301 U.S. 619 (1937).
Henrietta v. Giuliani, 119 F. Supp. 2d 181 (E.D.N.Y. 2000).
Hill v. Michigan, 2001 WL 857200 (6th Cir. 2001).
Hill v. Moorman, 525 So. 2d 681 (La. App. 1st Cir. 1988).
Hillman v. Columbia County, 474 N.W.2d 913 (1991).
Hodgson v. Minnesota, 497 U.S. 417 (1990).
Homere v. State, 361 N.Y.S.2d 820 (N.Y. Ct. Cl. 1974).
Honig v. Doe, 484 U.S. 305 (1988).
Horak v. Biris, 474 N.E.2d 13 (Ill. App. 2nd Dist 1985).
Houck v. Garroway, 293 A.D.2d 782 (N.Y. App. 3rd Dept. 2002).
Hudgens v. U.S., 424 U.S. 507 (1976).

Humphrey v. State, 2002 WL 321941 (Ala. Crim. App. 2002).
Hunt v. State, 904 S.W.2d 813 (Tex. App. 1995).
Huntley v. New York, 62 N.Y.2d 134 (N.Y. 1984).
Hutson v. Haggard, 475 S.W.2d 330 (Tex. App. 1971).
Idaho v. Coeur d'Alene Tribe of Idaho, 521 U.S. 261 (1997).
Idaho v. Wright, 497 U.S. 805 (1990).
Illinois v. Gates, 462 U.S. 213 (1983).
Immigration and Naturalization Service v. Chadha, 462 U.S. 919 (1983).
In re Adoption of Amy S. S., 486 N.Y.S.2d 912 (N.Y. 1985).
In re Adoption of Baby Z., 724 A.2d 1035 (Conn. 1999).
In re Adoption of C.C.G., 762 A.2d 724 (Pa. Super. 2000), *order vac.,* 803 A.2d 1195 (Pa. 2002).
In re Adoption of Carl, 184 Misc. 2d 646, 709 N.Y.S.2d 905 (N.Y. Fam. Ct. 2000).
In re Adoption of Coppersmith, 761 N.E.2d 1163 (Ohio Ct. App. 2001).
In re Adoption of Dobbs, 531 P.2d 303 (Wash. Ct. App. 1975).
In re Adoption of Luke, 640 N.W.2d 374 (Neb. 2002).
In re Adoption of M.D.L., 682 S.W.2d 886 (Mo. Ct. App. 1984).
In re Adoption of M.J.H., 501 A.2d 648 (Pa. Super. Ct. 1985), *appeal denied,* 522 A.2d 1105 (Pa. 1987), *appeal dismissed,* 108 S. Ct. 49 (1987).
In re Adoption of M.T.S., 489 N.W.2d 285 (Minn. 1992).
In re Adoption of Meaux, 417 So. 2d 522 (La. App. 3rd Cir).
In re Adoption of Stephen, a Minor, 645 N.Y.S.2d 1012 (N.Y. Fam. Ct. 1996).
In re Adoption of T.K.J. and K.A.K., 931 P.2d 488 (Colo. 1996).
In re Adoption of Tammy, 416 Mass. 205 (Mass. 1993).
In re Adoption of Two Children by H.N.R., 662 A.2d 535 (N.J. Super. Ct. 1995).
In re Adoptions of B.L.V.B. and E.L.V.B., 628 A.2d 1271 (Vt. 1993).
In re Aleese W., 2002 WL 1492166 (Conn. Super. Ct. 2002).
In re Amber B., 236 Cal. Rptr. 623 (Cal. App. 1st Dist. 1987).
In re Angel Lace M., 516 N.W.2d 678 (Wis. 1994).
In re B.W., 498 So. 2d 946 (Fla. 1986).
In re Baby Girl Clausen, 502 N.W.2d 649 (Mich. 1993).
In re Baby Girl P., 2002 WL 1343814 (N.H. 2002).
In re Baby M., 537 A.2d 1227 (N.J. 1988).
In re Brianna D., 798 A.2d 413 (R.I. 2002).
In re Burton, 11 Ohio St. 3d 147, 464 N.E.2d 530 (Ohio 1984).
In re Catrice S., 470 S.E.2d 856 (S.C. Ct. App. 1996).
In re Christine C., 236 Cal. Rptr. 630 (Cal. App. 5th Div. 1987).
In re Christine M., 157 Misc. 2d 4, 595 N.Y.S.2d 606 (N.Y. Fam. Ct. 1992).
In re Christopher F., 701 N.Y.S.2d 171 (N.Y. App. 3d Dept. 1999).
In re Claire C. Conroy, 98 N.J. 321, 486 A.2d 1209 (N.J. 1985).
In re Custody of Peal, 290 S.E.2d 664 (N.C. 1982).
In re Custody of Peterson, 491 N.E.2d 1150 (Ill. 1986).
In re Daniel R. R., 874 F.2d 1036 (5th Cir. 1989).
In re Doe, 2002 WL 31513378 (Hawaii 2002).
In re Dutchess County Department of Social Services, 522 N.Y.S.2d 210 (N.Y. App. 2d Dept. 1987), *appeal denied,* 532 N.Y.S.2d 368 (N.Y. 1988).

In re E.M., 137 Misc. 2d 197(N.Y. Fam. Ct. 1987).
In re Erica D., 742 N.Y.S.2d 112 (N.Y. App. 2d Dept. 2002).
In re Fletcher, 558 S.E.2d 498 (N.C. Ct. App. 2002).
In re Francisco S., 26 P.3d 562 (Cal. App. 2d Dist. 2000).
In re G.S., 2002 WL 31491370 (Mont. 2002).
In re Gault, 387 U.S. 1 (1967).
In re I.B., 2002 WL 531924 (Iowa App. 2002).
In re Involuntary Discharge or Transfer of J.S., 512 N.W.2d 604 (Minn. Ct. App. 1994).
In re J.J., 64 Ohio App. 3d 806, 582 N.E.2d 1138 (Ohio Ct. App. 1990).
In re J.J.J., 718 P.2d 948 (Alaska 1986).
In re J.L.H. and P.L.L.H., 316 N.W.2d 650 (S.D. 1982).
In re Jacob, 636 N.Y.S.2d 716 (N.Y. 1995).
In re K.P., 514 P.2d 1131 (Colo. 1973).
In re Karen Quinlan, 70 N.J. 10, 355 A.2d 647 (1976), *cert. denied, sub nom., Garger v. New Jersey,* 429 U.S. 922 (1976), *overruled for other reasons, In re* Claire C. Conroy, 98 N.J. 321, 486 A.2d 1209 (N.J. 1985).
In re Levin, 625 So. 2d 756 (La. Ct. App. 1993).
In re Linda K., 521 N.Y.S.2d 705 (N.Y.A.D. 2d Dept. 1987), *appeal denied,* 526 N.Y.S.2d 437 (1988).
In re M.B., 3 P.3d 780 (Wash. App. Div. 1 2000).
In re M.M.D. & B.H.M., 662 A.2d 837 (D.C. 1995).
In re Marriage of Buzzanca, 72 Cal. Rptr. 2d 280 (Cal. App. 4th Dist. 1998).
In re Marriage of Hunt, 476 N.W.2d 99 (Iowa. Ct. App. 1991).
In re Meggan C., *New York Law Journal,* December 17, 1987: 1–32.
In re Michael M., 614 A.2d 832 (Conn. App. Ct. 1992).
In re Napier, 532 P.2d 423 (Okla. 1975).
In re Naquan J., 727 N.Y.S.2d 124 (N.Y. App. 2d Dept. 2001).
In re Nicholas E., 720 A.2d 562, 1998 Me. 243 (Me. 1998).
In re Nicholas H., 46 P.3d 932 (Cal. 2002).
In re People in Interest of K., 514 P.2d 1131 (Colo. 1973).
In re Petition of Doe, 638 N.E.2d 181 (Ill. 1994), *sub nom., In re* Petition of Kirchner, 649 N.E.2d 324 (Ill. 1995).
In re Petition of K.M. & D.M., 653 N.E.2d 888 (Ill. App. 1st Dist. 1995).
In re R.A., 146 Vt. 289, 501 A.2d 743 (Vt. 1985).
In re R.P., 498 N.W.2d 364 (S.D. 1993).
In re Richard A., 146 N.H. 295, 771 A.2d 572 (N.H. 2001).
In re Robinson, Esq., 639 A.2d 1384 (Vt. 1994).
In re Ronald D., 673 N.Y.S.2d 559 (N.Y. Fam. Ct. 1998).
In re S.M.H., 2002 WL 1374508 (Mich. App. 2002).
In re S.O., 126 Cal. Rptr. 2d 554 (Cal. App. 4th Dist. 2002).
In re Sara M., 239 Cal. Rptr. 605 (Cal. App. 3d Dist. 1987).
In re Scott County Master Docket, 618 F. Supp. 1534 (D. Minn. 1985), *rev'd* by *Myers v. Morris,* 810 F.2d 1437 (8th Cir. 1987).
In re Shammo, 2002 WL 1173623 (Ohio App. 5th Dist. 2002).
In re Shandra C. C., 672 N.Y.S.2d 490 (N.Y. App. 3d Dept. 1998).
In re Smith, 112 Cal. App. 3d 956 (Cal. Ct. App. 1980).

In re T.L., 1996 WL 393521 (Mo. Cir. Ct. 1996), unpublished.
In re Urcuyo, 185 Misc. 2d 836, 714 N.Y.S.2d 862 (N.Y. Sup. 2000).
In re Winship, 397 U.S. 358 (1970).
In re Yetter, 62 Pa. D. & C.2d 619 (Pa. Com. Pl. 1973).
Irving Independent School District v. Tatro, 468 U.S. 883 (1984).
J.B. v. State, 2001 WL 311172 (Utah App. 2001).
J.D. v. N.D., 170 Misc. 2d 877, 652 N.Y.S.2d 468 (N.Y. Fam. Ct. Westchester County 1996).
Jaffee v. Redmond, 518 U.S. 1 (1996).
Jahnke v. State, 682 P.2d 991 (Wyo. 1984), *rev'd for other reasons, Vaughn v. State,* 962 P.2d 149 (Wyo. 1998).
Jeanine B. by Blondis v. Thompson, 967 F. Supp. 1104 (E.D. Wisc. 1997).
Jeanine B. v. Thompson, 877 F. Supp. 1268 (E.D. Wisc. 1995).
Jehovah's Witnesses of Washington v. King County Hospital, 278 F. Supp 488 (W.D. Wash. 1968), *aff'd,* 390 U.S. 598 (1968).
Jenkins v. County of Orange, 212 Cal. App. 3d 278 (Cal. App. 1989).
Johnson v. Calvert, 5 Cal. 4th 84, 851 P.2d 776 (Cal. 1993), *cert. denied,* 510 U.S. 874 (1995).
Johnson v. State, 58 S.W.3d 496 (Mo. 2001).
Johnson v. State, 469 S.E.2d 152 (Ga. 1996).
Johnson v. United States, 333 U.S. 10 (1948).
Joseph A. v. New Mexico Department of Human Services, 575 F. Supp. 346 (1983).
Juan F. v. Weicker, 37 F.3d 874 (2d Cir. 1994), *cert. denied,* 515 U.S. 1142 (1995).
K.B. v. Mills, 639 N.W.2d 261 (Mich. Ct. App. 2002).
K.H. ex rel. Murphy v. Morgan, 914 F.2d 846 (7th Cir. 1990).
Kansas v. Crane, 534 U.S. 407 (2002).
Katz v. United States, 389 U.S. 347 (1967).
Katzenbach v. Morgan, 384 U.S. 641 (1966).
Kerrville State Hospital v. Clark, 900 S.W.2d 425 (Tex. Ct. App. 3rd Dist. 1995), *rev'd for other reasons,* 923 S.W.2d 582 (Tex. 1996).
Kimel v. Florida Bd. of Regents, 528 U.S. 62 (2000).
King v. Olmstead County, 117 F.3d 1065 (8th Cir. 1997).
King v. Pine Plains Central School District 918 F. Supp. 772 (S.D.N.Y. 1996).
Kirby v. Illinois, 406 U.S. 682 (1972).
Klopfer v. North Carolina, 386 U.S. 213 (1967).
Knock v. Knock, 621 A.2d 267 (Conn. 1993).
Koramatsu v. United States, 323 U.S. 214 (1944).
Krank v. Krank, 529 N.W.2d 844 (N.D. 1995).
Kromm v. Literal, 2002 WL 59608 (Wash. 2002).
Kubik v. State, 664 N.Y.S.2d 365 (N.Y. App. 3 Dept. 1997).
Kuhn v. Kuhn, 1998 WL 673629 (N.D. Ill. 1998), *aff'd,* 1999 WL 519326 (N.D. Ill. 1999).
Kulak v. City of New York, 88 F.3d 63 (2nd Cir. 1996).
Kumho Tire Company v. Carmichael, 526 U.S. 137 (1999).
Lake v. Cameron, 364 F.2d 657 (D.C. Cir. 1966).
Lane v. Candura, 6 Mass. App. Ct. 377, 376 N.E.2d 1232 (Mass. App. Ct. 1978).
LaShawn A. v. Dixon, 762 F. Supp. 959 (D.D.C. 1991), *aff'd* by *LaShawn A. v. Kelly,* 990 F.2d 1319 (D.C. Cir. 1993), *cert. denied* by *Kelly v. LaShawn A.,* 510 U.S. 1044 (1994).
LaShonda D. v. Monroe County Board of Education, 526 U.S. 629 (1999).

Lassiter v. Department of Social Services, 452 U.S. 18 (1981).
Learning Disabilities Association of Maryland, Inc. v. Board of Education of Baltimore County, 837 F. Supp 717 (D. Md. 1993).
Ledbetter v. Ross, 725 N.E.2d 120 (Ind. Ct. App. 2000).
Lehnhausen v. Lake Shore Auto Parts Co., 410 U.S. 356 (1973).
Lehr v. Robertson, 463 U.S. 248 (1983).
Lessard v. Schmidt, 349 F. Supp. 1078 (E.D. Wis. 1972), *judgment vacated by* 414 U.S. 473 (1974), *on remand,* 413 F. Supp. 1318 (1976).
Leszinske v. Poole, 798 P.2d 1049 (N.M. Ct. App. 1990) *cert. denied,* 797 P.2d 983 (N.M. 1990).
Lewis v. Thompson, 252 F.3d 567 (2d Cir. 2001).
Linda P. v. Thomas, 659 N.Y.S.2d 55 (A.D. 2 Dept. 1998).
Lindsey v. Normet, 405 U.S. 56 (1972).
Liscio v. Woodland Hills School District, 734 F. Supp. 689 (W.D. Pa. 1989), *aff'd,* 902 F.2d 1561 (3d Cir. 1990).
Lofton v. Kearney, 157 F. Supp. 2d 1372 (S.D. Fla. 2001).
Lothman v. Lothman, 464 P.2d 1006 (Ariz. Ct. App. 1970).
Loveheart v. Long, 762 S.W.2d 32 (Mo. 1988).
Loving v. Virginia, 338 U.S. 1 (1967).
Lynch v. Dukakis, 719 F.2d 504 (1st Cir. 1983).
Lyng v. Castillo, 477 U.S. 635 (1986).
M'Naghten's Case, 8 Eng. Rep. 718 (1843).
M.R. v. Cox, 881 P.2d 108 (Ok. App. 1st Div. 1994), *cert. denied,* 514 U.S. 1019 (1995).
Maag v. Wessler, 960 F.2d 773 (9th Cir. 1991).
Maher v. Roe, 432 U.S. 464 (1977).
Mapp v. Ohio, 367 U.S. 643 (1961).
Marisol A. v. Giuliani, 929 F. Supp. 662 (S.D.N.Y. 1996), *cert. denied,* 520 U.S. 1211 (1997), *aff'd,* 126 F.3d 372 (1997).
Martinez v. School Board of Hillsborough County, 675 F. Supp. 1574 (M.D. Fla. 1987), 692 F. Supp. 1293 (M.D. Fla. 1988), *vacated,* 861 F.2d 1502 (11th Cir. 1988), *on remand,* 711 F. Supp. 1066 (M.D. Fla. 1989).
Martino v. Family Service Agency of Adams County, 445 N.E.2d 6 (Ill. Appl. 4th Dist. 1983).
Maryland State Board of Social Work Examiners v. Chertkov, 710 A.2d 391 (Md. Ct. Spec. App. 1997).
Maryland v. Craig, 497 U.S. 836 (1990).
Mathews v. Eldridge, 424 U.S. 319 (1976).
Matthews v. Weinberg, 645 So. 2d 487 (Fla. Dist. Ct. App. 1994).
McDonald v. McDonald, 608 N.Y.S.2d 477 (N.Y.A.D. 2d Dept. 1994).
McDonnell v. County. of Nassau, N.Y. Sup. Ct., Nassau County. No. 11152/73, unreported (1986).
McKeiver v. Pennsylvania, 403 U.S. 528 (1971).
McKenzie v. Smith, 771 F.2d 1527 (D.C. Cir. 1985).
McNeal v. Harper, 816 F. Supp. 421 (E.D. Va. 1993).
Meador v. Cabinet for Human Resources, 902 F.2d 474 (6th Cir. 1990).
Medina v. California, 505 U.S. 437 (1992).
Melton v. State, 790 S.W.2d 322 (Tex. Crim. App. 1990).

Meyer v. Nebraska, 262 U.S. 390 (1923).
Michael H. v. Gerald D., 491 U.S. 110 (1989).
Michael J. v. Los Angeles County, 247 Cal. Rptr. 504 (Cal. App. 2d Dist. 1988).
Michael M. v. Superior Court of Sonoma County, 450 U.S. 464 (1981).
Michaud v. Wawruck, 551 A.2d 738 (Conn. 1988).
Milburn v. Anne Arundel County D.S.S., 871 F.2d 474 (4th Cir. 1989).
Miller v. City of Philadelphia, 954 F. Supp. 1056 (E.D. Pa. 1997).
Milwaukee County v. White, 296 U.S. 268 (1935).
Minor v. United States, 396 U.S. 87 (1969).
Miranda v. Arizona, 384 U.S. 436 (1966).
Mississippi Band of Choctaw Indians v. Holyfield, 490 U.S. 30 (1989).
Mohr v. Commonwealth, 653 N.E.2d 1104 (Mass. 1995).
Monell v. Department of Social Services, 436 U.S. 658 (1978).
Moore v. Department of Human Resources, 469 S.E.2d 511 (Ga. Ct. App. 1996).
Morrissey v. Brewer, 408 U.S. 471 (1972).
Mullane v. Central Hanover Bank and Trust Co., 339 U.S. 306 (1950).
Murray v. Murray, 598 So. 2d 921 (Ala. Civ. App. 1992).
Nasser v. Parker, 455 S.E.2d 502 (Va. 1995).
New Jersey Coalition Against War in the Middle East v. J.M.B. Realty, 138 N.J. 326 (1994).
New Jersey v. T.L.O., 469 U.S. 325 (1985).
New Mexico Department of Health v. Compton, 131 N.M. 204, 34 P.3d 593 (N.M. 2001).
New York State Ass'n for Retarded Children, Inc. v. Rockefeller, 357 F. Supp. 752 (D.C.N.Y. 1973).
New York v. United States, 505 U.S. 144 (1992).
Newkirk v. Commonwealth, 937 S.W.2d 690 (Ky. 1996).
Newmark v. Williams, 588 A.2d 1108 (Del. 1991).
Nicholson v. Williams, 203 F. Supp. 2d 153 (E.D.N.Y. 2002).
Nicini v. Morra, 212 F.3d 798 (3d Cir. 2000).
Nigro v. United States, 276 U.S. 332 (1928).
Norfleet v. Arkansas Dept. of Human Services, 989 F.2d 289 (8th Cir. 1993).
Norman v. McDonald, 930 F. Supp. 1219 (N.D. Ill. 1996).
O'Connor v. Donaldson, 422 U.S. 563 (1975).
O'Connor v. Ortega, 480 U.S. 709 (1987).
O'Shea v. United States, 623 F. Supp. 380 (E.D.N.Y. 1985).
Oelsner v. New York, 66 N.Y. 2d 636 (N.Y. 1985).
Ohio v. Roberts, 448 U.S. 56 (1980).
Olmstead v. Zimring, 527 U.S. 581 (1999).
Owasso Independent School District v. Falvo, 534 U.S. 426 (2002).
Palmore v. Sidoti, 466 U.S. 429 (1984).
Parham v. J.R., 442 U.S. 584 (1979).
Parker v. Gladden, 385 U.S. 363 (1966).
Pavlik v. Kornhaber, 761 N.E.2d 175 (Ill. App. 1st Dist. 2001).
Payne v. Tennessee, 501 U.S. 808 (1991).
Pennhurst State School and Hospital v. Halderman, 451 U.S. 1 (1981).
Pennsylvania Association for Retarded Children v. Commonwealth of Pennsylvania, 334 F. Supp. 279 (E.D. Pa. 1972).

People v. Beckley, 456 N.W.2d 391 (Mich. 1990).

People v. Bledsoe, 681 P.2d 291 (Cal. 1984).

People v. Bowker, 249 Cal. Rptr. 886 (Cal. App. 4th Dist. 1988).

People v. Christel, 537 N.W.2d 194 (Mich. 1995).

People v. Colberg, 701 N.Y.S.2d 608 (N.Y. Cty. Ct. 1999).

People v. Doe, 138 N.Y.S.2d 307 (N.Y. County Ct. 1955).

People v. Emerick, 2002 WL 384489 (Cal. App. 3d Dist. 2002).

People v. Erickson, 67 Cal. Rptr. 2d 740 (Cal. App. 5th Dist. 1998).

People v. Fortin, 289 A.D.2d 590 (N.Y.A.D. 2d Dept. 2001).

People v. Jackson, 18 Cal. App. 3 Dept. (1971).

People v. Jeff, 251 Cal. Rptr. 135 (Cal. App. 5th Dist. 1988).

People v. Liberta, 485 N.Y.S.2d 207 (1984), *cert. denied, Liberta v. New York,* 471 U.S. 1020 (1985).

People v. McAuliffe, 632 N.Y.S.2d 253 (N.Y. App. 3 Dept. 1995).

People v. Munoz, 2001 WL 1397287 (Cal. App. 4th Dist. 2001), unpublished.

People v. Nelson, 561 N.E.2d 439 (Ill. App. 5th Dist. 1990).

People v. Petitt, 613 N.E.2d 1358 (Ill. App. 2d Dist. 1993).

Perez v. State, 925 S.W.2d 324 (Tex. App. 1996).

Perez v. United States, 402 U.S. 146 (1971).

Perkins v. General Motors, 129 F.R.D. 655, (W.D. Mo. 1990), *aff'd,* 965 F.2d 597 (8th Cir. 1992), *cert. denied,* 113 S. Ct. 654 (1992).

Phipps v. Saddleback Valley Unified School District, 204 Cal. App. 3d 1110 (Cal. App. 4th Dist. 1988).

Pierce v. Society of Sisters, 268 U.S. 510 (1925).

Pike v. Honsinger, 49 N.E. 760 (N.Y. 1898).

Planned Parenthood of Southeastern Pennsylvania v. Casey, 505 U.S. 833 (1992).

Playboy Enterprises v. Welles, 60 F. Supp. 2d 1050 (S.D. Cal. 1999).

Plessy v. Ferguson, 163 U.S. 537 (1896).

Plyler v. Doe, 457 U.S. 202 (1982).

Popovich v. Cuyahoga County Court of Common Pleas, 276 F.3d 808 (6th Cir. 2002).

Posik v. Layton, 695 So. 2d 759 (Fla. Dist. Ct. App. 1997).

Prince v. Massachusetts, 321 U.S. 158 (1944).

Printz v. United States, 521 U.S. 898 (1997).

Prinz v. State of Ohio Counselor and Social Worker Board, 2000 WL 43707 (Ohio Ct. App. 2000).

Proctor & Gamble v. Haugen, 179 F.R.D. 622 (C.D. Utah 1998), *rev'd in part on other grounds,* 222 F.3d 1262 (10th Cir. 2000).

Public Citizen v. United States, 491 U.S. 440 (1989).

Puissegur v. Puissegur, 220 So. 2d 547 (La. Ct. App. 1969).

Quilloin v. Wolcott, 434 U.S. 246 (1978).

Ray v. School District of DeSoto County, 666 F. Supp. 1524 (M.D. Fla. 1987).

Reep v. Commissioner, 593 N.E.2d 1297 (Mass. 1992).

Rettig v. Kent City School District, 720 F.2d 463 (6th Cir. 1983), *cert. denied,* 467 U.S. 1201 (1984), *rehearing denied,* 467 U.S. 1257 (1984).

Reynolds v. Giuliani, New York Law Journal, 224, no. 20 (2000): 35.

Richard P. v. Vista Del Mar, 165 Cal. Rptr. 370 (Cal. App. 2d Dist. 1980).

Richardson v. Knight, 521 U.S. 399 (June 1997).
Riggins v. Nevada, 504 U.S. 127 (1992).
Rinderer v. Delaware County, 703 F. Supp. 358 (E.D.Pa. 1987).
Rivers v. Katz, 67 N.Y.2d 485, 495 N.E.2d 337 (N.Y. 1986).
Riverside v. McLaughlin, 500 U.S. 44 (1991).
Robertson v. Granite City Unified School District, 684 F. Supp. 1002 (S.D. Ill. 1988).
Robinson v. California, 380 U.S. 400 (1965).
Roe v. Catholic Charities of the Diocese of Springfield, Illinois, 588 N.E.2d 354 (Ill. App. 5th Dist. 1992), *appeal denied,* 602 N.E.2d 475 (Ill. 1992).
Roe v. Wade, 410 U.S. 113 (1973).
Roland M. v. Concord School Committee, 910 F.2d 983 (1st Cir. 1990), *cert. denied,* 489 U.S. 912 (1991).
Romer v. Evans, 517 U.S. 620 (1996).
Rosebush v. Oakland County Prosecutor, 195 Mich. App. 675, 491 N.W.2d 633 (Mich. Ct. App. 1992).
Rouse v. Cameron, 373 F.2d 451 (D.C. Cir. 1967), *appeal after remand,* 387 F.2d 241 (D.C. Cir. 1967).
Rowe v. Bennett, 514 A.2d 802 (Me. 1986).
Rowe v. City, 279 F.3d 1271 (11th Cir. 2002).
Rowles v. Rowles, 668 A.2d 126 (Pa. 1995).
Rubano v. DiCenzo, 759 A.2d 959 (R.I. 2000).
S.E.G. v. R.A.G., 735 S.W.2d 164 (Mo. Ct. App. 1987).
Sacramento County v. Christine I., 239 Cal. Rptr. 605 (Cal. App. 3d Dist. 1987).
Saenz v. Roe, 526 U.S. 489 (1999).
San Antonio Independent School District v. Rodriguez, 411 U.S. 1 (1973).
*Santa Cruz v. Northwest Dade Community Health Center,*590 So. 2d 444 (Fla. App. 3d Dist. 1991), *review denied,* 599 So. 2d 238 (Fla. 1992).
Santobello v. New York, 404 U.S. 257 (1971).
Schaefer v. Schaefer, 183 Or. App. 513, 52 P.3d 1125 (Or. Ct. App. 2002).
Schaefer v. Wilcock, 676 F. Supp. 1092 (D. Utah 1987).
Scherer v. Waterbury, 2002 WL 254535 (Conn. Super. Ct. 2002), unpublished.
Schrempf v. New York, 66 N.Y.2d 289 (N.Y. 1985).
Schuster v. Altenberg, 424 N.W.2d 159 (Wis. 1988).
Seamons v. Snow, 84 F.3d 1226 (10th Cir. 1996).
Sean R. by Dwight R. v. Board of Education of Woodbridge, 794 F. Supp. 467 (D. Conn. 1992).
Sei Fujii v. State, 242 P.2d 617 (1952).
Sells v. United States, ____ U.S.______, 123 S. Ct. 2174 (2003).
Seminole Tribe of Florida v. Florida, 517 U.S. 44 (1996).
Shapiro v. Thompson, 394 U.S. 618 (1969).
Sherfey v. Sherfey, 2002 WL 63800 (Ky. 2002).
Sherman v. Four County Counseling Center, 987 F.2d 397 (7th Cir. 1993).
Simmons v. Simmons, 649 So. 2d 799 (La. App. 2 Cir. 1995).
Sims v. Medical Center of Baton Rouge, 1997 WL 527330 (E.D. La. 1997).
Skinner v. Oklahoma, 316 U.S. 535 (1942).
Skinner v. Railway Labor Executives' Association, 489 U.S. 602 (1989).

Slattery v. City of New York, 686 N.Y.S.2d 683 (N.Y. Sup. Ct. 1999).
Smallwood v. State, 716 So. 2d 684 (Ala. Civ. App. 1998).
Smith v. Doe, 123 S. Ct. 1140 (2003).
Smith v. O.F.F.E.R., 431 U.S. 816 (1977).
Smith v. Solgon, 561 S.E.2d 850 (Ga. Ct. App. 2002).
Society for Good Will to Retarded Children, Inc. v. Cuomo, 737 F.2d 1239 (2nd Cir. 1984), *rev'd on other grounds,* 902 F.2d 1085 (2d Cir. 1990), *on remand,* 745 F. Supp. 879 (E.D.N.Y. 1990).
Southeastern Community College v. Davis, 442 U.S. 397 (1979).
Soutiere v. Soutiere, 657 A.2d 206 (Conn. 1995).
Sparks Regional Medical Center v. Smith, 976 S.W.2d 396 (Ark. App. 2nd Div. 1998).
St. Louis Developmental Disabilities Treatment Center Parents Association v. Mallory, 591 F. Supp. 1416 (W.D. Mo. 1984), *aff'd,* 767 F.2d 518 (8th Cir. 1985).
Stanford v. Kentucky, 492 U.S. 361 (1989).
Stanley v. Illinois, 405 U.S. 645 (1969).
Stanley v. Litscher, 217 F.3d 340 (7th Cir. 2000).
State ex rel. C.J.K., 774 So.2d 107 (La. 2000).
State of Tenn. Dept. of Children's Svcs. v. T.S.W., 2002 WL 863289 (Tenn. Ct. App. 2002).
State v. Ashford, 2001 WL 137595 (Ohio App. 2002).
State v. Bales, 2002 WL 31814849 (Tenn. Crim. App. 2002), unpublished.
State v. Black, 745 P.2d 12 (Wash. 1987).
State v. Carol M.D. and Mark A.D., 948 P.2d 837 (Wash. Ct. App. 1997).
State v. Chamberlain, 628 A.2d 704 (N.H. 1993).
State v. Cressey, 628 A.2d 696 (N.H. 1993).
State v. Daniel T., 95 Misc. 2d 639 (N.Y. Crim. Ct., Kings County 1978).
State v. Danielski, 350 N.W.2d 395 (Minn. 1984).
State v. Dickerson, 789 S.W.2d 566 (Tenn. Crim. App. 1990).
State v. Doan, 498 N.W.2d 804 (Neb. Ct. App. 1993).
State v. Foret, 628 So. 2d 1116 (La. 1993).
State v. Fortin, 109 Wash. App. 1064 (Wash. App. Div. 1 2001), unpublished.
State v. Huey, 699 P.2d 1290 (Ariz. 1985).
State v. J.Q., 599 A.2d 172 (N.J. A.D., 1991), *aff'd,* 617 A.2d 1196 (N.J. 1993).
State v. James, 850 P.2d 495 (Wash. 1993).
State v. Jaquez, 2000 WL 241260 (Wash. Ct. App. 2000).
State v. Jones, 393 S.E.2d 585 (N.C. Ct. App. 1990).
State v. Lawrence, 541 A.2d 1291 (Me. 1988).
State v. Liddell, 685 P.2d 918 (Mont. 1984).
State v. Marks, 647 P.2d 1292 (Kan. 1982).
State v. McCoy, 366 S.E.2d 731 (W. Va. 1988).
State v. McQuillen, 689 P.2d 822 (Kan. 1984).
State v. Michaels, 625 A.2d 489 (N.J. Super. App. Div. 1993), *aff'd,* 642 A.2d 1372 (N.J. 1994).
State v. Ortiz, 831 P.2d 1060 (Wash. 1992).
State v. P.Z., 703 A.2d 901 (N.J. 1997).
State v. Plaskett, 27 P.3d 890 (Kan. 2001).
State v. Riker, 869 P.2d 43 (Wash. 1994).
State v. Saldana, 324 N.W.2d 227 (Minn. 1982).

State v. Sanders, 832 P.2d 1326 (Wash. Ct. App. 1992).
State v. Sharp, 418 So. 2d 1344 (La. 1982).
State v. Taylor, 552 N.Y.S.2d 883 (N.Y. 1990).
State v. Vega, 788 A.2d 1221 (Conn. 2002).
State v. Waddell, 527 S.E.2d 644 (N.C. 2000).
State V. Williams, 525 N.W.2d 538 (Minn. 1995).
Steward v. Davis, 301 U.S. 548 (1937).
Superintendent of Belchertown State School v. Saikewicz, 370 N.E.2d 417 (Mass. 1977).
Suter v. Artist, 503 U.S. 347 (1992).
Swann v. Charlotte-Mecklenburg, 402 U.S. 1 (1971).
T.E.P. v. Leavitt, 840 F. Supp. 110 (D. Utah 1993).
Tanner v. Oregon Health Sciences University, 971 P.2d 435 (Or. Ct. App. 1998).
Tanous v. United Behavioral Health Care, 2002 WL 378508 (D. Neb. 2003).
Tarasoff v. Regents of the University of California, 526 P.2d 553 (Cal. 1974).
Tarasoff v. The Regents of the University of California, 551 P.2d 334 (Cal. 1976).
Taylor ex rel. Walker v. Ledbetter, 818 F.2d 791 (11th Cir. 1987).
Tenuto v. Lederle Laboratories and Bishop, slip op. 08771 (N.Y. 1997).
Thompson v. Alameda County, 614 P.2d 728 (Cal. 1980).
Thurman v. City of Torrington, 595 F. Supp. 1521 (D.C. Conn. 1984).
Timothy S. v. Stumbo, 916 F.2d 312 (6th Cir. 1990).
Tinker v. Des Moines Independent School District, 393 U.S. 503 (1969).
Tony L. By and Through Simpson v. Childer, 71 F.3d 1182 (6th Cir. 1995).
Topel v. Long Island Jewish Medical Center, 55 N.Y. 2d 682 (N.Y. 1981).
Troxel v. Granville, 535 U.S. 57 (2000).
Tucker v. Toia, 390 N.Y.S.2d 794 (1977).
Turner v. Safley, 482 U.S. 78 (1987).
United States v. Agurs, 427 U.S. 97 (1976).
United States v. Bagley, 473 U.S. 667 (1985).
United States v. Bailey, 115 F.3d 1222 (5th Cir. 1997).
United States v. Bighead, 128 F.3d 1329 (9th Cir. 1997).
United States v. Bonnet, 882 F.2d 1360 (8th Cir. 1989), *rev'd for other reasons,* 110 S. Ct. 3267 (1990).
United States v. Butler, 297 U.S. 1 (1936).
United States v. Carbullido, 307 F.3d 957 (9th Cir. 2002).
United States v. Cardoza-Hinojosa, 140 F.3d 610 (5th Cir. 1998).
United States v. Chavez, 204 F.3d 1305 (11th Cir. 2000).
United States v. Darby, 312 U.S. 100 (1941).
United States v. Ecker, 543 F.2d 178 (D.C. Cir. 1976), *cert. denied,* 429 U.S. 1063 (1977).
United States v. Ellis, 935 F.2d 385 (1st Cir. 1991).
United States v. Garcia, 94 F.3d 57 (2d Cir. 1996).
United States v. Gillespie, 852 F.2d 475 (1988).
United States v. Henderson, 680 F.2d 659 (9th Cir. 1982).
United States v. Hiebert, 30 F.3d 1005 (8th Cir. 1994), *cert. denied,* 513 U.S. 1029 (1994)
United States v. Houston, 215 F.2d 1172 (10th Cir. 2000).
United States v. Johnson, 956 F.2d 894 (9th Cir. 1992).
United States v. Julian, 486 U.S. 1 (1988).

United States v. Juvenile Male No. 1, 86 F.3d 1314 (4th Cir. 1996).
United States v. Knott, 894 F.2d 1119 (9th Cir. 1990), *cert. denied*, 498 U.S. 873 (1990).
United States v. Lane, 815 F.2d 1106 (7th Cir. 1987)
United States v. Lopez, 514 U.S. 549 (1995).
United States v. Microsoft Corp., No. Civ. 98–1232 (D.D.C., filed May 18, 1998).
United States v. Morrison, 529 U.S. 598 (2000).
United States v. Mussari, 95 F.3d 787 (9th Cir. 1996).
United States v. Paradise, 480 U.S. 149 (1987).
United States v. Provenzano, 469 U.S. 14 (1984).
United States v. Salerno, 481 U.S. 739 (1987).
United States v. Taylor, 90 F.3d 903 (4th Cir. 1996).
Urbaniak v. Newton, 277 Cal. Rptr. 354 (Cal. App. 1st Dist. 1991).
Vacco v. Quill, 521 U.S. 793 (1997).
Vander Malle v. Ambach, 667 F. Supp. 1015 (S.D.N.Y. 1987).
Vaughn v. Ruoff, 253 F.3d 1124 (8th Cir. 2001).
Vogel v. Vogel, 637 N.W.2d 611 (Neb. 2002).
Vonner v. State, 273 So. 2d 252 (La. 1973).
Walker v. Ledbetter, 818 F.2d 791 (11th Cir. 1987).
Walton v. Alexander, 44 F.3d 1297 (5th Cir. 1995).
Washington v. Glucksberg, 521 U.S. 702 (1997).
Washington v. Harper, 494 U.S. 210 (1990).
Wayte v. United States, 470 U.S. 598 (1985).
Webster v. Reproductive Health Services, 492 U.S. 490 (1989).
Weinberger v. Wiesenfeld, 420 U.S. 636 (1975).
Weinschel v. Srople, 466 A.2d 1301 (Md. Ct. Spec. App. 1983).
Werdein v. Johnson, 633 N.Y.S.2d 908 (N.Y. App. 4th Dept. 1995).
West Virginia Board of Education v. Barnette, 319 U.S. 624 (1943).
Westside Mothers v. Haveman, 2002 WL 987291 (6th Cir. 2002).
Whalen v. Roe, 429 U.S. 589 (1977).
Whisman v. Rinehart, 119 F.3d 1303 (8th Cir. 1997).
White v. Illinois, 502 U.S. 346 (1992).
White v. Keller, 438 F. Supp. 110 (D.C. Md. 1977), *aff'd*, 588 F.2d 913 (4th Cir. 1978).
White v. Western School Corp., IP 85–1192-C, *slip op.* (S.D. Ind. 1985).
Wilkins v. Arkansas Dept. of Human Services, 2001 WL 419201 (Ark. Ct. App. 2001).
William v. Townsend, 629 N.E.2d 252 (Ind. App. 5th Dist. 1994).
Wisconsin v. Mitchell, 508 U.S. 476 (1993).
Wisconsin v. Yoder, 406 U.S. 205 (1972).
Wogelius v. Dallas, 504 N.E.2d 791 (Ill. App. 1st Dist. 1987).
Women of the State of Minnesota v. Gomez, 542 N.W.2d 17 (Minn. 1995).
Wyatt v. Stickney, 325 F. Supp. 781 (M.D. Ala. 1971), *aff'd*, 503 F.2d 1305 (5th Cir. 1974).
Wyman v. James, 400 U.S. 309 (1971).
Yakus v. United States, 321 U.S. 414 (1944).
Youngberg v. Romeo, 457 U.S. 307 (1982).
Youngstown Sheet and Tube v. Sawyer, 343 U.S. 579 (1952).
Yula v. State, 127 N.Y.S.2d 147 (N.Y.A.D. 3d Dept. 1954).
Yvonne L. v. New Mexico Dept of Human Services, 959 F.2d 883 (10th Cir.)

Zablocki v. Redhail, 434 U.S. 374 (1978).
Zavatsky v. Anderson, 130 F. Supp. 349 (D.Conn. 2001).
Zelman v. Simmons-Harris, 536 U.S. 639 (2002).
Ziegler v. Ziegler, 28 F. Supp. 2d 601 (E.D. Wash. 1998).
Zinermon v. Burch, 494 U.S. 113 (1990).

Bibliography

Adams, Barry and Beth Williams. "Student Raped at West High During School." *Wisconsin State Journal,* September 19, 2002.

Adams, Roger et al. "§ 25 General Matters." In *American Jurisprudence,* 2d ed. St. Paul, Minn.: West, 2002.

Advisory Committee. 1994. *Model Code on Domestic and Family Violence—Sec.* 403: Presumption Concerning Residence of Child. Reno, Nev.: National Council of Juvenile and Family Court Judges, 1994.

Alderman, Ellen and Caroline Kennedy. *The Right to Privacy.* New York: Alfred A. Knopf, 1995.

American Academy of Child and Adolescent Psychiatry. "Guidelines for the Clinical Evaluation of Child and Adolescent Sexual Abuse." *Journal of the American Academy of Child and Adolescent Psychiatry* 27 (1988): 655–72.

American Bar Association. *Model Code of Professional Responsibility.* Chicago: American Bar Assocation, 2001.

———. *Model Rules of Professional Conduct.* Chicago: American Bar Association, 2001.

American Law Institute. *Principles of the Law of Family Dissolution: Analysis and Recommendations.* Washington, D.C.: American Law Institute, 2002.

American Psychological Association. "Guidelines for Child Custody Evaluations in Divorce Proceedings." *American Psychologist* 49 (1994): 677–702.

Anderson, James E. *Public Policymaking,* 3d ed. New York: Houghton Mifflin, 1997.

Angelari, Marguerite. "Hate Crime Statutes: A Promising Tool for Fighting Violence Against Women." *American University Journal of Gender and the Law* 2 (1994): 63–105.

Apple, R. W. Jr. "Politics: The Issues—Interview with Newt Gingrich." *New York Times,* June 25, 1996, p. 18A.

Babb, Barbara A. and Judith D. Moran. "Substance Abuse, Families, and Unified Family Courts: The Creation of a Caring Justice System." *Journal of Health Care Law and Policy* 3 (1999): 1–16Banach, M., and F. P. Bernat. "Liability and the Internet: Risks and Recommendations for Social Work Practice." *Journal of Technology in the Human Services* 17, no. 2/3 (2000): 153–71.

Bartholet, Elizabeth. "International Adoption: Current Status and Future Prospects." *Future of Children* 3, no. 1 (1993): 89–103.

Bauer, Gary L. Testimony before the Senate Judiciary Committee. 1996 WL 387291.

Beck, Seanna M. "Overview of the Fourth Amendment." *Georgetown Law Journal* 89 (2001): 1055–67.

Bell, Mark. "Mainstreaming Equality Norms into European Union Asylum Law," *European Law Review* 26, no. 1 (2001): 20–34.

Berek, David A. "The Nuts and Bolts of the Health Care Power of Attorney." *Chicago Bar Association Record* 14 (2000): 28.

Besharov, Douglas J. 1998. "Practice Commentary." McKinney's New York's Family Court Act 168. St. Paul, Minn.: West, 2002.

———. "Protecting the Innocent: The McMartin Preschool Case." *National Review* 42 (1990): 17–26.

Black, Henry C. *Black's Law Dictionary,* 7th ed. http://www. westlaw.com. St. Paul, Minn: West, 1999.

Blocker, Kevin. "Teen Sentenced to 22 Years in Prison; Boy Killed Man in Mistaken Belief That He Had Stolen His Cell Phone." *Spokesman (Spokane, Wash.) Review,* September 10, 2002.

Blom-Cooper, Louis. "Article 6 and Modes of Criminal Trial." *European Human Rights Law Review* 1 (2001): 1–14.

Blum, George L. "Property Rights Arising from Relationship of Couple Cohabiting Without Marriage." *American Law Reports—Fifth* 69 (1999): 219–96.

Bower, Jeanette W. and Rita Laws. *Support for Families of Children with Special Needs: A Policy Analysis of Adoption Subsidy Programs in the United States.* St. Paul, Minn.: North American Council on Adoptable Children, 2002.

Brennan, William J. "The Bill of Rights and the States: The Revival of State Constitutions as Guardians of Individual Rights." *New York University Law Review* 61 (1986): 535–53.

Broughton, Richard J. "On Horror's Head Horrors Accumulate: A Reflective Comment on Capital Child Rape Legislation." *Duquesne Law Review* 39 (2000): 1–42.

Bruck, Maggie and Stephen J. Ceci. "Amicus Brief for the Case of *State of New Jersey v. Michaels* Presented by Committee of Concerned Social Scientists." *Psychology, Public Policy, and Law* 1 (1995): 272–322.

Burgess, Ann W. and Lynda L. Holmstrom. "Rape Trauma Syndrome." *American Journal of Psychiatry* 131 (1974): 981–96.

Caher, John. "Legal Resident Aliens Win Medicaid Dispute; Statute Violated Federal and State Constitutions." *New York Law Journal* 225, no. 108 (June 6, 2001): 1.

California Rules of Court, Special Rules for Trial Courts, Rule 1257.3 *et seq.* St. Paul, Minn.: West, 2002.

Callahan, Lisa, Connie Mayer, and Henry J. Steadman. "Insanity Defense Reform in the United States–Post-Hinckley." *Mental and Physical Disability Law Reporter* 11 (1987): 54–59.

Campbell, Ardis L. "Determination of Status as Legal or Natural Parents in Contested Surrogacy Births." *American Law Reports—Fifth* 77 (2000): 567.

Campbell, Suzanne B. "Taking Race out of the Equation: Transracial Adoption in 2000." *Southern Methodist University Law Review* 53 (2000): 1599–1626.

Canedy, Dana. "Boys' Case Is Used in Bid to Limit Trials of Minors as Adults," *New York Times,* October 6, 2002.

Carney, Joseph T. "American's Mentally Ill: Tormented Without Treatment." *George Mason University Civil Rights Law Journal* 3 (1992): 181–202.

Ceci, Stephen J. and Maggie Bruck. "Suggestibility of the Child Witness: A Historical Review and Synthesis." *Psychological Bulletin* 113, no. 3 (1993): 403–39.

Ceci, Stephen J. and Richard D. Friedman. "The Suggestibility of Children: Scientific Research and Legal Implications." *Cornell Law Review* 86 (2000): 33–108.

Center for Faith-Based and Community Initiatives. *What Is Charitable Choice?* Washington, D.C.: U.S. Department of Health and Human Services, 2002.

Chamberlin, Christine. "Not Kids Anymore: A Need for Punishment and Deterrence in the Juvenile Justice System." *Boston College Law Review* 42 (2001): 391–419.

Chemerinsky, Erwin. "The Supreme Court, 1988 Term: Foreword: The Vanishing Constitution." *Harvard Law Review* 103 (1989): 43–104.

Cole, Sarah Jane. "Speedy Trial." *Georgetown Law Journal* 89 (2001): 1377

Conroy, Robert J. and Mark D. Brylski. "Access to Medical Records Versus Patient's Privacy Interests." *New Jersey Lawyer* 173 (1995): 25–28.

Cook, Joshua. "Good Lawyering and Bad Role Models: The Role of Respondent's Counsel in a Civil Commitment Hearing." *Georgetown Journal of Ethics* 14 (2000): 179–95.

Coolidge, David Oregon. "The Hawaii Marriage Amendment: Its Origins, Meaning and Fate." *University of Hawaii Law Review* 22 (2000): 19–118.

Costin, Lela, B. 1983. *Two Sisters for Social Justice: A Biography of Grace and Edith Abbott.* Chicago: University of Illinois Press.

"Cost of Adopting," *National Adoption Information Clearinghouse,* 2000, http://www.calib.com/naic/pub/s_cost.cfm (March 10, 2003).

Das, Devaleena and Stephen Bradford Ballas. "Sentencing Guidelines." *Georgetown Law Journal* 89 (2001): 1655–1713.

Davis, Allen F. *Spearheads for Reform: The Social Settlements and the Progressive Movement, 1890–1914.* New York: Oxford University Press, 1967.

Defense of Marriage Act. 142 Cong. Rec. S10100–2, 104th Cong., 2d sess., September 10, 1996.

Derrick, John H. "Medical Malpractice: Liability for Failure of Physician to Inform Patient of Alternative Modes of Diagnosis or Treatment." *American Law Reports—Fourth* 38 (1985): 900–24.

DeVita, Carol J. "Nonprofits and Devolution: What Do We Know?" In Elizabeth T. Boris and C. Eugene Steuerle, eds., *Nonprofits and Government: Collaboration and Conflict.* Washington, D.C.: Urban Institute, 1999.

Diller, Matther. "The Revolution in Welfare Administration: Rules, Discretion, and Entrepreneurial Government." *New York University Law Review* 75 (2000): 1121–1220.

Donaldson, Russell G. "United Nations Resolution as Judicially Enforceable in United States Domestic Courts." *American Law Reports* 42 (2000 Supplement): 578–606.

Doris, J., R. Mazur, and M. Thomas. "Training in Child Protective Services: A Commentary on the Amicus Brief of Bruck and Ceci." *Psychology, Public Policy and Law* 1 (1995): 479–91.

Duncan, William C. "Domestic Partnership Laws in the United States: A Review and Critique." *Brigham Young University Law Review* (2001): 961–92.

Duquette, Donald N. "Legal Representation for Children in Protection Proceedings: Two Distinct Lawyer Roles Are Required." *Family Law Quarterly* 34 (2000): 441–66.

Dworkin, Ronald. *A Matter of Principle.* Cambridge, Mass.: Harvard University Press, 1985.

Ellman, Mark, Paul M. Kurtz, and Katharine T. Bartlett. *Family Law: Cases, Text, Problems,* 2d ed. Contemporary Legal Education Series 1991. Charlottesville, Va.: Michie, 1991.

"FBI Overview." Anti-Defamation League, http://www.adl.org/seach/query.asp (March 10, 2003).

Field, Martha A. "Sources of Law: The Scope of Federal Common Law." *Harvard Law Review* 99 (1986): 883–984.

Fields, Jason and Lynne M. Casper. "America's Families and Living Arrangements: Population Characteristics—2000." *Current Population Reports.* Washington, D.C.: U.S. Census Bureau, 2001.

Gallagher, Brian D. "The Right of the People . . .": The Exclusionary Rule in Child Abuse Litigation." *Thomas M. Cooley Journal of Practical and Clinical Law* 4 (2000): 1–26.

Galowitz, Paula. "Collaboration Between Lawyers and Social Workers: Re-Examining the Nature and Potential of the Relationship." *Fordham Law Review* 67 (1999): 2123–54.

Gibelman, Margaret and Philip H. Schervish. (1997). *Who We Are: A Second Look.* Washington, D.C.: National Association of Social Workers.

Gifford, Eric P. "42 U.S.C. § 1983 and Social Worker Immunity: A Cause of Action Denied." *Texas Tech Law Review* 26 (1995): 1013–40.

Goishi, Miye A. "Unlocking the Closet Door: Protecting Children from Involuntary Civil Commitment Because of Their Sexual Orientation." *Hastings Law Journal* 48 (1997): 1137–82.

Goldberg, Carey. "Spouse Abuse Crackdown, Surprisingly, Nets Many Women." *New York Times,* November 23, 1999, pp. 16A, C1.

Goldman, Maurice. "The Violence Against Women Act: Meeting Its Goal in Protecting Battered Women." *Family and Conciliation Courts Review* (1999): 375–86.

Goldscheid, Julie. "Gender-Motivated Violence: Developing a Meaningful Paradigm for Civil Rights Enforcement." *Harvard Women's Law Journal* 22 (1999): 123–41.

Goldscheid, Julie and Risa E. Kaufman. "Seeking Redress for Gender-Based Bias Crimes—Charting New Ground in Familiar Legal Territory." *Michigan Journal of Race and Law* 6 (2001): 265–83.

Goldstein, Joseph, Anna Freud, and Albert J. Solnit. *Before the Best Interests of the Child.* New York: Free Press, 1979.

———. *Beyond the Best Interests of the Child.* New York: Free Press, 1973.

Goldstein, Joseph, Anna Freud, Albert J. Solnit, and Sonja Goldstein. *In the Best Interests of the Child.* New York: Free Press, 1986.

Goodmark, Leigh. "Can Poverty Lawyers Play Well with Others? Including Legal Services in Integrated, School-Based Service Delivery Programs." *Georgetown Journal on Fighting Poverty* 4 (1997): 243–67.

"Grand Jury." *United States' Attorney Manual,* 4th ed. Washington, D.C.: U.S. Department of Justice, 1997.

Grob, Gerald N. "Government and Mental Health Policy: A Structural Analysis." *Milbank Quarterly* 72 (1994): 491–92.

Guggenheim, Martin. "A Paradigm for Determining the Role of Counsel for Children." *Fordham Law Review* 64 (1996): 1399–1433.

Gulbis, Vitauts M. "Annotation: Propriety of Awarding Joint Custody of Children." *American Law Reports—Fourth* 17 (1993): 1013–72.

Halle, Tamara. "Charting Parenthood: A Statistical Portrait of Fathers and Mothers in America." 2002. <<www.childtrendsdatabank.org>> (March 6, 2003).

Harris, Brett R. "Counseling Clients on the Internet." *Practicing Law Institute* 685 (2001): 135–225.

Hasenstab, Dan. "Is Hate a Form of Commerce? The Questionable Constitutionality of Federal 'Hate Crime' Legislation." *St. Louis University Law Journal* 45 (2001): 973–1017.

"Health: Lawmaker Asks Thompson to End Work on Administrative Simplification Mandate." Editorial, *BNA's Health Care Daily Report,* May 16, 2001.

Hildebrand, Heidi. "Because They Want to Know: An Examination of the Legal Rights of Adoptees and Their Parents." *Southern Illinois University Law Journal* 24 (2000): 515–540.

Holder, Angela R. "Circumstances Warranting Court-Ordered Medical Treatment of Minors." In *American Jurisprudence,* 2d ed. St. Paul, Minn.: West, 2002, vol. 24, p. 169.

Hughes, Michelle M. "Rights of Mentally Impaired Persons." In *American Jurisprudence,* 2d ed. (St. Paul, Minn.: West, (2003), vol. 53, 93–98, sec. 93.

Humphreys, K. and E. Klaw. "Can Targeting Nondependent Problem Drinkers and Providing Internet-Based Services Expand Access to Assistance for Alcohol Problems?" *Journal of Studies on Alcohol* 62, no. 4 (2001): 528–32.

Justice Research and Statistics Association. *Domestic and Sexual Violence Data Collection: A Report to Congress Under the Violence Against Women Act.* Washington, D.C.: National Institute of Justice, Bureau of Justice Statistics, 1996.

Karnezis, Kristine C. "Patient's Right to Refuse Treatment Allegedly Necessary to Sustain Life." *American Law Reports—Third* 93 (1979 plus supplement): 67–101.

———. "Restricting Access to Judicial Records of Concluded Adoption Proceedings." *American Law Reports* 83 (2000): 468–78.

Kaufman, Leslie. "Burden Grows on Services for Teenagers." *New York Times,* October 28, 2002.

Kaye, Judith S. "Brennan Lecture: State Courts at the Dawn of a New Century: Common Law Courts Reading Statutes and Constitutions." *New York University Law Review,* 70 (1995): 1–35.

Keating, Gregory C. "Settling Through Consent Decree in Prison Reform Litigation: Exploring the Effects of *Rufo v. Inmates of Suffolk County Jail.*" *Boston College Law Review* 34 (1992): 163–201.

Kelso, R. Randall and Charles D. Kelso. "How the Supreme Court Is Dealing with Precedents in Constitutional Cases." *Brooklyn Law Review* 62 (1996): 973–1038.

Kerian, Christin E. "Surrogacy: A Last Resort Alternative for Infertile Women or a Commodification of Women's Bodies and Children?" *Wisconsin Women's Law Journal* 12 (1997): 113–66.

Killmer, Darold W. and Mari Newman. "VAWA: A Civil Rights Tool for Victims of Gender-Motivated Violence." *Colorado Lawyer* 28 (1999): 77–81.

Klein, Catherine F. and Leslye E. Orloff, "Providing Legal Protection for Battered Women: An Analysis of State Statutes and Case Law." *Hofstra Law Review* 21 (1993): 801–1189.

Krauss, Clifford. "Canadian Leaders Agree to Propose Gay Marriage Law." *New York Times,* June 18, 2003, p. 1A.

Kussmann, Patricia C. "Right of Indigent Parent to Appointed Counsel in Proceeding for Involuntary Termination of Parental Rights." *American Law Reports—Fifth* 92 (2000): 379–402.

LaFave, Wayne R. and Austin W. Scott. *Substantive Criminal Law*. St. Paul, Minn.: West, 1986.

Landis, Debra T. " 'Guilty but Mentally Ill' Statutes: Validity and Construction." *American Law Reports—Fourth* 71 (2000): 702–53.

Levine, Joseph. "Internet: A Framework for Analyzing Online Human Service Practices." *Journal of Technology in the Human Services* 17, no. 2/3 (2000): 173–92.

Lucas, Melinda. "Adoption: Distinguishing Between Gray Market and Black Market Activities." *Family Law Quarterly* 34 (2000): 553–64.

McCord, David. "Syndromes, Profiles and Other Mental Exotica: A New Approach to the Admissibility of Nontraditional Psychological Evidence in Criminal Cases." *Oregon Law Review* 66 (1986): 19–108.

McEwen, Angie G. 1999. "So You're Having Another Woman's Baby: Economics and Exploitation in Gestational Surrogacy." *Vanderbilt Journal of Transnational Law* 32 (1999): 271–304.

Martin, Margaret Hoefner. "Restitution." *Georgetown Law Journal* 89 (2001): 1731–37.

Masson, Erin M. "Admissibility of Expert or Opinion Evidence of Battered-Woman Syndrome on Issue of Self-Defense." *American Law Reports—Fifth* 58 (1998): 749–82.

Meier, A. S. "Offering Social Support via the Internet: A Case Study of an Online Support Group for Social Workers." *Journal of Technology in the Human Services* 17, no. 2/3 (2000): 237–66.

Mickenberg, Ira. "A Pleasant Surprise: The Guilty but Mentally Ill Verdict Has Both Succeeded in Its Own Right and Successfully Preserved the Traditional Role of the Insanity Defense." *University of Cincinnati Law Review* 55 (1987): 943—96.

Milks, Harriet Dinegar. "Wrongful Adoption Causes of Action Against Adoption Agencies Where Children Have or Develop Mental or Physical Problems That Are Misrepresented or Not Disclosed to Adoptive Parents." *American Law Reports—Fifth* 74 (1999): 1–33.

Miller, Robin Cheryl. "Construction and Application of State Patient Bill of Rights Statutes." *American Law Reports—Fifth*. 87 (2001): 277–326.

———. "Damage Action for HIV Testing Without Consent of Person Tested." *American Law Reports* 77 (2000): 541–68.

"Model Standards of Practice for Family and Divorce Mediation." *Family and Conciliation Courts Review* 39 (2001): 121–34.

Moskowitz, Seymour. "Saving Granny from The Wolf: Elder Abuse and Neglect—The Legal Framework." *Connecticut Law Review* 31 (1998): 77–164.

Myers, John E. B. "New Era of Skepticism Regarding Children's Credibility." *Psychology Public Policy and Law* 1 (1995): 387–98.

Myers, John E. B., Karen J. Saywitz, and Gail S. Goodman. "Psychological Research on Children as Witnesses: Practical Implications for Forensic Interviews and Courtroom Testimony." *Pacific Law Journal* 28 (1996): 3–91.

Myers, Joseph A. Testimony before the Senate Committee on Indian Affairs. Federal Document Clearing House. 1996 WL 50663.

Nadel, Andrea G. "Annotation: Primary Caretaker Role of Respective Parents as a Factor in Awarding Custody of Child." *American Law Reports—Fourth* 41 (1993): 1129–82.

National Academy of Sciences, National Research Council, Committee on Maintaining Privacy and Security in Health Care Applications. *For the Record: Protecting Electronic Health Information* Washington, D.C.: National Academy of Sciences Press, 1997.

National Association of Social Workers. *Code of Ethics*. http://www.socialworkers.org/pubs/code/code.asp (July 21, 2003).

New York State Office of Mental Health. "Kendra's Law: The Process for Obtaining Assisted Outpatient Treatment," 2002, http://www.omh.state.ny.us/omhweb/omhq/q1299/ kendras_law_the_process.htm (February 12, 2003).

Note. "Discrimination Against the Poor and the Fourteenth Amendment." *Harvard Law Review* 81 (1967): 435–52.

O'Connor, Carolyn O. "Illinois Adolescents' Rights to Confidential Health Care." *Illinois Bar Journal* 82 (1994): 24.

Oedekoven, Byron. 1996. "Youth Violence Programs." Congressional testimony. Federal Document Clearing House. 1996 WL 7137245.

Office of Juvenile Justice and Delinquency Prevention. "Offenders in Juvenile Court." *Juvenile Justice Bulletin* (2000), http://ojjdp.ncjrs.org/jjbulletin/jjbul_000.html (July 13, 2003).

Owens, Wally. "*State v. Osby*, The Urban Survival Defense." *American Journal of Criminal Law* 22 (1995): 809–21

Perrin, Timothy L. "Expert Witnesses Under Rules 703 and 803(4) of the Federal Rules of Evidence: Separating the Wheat from the Chaff." *Indiana Law Journal* 72 (1997): 939–1014.

Peters, Ellen Ash. "Common Law Judging in a Statutory World." *University of Pittsburgh Law Review* 42 (1982): 995–1011.

Petrila, John. "Ethics, Money, and the Problem of Coercion in Managed Behavioral Health Care." *St. Louis University Law Journal* 40 (1996): 359–404.

Pierce, Christina T., Patricia Gleason-Wynn, and Marilyn G. Miller. "Social Work and Law: A Model for Implementing Social Services in a Law Office." *NAELA (National Association of Elder Law Attorneys) Quarterly* 13 (2000): 3–7

Practicing Law Institute. *City Attorney Ethical Issues* 188 (2001): 38–389.

President's Commission on Indian Reservation Economies. Executive Order 12401. 1984.

President's Commission on Privatization. Executive Order 12607. 1988.

President's "Private Sector Survey on Cost Control." Executive Order 12369. President's Commission on Housing, Executive Order 12310 (1982).

"Quest for Health Information Privacy Law Likely to Be Long and Full of Pitfalls." Editorial. *Health Legislation and Regulation* 23, no. 24 (1997), 1997 WL 8740348.

Ramsey, Sarah H. "The Wingspread Report and Action Plan: High-Conflict Custody Cases—Reforming the System for Children." *Family Court Review* 39 (2001): 146–56.

Ratner, Steven M. "Revisiting Health Care Proxies and Living Wills." *New York Law Journal* 226, no. 117 (December 18, 2001): 6–7.

Rennison, Callie Marie and Sarah Welchans, *Intimate Partner Violence*. Washington, D.C.: U.S. Department of Justice, Bureau of Justice Statistics, 2000.

Restatement (Second) of Torts § 4. St. Paul, Minn.: American Law Institute, 2002.

Restatement of the Law—Conflicts of the Law §283.2. Validity of Marriage. St. Paul, Minn.: American Law Institute, 2002.

Rhoades, Heather J. "*Zamstein v. Marvasti:* Is a Duty Owed to Alleged Child Sexual Abusers?" *Connecticut Law Review* 30 (1998): 1411–43.

Robinson, Paul H. "Punishing Dangerousness: Cloaking Preventive Detention as Criminal Justice." *Harvard Law Review* 114 (2001): 1429–56.

Rosato, Jennifer L. "Let's Get Real: Quilting a Principled Approach to Adolescent Empowerment in Health Care Decision Making." *DePaul Law Review* 51 (2002): 769–803.

Roy, Robert. "Modern Status of Views as to Validity of Premarital Agreements Contemplating Divorce or Separation." *American Law Reports—Fourth* 53 (1987): 22–126.

Rugani, Robert R. "The Gradual Decline of a Hearsay Exception: The Misapplication of Federal Rule of Evidence 803(4), The Medical Diagnosis Hearsay Exception." *Santa Clara Law Review* 38 (1999): 867–904.

Russel, R. A. "Role Perceptions of Attorneys and Caseworkers in Child Abuse Cases in Juvenile Court." *Child Welfare* 67 (1988): 205–16.

St. Joan, Jacqueline. "Building Bridges, Building Walls: Collaboration Between Lawyers and Social Workers in a Domestic Violence Clinic and Issues of Client Confidentiality." *Clinical Law Review* 7 (2001): 403–67

Scheinkman, Alan D. "Introduction to the Practice Commentaries." McKinney's New York Adoption Law—Private Adoption § 115-c. St. Paul, Minn.: West, 2003.

Schlam, Lawrence. "Children Not in the Physical Custody of One of [Their] Parents: The Superior Rights Doctrine and Third-Party Standing Under the Uniform Marriage and Dissolution of Marriage Act." *Southern Illinois University Law Journal* 24 (2000): 405–52.

Schneider, Andrea Kupfer. "The Intersection of Therapeutic Jurisprudence, Preventive Law, and Alternative Dispute Resolution." *Psychology, Public Policy and Law* 5 (1999): 1084–1102.

Schwartz, Paul M. "The Protection of Privacy in Health Care Reform." *Vanderbilt Law Review* 48 (1996): 295–347.

Schwartz, Steven J. "Damage Actions as a Strategy for Enhancing the Quality of Care of Persons with Mental Disabilities." *New York University Review of Law and Social Change* 17 (1990): 651–87.

Skolnick, Arlene. *Embattled Paradise: The American Family in the Age of Uncertainty.* New York: Basic Books, 1991.

Slaughter, Leslie. 1998. Testimony before the House of Representatives Education Subcommittee. Federal Document Clearing House. 1998 WL 210930.

Smith, Joel E. "Appointment of Counsel for Indigent Husband or Wife in Action for Divorce or Separation." *American Law Reports—Third.* 85 (1978): 983–92.

Snyder, Howard and Melissa Sickmund. "Juvenile Courts and Juvenile Crime." In *Juvenile Offenders and Victims: 1999 National Report.* Washington, D.C.: National Center for Juvenile Justice, Office of Juvenile Justice and Delinquency Prevention, 1999.

———. *Juvenile Offenders and Victims: 1999 National Report.* Washington, D.C.: National Center for Juvenile Justice, 1999.

Sokoloff, Burton Z. "Antecedents of American Adoption." *Future of Children* 3, no. 1 (1993): 21, citing J. H. Hollinger, ed., "Aftermath of Adoption: Legal and Social Consequences." In *Adoption Law and Practice.* New York: Mathew Bender, 1991.

Solomon, Gary. "Child Abuse, Neglect and the Foster Care System 2002: Effective Social Work and the Legal System; The Attorney's Role and Responsibilities." *Practicing Law Institute: Litigation and Administrative Practice Course Handbook Series* 189 (2002): 303–56.

Sprague, Marcia and Mark Hardin. "Coordination of Juvenile and Criminal Court Child Abuse and Neglect Proceedings." *University of Louisville Journal of Family Law* 35 (1996–97): 239–324.

Stein, Theodore J. "The Adoption and Safe Families Act: Creating a False Dichotomy Between Parents' Rights and Childrens' Rights." *Families in Society* 81, no. 6 (2000): 586–92.

———. "Child Custody and Visitation: The Rights of Lesbian and Gay Parents." *Social Service Review* 70, no. 3 (1996): 556–602.

———. *Child Welfare and the Law*. Washington, D.C.: Child Welfare League of America, 1998.

———. *Social Policy and Policymaking by the Branches of Government and by the Public-at-Large*. New York: Columbia University Press, 2001.

Stirrup, Heidi. Testimony before the Senate Committee on Finance. Federal Document Clearing House, 1996 WL 90840.

"Summary of Laws Regarding International Adoptions Finalized Abroad 50 States and 6 U.S. Territories." National Adoption Information Clearinghouse. http://www.calib.com/naioc/pubs (August 20, 2003).

Surgeon General of the United States. "Mental Health." 2000. http://www.surgeongeneral.gov (January 28, 2003).

Sypherd, Stephen S. and Gary M. Ronan. "Substantive Rights Retained by Prisoners." *Georgetown Law Journal* 89 (2001): 1898–1938.

Task Force on Life and the Law. *Assisted Reproductive Technologies: Analysis and Recommendations for Public Policy*. Albany: New York State Department of Health, 1998.

Task Force on Pediatric AIDS. American Academy of Pediatrics. "Guidelines for Human Immunodeficiency Virus (HIV)-Infected Children and Their Foster Families." *Pediatrics* 89 (1992): 17–24.

Task Force on Pediatric AIDS. American Academy of Pediatrics. "Pediatric Guidelines for Infection Control of Human Immunodeficiency Virus (Acquired Immunodeficiency Virus) in Hospitals, Medical Offices, Schools, and Other Settings." *Pediatrics* 82 (1988): 22–28.

Tatara, Toshio et al. *The National Elder Abuse Incidence Study*. Washington, D.C.: American Public Human Services Association and Westat, 1998.

Taylor, Ann. "Globalization and Biotechnology: UNESCO and an International Strategy to Advance Human Rights and Public Health." *American Journal of Law and Medicine* 25 (1999): 479–541.

Taylor, Mary E. "Parent's Use of Drugs as Factor in Award of Custody of Children, Visitation Rights, or Termination of Parental Rights." *American Law Reports—Fifth* (1994): 534–701.

Tondo, Carrie-Anne, Rinarisa Coronel, and Bethany Brucker. "Mediation Trends." *Family Court Review* 39 (2001): 431–45.

Trainor, Elizabeth. "Sufficiency of Evidence to Establish Parent's Knowledge or Allowance of Child's Sexual Abuse by Another Under Statute Permitting Termination of Parental Rights for 'Allowing' or 'Knowingly Allowing' Such Abuse to Occur." *American Law Reports—Fifth* 53 (1997): 499–529.

"Transracial Adoption." *National Adoption Information Clearinghouse*, 2002, http://www.calib.com/naic/ (August 20, 2003).

Trubek, Louise G. and Jennifer J. Farnham. "Social Justice Collaboratives: Multidisciplinary Practices for People." *Clinical Law Review* 7 (2000): 227–72.

"United Nations Millennium Declaration." *U.N. Chronicle* 37, no. 3 (January 1, 2000), available at 2000 WL 25574373.

U.S. Census Bureau. "Health Insurance Coverage—2001." *Current Population Survey: Annual Demographic Supplements*. Washington, D.C.: U.S. Government Printing Office, 2002.

U.S. Census Bureau. "Summary of Public School Finances for Elementary-Secondary Education by State: 1999–2000." http://www.census.gov (May 24, 2003).

U.S. Centers for Disease Control. "1995 Revised Guidelines for Prophylaxis Against Pneumocystis *carinii* Pneumonia for Children Infected with or Perinatally Exposed to the Human Immunodeficiency Virus." *Morbidity and Mortality Weekly Report* 44 (1995): 1–17.

U.S. Department of Justice. *Statistical Yearbook of the Immigration and Naturalization Service*. Washington, D.C.: U.S. Government Printing Office, 1999, table 15.

U.S. General Accounting Office. *Child Support: Need to Improve Efforts to Identify Fathers and Obtain Orders of Support*. Report GAO/HRD-87–37. Washington, D.C.: U.S. General Accounting Office, 1997.

U.S. General Accounting Office. *Drug Courts: Overview of Growth, Characteristics, and Results*. GAO/GGD 97–106. Washington, D.C.: U.S. General Accounting Office, 1997.

U.S. General Accounting Office. *Foster Care: HHS Should Ensure that Juvenile Justice Placement Are Reviewed*. Report GAO/HEHS-00–42. Washington, D.C.: U.S. General Accounting Office, 2000.

U.S. General Accounting Office. *Mental Health Parity Act: Despite New Federal Standards, Mental Health Benefits Remain Limited*. Report GAO/HEHS-00–95. Washington, D.C.: U.S. General Accounting Office, 2000.

U.S. General Accounting Office. *Nursing Homes: Additional Steps Needed to Strengthen Enforcement of Federal Quality Standards*. GAO/HEHS-99–46. Washington, D.C.: U.S. General Accounting Office, 1999.

U.S. General Accounting Office. *Nursing Homes: Complaint Investigation Processes Often Inadequate to Protect Residents*. GAO/HEHS-99–80. Washington, D.C.: U.S. General Accounting Office, 1999.

U.S. General Accounting Office. *Nursing Homes: More Can Be Done to Protect Residents from Abuse*. Report GAO-02–312. Washington, D.C.: U.S. General Accounting Office, 2002.

U.S. General Accounting Office. *Nursing Homes: Sustained Efforts Are Essential to Realize Potential of the Quality Initiatives*. GAO/HEHS-00–197. Washington, D.C.: U.S. General Accounting Office, 2000.

U.S. General Accounting Office. *Student Discipline: Individuals with Disabilities in Education Act*. Report No. GAO-01–210. Washington, D.C.: U.S. General Accounting Office, 2001.

U.S. General Accounting Office. *Violence Against Women: Data on Pregnant Victims and Effectiveness of Prevention Strategies Are Limited*. Report GAO-02–530. Washington, D.C.: U.S. General Accounting Office, 2002.

U.S. Immigration and Naturalization Service. "Information Sheet Regarding the Intercountry Adoption Act of 2000," http://www.bcis.gov/graphics/index.htm (July 14, 2003).

U.S. Senate. "Violence Against Women Act." Report 103–138, 103d Cong., 1st sess. September 1993.

U.S. Senate Committee on the Judiciary. U.S. Senate. *Separation of Powers Annual Report*, 93d Cong., 2d sess. S. Rept. No. 93–1195, September 1974.

U.S. Senate Committee on National Emergencies and Delegated Emergency Powers. U.S. Senate. *Executive Orders in Times of War and National Emergency*, 93d Cong., 2d sess., S. Rept. No. 93–1280, October 1974, 4.

"Unpublished Tables—Marital Status and Living Arrangements—1998 Update," *U.S. Census Bureau* <<www.census.gov/prod/99pubs>> (March 4, 2003).

Vento, Carol Schultz. "Construction and Application of Indian Child Welfare Act of 1978 (ICWA) 25 U.S.C.A. §§ 1901 *et. Seq*. Upon Child Custody Determinations." *American Law Reports—Fifth* 89 (201): 195–235.

Waldman, Mitchell. "Adoption. § 80. What Constitutes Abandonment, Desertion, or Neglect, Generally." *American Jurisprudence*. St. Paul, Minn.: West, 2002, vol. 2, p. 75.

Waldman, Mitchell J. and Joseph E. Conley. "§53: Social Workers and Similar Workers." In *American Jurisprudence*, 2d ed. St. Paul, Minn.: West, 2002.

Walker, Lenore E. A. "Battered Women Syndrome and Self-Defense." *Notre Dame Journal of Law, Ethics, and Public Policy* 6 (1992): 321–34.

Walker, Nancy E. "Forensic Interviews of Children: The Components of Scientific Validity and Legal Admissibility." *Law and Contemporary Problems* 65 (2002): 149–78.

Walker, Nancy E. and Matthew Nguyen. "Interviewing the Child Witness: The Do's and the Don't's, the How's and the Why's." *Creighton Law Review* 29 (1996): 1587–1606.

Warren, H. D. "Court's Duty to Advise or Admonish Accused as to Consequences of Plea of Guilty, or to Determine That He Is Advised Thereof," *American Law Reports* 97 (1964): 549–83.

Watson, Kenneth E. 1996. "Juvenile Justice and Delinquency." Federal Document Clearing House. 1996 WL 10163920.

Weil, Michael. "Research on Issues in Collaboration Between Social Workers and Lawyers." *Social Service Review* 56 (1982): 393–405.

Weithorn, Lois A. "Protecting Children from Exposure to Domestic Violence: The Use and Abuse of Child Maltreatment," *Hastings Law Journal* 53 (2001): 1–152.

White, Michael, Edward J. Loughran, Donna Wulkan, and Jerome G. Miller. "Systematic Critique and Transformation." *District of Columbia Law Review* 3 (1995): 403.

Wood, Rebecca. *A Summary of States' Activities in Support of Marriage and Promoting and Maintaining Health Intact Families*. Albany: New York State Office of Temporary and Disability Assistance, n.d.

Wooster, Ann K. "What Constitutes Services That Must be Provided by Federally Assisted Schools Under the Individuals with Disabilities Education Act?" *American Law Reports—Federal* 161 (2000): 1–110.

Wright, Alice M. "What Voluntary Acts of Child, Other Than Marriage or Entry into Military Service, Terminate Parent's Obigation to Support?" *American Law Reports* 55 (1998): 557–89.

Wydra, Heather A. "Keeping Secrets Within the Team: Maintaining Client Confidentiality While Offering Interdisciplinary Services to the Elderly Client." *Fordham Law Review* 62 (1994): 1517–1545.

Zawisza, Christina A. "Child Welfare Managed Care in Florida: Will It Be Innovation or Abdication?" *Nova Law Review* 25 (2001): 619–39.

Index

CPSIA information can be obtained
at www.ICGtesting.com
Printed in the USA
LVOW04*0635301215
467615LV00002B/2/P